INFORMATION TECHNOLOGY:
Strategic Decision Making for Managers

HENRY C. LUCAS, JR.

Robert H. Smith Professor of Information Systems
Robert H. Smith School of Business
University of Maryland

To Scott and Jonathan

Production Manager   *Pam Kennedy*
Acquisitions Editor   *Beth Lang Golub*
Associate Editor   *Lorraina Raccuia*
Editorial Assistant   *Ame Esterline*
Associate Production Manager   *Kelly Tavares*
Production Editor   *Sarah Wolfman Robichaud*
Managing Editor   *Kevin Dodds*
Illustration Editor   *Wendy Stokes Hodge*
Cover Design   *Jennifer Wasson*

This book was set in Times by Leyh Publishing LLC and printed and bound by Malloy Lithograph. The cover was printed by Lehigh Press, Inc.

This book is printed on acid free paper. ∞

To order books or for customer service please call 1-800-CALL WILEY (225-5945).

ISBN 0-471-65293-8

Printed in the United States of America

10 9 8 7 6 5 4 3 2

BRIEF CONTENTS

CONTENTS

PREFACE

This book is based upon the belief that information technology is one of the key drivers of business in the twenty-first century. This technology is providing new sources of revenue and opportunities to dramatically change a firm's cost structure. Information technology (IT) enables organizations to develop radically new structures such as value networks, in which a focal company undertakes key core activities itself and outsources noncore tasks to partners in the network. The technology has led to new business models and new types of businesses. IT has become intertwined closely with corporate strategy.

Some argue that IT is not important, that everyone has access to the same technology so it cannot provide a competitive advantage. Although this argument sounds reasonable in the context of a resource-based view of strategy, it misses several major points. First some firms gained a significant first mover advantage with IT and maintained that advantage as competitors tried to adopt their business models. Think of organizations such as eBay or Monster.com, the successful online employment service. Second, acquiring technology is not enough to provide an advantage; the organization must manage IT obtain a return from its technology investments.

This book is about the need to manage IT, to execute one's plans successfully. Dell's business model is public; anyone can copy its Web site logic and direct distribution model. Yet no one has duplicated the strategy to compete with Dell. Other competitors face significant management challenges trying to move from a retail distribution model to Dell's model. For a variety of reasons, they cannot execute a strategy to make such a major change. Management knowledge and skills are key resources for competitive advantage, and in fact may provide the major core competence of an organization in post-industrial society.

The objective has been to weave together a number of themes about information technology to motivate the reader to take an active role in managing technology. This task does not fall only to the chief information officer and his or her staff; effective IT management depends on all employees in an organization. Technology changes strategy given the presence of the Internet and a hypercompetitive economy. IT leads to new business models; managers need to understand their own and proposed business models, and why eBay's model makes sense where WebVan's did not, for example.

The text argues that one of the most exciting contributions of IT is the options it provides for structuring organizations. Firms literally change their organization structures to become more competitive with the help of technology. In addition this technology transforms markets and industries. Some of these changes create major challenges for incumbents, such as what file sharing software such as Napster and KaZaA did to the music industry. Overall, however, the prognosis is positive as IT leads transformations that provide customers with new services, and firms with new sources of revenue and new lower-cost structures.

It appears that many IT investments are made without a formal investment analysis. Managers often find this practice objectionable, yet in numerous examples, companies have justified quite large investments in technology without looking at ROI. The chapters explore this question of value in some detail and offer a taxonomy of the different kinds of value obtainable from IT. The book offers guidelines on how to evaluate IT investments and presents both net present value and real options approaches. (A student problem set built around the HBS Publishing Whirlpool Europe case is available on the books' Web site.)

The book looks at some major managerial decisions about technology and reviews the particular problem of what to do with legacy systems. Any system becomes a legacy system after it is implemented, and the manager will still face this problem even if no mainframes are left in the organization. The text also addresses how a manager goes about choosing a source of processing and services. You can handle all technology internally, or you can outsource all or part of it to a third party.

The implementation of new technology initiatives is a major part of executing your plans for technology. The book devotes a chapter to looking at this important task, and especially to the manager's role in seeing that innovations succeed. An important management consideration is how to structure the IT organization itself. A chapter presents contemporary thinking on this problem and describes how different companies currently organize the IT function.

Management has the responsibility for control within the organization, and of late many firms have experienced serious control problems. We look at the control that systems provide, and at the need to control systems themselves.

One part of the text is devoted to understanding the technology so that a manager can be conversant with it. It provides a discussion of the legacy environment through an example of a company that is definitely behind the technology curve. Modern technology is incredibly powerful, and three components make it so: computer devices, databases, and networks. A chapter explores each of these technologies so the manager is aware of what is possible.

The next part of the book explains various applications of technology and how each provides value to the organization. Other chapters cover electronic commerce, ERP and CRM systems, decision and intelligent systems, and knowledge management. A look at business processes assesses the pros and cons of implementing a suite of ERP or CRM products.

The last part of the book examines broader concerns. One chapter deals with the digital divide in the United States and among the world's countries. Business should be interested in a global digital divide because the world needs workers who can integrate technology with their jobs, and everyone involved in e-commerce needs customers. A customer who does not have access to technology or does not know how to use it is lost to the online vendor.

The final chapter addresses some ethical concerns about technology and takes a look at what is coming. It also summarizes some of the key management decisions that have been discussed in the rest of the book.

The overall objectives of the book are to convince the reader of the transformational power of information technology, and the need to actively manage the technology to obtain the full benefits from investing in IT.

ACKNOWLEDGMENTS

This text benefited from the many contributions of my friend and colleague, Ritu Agarwal. We worked together for several years to develop a course in information systems that fits into the time allotted to IS in the MBA core. This joint work, especially Ritu's contributions, shaped the content and approach of this text. Thanks also go to Likoebe Maruping for his help in reviewing the manuscript. I am particularly grateful for Stacy Calo's cheerful assistance in seeking permissions and integrating the references and bibliography. I also want to thank my wife, Ellen, for her encouragement through all stages of creating this book.

I would also like to thank the following reviewers for their helpful and insightful comments: Chandra Amaravadi, Western Illinois University; Paul Cheney, University of Central Florida; Gerald Evans, University of Montana–Missoula; Randy Guthrie, California State Polytechnic University–Pomona; Joseph Harder, Indiana State University; Howard Kanter, Depaul University; David Little, High Point University; William McHenry, University of Akron; Roberto Mejias, Purdue University; Dinesh Mirchandani, University of Missouri–St. Louis; Mahesh S. Raisinghani, University of Dallas; and Maria Roldan, San Jose State University.

CHAPTER 1

TECHNOLOGY TRANSFORMS THE ORGANIZATION

A Manager's Perspective

Information technology (IT) divides managers into three types. The first group consists of individuals who "get it." They understand what technology can do, and they want to take maximum advantage of it. Managers like Michael Dell of Dell Computer, John Chambers of Cisco, and Jack Welch, who recently retired as chairman of General Electric, all belong in this category. They believe in technology and they encourage the people working with them to exploit IT to change the way their companies do business.

A second group of managers includes those who understand the technology, but are not quite as committed to it as the first category of managers. These individuals use IT to augment their existing ways of doing business, and in doing so make more local changes to their firms. A company like Grainger is a good example of a leading firm that uses the Internet as a very successful sales channel to provide new sources of revenue.

The third group of managers consists of those who are highly skeptical of information technology. They provide little IT leadership and look at money spent on technology as an expense rather than an investment. John Roberts's predecessor at Victor Electronics is an example of this third category of manager. He minimized spending on technology, and as a result, missed many opportunities. Victor avoided any kind of commitment to electronic commerce, even as customers and competitors embraced it.

The goal of this book is to encourage you to join the first category of managers who believe in the technology and are willing to use it to create a real electronic business. Those who "get" technology are the managers who will build successful organizations in the twenty-first century.

TECHNOLOGY TRANSFORMS BUSINESS

- General Motors spends more than $1.5 billion on technology to tie together its design centers around the world and dramatically reduce the time to market for a new vehicle. Its objective is to make General Motors seem like a small company, despite having more than 300,000 employees.

- Cisco Systems decided to turn over production to contract electronic manufacturers; it uses the Internet to take 90 percent of its orders and to handle customer service requests. The company routes orders to its manufacturing partners, who ship directly to the customer.

■ Dell Computer refined a direct sales model combined with a lean supply chain. The company achieved an amazing five days for accounts receivable; most customers pay before Dell builds their computer.

■ PepsiCo uses data mining and statistical analysis to develop new marketing strategies, which help it take market share from Coke.

These and countless other examples show how the big three of technology—computers, databases, and especially networks—are changing the way organizations operate, as well as changing their business models and their structures. This book is about the management of information technology, a crucial responsibility for the twenty-first-century manager. The text presents a number of themes:

1. *Transformation.* Information technology is transforming organizations, markets, industries, and national economies.

2. *Strategy.* Organization strategy and technology strategy are inextricably intertwined.

3. *Value.* Investing in information technology offers value, but different kinds of investments have differing probabilities of payoffs; it is difficult to estimate the return from IT investments a priori.

4. *Management.* The most significant issues with information technology are managerial in nature, not technological. Management skills and processes are the key to obtaining the maximum return from a firm's investments in IT.

See Table 1-1.

Value Proposition

Information technology as a whole can help a firm become more competitive through changes in strategy and direction, and improvements in efficiency and effectiveness. The technology enables the organization to dramatically improve its business model and change its structure. In each chapter, we begin by reviewing the IT value proposition that

TABLE 1-1 Major themes of the text.

Key Theme	Issues
Organizational transformation	Technology is bringing about dramatic changes in organizations, markets, industries, and economies
IT and corporate strategy	Strategy and technology are now inseparable
Value	How to demonstrate value from investing in information technology
Management of technology	Incredibly powerful technology is available; the limits on its use are managerial, not technical

is best illustrated in the material that follows. Transformational technology provides value in the following forms:

- A firm that is more competitive
- Greater efficiencies in operations
- A more effective organization
- An improved work environment for employees

You can measure some of these benefits with metrics such as:

- New lines of business
- Market share
- Sales per employee
- Gross margins
- Employee satisfaction
- Employee turnover

Many different kinds of value come from investing in IT, and we review them throughout this textbook. If you fail to invest in IT, it is not possible to obtain any benefits from it. You want to avoid being in the position that John Roberts finds himself in at Victor Electronics.

Victor Electronics

John Roberts, CEO of Victor Electronics, was visibly annoyed as he tossed a consulting report he had been reading on his desk. The report was very critical of the information technology in place at Victor, which did not please Roberts, nor did it surprise him greatly. Where the report failed, in his thinking, was that it offered a large number of things that Victor could do without putting any priorities on them.

"I hired these people knowing that we have problems, and I expected them to diagnose the problems and develop a plan for us. Instead, they've taken the easy way out and given us a laundry list of problems and possible solutions, but no recommendations on what we should do first, and not a hint of the value they see in each option they've suggested," fumed Roberts.

Victor Electronics is a manufacturer of electronic components used in all kinds of equipment, from Nintendos and Xboxes to the latest computer. The company's sales fluctuate with the sales of computers and cell phones, but recently Victor passed the $2 billion a year mark in revenues. Investors and stock analysts generally regard Victor as a leader in its field, and in their view, the company is well managed. Roberts, who became CEO six months ago after being hired from a competitor, thought otherwise.

"This company has always done things on a shoestring," he told his senior management committee, "and now we are going to have to face the consequences." Our plants are not in too bad shape, but our information technology is a good ten years behind what leading companies are doing right now."

Ellen Collins, the VP of Finance who had come from Robert's old company, said "John, technology is very expensive, and IT projects carry a lot of risk. You and I had some spectacular overruns before we came to Victor."

John replied, "Yeah, I know that we went way over budget, and that some of our projects were late, but a lot of what we invested gave us the option to do different things, options that we don't have at Victor because of chronic underinvestment in IT."

"It's not just underinvestment, John, it's a real lack of trust and faith that you can get value from IT. I don't know the whole history, but I gather that Victor has had a lot of trouble pulling off IT projects."

"Ok, I'll grant that, but you don't give up! You try to figure out how to be successful. Do you know what I found? The first month I was here I walked through our main factory here in the United States and talked to people at each stage of production," John said, "and the production controllers who were scheduling all the work in the factory were doing their jobs manually, with a couple using Excel spreadsheets! Can you believe it, Excel spreadsheets to schedule a plant that produces over $250 million of products in a year."

Ellen responded, "Ok, you did tell me that story, and I agree, but, hey, the company is viewed as successful. And look at the money we have in the bank. We've been profitable every year, except for 2002 when the downturn in telecom hit everybody."

John shook his head, "Ellen, it's great that we make money, but I promised myself if I ever became a CEO I wouldn't just manage for quarterly profits and the stock price. We're responsible for the health of this company, and that means its well-being two years down the road to five or ten years ahead."

"So what are we going to do?"

"That's what I'm trying to figure out. We have ten plants throughout the world, and three major sales offices. Victor has grown from a small Southern company to a multinational. I'm going to make us a global firm, and that means spending some money on technology to help us get there. I think that we can install some systems and use the Internet to increase our market share, but we are going to have to invest. Your predecessor as VP of Finance didn't like to spend any money. That's what he thought everything was, an expense. I think he missed the part in his finance classes about *investment*."

"John, I came to work at Victor because I trust your instincts on how to run a company, but what are we supposed to do? Victor wasn't big on hiring the best people either."

"Yes, and I had to let a few of them go, though we'll try to bring some of the others up to speed with some coaching and training. That reminds me, what do the resumes look like for hiring a new Chief Information Officer. I need someone good as CIO if we're going to accomplish what I want in technology."

"There are a couple of possibilities—I'll check your schedule and invite them in to interview. But John, what are you planning to do? How much do you want to invest? I need to figure out what kind of demands you'll be placing on our capital budget."

"I wish I could tell you. I thought this consulting report might help, but all it does is paint an even more pessimistic picture of where we stand than I imagined. When we get a new CIO on board, the first order of business is going to be to start a planning effort so we can decide on where we want to be and what it takes to get us there. Then I'll be able to talk with you about the capital budget. I want to change this company, to get Victor ready for the next decade, and the first step is to get the technology in place that will let us transform this place."

ON BEING A MANAGER

The purpose of this book is to provide insights about the management of information technology to help you contribute to the success of your firm. Several experts divide

MANAGEMENT PROBLEM 1-1

Mary Allen and Carl Gordon are principals in a major consulting firm that has a significant amount of its practice in information technology. Mary and Carl spoke about the consulting business from their viewpoint. Mary began, "Consulting is not at all what I thought it would be when I started in the field ten years ago."

Carl asked, "How is it different from what you expected? Do you like it now, or are you thinking about a career change?"

She responded, "I'm not sure if like is the right word, it's just different. My vision was that we would be called in as experts, work with top management of the firm, and come up with recommendations. The client would accept our recommendations and we would work with them to implement them."

Carl laughed, "That would be great—I think maybe I had one case like that five years ago. You have to realize that clients call us in for a lot of different reasons, only some of which they tell us about. I've seen power struggles where I was hired for a job because the client's rival manager in another part of the company had a consultant. I've seen managers hire us because they heard about some solution we had for another company, and they wanted us to come up with the same solution for them."

"So why do consultants have such bad reputations?" Mary asked.

"I think it's because we do the job we think we were hired to do, and maybe that isn't what the client wanted. And a lot of the time the client wants us to succeed, but no one else in the organization really cares so they don't work with us, and sometimes they feel threatened and actually work against us."

Mary said, "Sure, but are we ever the cause of the problem?"

"Sure," Carl responded, "we make mistakes just like anyone else. It's usually not a technical mistake, but a poor recommendation because we don't really understand the entire situation. And sometimes a consultant is under pressure to get a follow-on job, so maybe they make a recommendation that is okay for the client and great for the consulting company."

How do you think managers can get the most return from a consulting engagement? How do you manage consultants and a consulting firm? What should your staff expect and how should they work with the consultants? What factors create friction in the relationship between consultant and client, and how can they be minimized?

companies into two kinds: those that know how to manage technology and use it to advantage, and those that are no longer in business. Business and the economy are never static, and the past years brought many changes including a movement toward globalization, the rise and fall of the dot-coms, and since the 1960s, the development of incredibly powerful information technology. It seems then that information technology (IT) is the most profound development shaping the business world, and that it will continue to be so for the foreseeable future.

The key to success with technology is not the technology per se, but the ability to manage it well. Management success with technology is mixed: some firms extract tremendous value from their investments in IT. In other unfortunate examples, companies fail to obtain the most basic returns from IT investments. What factor is responsible for these differences? It is virtually impossible to assign a single cause to success or failure, but observations suggest one important condition for success, even though there are no guarantees. When you visit or read about companies that seem to "get technology," who are successful in extracting value from IT, they have strong technology leadership. This leadership is not just the CIO, it includes the chief executive officer (CEO) and the chief operating officer (COO). In fact, the most successful companies have the CEO and COO leading the IT effort, with the CIO helping them to develop IT strategy and to implement the technology.

This book looks at examples of forward-thinking managers who put faith in the technology, and in the ability of their employees and company to successfully deploy it. Cisco is one of the most frequently cited examples of a company that obtained tremendous value from its investments in IT. You can say that Cisco is successful on the Internet because it sells a technology-based product, communications equipment for the Internet, to a technologically oriented customer. Certainly this set of circumstances helps, it is more important that the chairman of Cisco challenged all senior managers to figure out how their organization could transform their business with the Internet.

The view in this book is that you, the manager, can and do make the biggest difference in information technology, because it is management and not technology that determines the return on IT investments. The text is designed to help you become a successful general manager of information technology, and to provide leadership for IT in the organization. This leadership from senior managers is the critical factor in successfully transforming organizations with technology.

Managerial Decisions

Managers are involved in a wide range of decisions about technology, decisions that are vital to the success of the organization. An estimated 50 percent of capital investment in the United States goes toward information technology. Because this technology is so pervasive, managers at all levels and in all functional areas of the firm are involved with IT. Managers are challenged with decisions about:

- *Strategy.* IT and corporate strategy are closely intertwined. The manager needs a business model and a strategy that takes into account the fact that IT is a fundamental driver of modern business. The firm continues to invest in technology as it becomes an integral part of its operations.

- *Value of IT.* The various kinds of IT investments differ in their ability to show a return. It is important to understand the nature of IT value, and to develop capital budgeting for IT initiatives.

- *Investing in Infrastructure.* The organization needs a process for making IT investment decisions. How should you set priorities and allocate scarce resources to competing requests for IT investment? How do you decide whether and when to replace existing legacy systems?

- *Deciding on Applications.* Vendors have developed packaged solutions for three major activities in the organization; these packages are called Enterprise Resource Planning (ERP), customer relationship management (CRM), and knowledge management systems. Does your firm need one or all of these solutions? If so, should you purchase or develop them?

- *The Role of Knowledge.* Knowledge is one of the key resources that a firm possesses, one that may give it a competitive advantage. What is the role of knowledge in the firm? How does it help manage better and change the structure of the organization? How does technology contribute?

- *E-Business.* All business is or will become e-business. The benefits of e-commerce to consumers and producers are so great that e-commerce is or will become a component of every firm's strategy.

- *Options for Service.* A modern organization can outsource all or part of its IT operations. What are the pros and cons of outsourcing? How do you manage an outsourced relationship?

■ *Change Management.* Implementing technology is all about change. Those who are satisfied with the status quo see no reason to adopt new technology. Managing change is one of the most important and most difficult management tasks.

■ *Managing Value Nets.* The capabilities provided by modern technology encourage firms to outsource various activities to partner firms; for example, you might hire a logistics firm to operate your warehouse. You are now faced with managing and coordinating work with an outside firm instead of your own employees. How do you manage in this environment?

This book is intended to prepare the reader to participate in making these decisions. See Table 1-2. Because the best solution depends on the organization, its history, resources, employee capabilities, and IT infrastructure, no given choice will be right for all decisions. As a result, the manager has to be involved in analyzing the decision problem, identifying possible alternatives, choosing a solution, and finally implementing it. The more you know about IT and its impact, the better prepared you will be to participate in making these decisions.

TABLE 1-2   Key management decisions related to IT.

Managerial Decisions Involving IT	Nature of the Decision
Strategy	How to develop strategy and technology interact to create competitive advantage.
The value of IT	How to estimate the value of an investment in IT; how to measure return.
Investing in infrastructure	Defining what is in infrastructure; developing budgets and investment guidelines.
Deciding on applications	How does the firm allocate scarce resources among competing needs for technology initiatives?
The role of knowledge	All organizations rely on knowledge in some way to survive and flourish; how do you gather, store and disseminate that knowledge?
E-business	If all businesses will become e-businesses, how does the firm move in this direction?
Options for service	The firm can obtain IT services from a variety of places. What should it outsource?
Change management	How do you successfully manage change in the organization? Technology initiatives are undertaken in order to change and improve the status quo.
Managing value nets	Value nets are networks of organizations that exchange products and services in order to operate effectively. How do you manage in this very different kind of organization structure?

INFORMATION TECHNOLOGY IN PERSPECTIVE

We are living in revolutionary times, a revolution brought on by dramatic advances in information technology. If the steam engine, a new form of power, and mechanization created an Industrial Revolution in the nineteenth century, computers and communications equipment produced a Technology Revolution in the last half of the twentieth century. The Industrial Revolution grew out of three principle innovations: (1) the substitution of machines for human skill and effort, (2) the substitution of inanimate for animal sources of power—the steam engine—creating an unlimited source of energy, and (3) the substitution of new raw materials, especially minerals, for vegetable and animal substances (Landes, 1998). The Industrial Revolution changed the nature of work and led to dramatically higher standards of living.

In the Technology Revolution, the rapid adoption of many innovations included mainframe computers, minicomputers, personal computers, networks, the Internet and World Wide Web, assembly language, higher-level languages, spreadsheet programs, word processors, packaged programs, and Web browsers. In the Technology Revolution, companies use IT as a new source of energy for processing and accessing information. This technology helps the organization collect, store, retrieve, and apply knowledge to solve problems; IT converts the raw material of information into useable knowledge. The Technology Revolution, like the Industrial Revolution, changed the economy as it creates new industries and ways of doing business.

Some call the computer "the machine that changed the world." Through computers, information technology has and will continue to revolutionize management. The contributions of IT include the following:

- Provides new ways to design organizations and new organization structures.
- Creates new relationships between customers and suppliers who electronically link themselves together.
- Presents the opportunity for electronic commerce, which reduces purchasing cycle times, increases the exposure of suppliers to customers, and creates greater convenience for buyers.
- Enables tremendous efficiencies in production and service industries through electronic data interchange to facilitate just-in-time production.
- Changes the basis of competition and industry structure, for example, in the airline and securities industries.
- Provides mechanisms through groupware for coordinating work and creating a knowledge base of organizational intelligence.
- Makes it possible for the organization to capture the knowledge of its employees and provide access to it throughout the organization.
- Contributes to the productivity and flexibility of knowledge workers.
- Provides the manager with electronic alternatives to face-to-face communications and supervision.
- Provides developing countries with opportunities to compete with the industrialized nations.

A major objective of this text is to communicate the excitement and opportunities provided by this revolution in information technology.

TRANSFORMING ORGANIZATIONS

How is technology changing organizations? One impact of IT is the use of information technology to develop new organizational structures. The organization that is most likely to result from the use of these variables is the T-Form or Technology-Form organization, an organization that uses IT to become highly efficient and effective (Lucas, 1996). Figure 1-1 presents the characteristics of a technology-enabled organization.

The firm has a flat structure made possible by using e-mail and groupware (programs that help coordinate people with a common task to perform) to increase the span of control and reduce managerial hierarchy. Employees coordinate their work with the help of electronic communications and linkages. Supervision of employees is based on trust because it involves fewer face-to-face encounters with subordinates and colleagues than in yesterday's organization. Managers delegate tasks and decision making to lower levels of management, and information systems make data available at the level of management where it is needed to make decisions. In this way, the organization provides a fast response to competitors and customers. Some members of the organization primarily work remotely without having a permanent office assigned.

FIGURE 1-1 The T-Form organization.

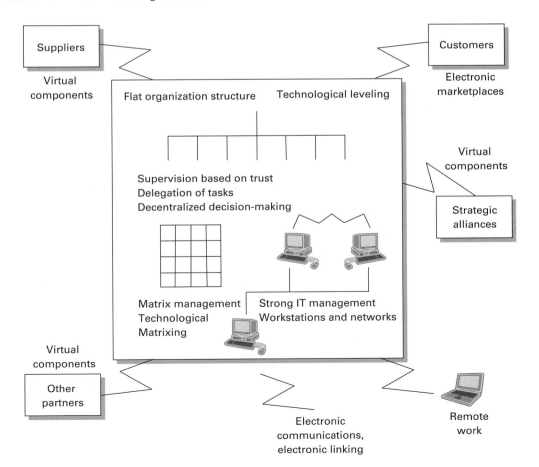

MANAGEMENT PROBLEM 1-2

One of the most important, ongoing tasks in the organization is planning and preparing for management succession. The publicity is often on the CEO and the board of directors who are supposed to worry about who can take over the top job in the company if the CEO were to leave suddenly or become incapacitated. But the job of planning managerial succession cannot stop at the CEO and board level. In a well-run company, a succession plan will be articulated for every managerial position. Each manager should be able to answer the question, "Who in your organization could take your place if you were no longer here?"

Naming a successor is only part of the answer. A successor needs to be groomed for a new position, and one of a manager's responsibilities is the advancement of his or her staff. A good manager will see that subordinates learn about more than their own jobs so that they can fill other roles, including the manager's own position, should the need arise. So a manager manages people and work, but a manager also is responsible for career development for the people who work for her or him.

Given the increasing importance of information technology in all aspects of operating a modern corporation, what kind of development should a manager provide for staff? What skills with respect to technology does a manager need? How much do the needed skills depend on your management level and the functional area in which you work? How can a manager best prepare for management succession?

The company's technological infrastructure features networks of computers. Individual client workstations connect over a network to larger computers that act as servers. The organization has an internal intranet, and internal client computers are connected to the Internet so members of the firm can link to customers, suppliers, and others with whom they need to interact. They can also access the huge repository of information contained on the Internet and the firm's own intranet.

Technology-enabled firms feature highly automated production and electronic information handling to minimize the use of paper, and they rely extensively on images and optical data storage. Technology is used to give workers jobs that are as complete as possible. In the office, T-Form companies convert assembly line operations for processing documents to a series of tasks that one individual or a small group can perform from a workstation. The firm also adopts and uses electronic agents, a kind of software robot, to perform a variety of tasks over networks.

These organizations use communications technology to form temporary task forces focused on a specific project. Technology like e-mail and groupware facilitate the work of these task forces. These temporary workgroups may include employees of customers, suppliers, and partner corporations; they form a virtual team that meets electronically to work on a project.

The organization is linked extensively with customers and suppliers. Numerous electronic customer/supplier relationships provide linkages to increase responsiveness, improve accuracy, reduce cycle times, and reduce the amount of overhead when firms do business with each other. Suppliers access customer computers directly to learn of their needs for materials, and then deliver raw materials and assemblies to the proper location just as they are needed. Customers pay many suppliers as the customer consumes materials, dispensing with invoices and other documents associated with a purchase transaction.

The close electronic linking of companies doing business together creates virtual components where traditional parts of the organization appear to exist, but in reality exist in a novel or unusual manner. For example, manufacturing firms are unlikely to maintain or store the traditional inventory of raw materials and subassemblies. This virtual inventory actually exists at suppliers' locations. Possibly the subassemblies will not exist at all; suppliers will build them just in time to provide them to the customer. From the customer's standpoint, however, it appears that all needed components are in inventory because suppliers are reliable partners in the production process.

This model of a technology-enabled firm shows the extent to which managers can apply IT to transforming the organization. The firms that succeed in the turbulent environment of the twenty-first century will take advantage of information technology to create innovative organizational structures. They will use IT to develop highly competitive products and services and will be connected in a network with their customers and suppliers. The purpose of this book is to prepare you to manage in this technologically sophisticated environment of intense global competition.

THE CHALLENGE OF CHANGE

A major feature of information technology is the change that IT brings. Those who speak of a revolution from technology are really talking about change. Business and economic conditions change all the time; a revolution is a discontinuity, an abrupt and dramatic series of changes in the natural evolution of economies. In the early days of technology, change was gradual and often not particularly significant. The advent of personal computers accelerated the pace of change, and when the Internet became available for profit-making activities in the mid 1990s, change became exponential and revolutionary. To a great extent, your study of information technology is a study of change.

In what way can and does technology change the world around us? The impact of IT is broad and diverse; some of the changes it brings are profound. Information technology has demonstrated an ability to change or create the following:

- Within organizations
  - Creates new procedures, workflows, workgroups, the knowledge base, products and services, and communications.
- Organization structure
  - Facilitates new reporting relationships, increased spans of control, local decision rights, supervision, divisionalization, geographic scope, and "virtual" organizations.
- Interorganizational relations
  - Creates new customer-supplier relations, partnerships, and alliances.
- The economy
  - Alters the nature of markets through electronic commerce, disintermediation, new forms of marketing and advertising, partnerships and alliances, the cost of transactions, and modes of governance in customer-supplier relationships.
- Education
  - Enhances "on campus" education through videoconferencing, e-mail, electronic meetings, groupware, and electronic guest lectures.
  - Facilitates distance learning through e-mail, groupware, and videoconferencing.

  ▦ Provides access to vast amounts of reference material; facilitates collaborative projects independent of time zones and distance.

■ National development

  ▦ Provides small companies with international presence and facilitates commerce.

  ▦ Makes large amounts of information available, perhaps to the concern of certain governments.

  ▦ Presents opportunities to improve education.

SIX IMPORTANT TRENDS

In the past few years, six major trends drastically altered the way organizations use technology. These trends make it imperative that a manager become familiar with both the use of technology and how to control it in the organization. These trends, discussed further in later chapters, are as follows (see Table 1-3):

1. *The use of technology to transform the organization.* The cumulative effect of the technology firms are installing is to transform the organization and allow new types of organizational structures. Sometimes the transformation occurs slowly as one unit in an organization begins to use groupware. In other cases the firm is totally different after the application of technology. This ability of information technology to transform organizations is one of the most powerful tools available to a manager today

2. *The use of information-processing technology as a part of corporate strategy.* Firms such as Cisco are implementing information systems that give them an edge on the competition. Cisco uses the technology to provide excellent customer service while keeping its own costs low. Customers at Cisco enter more than 90 percent of their orders online; Cisco automatically routes these orders electronically to contract electronics manufacturers who build its equipment. Networks are an integral part of the way the firm operates and coordinates with customers and suppliers. Organizations that prosper in the coming years will be managed by individuals who are able to develop creative, strategic applications of the technology as Cisco has done.

TABLE 1-3 Important trends in IT and IT management.

Six Important Trends
1. The use of information technology to transform organizations
2. Technology as a part of corporate strategy
3. IT as a pervasive part of the work environment
4. The use of technology to support knowledge workers
5. The evolution of the computer from a computational device to a communications medium
6. The tremendous growth of the Internet and the Web

The Netcentric Organization

Firms that take advantage of all the opportunities that information technology have to offer look quite different from traditional firms; computers, databases, and telecommunications define a "Netcentric" firm. This firm is involved in multiple networks including networks that are both technical and organizational in nature. The following figure depicts how one version of a Netcentric firm might look.

IT networks involve connecting various kinds of computers together via communications lines or a wireless technology such as radio frequency or satellite communications. The Internet is the network that most of us know best, but the Internet is actually a network of networks, thousands of individual networks that the Internet connects to each other. Your university has a large network that spans the campus, connecting computers in different buildings to each other and to the Internet. Most businesses have similar kinds of networks that facilitate the sharing of data and programs.

One of the most important contributions of computer networks is the opportunity they provide for communications. Firms can send data to each other, for examples, an order for a product, a shipping notice that the product is on the way, and so on. Employees send messages within the firm and to individuals at other firms over these same communications networks.

This technology communications infrastructure creates two kinds of organizational networks. The first is the network within the firm that lets managers create "virtual" teams and task forces and virtual departments. Virtual teams do not have to be in the same location, and members of the team may never meet in person. Because the computer network makes it so easy to communicate through voice and video, employees can work on the same project when separated by great physical distances that place them in different time zones. In this way, the internal structure of the organization becomes more dynamic and fluid,

(Continues)

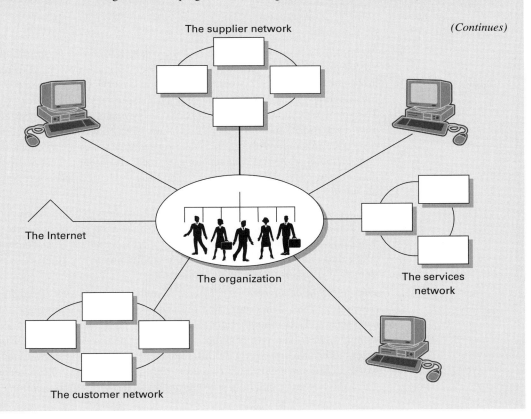

The supplier network

The Internet

The organization

The services network

The customer network

SIDE BAR 1-1 *(CONTINUED)*

allowing employees within the firm to form an internal organizational network.

Similarly, the computer network encourages the firm to communicate electronically with suppliers, customers, and service organizations, such as a law firm or a bank. These various partners form a second organizational network, and it is likely that they are connected to each other as well as to the focal firm in the diagram. Each organization is a member, then, of many logical networks of firms, and the composition of the network changes as one firm drops off and another joins a network. In this manner the network is constantly reorganizing itself.

In addition to improving the communications between the focal firm in the figure and its partner firms, the close relationship that develops among networked firms can influence the business model of the focal firm. Managers in a firm may decide to eliminate some of the functions that a traditional firm might perform, and turn these operations over to a partner firm. This approach is sometimes described as forming an

alliance with another firm or outsourcing an activity to it. The alliance is an ongoing operational one and must be carefully managed.

A good example of this use of networks is a company that sells a product, but relies on partner firms to do all of its manufacturing. The focal firm receives orders electronically from customers, checks that the order is correct, and routes it electronically to a contract manufacturer. The contractor builds the product, ships it to the customer directly, and sends an electronic notice to the focal firm. This firm then bills the customer electronically and receives an electronic payment. Similarly, the contract manufacturer bills the focal firm over the network, and it pays electronically.

The Netcentric organization takes many different forms. The one aspect that is common among such firms is the pervasive presence of computer networks that facilitate the creation of organizational networks, networks that have the potential to dramatically improve the efficiency and effectiveness of the firm.

3. *Technology as a pervasive part of the work environment.* From the largest corporations to the smallest business, we find technology is used to reduce labor, improve quality, provide better customer service, or change the way the firm operates. Factories use technology to design parts and control production. The small auto repair shop uses a packaged personal computer system to prepare work orders and bills for its customers. The body shop uses a computer-controlled machine with lasers to take measurements so it can check the alignment of automobile suspensions, frames, and bodies. This text provides many examples of how technology is applied to change and improve the way we work.

4. *The use of technology to support knowledge workers.* The personal computer has tremendous appeal. It is easy to use and has a variety of powerful software programs available that can dramatically increase the user's productivity. When connected to a network within the organization and to the Internet, it provides a tremendous tool for knowledge workers.

5. *The evolution of the computer from a computational device to a medium for communications.* Computers first replaced punched card equipment and were used for purely computational tasks. From the large, centralized computers, the technology evolved into desktop, personal computers. When users wanted access to information stored in different locations, companies developed networks to link terminals and computers to other computers. These networks grew and became a medium for internal and external communications with

other organizations. For many workers today, the communications aspects of computers are more important than their computational capabilities.

6.   *The growth of the Internet and World Wide Web.* The Internet offers a tremendous amount of information online, information that you can search from your computer. Networks link people and organizations together, greatly speeding up the process of communications. The Internet makes expertise available regardless of time and distance, and provides access to information at any location connected to the Net. Companies can expand their geographic scope electronically without having to open branch offices. The Internet leads naturally to electronic commerce, creating new ways to market, contract for and complete transactions.

What do all these trends mean for the management student? The manager must be a competent user of computers and the Internet, and learn to manage information technology. He or she must have a vision for IT in the firm, and develop a strategy for technology to help the firm execute its overall strategy to compete. You will have to recognize opportunities to apply technology and then manage the implementation of the new technology. As we shall see, senior management of the firm is responsible for the contribution IT makes and its overall success in the organization.

A PREVIEW OF THE BOOK

Modern information technology is pervasive in the organization and the economy, so a book about managing IT needs to address many different topics, including the following:

■   The use of technology to design and structure the organization.

■   The firm's use of the Internet to improve business and organizational processes.

■   The creation of alliances and partnerships that include electronic linkages. In a growing trend, companies connect with their customers and suppliers to create networks, or "value nets."

■   The selection of systems to support different kinds of workers. Stock brokers, traders, and others use sophisticated computer-based workstations in performing their jobs. Choosing a vendor, designing the system, and implementing it are major challenges for management.

■   The adoption of groupware or group decision support systems for workers who share a common task. In many firms, the records of shared materials constitute one type of knowledge base for the corporation.

■   Routine transactions processing systems, especially Enterprise Resource Planning applications, or ERP. These applications handle the basic business transactions, for example, the order cycle from receiving a purchase order through shipping goods, invoicing, and receipt of payment. These routine systems must function for the firm to continue in business. More often today managers are eliminating physical documents in transactions processing and substituting electronic transmission over networks.

■   Personal support systems. Managers in a variety of positions use personal computers and networks to support their work.

- Reporting and control. Managers have traditionally been concerned with controlling the organization and reporting results to management, shareholders, and the public. The information needed for reporting and control is contained in one or more databases on an internal computer network. Many reports are filed with the government and can be accessed through the Internet and the World Wide Web, including many 10K filings and other SEC–required corporate reports.

- Automated production processes. One of the keys to competitive manufacturing is increasing efficiency and quality through automation. Similar improvements can be found in the services sector through technologies like image processing, optical storage, and workflow processing in which paper is replaced by electronic images shared by staff members using networked workstations.

- Embedded products. Increasingly, products contain embedded intelligence. A modern automobile may contain six or more computers on chips, for example, to control the engine, the climate, compute statistics, and manage an antilock brake and traction control system. Washing machines today contain more logic than the first computers!

The book is divided into four sections. The first deals with issues in the management of the technology, while the second is focused on key management decisions about IT. How does the firm evaluate proposed investments in information technology? How do you choose among alternatives for investment? What is the real value from investing in IT? The third section of the book presents some of the key applications of IT with particular emphasis on how each application can provide value to the organization. The last section of the book looks at the implications of haves and have nots in technology, and some ethical challenges of IT. The three major themes of the text are how one makes decisions about IT, how to manage IT given these decisions, and where one finds value from information technology.

CHAPTER SUMMARY

1. Information technology is responsible for a revolution that will equal or exceed the impact of the Industrial Revolution on business.

2. Managers, no matter what their primary functional interest, marketing, finance, production, or human relations make decisions about technology.

3. Firms that succeed in the twenty-first century will use technology to create their structure, to manage themselves, to market goods and services, and to communicate with a variety of external organizations.

4. You will use the Internet routinely and encounter networks of computers within companies connecting a variety of organizations.

5. Managers are responsible for finding creative, strategic uses of information technology, applications that will give them an edge over the competition.

6. You will face a number of challenges in managing the technology and in seeing that the firm obtains a return from its investments in IT. In all these efforts, you will be using technology to bring change to the organization, its employees, customers, suppliers, and its marketplace.

KEYWORDS

Application	Integration	Strategy
Communications	Internet	System
Computer	Interpretation	T-Form organization
Data	Investment in IT	Technology infrastructure
Decision making	Network	User
Implementation	Output	Value
Information	Processing	
Information technology (IT)	Program	

RECOMMENDED READINGS

Applegate, L., Austin, R., and McFarlan, F. W. 1999. *Corporate Information Strategy and Management,* 6th ed. Homewood, IL.: Irwin-McGraw-Hill. (An excellent discussion of the issues managers face in dealing with the technology.)

Chan, Y. E. 2002. Why haven't we mastered alignment? The importance of the informal organizational structure. *MIS Quarterly Executive, 1*(2), 97–112. (The author discusses how senior managers align IT strategy with organizational strategy through informal structures.)

Cooper, B. L., Watson, H. J., Wixom, B. H., and Goodhue, D. L. 2000. Data warehousing supports corporate strategy at First American Corporation. *MIS Quarterly, 24*(4), 547–567. (A detailed case study of how a technology implementation led to organizational transformation.)

Landes, D. 1998. *The Wealth and Poverty of Nations: Why Some Are So Rich and Some So Poor.* New York: W.W. Norton. (The author believes nations that strive for high levels of education, gender equality, and that embrace technology create the highest standards of living.)

Litan, R., and Rivlin, A. (eds). 2001. *The Economic Payoff from the Internet Revolution.* Washington DC: Brookings Institution Press. (An interesting study attempting to determine the contribution of the Internet to economic growth.)

Randall, D., et al. 1999. Banking on the old technology: Understanding the organizational context of "legacy" issues. *Communications of the AIS, 2, 8.*

DISCUSSION QUESTIONS

1. What factors are responsible for the explosion of information technology that has occurred over the past several decades?

2. What role does the manager play in the management of information technology?

3. Why does the introduction of information technology in an organization create special challenges?

4. What are the characteristics of a technologically enabled organization?

5. What is the difference between using technology for computations and for communications?

6. Can you think of definitions of information systems other than the one presented in this chapter? What are the advantages and disadvantages of these definitions compared with the one provided?

7. Why is information often interpreted in different ways? Can you think of examples in which the same information is interpreted in different ways by different individuals?

8. What is the value of information? How would you try to assess the value of information to a decision maker?

9. What different types of information exist? Develop categories for describing or classifying information, for example, timeliness and accuracy. Develop an example or two of information that would fall into each category.

10. Why has Cisco been used as an example of the successful deployment of technology?

11. How would you define successful change? How would you measure it?

12. Describe an example in which the failure of an information system led to a major disaster. What can we learn from such a catastrophe?

13. To what extent do organizations now depend on the success of information technology to stay in business?

14. What factors would you consider if you were placed on a design team to develop a new information system? What would be your major concern about the project?

15. What are the pros and cons of not providing workers, such as those on the salesforce, with a physical office, but instead equipping them with information technology for communications purposes, for example, notebook computers and Internet connectivity?

16. What is the major flaw in the consulting report John Roberts at Victor Electronics received?

17. Why does Roberts want to make major changes in IT at Victor? What factors do you think led to the situation he found at Victor?

CHAPTER 2

A DYNAMIC MODEL OF IT STRATEGY IN A NETCENTRIC ECONOMY[1]

A Manager's Perspective

The late professor Herbert Simon, a Nobel Laureate from Carnegie-Mellon University, observed that programmed activities drive out the nonprogrammed. Programmed activities represent routine; for a manager, routine is answering e-mails, writing memos, reviewing performance, and spending time on the telephone. Many managers would say they spend a lot of time "fighting fires," trying to solve an immediate crisis. When a customer calls with a problem, you want to respond right away. The result of these programmed activities is that you do not have as much time for planning as you might like. Of course, every senior manager realizes that having a corporate strategy is important, but the time to develop one may be a luxury that he or she cannot afford.

In the case of strategy, time spent is not really a luxury. Developing a strategy forces managers to define their objectives and their vision for the organization. The strategy describes how to achieve those objectives. General Electric has a goal of being first or second in every market in which it competes. Each business unit must develop a strategy for how to achieve that objective. In today's world of the Internet, strategy is intertwined with information technology for just about every company. A manager needs to understand technology and strategy to be successful in a "netcentric" economy, an economy made up of networked computers and networked organizations.

VALUE PROPOSITION

The value from information technology (IT) is the ability to change the firm's strategy. IT can:

- Enable new strategies
- Provide new ways to reach customers
- Expand the markets in which the firm participates

The metrics for evaluating strategy are concerned with the overall performance of the firm and include the following:

- Market share
- Number of markets in which a firm participates
- Number of new markets
- Sales growth
- Size of the average sale
- Sales per employee

19

Thinking Strategically

What is strategy? In business, a strategy is an approach to achieving a series of objectives. In the best of circumstances, senior management has a vision for the firm, and a corporate strategy describes how the firm will achieve that vision. Various strategic business units (SBUs) formulate strategic plans that tie into the corporate plan: What does the unit have to achieve to make a contribution to the corporation? A strategy helps to focus the organization and to ensure that all SBUs and employees are working to achieve the mission of the firm. In practice, many firms do not seem to have strategies that are well known by employees. Possibly managers have a plan and do not want to reveal it for fear the competition will learn about their strategy, or it may be that management has not developed a strategy at all.

One goal is to have information technology contribute to the strategy of the firm, which means that senior IT management must be privy to the firm's strategy. This statement may sound obvious, but in many companies the senior IT manager is kept in the dark about corporate strategy.

The major change in strategy that has happened in the last decade is the fact that corporate strategy and IT strategy have become totally intertwined. A credible corporate strategy today will include IT as an integral component; this strategy will set forth the objectives of the firm for competing in the age of electronic commerce and the Internet, and how it plans to achieve these objectives.

Strategies often describe how a firm is to respond to a threat to its business model. Some examples of threats would include pharmaceuticals companies that are threatened when the patent runs out on a "blockbuster" prescription drug, one with $1 billion of sales or more, and no replacement product is in sight. General Motors faced the threat of imported cars for thirty years, and until recently, steadily lost market share. The Internet stimulated a large number of new ways to do business that threatened many existing approaches to business. Consider the industries listed in Table 2-1.

If any of these events happen to your company, it would face a strategic crisis, requiring you to formulate a new strategy to respond to the threat. The future success and even the viability of your business hangs in the balance. In the last five years, firms in all of the industries described in the preceding table faced such a strategic crisis. Only some of them found a new strategy to compete.

The Internet, the World Wide Web, electronic commerce, free markets, the stock market, venture capitalists, and the tremendous creativity of individuals in the United States and around the world created these threats along with many new opportunities. This chapter presents a model of corporate strategy that describes how the firm can take advantage of new technologies, responding both to the threats and opportunities they provide. The model is equally applicable to the Internet start-up and the traditional firm trying to cope with challenges new technology brings to its business. Firms that fail to understand how models of strategy apply to a new economy dominated by the Internet are unlikely to survive in the twenty-first century.

WHAT IS ELECTRONIC BUSINESS?

The new strategies all involve some form of electronic or e-business. An e-business recognizes that IT is a fundamental driver of success; it uses technology extensively in all of

TABLE 2-1 Industries and threats.

Industry	Threat
Stock brokerage	Someone figures out how to let the trading public and institutions bypass brokers and interact directly with the stock markets. (Merrill Lynch versus E*TRADE)
Book retailing	A competitor is able to do a brisk volume selling books without any stores. (Borders versus Amazon)
Auto manufacturer	A competitor figures out how to build a custom automobile in five days. (Toyota versus General Motors)
Grocery retailer	An innovator offers a shopping service where the customer does not have to come to a store to get groceries. (Safeway versus Giant and Peapod)
Book publisher	A technological shift eliminates the need for paper copies of your publications, and makes it possible for authors to publish without the services of a traditional publisher. *(The Wall Street Journal* versus *The Wall Street Journal Interactive Edition*, printed books versus e-books)
PC vendor	A competitor invents a supply chain that lets it receive payment from customers before assembling the computer, resulting in almost zero inventory. (IBM versus Dell)
Manufacturing company	Another company in your industry figures out how to take most of its orders without human intervention and route them automatically to companies that manufacture its products. (Lucent versus Cisco)
Music industry	A new technology is developed that potentially eliminates the need for a record label and record stores. (CDs versus MP3 versus Napster-like sites, iTunes and the iPod)

its operations. If the company has direct sales to customers, it undoubtedly features an online store and qualifies as e-commerce. A consulting firm might be an e-business, but not in e-commerce because its contacts with clients are all in person. Even though many people think of e-business and e-commerce as synonymous, they are not technically so.

Table 2-2 shows that electronic business encompasses all of the various ways a firm can use technology in strategy and operations. Electronic commerce is one aspect of electronic business, and it involves using networks, primarily the Internet, for the sale and purchase of goods and services. Individuals and firms purchase items online from vendors who have Internet stores or electronic data interchange (EDI) capabilities.

It is difficult today to avoid being bombarded by stories about electronic commerce; popular business periodicals as well as the *New York Times* print special sections on e-commerce. A casual glance at the headlines would lead one to believe that e-commerce is simply selling products and services over the Internet. However, e-commerce involves much more than a Web site and the ability to enter orders for goods or services online.

Electronic commerce consists of two broad categories: business to consumer (B2C) and business to business (B2B). The first excitement about e-commerce came from B2C; everyone can relate to buying consumer products such as books and music CDs over the Internet. This business model offers tremendous convenience for the customer who can

TABLE 2-2 E-business and e-commerce.

Nature of Business	Description	Example
Electronic business	Pervasive use of technology in the firm	E-mail, electronic conferencing, automated transactions processing, ERP, CRM, knowledge management systems, etc.
Electronic commerce		
Sell side		
To consumers (B2C)	Internet online store	Amazon.com
To other businesses (B2B)	Electronic connection vendors to customers	Wal-Mart Internet EDI with vendors
Buy side (B2B)	Business purchasing goods from suppliers online	Procurement auctions, free markets

shop from home; it is especially well-suited to commodity products such as books and music CDs that do not require an examination of the product, and the offerings from each vendor are identical. A motivated consumer can base a purchase on price and service. B2C electronic commerce should reduce consumer search costs and reduce the amount of friction in the marketplace.

The largest potential for electronic commerce is B2B, companies buying goods from their suppliers. These purchases dwarf consumer sales. For example, a consortium of automobile manufacturers established a Web site, Covisint, for purchasing a substantial portion of their supplies. General Motors and Ford buy about $80 billion and $70 billion of parts a year, respectively. One optimistic auto executive thinks Covisint could have an annual sales volume of $500 billion within three years. If the firms complete only 25 percent of their purchases on this electronic exchange, the numbers are still huge. Unfortunately, Covisint was not as successful as first predicted, probably due to the intense competition in the auto industry and the difficulty of getting manufacturers to cooperate. In 2004 FreeMarkets, a B2B firm, acquired Covisint. B2B electronic commerce has not grown as fast as expected, but its potential is immense.

Taking an order on the Internet may let a company say that it is in e-commerce, but true electronic business is more than setting up a Web site and letting a customer order products or services via the Internet. The real advantage of technology is in becoming an e-business, a fully electronic firm, integrating the Internet through all aspects of the firm's value chain. For a manufacturing company, being an e-business means that customers query a Web site for product availability and delivery schedules; behind the Web site supply chain management software consults online inventory files and a production planning system to return a promised shipping date to the customer. If the product is to be manufactured rather than shipped from inventory, the customer can use the Web site to inquire about progress.

The firm uses the Internet to market its products. For example, it might have product catalogs available on the Internet, and programs that help engineers determine how to best use its products. The firm might run auctions on the Internet to dispose of obsolete or discontinued products. The manufacturing company uses the Internet to communicate among its plants, and to interact with its suppliers. A fully electronic business uses the technology to process payments and receipts. The firm takes advantage of the option offered by technology to develop a flat organization structure, increasing the span of control and delegating more responsibility to employees.

Relatively few organizations have achieved this vision for electronic business, but it is the direction in which leading firms are moving. An electronic business is highly efficient and flexible; it is able to respond quickly to customers and to changes in market conditions. All segments of the economy are becoming more competitive making a fast response an important part of a firm's strategy.

Hypercompetition

Electronic commerce and the Internet economy stimulate much greater competition than existed in the economy in the past. A hypercompetitive economy leads to the rapid creation of new, firm-specific resources. Not only do companies generate resources and assets quickly, they find that these investments depreciate rapidly. Investments in technology are a good example: Estimates are that a personal computer depreciates at a rate of 10 percent a month.

Despite rapid obsolescence and depreciation, many firms remain rich in resources; some of these firms have large cash flows while others have the benefit of abundant venture capital and high stock prices. With these financial resources, it is easy for firms to innovate and develop new strategic assets. New start-ups and dot-com companies expect to function in a hypercompetitive economy, while some traditional firms were caught unawares by electronic commerce and the Internet economy. It is safe to say that many, if not all, firms today face a complex and frequently changing environment; they do business under conditions of hypercompetition.

Hypercompetition puts pressure on management in developing strategy and in the execution of the firm's business model. Time is critical in a hypercompetitive environment where businesses must respond quickly to competitors. It is unlikely that a firm where managers make leisurely decisions will be competitive in this setting.

The manager is interested in strategies that allow the firm to sustain a competitive advantage. In a slower-paced economy, one might consider a strategy to be a success only if it conferred a competitive advantage that lasted several years. In a hypercompetitive economy a successful strategy is one that lets you sustain a competitive advantage for a year or more.

A DYNAMIC MODEL OF COMPETITIVE ADVANTAGE

Figure 2-1 presents a dynamic resource-based model of competitive advantage for firms operating in the hypercompetitive environment of the Internet and electronic commerce. This section is an overview of the model, and the next section reviews past work on strategy that influenced its development before getting into the details of the model.

The starting point for developing strategy in Figure 2-1 is to identify the resources that give a firm a competitive advantage. In order to confer such an advantage, a resource must be rare, valuable, inimitable, and nonsubstitutable. If something is rare, it means few other available resources are like it, so it is difficult for a competitor to acquire that resource. Airline computerized reservations systems (CRS) are complex and rare; only a small number of fully featured systems exist. A competitive resource has to be valuable

FIGURE 2-1 A dynamic resource-based model of competitive advantage for the hypercompetitive, Internet economy.

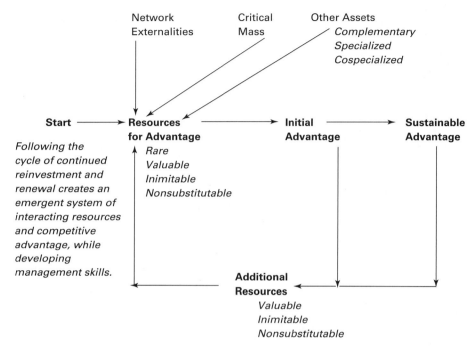

SOURCE: From *Strategies for Electronic Commerce and the Internet,* Henry C. Lucas, Jr., © 2002, The MIT Press.

as well as rare; a resource is valuable to the extent that it provides value to its owner. The CRS is extremely valuable for a number of reasons, one of which is the large, positive revenue stream it generates. A valuable resource, then, is one that enables a firm to implement strategies that increase its efficiency or effectiveness. The more expensive it is for a competitor trying to acquire a similar resource, the greater is the value of that resource.

A strategic resource also has to be inimitable or else a competitor can create a copy or near copy of it. In theory, one could develop a new computerized reservations system. However, to reach the level of the top three or four systems, given their links to the travel agencies, would be prohibitive in time and cost. Most imitations are not serious threats to industry leaders. In a similar vein, a strategic resource is nonsubstitutable—a competitor cannot easily find a similar resource to use in place of your strategic resource. In order to avoid paying booking fees, airlines developed Web-based reservations systems for just their own flights, which they promote as a substitute for the more complex computerized reservations systems that contain flight information for almost all airlines.

The model says that once the firm creates or develops a resource or bundle of resources, it can use those resources to obtain an initial advantage in the marketplace. In a highly competitive economy and in a period of rapid technological innovation, it is possible that some of these strategic resources will lose one of the characteristics that makes them strategic. For example, a technological breakthrough makes it possible for an innovator to create a substitute where one was not possible before.

MANAGEMENT PROBLEM 2-1

Martin Levinson is the CEO of U.S. Global Insurance (USGI), one of the leading insurance companies in the world. The company writes all lines of insurance, including many specialized and unique policies. For example, it might write insurance to cover the loss in revenue if a major toll bridge had to be closed because of an accident such as a ship knocking down part of the bridge. Levinson is known as a somewhat autocratic leader, and most decision making at USGI is concentrated at the top. Levinson took over the company twenty-five years ago, and has led it through years of growth to be one of the largest firms in the industry.

He was asked by a consultant about his strategy for growth and whether USGI had a strategic plan. Martin responded that of course, there was a plan, but it was only in his head. He was not going to put it on paper where a competitor might be able to get a copy.

USGI is a publicly held firm, which means that it must file a number of reports with the Securities and Exchange Commission. The performance of the company is published in quarterly reports, which announce any important news such as a merger or acquisition. The full range of information available about a public company makes it unrealistic to hide its strategy completely from competitors. The question is how difficult it is for one company to figure out another's strategy by reading annual reports and quarterly SEC filings.

Does Martin Levinson's position make any sense? Can he hope to keep USGI's strategy a secret? What problems does it create within the firm for the strategy to be in his head rather than circulated through the company? How much input do managers at USGI have in planning, and what problems does it create for them to be excluded?

A large brokerage firm such as Merrill Lynch has hundreds of offices and once employed about 17,000 financial consultants (retail stock brokers). This formidable presence represented a strategic resource for the company, giving it huge coverage in the marketplace. The Internet is a technological innovation that makes it possible for an online broker to reach everyone connected to the Net (well over 600 million people worldwide), with few brokers. Merrill's strategic resource is rapidly becoming a liability.

The model in Figure 2-1 contains a feedback loop in recognition of the fact that in today's world, it is increasingly difficult to sustain an initial advantage. A firm will most likely need to add new resources to its existing bundle of resources to build and sustain a resource-based advantage.

After a review of some other views of strategy, the discussion will return to look at additional details of the model in Figure 2-1.

Value Chains and Competitive Forces

The Internet has actually been around since 1969 when it was a Defense Department network known as the ArpaNet. University faculty and industrial researchers were the primary users of the Net; they exchanged files and electronic mail messages. The sponsorship of the Net moved to the National Science Foundation (NSF) and it became the Internet. In 1995 NSF phased out of financing the Net to concentrate its efforts on "second-generation" networking. At this point, it became possible to use the Internet for profit-making activities, something prohibited when NSF was its main sponsor. The rest is history.

The dominant force in corporate strategy in the 1980s was Michael Porter at Harvard. Although it is not correct to say that Porter's models predate the Internet, they do predate the ability to use it for profit. The years since 1995 have been exciting and tumultuous; the Net is responsible for many new businesses and new business models, the subject of a later chapter. It would be unfair to criticize strategy models because Porter developed them at a time when no one foresaw the impact of the technology. In fact, these models still have widespread applicability. Students have prepared insightful analyses of the threats to traditional businesses from the Internet using the value chain and five forces model developed by Porter nearly twenty years ago.

The Value Chain

Porter (1985) introduced the *value chain* into the vocabulary of managers. See Figure 2-2. The value chain divides activities into two types: primary and support. Primary activities are associated with the mission of the firm; they are the processes that create products and services. Inbound logistics refers to obtaining materials required for successful operations. Operations involves manufacturing or creating a service, and outbound logistics delivers the product or service to customers. Marketing and sales are included as primary activities because they are central to customer demand. Service is responsible for after-sales support of a product.

Support activities are represented by the firm's infrastructure. Human resource management is concerned with recruiting, training, and advancing the careers of people who work for the firm. Technology development is a function that includes both information technology and research and development. Technology also applies to the support of the value chain through all of its steps. Finally, procurement deals with obtaining the raw materials needed to produce a product or service.

Today, a firm might look at the distinction between primary and support activities a little differently. For example, supply chain management is concerned with procurement, inbound logistics, operations, and outbound logistics. Technology applies to all of the activities described in Figure 2-2, and the firm's infrastructure is increasingly characterized by its technology architecture.

The value chain is one way to analyze the impact of the Internet and electronic commerce on a traditional firm and to think about ways to build new business models. For years, the book retailer had a procurement department that evaluated and ordered books

FIGURE 2-2 The value chain.

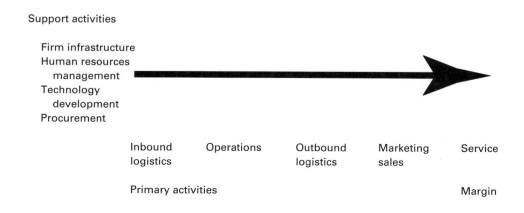

Support activities

Firm infrastructure
Human resources
   management
Technology
   development
Procurement

| Inbound logistics | Operations | Outbound logistics | Marketing sales | Service |

Primary activities

Margin

from publishers to be shipped to the retailer's warehouses. The inbound logistics operation at the warehouse involved receiving books and then placing them in the proper location for retrieval. When a store ordered or reordered a book, the warehouse removed the appropriate number of copies from the shelf and combined all requests from the store into a single shipment. Marketing and sales used various advertising media to encourage customers to visit a store and buy books.

When Amazon.com came up with a new model, it changed the value chain in several important ways. At first, it subcontracted most inbound logistics and operations, retaining only the order processing, billing, and customer service functions. By 1999, Amazon began building its own warehouses in order to have more control over logistics. The major change to the value chain, however, was the fact that Amazon.com has no physical stores as a part of its operations.

This simple change in the value chain has a profound impact on the organization and its cost structure. The firm infrastructure at Amazon is considerably smaller than a traditional retailer, as is the effort devoted to managing it. It requires far less real estate, no investment to build or remodel stores, and no store sales personnel when compared to the value chain at Borders. Human resources has fewer people to hire and train than a bricks-and-mortar bookseller, and technology development focuses on the Web site for taking orders and not on sales systems for retail stores.

Comparing value chains can highlight the differences among business models, especially models that are built around the Internet and Web. Examples in the rest of the book will show the dramatic effect that these technological innovations have had on a variety of firms' value chains.

The Five Forces Model

Porter's second contribution is the five forces model of competition. See Figure 2-3. This model describes the forces that shape a firm's competition. The forces are competitive rivalry, the threat of new entrants, the bargaining power of suppliers, the bargaining power of buyers, and the threat of substitutes.

An existing firm always faces concerns about new entrants who might take some of the market. The threat of new entrants sometimes keeps prices down; an industry with abnormal returns will attract other firms. A variety of conditions attract a new entrant. If a number of competitors are already in the market and no one firm is dominant, then entry will be easier. A single firm cannot cut prices to drive out the new entrant. If it takes relatively little investment to start a business, then entry will be encouraged. If the technology required is well known or can be easily obtained, it will be easier to enter an industry. It is relatively easy to start a garage, because the equipment to repair a car is readily available. On the other hand, it is quite difficult to start a pharmaceuticals company. Many drugs are protected by patents, so a new firm may spend years in R&D before it has a product to sell.

The Internet has done much to encourage entry. If one looks at the factors that promote new entrants, the Internet has helped many new companies get started. The technology of the Internet is described in widely published standards. Vendors make inexpensive equipment that conforms to these standards, so that assembling the technology for a Web site is inexpensive and mostly available off the shelf. In addition to the software packages

FIGURE 2-3   Porter five forces model.

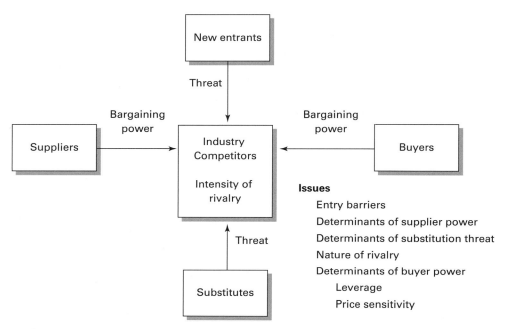

for setting up a store on the Web, a number of outsourcers can set up and manage a firm's Web site. One needs little in the way of a physical presence to start a business on the Internet. This technology raises the threat of new entrants for a variety of firms.

The bargaining power of customers also affects competition. In some situations, a customer can force a company into action it might prefer not to take. General Motors spends more than $80 billion a year on its purchases. A small company must follow GM's requirements to do business with the firm; it is the automaker who sets the terms. GM used this power to force its suppliers to adopt electronic data interchange (EDI), and is now encouraging them to move EDI functions to the Internet. A small company is at the mercy of a giant such as General Motors; in this case the buyer has almost total power over the firm, especially if the firm needs sales to GM to survive.

Sometimes suppliers also have an advantage over their customers, though it happens less often. It is most acute when few or no substitutes are available for what the supplier has to offer. Until AMD developed competitive chips, the PC industry depended almost entirely on Intel to provide hardware, and it has had to rely on Microsoft for software. Both Intel and Microsoft have tremendous bargaining power as suppliers (and probably as customers, as well).

The threat of substitutes is always present. As palladium prices increased, an electronics components manufacturer invested millions of dollars in new equipment to substitute a less noble metal for component leads. Automobile manufacturers substitute plastics and aluminum for steel. The recreational boat industry converted almost entirely from wood to fiberglass, and is in a transition to composite fibers for some parts of the vessel.

The Internet and electronic commerce affect the five forces in the model in important ways. The first impact, as described previously, is to lower entry barriers. The Internet makes it easy to start a new firm with minimal investment. The investment community was obsessed with Internet start-ups in the late 1990s, and capital was not a problem for the first movers on the Internet. The Net and electronic commerce are creating a huge number of substitutes for traditional businesses. One can trade stock without a broker, publish a book without a publisher, and record and distribute music without a record label. Internet substitutes for existing business models appear endless.

Several new business models on the Internet involve brokerage and auction services. These new types of markets change the way buyers and suppliers interact, and thus represent a new balance of power. It is safe to say that technological innovation like the Internet and electronic commerce affect all the forces in the Porter model.

Core Competence

Another important view of strategy stresses the *core competencies* of the organization (Prahalad and Hamel, 1990). The theory states that management's task is to create an organization "capable of infusing products with irresistible functionality, or better yet, create products customers need but have not yet even imagined."

Management must combine corporate-wide technologies and production skills into competencies for competition. Core competencies are the collective learning in the organization about how to integrate multiple technologies and coordinate diverse production capabilities.

Identification of a core competence involves three tests:

1. It should provide access to a wide variety of different markets.
2. It should make a significant contribution to the end product, especially the benefits the customer perceives.
3. It should be difficult to imitate.

Prahalad and Hamel argue that the best a company can hope for is to be a world leader in five or six competencies. Core competence can take years to build, and companies that fail to invest in them are not likely to enter an emerging market.

Management needs to develop a corporate strategy for organizing and deploying core competencies. This strategic architecture then acts as a road map in identifying which core competencies to build and their required technologies. One option is to outsource all of the activities that are not core (Quinn and Hilmer, 1994). Under this approach, management concentrates on just the firm's core competencies, and leaves all other activities to others. Cisco is an excellent example of a firm that follows this business model.

Managers often focus on core competence in downsizing and shedding business units. It is not clear whether these managers understand that competencies are intangible and are based on learning, knowledge, and management skills. You may have numerous core competencies in one business area and not be the number one in the market, possibly because the firm has underinvested in the business.

The resource-based model considers a core competence as a resource; later in many of the examples given, it will turn out that management skills at a business process or technology are a key resource for competitive advantage. It is interesting to note that Internet start-ups and dot-coms are developing their competencies much more quickly than

Prahalad and Hamel envisioned. Cisco converted to a major Enterprise Resource Planning software system in less than a year, and then moved aggressively to a business model based on the Web.

Resource-Based Views of Strategy

The model in Figure 2-1 is drawn from a resource-based view of competitive advantage, an approach to strategy that has been discussed for a number of years. Two of the most articulate presentations of this view may be found in papers by Barney (1991) and Peteraf (1993). The theory defines firm resources as "all assets, capabilities, organizational processes, firm attributes, information, knowledge, etc. controlled by a firm." Some authors in the field divide resources into three categories: physical, human, and capital. It should be noted that this view of competitive advantage in Figure 2-1 is based on combinations of resources, rather than a single resource that creates an advantage.

A firm has a competitive advantage when it creates a successful strategy that cannot be duplicated by a current or potential competitor. The advantage is sustained if competitors are unable to duplicate the benefits of the strategy, so it is important for resources to be immobile. Often a firm creates a bundle of resources by following some unique path, a path that it might not even understand itself. Thus, the strategy can be considered *path dependent*. If the firm with the strategic advantage cannot identify the path it followed, a competitor is likely to have trouble imitating its strategy.

Combine path dependence with the concept of *causal ambiguity*, and it can be difficult to imitate strategy. Causal ambiguity refers to the difficulty of determining cause-and-effect relationships. If a particular product or service is a success, can the firm identify all of the factors responsible? If a firm is profitable overall, can it determine the reasons for its success? Often, the answer to these questions is No or Maybe. If the firm with a successful strategy does not understand the path it followed or the cause of its success, competitors maybe equally confused in trying to imitate it.

An important consideration is that a competitive advantage from resources does not necessarily last forever. The theory states only that a resource-based advantage will not be competed away through the duplication of resources by other firms. "Revolutions" may still happen in an industry so that resources that once sustained an advantage for a firm are no longer valuable. "What were resources in a previous industry setting maybe weaknesses, or simply irrelevant in a new industry setting" (Barney, 1991, p. 103). How valuable are hundreds of branch brokerage offices today compared to pre-Internet days?

Authors call structural revolutions in an industry *Schumpeterian shocks*, after the noted Harvard economist. The Internet and Web seem to qualify as major shocks to business and the economy. Resources that once gave a firm an advantage may no longer do so; in fact some of those resources may now be liabilities.

The ability of a firm to gain a first mover advantage by implementing a strategy before its competitors depends on its ability to control resources that are not controlled by other firms. In the Internet world, obtaining such control is difficult. No one has control over understanding the technology, access to the network, or a business model, though some entrepreneurs have tried to patent aspects of e-commerce. Resource theorists discuss resource *mobility*, which can be thought of as the ease with which one can obtain a resource. If resources are highly mobile, they are easily acquired and a firm cannot obtain a strategic advantage from them. Most of the resources associated with information technology, the Internet, and the Web are highly mobile.

One characteristic of technology may help protect resources that are based on IT: complexity. If a resource is sufficiently complex, it can confer a competitive advantage because others cannot easily duplicate it. The first movers in e-commerce had to develop complex systems to provide storefronts for ordering and to connect the Web with mainframe, legacy transactions-processing systems. However, in the IT industry, vendors frequently develop software products to automate development and to hide complexity. Today one can find many ways to build a storefront, for example, by using software from several vendors, or outsourcing development and operations to EDS or IBM Global Solutions. Resource complexity in information technology may provide a short-term resource-based advantage, but it is unlikely to do so in the long run.

In summary, Barney (1991) contends that firm resource heterogeneity (difference) and resource immobility combine to make resources rare, valuable, inimitable, and nonsubstitutable. He also suggests that one cannot expect to purchase or acquire strategic resources on the open market; they must come from within the firm. In the context of the Internet and electronic commerce, then, how does the firm obtain and sustain a resource-based advantage?

THE DYNAMIC MODEL

Figure 2-1 provides a resource-based view of competitive advantage in the Internet economy. This model is dynamic and contains a feedback loop to illustrate the fact that strategy and resources are not static. The firm must constantly develop and enhance resources that have the potential to provide a sustainable advantage (Teece, Pisano, and Shuen, 1997). Particularly under today's conditions of hypercompetition and the speed with which events happen in the Internet economy, the firm must build and reconfigure resources to compete.

Several aspects to this model need further explanation in light of the preceding discussion on more general theories of resource-based advantage. In particular, ideas of network externalities, critical mass, and assets to enhance resources require an explanation. It is also important to understand the idea of lock in and switching costs, and to think of resources as a system in which new assets and resources emerge from the interaction among a firm's stock of resources.

Externalities and Critical Mass

Economists have developed a rich literature on *network externalities*; they explain the diffusion of many different kinds of products and services. Figure 2-4 depicts the idea behind network externalities: as the number of users of a product grows, the product's value to an individual increases.

If you are the only person in the world with a personal computer and e-mail program, the value of e-mail to you is pretty low, nearly zero. As a few friends buy computers and e-mail programs, and you start to exchange messages, the value of your investment in a PC and e-mail program increases, even though you have done nothing yourself to cause this increase. As thousands and then millions of people become users of e-mail, its value for you accelerates almost exponentially until it levels out when everyone you want to communicate with has e-mail capabilities.

Network externalities are important for a number of electronic commerce initiatives. An electronic hub that matches buyers and sellers of equipment becomes more valuable

FIGURE 2-4 Network externalities and critical mass.

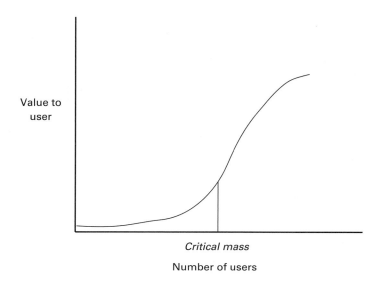

to each buyer as more sellers participate. The site is more valuable to sellers if it attracts more buyers, so both groups gain as the site grows.

Figure 2-4 also shows an estimate of a point called the *critical mass of an initiative*. This term is borrowed from nuclear physics; when a critical mass of fissionable material collects, a chain reaction begins releasing nuclear energy. In the diffusion of an innovation, a critical mass is reached when the product or service becomes so attractive that large numbers of users decide to participate. Critical mass is important because a nuclear reaction sustains itself after reaching it. For technological innovations, a critical mass means that an accelerating number of users participates with little promotion by those offering the service. Because the incremental or marginal costs of serving another customer are low on the Internet, achieving a critical mass is important to Web sites. Their business increases dramatically, but their costs do not rise in proportion.

Other Assets

Of the many different ways to look at the Internet and the Web, one is based on theories of innovation. Adding aspects of this theory to the model of Figure 2-1 provides a richer understanding of strategic advantage in an Internet economy. An economist named David Teece (1987) suggested that for an innovation to succeed, it needs additional assets, including those that are complementary, specialized, or cospecialized.

A complementary asset is different from the innovation, and helps the innovation to succeed. Teece uses the example of the name "IBM" as a complementary asset to the PC when it was introduced in 1981. Because IBM, at that time the leading computer vendor, and a vendor known for large computers, was selling a small computer for the desktop, it must be all right to buy one. In today's world, a complementary asset might be a special relationship you have with a firm that provides services. Calyx and Corolla, a nationwide

MANAGEMENT PROBLEM 2-2

Some managers like to build companies that have many unrelated businesses in order to diversify and reduce uncertainty. After all, most personal financial advisors recommend that investors should hold a diversified portfolio; you should not invest exclusively in one kind of instrument, or certainly not in one company. Many investors were hurt by bankruptcies in 2002 because their company pension plans required them to invest in their employer's stock. When the employers went bankrupt, employees lost their jobs and their pensions because of a lack of diversification.

What is good advice for an individual may not always be good advice for a corporation. Finance experts argue that a firm should not diversify into a variety of businesses precisely because an investor can.

It is more difficult for the investor to put together a diversified portfolio if a large number of conglomerates in the market have diversified already. Some management experts also question whether managers can have the skills to manage a variety of different businesses. In difficult business conditions, companies may often sell off unrelated subsidiaries in order to return to their core competencies.

What do you think the pros and cons of diversification are for managers? Would you prefer to work in a conglomerate or a highly focused company? Are managers correct in saying that they are returning to their core competencies when they sell unrelated businesses? What core competencies are they talking about?

floral distributor, worked for many months to reach an agreement with FedEx to deliver flowers overnight. FedEx became a complementary asset for Calyx and Corolla.

A specialized asset is one that the innovation must have to succeed. Alternatively, the specialized asset may depend on the innovation. A specialized asset for an e-commerce vendor is an Internet service provider (ISP). ISPs in the form of mass market communications services existed before commerce appeared on the Internet. For example, America Online (AOL), CompuServe, Prodigy, and others existed before the Internet could be used for profit-making activities. Merchants on the Internet depend on their e-customers having access to the Web, and thus portals and ISPs become specialized assets for them.

Cospecialized assets exhibit mutual dependence with an innovation. An operating system for a computer, such as Microsoft Windows 2000, and a browser, such as Internet Explorer, depend on each other. Most users of a PC want to access the Web; they need a browser for that purpose. The browser runs on a computer and interacts with an operating system, so it in turn depends on a version of Windows.

A firm may be able to use its resources to create a highly specific or specialized asset that confers a competitive advantage. Several major airlines added resources to their computerized reservations systems, expanding them to become "travel supermarkets." These specialized assets would be costly and time-consuming to recreate, even if an imitator was able to deal with their complexity.

Lock In and Switching Costs

A traditional approach to maintaining a competitive advantage is described by economists as lock in and high switching costs. If a firm offers a product or service that "locks in" customers, it may be able to sustain an advantage. By becoming a standard in the industry, Microsoft locked in a huge number of customers for its operating systems. In addition, it created Microsoft Office applications, which are highly integrated and work seamlessly with its operating systems. This kind of lock in creates high switching costs. One pays a

SIDE BAR 2-1

The New York Stock Exchange

The NYSE is a not-for-profit corporation and self-regulatory organization that, since the 1934 Securities Exchange Act, has been overseen by the Securities and Exchange Commission (SEC). The Exchange is controlled by its 353 member firms, which are the broker-dealer and specialist firms that own the NYSE's 1,366 seats. The role of the Exchange is to provide a fair and cost-effective market, which in turn encourages liquidity and attracts issuers (companies) to list their stock on the NYSE and become a Big Board, or NYSE-listed company. As of March 28, 2002, there were 2,784 listed companies with 343 billion shares and $16.3 trillion in total market capitalization. The 37,000 square foot floor accommodates about 3,000 traders, 481 of whom are specialists using their own capital to trade. The rest are floor brokers, handling orders for clients, clerks, or exchange officials.

During the past fifty years, the NYSE has faced competition for trading and company listings from a variety of sources. First, it competes with the regional exchanges for trade executions of NYSE-listed stocks. A broker may see a better price on a regional exchange and route an order there for execution. The other market for companies to list their stock is the NASDAQ Stock Market, and the NYSE faces competition for listings from the NASDAQ. In the mid-1990s, the Exchange also faced competition from electronic communications networks (ECNs), such as Instinet, and electronic markets that the SEC is allowing to become stock exchanges in their own right. While ECNs handled 45 percent of all NASDAQ trades, and 36 percent of NASDAQ shares volume in July 2002, just 1.5 percent of trading of NYSE-listing shares went through ECNs in fourth quarter of 2001.[2]

During its long history, the NYSE has developed a number of important tangible and intangible resources including:

Type	Resource	Measures
Tangible	A roster of listed firms	Number and share of all U.S. listings
Tangible	Market capacity	Maximum volume, peak load in messages per second (MPS), order turnaround

Type	Resource	Measures
Tangible	Trading infrastructure	Downtime, accuracy, error rates, order turn-around, execution quality
Intangible	Market quality	Bid-ask spread, trading volume, quotation size
Intangible	Technological innovation	Online comparison systems, off-hour trading facilities, wireless order management, 3D trading floor, e-Commerce initiatives (NYSE direct+)

- *Listings.* The NYSE has the world's leading roster of listed firms, including most of the largest and most successful U.S. corporations. These listed firms constitute a resource that is rare, valuable, and inimitable. However, it is possible to trade shares of NYSE-listed firms in other market centers. Even though firms choose to have a primary listing on the NYSE, substitute venues for trading are available. Hence, the resource does have a substitute.

- *Capacity.* The NYSE has the capacity to process large volumes of trading messages, hence to transact a substantial number of trades. Although enhanced system capacity and fast order handling are valuable, it is unlikely that they will confer a sustained competitive advantage.

- *Trading infrastructure.* The Exchange has built, using technology, a smoothly functioning trading infrastructure consisting of specialists, brokers, computer systems, communications networks, and market data reporting systems. However, NASDAQ and electronic exchanges have imitated enough of this infrastructure to be successful.

- *Market quality and fairness.* The New York Stock Exchange is generally regarded as providing a high-quality market with liquidity. However, it is possible for other exchanges to

(Continues)

SIDE BAR 2-1 *(CONTINUED)*

offer quality marketplaces, although they need to convince users of their benefits to attract trading volume away from the NYSE.

■ *Technological innovations.* The introduction of the stock ticker in 1867 marked the beginning of an increasingly important role for IT in the NYSE markets. Over the past twenty years, the NYSE focused on technological innovation that includes automatic order routing and processing, online order comparisons, wireless order management, off-hours trading facilities, and lately, Internet delivery initiatives. The NYSE's ability to develop innovative, usable, and readily adopted systems is rare, valuable, and appears to be extremely difficult to imitate, although not impossible.

Does the NYSE have any competitive advantage based on these resources? Each of the previously mentioned resources taken alone does not appear to confer a sustained competitive advantage; the combination of both tangible and intangible resources may do so. Market capacity, trading infrastructure, its roster of listed firms, market quality, and technological innovation are a system of resources from which a sustainable competitive advantage may emerge.

The New York Stock Exchange offers a convenient, efficient, and liquid market to trade the stocks of the firms in which a large number of individuals and institutions want to invest. The NYSE has long had a critical mass of buyers and sellers, and its trading infrastructure makes it easy to execute transactions on the Exchange. The established liquidity and the inertia in industry practices helps sustain the Exchange, but history shows that markets will shift to new locations when the established market becomes unattractive. This combination of resources at the NYSE is rare, valuable, and relatively inimitable and nonsubstitutable.

The components of the Exchange's IT strategy for the last eighteen years include investment in the following areas:

1. Enhancing and extending strategic resources by providing sufficient capacity for processing trade transactions.

2. Enabling efficient trade execution.

3. Providing a high-quality market for securities.

4. Reducing labor expenses and demands for costly physical space.

5. Competing effectively with new types of electronic markets.

IT at the Exchange provides for efficient trade execution and adequate trading capacity. IT also helps ensure a high-quality securities market, and reduce labor expenses and the demand for physical space. All of the Exchange's resources, when viewed as a system, enable it to compete successfully with other exchanges, especially electronic communications networks such as Island and Instinet, which announced a $508 million merger in mid-2002.

The U.S. securities industry's back-office crisis in 1969 accelerated the NYSE's computerization plans. Increased trading volumes and a paper-based settlement system forced the NYSE and other U.S. stock markets to close for trading on Wednesdays for six months through mid-1970. On these days, brokers and traders helped back-office clerks to process trades and sort out unsettled transactions. The continuing growth of trading volumes and additional listings in the 1970s led the NYSE to consider its alternatives for expanding its trading capacity. Rather than undertake costly expansion of its physical floor, the NYSE chose to invest in IT to increase the capacity of the market. The systems introduced between 1977 and 1987 enabled the Exchange to remain open for trading and to process record volumes during the October 1987 market crash.

During the 1983–1987 period, the Exchange developed a number of systems to speed transactions processing and provide adequate capacity to handle the growth in volumes and new listings. Its IT strategy was to provide enough processing capacity and systems to ensure that the market could function properly with volumes three time those of an average day.

The early projects to develop e-market capabilities at the NYSE's included the (1) Common Message Switch (CMS, 1977), the (2) Designated Order Turnaround system (DOT, 1976), which became SuperDot (November 1984), and (3) Display Book and (4) Broker Booth Support System (both in 1993). These systems are described in Table 2-3.

NYSE Major IT Investments

The Exchange's IT strategy from about 1988 to 1994 was to maintain the status quo with its major initiative being broker booth support. After 1994, the NYSE

(Continues)

SIDE BAR 2-1 *(CONTINUED)*

TABLE 2-3. NYSE major IT investments.

Category	System	Descriptions	Specific Functionality
Order Processing	Common Message Switch (CMS, 1977)	A message forwarding device that links member firms to Exchange systems	Receive/forward messages
	DOT and SuperDot (1984)	An order-processing system that receives incoming orders from member firms and routes them directly to specialist post or broker booth	Process incoming orders; assign an order reference number
			Route orders to trading posts
			Match buys and sells for the opening and report imbalances to specialists
			Provide a "circuit-breaker"
	Direct+	Direct execution of market orders up to 1,099 shares at the bid or ask price	Execute orders electronically without human intervention
			Limit size
			Allow investor to submit only one such order every thirty seconds
Broker Support	Broker Booth Support System (BBSS, 1993)	An order management system that enhances brokers' processing capability on the trading floor	Integrate many different applications, services, and functions into a single unit
			Handle booth-routed orders
			Monitor, report, and research orders
	e-Broker (1997)	A wireless handheld device that connects floor brokers to their booth and off-floor locations	Improve communication between floor brokers and booths
Specialist Support	Display Book (1993)	An electronic workstation that displays all limit orders and incoming market orders	Sort the limit orders and display them in price/time priority
			Improve the speed and efficiency of reporting executed orders

SOURCE: *NYSE FactBook,* 1997, and NYSE's Web site.

(Continues)

invested more heavily in IT as trading volume accelerated and it faced competition from the NASDAQ, which was becoming known for the IPOs of attractive new technology listings, and the ECNs. The Exchange also saw transactions rising dramatically in the buoyant capital markets and the expanding economy of the 1990s. In this period continuing to the present, the NYSE's IT strategy has been to use technology aggressively to meet competition from a number of sources as well as demands for trading capacity.

The cycle time for completing a trade decreased dramatically in the last eighteen years. SuperDot routes orders directly to the floor specialist, bypassing the floor broker and eliminating the need to communicate an order to a person who must walk to the specialist's booth. The Broker Booth Support System electronically routes complex orders to floor traders. Display Book reduces the time a specialist requires to complete a trade. In addition, the Exchange's overall IT infrastructure makes possible online trading via the Internet by providing real-time quotes, instant trade confirmations, and a short trade cycle. In 2001 the NYSE implemented the Direct+ system, which lets investors trade market orders electronically at the bid or ask price. No specialist is involved in these trades; however, investors were limited at first to 1,099 shares, and an investor can only enter an order every thirty seconds.

A NYSE system called OpenBook provides a real-time view of the aggregate limit-order volume at every bid and ask price for every NYSE-listed security (http://www.nyse.com). This proprietary data product is used by market professionals as they try to assess liquidity in a particular stock. Some 950 firms and 26 vendors who sell data currently subscribe to the system. OpenBook is a good example of a technology that extends the NYSE's network externalities. OpenBook provides important information to market participants and, by doing so, encourages them to trade on the NYSE rather than in an alternative market.

The Exchange's investments in IT over the last eighteen years prepared it to deliver on many of the promises of electronic commerce including direct access, real-time quotes, market information, and the new automated execution system just announced. Reduced trade cycle times facilitate e-commerce, while all of the Exchange's technology helps it meet the challenges of electronic markets. *The Wall Street Journal* compares the NYSE and the troubled London Stock Exchange:

The New York Exchange is one of the few international markets to survive…combining new technology with an old-time trading floor. The others, including London in 1987, have shut their trading floors in favor of computers. Since then, London has been unable to stay ahead of rivals in technology.[3]

So far, NYSE investments in information technology have allowed it to remain a leading exchange by (1) facilitating electronic trading, and (2) continually enhancing strategic resources to compete with regional exchanges, the NASDAQ, and electronic exchanges.

At the end of 2003, a scandal at the NYSE resulted in new leadership. The incoming chairman of the Exchange is investigating a move toward more trading with electronic systems than from the physical floor. It is interesting to note that the investment the NYSE made over time in its technology makes it possible for such a strategic change in direction. The NYSE already has Direct+, which allows certain trades to be conducted electronically. Now, it plans to increase the size and relax other constraints on using the system in order to compete with all electronic markets. This shift may require additional capacity, but the infrastructure is there to support this new direction.

The NYSE is an example of how an established organization applied investments in information technology to reinforce strategic assets and remain competitive over a long period of time. Even though each resource alone may not be rare, valuable, inimitable, or nonsubstitutable, the combination of those individual resources with appropriate technology can produce a system that helps an organization remain competitive. IT investments provided a modern trading infrastructure, which reduced the time for clearing and facilitated increasing trading volumes. The upgraded IT infrastructure improved the quality of the market and helped reduce bid-ask spreads. All of these outcomes continue to attract investors and listed companies to the NYSE.

SOURCE: Adapted from H. C. Lucas, Jr., W. Oh, G. Simon and B. Weber, "Information Technology and the New York Stock Exchange's Strategic Resources from 1982–1999," Working Paper, College Park: Smith School of Business, September 2002.

price for not using Office; you must convert all of the office documents you receive to your own software, something that is easy in theory, but not always easy in practice. One strategy is to use resources in such a way that you create lock in and high switching costs for customers.

Additional Resources

Competitive advantage happens in two stages: The firm first obtains an initial advantage, and then it must try to sustain that advantage. Teece (1987) describes this effort as an attempt to appropriate the value from an innovation for yourself, and speaks in terms of "regimes of appropriability." An innovation with high appropriability is one where the innovator is likely to "take" and retain the benefits. With low appropriability, someone else has a good chance of obtaining those benefits you fail to appropriate for yourself. If you have an advantage based on rare, valuable, inimitable and nonsubstitutable resources, then you should have a high regime of appropriability. One way to sustain an advantage is to protect assets (resources) so that their benefits cannot be appropriated by others.

How does one protect innovations? Traditionally companies employed patents and trade secrets to protect their innovations. Path dependence and causal ambiguity, discussed earlier in the chapter, offer only weak protection against those who seek the benefits of your labors. Do any of these strategies work in the Internet world? Unfortunately, it is difficult to obtain a patent or to protect a business model. Everything is highly visible on the Internet, and it is relatively easy to copy an innovation without infringing on a patent.

Priceline.com calls itself a "demand aggregator." It allows you to indicate how much you wish to spend on an item such as an airline ticket, and provides that demand to airlines who decide whether they are willing to sell a seat at the bid price. Until recently, the company was quite successful and was selling 50,000 airline tickets a week. Priceline received a patent on its model for bidding, and sued Microsoft to force it to stop offering a similar service.

Amazon.com is one of the largest merchants on the Internet. On its site, the company offers something called "one-click checkout." If you have previously supplied information such as shipping and billing addresses, credit card number, and so on, you can click on one button to check out. Amazon has a patent on the concept, and has sued its major rival, Barnes & Noble, to prevent it from using one-click checkout. Although an interesting attempt to protect an innovation, it is difficult to see that one-click checkout would dramatically affect each firm's competitive position.

So for most firms, the question remains, how do you sustain an initial advantage? The model in Figure 2-1 suggests that to maintain the benefits of your innovation and your business model, it is necessary to continually add resources so that you protect and enhance existing resources that are rare, valuable, inimitable, and nonsubstitutable. By continually building on resources that first provide an advantage, it is possible to sustain that advantage.

A System of Resources[4]

What the firm creates with this strategy is a system of resources that interact with each other; a few resources emerge from that system to sustain an advantage. The interaction of resources creates new assets and resources that enhance one's competitive position. Port of Singapore Authority (PSA) developed resources that interact with those provided by the Singapore government to create a highly specialized resource in the form of an automated customer-oriented transshipment port. PSA also exhibits one of the most valuable resources that can emerge from a system of resources: management skills. Port personnel have become skilled in developing operations and information technology in operating a port, something difficult for others to imitate.

The model suggests that you can obtain and sustain a competitive advantage even in the hypercompetitive world of the Internet and electronic commerce. However, to do so requires continued investment and the addition of new resources. As shown in Figure 2-1, it takes investment in technology and infrastructure, which may require the expansion of the scale and scope of operations.

Knowledge and Skills

As the organization builds its system of resources and creates assets for competitive advantage, managers gain knowledge and new skills. Consider a company such as E*TRADE. The firm's staff learned how to build a Web site for high-volume securities trading. This technology includes more than the customer's view of the site. E*TRADE routes trades to markets for execution, provides clearance and settlement, and handles customer records. The E*TRADE staff has developed knowledge about electronic trading and the skills to implement a trading system. Management knowledge and skills emerge as an important resource in their own right because they are difficult for a competitor to acquire.

Recognition of the importance of knowledge and skills in obtaining and sustaining a competitive advantage continues to grow (Conner and Prahalad, 1996). This view is in many ways an extension of the idea of core competence, which was introduced as "collective learning" about how to integrate multiple technological and production capabilities. In a significant number of companies, the knowledge and skill that emerge from building resources for advantage turn out to be key resources themselves.

CHAPTER SUMMARY

This chapter introduced a dynamic resource-based model of competitive advantage in the Internet economy. In Figure 2-1, the firm begins by creating resources that are rare, valuable, inimitable, and nonsubstitutable. Network externalities may contribute to creating resources with these characteristics, especially after a product or service achieves critical mass in the marketplace. The innovative firm may also find that complementary, specialized, or cospecialized assets are required to be successful. Path dependence and causal ambiguity can help to confuse competitors, though innovations that make use of the Internet are hard to hide and to protect.

The objective of the firm is to create an initial advantage, sustain that advantage, and to appropriate the benefits from its innovative activities. The model is dynamic because of its feedback loop: It is unlikely that gaining an initial advantage in the Internet economy will lead to a sustained advantage. Instead, the firm must continue to add additional resources to create a system, a system of interacting resources. From this system and its interactions

emerge enough resources that are rare, valuable, inimitable, and nonsubstitutable to sustain an advantage. This cycle continues in a never-ending loop if the firm is successful. The model suggests a way for you to formulate and analyze competitive strategy in the hypercompetitive Internet economy.

A firm cannot succeed with a strategy alone. Management must first devise a business model, and today, most business models feature the use of the Internet in some way, along with electronic commerce. The next step is to develop a strategy, hopefully with the help of the model presented in this chapter. You also need to develop an appropriate organization structure to facilitate your business model and to realize the firm's strategy.

The final step is to execute your business model and strategy. While all of this happens, you must respond to changes in the economy, environment, and the technology, and of course, to the actions your competitors take. Executing the business model is a complex challenge; it requires highly capable managers who demonstrate leadership and motivate employees. Ideas and recommendations can come from a variety of sources, but success depends on skilled managers as well as effective business models, strategy, and the right organization structure.

KEYWORDS

Appropriability	Electronic commerce	Rare
B2B	First mover advantage	Resource
B2C	Five forces model	Resource-based advantage
Bargaining power	Fulfillment	Specialized assets
Causal ambiguity	Hypercompetition	Substitutable
Competitive advantage	Inimitable	Sustained advantage
Complimentary assets	Lock in	Switching costs
Core competence	Network externalities	System of resources
Cospecialized asset	New entrant	Threats
Critical mass	Nonsubstitutable	Value chain
Dynamic strategy	Path dependent	Valuable

RECOMMENDED READINGS

Chesbrough, H. W., and Teece, D. J. 2002. Organizing for innovation: When is virtual virtuous? *Harvard Business Review*, *80*(8), pp. 127–135.

Hagel III, J., and Brown, J. S. 2001. Your next IT strategy. *Harvard Business Review*, *79*(9), pp. 105–113.

Mukhopadhyay, T., and Kekre, S. 2002. Strategic and Operational Benefits of Electronic Integration in B2B Procurement Processes. *Management Science, 48*(10), October, pp. 1301–1313. (An empirical study that provides evidence on the benefits from e-commerce.)

Prahalad, C. K.,, and Krishnan, M. S. 2002. The dynamic synchronization of strategy and information technology. *Sloan Management Review*, *43*(4), pp. 24–33.

Shapiro, C., and Varian, H. R. 199a. *Information Rules: A Strategic Guide to the Network Economy*. Boston, MA: Harvard Business School Press.

Weill, P., Subramani, M., and Broadbent, M. 2002. Building IT infrastructure for strategic agility. *Sloan Management Review*, *44*(1), pp. 57–65.

DISCUSSION QUESTIONS

1. Define *strategy*. What does *strategy* mean in a business setting?

2. What should management develop before trying to create a business strategy?

3. What are the advantages and disadvantages of making the firm's strategy known throughout the company?

4. Describe the major components of the dynamic strategy model presented in this chapter?

5. What are network externalities? Give an example. Why are network externalities important for new business ventures, especially those on the Internet?

6. What is critical mass in the model? Why is critical mass important for new business ventures, especially those on the Internet?

7. What is a value chain? How does the Internet change the traditional value chain for a manufacturing firm?

8. Describe Porter's five forces model. What is the impact of the Internet and electronic commerce on the forces in the model?

9. How does the Internet change barriers to entry for new businesses?

10. What are regimes of appropriability? Do IT innovations have a high or low regime of appropriability? Why?

11. Describe how a system of resources might interact to produce a new resource that is rare, valuable, inimitable, and nonsubstitutable.

12. Why does the model in Figure 2-1 stress the need for continued investment in IT?

13. Given the intense competition on the Internet and the low barriers to entry for Internet business initiatives, would you ever advise a firm not to compete with technology? Why or why not?

14. How does organization structure interact with a firm's strategy?

15. What is the role of a business model in developing corporate strategy?

16. What is a core competence? How is core competence related to the resource-based model of strategy?

17. How can knowledge be a firm resource? How can one take advantage of this resource?

18. How can a firm take maximum advantage of the Internet and what it has to offer? What would a Web-enabled firm look like? What kind of structure might it have and how would it look to customers and suppliers?

ENDNOTES

1. Condensed discussion of IT and strategy and figures from *Strategies for Electronic Commerce and the Internet*, Henry C. Lucas, Jr., © 2002 The MIT Press.

2. Nasdaq.com, and "Equity Trading Market Share Quarterly," Salomon Smith Barney, February 8, 2002.

3. I am indebted to Professor Ron Weber of the University of Queensland, Australia, for his insights about systems of resources and new resources that emerge from them.

4. *The Wall Street Journal,* November 2, 2000, p. C1.

CHAPTER 3

NEW BUSINESS MODELS[1]

A Manager's Perspective

The term business model became popular during the dot-com craze as entrepreneurs and venture capitalists tried to convince the world that they were doing something entirely new and different on the Internet. Despite this heritage, the idea of a business model is helpful in understanding a firm and what it does. One part of a business model is the firm's revenue model: how it plans to generate revenue to cover its costs and make a profit. During the heady days of the dot-com run-up, investors did not seem concerned at all that new enterprises were giving away services and seemingly had no concrete idea of where they would find revenue. A number of dot-coms said their funds would come from advertising because so many people would be visiting their sites. When looking at a new business opportunity, be sure to ask what the business and revenue models are!

VALUE PROPOSITION

Technology makes it possible to develop new business models or to expand an existing model. The value of the technology includes the following:

- New business models
- Extensions to existing models
- The possibility of serving new customers
- The potential for entering new markets
- Sales growth

You can measure the impact of IT on business models by evaluating the following:

- Market share
- Number and type of new markets the firm has entered
- Sales growth
- Size of the average sale
- Sales per employee

When Business Conditions Change

In May 2001, domestic passenger traffic at the nation's five largest airlines fell 10 percent compared to levels in May 2000; at the same time traffic at the five largest discount air carriers increased 11 percent. Much of the airline industry's distress was blamed on the tragedy of September 11. However it may be the case that the business model of the major air carriers in the United States no longer works. Traditional carriers have evolved a business model with high fixed costs; most of them have built expensive hub-and-spoke route systems. Their problems are compounded by expensive labor contracts and labor costs that run about 40 percent of revenue, a figure that can be compared to 25 to 30 percent at discount airlines. These discount airlines now provide about 20 percent of U.S. airline capacity.

The familiar hub-and-spoke system, which has developed since the late 1970s, feeds passengers from smaller markets into larger ones where the airline operates a number of flights between hubs. The original hub-and-spoke model featured waves of airplanes, up to forty or fifty, arriving at hub airports within twenty minutes of each other. Passengers move quickly to connecting flights, and the planes all leave again in a small window of time. Ground crews have nothing to do until the next wave arrives. This operation requires a large number of gates and big ground crews to handle the peaks when a wave of planes arrives and leaves again.

What kind of revenue model do the major airlines have in place to support this operation? This costly system depends on business travelers who are willing to pay high fares to travel with little advanced notice. The airlines discount seats not demanded for business travel according to complicated formulas that are designed to maximize the revenue from each flight.

Three major trends have put the major carriers' business model in jeopardy. The first is the growth of low-cost airlines such as Southwest and JetBlue. The second trend is a reluctance by corporations and individual business travelers to pay the high fares of the major carriers compared to the fares of the discount airlines. Unrestricted tickets aimed at business travelers are, on the average, four times more expensive than leisure fares. Finally, the Internet makes it possible for travelers to easily search for and compare fares for a given destination for all airlines that offer service in that market. Web sites such as Travelocity and Expedia search for flights between two cities and display the lowest-cost itineraries. Even though all travel sites do not include the discount carriers, these carriers have their own Web sites and sell a significant number of their tickets through them. As a result, in a few minutes a traveler can search for and compare fares across a number of different airlines.[2] All of these changes are being noticed by corporate travel offices; McDonald's has switched its business from Carlson Wagonlit, a traditional travel agency, to Orbitz, a Web agent. Most McDonald's employees now have to make their flight and hotel reservations online.[3]

The major carriers are trying to revise the original hub-and-spoke model. USAirways filed for bankruptcy in July 2002 to gain relief from creditors and to restructure its approach to operating an airline. Shortly thereafter, American, the largest U.S. carrier, announced a major change in its hub-and-spoke system along with 7,000 layoffs. The focus at American is now efficiency rather than revenue. American will drastically reduce first class service, and phase out several models of airplane to reduce maintenance and training costs. The major operating change is to smooth the flow of aircraft at major hubs to eliminate the "waves of planes" approach. Passengers will have longer to wait for connecting flights, but American will be able to utilize gates and personnel much more efficiently by eliminating peaks. Preliminary estimates are that American can offer the same service with seventeen fewer aircraft.

It is an interesting footnote that the airline credits the Internet with bringing about some of these changes. The airline reservations systems list flights according to elapsed time, while Web sites selling tickets generally list flights by price. American is changing its operations to match the emphasis of the Web sites that sell tickets.[4] However, it is still at a major price disadvantage compared to the discount airlines that rely predominantly on the Internet for ticket sales. It is estimated that conventional ways of selling tickets, through their own agents, airline computerized reservations systems, or travel agents costs $15 to $20 per passenger. Tickets booked through the Web site of a newly starting low-fare airline will cost it $0.50 each to process.[5]

The airline story presents different business models: one model aimed at price discrimination between business and leisure travelers, and the other a consistent low-cost model for all travelers. (American is trying a new model between these two.) The differences between these models are profound and permeate all aspects of an airline's operations and marketing. Companies structure their organization and operations following their business model. Consider the stark differences in the operations and structure of the traditional versus discount airlines just described. This chapter discusses different kinds of business models with a particular emphasis on the kind of model necessary for organizations to take advantage of the opportunities offered by information technology.

NEW BUSINESS MODELS

A business model is a description of how an organization functions, a general template that describes its major activities. It identifies the firm's customers and the products and services it offers them. In what markets does the firm compete? A model also provides information about how the firm is organized and how it generates revenues and profits. What are its key business processes? Business models combine with strategy to guide major decisions at a firm. The business model describes products and services, customers markets, and business processes, while strategy is concerned with how to achieve the objectives of the business model.

Your business model might be to create a site on the Internet for people to use buying and selling houses, and your goal is to exceed the business of a competitive site operated by traditional realtors. Your strategy describes how you will execute your business model to achieve the goal of a larger market share than the traditional realtors' site. Following the advice in Chapter 2, you would develop a strategy by looking at existing resources and determining what added resources would help you compete. You then follow the dynamics of the model in Figure 2-1.

The dominant business model before the Internet was a manufacturing or services company that sold its product/service to customers. The company had a physical location, its own employees, and used information technology in a variety of ways to make internal operations more efficient. A few leading companies soon figured out how to obtain an advantage from IT and actually used technology to generate revenue. Organizations that were most effective in using technology created networks to link themselves with their customers and suppliers, making it easier to do business with them.

The Internet and the World Wide Web stimulated a torrent of creativity; the technology enabled a number of new business models. Some firms changed their existing model to adapt to this new technology. Other organizations seemed confused by these changes and unable to cope with them. Entrepreneurs on the Internet also created entirely new models that could not exist without this technology. The purpose of this chapter is to explore these business models. Choosing a business model is key for a new firm, and changing one's business model is an important aspect of strategy for the traditional firm that is threatened by a competitor on the Internet.

The Internet

The Internet provides a worldwide communications infrastructure that brings together individuals and firms. With a minimal communications capability, individuals and firms all over the world can access the Internet with browsers, and provide content by setting up a server. For the first time, standards and the Internet make it possible for everyone in the range of a telephone to connect to the same computer network.

In 1995 government funding for part of the Internet ceased, and it became possible to use it for profit-making activities. The capabilities of the Internet unlocked thousands of creative ideas for products and services; the presence of abundant venture capital turned many of these ideas in to reality.

Figure 3-1 is a simplified map of the Internet and some of the many organizations associated with it. The Internet is the basic infrastructure of hardware and software that spans the globe. The World Wide Web, or just Web, is another set of software standards for presenting information. The standards let developers create Web sites so that anyone with a Web browser (that follows those standards) can access information on the site.

Portals are locations someone browsing the Web is likely go as a starting point for a session or to answer a question. A popular portal like Yahoo! has millions of visitors, and

FIGURE 3-1 Web map.

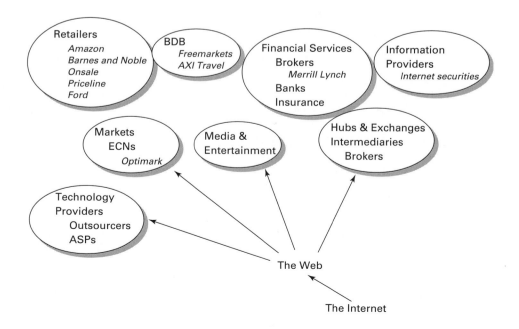

is able to attract companies to advertise on its site. The result is tremendous competition among portals for customers, with America Online (AOL) being one of the most aggressive competitors. Portals compete by providing services to attract users; the major portals also provide shopping opportunities, which are both a service and a revenue producer for the portal. Other services include stock quotations, directions and maps, search engines, and similar features to encourage users to frequent the portal. Business commentators expect that only a handful of portals will survive these "portal wars."

Figure 3-1 also shows different companies and the kinds of business they do on the Internet. Business-to-customer (B2C) transactions generated the first excitement about the commercial use of the Internet. Amazon.com is responsible for much of the "buzz" about selling on the Internet. This firm was successful in attracting publicity long before it opened for business. In a consumer-oriented society, what could be more exciting than the possibility of comparison shopping and ordering from a computer in one's home or office?

The business-to-consumer companies include many name brands as conventional merchants adopt the Internet as another sales channel. Firms like L.L.Bean and Lands' End have made many products available for sale on their Web sites. Barnes & Noble responded with bn.com to compete with Amazon.com, though it took a long time for the response.

Financial services providers are also in the B2C business. The Internet and electronic commerce affect brokerage firms, banks, and insurance companies. Retail customers (individuals rather than institutions) flocked to the Internet to save commissions on stock trades. An estimated 40–50 percent of all retail stock trades will soon occur on the Internet. A number of services on the Internet also collect premium and policy information and publish it on the Web for individuals planning to purchase insurance. Banks are interested in processing transactions over the Internet as a way to provide better service and reduce processing costs. A new kind of financial services is provided by an *aggregator* who accesses all of an individual's various financial accounts on different Web sites, and produces a single financial statement showing all assets and liabilities.

SIDE BAR 3-1

What to Do with a Portal

CIGNA, the insurance and retirement services company, uses a Web portal to provide better service for its customers. The company handles more than 30 million inquiries a year. The CIGNA Web portal helps more than 14 million of its members find the information they are seeking from the company. The portal lets customers review medical claims and manage their health plans, execute online transactions such as order medications, and access a summary of their retirement plans. Yahoo! provides CIGNA with the portal.

The need to provide services to 60,000 employers led CIGNA to a portal as a solution. To create the portal, CIGNA dealt with a host of legacy systems that spanned different departments of the company. A broad-based task force spent months studying the portal concept and CIGNA's resources. The company used Web services, middleware, XML, and Java to connect various databases so that customers could access them through the portal. A typical call center interaction runs $3 to $7, while a visit to the portal costs CIGNA 5 to 15 cents. The company is also saving $9 million a year by not printing handbooks and directories.

CIGNA shows how a customized portal can help support customers and provide better service. It also appears that a portal can save money for the company as it moves more and more customers to a self-service model of interaction.

SOURCE: *Internet World* (April 2003).

The Internet presents a challenge to those who make and sell one of the most important and expensive retail products, the automobile. Buying services such as Autobytel and CarsDirect.com work through dealers to bring the consumer a low price, or at least competing bids. The automakers would like to take advantage of electronic commerce, but in most states they cannot "own" dealers or deliver cars unless it is through a dealer. Ford and General Motors (GM) are working on plans to allow the customer to specify and order a vehicle on the Internet through dealers. One problem is that dealers offer different prices and do not have to follow the manufacturer's suggested price.

Business-to-business (B2B) activity is likely to dwarf business-to-consumer purchases. With companies like the automakers buying tens of billions of dollars worth of parts and supplies each year, shifting a small percentage to the Internet would make B2B far exceed B2C commerce. Internet purchasing allows companies to reduce the cycle time for their entire supply chain, so electronic commerce offers more than just a purchasing cost savings. A company such as Cicso is built around the B2B capabilities of the Internet, both for accepting customer orders and for passing these orders to its contract manufacturers who actually build its products.

Information providers sell information to customers, or they provide it free and obtain revenue from referrals and advertising. Information is a great Internet product because the marginal cost of producing a copy is nearly zero. Thus, once the vendor creates the basic information and infrastructure for providing it, additional sales cost nearly nothing and revenues flow directly to the bottom line.

Hubs are exchanges. For example, the site Detroit automakers established to conduct bids and purchase supplies is a hub. Vertical hubs involve firms from the same industry or the same commodity. Covisint is a hub for the auto industry, while Avendra is a purchasing exchange for hotel supplies. A vertical hub might be used for a product such as steel. Horizontal markets apply to a single firm offering its services to multiple customers, for example, a financial services company. Exchanges can be public or private depending on whether one has to be a member of a group or whether anyone can use the hub. The hub e2open.com is available to anyone in the electronics industry. An exchange that has many buyers and sellers and that is both vertical and horizontal becomes an electronic market.

New markets have also been established on or with help from the Internet, such as markets for securities trading. These electronic communications networks (ECNs) create significant challenges for the traditional stock exchanges and government regulators. Electronic brokers often execute trades through this "third market," claiming that it offers greater efficiency than the established exchanges. Electronic markets illustrate both network externalities and critical mass; an adequate supply of buyers and sellers is necessary to create liquidity in the marketplace.

The Internet generated a new industry of companies who provide technology and services. *Outsourcers* are companies that develop a strong core competence in some service and provide that service to others. CSC Corporation (Computer Sciences) and EDS (Electronic Data Systems) are two outsourcers for technology services. Solectron and Celestica are contract electronic manufacturers that existed long before the Internet; these firms build electronic products like computers, routers, and cellular phones, for a "manufacturer." Applications services providers (ASPs) run applications on their computer systems so that their customers do not have to install and operate the software internally. ASPs host many business Web sites for their customers

The Internet is also an entertainment medium. AOL and other portals provide a number of entertainment services including games and chat rooms. Supposedly the first and possibly

A large number of e-commerce firms adopted a simple e-business model. They would become intermediaries creating a market in some field such as chemicals or airline parts. Buyers would flock to their sites because they could compare prices among a number of suppliers and choose the lowest-price vendor. Sellers might not be happy, but they would have no choice but to compete in the electronic market if that is where their customers were shopping.

Sometimes simple models are powerful, and sometimes they fail because of the complexities they fail to include. In a number of these electronic markets, the model did not work.

What do you think went wrong? Why were so many good ideas easily turned into new dot-com companies that eventually failed? What did these firms need to succeed and why were they not able to achieve it? How is purchasing more complex than the simple model described? What kind of relationships do many industrial buyers and sellers enter into? How could you protect your e-business model? Do you think this model is dead, or might it return someday in a more sophisticated version? What has to be added to the model for it to succeed?

the most profitable Web businesses are those that feature adult entertainment, though little is written about these services. The merger of AOL and Time-Warner was originally about entertainment delivery and content, including what is likely to happen via the Web.

Three components of technology combine to create something greater than the sum of its parts. These components are computers, databases, and telecommunications. Computers provide vast processing power to perform computations and manipulate information. Databases are huge repositories of information and data that computers access and manipulate. Telecommunications ties everything together. A client PC in New York can extract information from a content server in France, and the server in France finds its data on a database server in Tokyo.

Through the Internet, people have global access to more than 3 billion pages of information. They also are all connected to each other; individuals and firms are linked via the Internet. This technology provides the capability to build previously inconceivable business models, unprecedented connectivity, the ability to transform business operations and structure, and the ability to enter into electronic commerce.

Electronic Commerce

The definition of electronic commerce provokes some controversy. Most articles assume that commerce is only electronic if it involves the Internet. For years, companies made millions of electronic purchases among themselves using electronic data interchange (EDI). Until the Internet became available for profit-making uses, this traffic occurred on private networks; the companies involved created the networks themselves or they used the services of value-added network providers (VANs). Much of EDI is sent in batches. For example, a computer at Ford determines what subassemblies are needed from suppliers to build its cars next week. The computer generates a batch of electronic orders and sends them to suppliers. The suppliers, via their own computer programs, accept and process the batch of orders. This process may continue through the payments cycle as well. This kind of transaction today would be called business-to-business or B2B commerce.

The first interest in electronic commerce on the Net came with retail sales, companies such as Amazon.com and CDNow presented new ways to shop. Most experts expect the new forms of B2B commerce and the transition of EDI to the Internet to dwarf retail sales on the Net. The Internet offers new models for both retail and business-to-business purchasing.

The Retail Sales Model

Figure 3-2 compares the traditional model of retail sales with a new business model found on the Net. The conventional model is pretty familiar: A manufacturer sells goods to a wholesaler who in turn distributes the merchandise to a retail store. Customers visit the store to make a purchase, paying with cash, a check, or credit card.

The Internet-based model for retailing makes some significant changes in the traditional retailing business model. The pure model eliminates the retail store, and the distributor becomes a fulfillment partner. Instead of receiving merchandise for distribution to a small number of stores, generally in bulk, the fulfillment partner must ship orders to the final customer. The customer does not visit the store, but instead orders over the Internet from the electronic merchant's Web site. The Web site processes the order and payment via a credit card, and sends the order to the fulfillment partner.

Of course, variations on the new Internet business model for retailing are numerous. Amazon.com found it necessary to build a series of warehouses around the country as it expanded its business and product lines. Conventional retailers are adding electronic

FIGURE 3-2 Retail business models.

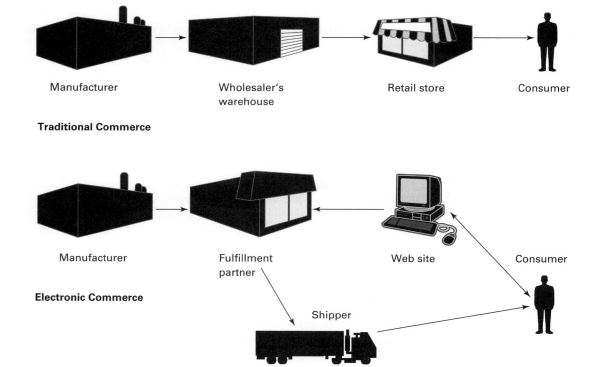

ordering capabilities, which present them with the task of maintaining both retail stores and a Web ordering business.

The differences between the two models are more profound than appear in Figure 3-2. The electronic commerce model features the following characteristics:

- No physical store, which means
  - No real estate purchase or lease.
- No retail store employees, including
  - No retail salaries or benefits.
  - No transportation between distributor and retail store.
  - The addition of a Web site.
  - The substitution of credit cards for cash and checks.
  - The substitution of a fulfillment partner for the distributor.
  - The addition of a shipping firm to deliver merchandise.

The end result is that the electronic retailer faces a considerably lower cost structure than the bricks-and-mortar retailer. The lack of a physical store and employees, and the elimination of shipments to stores all contribute to lower overhead. If the Web site actually places orders with the supplier/manufacturer, then it becomes a *virtual store* with no more overhead than its Web site. The company needs some technical support, customer service, accounting, advertising, and procurement personnel. Many of its business processes, then, are contracted out to others, minimizing overhead.

The lower cost structure is the reason that traditional retailers are threatened by electronic commerce. If their strategy is to keep retail stores, most feel they must also allow online ordering. (Most of the large department stores and category firms like Toys "R" Us have Web sites for ordering.) However, they end up with a formidable challenge of mastering a new business model and paying the overhead of the traditional retailer.

This discussion stresses the pure online store, but many traditional companies have adopted a bricks-and-clicks model in which they maintain a physical store and an online store simultaneously. Companies such as Grainger, L.L.Bean, Lands' End, and many others use the Internet as a sales channel. These companies enjoy a number of advantages. First, they are known brands that already have customers; success does not depend on attracting someone to a new business. Second, they have assets and financing to support the start-up online store. Sometimes they can use their physical stores in conjunction with the online store, for example, by having customers order online and pick up the product at a store, or at least be able to return products shipped to them at a retail store. The approach of the traditional firm to having both a real store and online presence is likely to continue; everyone selling to the public will feel pressure to have an online presence as well as a physical one.

Business-to-Business Electronic Commerce

Because many companies and industries make heavy use of EDI, the change to B2B electronic commerce on the Internet may seem at first to be less dramatic than the changes associated with retail e-commerce. However, most experts predict that the value and volume of B2B e-commerce will vastly exceed retail electronic commerce. If you think about the number of components that an automobile manufacturer must order to build a car, compared to the one order that the end customer places for the car, the reason for this forecast is more evident. In the tremendous volume of business-to-business transactions, each transaction often requires more messages than the final retail sale. It is not unusual for a B2B purchase to have an acknowledgment, a change order, an acknowledgment of the change, a shipping notice, notice of receipt, payment due, payment sent, and other miscellaneous messages associated with it. It is easy to see that B2B commerce will result in more traffic and more dollar volume on the Net than retail sales.

Figure 3-3 compares the two B2B business models: the traditional and electronic. The traditional purchasing process involves a procurement staff that negotiates with suppliers. A firm may provide an order for a specified period of time. For example, in the electronics industry manufacturers often negotiate a price with suppliers for a commitment to buy so many components a year. Then during the year the manufacturer provides forecasts and firm orders for the week, which the supplier ships under the blanket contract signed for the year. Other purchasing situations may require negotiation for each transaction.

In electronic B2B commerce, a smaller purchasing staff visits a market on the Web to procure the items it wishes to buy. One major advantage is that the buyer is able to comparison shop among a number of suppliers quickly using the Web, or through an auction offered by a company such as FreeMarkets.com. The Internet should facilitate price discovery and finding the lowest prices available for the buyer. After locating the supplier, the purchasing process continues much as already described. The end result should be a smaller, more effective purchasing group and better prices for supplies.

FIGURE 3-3 B2B models.

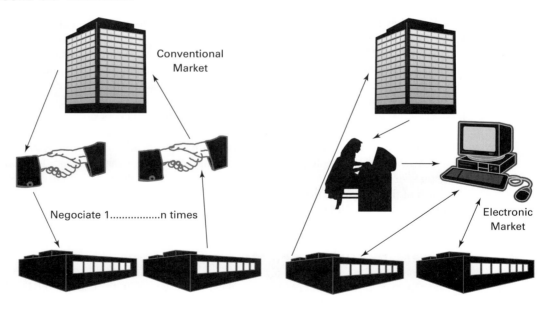

Conventional Market

Negociate 1.................n times

From 1.................n suppliers

Traditional B2B Commerce

Electronic Market

1.................n suppliers

Electronic B2B Commerce

Lean and Agile Manufacturing, Mass Customization

The mass manufacturing model, sometimes called *Fordist*, comes from the original assembly line set up by Henry Ford. Ford produced thousands of cars with no or limited options in any color as long as it was black. This model of manufacturing changed throughout the years, with a number of new variations. However, the most dramatic changes are still to come because of information technology.

Figure 3-4 presents the Dell model of manufacturing, a model so popular that Michael Dell has consulted for the Detroit automakers. Dell receives orders via phone and the Internet, currently more than half of its orders come via the Net. As shown in the Figure, Dell does not produce a computer until it has a firm order; the company orders from suppliers as it needs parts. The components that belong with the computer that Dell does not build into the machine (e.g., an external Zip drive) ship from their manufacturer directly to the customer; Dell never handles these parts. As a result, the company operates with little or no in-process inventory and no finished goods inventory. No distributors carry Dell products on their shelves, and no obsolete models sell at close-out prices. Dell also is paid for noncorporate accounts as soon as it books the order via the customer's credit card.

Even with this lean production model, Dell is able to offer a number of different computer models with different features. Given today's technology, the company appears to be about as lean as possible in terms of overhead and the manufacturing process. To encourage corporate sales, Dell sets up purchasing agreements with companies, universities, and government agencies. It develops custom Web pages to facilitate ordering by employees of these organizations.

FIGURE 3-4 The Dell business model.

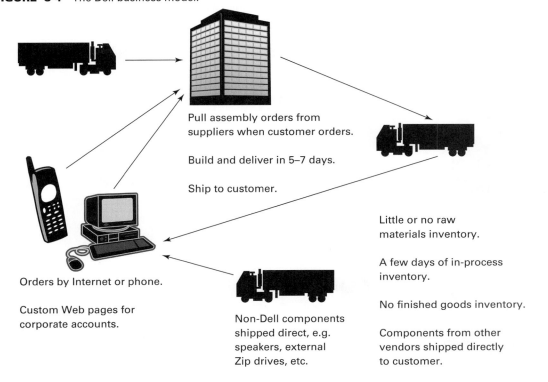

Pull assembly orders from suppliers when customer orders.

Build and deliver in 5–7 days.

Ship to customer.

Little or no raw materials inventory.

A few days of in-process inventory.

No finished goods inventory.

Orders by Internet or phone.

Custom Web pages for corporate accounts.

Non-Dell components shipped direct, e.g. speakers, external Zip drives, etc.

Components from other vendors shipped directly to customer.

Figure 3-5 presents another lean manufacturing model from Cisco, an extremely successful manufacturer of communications equipment for networks. To a large extent, Cisco is a virtual manufacturer. The company's strength is in design and marketing. Because its customers tend to work with technology, they are quite comfortable ordering products over the Web. About 90 percent of Cisco's orders come via the Internet. Cisco routes many of these orders to contract electronics manufacturers who build Cisco products to its specifications. An incredible 70 to 80 percent of customer service requests are handled by Cisco's extensive technical help information on the Web. Through its Internet links and virtual manufacturing, Cisco offers another lean manufacturing business model.

New Businesses on the Web

The Portal. The world now uses a whole new series of businesses that did not exist before the creation of the Internet. A portal such as Yahoo! is the place that a person browsing the Web accesses to begin a session on the Net. Yahoo! is a good example of a portal that started as a search engine to locate content on the Web. However, as mentioned earlier in the chapter, the way a portal supports itself is through advertising and referrals to other sites. The more people that access the portal, the more attractive it is to advertisers and the more it can charge for ads. As the portals expanded from search engines to offer other services, they found new ways to generate revenue. If you click on "Shop" at Yahoo! and follow a Yahoo! link to a store where you purchase something, Yahoo! gets a commission.

An Internet service provider (ISP) such as America Online is extremely successful because 25 million people who use AOL visit its portal when they log on to the Web. Portals exhibit both network externalities and critical mass. One of America Online's most popular features is its chat facility. If someone with whom you wish to converse is online at the same time you are, the two of you can interact via your terminals. As more people use AOL, the service becomes more valuable.

FIGURE 3-5 The Cisco business model.

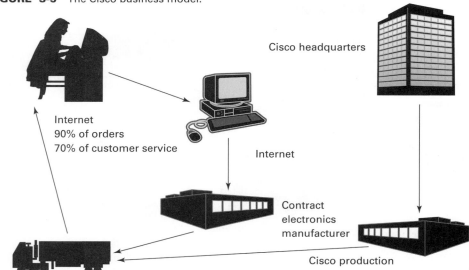

Internet
90% of orders
70% of customer service

Cisco headquarters

Internet

Contract electronics manufacturer

Cisco production

The Hub or Exchange. The hub is a kind of electronic broker or intermediary. Although the Web threatens many intermediaries such as stock brokers and real estate agents, it provides opportunities for intermediaries of a different kind. A hub connects two groups that wish to interact. For example, a person might create a hub that matches shipping companies with excess capacity in containers with shippers who have less than container-sized loads. A shipper lists containers, the amount of space, and their destination on the hub Web site. A customer accesses the hub's Web pages to locate a suitable container going to the desired location and makes arrangements to rent space in it. The hub also benefits from network externalities and critical mass. The hub is also a name sometimes used to describe exchanges that are vertical or horizontal marketplaces, as mentioned earlier in the chapter.

The hub or exchange creates a network of firms. A group of hotel chains including Marriott and Hyatt have formed a vertical exchange called Avendra. This exchange sees itself as a contracting agent, negotiating prices with suppliers and making their products available for hotels via the Internet. Avendra and all of its suppliers and hotel customers comprise a constantly changing network of organizations. Each supplier is a member of other networks, and the hotels are all members of a network of similarly branded hotels. Electronic commerce and the Internet help create many new network relationships.

The Service Provider. America Online is a portal, but it is also an Internet service provider (ISP). This new industry is dedicated to serving companies and individuals, making it easier for them to use and build applications on the Web. AOL has a private network that customers access around the world. This private network connects to AOL's computer center in Vienna, Virginia. Vienna, in turn, is connected to the Internet so that AOL's customers can access the Web. AT&T Worldnet, Comcast for cable modem users, and many other firms provide Internet access.

SIDE BAR 3-2

The Google Story

One of the new businesses created by the Web is the search engine, and Google is the most successful of this group of systems. Instead of simply searching an index, Google uses a page ranking algorithm to determine the popularity of a page. The PageRank algorithm determines the quality of a page by the pages that link to it. The algorithm backtracks to see how popular in turn the pages are that point to the one being ranked. Once a month Google's spiders crawl the Web to update its index. The search engine runs on a giant cluster of more than 10,000 Linux systems. (Google no longer publishes its server statistics, but one estimate runs as high as 54,000 servers with 100,000 processors.) Google's popularity is impressive. It now indexes 3 billion pages of Web content in more than twenty languages. The number of daily Google searches has grown to 150 million, 1,000 times more than when the service was introduced.

How does Google generate revenue when its search site is free? One way is to sell its search engine to individual Web sites so that employees and customers can find items on the site. A large company might have tens of thousands of Web pages and users need help in locating specific items of interest. A second stream of revenue comes from advertisers; Google displays an appropriate ad given the search request. This customized advertising is much more directed than a pop-up ad that everyone on a site sees. More than 100,000 advertisers use this feature. An importer of Italian suits saw her sales go from ten suits a month to 120 after buying ads that cost 21 cents to $1.50; Google displayed the ads when a user searched for "Armani" or "Hugo Boss." The importer expects to spend $60,000 in the coming year on Google ads.[6] Google also started an e-commerce site called Froogle.

Sources: *New York Times,* April 13, 2002; *Scientific American,* June 2003; and *PC Magazine,* May 6, 2003.

MANAGEMENT PROBLEM 3-2

WebVan is probably the most famous of the dot-com business models that did not succeed. A great deal of publicity centered on how it would revolutionize grocery shopping, and investors rushed to offer money, expecting tremendous returns on this unique model. The model was seriously flawed, however, which many investors saw the minute it was proposed. The idea of shopping on the Internet has not vanished; some existing grocery chains are experimenting with it, most notably Sainsbury in the United Kingdom.

What do you think the major flaws were in the WebVan model? What role did consumer research play in the planning for WebVan? What problems did WebVan need to overcome in order to be successful? What are the differences between a traditional retailer such as Sainsbury and WebVan when it comes to Internet grocery shopping? Compare and contrast a dot-com such as WebVan with a bricks-and-mortar company that offers Internet grocery shopping. Do you think the latter will be successful where WebVan failed?

This class of company also includes Internet service providers' Web hosting companies, which develop and host applications for a customer. Suppose that a firm wants to have a home page and the ability for customers to order products from it. An ISP will design the home page, implement electronic commerce software, and host the entire operation on its servers. IBM provides services through huge *server farms*, professionally managed locations that offer Web hosting.

The applications service provider (ASP) is a similar business, but it also offers the use of a particular application to a customer. If a firm is too small to implement a complete enterprise resource planning (ERP) system, it can access the parts it needs through an ASP for a monthly charge. This service also appeals to the company with limited in-house expertise for implementing IT applications. Because these applications are all based on the Internet, the communications infrastructure is in place. An ASP can easily provide a salesforce automation package that a sales representative traveling anyplace in the world with Internet access can use.

New Markets

All one needs for a market is a central meeting place, and the Internet provides the mechanism for such a meeting; a market creator needs a Web site. Many times, a buyer and seller do not need to interact directly or at the same time. Because the Internet is available around the clock, this technology removes time and location requirements that affect many physical markets.

Long before the Internet existed, people participated in auctions. The sealed bid auction is common in construction. An organization wishing to undertake a construction project sends the plans for that project to prospective construction firms and requests a sealed or secret bid be submitted by a certain date. Usually the lowest bidder gets the job. Many government contracts, both local and federal, use the sealed bid auction in an effort to obtain a facility at the lowest possible price.

Other kinds of auctions employ open outcry in which an auctioneer works with an audience of potential bidders. The auctioneer opens bidding at the owners' reserve price, the minimum the owner is willing to accept for the item for sale. The auctioneer encourages bidders to raise their bids until finally only the highest bidder remains. Other auction types include used car auctions attended by automobile dealers, livestock auctions, and of course art and estate auctions.

The Dutch auction is slightly different from the open outcry; it developed in the Dutch flower markets. Here the auctioneer begins at a high price and decreases the price rapidly until a bidder stops the process and buys at that moment's price. The Dutch flower growers believe that this kind of auction favors the seller rather than the buyer.

Except for the sealed bid auction, these auctions require a bidder to be physically present, connected by telephone, or to have a representative at the auction. The Internet removes this time and place requirement for an auction to be held. Instead, a seller can post the items to be auctioned on a Web site, and potential bidders can visit the site at their leisure to review the item and decide whether to bid. One of the most popular sites for retail auctions is eBay, which has had phenomenal success. For B2B purchases, FreeMarkets offers an auction service that it claims reduces purchasing costs for companies using its site and services.

Priceline.com has been successful with its reverse auction that its founder, Jay Walker, calls "demand aggregation." A buyer indicates on Priceline.com's Web site that he or she is willing to pay $X for an airline ticket on a certain date between two cities. Priceline has agreements with a large number of airlines who provide seats at clearance prices. Priceline determines whether such a seat is available. The buyer must be willing to be flexible in terms of time of day and connecting cities. In addition to airline tickets, the site offers a number of other products on which one can enter a bid.

The Internet extended this auction format to a large number of people and companies who could not have participated before. Network externalities and critical mass apply here as they do to other Net businesses. Because anyone on the Internet can access eBay, a potential seller has millions of potential bidders. Users of the Net know that they can go to this place to find items they might wish to bid on. The more sellers and bidders, the more valuable the site becomes to both groups.

You Need a Revenue Model

Some of the dot-coms had great ideas for business models, but they forgot that they needed to generate revenue as well. The revenue model for Amazon is easy; it is the same model that retailers have used throughout the years of a markup on a product sold. However, Amazon soon moved to let others sell on its site for a fee, modifying its original model. eBay earns revenue by charging sellers on its site, as do many auction sites. Priceline buys airline tickets and hotel rooms at a low price and sells them to customers at a markup, generating its revenue.

An early, pervasive model for the Internet was to generate revenue through advertising; Internet users are used to getting information for free, which can be provided through advertising support. A number of sites tried this approach and ended up bankrupt because advertisers found that they were not getting a return. Today, advertising on the Web is much more targeted; for example, advertisers pay Google to display an ad based on a user search that looks relevant to their product or service. Portals such as Yahoo! and Google earn considerable revenues today from advertising. When developing a business model, do not forget to think about how this model will generate revenue.

SIDE BAR 3-4

Turning the Phone System Upside Down

Telecommunications is a $300 billion a year industry that is threatened by Voice over Internet Protocol (VoIP). This technology converts phone calls into digital packets for transmission over the Internet; equipment translates the packets back into normal speech at their destination. Some systems involve the use of current phones, but others cut traditional phone lines completely out of the process.

Traditional phone companies face federal regulation while Internet communications companies do not. AT&T charges 86 cents a minute for a call from the United States to Botswana, while Vonage Holdings, an Internet phone company, charges 14 cents. The call is free if both callers are Vonage customers. Traditional phone companies have a tremendous investment in fixed assets in the form of communications networks.

As a defensive move, they are investigating Internet phone services. Qwest, Verizon, and SBC Communication are all looking into Internet phone services. If the traditional companies transition to VoIP, it will make much of their infrastructure obsolete and destroy much of their scale advantage. It is difficult to imagine a bigger threat to one's business model.

How serious is the threat? Vonage provides an adapter to turn a broadband line into an Internet phone. The company claims 70,000 customers and says it is adding more than 10,000 each month. Three million people have downloaded free software from Skype Ltd., which allows unlimited calls worldwide at no charge to other users of the company's software.

SOURCE: *The Wall Street Journal*, November 28, 2003.

Electronic Commerce: Pervasive Technology

The business models described in this chapter are templates that focus on the visible part of the firm; they suggest broad categories of e-commerce such as B2B or B2C. In reality, the model for many organizations is more complicated. For the truly electronic business, all aspects of its strategy and operations involve information technology. A good example of the pervasiveness of technology beyond e-commerce is the auto industry.

For many years, the Big Three automakers used technology heavily in their manufacturing operations. In fact, it was an industry group of auto manufacturers that encouraged early efforts at electronic data interchange. Detroit insisted for a number of years that its suppliers accept orders electronically, though EDI takes place using batch transmission over private networks rather than the Internet. Some of the manufacturers allow suppliers to access their production planning systems to anticipate when to deliver products to factories. Chrysler pioneered this kind of just-in-time production and electronic data interchange necessary technology for JIT to work in U.S. auto plants.

Now GM, Ford, DaimlerChrysler, Nissan, and Renault are cooperating in using Covisint, a Web site for purchasing supplies. They hope to save up to 10 percent of the cost of a car by purchasing through the Internet. In addition, these companies expect to gain revenue as they encourage their suppliers to use the site for their own purchases. Eventually will all automobile EDI shift to the Internet?

Because the automobile business is large and complex, the Internet and electronic commerce are having an impact in areas other than purchasing and manufacturing. Automakers do not really know the details of consumer demand; they build cars on speculation and send them to dealers. The car sits on the dealer's lot until a customer buys it; Detroit does not know what accessories the customer might really have wanted because many buyers are not willing to enter a custom order and wait for delivery. The automakers would like to reduce the cycle time from placing an order until delivery. Although it looks possible to shorten this time, reducing it to a few days is highly unlikely. A typical car requires more than 10,000 parts, and the source of many of these parts is subcontractors. To shorten delivery times, Detroit will have to coordinate production among a number of suppliers and find a way to reduce the time it takes to physically deliver a car from the plant to a dealer or customer.

One way to shorten cycle times is to have the customer specify and order a car over the Internet, to utilize electronic commerce for the purchase of cars. About 55 percent of new car buyers today do some research on the Internet before visiting a dealer. Sites such as Edmunds.com refer you to Autobytel to get a quote from a participating dealer while Carsdirect.com will deliver a new vehicle to your door. All of these alternatives provide a challenge for Detroit and its traditional dealership structure. It is clear that e-commerce is changing the way people buy cars, and the role of dealership is evolving. It is difficult to forecast the final outcome, but the end result should benefit the consumer.

The impact of the Internet on purchasing may create some problems as well as challenges for Detroit, but the automakers are excited about putting the Internet in the car. All of the manufacturers envision people having Internet access while driving, the ability to get and send e-mail (using voice recognition technology), inquire about traffic, obtain routing and recommendations on hotels and restaurants, and access a wide range of services. The auto companies have a vision of millions of customers in their cars using them as an Internet service provider. Fees of $10 to $20 a month for this service would add a lot to anyone's bottom line!

Detroit provides a scenario for an electronic business, though it is not quite there yet. The potential exists for customers to specify and purchase their product using electronic commerce on the Internet. The companies will use B2B commerce sites to purchase and acquire their raw materials. The Internet allows them to coordinate production with suppliers, and offers an attractive service to bundle with their final product. It is also a way to stay in contact with customers throughout the life of the car. This example illustrates how the real benefits from the Internet come not just from electronic commerce, but from integrating technology through the firm's entire value chain.

ANALYZING BUSINESS MODELS

This chapter presented a number of new business models, most of them enabled by the Internet. How does one distinguish among different kinds of models? Two researchers developed a series of atomic elements to characterize different business models (Weill and Vitale, 2001). Their model includes the following elements:

- The firm of interest
- A supplier
- A consumer
- Allies
- Electronic relationships
- Primary relationships
- The flow of money
- The flow of product
- The flow of information

These authors used these elements to describe different kinds of the businesses, including the traditional business model, the content provider, electronic broker, the direct-to-customer model, the full-service financial provider, the intermediary, and the portal (Weill and Vitale, 2001). The purpose of this scheme is to describe electronic business models, but it also describes almost any kind of traditional business.

Why do you need to describe and analyze business models? One reason is to evaluate the value proposition of existing and proposed businesses. Consider, for example, the business model of WebVan. This company proposed to deliver to customers groceries ordered over the Internet to their homes. This business model contained several flows of information including the flow from customers to WebVan, and the flow from WebVan to its suppliers. The flows of money went from customers to WebVan and WebVan to its suppliers; product flow moved the opposite direction from suppliers to the WebVan warehouses and finally to customers. The various information flows were or could have been electronic.

The problem with the model arose because it assumed that customers would be willing to pay higher prices than charged by a grocery store for the convenience of home delivery, and they would be able to plan in advance what to buy. The founders of WebVan also discounted any need for customers to inspect the merchandise they were ordering as easily as they could in the grocery store. Many of the e-business models described earlier in the chapter involve information goods characterized by little or no physical movement of the customer's purchase. B2C businesses on the Web usually ship their products through existing freight companies such as FedEx or UPS. WebVan required a costly physical infrastructure in each city where it wanted to do business. For example, WebVan needed a warehouse to stock groceries for delivery to its customers. In addition the company had to pay for its own fleet of trucks and drivers in order to meet guaranteed delivery time windows.

After attracting a significant amount of venture capital, WebVan went bankrupt due to less demand than expected and its high cost structure. WebVan is an illustration of the importance of analyzing one's business model to see if it offers a viable value proposition.

CHAPTER SUMMARY

This chapter discussed the concept of a business model, a template that describes the kind of business a firm is in. The dot-com era led to the development of new business models, many of which failed in a spectacular manner. A number of factors explain why so many seemingly good ideas met their demise, including the major push provided by the investment community and stock analysts, and the tremendous publicity surrounding the Internet. It seemed that traditional companies were on the way out, soon to be eclipsed by firms whose business model involved the Internet. Today the traditional firms, for the most part, continue in business while many dot-coms are no longer here.

Some of the entrepreneurs who started Internet companies lacked knowledge of business processes, and many overestimated how quickly customers would adapt to the Net. Some managers did not analyze reasons why customers might not use their site. To some extent, these new businesses suffered by being pioneers. In the 1990s, a small percentage of the population had access to the Internet compared to those who had access to physical stores or the telephone for ordering. Many of these failed models will be back with changes that overcome their earlier flaws. More will form alliances with traditional business models; for example, Peapod is now a part of Royal Ahold, the Dutch Supermarket chain. The message of the chapter is that you need to understand your existing business model and think carefully about new ones. The Internet is a tremendous resource, but using it as a part of your business does not guarantee success.

SIDE BAR 3-3

When Technology Threatens Your Business Model

Eastman Kodak Company has enjoyed a lucrative franchise in camera film, ranging from film products for the casual photographer to the professional, and products from cameras to X-rays. As more and more photography has gone digital, Kodak's stock has dropped in value, and several CEOs tried to improve the company's outlook. In the fall of 2003, Kodak announced that it was going to stress its digital business and admitted that the film business would never generate the kind of profits it had in the past. By early 2004, Kodak decided to stop making film cameras, though it will continue to manufacture and distribute film. The company cut its annual dividend from $1.80 per share to $0.50 in order to retain earnings to invest in its digital businesses.

Digital photography has revolutionized the way people record images. You can take photos and erase the ones you do not like, load them onto your computer, and view them one at a time, or in a slide show. Digital pictures are burned into CDs, and travel to friends and relatives instantaneously on the Internet. The quality of digital cameras has become good enough for professionals, especially reporters who can transfer their pictures over a network to their publications. Modern medical imaging equipment uses digital storage and viewing rather than film.

The CEO of Kodak hired a number of newcomers into senior management from companies such as Lexmark and Hewlett-Packard (HP) to help the company move into digital businesses. But what will replace the revenue stream from lucrative sales of film? Kodak estimates that unit sales of film will drop 12 percent a year through 2006. Kodak's CFO thinks that film prices will decline 4 to 5 percent a year during this period. In a first for the company, it will start manufacturing private label film. Kodak eliminated 30,000 jobs during the last six years, and will probably shed more employees.

The company wants to grow its digital products market to $9.5 billion in sales by 2006, up from $3.5 billion in 2002. Currently, Kodak loses money on digital products, but it expects to start making a profit. It now competes with HP, Sony, Canon, Seiko, Epson, and Lexmark. The company is working on innovative new products, such as a color printer for photos that uses a dry or thermal ink process instead of the wet inks in an inkjet printer. Kodak is also installing self-service photo printing kiosks in retail stores so that customers can print their digital photos without waiting. The company will go into commercial printing, and will sell consumer ink jet printers as well. Kodak is also purchasing companies that fit within its digital strategy and expects to spend $3 billion on acquisitions through 2006.

Kodak embarked on a high-risk strategy because information technology severely affected its traditional business model. What alternatives does the company have? Has it waited too long? How does a large company make a major shift in strategy such as the one that Kodak is undertaking? The lesson from Kodak is that you must anticipate threats to your business model, and be ready to make significant changes in it. Information technology can force dramatic changes in any organization.

SOURCES: *The Wall Street Journal*, September 25, 2003; and *New York Times*, September 26, 2003.

KEYWORDS

Agile manufacturing	Exchange	Outsourcing
Auction	Hub	Portal
Business model	Information providers	Service provider
Content provider	Internet	Traditional models
ECN	Mass customization	

RECOMMENDED READINGS

Feeny, D. 2001. Making business sense of the e-opportunity. *Sloan Management Review*, *42*(2), pp. 41–51.

Venkatraman, N., and Henderson, J. C. 1998. Real strategies for virtual organizing. *Sloan Management Review*, *40*(1), pp. 33–48.

Weill, P., and Vitale, M. 2002. What IT infrastructure capabilities are needed to implement e-business models? *MISQ Executive, 1*(1) pp. 17–34.

Weill, P., and Vitale, M. 2001. *Place to Space.* Boston: Harvard Business School Press.

DISCUSSION QUESTIONS

1. What are the components of a business model?

2. Compare and contrast Dell's business model with a traditional manufacturing model.

3. Why do you think Cisco has been so successful with its business model?

4. What sources of revenue are available to a company?

5. Describe a generic business-to-consumer model.

6. Describe a generic business-to-business model.

7. What are the benefits of an electronic exchange? Why do you think these exchanges have been less successful than originally forecast?

8. What are the revenue sources for a portal on the Internet?

9. Compare the business model of the traditional airline with a discount airline.

10. How has the Internet affected airline business models?

11. Do you think, as some experts suggest, that the Internet will replace most intermediaries? What are the opportunities for new intermediaries because of the Internet?

12. Why is the business model of a content provider a natural fit with the Internet?

13. Using the atomic business model elements described in this chapter, construct a model of a traditional business such as General Motors. Then use these elements to construct a model of an electronic business such as Amazon.com.

14. In the early days of the Internet, dot-com companies felt they had superior models to existing bricks-and-mortar companies not on the Internet. Yet many dot-coms failed spectacularly while traditional firms are still around and doing well. What do you think is responsible for this outcome?

15. Describe different kinds of auctions. Are auctions the most efficient markets? Take a position on this question and defend it.

16. Describe eBay's business model. Why has this company been so successful? What is its revenue model?

17. Do government agencies have a business model? How do you characterize their mission and operations?

ENDNOTES

1. Condensed discussion of new business models and figures from *Strategies for Electronic Commerce and the Internet*, Henry C. Lucas, Jr., © 2002 The MIT Press.

2. *The Wall Street Journal*, June 18, 2002.

3. *The Wall Street Journal*, October 28, 2003.

4. *The Wall Street Journal*, August 13, 2002.

5. *New York Times*, February 8, 2004.

6. *New York Times,* April 13, 2002.

CHAPTER 4

ORGANIZATIONAL TRANSFORMATION WITH IT

A Manager's Perspective

In the early days of technology, companies automated manual processes, generally saving labor and reducing the cycle time for processing. A few managers and academics were concerned about the impact of technology on the organization. How would information systems change people's jobs and the nature of work? What would be the overall impact on the firm? Would there be a reduction in the layers of management? Would workers who remained at the company find their jobs expanded or diminished by computers? For the most part, studies of the impact of computers on organizations produced mixed results.

As technology moved beyond computerizing manual processes, and especially when the Internet enabled fast, easy electronic communications between organizations, the question of technology impact changed. Instead of looking at technology after the fact, you can think about IT as a way to help design an organization. Technology can supplement or substitute for traditional approaches to organization design. Companies such as Dell and Cisco use IT in a way that makes their structure and operations different from other firms. Every manager is involved in the design of the organization; routine work assignments, work procedures, the formation of task forces, and similar activities create the organization. Information technology gives you an incredible range of options for organization design and innovation.

VALUE PROPOSITION

Technology's greatest impact may well be its effects on organizational transformation, though the impact is difficult to measure. IT-enabled transformation can:

■ Improve the effectiveness of the organization

■ Lead to new organization structures and relationships with other firms

■ Reduce overhead

■ Lead to high levels of employee satisfaction

Some of the impact of organizational transformation can be measured by:

■ Market share

■ Sales per employee

■ Sales growth

■ Administrative costs

■ Employee satisfaction

■ Employee turnover

TRANSFORMING ORGANIZATIONS

Previous chapters described the similarities between the Industrial Revolution and the revolution in information technology of the last fifty years. Differences in these two major events in history are also profound. The Industrial Revolution changed the physical environment. An industrial economy needed factories so that workers could build products under one roof. Factories needed employees, so industrialists put them in cities where they could find a concentration of workers. People moved from farms to cities to work in these factories. The physical location of work, the nature of the work, and the physical appearance of cities all changed. In fact, the Industrial Revolution started a migration of workers from remote areas to urban centers that only recently showed any signs of being reversed.

The revolution in information technology is different because it is quiet and gradual; its impact on the physical landscape remains limited. Instead, major changes show up in the way firms operate, the nature of work, and the relationship among organizations. The technology is changing the basis for competition and the relationships among the players in certain industries. Entrepreneurs use IT to create new industries that provide previously unavailable goods and services to customers.

Organizational transformation is one of the most exciting parts of IT, and one of the most disconcerting. Organizations have undergone major changes with or as a result of the technology, and these changes at times have been traumatic. Brokerage firms laid off thousands of employees, due partially to the recent tribulations of the stock market, but also due in part to online stock trading on the part of retail customers. At the same time, IT creates new businesses; portals such as Yahoo! and search engine firms such as Google produce new jobs for the economy.

The technology transformed existing industries and created new ones. Table 4-1 lists some of the industries where IT has been responsible for significant transformations. This section highlights a few of the impacts of technology. Examples throughout the rest of the book illustrated other IT-stimulated transformations. The biggest fear is to be the victim of change, rather than being in a position to plan change. Looking at companies and industries that experienced a transformation provides an understanding of the capabilities of technology that you can apply it in your organization. The following examples should help prepare you for new kinds of IT transformations.

Retail Stock Trading[1]

In the mid-1990s, Internet-based online brokers offered easy-to-use technology-mediated interfaces between individual investors and the stock exchanges: The number of online accounts grew from 7 million in 1998 to more than 21 million in April of 2001. Online brokers represented 28 percent of U.S. individual investor trades in the first quarter of 2002.

Until 1975, government regulators fixed brokerage commissions in the United States, which were identical across brokers and produced a brokerage market that was uncompetitive on price. The retail brokerage industry's core product, the stock trade, is largely an undifferentiated commodity. Established brokers competed by offering proprietary bundles that include complementary components to the trade, such as research and personalized investment advice, to differentiate themselves.

Deregulation in 1975 launched discount brokerage firms that charged lower commissions, but did not provide investment advice. Customers choosing to make their own

TABLE 4-1 IT transforms organizations and industries.

Industry	Fundamental Restructuring	Major Changes	Growing Impact	Where Discussed
Electronic retail stock brokerage	Expand self-directed investor market segment	Unbundling of services and trade execution	More price convergence for costs of a trade	This section
Digital goods, music, movies, newspapers	Downloading music from the Internet; video next	Search for a new revenue model; legal downloading	Movies coming soon	This section
Telecommunications	Internet model for data and voice	Flat rate independent of distance	The race to the consumer: wireless, fiber, cellular?	Verizon Side Bar, this chapter
Travel	Internet reservations, ticketing, and boarding pass	Yield management leverages CRS information	IT in all aspects of operations	Chapter 18, Decision Support Systems
Manufacturing	Outsourcing, IT for coordination	Going offshore	Lower prices, U.S. job losses	Dell and Cisco Side Bars, this chapter
Auto retailing	eBay as nationwide used car market	Informed customer	Slow impact on new car sales	This section
A new marketplace	eBay	Online community built around an electronic auction or fixed-price market	From individual to corporate participants	This section

investment decisions could save by using execution-only, discount brokers. The end of fixed commissions led to two market segments for trading securities: (1) traditional investors who wanted all of the services provided by a full-service broker, and (2) self-directed investors who only needed trade execution services from a discount broker.

In the mid 1990s, the first electronic or e-brokers appeared. The use of IT and the Internet provided online brokers with a significantly lower cost structure than full-service brokers. For example, online brokers require no costly physical branch offices and need far fewer human brokers. During this time, the Internet helped to expand the self-directed brokerage market segment in two ways. First, online brokers began to charge dramatically reduced commissions below the established discount brokers' fees and far below traditional full-service brokers. Second, the large amount of content on the Internet made it easy for investors to conduct research, themselves, often for free, reducing the appeal of the full-service broker's bundle. Online brokers enabled consumers to create their own bundles, for example, combining research and advice from a traditional broker with trading at an online broker site.

Online trading is possible because of the Internet and the infrastructure it provides. An online broker needs only to establish a Web site to reach millions of potential customers, without the need to create a private, proprietary data network. The Internet also facilitated the development of electronic communications networks (ECNs) or electronic securities markets. These markets follow a practice of paying for order flow in order to attract business and provide liquidity. Online brokers in general were thought to route most of their orders to ECNs, and to receive payment for order flow in return. This payment for order flow provided an additional stream of revenue for the online broker, helping to keep its commission costs down.

Online brokers and the content on the Internet put pressure on full-service brokers with their bundled services. Self-directed investors were only interested in having their trades executed. The published price of a trade was the commission charged by the broker; a self-directed investor would throw away anything else that came in a trade bundle. The Internet helped make the commodity part of a bundle, the trade itself, more transparent, and stimulated the growth of the self-directed market segment for brokerage services.

The Internet also began to disintermediate the industry. In the United States, regulations require that a registered brokerage firm must act as an agent between the investor and the financial markets; for example, investors are prohibited from accessing the New York Stock Exchange, the NASDAQ Stock Market, or the U.S. regional exchanges directly. Upon receipt of a customer order, the brokerage firm routes an order to a market of its choosing. For instance, an order for an NYSE-listed stock may be routed to the NYSE itself, or to a regional market such as the Chicago Stock Exchange, or to a third market dealer that trades the stock using its own capital. Because of regulation, it would be difficult to completely disintermediate the brokerage industry, for example, by allowing investors to trade with each other, or to trade securities on eBay. However, online brokerage firms have disintermediated the human broker; a customer of one of these firms enters an order directly in to his or her computer. Without human intervention, the online broker's computers route the order to a market for execution.

At first, full-service brokers, led by Merrill Lynch, fought the trend toward online stock trading. Before the rise of online stock trading, Merrill Lynch occupied a comfortable position as the largest brokerage firm in the world. Merrill had more than 60,000 employees in forty countries, as well as a relationship with more than 5 million households. As a full-service firm, Merrill offers far more than retail brokerage services; it provides institutional trading and investment banking services, among others. The company has more than $1.5 trillion in assets under management and institutional trading tops $30 billion a day. The company is the world's leading underwriter of debt and securities, and is first in mergers and acquisitions. Merrill has an extremely large research group of nearly 800 analysts in twenty-six countries.

Merrill's business model defined the full-service brokerage industry: a research department produces research products for the brokerage workforce. Brokers provide clients with research and encourage them to place trades with Merrill Lynch. The firm earns revenues from commissions, underwriting, fee-based account management, and from a number of other sources. Online brokers on the Internet threaten this business model.

Merrill executives saw the publicity and interest in e-brokers, but they did not "get the Internet" as Schwab did. On September 23, 1998, *The Wall Street Journal* printed an article quoting John "Launny" Steffens, a Merrill vice chairman in charge of the firm's 17,000 retail stock brokers. According to the article:

Steffens…has waged an unusually public campaign over the last few months to dramatize what he calls the dangers of buying and selling stocks unassisted over the Internet…Mr. Steffens has badmouthed low-priced cyber-trading, saying it encourages people to trade too much at the expense of long-term returns.…"The do-it-yourself model of investing, centered on Internet trading, should be regarded as a serious threat to Americans' financial lives. This approach to financial decision-making does not serve clients well and it is a business model that won't deliver lasting value."

For 100 shares of IBM at that time, Charles Schwab would charge $29.95, and it would charge the same for 1,000 shares. Merrill would have charged about $100 for 100 shares and nearly $1,000 for buying 1,000 shares.

Merrill's first response to electronic trading was to offer the public free access to its stock research over the Web for a four-month trial period. Steffens announced this initiative on October 15, 1998. Merrill had provided access to research for its clients on the Internet earlier; this effort was intended to generate new leads by making research available to the public.

Why did Merrill hesitate so long? One view is that 17,000 brokers have a lot of influence in the company; these individuals are used to six-, and sometimes, seven-figure incomes. Trading on the Internet has the potential to drastically reduce commissions and incomes. However, *The Wall Street Journal* estimated that in 1998, only about $2 billion of Merrill's $17.5 billion in revenues came from commissions paid by individual investors.

On June 1, 1999, Merrill announced that it would offer online trading at fees of $29.95, matching Schwab and worrying its 17,000 brokers. The Web service allowed individuals to set up online accounts to trade stocks, bonds, and mutual funds, and eventually stock options. Customers could obtain complete reports of their holdings and transactions, pay bills, and handle other financial tasks through Merrill.

Although Merrill's assets continued increasing 15 percent annually, this amount pales in comparison to Schwab's growth rate of almost 40 percent per year. Merrill Lynch will trade for a fixed commission, but the firm wants to convert customers to a new account called "Unlimited Advantage." For a percentage of the assets in the account, starting at a minimum $1,500 fee per year, Unlimited Advantage account holders can access all of Merrill's online services and are able to make as many trades as they want, electronically or through a broker. At the time of the announcement, fewer than 10 percent of Merrill's retail customers had fee-based accounts.[2]

What motivated the change? How did Merrill decide to overcome the resistance of its brokers? A cover story in the November 15, 1999, issue of *Business Week* offered a behind-the-scenes analysis of Merrill's conversion to an e-broker. The first indication of a problem came late in 1998 when Schwab's market value exceeded Merrill's. By every other metric, Merrill was considerably larger than Schwab. But investors feared Merrill did not understand the Internet. As customers flocked to e-brokers, the firm faced an 85 percent compression in its margins, much more than retailers of toys and books. Not only did this change concern the retail brokerage division, the huge corporate division began to panic as well. This one event, the change in position based on market capitalization of Merrill and Schwab, broke the inertia that had stifled efforts at innovation.

Several key executives and strategists at Merrill (including Steffens) became convinced that Merrill had to embrace the Internet, and change its business model accordingly. Bringing about such change is difficult in a firm that is on top of the industry and extremely successful. The change in Schwab's business model to embrace the Web was

SIDE BAR 4-1

Dell Computer: A Netcentric Firm

Dell is currently the second-largest computer systems company worldwide, and it claims to be the fastest growing. Its sales are now more than $30 billion a year. The company has 33,200 employees and ranks number one in the United States in PC sales.

In 1983, Michael Dell, then an eighteen-year-old freshman at the University of Texas at Austin, spent his spare time formatting hard disks for IBM PC upgrades. Within a year, he dropped out of college to manage his business, a venture with sales of $6 million by 1985 (Rangan and Bell, 1998). That year Dell moved from upgrading computers to assembling its own brand; sales increased to a rate of $70 million a year. In 1990 sales hit $500 million and Dell had secured a place as a major supplier to *Fortune* 500 companies, offering a broad product line of office and home desktop computers and laptops.

In 1992 Dell had its first loss, generated partially by its efforts to sell products through retail channels. The company also experienced quality problems with laptop computers. Dell acted quickly to exit the retail channel and to withdraw from the laptop market until it could offer a machine up to its quality standards.

With its decision to abandon retail sales, Dell became a direct seller; its model is to be an efficient, made-to-order, high-velocity, and low-cost distribution system. From 1992 until it launched its Web site in 1996, customers ordered via toll-free phone numbers, fax, or the mail. With only one way to sell its products, Dell concentrated on a direct, lean manufacturing model.

After order entry personnel check an order for completeness and accounting does a credit check, the order goes to manufacturing. There the order is broken down electronically into a list of parts needed to build the computer; this process generates a specification sheet with a bar code linking the spec sheet to the original order. If a customer calls to check order status, his or her order number is linked to the spec number and Dell can tell where the computer is in the manufacturing process. The spec sheet contains a bill of materials, special instructions, and the software to be loaded on the new computer, and it travels with the computer chassis during manufacture.

The spec sheet is generated from a computer file that has information about the specific components installed and the employees performing assembly at each step in building the computer (Kraemer et al., 2002). Workers use the spec sheet to assemble the computer, beginning with the motherboard, which has the central processor the customer ordered, and the amount of RAM specified. Factory workers put other assembly parts into a bin, disk drives, CD-ROMS and so on, and they forward the motherboard and parts bin to an assembly cell.

The five-person assembly cell is responsible for the final assembly of the PC. Members of the cell constitute a team; their job is to assemble a properly configured computer and test it before the machine leaves their area.

The next stop for the computer is the software loading area where the operating system, applications, and the customer's custom software are loaded onto the disk. (Corporate accounts provide proprietary software that Dell downloads to their computers.) Dell uses an Ethernet connection and fiber optics to download software in about ten minutes, software that used to take forty-five minutes to load using standard cables.

After software is download, the PC goes to an area where it is powered up and "burned-in" for four to eight hours. After passing this test, workers put the computer in a box and send it to the packaging area where other components are packed, like the keyboard, mouse, and manuals.

Dell does not handle the monitor that goes with the system. Instead, it sends an e-mail message to a shipper who pulls the appropriate monitor from supplier stocks, and schedules its arrival for the date the PC is to arrive at the customer's location. This process saves about $30 in shipping costs and reduces the number of times someone handles the monitor; it reduces Dell's overhead as well.

Dell viewed the Internet as a natural step given its direct sales model. In the early 1990s the company began experiment with the Internet, prompted by its customers to deliver online technical support and order status information. Dell established a small group to explore the use of the Net for communicating with customers. The group found that most *Fortune* 500 companies provided employees with Internet access while slightly fewer had intranets.

In July 1996, Dell opened up its Web site for ordering and immediately began selling $1 million of computers a week through the Net. Customers could order and

(Continues)

SIDE BAR 4-1 *(CONTINUED)*

Dell Computer: A Netcentric Firm

track their computers through links from dell.com to shipping partners. The site also contains service and support data, some 35,000 pages of information, which is the same information Dell's technical representatives use.

Sales on the site grew rapidly, within six months the rate was $1 million a day. Three months later sales hit $2 million a day, and in six more months $3 million. By January of 1999, sales at the Dell Web site were at the rate of $10 million a day and by December, over $35 million a day. As of this writing, 50 percent of Dell's sales, averaging $50 million a day, are through the Web, 40 percent of technical support activities take place on the Web, and 50 percent of order status inquiries are online.

Web pages help direct customers to their appropriate category: individual/home users, small businesses, and large organizations. The customer chooses a computer model, and the site helps with the configuration. A base system includes CPU, memory, and recommended components. However, the user can change the components and reprice the computer; the user can try a variety of configurations before choosing to submit an order.

Dell also established custom Web sites for its "premier" partnerships with more than 200 of its largest customers; these sites contain more than 19,000 pages. The sites reflect negotiated prices with each customer. Because Dell handles all PC sales to some customers, it knows the configuration and location of each of its clients' computers worldwide. Corporate customers access Dell's site to learn how much they have spent and what products are in place.

The Web site also helps Dell manage demand. When a West Coast dock strike stopped the flow of CRTs into the United States, Dell started offering its standard configurations on the Web with a flat panel monitor. Customers accepted that monitor over an optional CRT, and Dell chartered 747s to fly monitors to the United States. It was able to survive the potential disruption of the dock strike, and customers were happier with their flat panels than they would have been with CRTs.

The original direct ordering strategy and the Internet have had a major impact on Dell's business model. Because Dell made the decision in 1992 to move to direct ordering, it was well positioned to adopt electronic commerce and to take advantage of the Internet. As a result, Dell's business model has become an example that many others are trying to imitate.

How lean is Dell's lean production? Dell uses a *pull* system to obtain parts from its suppliers who warehouse their components within fifteen minutes of the Dell factories. Suppliers must ensure two hours of inventory in the plant at all times. Dell reduced its number of suppliers to forty-seven from more than 200 in 1992 (twenty-five suppliers account for 85 percent of parts and materials). Dell provides suppliers with real-time access to its production systems, allowing them to track demand and resupply factories faster than if they had to wait for Dell to issue an order.

Dell also worked with its suppliers to reduce defects per 100 units to 1.53 percent. Dell believes that components fail because they are touched too much in production; the company reduced the number of machine touches during assembly from 126 to 56 by redesigning assembly processes. Dell outsourced its inbound logistics to one firm, and its outbound transportation operations to another.

Remember that Dell does not start ordering components and assembling a computer until it has a firm order. A company building to a forecast and selling through retail sores may have thirty to forty-five days of inventory in plant and another forty-five days in the distribution channel. Dell has an average of eleven days of inventory, including inbound supplier goods in transit, outbound customer goods in transit and spare parts. It is estimated that PC components fall 30 percent in value a year, and that a PC sitting on a shelf loses about 10 percent a month of its value in obsolescence. Dell avoids all of these costs because it owns minimal inventory and it does not build computers on speculation.

Dell's cycle time for building a computer is impressive. In 2000, the company connected its suppliers to Dell over the Internet so they can see the parts Dell needs. Its most efficient plants order only the supplies needed to keep production running for two hours. The company notifies suppliers electronically of what it needs for the next two hours, and they must deliver from nearby warehouses. In some cases, a plant finishes and loads a PC for shipment just fifteen hours after a customer order, down from thirty hours before the Internet hookups with suppliers.[3]

(Continues)

SIDE BAR 4-1 *(CONTINUED)*

Dell Computer: A Netcentric Firm

From beginning of the build process to loading on the delivery truck is an estimated seven hours. At the new Austin plant, workers can sometimes build a PC, load software, test the machine, and package it in five hours. As a result, Dell's inventory turns over nearly 42 times a year, compared to an average of 14.3 times in the industry as a whole. Its "days cost of goods sold in inventory" is nine compared to an average of twenty-five in the industry.

Dell's cash conversion cycle is at five days because it frequently receives payment from a customer before it has to pay suppliers for the components of the computer. For retail transactions, Dell converts the order into cash within twenty-four hours. Compare this cash cycle to the build to forecast manufacturer who must buy components to build a PC, send the PC into a distribution channel for sale, and wait to receive payment.

Dell also knows its customers because all orders come from a customer, not a wholesaler or a retail store. The manufacturer selling at retail has no idea who bought the machine unless the customer completes all of the information on a warranty card and returns the card to the manufacturer. Even then, Dell knows more because the warranty card does not include the actual price the customer paid for the PC.

One of the reasons Dell can follow its business model is because technology, both from the Internet and from its internal systems, allows it to substitute information for physical parts and buffer stocks. IT processes the order and makes it possible to track production and shipping. The technology produces a bill of materials and instructions for assembling the computer. Dell interfaced its internal systems to the Web so that customers can follow production and shipping. Overall, the statistics suggest that Dell has 40–50 percent of all transactions coming via customer entry on the Web. How many employees, how much labor does having customers perform these functions save? Estimates are that Dell has a 6 percent cost advantage on manufacturers who follow the traditional build-to-forecast model.

In 2002 Dell announced that it would start manufacturing "white boxes," computers that do not have its own brand name for sale in retail discount stores. Dell says that it will continue to manufacture using its lean, minimum inventory systems, so the private labels that resell the computers evidently will have to maintain inventory. Dell is also pushing more into the server market in competition with Sun and the Linux operating system.

SOURCE: From *Strategies for Electronic Commerce and the Internet,* Henry C. Lucas, Jr., © 2002, The MIT Press. Used by permission of The MIT Press.

relatively small; for Merrill the changes loomed large. It expected to lose $1 billion in equity commissions, but hoped to make it up in fees and assets under management. Merrill also feared the loss of key brokers to rival firms, but this fear may be misplaced as others adopt Merrill's or E*TRADE's model. In a few years, few customers will be left for the full commission broker who will have to adapt to low commission trades or fee-based services in order to survive.

The full-service brokerage firms now offer accounts similar to Merrill's, and at a competitive price. The self-directed investor pays less than the investor who wants full service from a human broker. Technology has changed the nature of retail stock trading and the full-service brokerage business model forever.

This story also illustrates the constantly changing nature of the business environment. Even though Schwab's online trading has been a great success, as has their business model, they suffered greatly during the downturn in the stock market in the 2000–2002 period. Schwab purchased U.S. Trust in order to provide financial advice for its wealthier clients, but this acquisition created some friction with its independent financial advisors who saw Schwab competing with them. Today Schwab has a "discount, online, full-service" business model that is different from the low-price online brokers and the higher-end full-service firms like Merrill. It must cater to a broad mix of customers while keeping its cost structure low, a more difficult proposition than when it was simply a discount broker.

What Hit the Content Providers?

Technological discontinuities in the form of major changes in technology that enable new business models threaten incumbent firms and the way they do business. The Internet and the Web pose a particular problem to firms that deal with digital content, which is the natural language of the Net. The first technology that shocked the content providers was peer-to-peer sharing with Napster. The recording industry watched sales of CDs drop, especially in stores near college campuses. Napster took advantage of the MP3 compressed format for digital music and created a dynamic index of computers whose users were willing to share their files. Within a year, Napster had 1 million users.

The key to Napster was the central server that maintained the index. The actual sharing of the MP3 files involved a direct computer-to-computer (peer-to-peer) transmission from the computer of the provider to the computer of the person doing the download. For the user, the service offered a trove of free music, and it forced the unbundling of albums. You had to buy the entire CD to get the one song you liked; on the Internet you could download that one song. Within a couple of years of its launch, universities had to restrict the use of Napster because it was taking up so much of the capacity of their networks. By the middle of 2000, Napster had 13 million users, and by the fall the Napster community was estimated at 32 million, with up to 1.5 million using the system simultaneously (Moon, 2002).

As you might guess, the recording industry was not pleased with Napster's success. Because users were not charged for downloaded music, the recording company and the artist were not compensated for a song or album a listener would have purchased but downloaded instead. The industry viewed Napster as a massive scheme to violate copyright protection for intellectual content, and they sued to stop the service. The courts agreed with the content providers and forced Napster to shut down, though its name has been purchased by another company.

Napster was vulnerable because of its server with an index pointing to computers whose users were willing to share MP3 files. The courts decided that the server index was intended to get around copyrights, and ordered it turned off. A second generation of peer-to-peer systems has made it much more difficult to stop sharing. Gnutella, KaZaA, and others are true peer-to-peer systems. The user wanting to download a file broadcasts a message over the Internet looking for a computer with that file that is available for download. These systems involve no central index or server to close down. As a result, it is much more difficult for the recording industry to defend its copyrights than it was with Napster. It should also be noted that this approach floods the Internet with requests for a song because no index serves to indicate where the song is available.

The industry has gone to court to get the records of Internet service providers to see whether it can prosecute individuals who are heavy users of peer-to-peer downloads of music. The copyright law is not very understanding of music file swapping; penalties are up to $150,000 per song. That means an average college sophomore with ten weeks of music on a hard drive faces more than $1 billion in liabilities! The Recording Industry Association of America is sending instant messages to users of file sharing software warning them of legal penalties, and the number of households downloading music from the Internet has been dropping. The strategy seems to be to threaten violators with harsh penalties, and then accept a small settlement. Two recent suits against college students who were running small music services modeled after Napster were dropped for $12,000 and $17,500. If the students failed to settle immediately, they were warned that the minimum settlement if the suit went to trial would be $50,000.[4] The recording industry is not winning

MANAGEMENT PROBLEM 4-1

Larry Bryant is the CIO for Summit Pharmaceuticals, a large, diversified ethical drug manufacturing company. In addition to its Life Sciences Division, which develops and markets drugs for humans, it has a large Animal Sciences Division that produces drugs for farm animals, horses, and household pets. The company has a number of different plant locations in United States and around the world, as well as R&D laboratories and sales offices. Over time the company has grown by its own sales efforts and through acquisitions.

From an IT standpoint, an organization chart emerged that Bryant says even he has a hard time understanding. "We have systems staff at the plants, some of the sales offices, and a whole lot of people at headquarters. Some report to local managers and others to divisional CIOs. All the division CIOs have a 'dotted line' reporting relationship to me, but they take most of their directions from the local manager where they work.

"We make this federated structure work, but it is hard on planning, and really difficult for me to know whether we are supporting the needs of the organization. Are we just catering to the whims of a local manager? Are his or her requests really good from the corporation's view? I don't know.

"Are we using our people in the most effective ways? Do they have the organization support and technical tools to do their jobs? How about advancement, do we have a career path for a systems person in a sales office in France?"

Bryant has asked your help to devise a new organization structure to make the IT group at more effective. Be sure to state your objectives for the organization change, and compare and contrast at least two options for Summit to consider. What implementation problems do you anticipate in moving to the organization structure you recommend?

many friends with its approach, but it may be successful in driving people to legal, for-pay downloading services.

It appears that music distribution is adopting a new business model built around the Internet. Apple Computer started a music site, first for Apple computers and then for PCs, that allows a user to purchase songs for $0.99. Some half dozen companies are following this lead, with Wal-Mart, Microsoft, and Sony about to enter the competition. Profit margins are incredibly thin, and most of these sites have to find other sources of revenue. Apple says its iTunes site helps it sell the iPod, its MP3 music player; the Apple service makes it easy to download songs and transfer them to the iPod. At first music labels fiercely resisted licensing their content for Web distribution; now they are rushing to join the bandwagon. Other options include subscription services that provide a variety of pricing schemes that let customers set up play lists and stream songs to their PCs, or let them download a song and burn a certain number to CDs.[5]

As broadband connections proliferate, the movie industry is concerned that it will end up in the same position as the music recording industry. Both of these groups show one possible response to a technological discontinuity, and that is to fight it. The current turmoil is reminiscent of the advent of consumer VCRs; the movie industry fought the sale and distribution of these devices and blank videotapes, fearing the large-scale pirating of movies. It turned out that videotapes of movies, and later DVDs, are so popular that most Hollywood movies make more money in video sales than they do from the box office.

The recording industry, while still fighting music sharing software, is finally trying to adapt to new technology by offering its own downloading services for a fee. AOL Time Warner, EMI, and Bertelsmann started MusicNet in 2001, and Vivendi Universal and Sony launched Pressplay. These services offer music streaming and downloads in a number of ways, usually with a monthly subscription of about $10. A group of retailers including Best Buy, Tower Records, and others started a download service called Echo in 2003. The retailers hope to get licenses from the studios to download music from their own Web sites. Also in 2003 Apple Computer announced iTunes, a download service for 0.99 cents a song, quickly reaching a million downloads. By early 2004, iTunes had sold more than 25 million songs on the Internet. iTunes and Apple's popular iPod look like an Internet music business that will succeed.

Subscribers to most of these services can stream music to their system and are allowed a specified number of downloads a month. Napster itself has been reborn as a legal service; Roxio purchased both Pressplay and Napster, and offers online music under the Napster label.

What does the future look like for digital music and movie content? Verizon announced plans to roll out fiber connections to individual homes and businesses, and other companies are exploring radio links to the home. One such company is successfully offering high-speed Internet connections via radio in Boston, and is expanding to other cities. It is clear that the future is broadband connectivity, which means that individuals will have the technology in place to download music and movies. The challenge is for the industry to come up with a business model that takes advantage of the technological infrastructure that will soon be in place. This model must provide incentives for customers to pay for content rather than obtain it free.

The implications for different businesses are profound:

- *Record stores*: These stores are seeing a decrease in the sale of CDs; the reaction of the large vendors to start their own music download service makes a great deal of sense. Expect to see a continued decline in CD sales.

- *Movie theaters*: Despite the advent of videotapes, consumers still seem to like to go to a movie in a theater to see it on the "big screen" and to interact with the audience. Movie theaters should survive the Internet, at least for the near term.

- *Video rental industry*: This group of vendors is in serious trouble; they are under assault from "on demand" cable movies where subscribers pay per view, and soon from the ability to download movies to a home computer and TV over the Internet. Verizon expects to become a content provider after it reaches a critical mass of broadband customers.

- *Recording industry*: This group is searching for a viable business model. One suggestion would be to support download services by granting licenses to every site requesting them. Current download sites do not offer access to all recorded music, yet most people will not want to pay subscription fees for multiple sites. Charging by the download with no subscription fee might be an alternative in the near term.

- *Movie industry*: The movie industry is resilient and will certainly survive to produce content. It, too, needs to develop a business model that encourages customers to pay for content rather than obtain it for free over the Internet.

The Internet has created a technological discontinuity for various types of content providers. Such major change is usually not welcome, but organizations that figure out a new business model and strategy can flourish under a new regime enabled by information technology.

SIDE BAR 4-2

Cisco: A Netcentric Company

Cisco Systems was founded in 1984 and went public in 1990. The company has been extremely successful selling networking equipment; it has grown with the rapid expansion of corporate networks and the Internet. One of its primary products is a router, a hardware and software package that determines where traffic is to go on corporate intranets and the Internet.

The Internet stimulated manufacturers to develop products for packet switching that follow the TCP/IP protocol. The browser and Web made it easy to post and retrieve information on servers, and companies developed intranets. The intranet uses Internet protocols, hardware, and software to create a private network within a firm. A company such as Ford has hundreds of applications that run internally on its intranet, helping to coordinate different groups. As an example, automakers "tear down" competing automobiles. By posting the results of a teardown on the Ford intranet, engineers from all over the world have access to review parts of other makers' cars. Because all of the components for an intranet existed and followed standards, it was easy for firms to build on this infrastructure.

The corporate intranet model, combined with explosive growth of the Internet, created a large demand for devices such as routers that work with the TCP/IP protocol. Cisco was in an enviable position with its Internet-based products.

Cisco's Web site describes its history this way:

> Since shipping its first product in 1986, the company has grown into a global market leader that holds No. 1 or No. 2 market share in virtually every market segment in which it participates. Cisco Systems shipped its first product in 1986. Since then, Cisco has grown into a multinational corporation with more than 20,000 employees in more than 200 offices in 55 countries. Since becoming a public company in 1990, Cisco's annual revenues have increased from $69 million in that year to $12.2 billion in fiscal 1999. As measured by market capitalization, Cisco is among the largest in the world.

Cisco has enjoyed incredible growth; the company focuses on large corporations, small to medium-sized business, service providers, and education. The company makes products for a variety of network applications, including hubs, switches, and a variety of routers. It also has a line of equipment for local area networks (LANs), which generally use Ethernet as their protocol. The company, like others in the technology sector, experienced difficult conditions in the last half of 2001 and through 2002.

Sections of the chairman's letter from the 2001 annual report provide insights on Cisco's strategy:

> In the early days of the Internet economy, we worked with our customers by sharing ideas and exploring possibilities enabled by a networked world. Today, we are helping our customers share and address their needs by linking our technologies to their business challenges. Ultimately, we are delivering value to them through solutions that take full advantage of the breadth of our networking expertise.

> Although our enterprise, service provider, and commercial customers have historically built separate networks, we are seeing a transition toward a Network of Networks with transparent integration across extranets, intranets, and the Internet. In short, they want Cisco products that work seamlessly across all networks. And they expect us to present a consistent product architecture and strategy with clear product roadmaps—all brought together with a differentiated technology message and compelling business value proposition.

> Together with the accelerating consolidation in the communication equipment industry, we believe these trends will play to our advantage, assuming we execute effectively. Cisco is well-positioned to succeed in this environment because of our financial staying power; the breadth of our products; our end-to-end architecture; the diversity of customers we serve around the world; and our Internet expertise, which is unique in our industry.

> The Internet has become an integral part of Cisco's order entry and manufacturing operations. Most of Cicso's production is outsourced to companies such as Flextronics, and 90 percent of its orders, worth $1 billion

(Continues)

Cisco: A Netcentric Company

a month, come in through the Net with more than half forwarded to the contract electronics manufacturers. The contractor ships to the customer, and Cisco never touches the product. Employees do not handle paper until a check arrives, and soon the check should be replaced with an electronic payment. Cisco figures that going on the Web cut $500 million in costs per year.

Cisco is a technology company whose customers are technologists. It is logical that they would adapt quickly to Web ordering and customer service by searching Cisco's Web site for technical information. This model of customer self-service with a network at the heart of a firm's operations is one that will spread rapidly to other companies, powered by some of Cisco's products.

SOURCE: From *Strategies for Electronic Commerce and the Internet,* Henry C. Lucas, Jr., © 2002, The MIT Press. Used by permission of The MIT Press.

eBay: Creating a New Business

The Internet with its worldwide reach provides a huge market with critical mass if you can motivate people to visit your Web site and do business. In 1995, a French-Iranian immigrant named Pierre Omidyar launched eBay (electronic Bay Area) to help his then-girlfriend trade a collection of Pez dispensers. Within a year, the site was hosting 15,000 auctions a day and logging 2 million hits per week. In 1997 Omidyar sought help from a venture capital firm, and in 1998 he turned over management to a new chief executive officer, Meg Whitman. By January of 2002, eBay had 37 million customers and was one of the few dot-coms that had been continuously profitable (Frei, 2002). As of this writing, the site claims to have 95 million users.

The great appeal of this new industry on the Web comes from several sources. First, it is a worldwide electronic auction; you buy and sell from your computer connected to the Internet. You need not to be in a physical location at one point in time to participate. Economists like auctions because they believe that each person bids their true value for the item being auctioned, resulting in an efficient market.

eBay does a number of things well to keep its group of buyers and sellers loyal. First, buyers rate sellers in order to overcome some of the problems of trusting an anonymous seller. eBay also monitors auctions and tries to prevent fraud. It listens carefully to its users, and tries to be responsive to them. These elements made it successful in building an online community of eBay buyers and sellers.

One comment made when eBay was starting was that it had unlocked billions of dollars of value in people's attics. It is true that one of the largest parts of eBay is the sale of collectibles, but it is a much broader market now. In fact, major manufacturers sell goods on eBay, just as do thousands of individuals.

One of the most interesting parts of the site is eBay Motors. One might predict a national market for used cars at the retail level would never succeed, except possibly for specialty antique and exotic autos. eBay managed to create such a market by carefully building and marketing eBay Motors. Whitman encourages dealers to list cars on the site and suggests that they try to sell late model vehicles that are not moving quickly from their lots. As a result, a buyer finds a large number of autos with low mileage that the dealer is not able to sell quickly, often at very attractive reserve (a *reserve* is the minimum a seller will accept for a product; it is not known to buyers). eBay also has an option where sellers can list a fixed price at which a buyer can purchase an item without bidding, by agreeing to the price.

eBay holds a tremendous advantage over the typical used car listing in a newspaper's classified advertising section. The Internet makes it possible for someone selling a car to include a large number of pictures of the vehicle, inside and out, on the site. A picture is truly worth a lot of words when you compare a product description on eBay with a comparable ad in your local newspaper. In most instances, an auto bid is contingent on seeing and inspecting the vehicle. Buyers on eBay seem to be willing to travel some distance to buy a car and bring it home.

What eBay created, then, is a national market for used cars at the retail level. The market is not complete; if you look at the cars being offered you find few plain vehicles. The selection shows a much larger percentage of Porsches and BMWs than one finds in a typical Sunday newspaper's classifieds, but eBay Motors is relatively young, and is expected to grow.

Beyond the motors section, eBay created a new business, a worldwide auction. Some individuals become full-time sellers on eBay. They purchase or make goods to be placed in the auction. Interviews show that some of these people quit jobs in order to work full time selling on eBay, so this Web business is supporting a lot of independent vendors by providing a market for them. eBay is another example of how technology can transform markets.

IT VARIABLES FOR DESIGNING ORGANIZATIONS

The preceding examples show major technology-induced changes in industries; these changes occur at the macro level and influence individual firms in the industry. At a micro level, technology makes it possible to create new forms of organizations. Managers design and redesign organizations all the time. The decision you make to open a branch office and give it responsibility for sales in a region is an organization design issue. If you undertake a new project by creating a task force that includes members from around the world and that will work virtually, you have designed a temporary organization.

One way to look at these micro issues of organization design is to consider different design variables. A variable is something that takes on different values, for example, one calculates the interest payment (P) on a simple loan by taking the interest rate (i) times the loan's outstanding balance (B), or $P = iB$. In this equation, P, i, and B are all variables that can take on different values. The interest rate might vary for different customers or types of loans. Obviously, the outstanding balance will differ among loans.

For organizations, design variables include the span of control, a number that can take on different values. An organization that has chosen a span of control of seven subordinates for each manager will be hierarchical while one that chooses a span of twenty will be much flatter.

Table 4-2 contains examples of key organization design variables that you can use to build organizations. This table contains two types of variables: those labeled conventional and a set of variables that come from information technology. Information technology is defined to include computers, communications, videoconferencing, artificial intelligence, virtual reality, fax, cellular and wireless phones, pagers, and so on.

The problem with conventional organization design literature is its failure to recognize the new design variables enabled by information technology. In the case of linking mechanisms, IT such as e-mail or groupware can be used instead of conventional solutions such as task forces or liaison agents. The new IT-enabled variables may be totally distinct from traditional design variables as we shall see when we examine *virtual corporations*.

TABLE 4-2   Conventional and IT design variables.

Class of Variable	Conventional Design Variables	IT Design Variables
Structural	Definition of organizational subunits	Virtual components
	Determining purpose, output of subunits	Linking mechanisms
	Reporting mechanisms	
	Linking mechanisms	Electronic linking
	Control mechanisms	
	Staffing	Technological leveling
Work Process	Tasks	Production automation
	Workflows	Electronic workflows
	Dependencies	
	Output of process	
	Buffers	Virtual components
Communications	Formal channels	Electronic communications
	Informal communications/ collaboration	Technological matrixing
Interorganizational relations	Make versus buy decision	Electronic customer/supplier relationships
	Exchange of materials	Electronic customer/supplier relationships
	Communications mechanisms	Electronic linking

IT-enabled variables may also be an extension of traditional variables, as in the case of linking mechanisms.

Table 4-2 arrays the conventional design variables drawn from the literature on organization design with new kinds of IT design variables. The first column of the table groups conventional design variables into four categories: structural, work process, communications, and interorganizational. Column 3 in the table presents new organizational design variables made possible through information technology. These variables are described in the following paragraphs.

Structural

Virtual Components

The organization can use IT to create components that do not exist in conventional form. For example, some manufacturers want parts suppliers to substitute for their inventory. The supplier is linked through electronic data interchange with the manufacturer.

Using overnight delivery, it provides parts to the manufacturer just as they are needed for production. The manufacturer now has a virtual raw materials inventory owned by the supplier until it arrives for production.

Electronic Linking

Through electronic mail, electronic or videoconferencing, and fax, it is possible to form links within and across all organizational boundaries. New work groups form quickly and easily. Electronic linking also facilitates monitoring and coordination, especially from remote locations.

Technological Leveling

IT can substitute for layers of management and for a number of management tasks. In some bureaucratic organizations, layers of management exist to look at, edit, and approve messages that flow from the layer below them to the level above. Electronic communications can eliminate some of these layers. In addition, a manager's span of control can be increased because electronic communications can be more efficient than phone or personal contact for certain kinds of tasks, particularly those dealing with administrative matters. Technology makes it possible to increase the span of control and possibly eliminate layers in the organization, leveling it in the process.

Work Process

Production Automation

The use of technology to automate manufacturing processes is well documented in magazines and newspapers. IT is also used extensively for automating information processing and assembly line tasks in the financial industry. In cases where information is the product of a firm, IT is the factory. For white-collar workers, intelligent agents that roam networks provide one type of automation.

Electronic Workflows

Interest in process reengineering prompted the development of workflow languages and systems. As organizations eliminate paper and perform most of their processing using electronic forms and images, workflow languages will route documents electronically to individuals and workgroups that need access to them. Agents that can traverse networks to find information and carry messages facilitate electronic workflows. Electronic workflows also contribute to the monitoring and coordination of work.

Communications

Electronic Communications

Electronic mail, electronic bulletin boards, and fax all offer alternatives to formal channels of communications.

Technological Matrixing

Through the use of e-mail, video and electronic conferencing, and fax, matrix organizations can be created at will. For example, a company could form a temporary task force from marketing, sales, and production departments by using e-mail and groupware to prepare for

MANAGEMENT PROBLEM 4-2

John Roberts knew that he faced a number of organization problems when he took the CEO's job at Victor Electronics. His predecessor was an autocrat, to put it mildly. Most managers were afraid to make decisions for fear of incurring his displeasure. As a result, Roberts has a group of managers who are capable, but who are not used to making any decisions on their own. The safest approach was to wait for orders from the top, and then execute those orders well. You were not criticized and the CEO didn't yell at you if you followed this strategy.

Roberts does not like this kind of organization. "What a waste of talent—we have a lot of good managers, and their potential is completely bottled up because they are used to someone in my position telling them what to do. I expect them to have different ideas than mine, and for there to be some conflict. But

we can talk about the alternatives and choose the best one together without shouting at each other."

He went on, "My problem as I see it is to create an organization structure to draw these managers out, to help them learn to be decision makers. Some may not make it, but I think most of them are capable. I can play with the overall structure of the organization, the reward structure, the way we approach problem solving, and a number of variables. What I want to come out with in the end is a more effective organization—and not a lot of layers of management."

Your assignment is to help Roberts design a more effective organization for Victor Electronics. Think about different alternatives for structure, and consider the organization design variables discussed in this chapter. Here is an opportunity to transform an organization to make it far more effective than it is now.

a trade show; participants would report electronically to their departmental supervisors and to the team leader for the show, creating a matrix organization based on technology.

Interorganizational Relations

Electronic Customer/Supplier Relationships

Companies and industries are rapidly adopting electronic data exchange (EDI), Internet and intranet technologies to speed the ordering process and improve accuracy. These technologies help the organization monitor and coordinate relationships with external organizations, for example, different virtual components.

It is interesting to note that no specific IT variable parallels the traditional variable "control mechanisms." Firms have used information systems to provide control after the organization has been designed. Examples include budgets, project management applications, and similar monitoring systems. Mrs. Fields Cookies uses a variety of traditional and IT variables in creating an organization with extensive controls. However, even in this case, no single IT control variable influences the design.

Building a T-Form Organization

The IT design variables in Table 4-2 can be used to create a new organization using information technology, a structure labeled the *T-Form organization*. The pure T-Form organization depends on managers who base supervision on trust in employees and their self-control. It is not possible to exert close physical supervision. Managers also have to trust partners in business alliances because both partners depend on each other. The details of how people define and execute their tasks are left up to the employee. Decision making is moved to the lowest level of the organization where people have the information and knowledge to make the decision. People and tasks are extremely important components of the T-Form organization.

The T-Form organization is a generic model for a technologically enabled organization. The same IT design variables can be used in a variety of ways to create distinct types of organizations, all of which have some of the characteristics of the T-Form. Figure 4-1 presents simple structural models of five different organizations.

Frito-Lay is a major producer of snack foods, including Fritos Corn Chips. The company invested heavily in handheld computers for its drivers and a satellite communications network to transmit transactions data to headquarters. The firm developed a data warehouse and provided decision support tools for district managers to use in planning their operations. The company vests decision rights heavily in senior and lower-level managers, leaving relatively little need for middle-level managers.

Mrs. Fields Cookies developed elaborate in-store systems to guide its store managers in all aspects of the business. The company uses e-mail and voice mail to communicate with the store manager. It also maintains a flat control structure with store controllers at headquarters closely monitoring sales results for each retail store.

VeriFone is a company that manufacturers devices to verify credit card payments and is active in offering electronic commerce solutions on the Internet. The firm views itself as a global corporation. A recent chairman compares it to a "blueberry pancake where all the blueberries [locations] are equal." VeriFone uses technology extensively for communications and coordination in the firm.

Calyx & Corolla is a start-up that we describe as a *snap-together* organization. The founder, Ruth Owades, studied the floral distribution industry and came up with a new business model. Her observation was that flowers spent a long time in distribution from

FIGURE 4-1   IT-enabled organization forms.

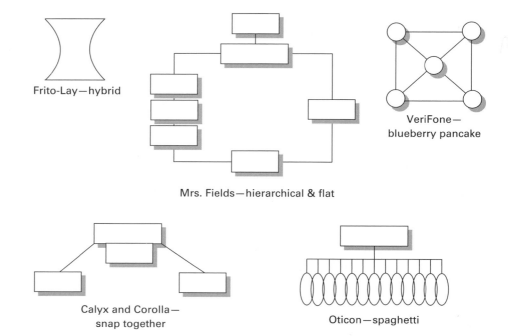

Frito-Lay—hybrid

Mrs. Fields—hierarchical & flat

VeriFone—
blueberry pancake

Calyx and Corolla—
snap together

Oticon—spaghetti

the time they were cut until they passed through wholesale florists to the local flower shop. She negotiated with growers to pick and arrange flowers according to the specifications in her catalogs, and with FedEx to ship the flowers overnight. Her core business process was to market the flowers and accept orders from customers. An order was routed to a grower who picked, arranged, and packed the flowers. The grower addressed the package and turned it over to FedEx for delivery. Calyx & Corolla itself had a computer system for order processing, and e-mail and fax to growers. Credit cards provided the accounts receivable, and customers could track their orders on FedEx's Web site.

Oticon is a Danish manufacturer of hearing aids that underwent a major restructuring when it lost considerable market share. The new chairman created a "spaghetti organization" in which an executive committee agrees on tasks that the firm must complete and assigns them to a team leader. The leader must put together a team to complete the task; technology facilitates the work of these virtual teams.

Table 4-3 shows how each of the firms in Figure 4-1 has used IT design variables to create a different structure. These structures help the firms enjoy the benefits described for the generic T-Form organization; they demonstrate the variety that is possible for the firm choosing to take advantage of technology for organization design.

Adopting the T-Form: An Example

An example illustrates how IT variables can be applied to the design of an organization. Assume that a traditionally structured manufacturing firm wishes to take advantage of new technology to become a T-Form organization.

SIDE BAR 4-3

Verizon: Technology Transforms a Business Model

Verizon is a telephone company that was formed by the merger of two "Baby Bells," Nynex in New York and Bell Atlantic, which served a number of states south of Nynex's territory. The company is immense and generates $22 billion a year in cash. It invests nearly $13 billion annually, and has a large debt of $54 billion from the merger and other investments. In addition to the traditional land-line business, Verizon is a major cellular and digital subscriber line (DSL) provider. The company is experimenting with setting up wireless access points in cities and providing free mobile connectivity to its DSL customers. Verizon has been successful with a local and long-distance flat-rate, all-you-can-call product.

Verizon has clearly branched out from plain old telephone service (POTS), and it has ambitions to change its business model further. The company announced a program to roll out a fiber connection to its customers in twenty-nine states over the next ten to fifteen years, at a cost of $20–$40 billion. Verizon is gambling that the cost of connecting subscribers by fiber will continue to decline. One assumes that Verizon will replace its existing DSL service with the faster cable offering. Given an increasing customer base with broadband service, Verizon plans to begin distributing video services within five years, competing with cable companies.

Verizon's transformation will take place over a number of years, and it represents a risky, bold strategy. Will fiber turn out to be the dominant technology to the home? What about WiFi or satellite? Will cable companies sit still; they have been competing with phone companies by offering phone service as a part of a cable TV, Internet access package. Which company will end up with the greatest market share? Technology stimulated these new business models, especially the Internet: Cable companies become phone providers, and telephone companies will offer content.

SOURCE: *Business Week,* August 4, 2003.

TABLE 4-3 Company structure and IT design variables.

Companies/IT Design Variables	Frito-Lay	Mrs. Fields	Verifone	Calyx & Corolla	Oticon
Virtual components		Presence of Mrs. Fields in each store	Extensive use of teams and alliances	Growers, FedEx, and credit card companies	Project teams
Electronic linking and communications	Extensive with route salesforce, district managers, factories, distribution centers	E-mail and voice mail; PCs in stores	Extensive within company	With growers	Within firm
Technological matrixing			Global teams to solve problems		Project teams
Technological leveling	At headquarters	For store controller organization	Minimum structure and hierarchy		
Electronic workflows				With growers, credit card companies	
Production automation		In-store systems			Redesign of factory
Electronic customer/ supplier relationships				With growers, credit card companies	

Currently, Victor Electronics has a traditional organization structure. At its headquarters is a small staff, and then a number of manufacturing plants operate in the United States and abroad as described in earlier chapters. The largest of these plants is responsible for most information technology in the company. The firm generally underinvested in technology and fell behind its competitors in the industry. Fortunately for Victor, its products are of high quality and the company has not needed to compete on information technology.

Suppose that management heard about the T-Form organization and would like to adopt it. What could the company do? Table 4-4 shows how management at Victor could use the IT design variables discussed in this chapter to restructure the company. Victor is currently being forced into becoming a *virtual supplier* by its customers who are moving to just-in-time production. Victor needs to develop the capability to inquire against and monitor its customers' production control and scheduling systems so that it can send products without the customer even having to order them.

TABLE 4-4 An example of design for Victor Electronics.

Class of Variables	Conventional Design Variables	IT Design Variables	Applied to Victor
Structural	Definition of organizational subunits	Virtual components	Manage virtual inventory for distributors; connect with customer production systems for JIT; use a common order entry system for a single point of contact; contract with overnight carrier for all distribution
	Determining purpose, output of subunits		
	Reporting mechanisms		Use more electronic communications to flatten structure, increase span of control
	Linking mechanisms	Electronic linking	Link production planning, order entry, and marketing; notebook computers for salesforce; eliminate private offices for salesforce
	Control mechanisms		Develop systems to make control information more widely available
	Staffing	Technological leveling	Reduce the number of layers in the organization by substituting electronic communications and groupware
Work process	Tasks	Production automation	Continue efforts at automation
	Workflows	Electronic workflows	Move toward total electronic tracking of order; use bar codes to coordinate production with an electronic traveler
	Dependencies		Coordinate with e-mail and groupware
	Output of process		
	Buffers	Virtual components	
	Formal channels	Electronic communications	Use e-mail and groupware, especially to communicate among distributed plants and headquarters
	Informal communications/ collaboration	Technological matrixing	Use e-mail and groupware to coordinate on production forecasts and special projects
Interorganizational relations	Make-versus-buy decision	Electronic customer/ supplier relationships	Develop a home page on the Internet containing product information; as soon as feasible, use it or a commercial online service to allow customers to inquire on availability; other options would be EDI and groupware
	Exchange of materials	Electronic customer/ supplier relationships	Same as above
	Communications mechanisms	Electronic linking	Establish electronic mail links with customers; consider commercial services, EDI, and/or groupware

SIDE BAR 4-4

Building a Value Network

The term *value net* describes the relationship that develops among companies and the firms to which they outsource various functions. One good example of how a value net evolves is Fidelity Investments, the largest American mutual funds firm, located in Boston. Fidelity manages a large number of 401(k) pension plans for large corporations. To service these accounts, Fidelity invested hundreds of millions of dollars for computer systems and call centers over a twenty-year period. The head of Fidelity recognized that many of these systems could be used for other applications such as payroll and health plan administration.

Fidelity began an outsourcing business for human resources functions. Today 10,000 of the company's 30,000 employees work in the outsourcing business for employee benefits, which serves customers such as IBM, British Petroleum, and Monsanto. This benefits work brought in a quarter of the company's $9.18 billion in revenue in 2001, and the company plans to grow the number to 50 percent of revenue in ten years. Fidelity invested $1 billion in this business since 1994.

Value networks will grow spontaneously as firms realize that activities that are a core competence for them can be offered to other firms. These networks will result in many complex relationships. For example, how would an organization chart look if Fidelity outsourced its IT to IBM while continuing to handle IBM's employee benefits?

SOURCE: *The Wall Street Journal*, January 3, 2002.

Electronic linking can be used to link production planning, order entry, and marketing. The salesforce does not need individual offices. Representatives can use notebook computers and home offices to concentrate on working with customers. Control can be enhanced by developing information systems that make control information available to various levels of management.

Technological leveling is accomplished by reducing layers of management and providing communications tools such as electronic mail and groupware to managers. Victor has a large number of administrative support staff members and others not involved in direct production in the factories. This support organization adds overhead and is an excellent candidate for leveling after analyzing the various job functions and determining where the technology makes savings possible.

In the factory, the company successfully moved toward production automation. Expanded efforts should focus on the creation of an electronic manufacturing environment. Orders arrive electronically from customers and each order generates a bar code to describe the customer and product. When production begins, a worker attaches a bar code to the physical tray that holds the product through the production cycle. At each stage a worker passes a wand over the bar code at a workstation to bring up a screen with instructions on what operation to perform. At the end of production after quality testing, the only paper necessary is a label for the shipper.

Electronic mail and groupware can be used for technological matrixing. They address the informal communications vital in managing a company. Victor can quickly form task forces and other informal groups to address problems. This approach is particularly valuable for communications among plants. For example, one U.S. plant sends "kits" of product to be completed to a plant in Mexico. Various problems between the plants can be resolved quickly using electronic communications rather than physical travel.

Technological matrixing also facilitates a reduction in managerial levels as it encourages employees to take the initiative in solving problems. Suppose that a customer contacts a marketing manager to ask if it would be possible to access Victor's production scheduling system to schedule products to be built for the customer. The marketing manager, using e-mail and groupware, can form a task force in a matter of minutes that includes personnel from production planning, marketing, information systems, and other interested areas. It then becomes unnecessary to pass this request through layers of management in different departments.

Victor needs to connect electronically to customers to provide them with a virtual inventory. It can also take advantage of more extensive electronic customer-supplier relationships. For example, Victor can put up a home page on the Web to describe its products and then allow its customers to order from the Internet.

The results of Victor Electronics' adoption of IT design variables include extensive use of electronic communications and linking, fewer management layers, and flatter organization structure. Fewer layers, combined with the availability of information at all levels in the organization, will push decision making down to lower levels of management. Easy electronic communications encourage employees to contact appropriate colleagues to solve a problem, rather than refer it up the hierarchy through a supervisor. Employees will be able to take on more responsibility and have an IT infrastructure to support them.

Some employees, especially the sales force, at Victor will no longer have offices. The firm will move toward complete electronic integration with customers and suppliers. Electronic mail for informal communications, EDI for routine transactions, and direct Internet links into customer information systems, will increase the firm's responsiveness to customers and suppliers. Electronic workflows in production will eliminate paper, and more importantly, provide better service. Production lots will not get lost if they are tracked electronically and production workers have accurate information about the tasks to perform for each order.

To accomplish this restructuring will take Victor a long time because it failed to keep up-to-date with technology. It will have to invest in a technological infrastructure and people to develop the kind of IT applications described. The company's product quality helped it attain a commanding market share, and adopting a T-Form organization will help it sustain this position and meet the threats of competitors who currently obtain more from their investment in IT than Victor.

A note of caution: IT is not the solution for every problem. Competent managers can use the IT design variables in this chapter to improve the organization. They can also use them to create significant problems; for example, in one company a manager only communicates with the staff via e-mail and rarely listens to any of them. It is likely that his strong staff will find other places to work. IT design variables are one approach to improving the organization; outstanding managers will use them with good taste to design efficient and effective organizations.

New Management Challenges

Organizations that take advantage of IT to develop innovative structures present challenges to managers who are responsible for their ongoing operations. In the traditional organization, a manager has authority from his or her position and from the incentives the manager controls. Managers have long had the ability to hire and fire subordinates, to evaluate their performance, and determine their salaries or wages. A custom in Western culture is the expectation that a subordinate will respond to assignments and requests from a manager to whom he or she reports.

The new organizations enabled by technology make heavy use of outsourcing, which are agreements with other firms to provide key products and services. A customer of Victor Electronics who manufactures a cellular phone is likely to do no real manufacturing, but to rely on a contract electronics manufacturer such as Solectron or Flextronics to build the phone. Firms then become part of a network of companies that provide services to

SIDE BAR 4-5

Where is Everyone and Everything?

As locator systems emerge from laboratories and move into business, they will change business processes and the way firms are organized. Locator systems for things are further along than they are for people. The technology is called radio frequency identification, or RFID. When interrogated by a radio signal, an RFID tag responds with information. The E-ZPass toll collection system on the East Coast is an example of this technology, though the tags for autos are quite large compared to tags used to track merchandise. The tag can provide more information than a bar code, and a passive tag currently sells for about $0.15 cents. (Hopes are that prices will drop to about $0.05 cents as the volume in use increases.)

Analysts predict that better tracking of goods will save about 5 percent of store inventories and reduce labor costs in warehouses by 7.5 percent. Of course, costs to introduce this new technology will be incurred. A retailer will need to invest in each distribution center and each store to read and manage data. A large chain may have to spend $35–40 million to integrate new information into existing logistics systems. It is likely that suppliers will have to absorb the costs of the tags, which will run into millions because so many of them will be needed.[6]

Wal-Mart mandated the use of RFID tags for its 100 largest suppliers for three distribution centers in Texas. The U.S. Defense Department will require major suppliers to use the tags by the end of 2004. General Electric's Power Plant Systems Group made RFID tags voluntary, but most of its suppliers are complying because they help goods get through customs faster, which is important on large projects. GE absorbed the costs for suppliers by providing them with the tags. The tags consist of small microchips that send radio frequency product identification information; GE's tags are battery powered, which makes them

"active" (passive tags respond to a query from a reading device). Active tags are much more expensive, on the order of $7 to $50, but they will work in places that do not have electricity. On the shipping date, suppliers send GE electronic data containing package information and each tag's unique ID. At each location (e.g. a port, a ship, or customs clearance), it is possible to check these data. The equipment for a large project can cover twenty acres, and employees take inventory by riding around in golf carts with handheld receivers that pick up RFID signals within 100 feet. The system cuts an estimated 75 percent of the time required to take inventory. Using a Web application, project managers can get the status of material in seconds.[7]

If you can locate things, then why not people? The technology exists to track employees in an organization, concerns about privacy remain an issue; employees may not want anyone to know exactly where they are! A setting where one generally finds consensus on the need for location information is the hospital. Mass General Hospital in Boston is using location devices to keep track of doctors and other medical personnel. A system like the one at the hospital tracks people wearing badges or devices that send radio or infrared signals to receivers in ceilings or walls. (GPS technology only works outdoors where GPS receivers have a clear view of low, earth-orbiting satellites.) This kind of system is based on wireless technology, and is being used to help people navigate in grocery stores, museums, and other places. In the hospital, knowing where surgeons, staff members, and equipment are located provides the advantage of making planning more efficient. One doctor explained how valuable it would be to walk to a workstation and ask for the location of the nearest defibrillator.

SOURCE: *New York Times*, October 30, 2003.

each other. How does a manager coordinate and influence behavior of a network partner? The employees of the partner firm do not report to the manager who cannot hire or fire them, nor can the manager influence those employees' salaries. The manager is in a new relationship of dependence on a partner firm, yet the manager lacks the traditional authority mechanisms that made subordinates responsive to managerial requests.

A few researchers addressed this problem, and one of them suggested that effective managers in this kind of environment will have many employees in boundary-spanning roles, that is, employees who coordinate with partners in the network. Leaders will try to include all stakeholders in making decisions, which will lead to the increased use of teams that cross functional and organizational boundaries. These managers will learn to use a wide repertoire of authority types and will figure out how to influence the behavior of others even though they have no direct reporting relationship to the manager. The manager will use different types of authority in different situations. For example, in a conflict situation the manager may use more traditional means such as the threat to no longer do business with a network partner (Schneider, 2002).

CHAPTER SUMMARY

Table 4-1 listed some of the industries and their transformations discussed in the chapter. The important points to remember follow:

1. Information technology interacts with organizations and can be used to change the structure of the organization and its subunits.

2. One desirable impact of IT occurs when technology contributes to organizational flexibility.

3. Older legacy systems often perform critical tasks for the firm. These systems usually run on mainframe computers and are large and complex. One management problem is deciding if and when to make massive investments to migrate these systems to up-to-date technology.

4. Some important considerations in studying the variety of organizational structures are uncertainty, specialization, coordination, and interdependence.

5. A number of IT-enabled variables can be used to design organizations. They supplement and sometimes replace traditional organization design variables.

6. These variables can be used to create the T-Form structure or applied to produce a range of structures including virtual organizations, negotiated organizations, and vertically integrated conglomerates. The variables may also be used in subunits of traditional firms.

7. It is important to remember that organizations and people play extremely important roles in the development and success of technology.

KEYWORDS

Competitive advantage	Flexibility	Production automation
Electronic communications	Legacy systems	Productivity
Electronic conglomerate	Middle line	Reciprocal interdependence
Electronic customer/supplier relationships	Mutual dependence	Sequential interdependence
Electronic linking	Operating core	Strategic apex
Electronic workflows	Organization	Support staff
	Pooled interdependence	Technological leveling

Technological matrixing

Technostructure

Time and space boundaries

Uncertainty

Virtual components

Virtual inventory

Virtual supplier

RECOMMENDED READINGS

Andal-Ancion, A., Cartwright, P., and Yip, G. 2003. Digital transformation of traditional businesses. *Sloan Management Review*, Summer, pp. 34–41. (Suggests ten drivers to determine the best strategy for integrating digital business with your existing business.)

Brown, C., Clancy, G., and Scholer, R. 2003. A post-merger IT integration success story: Sallie Mae. *MIS Quarterly Executive*, 2(1), pp. 15–27.

Brown, C., and Vessey, I. 2003. Managing the next wave of enterprise systems: Leveraging lessons from ERP. *MIS Quarterly Executive*, 2(1), pp. 65–77.

Capelli, P. 2001. Online recruiting. *Harvard Business Review*, 79(3), pp. 139–146.

Darwall, C. 2001. *Cisco Systems, Building Leading Internet Capabilities*. Boston: Harvard Business School Press. (The story of how Cisco encouraged the use of the Web in all of its activities.)

Frei, F. 2002. *eBay (A): The Customer Marketplace*. Boston: Harvard Business School.

Ghoshal, S., and Gratton, L. 2002. Integrating the enterprise. *Sloan Management Review*, Fall, pp. 31–38. (How technology helps companies integrate horizontally.)

Kraemer, K., and Dedrick, J. 2002. *Dell Computer: Organization of a Global Production Network*. Irvine: CRITO, Working Paper.

Lucas, H.C., Jr. 1996. *The T-Form Organization: Using Technology to Design Organizations for the 21st Century*. San Francisco: Jossey-Bass. (The story of the T-Form organization.)

Sawhney, M., and Prandelli, E. 2000. Communities of creation: Managing distributed innovation in turbulent markets. *California Management Review*, 42(4), pp. 24–54.

Schneider, M. 2002. A stakeholder model of organizational leadership. *Organization Science*, 13(2), pp. 209–220. (A look at the challenges of managing in a networked environment.)

DISCUSSION QUESTIONS

1. What kind of technology is least flexible? Most flexible?

2. The information services department is often considered to provide a support function. Can a support department really be powerful? What are the different kinds of power in an organization?

3. What kinds of management problems result from a lack of organizational flexibility?

4. What organizations are completely dependent on information technology for their operations?

5. What kinds of employees are most likely to be replaced by information technology? How does your answer depend on the type of system and the decision levels affected?

6. How would you measure the extent of unemployment created by the implementation of IT? What factors tend to mitigate the problem of increased unemployment if it actually occurs?

7. What signs might indicate the need to restructure or redesign an organization?

8. Is information technology creating more centralization in organizations? How do you define centralization? Why should technology have any effect at all on the degree of centralization?

9. How would you recognize a company that is using IT successfully? What signs would you expect to find?

10. How can IT be used to create *virtual* organizations?

11. How should managers introduce organizational changes that employ technology? What are the risks?

12. What alliances were key for the nationwide floral company described in this chapter?

13. Consider a typical manufacturing organization and describe the dependencies that exist among departments.

14. Why should users be involved in the design of systems? How much influence should they have?

15. What are the risks for a small company connecting itself electronically with major customers?

16. What are the problems with legacy systems? What are their implications for management?

17. How can IT be used to help design an organization?

18. What are the IT-enabled organization design variables? How do they supplement or replace conventional design variables?

19. What tools does the manager have available to influence IT in the organization?

20. As a user, to whom do you think the information services department should report? Should it be responsible to the finance department?

21. Should an organization that invests in developing an electronic market be free to build biases into the market that favor its own products and services?

22. Early forecasts suggested that middle managers would be reduced in number and stature as a result of information technology. Has this prediction been realized? Why or why not?

23. Does technology have an impact beyond the organization, for example, on stockholders or customers? What effects occur, and what problems are created for these groups?

24. What is the role of the traditional organization given the kind of structures that IT makes possible?

ENDNOTES

1. Section on Merrill Lynch from *Strategies for Electronic Commerce and the Internet*, Henry C. Lucas, Jr., © 2002, The MIT Press.

2. *New York Times,* October 8, 1999.

3. *Business Week,* September 18, 2000.

4. *Business Week,* September 8, 2003.

5. *The Wall Street Journal*, November 19, 2003.

6. *New York Times,* November 10, 2003.

7. *Informationweek*, October 27, 2003.

CHAPTER 5

GLOBALIZATION AND IT IN INTERNATIONAL BUSINESS

A Manager's Perspective

One of the most significant business trends of the last two decades is globalization. Information technology, especially the Internet, makes it possible to coordinate geographically dispersed business units. Variations of the global firm range from an alliance or affiliation with a foreign company, to a completely global firm such as VeriFone, where the CEO responsible for the firm's greatest growth did not like the concept of a headquarters location. His ideal was for all locations to be equal. The advantage in this type of organization structure arises when each local entity makes the decisions that affect its customers and geographic territory without the delay of checking with headquarters. A sales team can agree to a modification to a product in the customer's office when the idea first comes up without the delay for an approval. The local staff knows local customs and customers so the global firm can be highly responsive. As you read about international business, think about how information technology contributes to going global.

VALUE PROPOSITION

Information technology can help a firm become global through the following contributions:

- Enhanced global competitiveness
- Reduced administrative and coordination costs for a global firm
- Improved efficiencies
- More effective performance in local markets

The contribution of IT to global business can be partially evaluated by examining the following factors:

- Local versus global market share of the firm
- Market share in local countries
- Sales per employee per country
- Sales growth per country
- Administrative and communications costs
- Number of employees by country over time

Victor Electronics, introduced in Chapter 1, is a U.S. company with foreign plants, not a multinational and certainly not a transnational firm. Victor has strategic business units in different locations around the world, but these units lack much autonomy. The headquarters location pretty much runs the company worldwide. Victor plants in different countries are locally managed, but they do no planning on their own. Headquarters responds to all requests for capital and equipment, and the plant's job is to fill orders that it receives from one of the three sales offices, one in Rockville, Maryland, for the United States, Singapore for Asia, and Manchester in the United Kingdom for Europe. Victor operates plants in North Carolina, New Mexico, Maine, Mexico, Malaysia, Spain, Brazil, Costa Rica, Puerto Rico, and China (under construction); see Figure 5-1.

John Roberts wants to make Victor into more of a *transnational firm.* "I think we can do a lot better if local country operations have more autonomy. Right now, our salesforce has to contact headquarters in North Carolina to offer any special prices. I'd like to see us move that authorization level first to the three sales offices for each area of the world, and eventually to country managers," Roberts told his staff.

He continued, "But we need a combination of technology and human interaction to make this happen. With e-mail, I could insist that all decisions come to me and that I approve everything. I think that would slow down decision making and lead to a lot of resentment among our managers in other countries. I'd like to see a sales representative meet with a client and have the tools to quote a price and discount right there. That means we have to

FIGURE 5-1 Victor's locations.

☆ Headquarters
    North Carolina
○ Sales Offices
    Maryland—US
    Singapore—Asia
    Manchester—Europe

☐ Plants

North Carolina	New Mexico
Maine	Mexico
Maylasia	Spain
Brazil	Costa Rica
Puerto Rico	China

know our costs, and that sales rep has to have a notebook or PDA that can calculate whether the order is profitable to us at the price he or she wants to quote. We aren't quite there yet."

GLOBALIZATION: THE FUTURE OF BUSINESS

Globalization has been one of the major trends in business in the last decade. It is estimated that 579 global corporations account for about 25 percent of the world's production. These companies range in size from $1 billion to $100 billion. The world's strongest economies are heavily trade oriented. The United States, until recently, actively promoted free or reduced tariff trade, though some labor groups and members of Congress oppose this campaign.

The European Economic Community (EEC) eliminated almost all barriers to trade and adopted a common currency, the euro. The United States, Canada, and Mexico completed the NAFTA free-trade pact that phases out most tariffs over a fifteen-year period. Emerging markets continue to expand in Eastern Europe and the Commonwealth of Independent Soviet States. Trade is growing with China and India, countries that liberalized their economies in the past few years. The consensus among economists is that free trade will eventually benefit all countries that participate, though concerns remain about the possible negative impact of greater world trade on some developing countries. Recently much attention focused, for example, on the effects of agricultural subsidies in wealthy countries on subsistence farmers in developing countries. Globalization can greatly complicate the task of managing IT in a firm. Yet, IT can greatly improve the management of firms with operations in many parts of the world.

THE IMPACT OF GLOBALIZATION ON BUSINESS

The impacts of globalization are numerous (Ives and Jarvenpaa, 1992):

- *Rationalized manufacturing.* Firms manufacture in locations with a comparative advantage for the type of manufacturing involved.
- *Worldwide purchasing.* Firms can purchase worldwide for their operations giving them a great deal of leverage over suppliers.
- *Integrated customer service.* A multinational firm is likely to have multinational customers and can provide all locations with the same level of customer service. Customer service for several U.S. manufacturers is provided from India; the lower cost of labor more than offsets communications costs.
- *Global economies of scale.* Size, if managed properly, provides for economies in purchasing, manufacturing, and distribution.
- *Global products.* Consumer firms have worked especially hard to market global brands such as Kellogg's cereals and beverages like Coke and Pepsi.
- *Worldwide rollout of products and services.* The firm can test products and services in one market and then roll them out around the world.
- *Subsidizing markets.* The profits from one country can be used to subsidize operations in another.
- *Managing risk across currencies.* With floating exchange rates, doing business in many countries can help reduce risks.

■ *The growing irrelevance of national borders.* Technology has far outpaced political progress in integrating different cultures. As electronic commerce plays an increasingly important role, the ability of national governments to control transactions will become more difficult.

One conclusion prompted by the preceding list is that global business creates greater uncertainty and complexity. To handle these challenges, the firm will need faster communications and information processing. It will have to rely more on IT to manage the organization.

INTERNATIONAL BUSINESS STRATEGIES

Four major types of international business strategies are portrayed in Figure 5-2.

Multinational

The multinational strategy focuses on local responsiveness. Subsidiaries operate autonomously or in a loose federation. The advantage of this type of approach is that the firm can quickly respond to different local needs and opportunities. This strategy reduces the need for communications because local subsidiaries can make many decisions. Heavy reporting requirements are necessary to convey the results from the subsidiaries to a head-quarters location for monitoring.

FIGURE 5-2 Global business strategies.

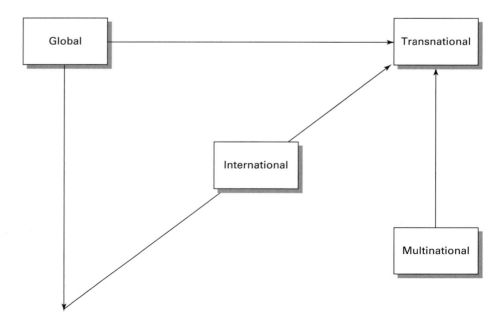

Global

A global strategy stresses efficiency based on a strong central control from headquarters. Economies come from standard product designs and global manufacturing. An extensive communications system is also necessary to centrally manage the global firm.

International

The international strategy is much like the multinational with autonomous local subsidiaries. However, these subsidiaries are dependent on headquarters for new processes and products. A good example is a pharmaceuticals company. The research labs in the headquarters company develop products for introduction around the world. Local subsidiaries stress product approval by local governments and local marketing.

Transnational

The transnational firm attempts to do everything. It seeks global efficiency while retaining local responsiveness. The firm integrates global activities through cooperation among headquarters and foreign subsidiaries. This difficult strategy tries to achieve local flexibility at the same time that it obtains the advantage of global integration, efficiency, and innovation.

The Globally Outsourced Firm

The trend toward outsourcing cuts across all types of global business. See Figure 5-3. For many years, the percentage of manufacturing jobs in the United States has been declining, with much of this work moving off-shore to lower-wage countries. If you look at the country of origin labels on most clothing, you will find that it comes from a foreign country, often located in Asia. Contract manufacturing companies build many of the electronic devices sold by name-brand vendors; for example, companies such as Solectron and Flextronics build a wide range of electronic devices. Cisco, Hewlett-Packard, and many others contract out all or a significant share of manufacturing to these contractors.

Just as companies moved manufacturing jobs to low-wage countries, a growing trend is developing toward moving service jobs abroad. Countries such as India, which have a well-educated, English-speaking workforce, are prime sites for outsourcing; India has an estimated two-thirds of the U.S. offshore outsourcing market for services. When you call a help desk for a computer vendor or software manufacturer, you are likely to be speaking with an engineer from India or Ireland. Many contract programming services send work overseas to countries such as India and Russia where a large supply of well-educated technical workers is available and wages are much lower than in the United States.

FIGURE 5-3 Global outsourcing.

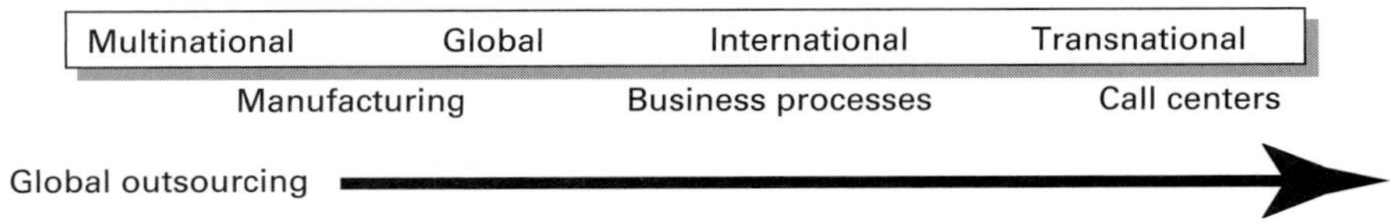

This trend is not confined to customer service or programming; businesses are also moving back-office functions such as payroll and human resources to countries that offer cheap labor. Procter & Gamble (P&G) was a pioneer when it created a Global Business Services (GBS) organization, a unit employing 8,000 P&G people at more than seventy locations, generating about $1.7 billion in sales. GBS provides key administrative functions, including finance, HR, IT, and procurement. P&G built three global offshore service centers in Manila, Philippines; Newcastle, United Kingdom; and San Jose, Costa Rica, to support GBS. Proctor & Gamble estimates that this offshore model resulted in savings of more than $200 million per year since it began. P&G investigated an agreement with Electronic Data Systems to run the whole GBS operation. Instead, the company decided on a best-in-class business process outsourcing (BPO) approach, treating each business function as a separate transaction. P&G recently outsourced its IT function to Hewlett-Packard in a contract worth more than $3 billion over ten years. The agreement includes servers, desktops, and 100 transitioned employees. The HR function has been put out to bid and is expected to be awarded this year in a deal that would be valued at $500 million over ten years.[1]

Outsourcing offshore reduces a company's labor costs and is efficient. One has to train overseas employees and coordinate their activities with locations in other countries. This practice also raises the political issue of exporting jobs that could be performed in the United States, especially if it is a time of relatively high unemployment. These problems have not kept manufacturing jobs in the United States, and we are likely to see increasing outsourcing of service positions as well.

Outsourcing creates a new kind of organization structure along with new challenges for management. Figure 5-4 is a hypothetical example of an electronics firm that outsources both manufacturing and business services. It is possible to end up with a complex network or web of changing relationships as outsourcers come and go, working for different parts of the firm. Offices in different countries may employ different outsourcers for the same function. Management has many of the same challenges in this environment as it does in trying to manage IT globally. How much independence in deciding on outsourcers do you allow local business units, and how much of the relationship with outsourcers should be centralized to obtain the best contracts and quality possible?

A few caveats must be considered when moving jobs offshore. A business always faces the risk of instability in foreign countries. Sometimes foreign partners fail to deliver; one computer vendor cancelled a 1,500-person customer service agreement with a firm in India due to poor performance. You can outsource tasks such as programming if the assignment is well specified. However, designing applications systems require extensive interactions with users, and it is difficult to think of this work going offshore. Language and cultural issues also become factors in trying to move activities such as finance or human resources offshore.

KEY ISSUES IN AN INTERNATIONAL ENVIRONMENT

Information Needs

An international corporation needs information to coordinate and control its diverse businesses. Reporting and early warning systems are especially important in this environment. Systems that summarize sales data and process accounting information are necessary, but

MANAGEMENT PROBLEM 5-1

Standard Foods is a major producer of foodstuffs, especially canned vegetables and fruits. The company contracts with growers for the produce, and has a number of canning plants in the United States and South America, which accept the produce, prepare it for canning, place it in the can, and label and ship the product to regional warehouses. The company sells products under its own label, and also prepares private label products for grocery chains.

Standard adopted information technology early on, which it used primarily for accounting and then for sales records. In the United States it has moved to efficient customer response (ECR) programs in which grocery stores send in scanner data electronically, and the company uses that data to determine what products and quantities to send to the store. A couple of chains are experimenting with vendor-managed inventory in which Standard becomes responsible for maintaining the inventory of its products on the store shelves, and the grocery store sells the products.

The CIO of Standard, Jaya Agarwal, is wondering how to move this technology to South and Central America and to Mexico. She is concerned about the communications infrastructure in some of these countries, as well as the educational level of the workforce. She must assess whether she can rely on the Internet to handle transactions, or whether Standard should build a private network to connect its warehouses to the grocery chains.

Agarwal has asked your help in figuring out how to move online in the rest of the Americas. What should Standard's communications strategy be? How should it proceed? Should the approach be to concentrate on one country, one grocery chain, or the entire region?

FIGURE 5-4 A globally outsourced organization.

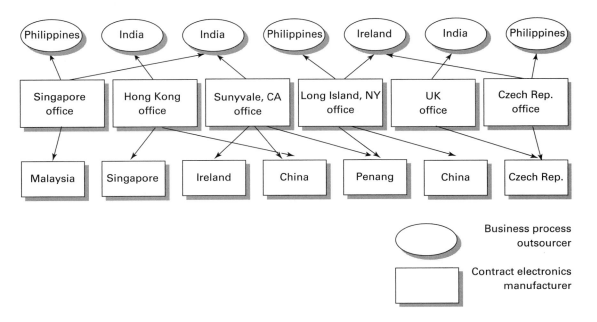

they only reflect what has happened in the past. These systems represent traditional uses of IT for reporting and control.

Technology offers the international firm many more active tools to help manage the business. Coordination is a major problem for the global firm. IT provides a number of approaches to improving communications and coordination, for example, e-mail, groupware, and videoconferencing. The emergence of groupware products is important to international business. These systems let workers in different locations create a shared electronic environment. Intranets encourage the sharing of information and provide for coordination as well. For example, design studios in different parts of the world can work on the developing the same, new automobile. Each studio posts its most recent design drawings on the company's Intranet, making them instantly available to designers in different locations. The Intranet provides the mechanism for coordinating the diverse design groups. The manager can use IT in a variety of ways to design the structure of the global organization.

Implementing International IT

The ultimate objective for the global firm is to process data anyplace in the world and share information without having to worry about the type of platform (hardware, software, operating systems, applications, etc.) used for processing. Firms may encounter a number of problems when trying to achieve this objective in an international environment.

The first problem is managing local development when the foreign unit does not coordinate with headquarters. The foreign subsidiary may be duplicating development efforts underway in other parts of the world. It also may not have a talented staff, and may end up with poorly conceived and designed systems. The question of headquarters-subsidiary coordination and management is a central one in pursuing an international corporate strategy.

The counterargument from the local company is that it knows the needs in its location. A distant headquarters unit cannot set specifications for foreign countries. This contention leads to the second development issue. How does the firm develop a set of common systems shared across different countries to take advantage of economies of scale? Headquarters does not want each country to develop its own accounting and sales reporting systems. Different countries have different laws and regulations, so it may be impossible to share programs among foreign locations without making special modifications for unique requirements in each country.

The third development problem is that when designing applications, real and perceived unique features are important in each country. Designers, especially those representing headquarters, must recognize what features are required for a system to work in a country and what features are there as an exercise in local independence. For example, Straub (1994) studied the use of e-mail and fax in Japan and the United States. He found that cultural differences predisposed managers in each country to a choice of communications vehicles. Straub suggests that high uncertainty avoidance in Japan and structural features of the Japanese language explain why Japanese managers have a lower opinion of the social presence and information richness of e-mail and fax, though American and Japanese managers rated traditional communications media like the telephone and face-to-face communications about the same.

Managers must also be aware that more and more firms want to build a worldwide communications network to take advantage of communications and coordination tools to

SIDE BAR 5-1

Global IT Organization

An international insurance brokerage business has grown through hundreds of acquisitions to form a global company. The firm has 2,500 IT employees and 50,000 employees worldwide. It operates 550 offices in more than 120 countries. In the insurance business, there is no product without information technology; you must keep track of money, payments, and risk.

The chief information officer (CIO) of the firm described a change in which the IT group moved from a centralized structure to a web of IT alliances with the IT groups in different countries. The basic trade-offs are local innovation versus coordination of the enterprise as a whole, and commonality in infrastructure. The CIOs of the business units report to the head of that

unit, and have a dotted line reporting relationship to the corporate CIO. The CIOs of the organization hold a monthly two-hour teleconference, and have an annual face-to-face meeting. The corporate CIO says that her most difficult decisions involve what should be centralized, and what should be left at the local level.

It is likely that many global firms experience the same problems with IT governance. The corporate CIO is interested in avoiding duplicate development efforts and wants to have standards for communications and sharing. The local business unit wants to be free to innovate and develop technology that meets its business needs. As a result the CIO is a negotiator as well as a manager.

move data freely around the world. This effort can be a major challenge because of different technical standards and regulations. Certain countries regulate the kind of telecommunications equipment that can be used on their network. In a number of foreign countries, postal, telegraph, and telephone (PTT) monopolies regulate communications and may restrict the ability to transmit data. Some underdeveloped countries may not have adequate communications capabilities to support private networks. Countries also may prohibit importing certain kinds of computer equipment in order to protect domestic competitors. Different kinds of communications networks and standards can greatly increase the difficulty and cost of building worldwide communications capabilities. One of the most attractive features of the Internet is that it has open standards and a presence in almost all countries. It is pervasive in Asia and the West and has much less penetration of Africa and the Middle East (except Israel).

A number of government requirements may impede the development of global information systems (Steinbart and Nath, 1992):

1. A requirement to purchase specific equipment in the foreign country that may not be compatible with the equipment other places the global firm operates

2. A requirement to do certain kinds of processing in the host country before data can be sent electronically to another country

3. Restrictions on the use of satellites and special requirements for building private networks

4. Limited access to flat-rate leased lines or a requirement that all transmission be made on variable cost lines

5. Restrictions on Internet access and efforts to censor Web sites

A sixth major issue arising from international IT efforts is transborder data flows. Moving data across a boundary may be curtailed by government regulation, ostensibly to protect its citizens and their privacy. Another impact of regulation is to reduce the economic power of foreign companies or limit the imposition of foreign culture on the host country. Many of the transborder regulations seem to be motivated by a desire to protect local industry. Countries may have a legitimate concern about the privacy rights of their citizens. This reason is probably cited most often for instituting data controls. To implement control, a country can establish regulations through its telecommunications ministry, levy tariffs, or require formal approval of plans to process data in the country.

Examples of barriers to data flows include the following:

■ Restrictive regulations that require processing of data originating in that country only, making it difficult to transmit and share data.

■ Exorbitant pricing of communications services by government-owned post, telephone, and telegraph (PTT) ministries. However, a wave of privatization is sweeping countries, and many PTTs are becoming private or quasi-private companies.

■ Security issues that took center stage as attacks on computers by various hackers throughout the world pointed out how difficult it is to secure networked computers.

As with any international venture, language and cultural differences can also present a challenge to developing IT on a global scale. Time differences can make communication difficult for different parts of the world, though fax and e-mail have eased this problem considerably. Some firms stress joint development teams with representatives from different countries to avoid problems stemming from developing a system in any one country or language. Foreign subsidiaries may be more willing to adopt an international system developed by a cross-cultural team.

MANAGING INFORMATION TECHNOLOGY INTERNATIONALLY

What can the manager do to solve the problems raised in the preceding section? Some of these impediments to IT require political action or deregulation, for example, the policies of foreign PTT utilities. In other instances, management needs to take action to solve problems and be involved in efforts to develop systems that will be used in multiple countries. Management must sell its vision for the firm's global technological infrastructure and resolve conflicts over IT requirements.

Roche (1992) presents a number of strategies for managing information technology in a global environment. These strategies are listed in Table 5-1.

TABLE 5-1   Strategies for managing global IT.

Concentrate on interorganizational linkages

Establish global systems development skills

Build an infrastructure

Take advantage of liberalized telecommunications

Strive for uniform data

Develop guidelines for shared versus local systems

Concentrate on Interorganizational Linkages

The strategy of moving firms toward more interorganizational systems by creating linkages with suppliers and customers can be extremely effective internationally. Setting up these linkages may be challenging because of differing telecommunications capabilities in different countries. In some regions phone systems do not work well and transmitting data over them is probably not viable. The Internet is one solution for quickly establishing these linkages.

Establish Global Systems Development Skills

Problems often arise in managing IT development projects when all participants are from the same country and work in the same location. Coordinating multinational project teams presents an even greater challenge. Language and distance make it difficult to coordinate. A New York bank has a development team with members in New York, Lexington, Massachusetts, and Ireland coordinated through groupware. In some foreign countries, hiring staff with the appropriate skills to work on technology can be difficult. Interviews with IT managers for multinationals in seven countries found dramatic differences in their accomplishments and their capabilities. Lack of personnel skills can be a major impediment to developing international systems; not all countries have educational programs to prepare individuals for systems analysis or programming jobs.

Build an Infrastructure

Justifying expenditures on infrastructure can also be extremely difficult. Infrastructure consists of hardware, software, network equipment, and the basic transactions-processing applications of the firm. It appears that investments in infrastructure do not have an immediate benefit, yet keeping an infrastructure up-to-date and operating is of critical importance. Even though the Internet provides an international communications infrastructure, a firm with a physical presence in a country needs a technology infrastructure in place to take advantage of the Internet and to perform local processing.

Take Advantage of Liberalized Electronic Communications

The trend toward deregulation in the United States is also sweeping foreign countries. France split France Telecom from the PTT and established it as a quasi-public organization. In the past two decades, France Telecom replaced an outmoded phone system and now it is trying to move users off its Minitel system and onto the Internet. Changes such as these facilitate the development of the international communications networks essential to managing in a global environment.

Strive for Uniform Data

One of the major problems in sharing data is identifying it. A story is told that a large computer vendor once looked at its logistics systems and found that "ship date" meant six or seven different things depending on the system involved. In one system it might be the promised ship date, and another the date the item left the loading dock. To obtain economies of scale from sharing data and systems, the firm must have a common vocabulary of terms and definitions.

Develop Guidelines for Shared versus Local Systems

Another important strategy needs to find its way to Roche's list: You need to develop guidelines for when a system should be shared and when a local, autonomous system is more appropriate. The obvious advantage of shared systems is economies of scale and the ability to share data. The problem with shared systems is that they tend to become large and complex. Also, individual locations and users have special needs that must be incorporated into the system. As the number of exceptions increases, the system becomes more cumbersome and difficult to program.

The advantage of a local system is that it can often be developed quickly in response to a local condition. If it later becomes necessary to coordinate this system with other applications, special interfaces will have to be created. If each location ends up needing a similar system and cannot share this one, the firm has paid for many systems when possibly one would have sufficed.

The benefits of standardization appeal to many firms, particularly for basic transactions-processing systems. A company that decides to purchase and implement an ERP package such as SAP will want to leverage its experience and the knowledge it acquires about the system across multiple locations and countries. If a company manufacturers or has inventory in different countries, it will want to know where products are that a customer has ordered. A standardized transactions-processing system around the world makes it much easier to communicate and share such information, just as it makes it easier to maintain financial databases and provide accounting information to management and the public.

TWO EXAMPLES

Standard Pharmaceuticals International

Standard Pharmaceuticals International (SPI) is the international division of a multinational drug company headquartered in the United States. The international division consists of thirty foreign subsidiaries located throughout the world. SPI is dependent on the U.S. parent company for all research and new products.

A major challenge for pharmaceuticals firms is to obtain government approval for the sale of new drugs. This process can take many years of testing and the submission of literally a truckload of documents to the Food and Drug Administration. The firm then must wait until the FDA approves or disapproves the sale of the drug.

Some foreign countries will accept U.S. FDA approval as sufficient to market the drug, but many will not. This practice means that the SPI foreign subsidiary must conduct clinical trials in its own country and submit the results to its government for approval. Once approved, the SPI subsidiary markets the drug to physicians and hospitals.

SPI's information services (SPIIS) department has a federal organizational structure. The head of the department reports to the SPI controller (based on historical precedent; it has been recommended that this individual report to the SPI president). Each country has its own information services (IS) manager who reports to the local controller. (In a similar vein, it has been recommended that the local IS manager report to the SPI local subsidiary president.) The headquarters IS group provides advice to the subsidiaries and tries to set standards. However, the local subsidiary staff does not report to the headquarters IS manager.

Because of the historical reporting relationship, it is not surprising that most of the applications at SPIIS involve finance, accounting, and sales reporting. The headquarters IS group developed a standard library of applications that most of the smaller subsidiaries adopted. Larger subsidiaries do not necessarily have the same equipment, and several of them have significant IS staffs and portfolios of applications.

Recently the parent company appointed a new president of SPI. This individual wants to change the strategy of the IS group with emphasis on supporting the sales and marketing departments. He commented, "I have yet to see how one gets a competitive advantage by closing the books each month two days before the competition."

SPIIS is trying to adjust to this change in strategic focus. One example of the problems they encounter is the sales representative notebook computer project. The sales and marketing department launched a separate effort from IS to develop applications for a notebook computer for sales representatives. The portable computer should provide information to the sales representative about his or her territory with access to a commercial database of prescription drug sales. These sales reps visit physicians in their offices and at hospitals to explain the company's new products and leave samples for the physician. The system should also keep track of sales calls and keep a record of drug samples left with the physician. (This record is often required by governments in order to limit the number of samples distributed.)

The marketing and sales groups tried to keep IS from becoming involved in this project because they felt IS was interested only in financial systems. The IS manager was concerned that the notebook computer team lacked adequate technological expertise and would waste a large amount of money.

Because of country differences, marketing tried different types of systems in different countries. In one country, marketing bought a package system and invested a reported $1 million before canceling the trial. The greatest success has been in France, where the Minitel system made it easy to implement all of the needed functions using existing technology. However, the emphasis in France is in moving off the old, slow Minitel and joining the rest of the world on the Internet.

SPI is caught in the dilemma of local system versus shared systems development. In addition, the president of the division wants to more than double sales revenues while keeping administrative expenses at current levels. Without providing more resources to the IS staff and investing in a worldwide network, it is unlikely that the president will be able to accomplish his goals.

VeriFone

Hatim Tyabji, the chairman who built VeriFone into a major force in payments systems, believed in a flexible organization structure and in the importance of being close to customers to provide a fast response to their needs (Galal et al., 1995). VeriFone faced strong competitors in its early days in the form of AT&T, GTE, Northern Telecom, and Mitsubishi, to name a few. In 1997 Hewlett-Packard acquired VeriFone in order to advance its efforts in electronic commerce, and in 2001 it sold VeriFone to an investment group. It is clear that the HP way did not match VeriFone's culture.

VeriFone's mission was "to create and lead the transaction automation industry worldwide." In the 1990s the company's products processed an estimated 65–70 percent of credit card transactions in the world. Much of the business was in custom software that

MANAGEMENT PROBLEM 5-2

The first thing Nancy Scott did when she was hired as CIO of Victor Electronics was to make a trip around the world to visit different locations and learn first-hand about the information technology resources in place. She returned home with the knowledge that she faced some major challenges. "Our CEO wants to create a truly global company, and right now we're more like a holding company with a group of foreign subsidiaries that pretty much do what they want to."

She continued, "We need to get some standardization in place to try and create a common infrastructure so that we can share data and applications easily. It also makes moving people around easier if each location isn't completely different from the others at Victor. In addition to issues in hardware and software,

we have the problem of figuring out what information Roberts and other managers need to run the company. Now they get sales data and, of course, accounting information at the end of each month. That's all history—they don't get much that looks forward."

Nancy Scott has asked your help to figure out where to start. What are the options for infrastructure given the disparate systems in place at Victor? Can the company impose a standard architecture, and at what cost in dollars and human capital? What kind of information does the CEO need from foreign subsidiaries? How does Roberts's desire to make the company more global and responsive to local demands fit with Nancy's idea of a standard company IT architecture?

ran in the verification "boxes" and on other parts of the transactions network. VeriFone offered more than 1,600 programs that run on its verification devices. The firm also formed alliances to verify and process payments on the Internet, including agreements with Netscape, several banks, and Discover.

VeriFone's ongoing structure was similar to most organizations. What made VeriFone unique, however, was the constant "organizing" that occurred within this structure, accomplished through cross-functional teams. Any employee could form a task force to address a problem. These teams come into and go out of existence regularly. They are *virtual* in the sense that they span different organizations and members may be in different locations. The constant formation, activity, and deactivation of teams provided the mechanism through which VeriFone constantly organized. In addition to teams within the firm, VeriFone formed alliances with other organizations. A virtual team might span organizational boundaries.

Although organizing was a key activity at VeriFone, a conventional organization chart showed reporting relationships and titles. The organization was originally relatively flat with the chairman having eight direct reports, and the executive vice president six. Tyabji's corporate model was a decentralized network of locations; he referred to this structure as the "blueberry pancake." "All berries are the same size; all locations are created equal" (Galal et al., 1995). His least favorite location was corporate headquarters. Regardless of formal structure, an employee could access any other employee directly through e-mail.

The focus was not on hierarchy and status. Rather, VeriFone defined the "right organization structure" as one locating employees near customers so that they continually put the customer first. The idea was that a customer in a country using VeriFone products could meet with a design engineer located in the customer's country; that design engineer could make changes in the product without approval from anyplace else. VeriFone operated in fifty-three locations with more than 2,900 employees.

The management culture and norms at VeriFone allowed it to operate in an organizing mode. Two of the key characteristics of VeriFone that emerged from discussions with company officials were "fast response" and "a culture of urgency." As one employee described it, they "never have time to rejoice" after finishing a project because something else was always waiting to be done. A lack of organizational hierarchy makes it easier to respond quickly.

Because of geographic decentralization and the existence of many virtual teams, an employee was often on his or her own. It was not unusual to be located in Atlanta and to report to a supervisor in Paris. VeriFone counted on individual initiative to achieve its goals. VeriFone believed, according to its stated corporate philosophy, that those who perform a job know best how it should be done. It is clear that this culture involves mutual trust. Employees trusted the company to support their actions and to encourage experimentation. VeriFone trusted its employees to take initiative and act in the best interest of the company. VeriFone tried to maintain this culture with a minimum of rules.

Communications was a key activity at VeriFone. A corporate philosophy of distributing power to the lowest level of the organization possible reduced the amount of communications required to operate. At the same time, the global nature of VeriFone's operations created significant demands for communications, especially for virtual project teams. Managers communicated with e-mail; no secretaries printed messages or entered responses. Executives in different countries might work together on the same spreadsheet in preparing a proposal. These executives could access information on bookings, shipments, and revenues from an online database with worldwide availability.

VeriFone used a broad array of different tools for communications. Travel, face-to-face meetings, and task forces are all communications mechanisms. Frequently task forces worked "around the world" with conference calls scheduled so that members took turns at getting up at 2 A.M. to participate.

VeriFone stressed the need for employees, while a part of a virtual firm, to interact physically on a regular basis. Large rooms in local offices facilitated group gatherings and the firm had annual meetings of different employees who work in similar functions. Every six to eight weeks, the senior management team met for a meeting in a different part of the world. (A recent VP of Human Resources lived in Dallas; the former CIO has homes in Hawaii and Santa Fe, while the chairman lived in the San Francisco Bay Area.) Senior managers felt it was important for employees to know each other so they could use information technology effectively. The cost of face-to-face communications was constant travel; Tyabji reported traveling more than 400,000 miles in a year while chairman. About one-third of the company's employees were on the road at any one time.

VeriFone suggests that the virtual organization does not necessarily want to substitute electronic for physical interaction completely: rather the electronic and face-to-face (FTF) communications complement each other. At VeriFone, occasional face-to-face communications enabled more regular and routine electronic communications with its advantage of reducing the constraints of time and space on interaction.

In addition to communications mechanisms, VeriFone believed in sharing information. The former CIO prepared a daily "flash" report that went to 300 VeriFone employees. The report was a method for evaluating progress. Recipients could easily access the data behind the interpretation so they were not dependent on one person's view of performance. The firm provided so much information that it, at one time, registered more than 10 percent of its employees as "insiders" with the Federal Trade Commission.

VeriFone also shared information and knowledge with its customers and alliance partners. Before e-mail became easily available through service providers, VeriFone had suppliers and alliance partners on its own e-mail system. Later VeriFone provided videoconferencing equipment for these firms. Before going public when it had to be concerned about releasing information, VeriFone shared its daily flash report with some partners.

VeriFone used appropriate technology, not necessarily the newest equipment. It spent about 60 percent as much as comparable electronics firms on information technology. Its e-mail system ran for many years on VAX computers using a text-based mail program. The daily flash report was character-based. Eventually the firm developed an intranet to facilitate information sharing. The responsibility for providing content on the intranet was distributed; for example, a new product group creates and maintains pages for its product.

For a VeriFone employee, the organizing character of the company, management culture and norms, and information sharing led to self-governance. The employee might not have extensive physical contact with a supervisor. This employee was encouraged to take the initiative in coming up with new ideas for improving VeriFone, its products, and its service to customers. Employees communicate using a variety of media with customers, alliance partners, and other VeriFone employees. Any employee might start a virtual, cross-functional team and be a member of several others. A major focus for employees is on responsiveness and fast response to conditions in the local environment.

However, information technology means that an employee will not be constrained to local solutions; VeriFone can marshal its global resources to solve local problems. An actual example helps to illustrate this global search. A customer told a sales representative in Greece, based on a VeriFone competitor's statements, that VeriFone lacked a certain product. The sales rep sent a single e-mail to ISales, which reached all sales reps worldwide, asking whether VeriFone had a product for this customer. A sales manager in San Francisco took on the task of heading this virtual task force. He collated 100 replies and constructed a PowerPoint presentation for the sales rep in Greece (while the rep slept). The sales manager had the presentation translated to Greek, and the sales rep took it to the client the next day. VeriFone won the account.

When HP purchased VeriFone, the concern was that the two organizations would not integrate well. In fact, VeriFone went from a historically profitable company, to a firm with losses. HP sold VeriFone to an investment firm, and the new managers of VeriFone hope to restore the company's culture from the days before HP acquired it. VeriFone reported that the firm became profitable again a short time after splitting off from HP. Although VeriFone's organization structure worked well for it, the question is whether it will work for other firms.

TRANSNATIONAL VIRTUAL FIRMS AND IT

VeriFone provides evidence that a transnational firm depends on information technology for information and knowledge sharing, communications, and coordination. However, technology alone is not enough to create either a transnational or a virtual corporation. Senior management determines the structure and culture of the firm. At VeriFone senior managers shaped an organization that encouraged local autonomy and fast response to the environment. The benefits of a virtual organization such as VeriFone in international business suggest it as a possible model for other firms.

BUSINESS MODELS AND IT MANAGEMENT

Based on their research, Ives and Jarvenpaa (1992) suggested that an international firm goes through the following stages in developing its management of information technology, which are outlined in Table 5-2.

TABLE 5-2 Information technology approaches in globally competing firms.

IT activities	APPROACHES			
	Independent operations	Headquarters driven	Intellectual synergy	Integrated global
Applications development	Total local autonomy	Modify a working U.S. application for global use	Joint high-level requirements analysis; implementation under local control	Multinational user/IS team designs and oversees implementation of the system
Applications maintenance	Total local autonomy	Centralized maintenance	Total local autonomy	Centralized maintenance on common core modules; localized maintenance on others
Systems software, hardware	Total local autonomy	Headquarters' (HQ) decision	Total local autonomy	Common worldwide architecture
Staffing senior IT positions at subsidiaries	Total local autonomy, a local employee	HQ's decision, often a U.S. expatriate	Advice from HQ's IT group, a local employee	Joint decision, a global search for eligible candidates
Control over IT operations	Total local autonomy	Run from centralized data center	Local autonomy, but incentives from HQ	Local systems run locally; common system run from local/regional data center
Relationship between subsidiary and HQ's IT heads	No formal relationship, little or no informal contact	Subsidiaries' IT heads report to HQ's IT head	Dotted-line relationship; considerable informal exchange	IT heads around the world are peers; considerable informal and formal exchange
Diffusion of IT innovation	Little or no diffusion across country boundaries	One-way, from HQ to subsidiaries	Two-way	Two-way, "centers of excellence" established around the world
Primary basis for common systems	Consolidated financial reporting requirements	Economies of scale in IT activities	Experience accumulated in other parts of a multinational firm	Global business drivers

Independent Operations

In the 1960s and 1970s, many multinationals gave considerable autonomy to foreign subsidiaries, which acquired hardware and software from local vendors. The applications implemented differed considerably across countries. Little interaction occurred with headquarters or the IT staff there. Headquarters might impose a chart of accounts or financial reporting standards on subsidiaries, however, these data were rarely transmitted electronically.

Headquarters Driven

During the 1980s, the focus of multinationals turned to efficiency in information technology operations. Headquarters based in the United States sought to implement worldwide applications at subsidiaries to reduce development and operating costs. The apparent motivation for this approach was efficiency, but local subsidiaries did not see much to be gained.

Intellectual Synergy

This approach to IT returns control to the local subsidiary. Headquarters tries to guide the choices of the subsidiaries. The firm might host worldwide planning conferences. If this model is working, the subsidiaries should request advice from headquarters. Headquarters tries to coordinate the subsidiaries to reduce duplicate development efforts and encourage resource sharing.

Integrated Global IT

This approach is often adopted because of pressure from global customers. The firm must provide more consistent customer service internationally. Systems design requires input from around the world. The firm must standardize its data and will probably consolidate data centers. Headquarters will specify certain applications as common systems, such as order entry. Only limited customization of these systems is allowed to fit a particular subsidiary.

Ives and Jarvenpaa suggested a relationship between approach to IT management and the business models presented earlier. (See Table 5-3.)

The multinational firm is expected to favor independent operations. A great deal of autonomy in information technology decisions is given to the local subsidiary. The focus of the strategy is on local response. The global business model stresses efficiency. You would expect to find a headquarters-driven technology strategy with this approach to business. Headquarters will try to coordinate and centralize to reduce duplication and encourage common systems.

TABLE 5-3 Business and IT management approaches.

Business Model	IT Management Approach
Multinational	Independent operations
Global	Headquarters driven
International	Intellectual synergy
Transnational	Integrated global IT

An international business model will probably be combined with an IT strategy of intellectual synergy. Subsidiaries depend on headquarters for guidance and for new knowledge. Headquarters tries to influence subsidiary technology policies through planning and sharing information.

The transnational firm is most likely to follow an integrated global IT strategy. Headquarters will define core systems that will provide uniform customer service in a global market. Management of the firm realizes that information technology is an important element in its strategy.

THE INTERNET, IMPERIALISM, AND DEVELOPING COUNTRIES

Earlier in the chapter, some of the barriers that countries sometimes put in place and that inhibit the free flow of information were mentioned. The representative of a developing Asian country, at a recent conference in Malaysia, stated that the "Information

---

SIDE BAR 5-2

Business Process Outsourcing

Outsourcing is no longer offshore data entry; service firms around the world are now providing high-level outsourcing services. Among this emerging group of business process outsourcing (BPO) firms is Evalueserve. This company has its headquarters in Bermuda and its main operational center near New Delhi, India's capital. It also has a U.S. subsidiary based in New York and a marketing office in Austria.

Evalueserve's cofounder and chairman, is based in Chappaqua, New York; his company supplies a range of value-added services to clients including some of the *Fortune* 500 and well-known consulting firms. Evalueserve provides services such as patent writing, evaluation, and assessment of their commercialization potential for law firms and entrepreneurs. It conducts market research services for financial services firms, including analysis of investment opportunities and business plans.

"Activities considered for offshoring have moved up the value chain and begun to touch core functions, such as highly analytical processes," says Stefan Spohr, a principal in the financial institutions group of A. T. Kearney, a global management consulting firm in Chicago. "More complex customer services are substituting simple data processing and call center activities." Spohr adds that the higher-end functions being performed offshore these days include information research, financial portfolio analysis, customer data mining, statutory reporting, and inbound insurance sales, among others.

Before setting up Evalueserve in December 2000, its cofounder was director of emerging business opportunities for IBM Research worldwide. Evalueserve has 175 professionals on its staff, many of whom are graduates of the Indian Institutes of Technology and the Indian Institutes of Management. The cofounder has an MBA from INSEAD and formerly worked for McKinsey & Co. in New Delhi.

The company does not disclose its revenues or name any of its clients. Evalueserve conducts between 50 percent and 80 percent of its work at an Indian facility, while the rest is done at the client's location. Projects undertaken by the company include:

Evaluating the commercial prospects of inventions in Russia and China.

Research for a hedge fund's database, and tracking financial statements of 2,300 companies.

Research and analysis of value-chain segments and industry developments for a market research firm specializing in information technology and telecommunications.

Market forecast studies for an OTC drug worldwide.

Evalueserve is an example of a new breed of BPO firm, one that provides almost any company with an opportunity to outsource work to a foreign country and create a type international business that cuts across traditional typologies of global firms.

SOURCE: Knowledge@Wharton.upenn.edu, 9/24/03.

Superhighway was the latest example of American imperialism." During this person's talk, he complained about a number of issues with new technology and the Internet:

- His government had to stop censoring newspapers and magazines when fax machines became easily available because people called on friends in foreign countries to fax the excised material to them.

- There was no way to authenticate information on the Internet; some recent civil disturbances were "perpetuated" through unverified information on the Internet. The Army set up a Web site to provide accurate information, but no one accessed it.

- It was important for his country and others to participate in the Internet and electronic commerce, but it was also important to find ways to avoid being influenced by Internet content.

Clearly modern information technology, and particularly the Internet, puts less democratic governments that wish to control and limit information in a difficult situation. The Internet makes it possible for companies in developing countries to do business with customers around the world, expanding their markets and increasing trade. However, this same technology makes vast amounts of information available to those with an Internet connection. More than the presence of information, the Internet culture emphasizes the free flow and availability of information. Many developing countries feature strong central governments that exercise considerable control over the economy. Leaders in these governments tend not to be in favor of providing transparency and full information to the public. How governments resolve this dilemma will determine whether they take part in the technology revolution, or fall behind the rest of the world.

CHAPTER SUMMARY

1. The four main international business strategies include the multinational, global, international, and transnational organizations.

2. IT can be used to facilitate international business, especially IT organization design variables that stress communications, knowledge sharing, and coordination. Headquarters-subsidiary coordination is one of the most significant challenges in managing an international business.

3. It can be difficult to implement international applications of the technology for a variety of reasons.

4. Many international firms find they need a global network, a technology infrastructure that ties together far-flung components of the firm. The Internet and intranets help in providing connectivity, information sharing, and coordination worldwide.

5. Firms building technology must trade off the advantages of local flexibility and freedom against the benefits and efficiency of common systems.

6. IT challenges in an international environment also encompass issues such as standards, uniform data, and dealing with the different quality and regulation of telecommunications in various countries.

7. The liberalization of trade and emerging economies in Eastern Europe suggest that international business will continue to be of major importance in the future.

8. Developing countries with strong central governments face a conflict between the need to participate in the growth of technology, especially the Internet, and their desire to control the economy and information.

KEYWORDS

European Economic Community (EEC)

Global

Headquarters driven

Integrated global IT

Independent operations

Intellectual synergy

International

Multinational

Outsourcing

Transborder data flows

Transnational

Virtual

RECOMMENDED READINGS

Adam, N., Awerbuch, B., Slonim, J., Wegner, P., and Yesha, Y. 1997. Globalizing business, education, culture, through the Internet. *Communications of the ACM*, *40*(2), pp. 115–121.

Carmel, E., and Agarwal, R. 2002. The maturation of offshore sourcing of information technology work. *MIS Quarterly Executive*, *1*(2), pp. 65–77.

Gwynne, P. Information systems go global. *Harvard Business Review*, *42*(4), p. 14.

Ives, B., and Jarvenpaa. S. 1992. Global information technology: Some lessons from practice. *International Information Systems*, *1*(3), July, pp. 1–15. (An insightful article that presents several of the models described in this chapter.)

Kirkman, B. L., Rosen, B., Gibson, C. B., Tesluk, P. E., and McPherson, S. O. 2002. Five challenges to virtual team success: Lessons from Sabre Inc. *Academy of Management Executive*, *16*(3), pp. 67–79.

Mbarika, V., Jensen, M., and Meso, P. 2002. Cyberspace across Sub-Saharan Africa: Moving from technological desert toward emergent sustainable growth. *Communications of the ACM*, *45*(12), pp. 17–21.

Newell, S., Pan, S. L., Galliers, R. D., and Huang, J. C. 2001. The myth of the boundaryless organization. *Communications of the ACM*, *44*(12), pp. 74–76.

Roche, E. 1992. *Managing Information Technology in Multinational Corporations.* New York: Macmillan. (This book contains a number of interesting case studies of global firms and how they manage IT.)

Townsend, A. M., DeMarie, S. M., and Hendrickson, A. R. 1998. Virtual teams: Technology and the workplace of the future. *Academy of Management Executive*, *12*(3), pp. 17–29.

DISCUSSION QUESTIONS

1. What motivated the current interest in global business?

2. Why might a country want to regulate the data collected within its borders?

3. One study reported that managers found concerns about regulations on transborder data flows to be unwarranted. Why do you suppose this issue has not surfaced?

4. What are the advantages of providing a subsidiary with a great deal of local autonomy?

5. What are the disadvantages of local autonomy for subsidiaries?

6. How should a manager determine whether a system should be common across a number of subsidiaries, or uniquely developed for each subsidiary?

7. Why do you suppose Standard Pharmaceuticals International primarily developed financial and accounting systems?

8. What can the president of SPI do to change the division's strategy toward marketing and sales support?

9. How can information technology support a marketing-oriented strategy in the drug industry?

10. What are the key features of VeriFone's structure?

11. What are the risks of a global IT strategy? What are its benefits?

12. What impediments do you see to worldwide networks for coordinating the activities of global firms? What is the role of the Internet in this process?

13. How can an international firm see that local staff members have enough expertise to develop and apply IT?

14. What are the problems of establishing common data elements in a global organization?

15. Why does a firm need common data elements and structures?

16. How can IT help coordinate a global firm? Where can it help save money while making the firm more responsive?

17. Roche advocates a number of interorganizational linkages in conducting international business. What problems do you see in connecting a global firm to its many customers in different countries?

18. What kind of business activities do you think are most amenable to common systems in different countries?

19. What are the advantages of making product design information available around the world? How might you use this capability to organize product development?

20. If company management or custom dictates a fairly independent and autonomous IT effort in subsidiaries, what approaches can management take to coordinate these activities?

21. What Internet access policies would you recommend to the government of a developing country?

ENDNOTES

1. *Optimize Magazine,* 2003, http://www.optimizemag.com/issue/020/leadership.htm.

CHAPTER 6

ASSESSING THE VALUE OF INVESTING IN IT: THE PRODUCTIVITY PARADOX[1]

A Manager's Perspective

Industry, educational institutions, and governments have invested huge amounts in information technology since the 1950s. In the early days of manual process automation, one could usually show a positive return on investment, which justified individual applications. As the technology became more pervasive, applications went beyond simple automation, and it became more difficult to quantify a return prior to the investment. Personal computers contributed significantly to the problem of figuring the returns from investing in IT: How could you measure and quantify the return from putting a PC on a manager's desk? What does the manager do with the machine? What would the manager do without it?

The productivity paradox became a major topic in the 1990s as a number of skeptics said that organizations were spending huge amounts on IT, but getting no visible payback from that investment. Academics conducted studies with mixed results. Some argued that it would be difficult to show overall IT contributions to the economy because of measurement problems and the challenge of finding causes for organization performance. The feeling was that enough examples of individual applications showed a return and that one could generalize from these applications to argue the investment was justified.

Finally, the chairman of the Federal Reserve at the time, Alan Greenspan, decided that IT and the Internet had in fact contributed to national productivity. His reasoning was not entirely satisfying, but having such a respected financial expert reach this conclusion was helpful for those who believed in the technology. Greenspan observed that during the mid to late 1990s, the U.S. economy was growing at a high rate with low unemployment, but inflation was very low. Macroeconomics had always said that these three conditions could not hold at the same time; strong inflationary pressures should be operating. Greenspan's reasoning was that huge investments in IT were finally paying off because productivity growth must be keeping inflation in check, and it must have been IT investments that led to increased productivity. What do you think?

VALUE PROPOSITION

What is the value of investments in information technology (IT)? What type of return comes from investing in IT? These two questions are critical because firms invest huge amounts in information technology; an estimated 50 percent of U.S. capital investment today is for IT. For top-ranked banks such as J.P. Morgan-Chase and Citibank, express carriers such as FedEx and UPS, and large brokerage firms, annual IT budgets approach or exceed $1 billion. (Only a portion of these budgets represents investment in new IT initiatives; the rest is for ongoing operations.)

Obtaining value from IT is important for organizations to survive and flourish in the highly competitive economy of the twenty-first century. Many believe that information technology holds the key to success as companies develop systems that provide them with a competitive advantage. IT also lets managers create dynamic, new organization structures to compete more effectively. Firms that create value through information technology will be the winners in the coming century.

The fundamental premise of this chapter is that information technology provides value, and that it is possible to show a return from certain kinds of investments in IT.

It is important to understand under what conditions one can expect to find a measurable return from IT investments. We also need to find creative ways to measure IT value. If we can accomplish these two tasks, it should be possible to predict what investments will lead to a return, and the nature of that return.

WHAT IS VALUE?

The most common meaning of value is monetary worth; in the marketplace buyers and sellers place a value measured in dollars on goods and services. When an investor seeks a return on capital, it is expressed as a percentage of the original investment. However, the term *value* sometimes holds only a remote connection with money. For example, a manager claims that a certain employee makes a valuable contribution to the firm. It might be possible to trace this contribution to the company's profits, but the comment is not made with that intent.

Because information technology is woven into the fabric of business, we adopt a broad definition of the value of IT investments. The marketplace establishes prices and the most familiar measure of value from investing in technology is dollars returned. However, computing a monetary value for a return from IT investments is not easy. In fact, in some cases, it almost appears impossible, at least at the time the firm is making the investment.

A good example is investing in IT infrastructure; a company might invest heavily to build a network of computers. The return from that network comes in literally hundreds of ways as individual employees use the network to do their jobs better, and IT staff members build applications of technology that take advantage of the network infrastructure. At the time the firm decided to invest in the network, it could only guess at the nature of activities the network might stimulate. A few years later, it is possible to study the return on the projects the network enabled, but it is a rare company that would devote the time and resources to such a post hoc analysis.

In searching for IT value, we seek all types of contributions from investments in technology. Some investments demonstrate traditional returns that can be expressed in monetary terms. Other examples require an effort to estimate an indirect return from an IT investment. Sometimes, it appears that an IT investment prevented a negative return, such as the case of a firm that develops a system to keep up with a competitor and avoid losing market share. In instances where technology becomes intertwined with the strategy of the corporation, the contribution of IT seems valuable, but exceedingly difficult to value.

Today we are confronted with an incredibly powerful technology that makes it possible to search vast amounts of data stored in locations around the world, a technology that offers services that could only have been imagined twenty years ago, and a technology that has the potential to revolutionize the way we structure organizations and conduct commerce. Only one embarrassing question left: *Has anyone obtained a return from investing in information technology?*

Challenging Conventional Wisdom and Practice

A large number of researchers have expressed concern at their inability to show a significant impact on productivity from the large investments organizations have made in information technology. One Nobel laureate economist supposedly said that "PCs are showing up all over the place, except in productivity statistics." In a 1993 article, Eric Brynjolfsson wrote about the *productivity paradox*, the fact that the benefits of IT spending have not shown up in aggregate output statistics.

He offers two possible explanations. First, the results of IT spending occur locally and cannot be expected to show up in aggregate statistics at the national level. Second, the benefits from IT investment often require restructuring or major cost cutting, and it is possible that firms have yet to undertake enough of this activity for it to be reflected in national statistics. Other suggestions look at the lack of finding of an impact of IT on national productivity as partly a measurement problem: The government tends to equate output to input in the services industry where seven out of ten American workers are employed. A Stanford economist, Paul David, suggests that it took more than forty years after the first electric motor was installed before managers designed plants to take advantage of this technology; IT may suffer from the same phenomenon.

Questions about the national productivity impacts of information technology are interesting for economists to debate. What is their relevance to the individual manager? The manager investing in IT is interested in the value obtained in his or her organization, possibly even his or her subunit of that organization. Although it would be nice for IT to have an impact on national productivity, the concern here is with value at the level of the firm and its subunits.

It will probably be difficult to consign the productivity paradox to history, but a study by the Brookings Institution may help convince some skeptics of the value of investing in IT as a country. The study by Litan and Rivlin (2001) focused on different sectors of the economy. The researchers felt that not enough appropriate data were available to use conventional macroeconomic models to estimate the impact of the Internet on the economy, so they commissioned different researchers to each look at an industry and estimate the impact of the Internet on growth in that industry. Litan and Rivlin combined the results to come up with an estimate that the Internet has contributed 0.25 to 0.50 percent to growth in the economy in year 2000 prices. In growth terms, this is a huge number. If the economy as a whole grows at 4 percent, then the study estimates the contribution of the Internet as 6.25 to 12.5 percent of the growth. The authors estimate the Internet in one year saves 1.2 to 2.5 percent of GDP measured in 2000 dollars.

It is interesting to note some of the Brookings' study conclusions:

- Much of the impact of the Internet may not be in e-commerce, but rather in making routine transactions more efficient across a wide variety of organizations, especially government and health care.

- The Internet shows great potential for improving efficiency in product development, supply chain management, and many other areas of business.

- The Internet will increase competition, possibly reducing profit margins.

■ The Internet makes a dramatic impact on consumer convenience, increasing choices and making it easier to accomplish a number of tasks.

This study only tried to estimate the impact of the Internet, not information technology as a whole; if we include all IT investment, then we would expect to see a more dramatic impact on the economy.

What About Successful Implementation?

The search for value from IT investments relies an underlying philosophical belief that technology investments are a good thing, and that firms only choose to invest in IT if they believe they will see a positive return from their investment. Another implicit belief says that the predicted benefits of an investment are realized after implementing new technology.

A key point of this chapter is that (1) not all investments in IT should be expected to show a measurable return, and (2) investments can have value to an organization even without measurable returns. Many organizations seem to hold a strong belief that every investment is made with the expectation of a positive return. One manager stated that his firm never undertook an IT investment without expecting benefits that exceeded its costs. This organization seems to be typical. A number of years ago when a manager in the field was asked if his firm only undertook an application of technology when the benefits exceeded the cost of the project, he responded that a positive return was definitely required. Then he was asked, "What if you really feel that you want to develop the application, but you can't show benefits that exceed costs." His response was, "We add on enough intangible benefits (better decision-making is a popular one) to justify the investment."

A panel of IT managers was asked if all of the projects they encountered were justified with a rigorous net present value analysis. No one on the panel raised a hand. One of the participants had been involved years before in a successful telephony program. He had worked on the tremendously successful MCI "Friends and Family" product. He asked the manager for this project what the information technology component was worth. The reply surprised him: "Zero." The MCI manager went on to explain that the advertising part of the project was also worth zero. Each of these components could not have worked without all the others. Together, the Friends and Family product was extremely successful. Individually, its components were not worth anything, but certainly the technology part of this initiative added value to the Friends and Family product. Situations such as this one make it difficult to identify the return from investing in information technology. They also point out that the technology does not necessarily stand alone; it is an integral part of products and services in modern firms. A change of any kind in the organization today is likely to involve a new investment in technology.

A major brokerage firm determined that it needed to develop a new broker workstation for its retail business. Retail brokers were using outmoded technology, and the retail business unit needed a new system for several reasons. First, the firm needed to demonstrate to its customers that its brokers were well informed and had access to the latest technology. A second important reason was to retain brokers; other firms recruit this company's brokers, and brokers tend to take their clients with them when they move to a new company. Finally, the brokerage firm felt it could increase its business with the new system. The initial request for funding from the business unit and the IT group was about $750 million. A source in the company said that the board of directors approved the request *without* an ROI estimate or any significant economic analysis. The retail business unit made an argument for the investment based on the need to stay competitive and on its ability to fund the project. They anticipated value from the workstation project and were willing to make a substantial investment in it. The project is estimated to have exceeded the original budget by a significant amount, but no one in the firm seems worried by the overrun.

One of the most controversial statements in this chapter, then, is that with some applications you cannot expect to obtain a measurable financial return from investing in information technology. At times, you will invest without the expectation of a return regardless of company policy or mythology about never making an investment without a positive net present value, or without concrete, identifiable benefits exceeding costs.

THE IT INVESTMENT OPPORTUNITIES MATRIX

Many different reasons motivate investment in IT, and other valid reasons support choosing not to undertake a project. Table 6-1 presents an investment opportunities matrix, which attempts to place different kinds of information technology investments into perspective. The first column of the table describes the kind of investment in technology that one can undertake. The second column provides an example, and the third offers comments on this investment type. The fourth column, Upside, discusses the possibility that you will obtain much larger return than predicted. An extraordinary return might result because an investment worked much better than expected, or a product with IT as a component became extremely popular like the Merrill Lynch Cash Management Account in the 1980s, or the airline CRS systems.

The last column in Table 6-1 provides an estimate of the probability of a return from the investment in this type of system. An estimated probability here of .5 means a 50 percent chance that you will get a return from this type of investment. The column presents ranges because the return depends on the specific IT investment you are planning to make. The second number in the column is an estimate for what you can expect in general for an investment in this type of IT.

The probabilities in the table are subjective; they are simply estimates based on encounters with a large number of applications and descriptions of IT investments. Providing such numbers is controversial; the objective is not to convince you that a particular probability estimate is the correct number. The point is that the probability of a return from each IT investment varies. You may want to supply your own numbers after reading more about the different types of investments. (It is easier to estimate the probability of a return for a specific IT investment that you are reviewing than to provide estimates for the categories in Table 1-1.)

Infrastructure. The transportation infrastructure consists of roads, interstate highways, rail lines, and airports to name a few components. Infrastructure tends to be expensive and not terribly exciting, but extremely important. Transportation infrastructure lets the economy function by moving goods from where they are produced to where they are consumed.

Technology today requires an underlying infrastructure. Experts differ as to what belongs in infrastructure. Most would include computers, communications networks, and some general purpose software such as database management systems. Given the rapid advance of technology, we would expect an organization to have a large number of desktop workstations (e.g., NationsBank, before its merger with Bank of America, had more computers than employees according to its chairman), computers that are dedicated as file

TABLE 6-1 IT investment opportunities matrix.

Type of Investment	Example	Comments	Upside	Probability of return
Infrastructure	Wide area network	Support current business—may allow for future investments	Little itself, but allows new programs	.2 to 1.0 (.5)
Required—no return Managerial control	OSHA reporting system, budgets	A cost of doing business	Almost none	0 to .5 (.2)
No other way to do the job	Computerized reservations system, air traffic control	Enable new task or process, provide better customer service, new products	Could gain more than forecast	.5 to 1.0 (.75)
Direct return from IT	Merrill Lynch, Chrysler	Structured, cost/benefit and NPV appropriate	A little if you can build on the investment	.7 to 1.0 (.9)
Indirect returns	CRS in travel agencies	Potential for considerable return, but indirect benefits hard to estimate	Could be substantial future benefits	0 to 1.0 (.5)
Competitive necessity	Bank ATMs Much EDI Electronic commerce	Need the system to compete in the business; what is the cost of not investing in technology?	Very little if you are following the industry	0 to 1.0 (.2)
Strategic application	Baxter, Merrill Lynch CMA	High risk-high potential; may be able to estimate return only after implementation	A high potential	0 to 1.0 (.5)
Transformational IT	Virtual organizations, Oticon	Must be combined with changes in management philosophy; good for fast response organization-risky to change structure, but high potential rewards	A high potential	0 to 1.0 (.5)

SOURCE: From *Information Technology and the Productivity Paradox: Assessing the Value of Investing in IT*, Henry C. Lucas, Jr., © 1999 Oxford University Press, Inc. Used by permission of Oxford University Press, Inc.

servers, computers that process transactions, and networks that link computers in the organization together. Connections to the Internet are also important. Increasingly, elements such as a home page on the Web and corporate information posted to Web pages constitute a minimal infrastructure. Groupware such as Lotus Notes might also be considered a part of infrastructure.

The gains from investments in infrastructure depend on the type of business. For many firms, information technology is vital to running the business. Banks, brokerage firms, and others that deal in services and transactions have long used technology as part of their production effort. Universities have a tremendous investment in infrastructure to provide technology for students and faculty. Infrastructure, then, is almost a requirement for many organizations to be in business today.

MANAGEMENT PROBLEM 6-1

The Detroit automakers were some of the prime movers behind the adoption of EDI in the industry. Because these companies have such huge purchasing requirements (reportedly more than $80 billion a year for GM, and not much less for Ford and DaimlerChrysler), any action that reduces purchasing costs has a potentially big bottom-line impact on profits. EDI works through standards. A company's current system probably does not conform to these standards, so it has to be translated into the standard to communicate. Fortunately software vendors offer packages that let the IT staff map current system outputs and inputs into the EDI standard.

Once systems are able to communicate using the standard, an automaker's computers can place orders electronically with suppliers. The auto company sends a batch of orders to a supplier, and the supplier accepts these orders and inputs them into its system. A large number of transactions are involved in purchasing a

product, including shipping notices, change notices, notices of receipt, and payment documents. Implementing EDI is not trivial, but it does appear to provide substantial benefits.

Most EDI takes place in batch mode; the buyer sends a group of orders to the seller. The seller processes them as a batch in its system. All of these transactions take place over a private network, and frequently they occur using a value-added network (VAN) operated by a computer services company.

It should save a great deal of money for communications costs to move EDI to the Internet. EDI can move as batch transactions, but the Internet offers the opportunity for online purchasing using XML as the standard. What are the pros and cons of moving in this direction? How would companies like the automakers save money converting from EDI to XML and the Internet? Do you recommend they do so?

Infrastructure may also enable an organization to take advantage of some opportunity. The firm that develops the capability to set up a Web page and post information to it is in a good position to create an intranet within the company. It is also better prepared for electronic commerce because it already has a presence on the Web. It can be argued that infrastructure investment is done as much for the opportunities it opens up as for the immediate needs for which it is justified.

The chance of getting a payoff that you can measure from infrastructure investments runs about 50 percent. However, like highways, railroads, and the air travel system, these kinds of investments are crucial to enabling you to do business. You may choose to do more than the minimum investment here, but that decision will be justified more on faith than hard numbers.

Required. How can a system be required? One source of many requirements is the government. Companies have developed applications to satisfy federal or state requirements, particularly for regulatory agencies such as the Occupational Safety and Health Administration (OSHA). It is difficult to see a return on this kind of investment, except possibly cost avoidance in situations where a fine is associated with noncompliance.

When the automakers first began to insist their suppliers be able to accept orders electronically, vendors saw little choice if they wanted to do business with Detroit. If you demanded an economic justification, you could determine the value of sales to the auto companies and compare that with the cost of EDI. However, most managers would probably not consider noncompliance unless they sold very little to Detroit. Investing in this technology was a cost of doing business.

Other kinds of required systems include managerial control, applications such as budgeting and accounting. IT used for these purposes is important in running the company,

SIDE BAR 6-1

Building a New Stock Trading Platform

The NASDAQ was established in 1971 as a screen-based market in which market makers post their bid and ask prices on a computer network that displays these quotes to all market participants. There can be more than one market maker per NASDAQ stock, and actively traded stocks such as Microsoft and Intel have more than fifty dealers' quotes and prices from five to ten electronic communications networks (ECNs) displayed. For many years, the NASDAQ was unique as an online market for stocks. It trades both NASDAQ-listed stocks and certain NYSE securities as well.

The advent of all-electronic exchanges, the ECNs, such as Island, provided stiff competition for the NASDAQ system. In addition, a number of exchanges around the world were abandoning their physical floors and moving to electronic markets. It was time to update the original system, and the price tag turned out to be $107 million and three years of work. For this amount, NASDAQ was able to develop its SuperMontage system. NASDAQ is contemplating a public offering of its own stock, and needs a modern system to make itself attractive to investors.

The new system provides more information and easier access to price information in the market. Though called a cosmetic change, it is important because it is the front end through which traders see the entire marketplace. The system is said to resemble some of the systems used for several years by the ECNs. These simpler, quicker systems have been taking business from NASDAQ. Of the total trading in NASDAQ-listed securities, ECNs have a 45 percent share and NASDAQ has 30 percent. Large brokerage firms have seen their percentage declining, and they now match only 25 percent of NASDAQ orders in-house.

Users of the NASDAQ system include hundreds of institutions, such as mutual funds, and about 830,000 individual investors. With the old system, a trader saw a list of symbols for brokerage firms and ECNs on the left of the screen for a security, and their best bids and offers on the right, organized chronologically in the order of posting. SuperMontage uses an order book that is organized to display more information. The system shows actual offers to buy and sell from investors, not just the quotes. On the TotalView screen below 2,200 to 4,000 shares of Applied Materials are for sale at $25.01 per share. The system allows investors with large orders to be anonymous or to keep their offers invisible from other investors to prevent influencing the stock price with their order. This listing provides more information about the depth of the market, the number of buy and sell orders, and the price and volume on the order book.

The SuperMontage system is regarded as critical to the future of the NASDAQ; it must stop the loss of business to ECNs for the market to remain viable. Given these considerations, how do you think NASDAQ management evaluated the investment in SuperMontage? Do you think that they undertook a detailed financial analysis? Into which category of the investment opportunities matrix does SuperMontage fall?

SYMBOL	**AMAT**	**Applied Materials (NNM)**	
LAST SALE	20.15 q	NASDAQ Bid Tick (+)	
NATIONAL BBO	20.15 q	20.16 q 8900 × 2000	

BID	Price	Total Depth	ASK	Price	Total Depth
	20.15	10700		20.16	3900
	20.14	59000		20.17	11100
	20.13	26300		20.18	15900
	20.12	12500		20.19	11200
	20.11	1600		20.20	14500

MPID	Bid	Size	MPID	Ask	Size
BTRD	20.15	2500	SIZE	20.16	2000
NITE	20.15	2400	ARCX	20.16	1900
SIZE	20.15	4000	SIZE	20.17	6000
CINN	20.15	2200	CINN	20.17	3100
ARCX	20.15	3600	BTRD	20.17	2000
BTRD	20.14	28500	SIZE	20.18	5000
SIZE	20.14	12500	SCHB	20.18	3500
NITE	20.14	7500	AMEX	20.18	5000
SCHB	20.14	1000	NITE	20.18	1100
GVRC	20.14	1000	BTRD	20.18	1000
AMEX	20.14	5000	DAIN	20.18	100
LEHM	20.14	2000	NOCI	20.18	100
SNDV	20.14	1500	GVRC	20.18	100
SIZE	20.13	10000	SIZE	20.19	5500
GVRC	20.13	8800	NOCI	20.19	3000
SCHB	20.13	7500	MONT	20.19	1500
RAMS	20.12	4000	BTRD	20.19	1000
TDCM	20.12	3000	JPHQ	20.19	100
SIZE	20.12	2000	SCHB	20.19	100
LEHM	20.12	1000	BEST	20.20	5000
MONT	20.12	1000	GVRC	20.20	4000
SWST	20.12	1000	NFSC	20.20	3000
NOCI	20.12	400	TDCM	20.20	1800
JPHQ	20.12	100	SCHB	20.20	500
PERT	20.11	800	NITE	20.20	100
GVRC	20.11	500	SNDV	20.20	100
LEHM	20.11	100	UBSW	20.21	5000
SIZE	20.11	100	GSCO	20.21	1100
PIPR	20.11	100	NITE	20.21	1000
SIZE	20.10	13500	TDCM	20.21	100
SCHB	20.10	3500	FBCO	20.21	100
TDCM	20.10	2000	LEHM	20.21	100
PRUS	20.10	500	RHCO	20.21	100
NOCI	20.10	100	WCHV	20.22	10000
SIZE	20.09	2500	GKMC	20.22	1000
FBCO	20.09	2400	LEHM	20.22	5000
BTRD	20.09	2200	BWNC	20.22	500
COWN	20.09	1800	GMST	20.22	500
NITE	20.09	1000	ADVS	20.22	200
SCHB	20.09	400	NOCI	20.22	100
UBSW	20.09	400	BTRD	20.22	100

SOURCE: *The Wall Street Journal*, August 29, 2002. TotalView Screen courtesy of NASDAQ.

but it is difficult to find a great deal of value, either cost savings or revenue generation, from investing in managerial control technology.

If you insist on economic justification, then the relevant numbers are likely to be opportunity costs. Consider the cost of not making the investment rather than considering what is saved or gained from a particular application. The upside here is almost negligible because you will probably invest in this technology and move on.

No Other Way. Although computerized reservations systems were mentioned previously, many more applications of technology would not be feasible manually. Once you are on the plane, the Air Traffic Control (ATC) system takes over. Unfortunately, even though we all depend on this system, severe management and underinvestment problems allowed the ATC system to become seriously outdated. However, obsolete equipment is easier to imagine than a manual replacement for it.

Think of the stock exchanges where hundreds of millions of shares trade hands every day. In the 1960s, the NYSE had to close one day a week to clear trades with a volume that is a fraction of today's volume numbers. Trading a billion shares a day on the NYSE does not stress the Exchange today. If you look at a plot of the amount of business done by commercial banks versus the number of employees, you will find a substantial growth in business with a reduction in employment. Information technology makes it possible to handle this kind of volume.

Many commercial vessels and pleasure craft use computers that display a nautical chart. A global positioning system (GPS) receiver uses a series of satellites to compute the vessel's position; it sends a signal to the computer to plot the position on the chart. Theoretically a navigator could make similar plots, but certainly not in the few seconds the system requires, and probably not with its three-meter accuracy. Trucking companies use this technology to track their fleets, and systems in automobiles plot routes and allow a service center to determine where a car in trouble is located.

States on the East Coast have implemented electronic toll collection at bridges and tunnels and toll roads. The manual, non-IT option is in place today with human toll takers and collection booths that do little to speed traffic flow. Getting motorists through the toll plazas faster reduces their travel times and increases the capacity and utilization of the bridge, tunnel, or roadway.

EZ Pass requires the motorist to attach a transponder to the windshield. When a car so equipped approaches a toll gate, a device at the gate reads the account number from the transponder, charges the toll, and gives the motorist a green light to proceed. A driver may have an automatic account in which his or her credit card is charged when the toll balance reaches $10, or a manual account in which one sends a check. In the case of the latter account, a sign lights at the toll plaza when it is time to add funds. Drivers receive an itemized monthly statement showing the date, time, and facility for which they were charged toll. The manual system of toll takers has reached capacity; it is very difficult to add more toll booths in most locations. The only feasible way to expand capacity is through an investment in information technology.

If the task for which you are investing must be done, and the only way is with information technology, then you probably have little choice in the matter. Some of these high-profile applications produce substantial benefits for the companies that innovate with technology. You may experience considerable upside potential if you are the first organization to develop this innovation. Certainly for first movers, the probability of obtaining a return from investments is higher; a typical number might be a 75 percent probability of obtaining returns.

A Direct Return. Applications of IT in this category are the textbook case. You can measure an expected return, evaluate the costs, and use a number of capital budgeting techniques to decide whether to invest. Merrill Lynch and Chrysler are the subjects of articles in which the authors were able to measure direct returns from investments in IT. In Merrill's case, the company developed a new application for the physical processing of securities involving imaging. Researchers who studied the system documented a variety of returns from it, including a payback from the initial investment. Chrysler implemented an extensive EDI program with suppliers; these electronic communications resulted in a reduction in the cost of building each vehicle.

These applications are well-structured, and estimating costs and benefits are relatively easy compared to other categories in the matrix. The probability of obtaining a return from investments in a system increases in cases where direct benefits were evident from the start. However, because you identified the returns to start with, the upside potential here is probably not too great unless you can build on the system with some new innovation.

An exception to these observations about the upside comes in situations with the potential to affect a large portion of an industry. Electronic data interchange has had a major impact on grocery and clothing retailers. Efforts are underway to develop a national standardized electronic health care record for U.S. residents. Such an investment should save a large number of lives, especially when coupled with hospital systems that control and monitor the delivery of medicines. Calculations of a return on investment for such a system are difficult if not impossible.

Indirect Returns. This relatively new category was identified in some recent research on airline CRSs in travel agencies. FedEx maintains a Web site where you can check on the location of packages. Before this service, the only way to check was to call a toll-free number and speak with an operator. FedEx expected direct returns from this system through reductions in the use of its toll-free number and the ability to handle more inquiries with the same or smaller staff. *Indirect benefits* accrue from this technology if customers develop more loyalty to FedEx because it is easy to check on their packages using the Internet. In a discussion of this example, a student also mentioned that she had been on hold for thirty minutes the last time she called, so the time the system saves the customer is an added indirect benefit.

This example shows how difficult it can be to measure indirect benefits. In the airline CRS case, it was years after the development of these systems before the airlines placed terminals in travel agencies. For FedEx, the challenge is in measuring increased customer satisfaction and loyalty and relating it to revenues and profits. The potential upside is great from investments in this category, but few applications result in significant indirect benefits. Given the difficulty of identifying indirect returns, and even of thinking what they might be, you probably are looking at a 50 percent probability or lower of obtaining returns from the indirect benefits of an investment in technology.

Competitive Necessity. Although sometimes ideas for new technological innovations do not spark an enthusiastic response from senior management, one argument that attracts notice is to say that "our competitors are developing a similar application," or worse, "our competitors have already implemented this system and are capturing market share."

One of the best examples of technology that is a competitive necessity is the bank automatic teller machine, or ATM. Several researchers studied ATMs to see whether banks reduced costs or increased revenues at the expense of competitors. Most of these investigators concluded that ATMs are simply a competitive necessity. A slight advantage may be attributed to the first bank that developed them, but all of that advantage disappeared with banks forming networks of ATMs to meet customer demand for widespread ease of access. It is difficult to imagine a bank today that does not offer ATMs.

At the time ATMs were first installed, they seemed to provide few direct benefits. However, as technology matures, it is possible that an investment in this technology will have a payoff. The chairman of NationsBank mentioned earlier in this chapter indicated that the bank had closed about 150 branches one year while installing between 600 and 1,000 new ATMs. If customers are ready to accept fewer branch locations, ATM technology, which first was a competitive necessity, may become a way to substantially reduce costs.

It is interesting to note that Calyx & Corolla, a company that uses technology heavily in its operations (for processing orders, communicating with growers, and tracking shipments), had no presence on the Web until the spring of 1997. However, its main competitors, FTD and 1-800 FLOWERS both had Web sites from which one could place an order. At this point, such a site is a competitive necessity for Calyx & Corolla.

The upside of investment in this category is probably small if you are following others in the industry. Unless you can come up with a new innovation, you are simply replicating what your competitors have. Any advantage you might gain from the system has already been competed away, leaving about 20 percent chance of obtaining a return from your investment in systems that are a competitive necessity.

Strategic Application. Beginning in the 1980s a great deal was written about the strategic use of IT. American Hospital Supply, which merged with Baxter International, only to be spun off again as Allegiance, provides a thirty-year history of integrating technology with strategy. After the publicity about Baxter and a few other companies, looking for strategic applications became very popular. Several companies, such as Baxter, Merrill Lynch with its cash management account, and Braun Passot, an office supply company in France, all provide success stories. Unfortunately, these stories include little evidence; one must make a lot of assumptions about the impact of the technology to be convinced that IT is responsible for the firms' successes.

A few of the strategic applications only became strategic after someone recognized that a rather ordinary system could be used for another purpose. For both Baxter and Braun Passot, technology made it easier for customers to place orders with the company. Each firm took advantage of this ability to provide better service and get closer to customers by devising new strategies based on technology. It is unlikely that they recognized their order processing systems as strategic applications when they were first implemented.

In cases where the strategic nature of a system becomes obvious only after installation, it is more difficult to include strategic considerations in justifying the investment. Strategic advantage is often stated in terms of increased market share, something that's difficult to predict because of the response of both the market and of competitors. Identifying a system as strategic in advance provides an estimated 50 percent chance of seeing the kind of returns in market share you hope to obtain from your investment.

Transformational IT. This type of investment is both exciting and difficult to implement. Here you use a combination of management and technology to change the basic structure of the organization. This kind of change, as discussed in Chapter 4, requires more than technology; management has to adopt a new philosophy as well. Management uses IT in creative ways to define new organization structures and modes of operation.

Examples of companies in this category include T-Form organizations, virtual organizations and networked companies. Even though the technology here is often simple, the

MANAGEMENT PROBLEM 6-2

In the early days of computing, companies automated many clerical tasks. The first big users of computers were in financial services, banks, and insurance companies. These companies process a tremendous volume of transactions: think of the statements that a bank produces each month, the number of checks that it encodes and runs through systems to maintain balances and a trail of transactions. Insurance companies maintain records of all policies, send bills and renewal notices, and process payments from customers. Prior to the advent of electronic computers, these banks and insurance companies had one choice: clerical workers did these tasks. Computers automated many of these tasks and saved a tremendous amount of labor. It is difficult to imagine a bank handling its records with clerks in today's financial environment.

With these early transactions-processing applications, it was easy to show that a company would receive a return from its investment in IT. One could

figure the amount of labor saved, and it generally showed a handsome return on the investment in a system. In most companies today, the routine transactions-processing tasks are already on a computer, so the easy savings have already been achieved. Additional systems that improve transactions processing will probably make the firm more efficient, which is certainly worth something. Online stores, e-commerce, the Internet, integrated supply chains, all of the systems that you probably find more exciting are more difficult to justify on a return on investment basis.

How do you think an organization today should evaluate potential IT investments? What criteria should it use? What kind of systems will the organization end up with if it insists on a positive ROI for each investment? How can a not-for-profit organization such as a university use financial measures to guide its IT investment decisions, or can it?

entire change program is risky. The estimate of a 50 percent chance of obtaining a return from investing in technology for the purpose of transforming the organization is low because firms introduce many, many applications without obtaining the changes they expect. Often the failure to obtain organizational changes occurs because management expects the technology to be enough to change behavior. A major change in the organization requires a significant management effort to create such a transformation.

Are Investment Types Independent?

The categories in the IT investment opportunities matrix are based on research and personal experience. The preceding discussion suggests that the different types of investments are independent and that a proposed IT innovation fits into only one category. It is quite possible that an IT investment will fit more than one category. Airlines developed the original computerized reservations system because these systems were thought to be the only way to handle the reservations process with the advent of jet planes. Later these systems became strategic and demonstrated indirect returns. If you can identify multiple categories into which a proposed investment fits, then it should increase the probability that the organization obtains a return from that investment. The manager then estimates the probability of a return, given that a proposed investment shows the potential for both direct and indirect benefits.

A more likely scenario is that a long-lived application of technology moves from one investment type to another as it matures and as the organization faces the decision to make additional investment in the application. It would have been difficult for airline managers to have foreseen the development of airline CRS in the late 1950s when they made their first investments in this technology. In the 1970s when American and United made an investment

SIDE BAR 6-2

Productivity in Services

Services dominate manufacturing and agriculture in the U.S. economy, and this fact has led to pessimism among economists that we can continue to see productivity improvements. A widely held view sees service as requiring hands-on activity that is hard to automate. It appears, however, that now technology is bringing significant gains to productivity in the services sector.

FedEx recently completed a $150 million project providing drivers with new handheld package-tracking devices. The wireless handhelds will cut about ten seconds per pickup per stop, and the company will save at least $20 million a year as a result. Countrywide Financial, a California mortgage lender, reduced the time to originate

a loan to about ten days, down from sixty days ten years ago. Its chief technology officer says the company has a goal of reducing underwriting time to twenty minutes. Airlines installed kiosks to replace passenger agents in the boarding process at airports. (Most airlines charge more for a paper ticket than an e-ticket.) Northwest installed 755 kiosks at 188 locations, and two-thirds of its passengers use the kiosks or else check in at home over the Internet. The estimate is that one kiosk does the work of 2.5 employees for 25 percent of the annual compensation of a single employee.

SOURCE: *The Wall Street Journal,* November 7, 2003.

to deploy terminals to travel agents, managers could make an argument for a direct return based on bookings fees. Managers probably did not anticipate the additional indirect benefits.

A PERSONAL VIEW

Figure 6-1 presents some conclusions about investments in information technology. Organizations invest in the categories of application delineated in the investment opportunities matrix and shown on the left side of Figure 6-1. The organization tries to convert each investment into a working application of IT. When implemented, that investment may create direct savings or generate additional revenue for the firm. Indirect returns and a major organizational change may also result from the investment. Unfortunately, other possibilities include partial successes and outright failures. The second-order impact of this investment may accrue to the consumer through better products and services. The

FIGURE 6-1 The payoff from investments in IT.

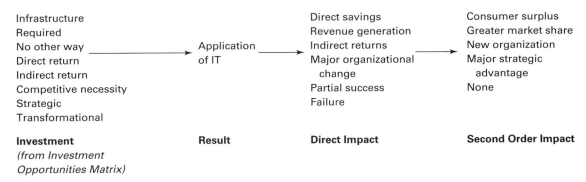

Investment (from Investment Opportunities Matrix)	Result	Direct Impact	Second Order Impact
Infrastructure Required No other way Direct return Indirect return Competitive necessity Strategic Transformational	Application of IT	Direct savings Revenue generation Indirect returns Major organizational change Partial success Failure	Consumer surplus Greater market share New organization Major strategic advantage None

SOURCE: From *Information Technology and the Productivity Paradox: Assessing the Value of Investing in IT,* Henry C. Lucas, Jr., © 1999 Oxford University Press, Inc. Used by permission of Oxford University Press, Inc.

investing firm may gain market share or a major strategic advantage. It may create an entirely new organizational form enabled by IT.

Successful investors spread their funds over a portfolio of applications from the investment opportunities matrix. These firms spend on infrastructure so they are ready when an opportunity comes along. Some applications in their portfolio will probably fail and others may be a partial success. However, certain applications provide a major contribution to the firm, the way shares of Microsoft purchased ten years ago enhance a stock portfolio.

CHAPTER SUMMARY

This chapter addressed the question of how one measures the value from investing in information technology. The different kinds of IT investments range from those that are a competitive necessity to those made in infrastructure. Each of the different types of applications has a different probability of providing a return to the firm. The return from a competitive application where you are a first mover is likely to be greater than for a competitive application where you are responding to other firms who already have the application in place.

It is important to estimate the return from any investment, and investments in IT present particular challenges for capital budgeting. Different kinds of investments in technology provide returns in a variety of ways. You will have to make estimates with little information to go on, for example, the possible indirect returns from an application that you expect to increase customer loyalty. One way to approach these estimates is to do several analyses, the one you expect, a worst case, and a best-case scenario.

A review of the evidence supports a conclusion that the total impact of investments in technology is more than the sum of their individual contributions. Applications of IT interact with each other, creating new benefits and opportunities. A medium-sized brokerage company is an early innovator with a Web site; it uses this experience to build an intranet for all of its research output. Suddenly, all research in the firm is available to any professional, and the firm dramatically reduces its publication costs. Management turns the intranet into an extranet by allowing key customers to have access to it; through this vehicle the company provides its research to customers and establishes a closer relationship with them. Soon the broker offers online trading over the Internet. The firm gradually finds its structure changing as more employees have direct links to clients, reducing the need for a hierarchy of management and for support staff. Applications of technology enhance each other and become woven into the fabric of the organization. It may even be difficult to identify specific applications as technological innovation becomes a part of doing business.

KEYWORDS

Competitive necessity	Investment opportunities matrix	ROI
Direct return	Measurement	Strategic application
Implementation	No other way	Transformational application
Indirect return	Productivity paradox	Value
Infrastructure	Required application	

RECOMMENDED READINGS

Brynjolfsson, E. 1993. The productivity paradox of information technology. *Communications of the ACM, 35*(12), pp. 66–77. (A clear explanation of the productivity paradox with IT.)

Jap, S. D., and Mohr, J. J. Leveraging Internet technologies in B2B relationships. *California Management Review, 44*(4), pp. 24–38.

Litan, R., and Rivlin, A. (eds.). 2001. *The Economic Payoff from the Internet Revolution.* Washington, DC: The Brookings Institution. (Reports evidence that the Internet has contributed to economic growth in the United States.)

Merchand, D. A., Kettinger, W. J., and Rollins, J. D. 2000. Information orientation: People, technology, and the bottom line. *Sloan Management Review*, *41*(4), pp. 69–80.

Stywotsky, A. 2001. Revving the engines of online finance. *Sloan Management Review*, *42*(4), p. 96.

Tyson, L. D. 1999. Old economic logic in the new economy. *California Management Review*, *41*(4), pp. 8–16.

Zack, M. H. 1999. Modifying codified knowledge. *Sloan Management Review*, *40*(4), pp. 45–58.

DISCUSSION QUESTIONS

1. What is the productivity paradox?

2. Why might investments in information technology not show up in national productivity statistics?

3. What are the ways in which the Internet can save costs for routine activities? Why might the Brookings study suggest that the largest impact of the Internet is not likely to be from electronic commerce?

4. What does *value* mean to you?

5. What return did Dell and Cisco receive from their investments in Web ordering systems?

6. What benefits might a company receive from investing in infrastructure? Why does a firm make investments in this category?

7. Using the model for Internet and e-commerce strategy from Chapter 2, explain how a company might benefit through strategic investments in technology.

8. Explain how an application might be a gain in one category of the investment opportunities matrix and move to another one over time.

9. Describe the characteristics of an investment that provides a direct return for a technology application.

10. Is it likely that all investment in new technology will be successful? If not, what are some circumstances in which projects might return less than originally forecast?

11. How can an investment in technology be a competitive necessity?

12. Describe how investments in information technology sometimes benefit customers more than the companies making the investment.

13. Explain how electronic toll systems make it possible to increase the physical capacity of a road or a bridge without adding new physical infrastructure.

14. Who developed the global positioning system? What kind of investment is the GPS system? Who are the major users, and what benefits do they receive from GPS?

15. Identify investments in information technology that might be required in some way. Does a firm usually have a choice in making these investments?

16. Why is it so difficult to identify possible indirect returns from investments in information technology?

17. Based on the discussion in this chapter, how many applications do you think provide a measurable return on IT investment?

18. Describe the ways in which information technology might contribute to economic growth.

19. How do you think managers should make decisions about whether to invest in suggested applications of information technology?

ENDNOTES

1. Condensed material and figures from *Information Technology and the Productivity Paradox: Assessing the Value of Investing in IT,* Henry C. Lucas, Jr., © 1999 Oxford University Press, Inc. Used by permission of Oxford University Press, Inc.

CHAPTER 7

MAKING THE IT INVESTMENT DECISION ^{1}

A Manager's Perspective

One the most difficult and time-consuming IT decisions for a manager is whether to invest in a proposed application of the technology. Although the ongoing management of IT should be more important, the investment decision seems to draw an inordinate amount of attention. Why? Maybe it is because the manager is putting funds at risk in a very public decision in the firm. Other reasons that managers focus on this decision include discomfort with how it is made. Each proposal for an IT application seems to be justified on different grounds, making it difficult to compare them. An ERP system is different from a network infrastructure investment or an investment to electronically integrate with supply chain partners. IT proposals also usually contain a large section on intangible benefits, which just adds to the uncertainty about payoffs. It is important to become comfortable with the IT investment decision because it is something that you will make many times in your career, and it is a necessity for applying technology in the organization.

When thinking about an investment in information technology, the manager needs to be aware that the estimates for the return on the investment may be too optimistic, as shown in the investment opportunities matrix. The manager also needs to consider whether the organization will be 100 percent successful in implementing the IT initiative.

GARBAGE CANS AND IT INVESTMENT

Investments in information technology are replete with uncertainty. These situations involve a great deal of complexity, including the need to fit unknown technology to processes in an organization that can be abstract and hard to understand. A garbage can model of IT value portrays the factors most organizations confront when making investments in technology. This model is depicted in Figure 7-1.

Floating around in the garbage can are the actors and the technology that combine to produce IT initiatives. A key group in implementing an IT initiative is the IT staff, the individuals who specialize in creating and deploying technology. Members of the IT staff include analysts, programmers, project managers, network and communications specialists, operations personnel, and individuals who offer help to users. A typical IT initiative also includes users. These people come from any level of the organization, and it is unfortunate that senior managers often delegate the user role to low levels in the firm.

Consultants may be involved in developing new information technology, partially because of the complexity of the technology and the large number of choices available.

FIGURE 7-1   A garbage can model of IT value.

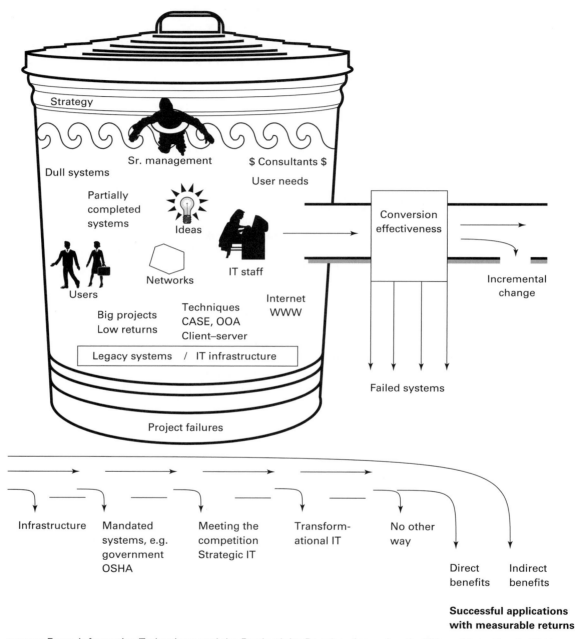

SOURCE: From *Information Technology and the Productivity Paradox: Assessing the Value of Investing in IT*, Henry C. Lucas, Jr., © 1999 Oxford University Press, Inc. Used by permission of Oxford University Press, Inc.

Senior management also takes part in a technology initiative, at least in theory. One expects senior managers to be responsible for what goes on in the organization. In general, the more this group gets involved in IT decisions and implementations, the better the results.

All of these actors work with both tangibles and intangibles that float by. The tangibles are easy to understand; they include the IT infrastructure of computers, networks, databases, and software. This technology is complex and all parts must work together. Whether you buy a software package or write programs from scratch, software must run on the hardware that you buy or already have installed. Computers execute millions of instructions per second; requests for service come in at random intervals and it can be difficult or impossible to recreate the exact scenario that resulted in a system failure. Computer scientists have proven that no program is ever fully debugged. Making the technology work is an extremely challenging task!

The intangibles that confront everyone working on an IT investment are user and organization needs, ideas, and strategy. One of the crucial stages in developing any system is requirements analysis, trying to figure out what users want the system to do. It is much more difficult than you think for people to explain their needs for technology; the task gets even harder when you are trying to undertake a major redesign of the way work is done. It is common to have individuals who are in similar functions describe needs and potential systems that are totally different from each other.

Ideas are what drive progress; some of the most creative and successful systems originated with user ideas. For many years, American Hospital Supply and then Baxter (after a takeover) ran its strategic order entry application with a separate IT operation in marketing, rather than through the traditional IS function. A sales representative had the idea for connecting a customer directly with the system in the 1960s. The company built on that idea to integrate technology with its products, selling value-added services in addition to hospital products. Users and managers suggest many of the innovative applications of technology on the Internet and World Wide Web. Ideas from a variety of sources are critical to finding innovative IT investments.

The last intangible is corporate strategy, as discussed extensively in Chapter 2.

The garbage can model can help one understand why not all IT investments are successful. Before applying this model, the chapter presents evidence to support the contention that, in the past, IT projects failed to meet expectations or failed outright.

Project Success and Other Outcomes

Suppose that your company just purchased a new truck. It would be hard to imagine that the investment in the truck would fail; that is, you would buy the truck and find that it could not carry the goods you planned to ship, or worse yet, that you could not drive the truck because it would not start, you could not steer it, or some other mechanical failure made it inoperative. How similar is this expectation to an investment in systems?

- In 1997, the GAO criticized the IRS's modernization project saying that the agency would have to scrap the project and start over. The IRS canceled one project to turn paper tax returns into electronic images after paying a contractor $284 million for it. In total, the agency admits that it has spent $4 billion developing modern computer systems that a top official said "do not work in the real world."

- The automated baggage handling system at the new Denver airport was blamed for expensive delays in opening the airport, some three times in seven months. The contractor, BAE, had a $175.6 million contract to build one of the most sophisticated baggage handling systems yet developed for the entire Denver airport. As might be expected, when delays occurred, much finger-pointing took place between the airport and the baggage contractor. Upon opening, the fully automated system was working for United, the largest tenant, while more conventional systems existed elsewhere (Montealegre and Nelson, 1996).

■ The joint effort between American Airlines Sabre Technologies and Marriott hotels to develop a major travel supermarket system was canceled among a flurry of lawsuits. The initial estimates for the cost of the project were $55.7 million; it was canceled due to significant management failures after three-and-a-half years and $125 million in costs (Ewusi-Mensah, 1997).

■ The Secretary of Transportation canceled a long-running, expensive air traffic control modernization project after the government spent billions of dollars on the project. Some experts suggest that IBM sold its Federal Systems Division, the prime contractor for the FAA, to isolate itself from this project. The design had a number of flaws, including a lengthy development time that rendered it obsolete. The original concept was for the ground controllers to inform pilots of their location as determined by ground radar. The satellite-based global positioning system became widely available during the system design and it could provide a more accurate location for the pilot than the controller from the ground. Providing the information directly in the cockpit reduces communications requirements and the processing load on the human controller.

The good news is that many examples of successful IT investments occurred as well. The investments in most peril are for large, multi-user projects. These projects generally involve the largest investments, and require many users and developers to work together successfully. At the opposite end of the investment spectrum, users routinely develop thousands of spreadsheets, small databases, and applications in systems such as Excel, Access, or Lotus Notes that are highly successful. However, most of these projects involve users working on their own without a formal project and budget. Their efforts are the results of an earlier investment in IT infrastructure that provides a workstation, software, and a network.

The Concept of Conversion Effectiveness

The garbage can model for IT value in Figure 7-1 sends various projects down the pipe toward a "return on investment" spigot. The first thing they encounter is a filter called *conversion effectiveness*, a concept suggested by Weill (1990). This filter is defined "as the effectiveness with which investments in IT are converted into useful outputs." Weill measured four components of conversion effectiveness including top management commitment, experience with IT, user satisfaction, and turbulence of the firm's political environment.

Although these components undoubtedly influence the conversion of the IT investment into a successful project, many more factors influence success. A partial list includes the following:

■ Size and scope of the project

■ Amount of unknown technology involved

■ Project management

■ Support and encouragement of managers, sponsorship

■ The urgency of the problem/opportunity addressed by the technology

- Norms in the organization
- User commitment and involvement
- Technical development environment
- Quality of the IT staff
- Strength of the project team
- Level of expertise of participants
- Type of technology employed
- Type of application
- Amount of custom code written
- Nature of packaged software included
- Use of external consultants
- Degree of understanding between users and developers
- Presence of a project champion
- Senior management involvement
- Amount of organizational change required
- Threat to existing personnel, vested interests
- User's views of the quality of the system

Many variables partially determine conversion effectiveness. A failure on any one of the items previously listed can doom a project, even if every other aspect of development is successful.

Estimates for the probability of successful conversion are the responsibility of IT staff members, consultants, outsourcing staff members, and other professionals with experience in the field. These individuals, given the nature of a proposed IT investment, should be able to estimate the probability of conversion success. They will base this estimate on their own past experience, the kind of technology the project requires, the capabilities of those working on the project, and other factors like those listed that experience suggests influence project success.

THE INFORMATION TECHNOLOGY INVESTMENT EQUATION

A couple of methods can be used to determine the influences on the return one can expect from investing in information technology. The first, from Chapter 6, is the investment opportunities matrix portrayed in Table 6-1. The right-most column of this table suggests that each opportunity does not necessarily have a probability of 1.0 for a return from an investment in IT. For the Chrysler EDI/JIT system to be discussed later, the probability of a return was quite high. For a budgeting system or a government report, the probability is low.

The discussion in Chapter 6 made the implicit assumption that an investment in IT would be successful, something that companies seem to do regularly. Rarely would a justification for a system suggest that the project might not meet 100 percent of its objectives on time and within budget! Based on this common practice, the estimates of the probabilities in Table 6-1 assumed successful conversion. Another assumption was that the estimates of a return given a particular investment type are independent of other events.

This chapter argues that the ability of the organization to implement technology introduces a probability of success once you make a decision to invest. The calculation of the probability of obtaining a return on an IT investment requires a weight for the probability that an investment type will show a return based on successful conversion.

Before looking at an example or any equations, consider the issue intuitively. When the chance is that a type of IT investment will not return the full forecasted amount, you should expect less of a return than the amount suggested by those proposing the project. If a project team forecasts a return of $100,000 and thinks there is less than a 100 percent chance of getting that return, then the team should expect to see less than the $100,000. The amount will be reduced because the team does not expect this type of investment to provide a full return. Perhaps the project with the forecast $100,000 return drops to an estimated return of $80,000 given the type of project.

This chapter introduces the idea of conversion effectiveness. If not completely successful in converting an IT investment into a working application, then a team would expect a further reduction in the returns from the investment. Then, the previous estimated return of $80,000 drops again because the project team is not sure of being completely successful in converting the IT investment into a successful application. This failure to achieve 100 percent conversion success might drop the estimated return to, say, $65,000.

This reduction in estimated return is due to (1) the contention in Chapter 6 that some types of IT investment are unlikely to show a full return, and (2) the discussion in this chapter about conversion effectiveness and a historical lack of total success in developing IT applications. The following examples and equations are important later during the discussion of possible ways to make decisions about IT investments.

Suppose that you are reviewing a proposed IT project to let customers track their orders over the Internet. Because several of your competitors already offer this feature, it is proposed as a competitive necessity. A task force studying this project estimates that you will save $500,000 per year on customer service expenses if some customers are able to answer their own inquiries. They also feel that their design is superior to that of the competition, and you will gain $250,000 in additional profits from increased market share. Examining the proposal, you estimate that there is a .5 probability that you will get the return suggested by the task force because (1) your design may not be that much better than the competition; (2) if all your competitors move to the net it is unlikely you will increase market share; and (3) it is not clear that a significant percentage of your customers will use the new service.

Can you now state confidently that the project has a .5 probability of being successful and generating a return? The preceding analysis assumes that you are 100 percent successful in developing this Internet initiative for your customers. Based on the examples in this chapter, the garbage can model, and the history of IT development in your own organization, is completely successful development likely? Given your doubts, you take the project proposal to three experienced and candid IT staff members and ask them to predict the probability that the company can implement the Internet initiative with all the features in the report. These three staff members come back with estimated probabilities of successful conversion of .7, .8, and .9, and you take the average at .8.

Now the two numbers indicate a .5 probability of a return given the type and characteristics of the proposed IT project, and a .8 probability that the firm can successfully convert that proposal into an application that has all of its features. The return and successful conversion are treated as independent events. The laws of probability theory say that the probability of two independent events happening is found by multiplying the probability of each event alone. Thus, the probability of a return given the type of application *and* successfully converting the proposal into a system is .5 multiplied by .8 which is .4.

Following this logic, you can get the probability of a successful return on an IT investment: multiply the probability of a return given a particular type of IT investment times the probability of conversion success. The calculation relies on the assumption that the probability of a return on an IT initiative based on the investment type is independent of the probability of converting the investment into a successful application.[2] This line of reasoning leads to the *IT investment equation:*

(1) *P*(Success/Return) = *P*(Return on Investment Type) * *P*(Conversion Success)

where *P* means "probability of." The IT investment equation says that the probability of obtaining a return on an investment in information technology is the probability the type of investment you are making has a return times the probability that you will be successful in converting the investment into a working IT application. Equation 1 calculates a number that is referred to in later chapters as the S/R index, the probability of a successful return.

A few examples will help to illustrate what the equation means. Table 7-1 contains four columns. The first is the type of investment. The second is an estimate by management and the IT staff of the probability of a return given the nature of the investment. The third column is the probability of a successful conversion of the investment into a functioning system. According to the reasoning described in the chapter and the IT investment equation, the product of these two probabilities gives the overall probability of obtaining a return from this investment.

TABLE 7-1 Examples using the IT investment equation.

Type of Investment	Management and IT staff estimate of probability of a return based on the type of project	Estimate of probability of successful conversion effort	Overall probability of a return: the S/R Index
Budgeting system	.5	1.0	.5
JIT/EDI system	.95	.75	.71
Infrastructure network	.5	.7	.35
Package tracking system	.2	1.0	.2
Groupware	.9	.8	.72
Web order entry	.9	.7	.63
Web home pages	0	1.0	0

SOURCE: From *Information Technology and the Productivity Paradox: Assessing the Value of Investing in IT*, Henry C. Lucas, Jr., © 1999 Oxford University Press, Inc. Used by permission of Oxford University Press, Inc.

The table illustrates how difficult it can be to obtain a return from IT investments. For a hypothetical budgeting system, management feels there is only a 50 percent chance the organization will obtain any return because the new application replaces an old budgeting system. It offers a nicer interface and better reports, but managers could not honestly say the system will help them make more money. The 50 percent figure is based on the belief that some labor savings will be realized. The IT staff thinks the package will be easy to implement and estimates a 100 percent chance of successful conversion. The probability, then, of a successful return on this investment is .5 x 1.0 = .5.

In the second example, management is sure from seeing the results at other companies, that an EDI/JIT system for its factories will produce a significant, measurable return. They are certain enough to estimate the probability at .95. The IT staff, however, is concerned with the scope of the project and is only willing to estimate a probability of .75 that it can implement the system so all the benefits occur. The probability of a successful return then is .95 x .75 = .71.

The rest of the table illustrates other hypothetical scenarios, an infrastructure investment, an overnight delivery firm investing in a package tracking system, order entry on the World Wide Web, and Web home pages. Note the probabilities and how each one has a substantial effect on the probability of a successful return from investing in IT. Anything less than a probability of 1.0 for a return on the type of investment and a probability of 1.0 for conversion success dramatically reduces the probability that you will be successful in obtaining a return on an IT investment.

Estimating Returns

Almost all IT initiatives involve some estimate of costs and benefits so that those making the decision to invest have a sense of the dollars involved. Managers are in the position of having to predict the return for specific investments in technology proposed by various actors in the organization. If you look at Table 7-1, the difficulty of making these estimates is evident.

For applications that offer a direct return, by definition estimates are not too difficult. When looking at a case of indirect benefits, you shall see how difficult it is to define and measure these kinds of benefits. It has been suggested that infrastructure investments provide the opportunity to undertake some initiative in the future; you are buying an option to invest again. Still, the following questions need to be answered: How much is that option worth? What is its price? Where is the market for it?

What is the estimated return for a system that is a competitive necessity? For technology when it is the only way to do the job? Some experts suggest that you should look at the *cost of not investing*. What would happen to a new bank that failed to deploy ATMs? Could it remain in business? Would it end up being unable to build market share? If a valued customer says you must implement an EDI package, the cost is clear: losing the customer's business. Does that amount of business become the return on the investment in IT?

You must continue to attempt to estimate the return from investments in technology in order to allocate scarce resources as effectively as possible. However, managers should realize the imprecision and difficulty of making these estimates. The investment opportunities matrix is intended to illustrate these problems.

MANAGEMENT PROBLEM 7-1

In the early 1990s, Cisco Systems decided that its old stove-pipe systems would not support a rapidly growing business. The IT group suggested that Cisco embark on a project to implement an ERP system to provide a standardized architecture throughout the company. The investment was Cisco's largest to date, and the CIO was concerned that the project succeed. The head of Cisco made the success of the system a key corporate goal for the year, and employees all pitched in to make the implementation a success. Cisco experienced some difficult moments, and it took some months for things to be running smoothly after the cutover. Cisco's timing was quite fortuitous; just after ERP implementation, the Internet became available for commercial, profit-making use. With its ERP architecture in place Cisco was in an excellent position to move its business to the Internet.

What are the advantages that a company such as Cisco would gain from having a standard ERP system? The ERP implementation turns out to have provided Cisco with an option to adopt the Internet. Do you think Cisco looked at the ERP investment in an options pricing framework? How do you think it was probably justified? What does this example say about using real options theory to evaluate IT investments? What are the requirements for this method to be applicable?

THE IT VALUE EQUATION

Managers usually do not think in terms of probabilities; they prefer dollar estimates. However, if probabilities are involved, the decision maker should weight the dollar estimates with the probability of actually realizing the dollars. If a geologist tells an oil company executive that the probability a field contains oil that is worth $100 million is 60 percent, what revenue should the executive *expect* to receive from the field? The executive's *expected value* is the probability the field has oil times the value of the oil, or .6 × $100 million, which is $60 million. In general, expected value is the amount expected times the probability that you will receive that amount.

In addition to estimating the probability of a return in the investment opportunities matrix, most companies would try to estimate the dollar returns from investing in technology. Typically these returns are cost savings, cost avoidance, or new sources of revenue. If you estimate that the EDI/JIT system in Table 7-1 will save the company $1 million in its first year, then the actual expected savings will be your estimated savings times the probability of a return times the IT staff estimate of conversion success, or $1 million × .95 × .75 = $712,500. This reasoning leads to the IT value equation:

(2) Expected Return = Estimated Return × *P*(Return) × *P*(Conversion Success) or
= Estimated Return × *P*(Success/Return) or
= Estimated Return × Equation (1)

where P means probability. The IT value equation shows that the expected return from an IT investment is rarely the amount estimated by those involved; it must be weighted by the probability of obtaining the return and the probability of successfully converting the investment into a working application.

Back to the Pipeline

The conversion effectiveness filter resulted in a lengthy digression from the garbage can model, but an important one. It provides a conceptual basis for understanding some of the problems in finding IT value. The type of investment and the firm's success in converting the investment into a working IT application determines whether a measurable financial value will be realized from investing in information technology. The rest of the pipeline exiting the garbage can in Figure 7-1 shows some types of investment that have a good chance of falling by the wayside. At the end of the spigot are the two types of systems where you can find quantifiable value, those with a direct return and those that provide indirect benefits.

Other types of investments may or may not provide much of a return (though they may still provide other types of value). The pipeline illustrates graphically the various categories in the investment opportunities matrix. Infrastructure and mandated systems such as managerial control applications have a tendency to leak from the pipeline. It is difficult to get investments to keep up with the competition, and many strategic applications, to the end of the line. IT that transforms a business or the entire organization has the potential for high returns, but those returns often defy measurement. Where you have no other way but technology, you may be able to identify a return by looking at infeasible alternatives, such as hiring a thousand clerks to do the job.

THE INVESTMENT DECISION

Traditional Net Present Value Analysis

Probably the most frequently used capital budgeting analysis is based on net present value (NPV). The concept takes into account the time value of money and the likelihood that an investment will pay returns over some period of time. The formula for present value, or PV, factor for a sum n periods in the future at interest rate i is:

$$PV = \frac{1}{(1 + i)^n}$$

To calculate the present value of a sum S, multiply it by the formula for present value. With present value, you are discounting future income to today taking into account the time value of money. If you have two investments that have different costs and different income streams, present value is a way to compare them.

Assume that two managers each suggest an IT investment. Project A requires an investment of $45,000 today, and will payoff $20,000 at the end of this year and $30,000 at the end of next year. Project B costs $30,000 today and will pay $50,000 at the end of the third year. To compare these two projects, the first thing needed is a discount or interest rate. Assume that the company's cost of capital is 10 percent. For Project A, you need to discount the two payoffs, $20,000 and $30,000.

> $20,000 at the end of year 1 has a PV of 20,000/1.10 = $18,182
> $30,000 at the end of year 2 has a PV of 30,000/(1.10 × 1.10) = $24,793

The sum of the two present values is $42,975; this amount is the income stream from Project A discounted to today.

Project B yields an income of $50,000 at the end of year 3:

> $50,000 at the end of year 3 has a PV of 50,000/(1.10 × 1.10 × 1.10) = $37,566

You can see that Project A has a higher present value from its payoffs than Project B, $42,975 compared with $37,566. Does that mean the company should invest in Project A? These numbers represent the returns on the investment; they have to be compared with a project's cost. The net present value does this comparison. Project A costs $45,000 today; its net present value is $42,975 – $45,000 = $-2,025. Project B has a NPV of $37,566 – $30,000 = $7,566; the firm should undertake Project B on the basis of estimated costs and benefits (disregarding other factors). In general, one should not make investments with a negative net present value because it is not earning the return specified in the interest rate used in the calculation.

The formula for net present value or NPV is:

$$NPV = -C + \sum_{t=1}^{T} \frac{A_t}{(1+i)^t}$$

where C is the initial investment cost (possibly a stream of investments discounted to the present time period), A is the income at time period t, i is the interest rate, and T is the project life.

Some problems arise in applying NPV to IT investments, however. It is difficult to estimate both the costs and the revenues or savings for an IT investment compared to investments such as the purchase of a new machine for a factory. Typically analysts do not factor in the probabilities that are associated with their estimates for costs and revenues when looking at IT projects. NPV analysis assumes that predicted benefits will actually occur; it does not allow for problems with conversion effectiveness. In general, NPV assumes that the interest rate is constant and has no variability. Because some types of IT investments, such as those for infrastructure, may have little payoff now and a highly uncertain benefit in the future, NPV is biased against funding these kinds of initiatives.

Net present value does not explicitly consider risk. This concept was introduced in the discussion about computing expected values before applying NPV. However, considerations of risk are outside of the model. Criticism against NPV includes its discrimination against longer-term and more risky programs because of this failure. The estimates of expected value come to a single number; an investment analysis that actually looked at the distribution of possible benefits and costs would be more realistic. Finally, NPV does not deal with the implications of *not* undertaking an investment. For a system that is necessary to meet the competition, its benefits need to be determined. These benefits are an estimate of the payoff as incremental revenue or the value of the market share lost if the firm fails to make an investment in technology.

An NPV Example

A number of years ago, Frito-Lay developed a handheld computer for route sales representatives, and management made a decision to fund the project based on a feeling that the benefits would outweigh the costs of the project.

It is possible to use the numbers in a case study of Frito-Lay (Applegate, 1993) and estimates from the managers to conduct a high level net present value analysis of the investment. (See Table 7-2.) The initial estimate for the cost of the project was $40 million, which consisted of costs for the handheld computers, installation in trucks, training, and upgrades in the communications system to transmit the data from each sales district to headquarters in Dallas. The IT staff estimated the new system would increase data center operating costs from $12 million a year to $15 million.

Table 7-2 shows a simple NPV analysis of these data for the investment cost and increased operating costs each year. The savings figures come from management's estimate

MANAGEMENT PROBLEM 7-2

The brokerage company described in the text developed a billion dollar broker workstation, as the project turned out. In the brokerage industry, customers tend to be loyal to their brokers rather than the broker's firm. When a broker leaves a company, his or her customers tend to follow. As a result, a lot of "raiding" goes on among firms trying to lure the top brokers. In the case of this specific system, the sales organization in the brokerage firm essentially said, "We made a lot of money in the last few years, and we can pay for it, and we plan to develop the system." The board of directors approved.

This kind of evaluation and approval is not what the chapter recommends. Was it justified? What are the benefits that a brokerage firm might get from a powerful broker workstation? How could it help individual brokers? How could it help the firm? On what basis do you think the brokerage firm should have evaluated the proposed project? If you were on the board, would you have voted in favor of the investment in the broker workstation project?

that it can increase sales by 10 percent a year through moving to micromarketing and regionalization. The company had sales of almost $3 billion at the time. Assuming a 10 percent increase in sales gives $300 million a year. If margins are 10 percent, which is a lower percentage than the average, the $300 million increase means $30 million a year in profits. Arbitrarily assigning half of the benefits to the handheld project provides $15 million a year in new revenue.

Table 7-2 shows cost and new revenue rows. Their difference in the next row is the net cash flow. It is helpful to compute and show the discount factor, because in many analyses the net cash flow will be different each year, so it will be necessary to roll back each year's net to the starting point of the analysis.

This high-level analysis shows a positive net present value of $5.5 million, though management evidently proceeded to authorize the investment without this kind of financial analysis. It turns out this investment yielded a large number of benefits to Frito-Lay. Later, a manager estimated that the company saved $40 million a year in "stales," products

TABLE 7-2 The Frito-Lay example.

Frito-Lay HHC Project (millions)	Year 0	1	2	3	4	5
Cost	40	3	3	3	3	3
New Revenue	0	15	15	15	15	15
Net Cash Flow	–40	12	12	12	12	12
Interest Rate =	10%					
Discount Factor	1	0.909	0.826	0.751	0.683	0.621
Discounted NCF	–40	10.909	9.917	9.016	8.196	7.451
NPV (5 year) =	$5.5					

SOURCE: From *Information Technology and the Productivity Paradox: Assessing the Value of Investing in IT*, Henry C. Lucas, Jr., © 1999 Oxford University Press, Inc. Used by permission of Oxford University Press, Inc.

that would have to be thrown out because they had been on the shelf too long. Clearly, this application had some direct, measurable savings. A rough NPV analysis would have supplemented management's intuitive decision, reduced their uncertainty about the investment, and possibly stimulated more enthusiasm for the project among managers.

A Controversial Approach: The Real Options Pricing Framework

It is often the case that today's investment in IT makes it possible to undertake a major initiative sometime in the future. For example, American Airlines invested in the Sabre system to solve its immediate problem of making reservations when it introduced jets into its fleet. This initial investment provided the foundation for a travel-related supermarket, and the deployment of terminals to travel agencies. This option is somewhat analogous to the option that one can purchase to buy a stock in the future, known as a call option.

A key insight from this analogy is that an option does not have to be exercised. If you have an option to buy shares of stock for $50 a share, and the value of the stock is $45 when the option is to be exercised, you will simply let the option expire. Your only cost is the cost of the option; you are not forced to buy the shares of stock. Similarly, a company may decide not to undertake an IT project it planned when the opportunity comes up to invest in it. Viewing an IT investment using the options framework is particularly appropriate for infrastructure investments; companies often invest in infrastructure to enable further applications of technology.

The options framework is particularly useful in two kinds of IT investment situations. The first was already discussed: The firm is deciding whether to make an investment that enables it to undertake another IT initiative in the future. This situation requires an analysis of both a current and a possible future investment. It can also involve a single decision situation where an options framework is helpful. Consider a decision of when, if at all, to undertake a new project. You might be interested in having the option to invest in an IT project one, two, and three years into the future. For both of these situations, different researchers suggest treating the IT investment as an option and using one of several options pricing models (OPM) for valuing the option. These models originated in the finance literature as ways to value stock options.

An investor buys a stock option to have the opportunity to buy (or sell) shares of a stock at some point in the future. The investor pays the asking price for the option. The option, itself, is for a specific number of shares. For a call option, the buyer has the right to buy this number of shares at the strike price of the option. If you buy a call option on 100 shares of XYZ stock with a strike price of $50 share, you have the right to exercise this option at its expiration date. If the shares of stock are selling at that date for $55, you will exercise the option, paying $50 for each share and immediately selling it for $55. If the share price is $49, then you would let the option expire.

The most famous pricing model was developed by Black and Scholes (1973); it arrives at a theoretical options price based on the following assumptions:

1. The interest rate is known and constant.

2. A stock price follows a random walk with a variance proportional to the square of the price.

3. The stock pays no dividends or distributions.
4. The option is exercised only at expiration.
5. There are no transactions costs.
6. One can borrow to purchase or hold at the interest rate in assumption 1.
7. No penalties come from selling short (i.e., selling without owning the security).

Given these assumptions, the model for the theoretical price of an option is as follows (Black and Scholes, 1973):

$$(1) \quad w(x,t) = xN(d_1) - c\, e^{-r(t^*-t)} N(d_2)$$

$$(2) \quad d_1 = \frac{\ln(x/c) + (r + .5\sigma^2)(t^*-t)}{\sigma\sqrt{t^*-t}}$$

$$(3) \quad d_2 = \frac{\ln(x/c) + (r - .5\sigma^2)(t^*-t)}{\sigma\sqrt{t^*-t}}$$

$w(x,t)$ = the value of an option on stock with price x at time t (for an IT project w is the value of the project whose underlying risky asset X is the expected revenues from the project)

c = the exercise (strike) price (for an IT project, the cost of development)

r = the continuously compounded risk-free rate of interest, usually the T-bill rate

$t^* - t$ = the duration of the option

σ^2 = the variance of the rate of return or the volatility of the stock (for an IT project, the variance in its expected return)

$N(d)$ = the cumulative normal density function

From a practical standpoint the data required for options pricing models are just as difficult to develop as for an NPV analysis. You have to estimate the variance in the expected return on the IT investment. In the case of an options trader, the variance is the variability of the underlying stock. The options specialist obtains this information from a firm that clears trades; this firm calculates several measures of variance, or volatility as it is known in options valuation. What is the basis for estimating this variability on a new investment in IT?

The analogy between the call option on a stock and an option on a real asset such as an IT investment is as follows in Table 7-3.

For the options trader, the specialist sets the strike prices of the option. For an IT investment, you must estimate the investment required to develop a project at the expiration date of the option, that is, at the time you might be undertaking the project. For an option three years in the future, the analyst must estimate how much investment would be required. Many variables influence this cost, including the pace of technological change. In three years, a package like SAP might come along, which dramatically changes the cost of an investment.

Options pricing models have been used in contexts other than the stock market. For example, companies employ them widely to value stock options for managers and report them to shareholders. It remains to be seen whether the problems with using an OPM for

TABLE 7-3 Comparison of stock and IT project outcomes.

	Call option on a stock	**Real option on IT project**
Underlying asset	Common stock on which option is purchased	An IT system that will be developed in the future
Current value	Current price of stock	Expected present value of returns from the IT project
Volatility	Stock price fluctuations in the market	Uncertainty (variance) in expected cash flow from the IT project
Exercise price	Price in the option at which holder may buy shares when exercising the option	Investment required in IT project
Exercise date	Date on the option when it can be exercised	Date for developing the IT project

SOURCE: From *Information Technology and the Productivity Paradox: Assessing the Value of Investing in IT*, Henry C. Lucas, Jr., © 1999 Oxford University Press, Inc. Used by permission of Oxford University Press, Inc.

IT investments will be resolved. The framework it offers for viewing certain IT opportunities, however, is valuable.

This model has a number of advantages, though its application in the context of IT projects is, to say the least, controversial. The advantages include the fact that the model fits the kind of decision problem described; a firm may find itself in a situation, especially with infrastructure expenses, of needing to invest now in order to have the option of undertaking another initiative in the future. The options framework is also useful when a firm is deciding on the timing of an IT investment; it might take an "option" on the initiative at one of several times in the future. The model does take the variability of expected returns, or risk, from the project into account, something that was stressed in the discussions of conversion effectiveness.

The controversy arises because some experts in finance argue that options pricing models should not be used for nontradable assets. The stocks underlying options trade as do the options themselves, whereas IT investments really do not "trade." Other questions include What is the value of a partially finished IT project, or what is its salvage value? Is there a market for such projects? In options valuation one can ignore the option's risk because the investor can always hold some quantity of the underlying asset to hedge this risk. The option plus the underlying asset provide a riskless asset's return. As a result, one can price the option from the price of the underlying asset, whose price itself reflects the risk and the investor's risk aversion. If one cannot hedge because the option has no underlying asset, then the option becomes like any other asset given its risk and return characteristics. An expert in financial options would argue that this asset should be valued as any other, based on its risk and return. The lack of an underlying asset then makes the use of options pricing inappropriate.[3] To overcome the problem of nontraded underlying assets, it is sometimes possible to construct a proxy, such as a combination of traded assets. If you wanted to calculate an option on an untraded gold mine, you could use gold futures contracts to proxy the return from the gold mine. In this way you construct a proxy in which to invest, an investment that should trade the same way the underlying nontraded gold mine would trade. Can one construct such a proxy for an IT project? The answer is clearly No, leaving a major violation of the options pricing model's underlying assumptions in applying it to IT projects.

It is not unusual in applying models to violate one or more of their assumptions. The issue is whether the violation is material, leading to incorrect conclusions and results. Unlike the options pricing specialist, the manager confronting an IT investment is not pricing a stock option for purchase or sale. Instead, this manager seeks guidance on making an investment.

On balance, used in combination with other information, the options pricing model may provide some insights into the investment decision. Making a decision solely "by the numbers" using either NPV or OPM is not recommended because of (1) the estimates of costs and future returns one is required to make, and (2) the fact that neither approach seems to fit precisely the context of IT investment decisions.

OPM Examples

A Hypothetical Hospital System. The easiest OPM model to understand and apply uses the Cox and Rubinstein binomial options pricing model instead of Black-Scholes (Kambil, Henderson, and Mohsenzadeh, 1993). In this hypothetical example, a hospital is evaluating handheld computers for use by nurses and physicians. The investment required to undertake this IT initiative totals $4 million, consisting of $1 million in hardware and LAN expenses, $2.5 million for the computers and applications programming, and $500,000 for training and implementation.

The task force studying the project identified a number of project risks and then estimated cash flows under different scenarios. The first scenario includes a $1.8 million annual savings starting in three years from reduced paper processing costs. The probability of this outcome is 40 percent. The pessimistic scenario resulted in higher costs and lower savings for an annual reduction of $600,000. The probability of the less successful outcome is 60 percent.

Using traditional PV techniques and a 20 percent cost of capital, the present value of the optimistic scenario is computed to be $6.25 million and the pessimistic scenario at $2.083 million. Weighting these outcomes by their probabilities produces an expected present value of

$$0.4(6.25) + 0.6(2.083) = \$3.75 \text{ million}$$

The expected net present value is $3.75 million – $4 million = –$250,000. Following the standard NPV decision rule, the hospital should not undertake the project.

The task force then thought about an alternative; they could fund a pilot project for $1.1 million to develop the LAN along with a limited test of the handheld computers. If the results turned out to be favorable, then the hospital would undertake the full project. The pilot project would not have positive cash flows since because little savings would result from a prototype. However, one could look at the pilot as an investment in a real option, the option to undertake the full application if successful. The pilot provides the opportunity, but not an obligation, to invest in the full handheld project in a year.

A year from the decision to undertake the pilot, management will be better able to assess the outcome from the full project. Earlier the expected value of the two scenarios was calculated to be $6.25 million and $2.083 million. If the option is to be exercised a

MANAGEMENT PROBLEM 7-3

In many proposals for implementing an enterprise resource planning (SAP) system, the cost of the packaged software itself has been 20 to 40 percent of the total project cost. The majority of the funds are for consultants. Systems such as SAP require the user to enter a large number of decisions about how the firm does business to set the parameters for the package. In addition, these packages require the firm to change many of its existing procedures. In theory, the consultants know how to help guide the process of setting up the software, and can help in implementing new work procedures to take advantage of it.

The CEO of one large company announced a few years ago that his firm would soon become the world's largest SAP customer. He stated publicly that SAP would drive $1 billion in cost out of the company. A few years later, it appeared that none of these statements would turn out to be correct.

How does the heavy percentage of the investment required for consultants affect the evaluation of a proposed SAP installation? How can a company estimate the impact of the procedural changes on workers and work processes? How does it compute cost estimates for these changes in work process? Finally, how does the organization estimate cost savings or revenue generation from a large, complex system such as SAP?

year from now, the value of each scenario one year in the future must be calculated. It is 1 plus the cost of capital to the firm, times the present value, or 1.2 times the figures given. These computations give a value from the two outcomes from the pilot of $7.5 million on the optimistic side and $2.5 million for a pessimistic scenario.

The Cox-Rubinstein model for the value of an option is:

$$C = \{ C_u [(r - d)/(u - d)] + C_d[(u - r)/(u - d)]\}/r$$

where C = the current value of the call

C_u = value of the option at the end of period if the stock price rises to uS

C_d = value of option at the end of the period if the stock price falls to dS

The underlying model assumes a stock of asset of current value S. After one period the stock can increase to a value $u*S$ with probability q or decrease to a value $d*S$ with a probability of $(1 - q)$. Given an exercise price of K, the value of a call option on this stock is C in the formula. At the end of this period, the value of the option is either max $[0, uS - K]$ with probability q, or max $[0,dS - K]$ with probability $1 - q$.

To evaluate this investment from an options pricing perspective, the values for S, u, and d are needed. S is a twin security that is to match the behavior of the project; it must have a value equal to the expected present value of the original project, $3.75 million. In one year the security S will either be worth $7.5 million under the optimistic outcome or $2.5 million under the pessimistic one. One year from the evaluation, the project is worth either $u*S$ = $7.5 million or $d*S$ = $2.5 million, which means $u = 2.0$ and $d = 0.67$.

Solving the Cox-Rubinstein equation for the option value C gives $1.18 million. This amount exceeds the present value of the investment required for the pilot, $1.1 million, so from a financial standpoint, the pilot project looks reasonable. Of course, this situation violated some assumptions of the options pricing model, the most serious being the fact that no real twin security S can track the value of the project. No market exists for the project, and the underlying asset cannot be traded. You can use the OPM model to provide additional information for making an IT investment decision, but it should not be the only factor considered. If both the NPV and OPM results were negative, then the message is that the project under consideration is not viewed positively from a capital budgeting standpoint. However, even with this outcome, some other reasons might justify the IT investment. For example, the strategic potential of the proposed IT initiative, or the need to keep up with competitors might convince management to invest.

Timing an Investment for Yankee 24. Another example of an OPM model for IT investments is a post hoc analysis of a decision by a bank network on when and if to enter the debit card business (Benaroch and Kauffman, 1999). The network, Yankee 24, had an option to enter the point-of-sale (POS) debit card business at several points over a four-year period. An interview with a number of officials involved in making the decision and subsequently implementing the debit card program revealed a number of interesting aspects, including the ability of the researchers to obtain actual estimates for some of the critical parameters in the model. Probably the most difficult and uncertain estimate is the volatility of expected revenues, which was set at 50 percent based on discussions with Yankee 24 personnel.

This opportunity raises another problem with options pricing models and the IT investment decision. Most of the models deal with European options, options that can only be exercised at one point in time. The Yankee 24 investment decision, as many other IT projects, could really take place at any point of time in the future. Such a timing pattern corresponds to an American option. The researchers used Black's approximation to evaluate the Yankee 24 decision problem as shown in Table 7-4.

The analysis is based on determining the prices of European options at the latest maturity date—in this case, year 4—and the price of a European option at each maturity date. Table 7-4 shows six-month intervals beginning in 1987. The American option price at each date is the maximum of the European option at year 4, or the European option at that date as shown in the Maximum row.

The table indicates that the best price is in year 3 from the options pricing analysis, so the financial analysis results in a recommendation to defer the entry into POS debit cards until the beginning of 1990. Looking at the discounted values in the third row of numbers, which is benefits less costs discounted, the maximum value is reached at year 2.5, and a dramatic drop occurs at year 3.5. These numbers suggest that a deferral of the investment for two and a half or three years makes sense. The options analysis agrees with this interpretation of the data on discounted costs and benefits.

It is interesting to note that Yankee 24 made the decision to defer its entry into POS services for three years, but without the benefits of the model. The reasons for this deferral included a desire to wait for the uncertainty about consumer acceptance of debit cards to be resolved and the need to wait for Yankee 24's switching capabilities to have enough slack to add POS services. A special report in 1989 also stimulated interest among merchants in the cost advantages of debit cards over other forms of payments. The POS business grew from no debit terminals in 1990 to about 27,000 by early 1993 (Benaroch and Kauffman, 1999).

It is interesting to compare the reasons for Yankee 24's entry with the options pricing model recommendations. It appears that the network did not have the capacity to begin debit card services in 1987, so that beginning at that time might not have been possible. While deferring their entry, management was able to gather more information about the likely acceptance of debit card services. Neither the qualitative nor OPM analysis could have foreseen the critical industry report that stimulated merchant demand for POS service.

TABLE 7-4 Yankee 24 POS debit card investment.

t (length of deferral period)	0.0	0.5	1.0	1.5	2.0	2.5	3.0	3.5	4.0
Calendar time	Jan. 87	July 87	Jan. 88	July 88	Jan. 89	July 89	Jan. 90	July 90	Jan. 91
Black-Scholes Parameter Values									
A_t (A_0 less revenues foregone during waiting)	$323,233	$342,216	$360,083	$376,230	$389,207	$395,566	$387,166	$344,813	$223,295
X_t (discounted investment cost, X_0; 3.5% interest/6 months)	$400,000	$393,179	$386,473	$379,883	$373,404	$367,036	$360,777	$354,625	$348,577
$A_t - X_t$	($76,767)	($50,963)	($26,391)	($3,652)	$15,803	$28,530	$26,389	($9,812)	($125,281)
Black's Approximation Results									
C_T (option maturing at time T)									$65,300
C_t (option maturing at time t)	$0	$32,024	$66,093	$96,830	$123,786	$144,565	$152,955	$134,873	$65,300
Maximum [max(C_T, C_t)]	$65,300	$65,300	$66,093	$96,830	$123,786	$144,565	$152,955	$134,873	$65,300
Suggested deferral time (in years)		0.5	1.0	1.5	2.0	2.2	3.0	3.5	4.0

SOURCE: Benaroch, M., and R. Kauffman, "A Case for Using Options Pricing Analysis to Evaluate Information Technology Project Investments," *Information Systems Research*, Vol. 10, No. 1 (1999) pp. 70–86. Table 2.

(Continues)

TABLE 7-4 Yankee 24 POS debit card investment. *(Continued)*

Year/ Month	Number of Transactions	Operational Revenues	Costs	Cash Flows
Jan. 87	0	$0	$0	$0
July 87	0	$0	$0	$0
Jan. 88	3,532	$353	$20,000	($19,647)
July 88	8,606	$861	$20,000	($19,139)
Jan. 89	20,969	$2,097	$20,000	($17,903)
July 89	51,088	$5,109	$20,000	($14,891)
Jan. 90	124,470	$12,447	$20,000	($7,553)
July 90	303,258	$30,326	$20,000	$10,326
Jan. 91	738,857	$73,886	$20,000	$53,886
July 91	1,800,149	$180,015	$20,000	$160,015
Jan. 92	4,385,877	$438,588	$20,000	$418,588

Assumptions:

1. Transactions volume—The New England market is 25 percent of the California market, and the POS debit transaction volume expected in New England is estimated based on the experience in California. Until the end of 1991 the total number of POS debit transactions in California was around 12 million, and by the end of 1992 the number of transactions per month rose to 10 million. These figures imply a 16 percent per month growth rate in transaction volume in California between 1985 and 1992. This growth rate is consistent with expert estimates of the growth rate expected between 1993 and 1996. Assuming that the New England and California markets are similar, except for size, we applied a similar growth rate. (A similar estimate would have been established based on the transaction volume in California between 1985 and 1987.) A base of 2,500,000 transactions for December 1992 is used, based on a corresponding 10,000,000 figure in California. The base figure is discounted back by the 16 percent growth rate per month, and the monthly transaction volumes are aggregated by year.

2. A — the present value of revenues less operational costs, where the discount rate of 12 percent approximates the rate used for capital budgeting of other electronic banking investments at the time. The yearly operational marketing cost is $40,000 ($20,000 every six months), and the revenue per transaction is 10¢. Once an entry decision is made, it takes one year to begin servicing customers.

3. X — initial (sunk) technical investment is $400,000.

4. s — volatility of expected revenues is 50 percent.

5. T — the maximum deferral period in years, from (early) 1987 to (early) 1992, is also the analysis horizon of 5.5 years.

rf — 7 percent annual risk-free interest rate.

SOURCE: Benaroch, M., and R. Kauffman, "A Case for Using Options Pricing Analysis to Evaluate Information Technology Project Investments," *Information Systems Research,* Vol. 10, No. 1 (1999) pp. 70–86. Table 2.

GUIDELINES FOR IT INVESTMENTS

Table 7-5 presents information for making decisions about IT investments. This spreadsheet combines information from the investment opportunities matrix, the IT investment equation and IT value equation, and capital budgeting techniques discussed in this chapter.

TABLE 7-5 A decision worksheet.

Name	Type	Cost	Estimated Return	Prob Return	Prob Conv	Prob S/R	Expected Value	Capital Budget Model	Upside
Budgeting system	Required	$20,000	$20,000	0.50	1.00	0.50	$10,000		None
JIT/EDI system	Direct	$300,000	$500,000	1.00	0.75	0.75	$375,000	$957,058	Expand $5 million savings
Infrastructure network	Infrastructure	$100,000	$75,000	0.60	0.80	0.48	$36,000	$120,678	Allow future applications
Delivery tracking	Competitive necessity	$750,000	$1,000,000	0.40	1.00	0.40	$400,000		Prevent market share loss
Groupware	Indirect	$100,000	$50,000	0.90	0.80	0.72	$36,000		Restructure firm?
Web order entry	Direct	$100,000	$500,000	0.90	0.70	0.63	$315,000	$1,055,929	Reduce costs $500,000
Web home pages	Competitive	$50,000	—	0.00	1.00	0.00	—		Experience for e-commerce
							—		
Proposed Intranet	Infrastructure	$160,000	$60,000	0.80	0.90	0.72	$43,200		Internal Intranet
								$144,813	Present value 5 yrs savings
								$(15,187)	NPV original proposal
								$37,608	Options Price experiment

SOURCE: From *Information Technology and the Productivity Paradox: Assessing the Value of Investing in IT*, Henry C. Lucas, Jr., © 1999 Oxford University Press, Inc. Used by permission of Oxford University Press, Inc.

Although Table 7-5 provides an example of the information management could use in making IT investment decisions, it is not recommended that a single decision criteria be used to determine the investment decision. Except in rare circumstances, management needs to look at all aspects of the decision. The table identifies each IT initiative in this hypothetical example and lists its type. (One initiative might fit in more than one type, which makes for a slightly more complicated analysis; however, the same approach applies.) The fourth column of the table is an estimated return from the project. The next two columns are probability estimates, the first being the probability that this project, given its type, will have a return. The second probability is for conversion effectiveness that indicates the risk of this initiative. These two probabilities provide a calculation of the likelihood that the organization can implement the project successfully to meet specifications.

The *S/R* index comes from the IT investment equation: It is the product of the probability of a return and the probability of successful conversion and represents the likelihood of a successful return. The expected value comes from the IT value equation; it is the estimated return times the probability of a return times the probability of conversion success (or the estimated return times the *S/R* index).

The Capital Budget Model column contains the results of applying a budgeting technique to the data in the table. Note that these techniques do not necessarily apply in every instance. The right-most column in Table 7-5 comments on the possible upside benefits of the investment.

Table 7-5 lists a variety of projects for a rather diversified holding company. The company convenes an IT steering committee as needed; one of its tasks is to approve suggested projects. IT steering committees usually consist of the top operating officer in the firm and the most senior managers of different functional areas such as finance, production, and human resources. The committee helps to set priorities and allocate resources to requests for new IT initiatives.

One can look at present IT investments from the budgeting system to Web home pages and the proposed IT investment for an intranet shown in Table 7-5 as a portfolio of IT projects. Management should try to balance this portfolio on several criteria. For example, it is unlikely that one will obtain great value if all conversion probabilities are very low, or if all expected values are small. The *S/R* index provides an overall evaluation of the opportunity to create value from IT. Comparing a proposed project with the existing portfolio provides a picture of its contribution to the firm's efforts to obtain value from IT.

In the past, the steering committee made decisions on all of the projects in Table 7-5 except the last one, the proposed intranet. A review of its past decisions will set the stage for discussing the new initiative for an intranet.

The budgeting system falls into the "required" category of application. Both the company's accounting firm and its controller argued strongly that the old budgeting system was no longer suitable. The cost of this system is rather low with an identified package costing $10,000; no more than another $10,000 would be required to implement the package. The controller estimated an annual savings of $20,000 in reduced clerical costs once the package is implemented. However, she lacked confidence in her estimate given this type of investment and the required nature of the application; she estimates a 50 percent probability of a return. The IT staff was confident that it could successfully install the system; they rate the probability of conversion success as 1.0. The steering committee approved the system because its cost was low and because the controller made a strong argument that such a system was required for the business.

The JIT/EDI system for one of the company's manufacturing subsidiaries required lengthy discussion due to the size of the investment. Based on visits to other companies using this approach, the IT staff felt that their company could expect to get all of the estimated returns (probability of a return = 1.0); they also estimated a 75 percent probability of successful conversion. Given a project with an expected annual value then of $375,000 ($500,000 × 1.0 × .75) and a $300,000 investment, the economics of the proposal were not in question. The Capital Budget column shows a PV of a little under $1 million using a five-year planning horizon and a 15 percent cost of capital; the NPV = $957,058 – $300,000 = $657,058. The major issue for the steering committee was the $300,000 investment and the demands this system would place on the IT staff. A system of this size, done in-house, might preclude some other IT initiatives, or force the firm to go outside for them. The steering committee approved this proposal because of its favorable financial projections and the upside possibility of even larger savings from expanding the system in the future.

The third project originated in two departments of a subsidiary; it is an infrastructure investment for a local area network linking the two departments, with connections to the Internet. The estimated cost is $100,000 and the expected annual value of the return is $36,000. This expected value comes from the product of a .6 probability of an estimated $75,000 return and a .8 probability of conversion success. The five-year NPV of a $36,000 annual savings at the firm's cost of capital is $120,678 – $100,00 = $20,678. However, the steering committee decided against funding this proposal despite the positive economic evaluation. Instead, it asked the departments proposing the LAN to work with their IT group to propose a network for the whole subsidiary rather than just two departments.

A competitor recently began tracking all of its products using scanners in its trucks and bar codes on all packages. The trucks return to their base each night and transmit their data to a central computer where customers can make inquiries about the status of their shipments. Company management proposed a similar system to remain competitive. Because the firm felt that technology vendors have a lot of experience with this kind of application, it estimated the probability of conversion as 1.0. The $1 million in estimated annual returns was a figure that inspired little confidence; weighting it with a probability of .4 gives an expected value for the project of $400,000. The estimated return was based on the VP of Marketing's estimate of lost market share if the company did not make this investment. Given the uncertainty on the benefits side, the IT staff did not feel comfortable applying a capital budgeting model. The IT steering committee approved the project based on the argument that package tracking had become a competitive necessity, and because it wanted to help this subsidiary grow.

Another subsidiary requested funding for a groupware initiative, a project that at best would only have indirect benefits. Arguments in favor of the investment stressed the opportunities groupware offered to restructure the organization. This subsidiary has a large, mobile staff of representatives who call on customers and make proposals to them. Groupware would reduce the cycle time for proposals and allow the company to decentralize more decision making to its representatives. Senior management felt that such IT support would help the subsidiary compete by providing a fast response to customers. Management admitted that its return estimate was a guess, so the steering committee looked at the project from the standpoint of its potential upside benefits for the subsidiary.

The proposal for a Web order entry application was an easy one to approve. The NPV = $1,056 million – $100,000 = $956,000 for five years at a 15 percent cost of capital. However, the steering committee was less concerned with the economic analysis than with the future; it sees the Internet as an important sales channel for many parts of the company. It was eager to encourage the first direct ordering initiative for the Web, and quickly approved the request.

Similarly, a subsidiary wanted to establish a home page and related pages on the Web. It argued for the investment, not on a return basis, but because its competitors already had Web sites. It viewed the proposal as a first step in moving toward electronic commerce. Because the steering committee had a policy promoting the use of the Internet, it approved this proposal as well.

The proposed intranet looks attractive compared to the projects already underway or completed. It has a high *S/R* index with a good probability of conversion success and of obtaining a return. The subsidiary requesting the intranet classified it as an infrastructure expense. The subsidiary would gain from making information available throughout its operations, and estimated that it could save $60,000 a year in paper and publishing costs. The NPV analysis shows a five-year value of $144,813 using a 15 percent cost of capital; the NPV = $144,813 – $160,000 = –$15,187. The NPV in this case is negative.

The subsidiary then recast its analysis of the intranet in an options pricing model. First the analyst determined that the company could develop a prototype for $30,000. This test intranet would give enough information to know whether the original proposal should be undertaken. At the end of the prototype development in a year, the company would need to invest another $100,000 to develop the full intranet. The analyst examined the $60,000 in estimated benefits and saw that this amount could be viewed as the combination of an optimistic scenario of $80,000, occurring with a probability of .6, and a pessimistic scenario of $30,000, having a probability of .4. Weighting each of these outcomes by the *S/R* probability index of .72, allowed a calculation of the value of the option the company would "buy" if it undertook the prototype. The value of the twin security representing the option is $144,813, the NPV of the two benefits scenarios. As in the earlier example, to compute the parameters of the options pricing model, the analyst looked at the future value of the scenarios in one year. The final results shown in Table 7-5 indicate the value of the option as $37,608, which is more than its cost of $30,000.

Given this additional information from the OPM, it is likely management will approve at least the prototype intranet. With the small amount of money at risk, the firm might decide to proceed with the full project because the evidence for benefits from intranets in general is positive. In addition, the steering committee consistently shows support for Internet-type initiatives.

CHAPTER SUMMARY

Decisions about investments in information technology are too important to be left to technologists. For major commitments to new IT initiatives, senior management of the firm needs to be involved in the decision. These managers should follow and monitor the progress of projects, providing advice and resources when problems arise. The kinds of applications discussed so far are critical to the firm; they have the potential to return enormous value and the potential to fail miserably. Some of these initiatives protect or even expand market share while others become intertwined with corporate strategy. By joining discussions and reviews of IT initiatives, the CEO communicates that these investments are important, encouraging users and managers at all levels to contribute to a project's success.

The examples showed that different criteria apply to project approval depending on the type of investment. In some cases quantitative analysis was appropriate; in others decision makers responded to qualitative factors. A survey of different companies and their actual practice in making IT investment decisions revealed a group of utilities that insisted on a positive net present value before undertaking any IT project. Although this rule probably sounds good to management and shareholders, Table 7-5 suggests that these companies may be missing a number of important opportunities (at least if they are being honest in their NPV analysis).

If a firm insists on a cost–benefit, NPV, or even options pricing analysis alone, it is likely to ignore proposed investments in several categories and some opportunities with considerable upside potential. In particular, it is difficult to come up with credible quantitative evaluations of infrastructure, initiatives with indirect returns, strategic applications, and investments that may transform the organization. Every proposal should be evaluated, but decision makers must use criteria that are appropriate for the type of investment proposed.

KEYWORDS

Black-Scholes options pricing model	Expected value	Net present value
Cox-Rubenstein options pricing model	IT investment equation	Options
	IT value equation	Real options
Conversion effectiveness	Garbage can model	Steering committee

RECOMMENDED READINGS

Applegate, L. 1993. "Frito-Lay, Inc.: A Strategic Transition (A) (Updated)," Boston: Harvard Business School.

Benaroch, M., and Kauffman, R. 1999. A case for using options pricing analysis to evaluate information technology project investments. *Information Systems Research*, 10(1), pp. 70–86.

Black, F., and Scholes, M.1973. The pricing of options and corporate liabilities. *Journal of Political Economy,* 81(3), pp. 637–654.

Cohen, M., March, J., and Olsen, J. 1972. A garbage can model of organizational choice. *Administrative Science Quarterly, 17,* pp. 1–18.

Dos Santos, B. 1991. Justifying investments in new information technologies. *Journal of MIS,* 7(4), pp. 71–90.

Ewusi-Mensah, K. 1997. Critical issues in abandoned information systems development projects. *Communications of the ACM,* 40(9), pp. 74–80.

Kambil, A., Henderson, J., and Mohsenzadeh, H. 1993. Strategic management of information technology investments: An options perspective. In *Strategic Information Technology Management,* R. Banker, R. Kauffman, and M. Mahmood (eds.), Harrisburg, PA: Idea Group Publishing.

Kumaraswamy, A. 1996. A real options perspective of firms' R&D investments. Unpublished Ph.D. Dissertation, Stern School, NYU.

Montealegre, R., and Nelson, H. J. 1996. "BAE Automated Systems (A): Denver International Airport Baggage-Handling System," Boston, Harvard Business School Press.

Weill, P. 1990. *Do Computers Pay Off?* Washington, DC: ICIT Press.

DISCUSSION QUESTIONS

1. How is an information technology investment different from the investment in a physical asset such as a truck?

2. Explain how the garbage can model of IT works.

3. What is the concept of conversion effectiveness? How does it impact the return on IT investments?

4. Why can you multiply two probabilities of a head or tail together in the case of tossing two coins, one after another?

5. Explain the concept of expected value. How does it apply to IT investments?

6. Describe the IT investment equation. What are its advantages and limitations?

7. What is the impact of using the IT investment equation on forecasts for the return on an IT investment?

8. Describe the IT value equation. What is its impact on forecasts for the dollar return on an IT investment?

9. What is net present value? How is it used in making many types of investment decisions?

10. How is NPV applied to IT investments? What are its assumptions and limitations in evaluating IT investments?

11. If a firm only uses NPV for evaluating IT investments, what kind of applications is it likely to develop?

12. What is an option? A call option? Can you figure out from a call option what a "put" option is?

13. What is the conceptual benefit of using an options pricing framework to evaluate IT investments?

14. Why might a finance professor object to using real options theory to evaluate an IT project?

15. How can you evaluate the variability or uncertainty in the returns on an IT project?

16. How does the OPM compare with NPV when considering IT investments?

17. How might the OPM help in determining the timing for IT investments?

18. Why can a firm not decide on all of its IT investments using the same criteria for each one?

19. What are the advantages of using a management committee to help make IT investment decisions?

20. What is the role of the chief information officer in choosing IT investments?

21. What is the role of the senior manager in the business unit requesting an IT application in deciding on the investment?

22. Should Frito-Lay have made the handheld computer investment? If the NPV for the project had been negative, what are some other reasons to invest?

23. Why is it more difficult to make a decision on IT investments than a decision to invest in a new plant or machinery?

24. How do the probabilities in the two equations about IT investments in this chapter change the original forecasts for the benefits from an application?

25. Is it realistic to expect firms to undertake the kind of analyses described in this chapter?

26. Would you recommend doing an investment analysis for a system that is a competitive necessity? How about a strategic system?

ENDNOTES

1. Condensed material and figures from *Information Technology and the Productivity Paradox: Assessing the Value of Investing in IT,* Henry C. Lucas, Jr., © 1999 Oxford University Press, Inc. Used by permission of Oxford University Press, Inc.

2. You could argue that the type of investment is correlated with project size; for example, a required government report is probably a much smaller project than a strategic application. However, this reasoning is not necessarily the case. An OSHA report in the chemical industry might require a substantial system for monitoring the exposure of all workers in the company to certain chemicals.

Being the first in your industry to set up a Web page to accept incoming orders might give you a first mover advantage from relatively simple technology. Projects of varying size and complexity may appear in any of the cells of the investment opportunities matrix. If a project is very large, and you think that size reduces the chances for success, then your estimate of the probability of successful conversion should reflect your concern.

3. I am grateful to Professor Yakov Amihud of NYU for his comments on the suitability of options pricing for IT investments.

CHAPTER 8

CHOOSING TECHNOLOGY

A Manager's Perspective

The price of having choices is the consideration of a lot of alternatives and then choosing just one. When the computer industry was young, it consisted of mainframes, and the manager had the option of developing the application within the company or hiring a consultant to develop it. A manager might also buy a package, but most packages were pretty unimpressive in the 1950s and 1960s. For processing power, the manager usually had an in-house computer, or could turn to a company called a service bureau that rented time on its computers. In the late 1960s, the facilities management industry emerged. As desktop PCs and local area networks proliferated, and with the coming of the Internet for profit-making use, the options for how to develop, implement, and operate applications of technology multiplied. An organization has no single right answer for what technology to choose; it depends on the organization, its staff, and the technology in place and what applications need to be developed. A manager needs to be aware of the alternatives in order to make an appropriate choice when confronted with the need for new technology and services.

Operating an IT unit in an organization can be described as a "business within a business." Large companies may have IT budgets of $1 billion annually, which is more than the sales of many companies. The person with a new initiative for IT will often leave the question of what technology is appropriate to the IT department, being unconcerned with the actual hardware or software involved. However, senior managers in the corporation have to manage the IT function within the organization, and they face a daunting array of choices. Each organization is different and will use unique criteria for choosing technology. This chapter provides some general guidelines so that managers can ask the right questions before making decisions about technology.

Victor Electronics is a fairly typical company today with a variety of technologies in place. Victor developed these technologies over many years, some of them are new and others have been installed for a number of years. It would be both too expensive and too disruptive to replace all older systems and technology at one time. Companies like Victor add new applications of technology and gradually update older ones. A CIO of a large firm mentioned in a video presentation that he had replaced the company's human resources system without being asked by the HR manager. The CIO felt the system was inadequate and was getting to the point where he could not support it. So the impetus for upgrading technology may come from a manager or from the IT staff.

Victor uses a range of typical applications for a manufacturing company, except that it is a little behind in systems modernization. On the hardware side, Victor's mainframe computer in Rockville, Maryland, processes all sales orders for the Americas. The sales offices in the United Kingdom and in Singapore each have midrange IBM AS/400 computers, a popular computer for distributed processing. The order system for the main-frame was written in COBOL and modified over the years. Victor purchased the AS/400 system for sales order entry and modified it heavily. As a result, the company cannot apply new upgrades from the software vendor; Victor made too many changes and does not have a good record of the modifications it made to the system. Currently Victor has no enter-prise resource planning (ERP), customer relationship management (CRM), or supply chain management (SCM) applications. Factory planners use a small custom-written system to schedule production; this application is of limited usefulness, and most of the schedulers work with Excel spreadsheets in planning production and loading the factories. Also, most professionals and managers at Victor have PCs connected to the corporate intranet.

Victor went to an applications service provider (ASP) to host a Web site when it did not have the resources or the knowledge on its staff to set up the site. A task force in the company is trying to decide what to do about e-commerce; most of its customers are satisfied with EDI for ordering, but Victor thinks that they will want full-blown e-commerce within the next three years.

THE INDUSTRY

The computer industry today consists of a large number of companies that offer a variety of components for implementing technology, and services to help clients solve their problems.

- The industry began with companies that sold hardware, the physical devices that execute software programs. These firms still exist today, but at least for one of the early leaders, IBM, the emphasis has changed from hardware to services. Computer hardware is rapidly becoming a commodity, and commodities are known for their low margins. Dell and the merged Compaq and Hewlett-Packard are leaders in personal computer hardware, and Dell has managed to remain profitable with commodity PC sales largely through innovative uses of technology and a direct sales model. Hardware today encompasses far more than computers; it also includes a variety of network devices such as hubs and routers. Cisco is a leading vendor of network equipment. Sun Microsystems sells a large number of servers that are used on the Internet, especially for electronic commerce applications.

- Most firms today would rather buy than build a new IT application; the cost of developing software is high, and it can take a long time to complete a develop-ment project. A number of firms offer packages for a large variety of applica-tions. The largest, dedicated packages are systems for ERP, applications that encompass all of the basic transactions processing activities of a firm. SAP, Oracle, and PeopleSoft (which bought J.D. Edwards) are among the firms that offer these packages. Other popular packages deal with customer relationship management, data analysis, and data mining. ERP is an example of a dedicated application; it is only designed to process transactions. Most people with a desktop computer use problem-oriented packages such as Excel or Word for word processing. In between these general purpose packages are programs that can be used to create custom applications; for example, a database management system features a number of components that help a developer create an application more quickly than possible with a conventional programming language.

■ The rapid proliferation of technology created a large service industry to help companies integrate technology with their strategy and operations. IBM has a consulting subsidiary, IBM Global Solutions, which competes with Electronic Data Systems (EDS), and Accenture is a firm with thousands of employees in forty-six countries working to implement IT solutions for customers. Services companies will develop a single application of technology or will contract to take over the operations of a company's entire IT effort, a process called outsourcing. In addition to taking on the responsibilities for a client's entire processing, outsourcers may specialize in a particular aspect of technology, for example, hosting a Web site or providing an electronic online store for a company.

TO BUY OR NOT: MAJOR APPLICATIONS

The Decision Context

The rest of this chapter discusses multi-user applications rather than the kind of processing you might do on a desktop using Microsoft Office. Multi-user systems are much more difficult to design and implement than a system a person creates for personal use. Suppose that Victor Electronics decides to develop an ERP application. A company of its size should consider a number of conditions when designing and programming such a system on its own. It is difficult to conceive of circumstances where Victor would not want to buy a package. The reasons in favor of a package are numerous:

■ The program exists already, and Victor can buy as many functions or modules as it may need.

■ The program code for the application has been heavily debugged as it is running at a number of client sites.

■ The time to implement will be much, much shorter than trying to undertake a custom development project.

■ It is possible to visit sites using the package to evaluate it.

■ A number of consultants who are familiar with the package are available to help guide implementation.

■ Most package vendors are in business for the long-term and will continually improve and update their products.

Of course, management must consider the potential negatives in looking to buy this package:

■ The cost will appear to be high, and probably at least 50 percent of the total cost will be for consulting help, not just the package.

■ The package will not perform functions exactly the way Victor does now; the company will have to pay a high price to change the package, or, more likely, will have to change some of its own procedures.

■   It can still take a year or more to implement a large package, particularly if Victor wants to install it at locations around the world.

Most companies today, including Victor, would make the decision to purchase the package, realizing that the package is no guarantee of success. However, the argument for debugged code, a short time to obtain benefits, and the promise of updates is usually persuasive.

Several choices of packages are available in the marketplace for the ERP application at Victor. When no obvious package is available, such as when the application is strategic or transformational, then the decision must be made whether to develop a system in-house, ask a consultant to develop it, or use some combination of the two. If an application is likely to provide a competitive edge, is a part of a major strategic thrust of the firm, or has the potential to transform what the organization does, then management needs to carefully control the development effort and the resulting system. You may need a consultant to provide expertise or resources, but the firm will want to maintain and modify the system.

Buying Applications Packages

Doing a little homework before shopping for a package and while evaluating them makes sense. The major difficulty with an applications package such as ERP is fitting the package to the organization. Employees will have to change procedures and learn how to use the new system, and they will have a lot of work to convert from whatever they are doing now to the new package. It is important to understand how the functions of the packages under consideration differ from the functions at Victor Electronics. One important criterion in deciding on a package is the extent of organizational and individual change required to successfully implement the package.

The most serious problem with purchasing packages arises if users insist that the organization customize the package for its unique situation. Although individual organizations always claim uniqueness, it is often easy to change routine procedures to suit a package. On the other hand, some legitimate reasons also favor maintaining uniqueness in the organization. Many systems developed on a custom-tailored basis fail completely or never reach their potential. It seems that packages are even less likely to succeed because they have a tendency to impose a system on a user. So the situation must be examined to see what can be done to lessen the implementation problems of packages.

The package vendors recognize this problem and generally design packages to allow some custom tailoring. Two ways are often employed for providing flexibility: the use of modules and the use of parameters. The first strategy provides a modular set of programs in the package. The user configures a custom applications package by selecting appropriate modules for a particular set of needs. Little or no programming is required on the part of the user. Packages also make extensive use of parameters or data values to indicate unique features for a particular user.

Often, the customizing features provided by the vendor of the package are insufficient for an organization. Less expensive packages may have to be accepted as is, but for more elaborate applications, the customer often finds it necessary to write custom code to modify the package. Sometimes the modifications are easy and require only the addition of some reports or the alteration of reports already in the package. Code modification can become quite extensive and may involve rewriting significant portions of the package. The major reasons not to modify the code include time and cost and the difficulty of installing updates to modified packages. The important thing to remember is that the cost of a package is usually not just the purchase price. The costs of transition, modification, and maintenance must be forecast and considered as well.

Establishing Criteria

The information technology department and a project team should agree on screening criteria for packages. Many times packages will be considered as alternatives to developing a system in-house. Table 8-1 lists some possible evaluation criteria for decisions on packages. The major reason for acquiring a package is the function it performs. You will want to know how many desired functions are included and what effort is required to modify the package. The integration of the package with other packages is often a key decision factor. If a company wants to develop a sophisticated production planning system using i2 software, then it needs to be sure that an ERP system under consideration includes an interface to the i2 application.

It is also important to consider questions about the user interface: How difficult is it to use the package? How much information does a user have to supply? Is it simple to prepare and understand the input? Is the package flexible, and can it be used if the organization's requirements change?

The evaluation is also concerned with the package's response time. Organizations are interested in how much present procedures will have to be changed to use the package. Just as with hardware, it is necessary to evaluate vendor support. Updates and improvements for the package should be forthcoming, so adopters of the package are dependent on the vendor's remaining in business.

With software packages, documentation is important; the IS staff will maintain the package and may modify it. Finally, cost is a major consideration. Remember, companies almost always underestimate how much projects cost. The VP of Finance of a large holding company mentioned that many of its subsidiaries had installed SAP's ERP system. The VP complained that these projects always took twice as long as predicted at the start, and cost twice as much as budgeted!

Making a Final Decision

This discussion is mostly interested in whether a package qualifies for consideration. Almost all these criteria are subjective, which means several individuals should rank a package on each criterion. The responses can then be averaged for each criterion and a

TABLE 8-1   Considerations in evaluating software packages.

■ Functions included	■ Response time
■ Integration with other packages, internal applications	■ Changes required in existing procedures
■ Modifications required	■ Vendor support
■ Installation effort	■ Updating from vendor
■ User interface	■ Documentation
■ Flexibility	■ Cost and terms

MANAGEMENT PROBLEM 8-1

Suppose that you are assigned the task of figuring out how to solve a particular information processing problem at your employer. One way to approach the assignment is to do some research on your own to see what kind of packaged solutions exist. You could also talk to IT staff members to get a rough design for a system as a way to help evaluate packages. At some point, you will have to talk to package vendors to find out about their offerings. And, at the end, you will need to evaluate the packages and make a recommendation on how to solve the problem.

What kind of information would you supply to the package vendors? What information do you want them to provide to you; how should they respond? What criteria can you develop for evaluating competing packages? Why would you be interested in a package compared to having a custom system developed?

score can be developed for the package. It may be desirable to divide the criteria into essential and nonessential groups. You can insist that a package get a passing score (established in advance) on each of the essential criteria to be considered for acquisition. Then examine the criteria to see whether the package passes enough of them to be considered.

If several packages are available, the ones that pass the screening test can be compared using ratings or through the scenarios described earlier. If the package under consideration is an alternative to designing an in-house system, use the criteria established by the project team to evaluate the package in comparison with other processing alternatives.

Enterprise Software Packages

Large applications such as SAP's R/3 and similar products from Baan, Peoplesoft, and Oracle are packages, but the tremendous scope of their impact makes decisions about them much more challenging than the decision to buy Microsoft Office. Enterprise software is designed to fulfill all the basic transactions processing needs of a firm, from entering orders through producing a product, accounting, financial statement preparation, and querying databases. Of course, you do not have to buy all of such a package, but many of the benefits from enterprise software come from its integration.

As an example, consider processing an order. A comprehensive enterprise software package accepts the order, checks inventory, notifies the customer, schedules production if a product is not available, and tracks the order until it can be filled. The package creates an accounts receivable entry when the order is shipped and makes the proper accounting entries when the customer pays the bill. All of this activity is reflected in the firm's financial statements.

These packages cost multiple millions of dollars to purchase and implement, and can easily take several years to get up and running. If you choose this alternative, the firm is committed to this package and to a costly implementation effort. What have you bought? Just as with any package, you have purchased debugged code, functions you probably would not have designed into a custom system, and a significantly shorter implementation time than custom development would allow. A decision to adopt SAP comes only once in many years, and you must comparison shop and study it just as you would any major business decision. Our comments on package programs still apply, but the scale of this acquisition decision demands significant research and management attention.

What If It's Free? Shareware for Everyone

A few figures in the computer industry feel that software should be free, though Microsoft and Oracle are not enthusiastic about this possibility. However, free software, called *shareware* or *open source,* has had some notable successes. One of the most popular shareware programs is an operating system called Linux. Linus Torvalds developed the core of the operating system, and then asked others to contribute to expanding the system over the Internet. A few pioneers began running their servers using Linux, and the system started to spread. Red Hat software was founded to provide tools, consulting, and training for Linux. IBM gave the product a huge boost when it adapted versions for its servers, and continued with the tradition of making the product available for free. Although Linux itself is free, a buyer often needs to purchase additional applets, documentation, and system support from a vendor.

Was this charity on the part of IBM? IBM and others would be delighted to break the grip that Microsoft has on the desktop with its Windows products, and to replace Unix from HP and Solaris from Sun with Linux. Given this kind of endorsement for the operating system, IT managers were more willing to try the product, since well-known companies offer support for Linux. An IT manager does not want to be dependent on someone to voluntarily contribute software that is critical for his or her applications.

Other examples of free software exist, though it is not as plentiful as the kind you have to pay for. Adobe developed its Acrobat software to make it easy to share information. Acrobat translates documents into a format called portable document format (PDF), and Acrobat Reader displays any PDF document on the screen. When the Web came along, Adobe worked hard to make Acrobat a standard for displaying content. What was their strategy? Adobe decided to give away the Reader free, through a download from its Web site. The company generates revenue by charging for Acrobat for anyone who wishes to publish content as a PDF file.

Large organizations no longer shy away from free software, something that is disconcerting to the major software vendors. Microsoft, in particular, clearly sees Linux as a major threat to its business because the Windows operating systems is key to Microsoft's franchise for PCs. Your computer comes loaded with Windows, so you buy Microsoft Office for Windows. If you have a Linux computer, you not only skip Windows, you also have to go to another vendor for word processing and spreadsheets because Office does not run on Linux. In this way, Linux threatens Microsoft's entire set of products, and is of great concern to the company.

LOOKING FOR SERVICES

The services industry began early in the days of computing; companies called service bureaus provided a variety of data services for companies. As computing power became cheaper, and managers felt they wanted more control of technology, the service bureau industry had to change to provide more than just processing power. Some of these companies went out of business, while others reinvented themselves; for example, one company became an expert in EDI and sold these services to clients. When the Internet exploded onto the scene, a number of start-ups offered services to help companies take advantage of this new technology. Traditional firms could not find trained IT staff members, and dot-com start-up firms sometimes needed expertise they did not have. These Web companies offer a variety of services from Web hosting to running an electronic store for clients.

1. *Consulting Services.* Technology consultants have been around since the development of the first computer. You can find consultants who work on any problem or challenge a firm might have with technology, from helping a firm develop a strategic plan to integrating disparate applications technologies, to operating all technology for a client. The use of consultants is sometimes controversial. A good consultant offers an external view of a problem, and can provide valuable insights for management, but management has to pay for this advice.

2. *Applications Integration.* The Internet has highlighted the need to integrate different applications in a firm. If Victor Electronics ever sets up an online store, it will either have to replace its existing order entry system, or integrate an old, legacy system with the Internet so it can process Web orders. Firms offer software and expertise for doing this kind of integration, a task undertaken many times as firms move to do more business on the Internet.

3. *Web Hosting.* Victor Electronics began with a Web hosting company to set up a corporate Web site. As their CIO said, "We don't have the expertise, or the staff time to get up a site. Using a Web hosting service is the only option that will get something going quickly as management has demanded." A hosting service will manage and monitor a firm's presence on the Web, generally operating it in the Web host's own computer centers. The hosting service provides around-the-clock monitoring for all Web servers, something expensive for a firm to do on its own. A number of smaller companies have gotten out of the hosting business, feeling that they cannot make a profit. The largest Web host is EDS, which generated $3.5 billion in revenue from hosting in 2001, followed by IBM Global Services (*Information Week,* June 24, 2002).

4. *Applications Services Providers (ASP).* Typically an ASP purchases major software packages and leases them to customers. This business became popular with the growth of the Internet because a client does not need a special, private network to use the packages. A browser and Internet connection will suffice for most applications. These packages include licenses for a certain number of *seats*, or simultaneous users. The ASP has to purchase enough licenses to cover its clients' usage of each package. An ASP wants to buy popular packages to appeal to customers who want to *rent* only the part of the package they need. An ASP might be a solution for Victor's dilemma over what to do about an ERP package, however, the decision would depend a great deal on costs. An ASP will offer a range of products, and some vendors such as Oracle have set up their own ASP-like models to rent their own products. It has been difficult to make the ASP business model work, and several ASPs have gone into and come back from bankruptcy. It remains to be seen whether this approach to providing services will succeed.

5. *The General Purpose Outsourcer.* The outsourcing industry began in the 1960s, and EDS was one of the first companies to enter this business. The first model was for the outsourcer to take over all processing for a client company, offering a fixed price for providing services. Usually the agreement covered only the

operation of existing applications, including a data center and possibly a communications network. If the client desired new applications, they had to be specified and a price negotiated. The appeal of outsourcing came from the thought that managers could get better control over costs by outsourcing. The costs would be fixed and often declining during the time of the contract. Some managers felt, erroneously, that they could also stop having to make decisions and manage IT in their firms. The outsourcing business is a major sector of the IT industry, even though it has been estimated that only about 3 percent of all IT is outsourced.[1] Outsourcing is discussed in more detail in the next section.

6. *Software for Rent.* A model similar to the ASP is the software utility. IBM on the high end, and Salesforce.com as a smaller company, no longer just sell a program, they rent it to the user. Just as you pay for electric power by how much you use, a company pays for software by how much it consumes. This concept of computing on demand is the latest big push of service providers. This idea appeals most to small firms because large companies have the problem of integrating their software across a number of systems. However, the growth of Web services to connect disparate programs should make this approach to computing more attractive. Salesforce.com wants to provide the servers for other software vendors and integrate their programs with its own. IBM claims that it generated $7 billion in orders for on-demand computing services in 2002, and that it applied these same techniques to its own internal computing for a comparable savings.[2]

THE PROS AND CONS OF OUTSOURCING

Outsourcing involves turning over some or all of your organization's IT effort to an outside firm specializing in operating, developing, and managing various aspects of information technology. These firms negotiate a contract with a company that wishes to give some or all of its technology function to the outsourcer. The kinds of services an organization might want to outsource vary.

Obviously, the outsourcing consultant would be delighted to assume all of a company's IT activities. This firm would operate existing applications, possibly on the outsourcer's computers or on the client's existing computers. The consultant would also gladly assume responsibility for running the client's communications network and for developing new applications.

Some clients chose to retain part of their IT functions and to partially outsource some activities. For example, a large brokerage firm outsourced part of its network management, keeping control of the part it felt was strategic. A major advertising agency outsourced its transactions processing and accounting applications while continuing to develop and manage systems designed to help the creative part of its business. Xerox outsourced its legacy (older IBM transactions processing systems) to EDS so that it could concentrate on developing a new client–server architecture in-house. The largest outsourcing contract to date is between J.P. Morgan Chase and IBM; it is a seven-year $5 billion agreement announced at the end of 2002. IBM had a good year in outsourcing picking up agreements with American Express for $4 billion over seven years, and Deutsche Bank for $2.6 billion over ten years.

Outsourcing is controversial: Some managers argue that it makes sense to let a firm that specializes in technology take over and act as an independent contractor. They feel it's probably not as efficient to manage something that is not their specialty. On the other hand, others are not comfortable turning over to an external organization technology that may be crucial to corporate strategy.

Loh and Venkatraman (1992) identified some of the factors that lead a firm to outsource:

- A firm that feels it is spending more on technology than it should (or more than the competition) may adopt outsourcing if it feels this option provides a lower-cost alternative than internal management. Even if the firm does not feel at a disadvantage compared to others, it may see outsourcing as a way to reduce IT-related costs in general. Several firms claim cost savings by turning their IT function over to an external firm. Another possibility is that large outsourcing agreements are motivated by companies trying to return to profitability by cutting employment. (A company outsourcing all of its IT operations generally gets an immediate cash inflow when it sells equipment to the outsourcer, and the outsourcer usually hires a large percentage of the company's staff, reducing its salary expense.)

- A firm with a high debt structure may not wish to invest in technology. It may view outsourcing as a way to lease technology instead of buying it.

- An organization may feel its IT function is not performing adequately. Outsourcing can be a way to arrange for a more professional and higher-performing IT operation in the company.

Kambil Turner (1993) added to this list:[3]

- An organization decides to return to its core competencies. Managing IT is not one of these competencies, so it outsources this task to another firm.

- The organization is interested in technology transfer from the expert outsourcing firm. It will learn from the outsourcer.

- A firm may outsource "commodity" processing to free its staff to develop new applications of technology.

Outsourcing accomplishes the preceding objectives in various ways. The outsourcing firm must have a high level of expertise in technology. In fact, the VP of a prominent outsourcing firm maintained in a recent class that the only advantage his firm had was its knowledge of how to manage information technology. A potential outsourcing client can buy the same computers that the outsourcer buys, and can hire many of the same people. The outsourcer's business is knowledge intensive, especially when many contracts today have clauses where the outsourcer and the client share cost savings. (In the old days, the outsourcer counted on making money from declining hardware costs; that same feat is difficult to do with most clients today.)

The outsourcer may also enjoy economies of scale. For example, the telecommunications outsourcer can probably provide network services for a number of clients with a smaller staff than the sum of the networking staffs from all of the clients. An outsourcer may centralize the hardware for several clients in one location, making better use of these assets.

A number of arguments can also be made against outsourcing. The outsourcing firm may have a high cost structure because of its need to employ highly skilled personnel. The need to have a contract with the outsourcing firm can lead to conflict and misunderstandings. Some companies are surprised at the cost of using an outsourcing firm to develop applications.

Probably the biggest deterrent to outsourcing is the question of control. Management that regards technology as a competitive factor in business may be reluctant to turn over control of it to an outside firm. The brokerage firm described previously examined the option of outsourcing all of its technology effort, but decided only one part of it was not sufficiently strategic to be outsourced.

Lacity and Hirschheim (1993) studied a number of firms that outsourced. Their criticism of outsourcing provides a cautionary note. Their study identified two myths of outsourcing.

Myth 1: Outsourcing vendors are strategic partners.

The outsourcing vendor cannot be a partner because the outsourcer's profit motive is not shared by the customer. The outsourcer makes more money if it is able to charge the customer higher fees. If the outsourcer can reduce service levels and collect the same fees, it also contributes to its profit margins. You might want to consider some kind of a cost reduction sharing arrangement with an outsourcer so that both the services firm and the client benefit from more efficient operations.

Myth 2: Outsourcing vendors are inherently more efficient than an internal IS department.

The outsourcer's argument here is that economies of scale help it to be more efficient. Today hardware costs do not favor huge installations. The cost performance ratio for smaller computers may be better than for mainframes. It is possible the outsourcer can do some tasks more efficiently because it has done them before or because it can afford to share highly paid specialists among a number of clients.

An outsourcing agreement will probably extend for a number of years in order to justify the transition effort involved. All experts in this field suggest that developing a contract between the outsourcer and the client is crucial. Because an agreement may be for five or ten years, the contract must be highly flexible. Business conditions and technology are expected to change during the life of the agreement. General Dynamics, which had an outsourcing agreement with Computer Sciences Corporation, was reported to have eight contracts covering divisions that might each evolve in a different way (McFarlan and Nolan, 1995).

After entering a relationship with an outsourcer, the company must still manage information technology. It will still need the equivalent of a CIO to manage the partnership and contract with the outsourcer. Xerox reportedly had at one point a dozen people managing its $3 billion, ten-year contract with EDS. The client still must look at emerging technologies and plan for its technology architecture. Creative applications are most likely to come from users rather than the outsourcer, and mechanisms for turning ideas into new applications of the technology are necessary. Outsourcing can be an excellent alternative for some companies, but no company should enter into an outsourcing arrangement with the idea it will no longer have to manage IT.

A study by Barthelemy (2001) estimated that companies are giving more than a third of their IT functions to outsourcers to run. He also found in a survey of 50 companies, that 14 percent felt their outsourcing had been a failure. One major concern is with hidden costs, even though clients thought they had identified all of the costs that belonged in the contract with the outsourcer. These costs include the following:

1. Searching for and finding the right vendor and negotiating a contract involve costs before the outsourcing services even begin. Outsourcers have standard

MANAGEMENT PROBLEM 8-2

A medium-sized manufacturing company entered into an outsourcing agreement with a local consulting firm. The manufacturing company had experienced years of turmoil in its IT group, and users and managers were openly hostile to technology efforts. Senior management at the manufacturing company felt that outsourcing might solve all of these problems because the outsourcer would bring in new expertise and take over the headache that running IT had become.

The outsourcer did provide new managers and some staff to supplement the firm's IT workers who transferred to its payroll. The outsourcer worked hard at improving relations; it set up a steering committee and had regular meetings with users. Of course, it had to run the systems that were already in place, and these poorly designed systems were part of the problem from the beginning. At one meeting between the head of IT and a major user, observers said that paper reports ended up being thrown around the room.

It is clear in hindsight that the manufacturing company had unrealistic expectations that a firm from the outside could quickly solve problems that were years in the making. The consulting firm was probably overconfident of its expertise, and did not understand fully the history at the manufacturing company.

What does this story say about outsourcing as an IT choice strategy? What should the manufacturing firm have done differently? What about the outsourcing consultant? What recommendations would you have for a company that is seriously considering an outsourcing solution for its IT services?

contracts, which not surprisingly, are biased toward them. A client usually has to seek legal advice and negotiate a special contract.

2. Transitioning to the vendor is a major undertaking. Usually the vendor hires some of the client's IT staff, and may transfer computers and applications to its own processing facility. A transition can be complex, as a European bank found when it outsourced a telecommunications network that covered fifty countries.

3. A major cost is managing IT even after some or all of it has been outsourced. The client company needs to monitor outsourcer performance and to negotiate any appropriate changes in the contract. The client still must respond to requests from managers for new applications of technology not covered in the contract with the outsourcer.

4. Costs for possible transitioning after the end of an outsourcing agreement are also a factor. One enters an outsourcing arrangement planning for the future, but there are times when a termination date is clear. For example, companies using outsourcers to run legacy systems while they developed new, replacement applications, have a termination date in mind. A cost will be incurred to transition from the outsourcer to another source of processing.

On Balance

If a firm enters into an outsourcing agreement, it is moving more toward a network organization, that is, an organization structure characterized by many companies interacting with each other and becoming highly interdependent. Some of these relationships go beyond the normal customer–supplier relationship. An outsourcer's performance is critical for the ability of a company to operate. Many believe that networks are the organization structure of the future, and IT outsourcing is just one example of a general trend toward outsourcing, with a firm retaining only functions that represent its core competencies. Because of the high level of interdependence between a firm and its technology, IT outsourcing is an example of the most difficult kind of relationship to establish. If IT outsourcing works, so should most other types of outsourcing that have been proposed.

A definitive recommendation on outsourcing is not possible, because each company is in a different situation. The many options range from outsourcing a small part of the IT function to turning it completely over to a large outsourcer. Outsourcing is a viable alternative for some firms, but it is not a panacea for every IT problem. Some experts believe outsourcing is a precursor of how firms will obtain their technology in the future. Whatever the outcome, do not think that a manager can stop making decisions about IT because the firm has outsourced.

A SCENARIO FOR THE FUTURE: THE COMPUTER UTILITY?

Time-sharing was a technology that developed in the 1960s. At that time almost all processing took place in batch mode, computer programs accepted a batch of punch cards and processed them against computer files, producing updated files and reports. It could take a long time for an individual to write and debug a program because only one or two runs on the computer a day might be possible. Researchers at several universities, including MIT and Dartmouth, developed the idea that a group of users could share a computer's resources, they would *share time* on the CPU. Eventually commercial firms started to provide time-sharing services to users who had trouble getting service from internal IT staff members. A popular book at the time hailed the rise of the "computer utility." Time sharing would become universally available like the electricity provided by the power company.

It is interesting to note that with the Internet and some forty-five years later, experts are talking once again about the rise of the computer utility. In today's world, the technology utility is based on the Internet, as might be expected. Companies such as IBM and AT&T offer Web services to customers, both businesses and consumers. Imagine a scenario in which all of the paperwork in buying a car is completed at a single client computer. The systems of insurance companies, inspection facilities, and the department of motor vehicles all share information. The buyer can complete all the transactions in one short session from a PC at home or in the dealership. In this example, the Web and XML standards make it possible for disparate systems to communicate with each other.

In the most radical scenario for Web services, large hardware installations in companies will disappear. Organizations and individuals will pay a monthly technology bill, just as consumers pay an electricity and phone bill each month. Companies will pay for just the technology they need to use (just as was claimed with time sharing). Web services as a form of outsourcing are unlikely to replace the technology in most organizations. However, it does seem likely that Web services will increasingly integrate applications, and that individuals may eventually subscribe to a Web services provider that integrates the applications they use.

The problem with this line of reasoning today, just as it was in the 1960s, is the incredible complexity of a modern IT operation. A company such as Victor Electronics runs thousands of jobs a night in many locations around the world. It could, with a great deal of effort and expense, convert to a series of standard packages provided by an ASP or Web services provider. However, it would still require some applications that are unique to the company, necessitating its own IT function of some kind. Suppose that Victor came up with a new loyalty program for companies that buy from it, a first in the industry. If it could find the functions of such a program on the Web already, Victor would have a hard time getting any kind of competitive advantage from offering the program. What it wants to do is to surprise the world and its customers and gain a first mover advantage for as long as possible. The services model is fine for existing and well-known applications, but how it will work with innovation, strategic applications, and applications that can transform the organization is the critical issue.

AN EXAMPLE

A major university faced an acquisition decision that involved both hardware and software, which presents an interesting case study of an acquisition decision most people in the school now think was a mistake.

The school was installing a fiber-optic backbone network on its campus. It needed to choose a vendor to provide the networking software for the system. In addition, the choice of network vendor would also determine what file servers to install. The computer center at the school sent proposals to a number of vendors; two returned acceptable proposals.

Vendor A is a computer manufacturer with a strong support organization. Its networking software is proprietary, though it is based on a major PC software vendor's networking system. This network required fairly expensive servers that ran the Unix operating system. Vendor B provided the networking software that was already in use at the school and is the market leader in networking PCs. The school staff also had experience with this software, because three or four of its networks were operating with it while the decision was made. Vendor B's network used PCs for servers, making hardware costs less than for Vendor A.

The computer center staff liked Vendor A, who it felt would provide extensive services and would better monitor and control their network. The staff convinced the dean responsible for making the decision that Vendor A was the best choice. Faculty with IT experience were in favor of Vendor B for the following reasons:

- The school had experience with the product from Vendor B. It would be throwing away most of that experience and starting from scratch with Vendor A.

- The system from Vendor A was more complex than Vendor B's. It required a great deal of memory on each client computer, which might make it difficult to run certain packages and the networking software simultaneously.

- It would be difficult to get outside help or hire people with experience with Vendor A's products since most professionals knew Vendor B's system.

- The more widely used system from Vendor B was better debugged than the newer product from Vendor A.

The decision was made to go with Vendor A. As you might expect, the implementation was a disaster. Students could not print in the PC labs, because the network had significant problems handling printing. The entire networking effort discredited technology in the school. Emotions were so high that an outside review panel was asked to report on the computer center. It concluded the school was in great difficulty from having chosen Vendor A's product. In fact, it turns out that the school had the largest installation of this product! In addition Vendor A has started to resell Vendor B's network software, raising the question of whether Vendor A would continue to support and enhance its own offering. Three years later, the school abandoned Vendor A and moved to Vendor B. Shortly thereafter, another firm bought Vendor A, and it eventually disappeared as a force in the industry.

This disaster happened because the evaluation failed to consider important intangibles, such as the school's experience with Vendor B and the difficulties of finding and training staff for the complex system offered by Vendor A. In addition, it appears the computer center staff did not do an adequate evaluation. They failed to visit sites using the systems from both vendors that would be comparable to the school's environment.

This example should serve as a warning that any business must be extremely careful in making major hardware and software acquisition decisions, especially those that affect the entire IT infrastructure of the organization. A firm must take into account intangibles and management considerations in addition to the technical features of technology.

CHAPTER SUMMARY

Table 8-2 presents some of the options open to management for acquiring new applications and for ongoing operations. Consultants and outsourcers can be found for almost any aspect of these activities, and it is likely that a firm will have combinations of these solutions. It will undoubtedly buy packages whenever it can. It may develop highly customized applications itself or with the help of a consultant. It will use consultants to help implement large packages such as ERP or CRM. The decision to outsource applications is a major one, and few companies outsource all aspects of this activity. It is likely, however, that some aspect of IT will be outsourced.

1. Evaluating technology is an ongoing task for most organizations; large numbers of services and packaged programs are available.

2. The computer industry offers a large variety of firms that sell hardware, software, and services.

3. Today, most organizations are interested in reducing the cost, time, and risks associated with custom applications development. The first strategy is to look for a package to accomplish a firm's processing objectives.

4. If a suitable package cannot be found, alternatives such as the use of a DBMS may work for implementing the application.

5. Outsourcing is becoming increasingly popular for developing applications and for running all or part of a firm's technology.

6. A number of trade-offs come with doing the task internally versus using an outsourcer. Management has more control over internal operations, but it must take an active management role in IT under this alternative.

7. Because companies are continually developing new applications, demand for hardware and software continues to increase. This demand means the firm is frequently faced with decisions on acquiring more computer equipment and more software.

8. The acquisition of large and midrange computers is fairly routine. If the firm has an architecture in place, that architecture may dictate what new computers to buy.

9. The IS staff will want to keep up with new technology in hardware and software, both to provide the firm with a powerful IT infrastructure and to make the task of supporting hardware and software manageable.

10. Because packages are such an attractive option, it is important to purchase packaged software with great care. For dedicated applications, a rough systems analysis and design to provide a benchmark for evaluating different packages are helpful. For general packages such as a word processor, the organization will probably want to adopt a single standard in order to make it easy to share documents and to ease support requirements.

TABLE 8-2 Options for acquiring applications and ongoing operations.

	Acquiring Custom Design	Applications Package	Ongoing Operations
Own staff	Develop according to your specifications; project risk, development time, new code	Responsible to help install package, possible modifications, extensive data collection and setup	Very typical; maintain infrastructure, provide 24/7 operations, help desks, backup
Consultants	Provide services to design, program, and implement a solution	Almost mandatory for large packages like ERP	Generally not applicable
Outsource	Will provide usually as separate contract from operations	Yes, but need extensive involvement of company personnel	Outsourcer eager to enter into long-term relationship; to operate all IT in the firm, must manage the relationship

KEYWORDS

Benchmark	Outsourcing	Utility
Computer utility	Performance evaluation tool	Web services
Enterprise software	Proposal	
Integration	Scenario	

RECOMMENDED READINGS

Barthelemy, J. 2001. The hidden costs of IT outsourcing. *Sloan Management Review*, Spring, pp. 60–69.

Bragg, S. 1998. *Outsourcing: A Guide to Selecting the Correct Business Unit, Negotiating the Contract, Maintaining Control of the Business*. New York: John Wiley & Sons. (A well-written book featuring various outsourcing strategies and business implications.)

Hirschheim, R., and Lacity, M. 2000. Myths and realities of information technology insourcing. *Communications of the ACM*, 43(2), pp. 99–107. (An insightful article into the advantages of insourcing over outsourcing information technology.)

Lacity, M. 2002. Lessons in global information technology sourcing. *IEEE Computer*, August. (Twelve lessons for those considering an outsourcing agreement.)

Walsh, K. 2003. Analyzing the application ASP concept: Technologies, economies, and strategies. *Communications of the ACM*, 46(8), pp. 103–107. (An informative article looking at the ASP concept.)

DISCUSSION QUESTIONS

1. What is the appeal of a package compared to writing a custom system?

2. What criteria should the firm use to decide on packages?

3. Why do you think ASPs had difficulty with their business models?

4. Why would management with an internal IS staff be interested in using a consultant that specializes in integrating systems?

5. What sources of processing are available to a manager?

6. What is the major difference between a problem-oriented applications package such as Excel and a dedicated ERP package?

7. Why has hardware become a commodity?

8. What is the outsourcing model? How does the outsourcer make money?

9. Why might an organization choose to outsource all of its information technology?

10. What are the major differences between outsourcing the development of an application and outsourcing the operation of some part of your information technology activities?

11. Most organizations today have computers and software from a variety of different vendors, all of which are supposed to work on a network. What are the potential problems with using products from many different sources?

12. How has the Internet changed the services business?

13. Make a list of the types of questions and information desired for a survey of other users of an enterprise software package under consideration for acquisition.

14. What is a *computer utility*? How might such a utility work today?

15. What can a firm do if a package does not fit the way it does business?

16. Why might integration services be needed with IT?

17. What applications might the firm want to retain if it is planning to outsource some of its IT activities?

18. Why should applications packages be seriously considered as an alternative to programming and implementing a system? What are the most significant problems with these packages? How can the ease of modifying the package be determined before its acquisition?

19. Compare and contrast the major sources of software. What are the advantages and disadvantages of each?

20. How can the vendor of an applications package make it more appealing to potential customers?

21. Why would a vendor such as Oracle take a chance on reducing the sales of its full package by offering only what the customer wants as an ASP?

22. A great deal of free or low-cost software is available for PCs. What are the advantages and disadvantages of *shareware*?

23. Why might a systems integrator be faster in developing a complex application than a firm's internal staff?

ENDNOTES

1. *Information Week*, June 24, 2002.

2. *New York Times,* November 13, 2003.

3. Kambil, A. and J. Turner, "Outsourcing of Information Systems As a Strategy for Organizational Alignment and Transformation," Unpublished paper. New York: Stern School, NYU, 1993.

CHAPTER *9*

IMPLEMENTING IT

A Manager's Perspective

My interest in implementation came from early work experiences when I observed organizations making significant investments in technology, and the people for whom the technology was intended resisting its use. Some of this resistance was obviously due to fears that IT would replace the worker. I remember speaking with one clerical employee who was telling me about his work and commented, "By telling you all of this, I'm probably talking myself out of a job." The results of custom-designed systems for the organization were often less than expected. Systems processed certain transactions incorrectly and did not fit the current business environment. What had gone wrong? Well in those days it could take a year or more to determine the requirements for a system and to program it. By the time the IT staff got around to implementation, the business had changed and those original specifications were out of date. Problems also arose in understanding what users of the system wanted and translating that into the system.

A CIO described a system in which his firm had invested heavily in developing and mentioned that he thought the average user worked with about 10 percent of the functions the system was capable of providing. This total does not sound very good, but think about your use of a spreadsheet package. How many of the total available functions do you use? Now that most managers prefer to buy rather than build, implementation should be easier, right? Unfortunately, easier is not the always the case. Because the advantage comes from accepting the package as is without making modifications, the user of the system is forced to change procedures and adapt to a system that he or she had no input in designing.

Will the Internet and the Web make implementation easier? The focus today is to move applications to the Web for a lot of reasons. Anyone using a Web-based system will do so with a browser, a familiar and easy-to-use piece of software. So in theory, it should be easier to implement Web-based systems. However, the browser presents the interface; it has nothing to do with the underlying processing logic of the system. Web-based systems should be easier to implement, but they offer no guarantee that anyone will use the system to its full potential. For these reasons, it is important to understand the implementation process, and to pay attention to it when developing new innovations with IT.

173

IMPLEMENTATION

What Is Implementation?

Implementation is part of the process of designing a system and is a component of change. New information systems change existing information processing procedures and often change the organization itself. Implementation refers to the design team's strategy and actions for seeing that a system is successful and makes a contribution to the organization.

This definition stresses the long-term nature of implementation. It is part of a process that begins with the initial idea for a system and the changes it will bring. Implementation terminates when the system is successfully integrated with the operations of the organization. Most of implementation is concerned with behavioral phenomena, because people are expected to change their work activities. Implementation becomes more important and difficult as systems design becomes more radical. If a firm undertakes a large systems project, it wants to make major changes in tasks to reduce costs and improve productivity in the organization.

Success or Failure

Researchers do not agree on an absolute indicator for successful implementation. One appealing approach is a cost–benefit study. In this evaluation, one totals the costs of developing a system and compares them with the dollar benefits resulting from the system.

In theory, this evaluation sounds like a good indicator of success, but in practice it is difficult to provide meaningful estimates. Obtaining the cost side of the ratio is not too much of a problem if adequate records are kept during the development stages of the system. However, an evaluation of the benefits of an information system eludes most analysts. Chapter 6 described a number of categories for classifying the benefits or value provided by an application of technology. These categories included:

- Infrastructure
- Required applications
- Applications where technology was the only solution
- Applications providing a direct return
- Applications with indirect returns
- Technology initiatives that are a competitive necessity
- Strategic applications
- Transformational information technology

For only a few of these categories is a direct, financial return likely to be demonstrated, which makes it difficult to perform a cost–benefit analysis to determine the success of a system.

As an alternative, several indicators of successful implementation can be applied to an individual application, depending on the type of system involved. In many instances, use of a system is voluntary. A manager or other user can view a report on the screen, but does not have to use the information on it or even look at the data. Systems that provide interactive retrieval of information from a database also can often be classified as voluntary. The use of such a system is frequently at the discretion of the user. A manager with a personal computer in his or her office is not required to use it. For the type of system in which use is voluntary, high levels of use indicate successful implementation.

For systems whose use is mandatory, such as a production control system or a computer that provides stock market quotations for a broker, the user's evaluation of the system can be employed as a measure of success. For example, one can examine user satisfaction, although it will probably be necessary to measure several facets of satisfaction, such as quality of service, timeliness and accuracy of information, and quality of the schedule for operations. An evaluation might also involve a panel of information processing experts reviewing the design and operation of the system. Managers might well consider a system to be successful if it accomplishes its objectives.

Finally, though it is difficult to do, estimates of the impact of a system on individuals and the organization can be derived by answering these questions: How has a system affected personal productivity and output quality? Can the organization point to added sales or increased revenues from a competitive application? Does IT show a demonstrable impact on performance, either for individuals or the organization?

RESEARCH ON IMPLEMENTATION

Most research on implementation is an attempt to discover factors associated with success. What independent variables are related to successful implementation as defined by the researchers? If any evidence shows a causal connection between independent and dependent variables, an implementation strategy can be developed around the independent variables. For example, suppose several studies using different research methodologies indicated that top management's requesting a new system and following through with participation in its design is associated with successful implementation. If sufficient evidence supported this finding, an implementation strategy should emphasize top management action.

Although individual studies of implementation address a number of independent variables, no real consensus in the field provides an explanation of successful implementation or a single implementation strategy. Table 9-1 lists some of the variables employed in implementation studies. Dependent variables used to measure implementation success generally can be classified as measures of use, intended use, or satisfaction with a system. The independent variables fall into several classes, as shown in the table.

A Model of Implementation

A number of different studies of systems implementation were reviewed in Lucas, Ginzberg, and Schultz (1991). Figure 9-1 is a model based on the most significant findings from the research in that study. The model suggests that the user's personal stake in the problems addressed by the system will be an important determinant of use. *Personal stake* refers to how important the domain of the system is for the individual. A marketing manager is expected to have a high personal stake in a market research system that addresses the brands managed. Personal stake is hypothesized to be influenced by the level of management support for a system. The most consistent finding across implementation studies is the importance of management support and leadership in successful implementation.

TABLE 9-1 Variables associated with implementation studies.

INDEPENDENT VARIABLES	
Information services department Policies Systems design practices Operations policies **Involvement** User origination of systems Involvement and influence Appreciation **User demographics** Personality type Business history Social history Past experience **User's personal stake** Problem urgency	**System characteristics** Quality Ease of use **Decision style** Cognitive style **Management** Actions Support Managerial style **Organization support** Ease of access **User performance**

DEPENDENT VARIABLES
Implementation Frequency of inquiries Reported use Monitored frequency of use User satisfaction

FIGURE 9-1 An implementation model.

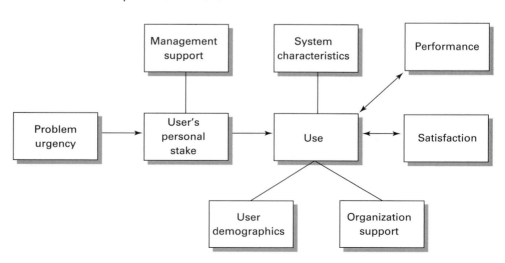

Problem urgency is likely to influence personal stake. The more urgent the problem is, the higher the personal stake.

Personal stake influences use directly when use is voluntary. System characteristics will also influence use. A poorly designed system may be virtually unusable. User demographics, like age and past computer experience, are also likely to impact system use. Organizational support refers to actions that make a system easy to use. For example, use of a system was found to increase with the ease of accessing the system. The model suggests that high levels of use should lead to high levels of satisfaction, and high satisfaction is likely to increase levels of use.

Although the evidence is not strong, it does appear that use of technology is related to either individual or firm performance in certain instances. This relationship is likely to be complex. For example, one study found that high-performing sales representatives used the output of a system to work with buyers in a store to figure out what to order. Low-performing sales representatives also used the output of the system, but they focused on information that might indicate what was wrong in their territories. A number of technology efforts appear to coincide with where a firm reduced costs or increased revenues. However, it is difficult to demonstrate causality in such situations because so many variables are changing at one time.

The Implementation Process

The aforementioned research deals with variables or factors associated with successful implementation. Another school of thought stresses the process of implementation as the most significant determinant of implementation success. The implementation process refers to the ongoing relationship among individuals involved in developing a system. A process model might look at various stages during implementation and describe how different parties work together during these stages.

Table 9-2 outlines the stages of the process model. This model emphasizes tasks that take place in design. Reading between the lines, however, reveals the need to concentrate on the relationship between designers and users. During the early stages, the individuals involved with the system must develop trust in each other's objectives and competence. The designers should want to help users, and users must be willing to spend time working with designers and on their part of the design. If those involved do not develop a cooperative relationship and instead become adversarial, the system is doomed.

A major objective during the design process is for users to accept ownership of the system. Professional designers, ironically, almost never use the systems they design. The user is left with a system at the end of a project. If the user does not "own" the system from a psychological point of view, the system is unlikely to be successful. Some research shows that the termination stage in the model is the most important. Here is where organizations learn whether users developed feelings of ownership and commitment to the system.

AN IMPLEMENTATION STRATEGY

An implementation strategy needs to take into account the crucial process issues in designing an information system as well as the factors that appear to influence success. Systems design can also be viewed as a planned change in activity in the organization. Earlier, the chapter stated that the reason for developing a new information system is to

TABLE 9-2 A process implementation model.

Stage	Activity
Initiation	The first contact between the users and designers
Exploration	Getting a feel for the problem
Commitment	Making a decision to proceed with a system
Design	Developing the logical design and specifications for the system
Testing	Verifying that the system works
Installation	Converting to the new system
Termination	Design team finished; users must now own the system
Operations	Routine operation plus enhancements and maintenance

create change. Dissatisfaction with a present situation stimulates the development of a new information system. Alternatively, a user sees how the technology can be used in a new way to improve the firm's competitive position.

For many years, articles and books on design stressed user participation in the design process based on research in psychology, which maintains that a change approach based on user participation is most likely to succeed. The first part of the strategy, then, is encouraging users to participate in and influence design. Some of the reasons for a participation strategy include the following:

- Participation builds self-esteem, which results in more favorable attitudes.
- Participation can be challenging and intrinsically satisfying, leading to positive attitudes.
- Participation usually results in more commitment to change. In this case, commitment means that a system will be used more.
- Participating users learn more about the change, and therefore get to control more of the technical qualities of the system and become better trained to use it.
- Technical quality will be better because participants know more about the problem domain than does the IS staff.
- Users retain much of the control over their activities and should therefore have more favorable attitudes.

User participation in the design of a system requires the efforts of both the IT staff and the users. The IT department has to encourage participation, while users have to be willing to participate and devote considerable effort to design work.

The Role of Design Teams

Teams consisting of managers, end users, and systems professionals design most applications today. How do users and professional systems analysts work together on a team? The first task delineated by the analyst might be a discussion of the functions the system is to perform. Working together, the team might develop high-level data flow diagrams for the

MANAGEMENT PROBLEM 9-1

Morgan Mines is a major copper producer with six open pit copper mines in the western United States. The mining business is capital intensive, requiring a large amount of equipment to dig the copper out of the ground, and smelters to extract and refine the copper, which makes up a small part of the total of what is mined. In the past twenty years, environmental concerns led to a heavy investment in technology to reduce pollution and to properly deal with the tailings after the company removes copper from the soil.

Mining may not seem a likely application for ERP, but extensive information requirements characterize this business. First, traditional accounting is necessary for production, manufacturing (smelting), and sales. Second, Morgan needs to keep track of inventories, both of work-in-process and finished goods, as well as repair and supply inventories. Because the mines are in remote locations, Morgan keeps a large spare parts

inventory in excess of 50,000 items at each mine. This inventory ranges from fasteners to huge tires for giant dump trucks that operate in the mine.

Morgan's largest division implemented an ERP package a year ago. It had the usual difficulties with implementation, but the system is operating successfully today. The idea was that the largest division would go first, and then the other division would follow. The CIO stated recently that even though the first effort had been a success, "the other divisions are still successfully resisting the implementation of the ERP system at their sites, even though we can demonstrate savings."

Why do you suppose the other divisions are resisting the ERP system? Develop a strategy to overcome this resistance and sell the divisions on the new system. What reasons are there in favor of implementation? How can Morgan strengthen the forces that encourage change?

system. The analyst, from knowledge of the capabilities of technology, presents alternatives for the user to consider. Users help conduct interviews to determine the requirements for a new system. They also contribute to and review the design of the system as it unfolds.

Although much of the research on implementation is focused on the custom design of systems, the same strategy applies to the selection and implementation of packaged solutions such as an ERP system. The last chapter advocated a design effort when planning on purchasing a package; the design involves determining the functions the firm needs to have in the software and assessing what the package offers. Implementation of a packaged system is more intense and more risky than for a custom system because the custom system is designed to fit the organization. For the package, it is likely that the organization will make changes in its processes rather than modify the package extensively. Implementation also begins quickly with a package, unlike a custom system that can take months or years to develop.

An Implementation Framework

A team approach that stresses cooperation and participation addresses the issues raised in the process model of implementation, but what about the factors discussed earlier in the chapter? A complete implementation strategy comes from merging the most important factors with the steps of the process model (see Table 9-3).

The combined model in Table 9-3 arrays the steps of the process model with the variables from the factor model of Figure 9-1. During initiation, one key to success is having a sponsor or champion for the system. Without the active support of a senior-level person in the organization, the chances for success are greatly reduced. Similarly, the factor model suggests that attacking urgent problems is a good strategy. It is difficult to develop enthusiasm for boring systems that are unlikely to have an impact on the firm. Management

TABLE 9-3 An implementation model.

	Management support	Problem urgency	User's personal stake	System characteristics	Use	User demographics	Organization support	Satisfaction	Performance
INITIATION	Having a sponsor is key	Attack the most important problems	Find users for whom the stake is high	Determine requirements and architecture	Who will use the system?	Not under the control of designers	Find the champions	One objective is satisfied users	Determine any performance objectives
EXPLORATION	Sponsor commits resources	Urgent problems help provide motivation	Show how system is important to user	Choose among alternatives	Who pays the costs of use?	In longer term may be able to choose team members	Be sure someone will provide the resources you need	Design for satisfaction	Is there likely to be an impact on performance?
COMMITMENT	Sponsor provides time for users to work on system	Dealing with key problems helps obtain cooperation	Involve the important stakeholders	Develop prototypes to aid in design	Who gains from use?	Look for users with successful history of working on IS projects	Get a commitment before starting	Consider user surveys	Be honest about what to expect
DESIGN	Sponsor helps make key policy decisions	Urgent problems demand quality designs	High stakes should lead to a lot of design input	Build the highest-quality system possible	Design to encourage use, e.g., good interfaces	Provide education where needed (prototypes help)	Make the system as easy to use as possible	Design for satisfaction	Try to understand what leads to performance, and design for it
TESTING	Sponsor reviews results	Test carefully	Let the stakeholder verify the results	Test exhaustively	Make sure system is usable	Let the worst critics help test	Get resources for testing	Let users plan tests, too	Test carefully if system impacts performance
INSTALLATION	Sponsor provides added resources	Plan installation to minimize disruptions	Users with a high stake should plan installation	Use extensively	Expect and prepare for use problems	Everyone will have to help	Be sure there is enough support	Try to plan a smooth installation	Install carefully if performance is an issue
TERMINATION	Sponsor rewards team	Is the problem solved?	Stakeholders should own the system	Transfer ownership to users	If successful, expect high use	With luck, there will be new supporters	Support users with help desks, etc.	High satisfaction should lead to user ownership	If successful, user will use system to enhance performance
OPERATIONS	Sponsor continues to provide resources	Continue to work on problems	High-stake users should continue their interest	A high-quality system is easy to use	Continue to refine to encourage use	Even the skeptics will use a good system	Provide ongoing organizational support	Obtain ongoing feedback from users	Monitor performance changes

wants to locate users with a stake in the problem and start to think about who users will be when the system is done. User demographics are not under a developer's control in the short run.

When exploring possible solutions, management needs to provide resources for support. It is also useful to think in cost–benefit terms, to understand who pays the costs to use the system and who gains. If users are expected to provide complex input but receive no benefits from the system because only senior management uses the data, users may exhibit resistance to the system. During exploration, the architecture for the system begins to emerge and can determine what kind of organizational support is needed to encourage use. During the commitment stage, the sponsor prepares the organization for the design effort, often by providing release time and resources for the design team. One good way to enlist support and to show how the systems design effort will solve problems is to develop a prototype of some or all parts of the system. User surveys to gain information for design also offer helpful input.

During design, the sponsor needs to be part of making key policy decisions. For example, if the planned application includes exchanging data with a business partner over the Internet, the target audience needs to be defined. How are suppliers and customers approached? Will senior management negotiate with potential partners? Remember the benefits of attacking urgent and important problems.

Testing is extremely important in preparing for installation. Management and as many users as possible should be involved in designing and verifying tests. Installation is challenging because any system is designed to change existing procedures. Tackling important problems increases the risks. A failed installation threatens some key component of the organization. Careful testing, a good cutover plan, and a lot of help from users become essential to a successful installation.

Termination marks the departure of the professional analysts and the completion of the design team's responsibilities. If the design team is successful, users will develop a sense of ownership of the system. The installed system will help solve an urgent problem for user stakeholders, and the organization will provide adequate resources to support the system. Users will be satisfied with the resulting system.

When the system is in *operational* status, it is not finished. As users work with the system, they will see ways to improve it. Business conditions are also likely to change, necessitating ongoing maintenance and enhancements. The organization must continue to support the system by expanding it as conditions warrant. The operations staff of the IS department must provide maintenance and should obtain periodic feedback from users.

This combined implementation model is based on implementation research and experience. It can help develop systems that are successful and that will be used. The threats to a successful system are many and varied. Following a conscientious implementation strategy is the best way to maximize the probability of a successful design project.

Emergent Change

The changes just described are all planned; managers determine in advance their objectives for change within the organization. However, individuals adapt technology in a number of diverse and interesting ways, constituting emergent change (Orlikowski, 1996). These kinds of changes occur in the absence of explicit intentions and objectives for change. In fact, such changes cannot be anticipated in advance because people adapt to the technology as they use it. Such emergent change can be a positive, unintended consequence of a new application.

Zeta Corporation, a leading software vendor, installed Lotus Notes to support its customer services department (CSD). The fifty representatives in this department answer phone inquiries from customers and try to solve the customer's problem. Notes is a groupware product that promotes sharing and coordination. Management encouraged CSD representatives to enter all of their calls, the nature of the problem and information about the solution into the Notes database. CSD members can access this database in a number of ways and can search it for past incidents that are similar to the one they currently face. Within a year the database contained 35,000 entries of problems and their resolution.

How did change emerge from this technology investment? First, CSD representatives found a similar problem in the database for 50 percent of their calls; past solutions let them respond quickly with the correct answer to these customers. With this level of access, the representatives quickly became highly dependent on the database and technology. Management noted the change in the way representatives solved problems and reorganized the department into senior and junior representatives based on experience and expertise. The idea was that junior staff members would field all calls and pass the difficult ones on to the senior staff. However, junior representatives were not comfortable assigning problems to senior colleagues, so management created the role of an intermediary who would review problems and decide when they needed a referral to a senior representative.

CSD employees noticed a decline in face-to-face contact, and began to find reasons for meeting each other. Some of the representatives became proactive, looking for open problems in the database when they were not too busy. The company expanded use of the system to two overseas offices, creating some problems at first when the foreign representatives did not completely understand the process for creating and using the database. As the groups adopted shared norms for the system, the problems disappeared.

When others in the company wanted access to the data, the CSD staff was concerned because the database contained so many details. To solve this problem, non-CSD employees were given access to "sanitized" reports. The CSD staff also began to publish technical notes for the company based on the database. Finally, Zeta used Notes to create a bug database to facilitate identifying and fixing problems with their products.

This example of emergent change is positive; CSD staff members found ways to integrate the Notes database with their jobs and to improve the quality of customer service. They expanded their use of technology to create a broader impact on Zeta than originally planned. In this case, information technology facilitated changes that emerged spontaneously from employees using the technology. Planning for emergent change is not possible, but support and encouragement help to take advantage of these changes as they become evident.

IMPLEMENTING IT-BASED TRANSFORMATIONS OF THE ORGANIZATION

The preceding discussion focused on the changes caused by an individual system within the organization. It requires even greater commitment to implement the massive changes required to use information technology to transform the organization and create new structures and relationships within the firm and with external organizations. Information technology can create a new kind of organization structure, which includes the following advantages:

1. A lean organization with the minimal number of employees necessary for the business to function
2. A responsive organization that reacts quickly to threats from competitors and changes in the environment
3. A minimum overhead organization
4. A structure with low fixed costs due to more virtual components, partnerships, and subcontracting
5. An organization that is responsive to customers and suppliers
6. An organization that is more competitive than firms with traditional structures
7. An organization that allows its employees to develop their capabilities and maximize their contribution to the firm

One of the major advantages of this kind of organization is its lack of a large number of hierarchical levels. The firm is flat with few levels of management. This organization is *responsive* because decisions are made quickly; layers of managers are not present to slow decision making. All of these features add up to lower overhead than the traditional bureaucratic organization. The end result should be a firm that is more competitive than traditional, hierarchical organizations due to its responsiveness and lower operating costs.

Costs that go along with these benefits include the following:

1. The organization has to invest in information technology.
2. The firm must be able to manage IT.
3. Employees need to learn new technologies and constantly update their knowledge.
4. Managers have a large span of control.
5. Managers must to supervise remote workers.
6. Firms need to manage close relationships with partners and companies in various alliances.

Another cost of using technology to transform the organization is learning new technology. Products and systems are constantly changing. A firm that does not upgrade and learn new systems eventually results in an environment where it is difficult to share with others. Additionally, of course, the firm forgoes the improvements in the new version of the packages.

The organization features a large span of control for most managers. The idea is to substitute electronic for face-to-face communications. Implicit in a large span of control is a degree of trust in subordinates. Electronics will not substitute for the close control one can exercise over subordinates when a manager has only five or six direct reports. A recent news story on Japanese management showed a large number of workers arranged in two rows of desks, each row facing the other. At the end of the row sat the workers' supervisor, with his desk perpendicular to the workers where he had them under constant view. Evidently a common feature of Japanese organizations, this physical structure is probably the ultimate in close supervision. This new organization is at the opposite end of the spectrum. It requires managers to place more responsibility with subordinates to do their jobs.

Closely related to the need to adopt a management philosophy stressing subordinate responsibility is the problem of managing remote work. Companies are likely to eliminate physical offices for employees who spend a great deal of time traveling or who work from a satellite office or home. Work-at-home experiments have shown that some managers feel uncomfortable trying to supervise subordinates they rarely see. Remote work also requires the manager to trust subordinates, and of course, requires subordinates to act responsibly. Some subordinates reacted negatively to losing their offices and to using part of their homes as offices. They feel the company is forcing its overhead costs onto them. Virtual offices will undoubtedly call for new managerial skills and relationships between managers and the people reporting to them.

The final management cost of a technology-based organization is handling relationships with external firms. These firms might be suppliers or customers, partners in a strategic alliance, or governmental agencies. These partners are a vital part of the business, but they do not report to business employees. Managers must interact in these cooperative arrangements without having the usual "tools" given a manager, such as reporting relationships and control over subordinates' salaries.

Analyzing the Costs and Benefits of Change

When trying to implement something new, it is helpful to compare the costs and benefits as in the preceding sections. Figure 9-2 contains a vertical line that represents an equilibrium in which costs and benefits balance each other. Moving the line to the right is progress toward the new organizational forms and moving it left is toward traditional, hierarchical firms. The benefits of the a new organization are on the left pushing toward the right with

FIGURE 9-2   Forces for changing organization structure.

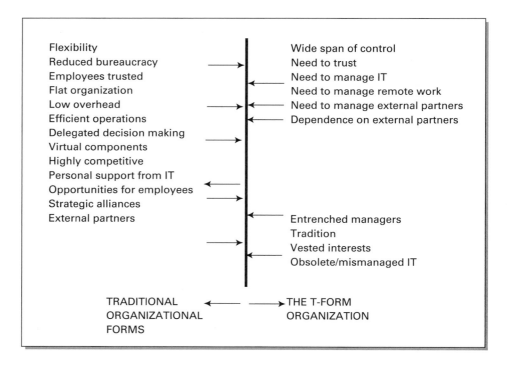

the costs on the top of the right pushing left. When managers see the benefits exceeding the costs, they will move toward a transformed organization.

The advantages of these new organizations are expected to far outweigh the costs because the new form fits start-ups well. A number of Silicon Valley companies employ virtual components and electronic linking and are well along the way in using IT design variables. A company makes a scanning system and software that is aimed at eliminating paper in the office. Their corporate office in Palo Alto is responsible for design, marketing, and sales. Subcontractors manufacture the product: the circuit board comes from Singapore, and a Boston firm makes the case, tests the product, and ships it to customers. Other partners help write the software. Sales representatives in the field do not have physical offices. They are linked by mail, voice mail, and cellular phones.

A number of factors influence how more traditional firms move toward a new structure. In addition to the costs and benefits of Figure 9-2, other forces act against change in hierarchical firms. These forces are "costs" to the current employees of the firm as the technology-based organization clearly threatens many vested interests. A minor restructuring of a department or workgroup will not equate the benefits of a new structure for the organization. The type of massive change needed includes all employees and units of the firm. The change process might start in one department or division, but as with other technologies, a critical mass is needed. Customers may be happy to use EDI with one division, though they may wonder why the rest of the company does not offer electronic linkages.

Massive changes are difficult to carry out because many forces act against them. Major change programs create a number of threats to those already in the firm. The first of the threats is to the entrenched bureaucracy. Middle managers and others have proven adept at protecting their jobs. The result of many IT-stimulated restructurings tends to mean fewer employees. The new organization structure will require the company to downsize. Clearly, downsizing is a threat to existing employees, and it is natural for them to oppose an organizational form that encourages a smaller firm.

A manager committed to using IT design variables will also ask fundamental questions about all of the tasks performed in the organization: Should the company continue to operate a transportation system or contract with outside carriers? Should the company eliminate all forms of payment except credit cards and do away with the accounts receivable department? Should the company contract out its IS operations? The threat of any of these partnerships or alliances is certain to arouse resistance on the part of current employees.

Motivating Organizational Change

Figure 9-2 also shows how these "costs" help to maintain the status quo, traditional organization. In fact, the cost–benefit assessment in Figure 9-2 is a helpful tool in understanding all kinds of change efforts.

It will be difficult in many traditional firms to create movement toward new forms of organization. A number of situations might motivate such a firm to change structures, however:

1. A merger or acquisition
2. A major crisis (e.g., substantial losses)
3. Bankruptcy
4. Rebellion by the board of directors
5. Legal or regulatory reversal

MANAGEMENT PROBLEM 9-2

Martha Spencer is the CIO of Stardust Hotels, a major chain with hotels in the United States, Europe, and Asia. The company has a number of important IT applications, including a reservations system that runs on a mainframe computer. Customers make reservations by calling an agent on a toll-free number, or as of last year, they can go to the Stardust Web site and make a reservation themselves. The hotel is looking into joining a purchasing exchange for all of the items that they buy during the year. Hotels buy a large variety of supplies, ranging from food for restaurants to soaps and shampoo for the rooms. In addition, necessary maintenance and replacement items include mechanical equipment, chairs, beds, and sofas.

The purchasing exchange requires its members to buy a product through the exchange if the exchange carries that product. Martha is wondering how this requirement will be viewed at the individual hotel properties. "Our hotel managers are pretty powerful; they run a small city and are resistant to dictates from headquarters. The new CEO of Stardust is interested in the Exchange—he thinks it is the way we will all be doing business in the future. He has offered to help us any way possible with implementation."

Given this level of support from the CEO, what would you have him do? If the CEO wants to be helpful, develop a role for him to play. What specific actions on his part facilitate implementation?

Mergers and acquisitions often result in new management teams. New managers might look at the firm and realize that integrating two companies is a good time to develop a new overall structure. Unfortunately, sometimes it takes a major crisis to motivate managers. A rebellion by the board of directors might be included here as well. The chairpersons of companies with significant problems have been asked to resign in record numbers in the past few years. Powerful chairpersons of large, well-known companies have suffered this fate. Being a new manager in a crisis situation provides a certain amount of leverage for changing the organization.

Bankruptcy is a traumatic event that may well provide the opportunity for a dramatic restructuring of a firm. Unfortunately, the bankrupt firm is at a bit of a disadvantage with efforts to partner and form alliances given the history that put it into bankruptcy in the first place. It may also lack the funds necessary to develop a technological infrastructure. Finally, a legal or regulatory reversal may also provide the motivation for a firm to use IT design variables to come up with a new structure.

It appears that a crisis may be the strongest motivation for reorganization. Possibly the second reason is competition. If a firm sees the competition performing significantly better after adopting a new structure, it may imitate the competitor.

A Change Program

A manager can go about trying to create a transformed organization in a variety of ways. The goal is to move the organization from one state, say a traditional, hierarchical organization, to another, newer structure. Change is one of the most difficult things to bring about, as pointed out in discussion earlier in the chapter. A number of forces acting against the manager who wishes to change a firm's structure. Figure 9-2 can be thought of as a force field that shows the forces acting for and against change. To bring about change, the manager can either increase the forces for change or decrease the forces opposing change.

Various approaches can be used to strengthen the forces for change, but each organization is different and a change program must be custom tailored. Table 9-4 describes

TABLE 9-4 Moving toward the new organizational forms.

Step	Action
Motivate the change	Explain reasons such as competition, falling sales; look for broad support from places like the Board; communicate with everyone in the organization
Develop a transition plan	Use a task force to develop the vision for the new organization; describe steps that must be taken to reach a new organization structure; take full advantage of IT design variables
Accumulate power and resources	Obtain support from key individuals and groups in the organization; be sure you have the influence and resources to bring about change
Manage anxiety	Communicate with employees; consider a groupware rumor mill application; provide outplacement and counseling; involve employees in designing the new organization
Build IT capabilities	Technology must be in place to enable the T-Form; there is often a lead time for implementing IT before you can make changes in the organization

the key steps and some recommended actions. It is based on some of the ideas of Nadler and Tushman (1988).

The first step is to motivate the change. In some cases, crises may provide enough motivation for action. In other situations, some less dramatic events might convince everyone that change is needed. It is helpful here to have broad support from the board of directors and others with influence in the firm.

Having a plan for the transition to a new organization form is important. It provides a roadmap for action and keeps employees aware of what is happening. Task forces for developing the plan are a good way to bring employees into this process and tap their knowledge for building the new organization. The results of the task force should be widely disseminated. Be sure to take maximum advantage of the IT design variables discussed in Chapter 4.

Employees will experience much anxiety with just the suggestion of a change in the status quo that could alter their jobs or eliminate them. Nadler and Tushman suggest that one job for management is to manage anxiety in the change process. Involving workers is one way to reduce, but not eliminate anxiety. Individuals will be aware of the company's plans, but they may also see changes that look threatening to them.

On balance, it is a good idea to stress open communications rather than keep plans secret. In today's business environment, a responsible firm will also provide counseling and outplacement services for employees who are no longer needed.

Making the transition to a technology-based organization requires that the firm have adequate technology in place. These capabilities may be developed in-house or obtained from outside vendors. Some businesses more than others will require electronic connections to buyers and suppliers. Some of these links can be purchased through value-added carriers and other service companies. Workstations in offices and networks connecting them are important. Increasingly, it appears that groupware and the Internet will become important ways of managing within the organization and a mechanism for linking to external partners.

The task here is to design the firm's technology so it will enable, not constrain, the ability to move toward a new organization. Once the technology is in place, one can use IT design variables to develop the structure of the organization. The following questions clarify the use of IT variables in the design. It is important to recognize that each organization will develop its own, unique structure.

1. What are the most significant processes in the organization (e.g. order fulfillment, manufacturing, etc.)?

2. To what extent should these processes be redesigned?

3. What opportunities do new technologies and IT design variables offer for improving these business processes?

4. Who are major partners, including customers, suppliers, and others (banks, accountants, law firms, etc.)?

   a. What are the opportunities for electronic linking and communications with these organizations?

   b. Where is it feasible to establish electronic customer/supplier relationships?

   c. What additional services can these partners provide? What opportunities are there to create virtual components?

5. How should the firm structure its strategic organization—by product, region, or a combination of factors?

6. What is the organization's competitive strategy? How do IT design variables help implement this strategy?

7. Given the major processes in this business, how does the organization assign personnel to be sure these processes are accomplished?

   a. Can technological leveling minimize the number of layers in the organization?

   b. Do production automation and electronic workflows have something to contribute to the business processes?

8. What kind of managerial hierarchy is necessary?

   a. Can technological leveling reduce layers and broaden the span of control for managers?

   b. Can technological matrixing be used to form temporary task forces and work groups instead of establishing permanent departments and reporting relationships?

The overall objective is to create an organization with a flat structure, flexibility, responsiveness, decentralized decision making, effective communications, links to business partners, and the other characteristics of the T-Form structure.

The major challenge facing managers in the twenty-first century will be to design organizations that take advantage of the IT design variables discussed here. Moving toward a new organization requires new ways of thinking for the start-up organization and massive changes for traditional organizations. Senior managers must decide whether the benefits claimed for this kind of organization are sufficiently compelling to confront the perils of changing the organization.

BEYOND STRUCTURAL CHANGE

The next step involves bringing about changes in interorganizational relations, the economy, education, and national development with the help of new technologies. This chapter discussed the impact of IT and the way firms use electronic communications and linking to change interorganizational relationships. Because these changes generally involve individuals who are not part of the organization, they require a somewhat different approach. The implementation framework in Table 9-3 has a column for Management Support, which mentions having a sponsor or champion. This individual is at a senior level of management; he or she provides the leadership necessary to create change. For developing new interorganizational relationships, such a champion initiates ideas, meets with managers of the other organizations involved, and obtains support within the organization for the change.

Information technology can also facilitate changes in education or national development. Here again a sponsor or champion is important for change. These types of changes take place in a political arena, making them highly uncertain and probably irrational. Changes at the national level involve multiple constituencies, competing political philosophies, and different personal objectives. The force field analysis in Figure 9-2 can provide a number of insights to help the sponsor identify various constituencies and the forces leading to their positions.

Changes enabled by technology at the level of the economy reflect all the other changes discussed. These changes will be emergent rather than planned given the decentralized nature of the economy. If IT does contribute to productivity, as thought likely, then overall productivity gains are emerging from the individual change efforts of thousands of firms in the economy. The economies of post-industrial nations are enjoying the benefits of information technology. The challenges of bringing these benefits to developing economies are extensive and difficult; such an effort will test everyone's implementation skills.

CHAPTER SUMMARY

1. Implementation is a change process that is designed to alter existing practice. With information technology, changes take place through individual applications and by using IT variables to redesign the organization.

2. The ability to use IT to change procedures and organizations, themselves, is one of the most exciting parts of technology. With IT, a manager can make a difference in how an organization functions and in its chances for success.

3. A great deal of research focused on the implementation of individual systems, but it is still too often the case that new applications fail completely or fail to achieve their potential.

4. The chapter reviews factors thought to be related to successful implementation and a process model for the stages of systems development and implementation.

5. Table 9-3 combines the factor and process models to provide guidelines for improving the chance of successful implementation for an individual application of the technology.

6. The chapter recommends a high level of user involvement and influence in the design of a system for a number of reasons, including the psychological commitment that involvement helps create and the knowledge that a user brings to the design project.

7. It is important to transfer psychological ownership of a system to the users of the application.

8. Emergent change is unanticipated; it emerges from individuals who adapt the technology and use it to change the way they work.

9. The problems of implementing change are multiplied when the change target is the entire organization.

10. IT organization design variables are some of the most exciting contributions of the technology; however, using these variables to adopt a new design is a formidable challenge.

11. A force field analysis of the forces encouraging and inhibiting change can help to plan for a new organization structure.

12. It will in general be easier to use IT design variables when creating a new firm than when trying to change the structure of an existing one.

13. The motivation for a traditional organization to adopt a technology-based structure is likely to come from a crisis, or from seeing competitors convert to new organization forms.

14. IT also enables changes in interorganizational relations, the economy, education, and national development.

15. Change is one of the most difficult assignments, but it is through change that management assures organizations will survive and flourish in the future.

KEYWORDS

Champion	Initiation	Process of design
Change	Installation	Responsive organization
Commitment	IT design variables	Satisfaction
Demographics	Lean organization	Span of control
Design	Management support	Successful implementation
Emergent change	Operations	System characteristics
Exploration	Organizational support	Termination
Force field	Participation	Testing
Impact of a system	Planned change	
Implementation	Problem urgency	

RECOMMENDED READINGS

Dutta, A., and McCrohan, K. 2002. Management's role in information security in a cyber economy. *California Management Review, 45*(1), pp. 67–87.

Lucas, H. C., Jr. 1996. *The T-Form Organization: Using Technology to Design Organizations for the 21st Century.* San Francisco: Jossey-Bass. (A book devoted to the design of technology-based organizations.)

McAfee, A. 2003. When too much knowledge is a dangerous thing. *Sloan Management Review*, Winter, pp. 83–89. (The author offers guidelines for senior management for implementing technology.)

Nadler, D., and Tushman, M. 1988. *Strategic Organization Design.* New York: HarperCollins. (An excellent book on traditional approaches to organization design.)

Orlikowski, W. 1996. Improvising organizational transformation over time: A situated change perspective. *Information Systems Research, 7*(1), pp. 63–92. (A well- written article that provides many insights on emergent change.)

Scott, J. E., and Vessey, I. 2002. Managing risks in enterprise systems implementations. *Communications of the ACM, 45*(4), pp. 74–81.

Venkatesh, V., Morris, M., Davis, F., and Davis, G. 2003. User acceptance of information technology: Toward a unified view. *MIS Quarterly, 27,* pp. 425–478. (A more academic technology acceptance model.)

DISCUSSION QUESTIONS

1. Why is implementation more than just the last few weeks of the systems life cycle?

2. What definitions and measures of successful implementation can you suggest other than the ones in this chapter?

3. What are the responsibilities of users in the systems design process?

4. How do the responsibilities of managers differ from those of other users during systems design?

5. What are the crucial differences between an internal information system and an interorganizational one from the standpoint of implementation? What are the key similarities?

6. What is the role of a consultant in helping to design information systems? How does this role change under the systems design policies suggested in this chapter?

7. What approaches are used to evaluate the benefits of information systems?

8. How would you measure the impact of an information system on decision making?

9. What factors mitigate the effects of massive change in the organization?

10. What might motivate a firm to use IT design variables to make a radical change in its structure?

11. What problems does user-oriented design create for users, their management, and the IT department?

12. Can user-oriented design work for a system encompassing large numbers of people, for example, a reservation system involving hundreds or thousands of agents? What strategy could be adopted in this situation?

13. What are the advantages of an organization with a large span of control? What are the disadvantages?

14. How does IT enable change in the economy?

15. What implementation strategy does the process model suggest?

16. Why do some authors think the hierarchical organization is doomed in the twenty-first century? What are the advantages of a flat organization structure?

17. How can information technology make major changes in education?

18. As a potential or present user of information systems, how do you respond to the idea of being in charge of the design of such a system?

19. Why are the relationships among system use, user satisfaction, and performance important?

20. Are the techniques suggested here applicable in other contexts? What situations can you suggest in which user control might be more successful than control by a group of technological experts?

21. How can you transform a huge firm such as General Motors with the help of information technology?

22. When does planning for successful implementation begin in designing an information system?

23. What is the role of the technological infrastructure in moving toward the T-Form organization?

24. How does information technology impact national development?

APPENDIX 9-1

The Technology Model

In 1989, a group of researchers led by Fred Davis developed the Technology Acceptance Model (TAM). This model is based on several theories in psychology, which gives it a good theoretical grounding. After testing the model in experiments, the authors reduced it to three key variables. The simplified model says that perceived usefulness (of an IT product) and perceived ease of use predict user acceptance, which is either a stated intention to use the IT product or actual use.

Because the model is based on accepted theory, it generated a great deal of academic interest and a number of studies to test and refine it. Many of these early tests were on college students and were run as experiments, leaving some questions about how the model might do in the work environment where one has to confront the culture of the organization, the wishes of supervisors and subordinates, and a task that has to be completed. Various researchers added variables to the model, and one group tried to formulate a unified model of technology assessment (Venkatesh et al., 2003). Their model may be found in Figure 9-3.

The unified model contains variables that overlap with the models presented in this chapter, including user demographics, social influence (management support), performance expectancy (performance), and of course, use. TAM includes a variable for voluntary use explicitly, while the chapter's model suggests choosing different outcome variables depending on whether use is voluntary or required.

What the unified TAM model does not include is an emphasis on the process of implementation, which is equally important to the factors in these models. TAM received a great deal of academic interest and many studies rely on it for their underlying theory. This model may be helpful to you in thinking about implementation and user acceptance of technology. The objective of all of these models is to focus managers and developers on the fact that successful implementation is not assured, even if a system is a technical success.

FIGURE 9-3 An unified model based on TAM.

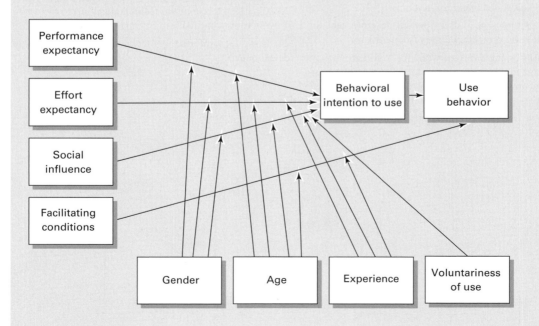

CHAPTER 10

STRUCTURING AND MANAGING THE IT FUNCTION

A Manager's Perspective

In a number of firms, management's strategy for the IT function was "benign neglect." One CEO even avoided talking to his CIO, saying that he did not like him and wanted to stay away from technology. (His comments say more about the CEO than the CIO.) Why is the technology function so hard to organize and manage? Most senior managers have risen through the ranks in other than IT jobs, though this trend is likely to change in the future. A clear lack of understanding of IT exists among senior managers, and as a result many managers seem to withdraw from technology instead of learning more about it. As companies move toward business models that involve technology for all aspects of their business, these conditions have to change. Two leading e-business companies are Dell and Cisco, both technology firms. One would expect their chairpersons to have a good grasp of IT issues. These netcentric firms appear to be a precursor of what all companies will look like in a few years. To get there, companies need senior managers who are knowledgeable about the technology, and who are comfortable structuring and managing the IT function.

Designing and managing the IT function is a challenge in most organizations. The IT subunit has a number of functions that differ significantly from each other. Work in IT ranges from creative and innovative in planning applications to factory-like in operations. The unit faces demands from multiple stakeholders including all levels of management, users, customers, and suppliers.

A consensus may not yet be present in the organization on the role of the IT function, and many managers have little understanding of what is involved in providing technology services. Steering committees, task forces, and systems development teams should be cross-functional and include members from different parts of the organization. It is a challenge for both IT and line management to develop an IT organization that is able to operate existing technology and develop new initiatives in cooperation with others in the firm.

OPPORTUNITIES FOR GREATNESS AND DISASTER

The information technology subunit of the organization encompasses a diverse set of activities. This unit may develop applications of technology that literally transform the organization. Other initiatives may make a major contribution to corporate strategy, provide a new source of revenue, or help the organization reduce cost. All of these outcomes are highly desirable, but difficult to attain.

In addition to the creative activities already described, the IT group operates and maintains the firm's technology infrastructure. In this role the staff provides ongoing service to managers and other users in the organization. In today's environment with companies linked together electronically and firms conducting business online with their customers, the IT staff must serve a variety of stakeholders in the organization.

Both the creative part and the routine activities of the IT group always hold the potential for disaster. Developing and implementing innovative uses of technology often prove challenging; a large number of projects fail for one reason or another. A lot has to go right in an IT development project, and it only takes the failure of one or two small components to doom an entire project. The services side can involve complex technology including networks of lines, routers, and other communications hardware, and complex programs that have the potential to fail. Computer science research shows that no program is ever fully debugged; many errors await discovery, even in program code that has run successfully for many years. A new set of conditions arises, and a program encounters an error in trying to deal with a situation that programmers never tested.

The IT subunit presents a difficult environment for management. The unit deals with both creative and routine operations at the same time, and each of its activities has a risk of failure. Firms have tried a number of different organization structures to better manage the IT group, and it is not surprising that a single, best organization structure has yet to emerge.

Centralization and Decentralization

Debate on the appropriate structure for the IT function historically focused on questions of centralization. Although generalizations are dangerous, centralized information technology structures generally result in the lowest cost to the organization. The trade-off is that low cost is often associated with poor service. If all IT expenditures require approval by a central group, users will have to spend more time and exert more effort in satisfying the central group than they would a local high IT manager. Centralized groups can develop a plan and a budget and see that all expenditures fit within the budget. This group coordinates purchases and attempts to create standards that will be used throughout the organization. Centralized staff also gain benefits from purchasing equipment and supplies for the entire corporation.

Decentralized information technology organizations, on the other hand, are associated with greater flexibility and better service. A local IT manager is expected to be more responsive to requests than a central organization. A local IT staff should be more familiar with the unique needs of users in their location. Decisions are made more quickly because justification of projects to a central staff is not needed, nor is central approval for decisions. Each organization must find a structure that works best for it, balancing the costs and benefits of each option.

A Political Model of Information Technology

Table 10-1 describes a political model of information technology in the organization, a somewhat tongue-in-cheek description of IT. Firms that practice technocratic utopianism are fascinated with the technology. An assumption in the firm somehow perpetuates the belief that technology will solve all problems. The firm will develop databases, desktop workstations, and networks, and purchase large amounts of software. This organization

TABLE 10-1   Information politics.

Technocratic utopianism	Reliance on technology; model the firm's IT structure and rely on new technologies
Anarchy	No overall information management policy
Feudalism	Management of IT by individual business units; limited reporting to the corporation
Monarchy	Strong control by senior management; information may not be shared with lower levels of the firm
Federalism	Management through consensus and negotiation about key IT decisions and structures

lacks a vision of how all of this technology will be used to further its objectives because it admires technology for technology's sake.

Anarchy results when technology is not managed. Management abrogates its responsibilities to control IT and lets a thousand flowers bloom. This strategy may encourage the bold to acquire computers and connect them, but as the firm matures, the lack of overall planning and standards will create tremendous problems. Many firms practiced this style of management in the early days of PCs, letting users purchase whatever equipment they pleased. As a result, these firms found it difficult and expensive to connect all their diverse computers to a network.

In the feudal model, powerful executives control technology within their divisions and departments. These executives determine what information to collect and choose the technology for their fiefdoms. They also make the decision on what information to forward to higher levels of management. This model is most often found when the firm stresses divisional autonomy. Because it is unlikely two chiefs will follow the same model, it again can be difficult to coordinate different feudal systems if senior management decides that such a network is an appropriate technology strategy.

In a monarchy, the CIO becomes the CIC, the chief information czar. Instead of playing the consultant role, the CIO establishes and enforces standards that will be followed throughout the corporation. The monarchy often emerges when the firm finds that it has suffered too long from the feudal model. A possible halfway point between feudalism and a monarchy is a constitutional monarchy, in which a document sets out the powers reserved to senior management and those that fall to the divisions.

In today's environment, the federal model is probably the most frequent structure. The firm tries to reach a consensus on what IT decisions belong at each level and how information should be shared. The emphasis is on what policies make the most sense for the corporation as a whole, not just for a specific department or division. Senior management recognizes that local divisions need some autonomy, and local managers recognize that information belongs to the company and may often be of great strategic value.

In most cases, it makes sense for infrastructure such as networks to be designed and operated centrally. If many opportunities arise to share systems across divisions, corporate management will encourage a strong role for a central IS group. Also, if the divisions have line managers who have little knowledge of IT, a central group may play a major role in helping the divisions. In the case of dissimilar divisions that experience little opportunity for sharing, the expectation is that the local unit assumes a lot of responsibility for IT decision making. A central IT group will provide some coordination, but most decisions will be left to local managers. This decentralization will be more pronounced if local managers are especially knowledgeable about information technology.

WHAT HAS TO BE MANAGED?

The general tasks of the IT subunit just described actually subsume a number of more detailed activities. A list of important tasks or processes in the IT function may be found in Agarwal and Sambamurthy (2002).

Relationships

The most important IT activity is maintaining relationships with a variety of stakeholders. Senior management is the first group that comes to mind; the head of IT, often called the chief information officer (CIO), needs to be a part of senior management and aware of the firm's strategy. Chapter 2 stressed that IT is an integral part of today's corporate strategy for electronic commerce and the Internet. Senior management can hardly exclude the CIO from strategy and planning sessions, and expect to have the technology in place to execute their plans. The task of the CIO then, as a member the senior ranks of management, is to suggest innovations that will advance the company's agenda.

Other managers and staff members in the organization are an equally important constituency for the IT group. These managers work with the IT staff to implement new innovations that make use of technology, and they interact with IT operations staff members who see that all of the firm's technology operates on a routine basis.

A more recent group of stakeholders for the IT subunit consists of individuals who do not work for the company, but who conduct business electronically with it. This constituency includes customers and suppliers. In an era of online Internet stores for selling products and services, and electronically integrated supply chains, these individuals who work externally to the organization form an important group. It is not a good idea to irritate customers with online stores that fail. A few years ago, several online electronic stock brokers had embarrassing outages when their computers or networks failed. These outages were not only inconvenient, they cost customers money when their trades were not executed.

Strategy

Chapter 2 discussed the role of IT in developing corporate strategy, especially given the benefits of the Internet. Beyond the Internet, the IT staff should help business units by showing how IT can support their strategic plans, and how IT might enable new strategies.

Infrastructure

Infrastructure consists of all of the hardware and networks in the firm, and sometimes includes routine processing systems as well. The infrastructure is what enables the firm to operate its current systems and undertake new initiatives. Although not particularly glamorous, it is key to a successful IT operation.

MANAGEMENT PROBLEM 10-1

In the early days of the technology, most IT departments reported to the head of finance. The reasoning was that the system kept a lot of records that related to accounting and financial reporting. Gradually, the technology moved into other areas of the business, but the department often stayed under finance. Nancy Scott, CIO of Victor Electronics, recalled her early experiences, "We would work for the controller or VP of Finance, and all this person cared about was financial applications. We'd get a request from marketing, and the controller would say you can go over there when you finish everything on my list. And, of course, you could never finish his list because it just kept growing."

What are the arguments for and against having the IT function report to Finance? Does it make sense to have IT reporting to any particular functional area? What are the alternatives? If you were the CEO, where would you like to have IT report? What if you were CIO?

Human Capital

Information technology is a knowledge business. The IT staff must be knowledgeable about technology and its possibilities, the organization itself, and the technology being used in the firm. Few organizations maintain enough documentation so that they could replace their entire operations staff and keep functioning. Information on how systems work, how the network operates, and how to help users with questions comes from the knowledge of IT professionals. Every manager needs to be concerned with human capital, both developing the skills of the staff, and recruiting and retaining talented people.

Innovation

The creative role of IT entails coming up with innovations that will advance the organization. The Internet has provided the platform for a huge number of IT innovations. Consider all the services now offered on the Web; a decade ago most of them did not exist, at least not online with easy access through an Internet connection and Web browser. The Internet inspired new business models and new ways for traditional firms to provide goods and services. It is Internet-stimulated innovation that is responsible for the greater visibility that IT has achieved in many organizations in the last few years.

Solutions Delivery

Traditionally, the IT function delivered services to its users. In the early days of the technology the IT staff designed, programmed, tested, and installed most of these solutions. Today, the staff is more likely to help determine the functional requirements for a new use of technology, and then help select a packaged problem solution for purchase. The staff will also help to configure and implement the solution, and often will integrate that solution with hardware and software already in place.

Provisioning for Service

The IT group is responsible for providing services to its constituency. It must outfit the data center through obtaining equipment and service to keep various data centers in the firm operating. Organizations today expect IT to maintain help desks to provide consulting help to users with questions. With most professionals in an organization having desktop computers, the IT group is responsible for providing, maintaining, and upgrading the hardware and software on these machines.

Financial Performance

Chapter 3 discussed some of the problems in computing a return on investments in IT, but many managers expect some financial analysis of a proposed application of technology. If the IT group outsources any part of its operations, the group must structure service-level agreements and negotiate financial terms with the outsourcer. The IT group will be subject to an operating budget, and it will be expected to help justify new investments in IT innovations beyond normal operations.

NEW ORGANIZATIONAL MODELS FOR IT

In their research, Agarwal and Sambamurthy (2002) identified three new models for organizing the IT function. It is interesting to note that these models do not address centralization or decentralization; they are orthogonal to this issue. Instead, they describe different management expectations about how all information technology should function in the organization. The three models include partner, platform, and the scalable models, and their basic characteristics may be found in Table 10-2.

The Partner Model

In the partner model the IT subunit is a "proactive partner in the innovation process." Senior IT management stimulates thought about the strategic uses of technology. This model requires extensive collaboration between business and IT managers; these managers

TABLE 10-2 Three models for the IT organization.

	Partner	Platform	Scalable
Strategic position	IT is an active business partner for innovation	IT provides infrastructure for an entire business	IT remains flexible and able to undertake new initiatives quickly
Characteristics	IT managers in divisions, corporate IT for leadership, matrix reporting in IT	Corporate IT supervises overall infrastructure, businesses "own" IT innovations, IT account manager in each business	Centralize IT to encourage commonality and reduce duplication, IT in business units
Most applicable	Senior executives lack in-depth knowledge of IT, firm needs to promote IT innovation, solid IT leadership	Global companies with diverse lines of business; company managers knowledgeable about IT	Cyclical businesses, global businesses with similar subsidiaries, e.g. oil retailer

SOURCE: Agarwal and Sambamurthy, 2002.

search for innovation and constantly consider future IT capabilities. It is likely that the CIO will report to the CEO and become a member of senior management. The role of the CIO is to help the firm develop a vision of how technology can advance its strategy.

A similar structure is appropriate for various divisional information technology officers; they partner with peers in different lines of business. It is likely that this model will include divisional information technology staff members who are located in individual business units to strengthen their relationships with divisional management. This structure looks similar to a federal IT organization; but the focus is on innovation rather than decentralization.

In this model it is likely that individual divisions are responsible for their own IT costs, while infrastructure and utility costs are considered shared services managed by a central unit. A charge-back scheme may or may not be in place to apportion the shared costs to each division.

The researchers feel that the partner model is appropriate for firms that want to promote innovation with technology, but where executives lack a deeper understanding of IT. The model encourages collaboration in developing new technology innovations. Both IT and line managers learn from each other as they collaborate. This model is also appropriate for multidivisional firms that are seeking to exploit synergies across their divisions. It is helpful if a history of trust exists between the IT function and its constituents because IT credibility is important in encouraging collaboration.

The Platform Model

The platform model concentrates on infrastructure and tools that enable others in the organization to come up with innovations. The IT function provides a global infrastructure and development tools as a platform for creating new applications. Infrastructure investment can be thought of as buying an option to undertake innovations in the future when the opportunity arises. IT is much less of a partner in the business in this model.

A company adopting this model is likely to create the position of account manager who acts as a liaison between the IT function and business units. Collaboration takes place at this level rather than with senior management, so the account manager assumes considerable responsibility for fostering innovation. If the firm allows a competitive market for IT services, the account manager must remain competitive so that the business units will use his or her facilities. The account manager's job includes learning the needs of managers in the business unit and planning ways to fulfill these needs. The account manager also coordinates the delivery of IT solutions to the business unit.

The platform model is thought to be most fitting for global, multidivisional firms with several lines of business. Each of these lines of business has its own, unique IT needs, so that local IT knowledge is important.

The Scalable Model

This model fits the organization that needs maximum flexibility, a firm that wants to acquire resources when an opportunity presents itself. The firm adopting this model might operate in a cyclical business that requires it to expand and contract resources. The IT function needs to be fast-moving and adept at developing new applications on short notice. With the scalable model, the firm outsources a large portion of its IT to take advantage of the resources of service providers. It is not possible to quickly scale up the number of employees in IT or to dramatically increase one's network and computing infrastructure. Instead, the scalable IT group relies on others for additional capacity when it is needed. Conversely, it is easier to exit from a business or discontinue processing an application when using an outsourcer. The IT staff develops a number of relationships with service providers and mechanisms to manage these relationships.

COORDINATION

The IT subunit faces a number of coordination challenges, especially when it relies on some outsourced service providers. IT needs to be integrated with multiple units and divisions in its own organization and to ensure that the firm's organizational network is well integrated. IT can achieve this type of coordination in a variety of ways, including traditional and electronic techniques.

Traditionally, the firm followed various rules and procedures. Systems embody many of these procedures and execute them routinely. When working with supply chain partners, a customer sends forecasts of demand to the suppliers, which helps coordinate the supply chain activities. Task forces within the firm generally cross multiple departments; for example, marketing and production form a committee to work on forecasts. Similar task forces cross organizational boundaries and coordinate the systems of companies that are connected electronically.

In highly networked companies, the IT group establishes coordination electronically. The entire order cycle starting with the customer entering an order over the Internet is a form of electronic coordination. The firm routes the order electronically to a fulfillment partner. The partner sends electronic notification of shipment to the customer, and looks at its partner's order entry backlog to plan its own production.

Within IT itself, coordination is important in all of its activities, particularly in managing different relationships in the firm. IT must coordinate its development efforts with consultants, package providers, and management and users in the organization. The most popular coordination mechanisms here are task forces and committees. In addition to meeting physically, these groups can make use of teleconferencing, videoconferencing, Web meetings, and groupware such as Lotus Notes to supplement face-to-face meetings.

The Chief Information Officer

The increased importance of IT to the firm has led to the creation of a chief information officer (CIO) position. This individual is, of course, in charge of information technology in the firm. However, the chief information officer is also an influential member of senior management and is usually a vice president or senior vice president in the firm. In addition to traditional information processing, this individual is responsible for voice and data communications and office technology. The job demands someone who can assume a role in planning, influencing other senior managers, and organizing information activities in the organization.

Many of the issues discussed in this text concern the CIO. He or she must worry about strategic planning for the corporation and how information technology can provide a competitive edge. The executive in this role must provide leadership and control over processing.

It is important that planning, systems development, and operations are all undertaken successfully. A large firm might spend in the hundreds of millions or even more than a billion dollars a year on information technology. A manager, not a technician, is needed to obtain a return from this kind of investment.

Earl and Feeny (1994) describe ways in which CIOs should try to add value to their organizations. They found two types of CEOs: those who see IT as a strategic resource and those who see it as a cost. Table 10-3 presents various issues in managing IT as seen by CEOs in these different positions. If you are the CIO of a firm whose CEO holds the views in the middle liability column, then the job will indeed be challenging. Earl and Feeny argue that the CIO must find a way to add value to the corporation from its use of IT so the CEO will view IT as an asset.

One role of the CIO is to determine whether success stories from other industries or from competitors are relevant to the company. At one chemical company, managers dismissed stories of competitive advantage from IT saying they were not applicable in their industry. Unfortunately, at the same time a competitor was developing technology that gave it a competitive advantage.

It appears the most successful approach to obtaining benefits from IT is not to identify *separate* IT and business strategies; rather business strategy subsumes IT strategy. The job of the CIO is to build relationships with other functional managers so IT requirements

TABLE 10-3 Perceptions of IT.

Issue	IT a Cost/Liability	IT an Asset
Are we getting value for money invested in IT?	ROI on IT is difficult to measure; the organization as a whole is unhappy with IT.	ROI is difficult to measure, the organization believes IT makes an important contribution.
How important is IT?	Stories of strategic IT use are dismissed as irrelevant to this business.	Stories of strategic IT use are instructive.
How do we plan for IT?	IT plans are made by specialists or missionary zealots.	IT thinking is subsumed within business thinking.
Is the IS function doing a good job?	There is general cynicism about the track record of IS.	The performance of IS is no longer an agenda item.
What is the IT strategy?	Many IT applications are under development.	IS efforts are focused on a few key initiatives.
What is the CEO's vision for the role of IT?	The CEO sees a limited role for IT within the business.	The CEO sees IT as having a role in the transformation of the business.
What do we expect of the CIO?	The CIO is positioned as a specialist functional manager.	The CIO is valued as a contributor to business thinking and business operations.

SOURCE: Reprinted from "Is Your CEO Adding Value?" by M. Earl and D. Feeny, *MIT Sloan Management Review*, Spring 1994, pp. 11–20, by permission of publisher. Copyright © 1994 by Massachusetts Institute of Technology. All rights reserved.

MANAGEMENT PROBLEM 10-2

Much of the discussion in this chapter applies to the traditional firm, one that existed long before the Internet. This firm manufactures a product or provides a service, and technology supports these activities. The firm is likely to have an intranet and possibly an online store. The IT function in this kind of firm will be relatively small compared to other groups such as production workers, or consultants in a consulting firm.

To consider how the models in this chapter apply to an Internet firm, think about Amazon.com or eBay. Here the technology is at the heart of the firm; these companies exist because of the Internet. eBay is one of the few profitable dot-coms, and the technology is essential to its operations. If their servers are down for even a few minutes, eBay loses a large amount of revenue.

Do the suggested models for the IT organization in this chapter fit an Amazon or eBay? How do you organize for IT in a company where the technology is one of the most significant parts of the firm, and where a large percentage of the company's workforce is employed? How would you recommend that these companies structure and manage their IT organizations?

become a part of business strategy. This approach means the CIO must be involved in planning and strategy meetings across the company.

To provide confidence in technology, the CIO must build a track record of delivering IT as promised, on time, and within budget. Users quickly become cynical when delivery dates, cost estimates, and functional specifications do not meet expectations. Rather than scattering the development effort, a well-run company focuses its IT efforts on opportunities and areas where the firm is weak. The task of the CIO here is to determine not how to use IT, but rather where it should be used to most benefit the organization.

The CIO has to be a promoter, marketing the potential of IT to transform the organization. A track record of delivering what has been promised will increase this manager's credibility as will good examples of organizations that have undergone technology-driven transformations. The CIO has a political role to play in this process, campaigning for the effective use of technology and appropriate levels of investment. Just as a politician must always consider his or her constituents, the CIO needs to focus on other managers and on users in the organization.

In addition to being a liaison with other managers in the firm, the CIO needs to find champions and sponsors for different initiatives. If a CIO cannot find someone in senior management to take responsibility for a new IT innovation, and do so enthusiastically, then the CIO should reevaluate the project. Too many examples tell of projects that have failed for lack of organizational support, and too many anecdotes of how committed non-IT managers championed projects through to a successful completion.

Table 10-4 summarizes the characteristics Earl and Feeny found among CIOs for firms that considered IT to be an asset rather than a liability. This table shows how the CIO can add value to the organization. The last item, a shared vision for IT is extremely important. The IT function cannot succeed without the enthusiastic cooperation of non-IT managers in the firm. Many IT activities involve people from across the organization, and the CIO must enlist other managers to provide staff for cross-functional teams that work on operational problems, systems development, strategy, and an overall plan for IT.

The CIO of a major, diversified company offered a description of his job. This CIO claims to add value by finding new business opportunities for the company and using technology to conduct business in new ways. The company manages IT in a feudal structure,

TABLE 10-4 The added value of the CIO.

1. Obsessive and continuous focus on business imperatives

2. Interpretation of external IT success stories as potential models for the firm

3. Establishment and maintenance of IS executive relationships

4. Establishment and communication of IS performance record

5. Concentration of the IS development effort

6. Achievement of a shared and challenging vision of the role of IT

SOURCE: Reprinted from "Is Your CEO Adding Value?" by M. Earl and D. Feeny, *MIT Sloan Management Review,* Spring 1994, pp. 11–20, by permission of publisher. Copyright © 1994 by Massachusetts Institute of Technology. All rights reserved.

so he takes responsibility for infrastructure like a worldwide network. IT managers in each division develop systems for their divisions and worry about the day-to-day operation of their systems. The role of the CIO will differ among companies, but first and foremost this person has to be a manager concerned with the business as well as someone who understands information technology.

It should be noted that in the last few years, CIOs have been under intense pressure to reduce costs, something that is difficult to do. Much of the IT budget is fixed and is not discretionary; the CIO ensures that the infrastructure of hardware, networks, and systems keeps running. A drop in a company's business of 10 percent translates into little reduction in the cost of IT because of the difficulty in turning off just 10 percent of capacity. (On the positive side, when business picks up, a concomitant increase in expenditures does not necessarily follow because a robust infrastructure will handle additional volume.)

The question is then what the CIO can actually cut. The discretionary budget is for new innovations and applications of the technology; the initiatives that have a chance of moving the company ahead, providing an advantage, and making users happy. So during times of retrenchment, the CIO may have to abandon the pursuit of projects that will offer the most help to the company.

A Vision and Plan for IT

One task of a CIO is to be sure the firm articulates a vision for what IT can accomplish and a plan to provide a guideline for management decisions about technology. A vision is a general statement of what the organization is trying to become. A vision might describe, possibly in scenario form, the environment seen by a user. "We will use information technology to support our strategies of providing the best customer service in the industry and becoming a global firm. Our first priority is to develop electronic links with customers and suppliers over the Internet. Product brand managers will be furnished with decision support tools to conduct their own analyses of global data. Product development engineers will have workstations capable of running the CAD/CAM software…" A vision might include a statement about the kind of technology architecture the firm hopes to provide, such as making all applications Web-enabled with all communications based on the Internet. The vision needs to be sufficiently compelling so it creates enthusiasm for the plan to achieve it.

Corporate and IT strategic planning should be one part of a planning effort. The IT plan expands the IT component of the strategic business plan and describes how to execute the agreed-upon strategy. This plan must combine the vision of IT with strategy to produce a document that guides IT decision making. Suppose the overall strategy of the company is to become the low-cost producer in its industry. This strategy is to be achieved by reengineering existing processes and installing automated production equipment in manufacturing plants. The vision of the firm in five years is to have process owners in charge of business processes that have extensive technology support. The overall architecture is client-server and Web-based applications, with the Internet connecting all plants and office locations. In addition, to pursue its low-cost producer strategy, the company will establish Internet links with key customers and suppliers.

Thus, the vision and strategy provide the goals for an IT plan, which describes how to achieve them. This operational plan depends on the company and its strategy, but in general it discusses hardware and software, communications, and individual applications. The plan in the preceding example would detail the equipment needed to move toward the client-server, Web-oriented model and a schedule for implementation. This section would also discuss networking, including the hardware and services required to provide communications.

A key role of the plan is to identify the most important new applications of technology and prioritize them. It is important to focus efforts on applications that contribute to achieving the vision and strategy of the company. For the preceding example, do not be too concerned about routine applications. Management decides that resources should be applied to developing an online store and an online auction for discontinued products. The plan would describe each of these projects in some detail including cost, time, and staff requirements for completion. If management decides it wants to undertake more applications than there is staff available, some of the development will have to be outsourced.

Having a plan makes managing IT requests easier for the CIO and for management in general. The rapid diffusion of technology has led to a flood of ideas and requests for how to use IT. The typical organization cannot afford to undertake every application suggested. A manager can evaluate applications against the plan and determine whether the suggestion helps to achieve the organization's vision and strategy and where it falls given the priorities of other projects. A well-prepared plan can create enthusiasm for IT, focus the technology effort on business imperatives, and help manage and evaluate technology. The plan is a fundamental management tool for seeing that IT makes the maximum contribution to the organization. Table 10-5 shares the contents of one corporate plan for information technology.

The best approach is for a representative group of managers to work together to develop a plan for information technology and the organization. A plan developed by a CIO alone will probably not be acceptable to other managers. The CIO should act as a resource, consultant, and tutor for the planning committee. The idea is for technology not to be a separate plan, but to be integrated, and to some extent subsumed, in a corporate plan.

WHAT THE CEO SHOULD DO

Surprisingly little research addresses the role of the CEO in managing information technology. Most of the evidence comes from anecdotes and stories about companies that

TABLE 10-5   Contents of an information systems plan.

- Executive summary
- Goals—general and specific
- Assumptions
- Scenario—vision of the firm
- Applications areas—status, cost, schedule, priorities
- Operations
- Maintenance and enhancements
- Organizational structure—pattern of computing
- Effect of plan on the organization—financial impact
- Implementation—risks, obstacles

seem to be successful in the application of technology. The Earl and Feeney study quoted earlier suggests that a CIO wants to work for a CEO that views IT as an investment and not just an expense.

A review of a number of teaching cases and articles about CEOs indicates that a CEO needs to take a number of actions for the CEO to ensure a successful IT effort. Many of these actions are fairly simple, but sometimes simple can be the most effective. The CEO should:

- Understand enough about technology so that IT becomes a part of corporate strategy.
- Look for e-business opportunities.
- Insist that the firm and its management develop a vision and plan for IT.
- Be aware of the possibilities for adopting new organization structures enabled by IT (e.g. becoming a network or a virtual corporation).
- Help set priorities within IT and the priority of IT given other corporate activities.
- Meet regularly with the CIO.
- Spend time understanding IT applications in the firm.
- Make a major systems effort a company goal for the year.
- Ask for regular reports on the progress on major IT initiatives, and take action when problems develop.
- Evaluate the impact of technology on the firm.
- Challenge managers at all levels of the firm to think about what technology can do for the firm and to look for e-business opportunities.

The essence of these recommendations is that the CEO provides leadership for the organization with an effective information technology. Some recent research also suggests that having a board of directors with outside members who have some background in technology helps in managing technology in the firm (Kambil and Lucas, 2002).

CHAPTER SUMMARY

It should be clear from the discussion that no one way is best for organizing the IT function in a modern organization. Companies find themselves in different situations, and senior executives have different ideas and attitudes about the possible contributions of IT to the organization. Just as in developing new systems, choosing an organization structure for IT entails a series of trade-offs.

Executives need to be aware of the options available to them for this organization design task, and they should be willing to experiment with different structures. Whatever structure is chosen, it is important to see that the various tasks in the IT unit described in this chapter are managed. IT is an integral part of the firm, and managers must incorporate this subunit into the overall organization.

KEYWORDS

Anarchy

Centralization

CEO

CIO

Coordination

Decentralization

Federal

Feudal

IT plan

Monarchy

Partner

Platform

Scalable

Vision

RECOMMENDED READINGS

Agarwal, R., and Sambamurthy, V. 2002. Principles and models for organizing the IT function. *MISQ Executive, 1*(1), pp. 1–16.

Brown, C., and Magill, S. 1998. Reconceptualizing the context-design issue for the information systems function. *Organization Science, 9*(2), pp. 176–194. (A difficult article that describes some of the considerations in the debate about centralizing or decentralizing IT decision making.)

Davenport, T. H., Eccles, R., and Prusak, L. Information politics. *Sloan Management Review, 34*(1), pp. 53–65. (An insightful article on how many different organizations approach IT management.)

DiRomualdo, A., and Gurbaxani, V. 1998. Strategic intent for IT outsourcing. *Sloan Management Review, 39*(4), Summer. (An article that discusses three motivations for outsourcing and the appropriate relationship with an outsourcer for each.)

Earl, M., and Feeny, D. 1994. Is your CIO adding value? *Sloan Management Review,* Spring, pp. 11–20. (An excellent discussion of the challenges and actions for a CIO.)

Kambil, A., and Lucas, H. C., Jr. 2002. The board of directors and the management of information technology. *Communications of AIS, 8,* Article 26.

Lacity, M., and Hirschheim, R. 1993. The information systems outsourcing bandwagon. *Sloan Management Review,* Fall, pp. 73–86. (A somewhat contrary view of the move toward outsourcing.)

Loh, L., and Venkatraman, N. 1992. Determinants of information technology outsourcing: A cross-sectional analysis. *Journal of MIS, 9*(1), pp. 7–24. (An interesting study of outsourcing.)

Sambamurthy, V. and Zund, R. 2000. Research commentary: The organizing logic for an enterprise's IT activities in the digital era—A prognosis of practice and a call for research. *Information Systems Research, 11*(2), pp. 105–114.

DISCUSSION QUESTIONS

1. What are the major activities of the IT unit in a firm?

2. What are the main arguments in favor of centralized IT management?

3. What are the advantages and disadvantages of decentralized IT?

4. What issues besides centralization are important in deciding how to structure the IT subunit?

5. When would a firm choose the partner model for IT management?

6. What is the major difference between the partner model and the platform model?

7. When is it appropriate to use a scalable model for IT management?

8. What is coordination and why is it important? What mechanisms exist to help IT coordinate its activities with the rest of the firm?

9. What is the role of the CIO in an organization?

10. Where do you think the CIO should report in the organization?

11. The term *CIO* has been described as really meaning "career is over." What do you think of this suggestion? Why might it have been true in some instances?

12. Why do some managers seem to see IT as an expense while others see it as an investment?

13. What challenges does outsourcing present to the IT staff?

14. Why do many companies outsource some but not all of their information technology activities?

15. What part of IT would you advise senior management not to outsource?

16. How does one get out of an outsourcing contract if conditions change?

17. What is the reason for an IT plan?

18. Why does it probably not make sense to have an IT plan that goes more than two or three years into the future?

19. What is the relationship between the IT plan and a corporate strategic plan?

20. How do various task forces help to coordinate IT activities within the company and with network partners? What are the major problems with task forces?

CHAPTER 11

MANAGEMENT CONTROL OF INFORMATION TECHNOLOGY

A Manager's Perspective

A lot of a manager's job is control in the organization. As a manager, you look for signs that something is going wrong, not because you are a pessimist, but because a deviation from a target value may indicate a serious problem. Consider a car that has a turbo-charger to increase engine power. One of the by-products of turbocharging is heat, so the engineers have two gauges on the instrument panel to allow the driver to monitor the engine. It also has a temperature gauge for water, which you find on many cars, and one for the temperature of the engine oil. If either of these rises too far, then the driver should shut off the engine to prevent damage, and seek help. Managers have gauges, too, with values frequently provided by information systems. A budget is a fundamental control mechanism in the firm; it helps the firm control costs. A sales forecast is another gauge; if sales do not meet forecast, then revenue will be less than planned, and it may be neces- sary to reduce expense budgets. Technology helps with control, and it needs to be con- trolled itself given the extreme dependence most organizations have on IT today.

MANAGEMENT CONTROL

One of the fundamental roles of management in an organization is control. What is control? How do managers control the organization? This chapter seeks to answer these questions, particularly with respect to information systems.

Control Theory

Process control offers a useful model for thinking about control in general. Consider Figure 11-1, which shows a typical control system. In this system, an adjustable standard sets desired performance. A sensor determines actual conditions, and a comparison device compares the standard with what actually exists. If the difference between reality and the standard is too great, the comparison device sends a signal to take action. The action taken in turn affects the sensor and standard, and the cycle continues until the comparison device finds agreement between sensor and standard and stops signaling for action.

A real example of this model may be found in an automobile's cruise control system. A driver sets the adjustable standard—the speed desired—using the cruise control button. A sensor determines the car's speed, and a control unit compares the desired setting and

FIGURE 11-1 A control system.

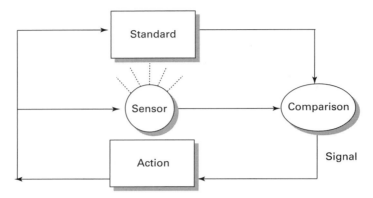

the current speed. If the difference between the two is too great, the cruise control system increases or decreases the throttle appropriately.

This example shows how a basic control system functions. In an organization, you can apply the same concepts. Managers set a notion of a standard, and they must become aware of deviations from the standard. Given that some indicator deviates from the standard, management must take action to bring the organization back into control.

Control in the Organization

Figure 11-2 shows some of the tools available to managers at different levels for controlling the organization. Top management can create control through the structure of the organization. For example, management can decide to decentralize and to have local managers responsible for comparing their performance with the goals the managers set for the year. As an alternative, top management can opt for a high degree of centralization so it can set policy and review all decisions.

The previous discussions of the T-Form organization suggest that in the future, management will have a more difficult time using traditional methods such as structure for control. Hierarchical structures are in retreat and managers will have to trust subordinates and come up with new ways to exercise their responsibility for control.

Top management also exerts control through the reward structure. Several brokerage firms suffered control breakdowns, partially because of a reward structure encouraging heavy risk taking in bond trading. The firms paid bond traders large bonuses based on performance because bond trading is highly competitive among firms. One firm found it lost well over $100 million in a few weeks when the market turned against its traders. A highly motivating reward system was accompanied by almost no managerial control over the traders. Two banks recently found losses of over $1 billion dollars in unauthorized trading, forcing one bank into a merger.

One form of managerial control that is used frequently and probably could have helped ameliorate the bond trader problem is the management committee. For many years, banks employed loan review committees. The lending officer adheres to a certain limit he or she

FIGURE 11-2 Tools of management control.

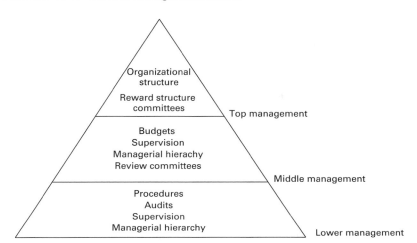

can approve on a loan. Any loan larger than the limit must be discussed and ultimately approved by the committee. The committee serves a review and control role in the firm.

The most frequent middle-management control device is the budget. Many managers in the organization receive periodic budget reports that inform them of actual versus targeted performance. Budgets are extremely important tools for controlling expenditures.

Middle managers are also expected to exert direct supervision over their subordinates, though more remote work makes this supervision difficult. When in doubt they can refer problems up through a managerial hierarchy. The entire structure of management serves to control the organization and keep it on course. Middle managers can also establish review committees to foster greater control.

At the lowest levels of management, various procedures indicate how operations should be done. Procedures were particularly evident in paperwork transactions processing departments. If one visited an accounts payable operation, it was possible to see clerks who carefully looked up each bill the firm received to find the purchase order that authorized the purchase. The clerk saw that the goods or services purchased actually arrived and delivery was satisfactory. Then the clerk authorized the payable and put all the documents relating to the payment into a voucher, which was filed for a number of years.

This kind of manual accounts payable operation is rapidly vanishing, which creates new control problems for the organization. Consider Chrysler's Pay as Built program where it calculates what it owes suppliers based on each day's production and sends an electronic payment. How does Chrysler know and how do its suppliers know the calculations and payment are correct? At some point in time, the number of components shipped to Chrysler should match the payments, but verifying these transactions could be a formidable task.

Regular, routine audits help to establish control by showing control is important and by sending the message that a form of quality control is exercised over all the firm's procedures, or at least those that affect the financial statements. Lower-level managers also have direct supervision responsibilities. They too can make use of the managerial hierarchy to obtain approvals or additional guidance.

Failure of Control

Often, a firm fails as a result of a control breakdown. The computer industry provides some notable examples of firms with few controls. In one case, while the single product the firm sold was in demand, it was possible for high sales to mask the lack of budgets and the absence of controls over expenditures. However, when demand for the product dropped, the failure to have a budget or to control expenditures pushed the firm into bankruptcy.

More recently, WorldCom filed for the largest bankruptcy in U.S. business history. The senior financial officers, who have since been arrested, are accused of inflating reported profits by burying expenses that should have been charged on the income statement in capital accounts so that the expenses would be depreciated over time. It is clear to everyone involved that this action is not proper accounting, and that the results misled investors about the company's earnings. In the WorldCom case, both senior and middle managers had to agree to make fraudulent accounting entries. What happened? Where were the controls that should have been in place to prevent erroneous charges? What was the company's public accounting firm doing on its audits? The answer to these questions should emerge in the next few years as investigations of the company continue.

Some business commentators feel that reward systems for senior managers cause these types of control failures. Stock options have become a popular way to motivate senior managers; if the price of the company's stock goes up, their options become more valuable, in some cases exceeding $100 million. The idea is to pay senior managers for performance, but did these options encourage managers to overstate performance? Top executives at WorldCom, Qwest, and Global Crossing made huge amounts of money on options before the stock price of their companies dropped precipitously. If these generous stock options encouraged these executives to overstate the company's performance, the companies need to review what controls can be implemented to prevent behavior that ultimately hurts shareholders' interest.

Information and Control

One contribution of information systems is to strengthen routine control systems; some of the control problems just described are new, and companies have yet to devise systems to prevent them. In general, a manager needs information about the deviation of actual from standard or targeted performance. Budget systems help managers identify exceptions and take action. Senior management may be able to take immediate action if sales are falling below projections. Managers may alter production schedules, emphasize different products, or begin to reduce expenditures.

Although information systems can help to improve managerial control, they create a tremendous control problem themselves. Information systems are complex. For example, it is likely no one person understands everything about a large system such as Sabre. Managers who do not necessarily understand the technology are responsible for seeing that information systems are under control.

CONTROL OF SYSTEMS DEVELOPMENT

An important area in which organizations face loss of control is in the development of new information systems. Each new system has a research flavor. It is difficult to predict how

SIDE BAR 11-1

A Few Control Problems

The following table shows some well-publicized examples of a breakdown in controls.

The combined total of all these problems is more than $3.5 billion in losses for the companies involved! Barings Bank had to merge with a Dutch company, which dismissed the senior management of the bank. General Electric sold Kidder Peabody, partially because of its trading losses, and the head of Daiwa Bank resigned after its loss became public.

In addition, a number of client companies are suing banks for losses they incurred trading derivatives. A derivative is a complex financial instrument whose value is linked to, or derived from, an underlying asset. This asset might be a stock or bond, a foreign currency, or a commodity to name a few.

Banks and brokerage firms are working to install systems to value complex derivatives, both to help them determine the prices of these instruments and to help control risk. Management wants to know the extent to which the firm is vulnerable if certain events happen, such as an increase in the prime rate or the devaluation of a foreign currency.

Name	Loss	Employer	Explanation
John Rusnak	$691 million	Allfirst (2002)	Trading losses over five years primarily in Japanese Yen; sentenced to seven-and-a-half years in jail.
Bing Sung	$162 million Problem in 1996, reported in 1998	RhumbLine (Boston Investment Advisor)	Charged with unauthorized options trading for the pension funds of AT&T and the state of Massachusetts.
Yasuo Hamanaka	$2.6 million	Sumitomo Corp. (1998)	Off-the-book copper trading, inventing fictitious deals to hide losses; pleaded guilty with prosecutors seeking a ten year sentence.
Toshihide Iguchi	$1.1 billion	Daiwa Bank (1995)	For eleven years hid bond trading losses trying to make up an original $200,000 loss.
Nicholas Leeson	$1.4 billion	Barings P.L.C. (1995)	Had control of trading records as well as doing trades; used futures contracts to bet on a rise in Japanese stocks. Barings forced to merge, Leeson sentenced to six-and-a-half years in Singapore.
Joseph Jett	$350 million	Kidder, Peabody (1994)	Fooled the accounting system into crediting him with $350 million in profits from fictitious trades, while real trading lost $100 million—he denies wrongdoing.
Victor Gomez	$70 million	Chemical Bank (1994)	Trader over-reached authority in trading Mexican pesos; loss occurred after devaluation of the peso.
Paul Mozer	$290 million	Salomon Brothers (1991)	Ignored new rules limiting the amount of securities a single dealer could buy at Treasury auctions by submitting false orders in the names of clients; served four months in jail and chairman of firm resigned.
Howard Rubin	$377 million	Merrill Lynch (1987)	Ignored instructions and took a risky position of $500 million in mortgage-backed securities.

long it will take and how much it will cost to develop something new. Because most systems contain components that are new, a great deal of uncertainty is inherent in development.

It is quite possible that the majority of information systems developed to date have suffered from being overbudget, from being beyond targeted completion time, or from not meeting their specifications. The vice president of finance for a large company told me that his rule was to double the time and the budget when he saw the proposal for any IT project. The task then, is for general management to control systems development.

The use of a package, if carefully selected, should reduce uncertainty because we can see the package and we know code exists that has been executed before installation. Visiting package clients who recently implemented it can provide some insights on what is involved, as can consultants who previously worked on package implementation.

Managers also help control development projects by attending review sessions and providing input. Projects slip for a number of reasons, including lack of user input, too few resources, too few individuals working on the project, and lack of management support. Managers who stay in close contact with the progress of a project are in a position to allocate new resources or to influence development priorities.

It is also important to be sure that the IT staff is concerned about project management. Many programmers and analysts view their profession as a craft-like trade. They feel that time spent managing a project is wasted and could be better spent in doing analysis or programming. Management must demonstrate that it wants projects to be controlled.

CONTROL OF OPERATIONS

In addition to controlling systems development, management must be concerned about controls over the operations of systems.

- At least twice before the collapse of the Soviet Union, air defense alarms signaled the launching of Soviet missiles aimed at the United States from both land bases and submarines. The first time, officers in charge of the system suspected something was wrong with the data. In flight, the missiles supposedly appeared on only one sensor and not on others. However, the defense command remained on alert status for more than five minutes, and fighter planes were sent aloft while the data were checked.

  The monitors were wrong. Through a human error, a connection was made between an off-line computer running a simulation exercise of the firing of land- and submarine-based missiles and the online computer monitoring air defense at the time. Because the test did not simulate data from all sensors, the officers in command were suspicious. What would have happened if the simulation were complete? (No details were released on the second incident.)

- Near the end of 1985, a computer problem at the Bank of New York nearly halted the Treasury bond market for twenty-eight hours. The computer program had a counter for the number of transactions that could reach as high as 32,000 items. On the day of the failure, the number of transactions exceeded 32,000 for the first time. The computer then stored each record on top of the last one, losing data and corrupting the database.

  This control failure rippled through the financial system. Because the Bank of New York did not know its position, it could not demand payment from

The year 2002 will be remembered in business as the year corporate governance failed in a number of large companies. WorldCom and Global Crossing declared bankruptcy, and several other well-known companies restated financial results for past years. Xerox paid a large fine to the SEC for accounting errors and incorrect financial statements. New legislation requires the CEO and CFO to sign and certify that financial statements are correct, and subjects them to possible prison terms for fraud if the company later has to restate the results they certified.

The problem for the CEO is that he or she usually does not get into how the company records transactions on its books; that job is delegated to the finance and accounting groups. In the case of WorldCom, $3.8 billion, and possibly as much as $11 billion, was incorrectly recorded as a capital charge rather than an operating expense. Because a capital investment is depreciated over a number of years, the result was to overstate profits each year; the company essentially postponed the recognition of expense items.

The CEO cannot audit the books, and yet must certify the financial statements as if she or he had. How can information technology help the CEO be sure that the financial statements he or she is asked to sign have been properly prepared? What kind of controls need to be in place to prevent a misstatement?

customers to settle trades. The bank had to borrow the cost of carrying the securities from the Federal Reserve and asked for $20 billion overnight. The interest on this loan was $4 million per day!

Because other banks were expecting to pay for the bonds, they had an extra $20 billion on hand overnight, causing the federal funds rate to plummet from 8 3/8 percent to 5 1/2 percent. When rumors of problems in the bond market emerge, traders buy platinum. The price for January platinum delivery rose $12.40 per ounce on a volume of nearly 12,000 contracts, a twenty-nine-year record at the New York Mercantile Exchange.

- A student at a major university introduced a virus or, more correctly, a worm, into one of the major networks connecting various computers. He is thought to have exploited a little-known opening in systems software to send a program to other computers. The program replicated itself and slowed the computers to a near standstill.

These examples all represent failure of control in the organization. For a control system to work, the organization must have a model of its desired states. Often, this model is in the form of routine procedures or generally accepted accounting practices. For problems such as controlling a sales representative, standards are less clear, as is our ability to influence behavior.

All levels of control in the organization are the responsibility of management. The Foreign Corrupt Practices Act makes operational control a legal as well as a normal management task. This act requires that publicly held companies devise and maintain a system of internal accounting controls sufficient to provide reasonable assurances of the following:

- Transactions are executed according to management authorization.
- Transactions are recorded as necessary to permit the preparation of financial statements according to generally accepted accounting principles.

- Records of assets are compared with existing assets at reasonable intervals, and action is taken when differences are noted.

- The Sarbanes-Oxley Act requires senior managers to sign the firm's financial statements and certify that the data in them is correct. There are severe penalties for managers who sign statements that turn out to be incorrect.

Information technology gives organizations the ability to process large numbers of transactions in an efficient manner. These same systems create significant control problems and challenges, however. With thousands of transactions processed in a short period of time, an error can spread through an immense number of transactions in minutes. Control failures can become costly and firms have been forced out of business because of their inability to control information processing activities.

Numerous opportunities for errors arise in processing. Figure 11-3 provides a diagram of the most difficult case: a client-server system with widespread connections outside the organization. The figure highlights eight areas where the system is vulnerable.

1. The operating systems for the client and server control the operations of the computers and allocate computer resources. Operating systems can and have been penetrated. They also have errors in coding, as does any other program. Someone who is unauthorized could gain access to a network through the operating system of the server, or possibly through a client machine. An intruder would masquerade as a legitimate client in order to gain access to the server's operating system.

2. Applications programs contain the logic of individual systems operated in the organization. These programs may have errors or may be incomplete in their editing and error checking for input and processing. The programs may execute

FIGURE 11-3 Components of a client server system.

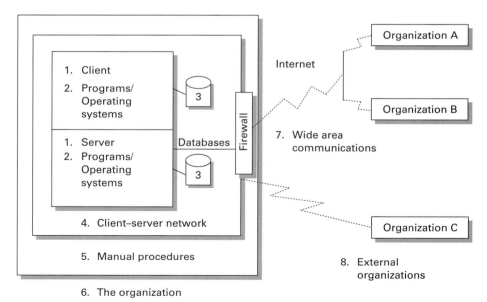

entirely on the client computer, or on some combination of the client and the server. The server might manage to replicate an error across all the clients using a certain program.

3. Databases exist on the server with local user data on the clients. Data are often proprietary or confidential within the organization. Measures need to be taken to make sure data are safe from accidents and that crucial data files on the server are backed up.

4. The entire network must operate reliably if transactions are to be processed effectively. If the network operating system is reliable and secure, outsiders will not be able to gain unauthorized access to company systems through the Internet.

5. Many applications have a number of associated manual procedures for the submission of input and the processing of output after it has been produced by the system. These procedures must be developed with adequate controls to ensure the accuracy and integrity of processing.

6. At a higher level than the individual user, the organization itself must be structured with control in mind. Management must take its responsibilities seriously and emphasize control.

7. Networks provide connectivity. Wide area communications links are subject to failure, penetration, and sabotage, especially the Internet, which opens the firm to access by millions of people.

8. Many systems are also available to external users from other organizations. These individuals may make mistakes or intentionally try to misuse a system. Controls must protect the system from these users and the users from themselves.

CONTROL AND ELECTRONIC COMMERCE

The extent of concern over security on the Internet varies. Some experts feel that Net security is a major issue, while others dismiss security as unimportant. The major issue concerns the transmission of credit card information to a merchant when you order merchandise over the Web. The concerns focus on the chances of your credit card number being intercepted and misused or that someone will figure out how to break into a computer file containing thousands or millions of credit card numbers and misuse them.

Some credit card companies have said that they will not hold a customer liable for unauthorized charges on a credit card number used in electronic commerce. Their objective is to encourage electronic commerce (and the use of their credit cards). Also, the major Web browsers support encrypted transmission of sensitive data. A server must run corresponding software so that the browser can communicate with it using encrypted data. (Encrypted data are coded in some way that is difficult for someone intercepting the message to decode without knowing the key that was used for encoding.)

Credit card companies have developed a standard called secure electronic transmission (SET), which offer stronger protection than the encryption currently in browsers. A number of firms offer secure payment schemes such as PayPal, which eBay purchased. It appears that sufficient options provide confidence in electronic commerce. Many credit card users report being relatively careless with the second copies of their credit card

SIDE BAR 11-2

Your Tax Dollars at Work

The major information technology modernization drive of the Internal Revenue Service (IRS) is one of the largest IT project failures in history. Some $4 billion dollars was invested in this effort, which produced little in the way of new functionality or service. In a study of the Tax System Modernization (TSM) project, Professor Barry Bozeman of the Georgia Institute of Technology, examined a number of alternative explanations for this massive failure. Pricewaterhouse Coopers Endowment for the Business of Government provided support for the study.

Even though TMS is widely considered to be a failure, information technology has taken major steps forward at the IRS. The agency now has a prize-winning Web site that contains a great deal of useful information and access to tax forms that can be easily downloaded and printed on a PC. The IRS is also working to create systems that can match all of the various 1099 forms for interest, dividends, and other payments with your tax return to check for underreported income. The IRS continues to expand its electronic filing program, a program that had serious problems when first introduced, but that now is much more successful.

What happened to the TSM program in the 1990–1996 time period? Despite complaints, the IRS has a history as a well-managed agency, and the TSM included capable and talented people and outside assistance. Professor Bosworth reviewed more than 100 IRS reports and more than 100 reports from oversight agencies and critics; he also interviewed a large number of IRS employees. From his work, Professor Bosworth developed a series of lessons learned and recommendations for managing large-scale IT projects.

Today's IRS collects more than $2 trillion in gross revenue each year, which is more than 95 percent of the federal government's total revenue. It employs more than 100,000 people to process in excess of 230 million tax returns. In 2001, 42.3 million taxpayers filed electronically, a number the IRS projects to increase to 73 million or about 50 percent of individual tax returns by 2007. The IT infrastructure for the IRS includes 40 mainframes, 872 mid-range computers, more than 100,000 personal computers (desktop, laptop, and PDAs), almost 2,800 vendor-supplied software products, and 50 million lines of IRS-owned and maintained computer code. Still, the IRS is most vulnerable in its master file of taxpayers, which is based on 1960s technology, magnetic tapes, and a number of near-retirement assembly language programmers.

The TSM began with a prestigious panel of advisors and heavy involvement by IRS personnel. The people working on the project developed a long list of new systems to be developed, and some of these systems spun out of control and had to be cancelled. The most embarrassing failure was the Document Processing System, which was projected to cost $1.3 billion. The system was supposed to scan paper returns and convert them into machine readable data for IRS computers. This DPS was a critical link in the modernization system; it would account for the bulk of front-end processing, taking care of all paper returns while other subsystems took returns from the phone and the Internet. This optical recognition system was to accept a large variety of IRS forms. The DPS system was scrapped after an expenditure of $284 million. The problem was that technology was insufficient for the IRS's need to read forms that included handwritten and typewritten information, and sometimes notes stuck to the form.

The good news is that the IRS has learned from the TSM experience. The Agency has a new strategic plan, and a new mission that is to provide the highest levels of taxpayer service possible, not just collect revenue (though Congress did impose the customer service goal on the IRS). The recent CIOs at the IRS have had considerable experience in government or industry, and the agency has more technical expertise available than in the past. It also has a prime contractor, Computer Sciences Corporation, to help develop and implement IT. The agency still lacks a high-performance, integrated IT system, but one of its goals is to create that system.

Today the agency is seeking to establish an overall IT architecture for a set of new systems that will accommodate all tax administration functions. To achieve this architecture, the agency plans to define a sequence of targeted and manageable-sized projects to implement the architecture. One of these steps has been the creation of the Web portals described earlier. The agency converted tape-based master files to a modern database for the simplest tax returns of the last five years, about 6 million in number.

A number of theories attempt to explain what went wrong with TSM, and it is possible that all of the following conditions in some way contributed to the failure of TSM and a $4 billion investment with little return.

(Continues)

SIDE BAR 11-2 *(CONTINUED)*

Your Tax Dollars at Work

1. *Task complexity and difficulty.* Although a large and complex task, Professor Bosworth does not feel that it was unattainable. It included demands for interoperability among systems, but other government agencies have such demands. The IRS has a huge master file, but so does the Social Security Administration, which makes monthly payments. The IRS has limited time deadlines—the government does not pay interest on your refund, so if it takes a month or two months to process it, the cost to the government is the same. Vendors of commercial database products have experience with large databases, and the computing power to process the data is certainly available.

2. *Insufficient technical resources.* During the TSM era, the IRS did lack in-house managers with a good understanding of information technology. However, the agency could have relied more on the private sector for technology expertise. Some evidence indicates that personnel problems probably did contribute to the failure of TSM.

3. *Inadequate contracting and outsourcing.* Reactions to outsourcing are mixed within the agency; some managers think it is the only way to go, and others feel contractors do not "pull their weight." In general, the people interviewed for this report agree that the IRS does not have a history of the effective use of outside contractors, and that this problem exacerbated the TSM project problems.

4. *Flawed organization culture.* Professor Bosworth's interviews showed that most see IRS management-level employees as insular and distrustful of outsiders. For many years the agency did not recruit outside the IRS, leading to a lot of insularity. A long-standing animosity between headquarters and the field is also not at all unusual in distributed organizations. A risk-averse attitude meant that some managers did not want to get involved modernizing critical systems. This kind of organization culture can undermine change, modernization, and efforts to introduce new technology.

5. *Failures of internal management and leadership.* One persistent problem with TSM was turnover. CIOs changed about every two years, and the project lasted through the terms of five commissioners. Lower-level IT employees also turned over almost completely during the project. Those working on the project felt hindered by senior management's lack of knowledge of IT. The agency also lacked experience in project management. All of these problems contributed to the failure of TSM.

6. *Public sector constraints.* Some problems that affected TSM came from the features of the civil service system, contracting, and procurement policies of the federal government, and other unique attributes of a public agency. Professor Bosworth feels one of the biggest problems was Congress providing the IRS with too many resources too quickly, and with too little oversight.

TSM is widely regarded as a failed project, and that is probably a fair assessment. The IRS did learn some things, and some equipment and software it purchased for the project is still being used. Professor Bosworth offers some lessons that apply beyond the IRS when considering large IT projects:

1. Be sure that you know how to manage a project, or get help to do so.

2. If you want to make major changes using IT, assess the culture first. You may need to change the organization before you can change the technology.

3. Beware of receiving a huge project budget; you need to plan and manage a large project.

4. If you contract out, you still have to provide management from within the organization. Outsourcing does not mean that managers in the organization no longer have responsibility for a project and its day-to-day management.

It is important to learn from our failures, or we will surely repeat them in the future.

SOURCE: B. Bozeman, *Government Management of Information Mega-Technology: Lessons from the Internal Revenue Service's Tax Modernization*, The PricewaterhouseCoopers Endowment for the Business of Government, March 2002.

MANAGEMENT PROBLEM 11-2

Terry Anderson is the CIO for Chicago Scientific, a company that manufactures and distributes scientific instruments for weather forecasting, among other products. Chicago Scientific makes a series of electronic recording barometers and thermometers. It also has a complete home weather station that includes instruments to tell wind direction and speed as well as humidity, air pressure, and temperature. The company sells through a number of outlets including a variety of catalogs, marine stores, and home centers.

Terry found a disorganized systems effort when he arrived, including a variety of PCs and a medium-sized computer. After a six-month study, Terry and a task force of managers decided that they should implement parts of an ERP system, and selected Oracle as the vendor. Chicago Scientific will start with Oracle financials, and then expand to some of the company's other ERP

modules. He wants the first part of the implementation to go well so that everyone in the company will gain confidence in the strategy and package.

Terry has a number of concerns about the project, "In many respects implementing a package is more risky than a custom system. With a custom system we always tried to design what our users wanted, now they have to adapt to the package. Also, with a custom system, it took some time to do the design and implement it—with a package we are ready to go right away."

How should Anderson and Chicago Scientific control the ERP implementation project? What kinds of tools are available to assist a project manager with this kind of task? How do you justify taking time and resources from the project in order to use a management tool?

charges, eventually discarding them without tearing them in pieces. It would be far easier to find these discarded copies than obtain an individual's credit card number as it travels over the Internet, particularly if it is encrypted in any way. The possibility of someone breaking into a server containing lists of credit cards is probably more serious, and vendors must be careful to protect such information.

SECURITY

The Internet opened up a myriad of opportunities for individuals who like to disrupt the lives of others. It also led to an industry of security firms and products devoted to trying to thwart the attackers. You undoubtedly run a virus checking program on your computer; these programs are widely available, some for free and some at a price. Companies that take credit cards online do so through an SSL or secure sockets layer server that employs cryptography to hide sensitive data. For an individual user that level of security may be enough, but for an organization, security is a major concern. A corporation may devote considerable resources to looking for attacks on its network and to stopping them. The tools used include firewalls, monitoring programs, and monitoring firms.

Most organizations connected to the Internet do so through a server that acts as a firewall between the organization's computers and the Internet. The internal network routes all Internet traffic through the firewall. The firewall computer's software contains rules about what messages are to be allowed to pass, and what messages and Web sites are to be blocked. The firewall means that the IT staff in a company in theory does not have to be concerned about the security of every computer on its network; instead it relies on the firewall to protect all computers on the network. This theory does not always work, for example, when a user connects a laptop that has picked up a virus on a trip to the company network *behind* the firewall. A partial solution is a host-based firewall, a layer of software inside your desktop computer that warns you of suspicious activity involving your machine.[1]

You can retain a company to examine a log of attempts to connect to your firm's network, and determine which of these are hostile threats versus ordinary business transactions. With this information, you can figure out how to better protect your network from attack. In addition to safeguarding against attack, you need to create a system that will recover gracefully after a security breach. You would like your system to "fail well" and come back up quickly with no damage.

AUDITING INFORMATION SYSTEMS

Accounting firms developed procedures for conducting an audit of information systems because so many of their typical clients' transactions are processed by computer. The auditors are most concerned about systems that affect financial statements, the balance sheet, and income statements. Auditors also render an opinion about the viability of the firm. If critical information systems are not well controlled, the future of the firm is in doubt.

The auditor examines a system as a whole, focusing on controls and their effectiveness. Typically the auditor runs programs to examine databases and transactions. These programs verify the logic used in processing. Many large organizations have internal auditors who continually examine information systems. Based on the preceding discussion of the places where an organization is vulnerable, the task of auditing a technologically complex system is not a trivial one. Many managers are concerned about the threats posed by a system that has a major breakdown but continues processing and producing erroneous results.

MANAGEMENT ISSUES

Many of you will eventually be responsible for systems in your functional areas of business. You are likely to confront the following issues in this role?

- *Backup.* It is extremely important to have backup for systems, including off-site data storage. After September 11, firms with backup data and systems were able to set up systems in other locations and get back in business. Firms without backup had a much more difficult time recovering from this disaster.

- *Security.* Personal computers present a host of security problems because they are so accessible. Users routinely leave diskettes, zip drives, or memory sticks containing important data lying around, and few users physically lock their computers or use start-up password protection programs. As a manager, you will have to decide how much security is necessary to safeguard the data and systems for which you are responsible.

- *Keeping to the budget.* The appetite that users have for technology seems to be insatiable. Yet, the organization cannot afford to buy all of the technology users want, at least not in any one year. The goal is to exert budgetary control at the same time as setting priorities for acquiring hardware and software and developing new systems.

■ *Project management.* As mentioned earlier, IT projects frequently lose control. If you have the ultimate responsibility for a development project, you will need to be sure the project is under control. Consider using a project management system to track and monitor progress so you end up with a finished system rather than any unpleasant surprises.

■ *Control over data.* The accuracy of data used in making decisions is always an important management consideration. As we develop more distributed databases, accuracy and consistency among different copies of the same data will become a critical issue for control.

CHAPTER SUMMARY

1. At the highest level, management control over technology deals with planning, organizing, and monitoring information processing.

2. At this highest level, management establishes plans and policies, assesses the technology, and looks for ways to apply information processing creatively.

3. Coordination across the corporation is one major control problem for senior management.

4. Middle-level managers in various divisions and locations share many of the same problems as top management. These local managers need to devise organizational structures and management policy for information processing in the areas for which they are responsible.

5. Both groups of managers also must relate to information processing managers. In some corporations, a chief information officer will provide coordination and help local management obtain more from its investment in computing.

6. All levels of management are responsible for operational controls, though usually the details will be left to middle and lower management in the firm.

7. Information processing systems process vital transactions for the firm. They must have adequate controls built in because they can go wrong in many places.

8. The information services department must have control over the ongoing operation of systems.

9. Management issues for controlling IT include backup, security, keeping within the budget, and project management.

10. As an individual and as a manager, you are concerned about malicious programs that can damage computers, networks, and, ultimately, the organization.

KEYWORDS

Audit	Electronic commerce	Security
Backup	Firewall	Systems development
Budget	Fraud	Virus
Control	Operations	Worm
Data	Reward structure	

RECOMMENDED READINGS

Austin, R. D., and Darby, C. A. R. 2003. The myth of secure computing. *Harvard Business Review, 81*(6), pp. 120–126.

David, J. S., Schuff, D., and St. Louis, R. 2002. Managing your IT total cost of ownership. *Communications of the ACM, 45*(1), pp. 101–106.

Lederer, A., and Prasad, J. 1992. Nine management guidelines for better cost estimating. *Communications of the ACM, 35*(2), pp. 50–59. (This paper discusses cost estimating, an important part of controlling projects.)

Meinel, C 1998. How hackers break in . . . and how they are caught. *Scientific American,* October. (The first article of several in this issue about computer break-ins and security.)

Scott, J. E., and Vessey, I. 2002. Managing risks in enterprise systems implementation. *Communications of the ACM, 45*(4), pp. 74–81.

Weber, R. 1999. *Information Systems Control and Audit.* Upper Saddle River, NJ: Prentice-Hall. (An excellent text on audit and control.)

DISCUSSION QUESTIONS

1. What are senior management's problems in controlling information processing?

2. Why should users worry about a virus?

3. How can users avoid getting a virus on their PCs?

4. What is the difference between a virus and a worm?

5. Why is control over systems important for users?

6. What are the issues in managing and controlling data given today's trends in technology?

7. Will controls ever completely protect systems?

8. What are the major control systems that exist in most organizations?

9. What are a manager's concerns with respect to a budget for IT activities in his or her department?

10. What kind of backup plan would you recommend for fellow students?

11. What are the threats to an interorganizational system?

12. To what extent do security concerns inhibit electronic commerce? What are some solutions?

13. Have computer systems made fraud easier? Do you think more or less can be embezzled from a computer system than from a manual system?

14. How is it possible to detect fraud if widespread collusion occurs among IS personnel and management?

15. Why do you think viruses are created and spread?

16. What problems can viruses cause a PC user?

17. What kind of file backup procedures are needed in the average organization?

18. Can a worm hurt a LAN that only operates within a company?

19. Why audit a system?

20. Why do companies create *firewalls* between their systems and the Internet?

21. Can an information system be over-controlled? What might happen under such conditions?

22. Describe how a virus actually works. What kind of files does it want to infect?

23. What do you think of computer break-ins? Are they harmless pranks or do they cause serious damage?

24. What devices does management use to control the organization?

25. How does organizational structure influence control?

26. How do budgets exert control?

ENDNOTES

1. *Technology Review,* September 2002.

CHAPTER 12

THE LEGACY ENVIRONMENT

A Manager's Perspective

Programmers used assembly language to program the first generation of computers, and assembly language was unique to each manufacturer's computer. That practice left no possibility of running an assembly language program for an IBM computer on a Univac computer. When the second generation of computers appeared, most companies happily converted their programs because the number of applications was small. We began to see movement toward higher-level languages away from assembly language, because programmers were more productive with these languages, coupled with the hope that programs could run on different machines. When the third generation of computers came along in 1964, computer vendors offered ways to simulate old computers on the new ones so customers could take their time converting to the new computers. No one understood how painful that process would be, and most users swore that they would never again go through that kind of conversion. Customers now want open systems using software that one computer vendor does not control. In theory open systems are easy, in practice even open software present difficulties—consider the different versions of Unix, which is one of the most open operating systems.

The fact remains that a system becomes a legacy system the day you implement it. You can stretch the life of a system for many years, which is why so many mainframe legacy systems are still around. If you invested in a system with millions of lines of code, and if a vendor such as IBM continues to make faster and faster computers to run the system, you feel little incentive to reprogram it. A tough management decision is when and how you need to upgrade or replace a legacy system. It is likely that you will be involved in such a decision more than once in your career.

The term *legacy system* carries a negative connotation, suggesting that one is working with old, outdated technology. One day a CIO from a successful dot-com company complained that he had to replace his legacy systems of two years ago! The company, in its rush to get started, built its Internet services quickly without paying much attention to the quality of the system; the emphasis was on speed and time to market. Now the company needed to go back and replace code written only months earlier. His comments drove home the point that code and computers become legacies at the moment of installation.

To most people, a legacy system is an older application running on an IBM mainframe computer. For many years, the mainframe was the workhorse of computing; it could handle the largest jobs short of the supercomputers required to solve massive scientific problems. Beginning in the 1960s, programmers wrote code for mainframe applications in COBOL, a computer language designed for processing business data. This kind of technology was expensive compared to client–server architectures, and was difficult to adapt to the Internet.

This chapter explores how and why legacy systems exist and looks at the challenges that an information technology architecture poses for management. To illustrate these issues, the chapter examines the IT architecture of Victor Electronics, a company with a number of legacy systems and a lot of questions about what to do next.

THE IT ARCHITECTURE AT VICTOR ELECTRONICS

Chapter 1 introduced Victor Electronics, a manufacturer of electronic components used in devices such as computers, cell phones, and game consoles. The company grew internally and through occasional acquisitions. John Roberts, the new chief operating officer, also brought in a new chief information officer, Nancy Scott, when he joined Victor.

Nancy spent her first few months on the job trying to understand the IT architecture at the company. "If you look at our IT architecture from the outside, it doesn't make much sense," she said. (See Figure 12-1.) "We have a huge mixture of equipment from different vendors, which is not all that unusual. Past management has not been interested in investing

FIGURE 12-1 Victor Electronics IT architecture.

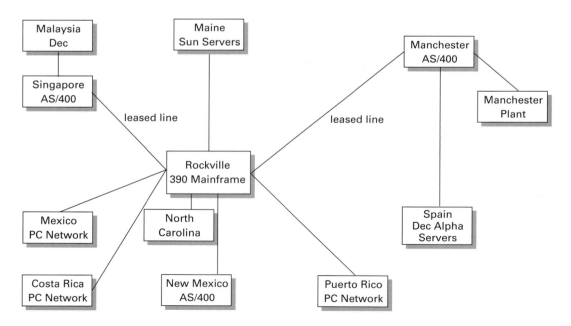

All locations have local connections to the Internet.
All lines not designated as leased are dial-up.

in IT, so they bought what was cheap at the time. We also responded to fashion in the computer industry just like everyone else. Finally, Victor bought some other companies, inheriting the IT architecture they had in place. Now, if you look at IT throughout the entire company, we are talking a lot of money. Is our architecture costing us more than it should? Is the architecture adequate to support what we want to do? Does it give us the option to undertake new initiatives?"

The Mainframe in Rockville

Without question, the biggest legacy system is in Rockville and uses an IBM 3090 series computer and associated software. Rockville is corporate headquarters and the sales office for the Americas; its computer also provides processing for the North Carolina plant, which is the largest Victor plant in the world. Dedicated, leased lines connect terminals in North Carolina to the Rockville facility. Most of the programming for this computer is in COBOL, and the major applications include order entry, financial statements and accounting, inventory, especially work-in-process and finished goods inventory, warehousing, and shipping.

Victor wrote the order entry system itself, in something called a fourth-generation language, a language that was designed to be at a higher level than COBOL, and therefore easier to use. These languages were very popular in the 1980s as a way to increase programmer productivity. Unfortunately, the language is no longer being used extensively, and the future of this system is not clear. The accounting and financial statement system is an application that Victor bought and installed last year, so it is fairly modern. The major production system started as an IBM package for work-in-process control. Over the years, Victor modified the package heavily, finally rewriting most of it in COBOL.

Victor also tried to write a series of programs to help allocate and plan production. This production control task is complex because Victor may allocate an order for a part to one of several plants or even split a large order among plants. Planning production involves looking at the capacity of each plant, and its order backlog, and then trying to determine the best place to manufacture. A group at Victor worked for two years on this problem, and eventually developed a system. However, the system proved difficult to use and not all that effective in scheduling, so the production planners requested that the IT staff turn it off. At the present time, production planners allocate production to plants using manual methods and an occasional Excel spreadsheet.

Rockville and all of Victor's locations do have local area networks, PCs for all clerical and professional workers, and many plant PCs for collecting data on production and work-in-process inventories. Most managers and other professionals have Internet connections as well.

Singapore

In 1964, IBM announced its third-generation computer, the 360, built with integrated circuits instead of transistors and other components on individual circuit cards. For the first time, a computer needed an operating system to run, and IBM expected most applications to be written in higher-level languages such as COBOL. The conversion from assembly language for second-generation computers to the IBM 360 turned out to be more difficult, more expensive, and to take longer than anyone predicted. As a result, an IBM mainframe today can execute the same instruction as the computers in the 1960s, along with other

SIDEBAR 12-1

Reports on the Death of the Mainframe are Premature

In 2003 IBM brought out a new mainframe named T-Rex, a jab at those who call mainframes dinosaurs. The official name of the line is the Z990 eServer, and IBM invested $1 billion to develop it. In a down market, mainframe sales dropped the least, and analysts think the IBM will increase its mainframe sales with the new series. IBM is encouraging users to adopt Linux for the operating system on this series. It is estimated mainframes account for only 3 percent of IBM's total sales, but that it derives 25 percent of its revenue and 45 percent of its profit from the sale of mainframes and their software.

Large processing jobs still run on mainframe computers: jobs such as handling social security payments, recording trillions of dollars in currency exchanges, settling trades on the NYSE, and similar activities. Winnebago Industries planned to buy servers with Intel chips to run e-mail for 1,500 employees at a cost of $75,000. Instead the company spent $25,000 and added e-mail to its mainframe. A regional department store chain found that it was adding a new server every month and every twelve servers required an employee to manage them. For half the cost of fifteen to twenty servers the company bought a ZSeries mainframe.

It is possible to run multiple copies of Linux at one time, creating a series of virtual servers on the mainframe. One organization runs twenty-six virtual Linux servers on a ZSeries mainframe to manage a variety of applications. The organization can run Linux on the mainframe for 40 percent of what it would cost to run the same programs on any other server, according to a spokesperson.

At the same time, other firms are moving away from mainframes to Linux servers from other vendors. Sabre Holdings is migrating its airfare-pricing applications from IBM mainframes to HP NonStop servers, and Galileo International, another CRS vendor, is replacing IBM mainframes with Sun servers for an airfare-pricing system that the company says will save tens of millions of dollars in programming and hardware maintenance costs. Sun Microsystems claims to have helped 1,000 customers move from IBM mainframes to Sun servers.

No agreement has emerged on the best hardware strategy, at least among the companies described here. The jury is still out, but it looks as if the mainframe is alive and well, and may even be enjoying some increased sales.

SOURCES: *The Wall Street Journal,* May 3, 2003; and *InfoWeek,* October 21, 2002.

---

instructions that have been added. One reason this architecture is considered legacy is because it has to be able to run the programs developed for earlier computers, and therefore carries forty years of history with it.

When it came time to bring out additional lines of computers, one development group within IBM wanted to replace the 360 with yet another architecture, one that would be easier for programmers to use and therefore more productive for customers. Those in IBM arguing for compatibility with the 360 won because of fears that customers would revolt if required to move to a new computer and reprogram everything once again. However, the new architecture advocates were allowed to develop a midrange computer, and the AS/400 is what came from their efforts. The computer contained a database management system that is integrated with the operating system, and features a relatively easy programming language to use called Report Program Generator (RPG). Organizations report great productivity with the AS/400, and it proved to be a popular computer for distributed processing, that is, for placing a medium-sized computer at different plant or office locations. Today IBM sells its iSeries servers as an upgrade path for AS/400 users; these servers run a version of the OS/400 operating system.

Victor, like many other companies with a headquarters location and a number of distributed offices and plants, invested heavily in the AS/400. The company hoped to share some synergies in application development by having different locations prepare applications that could be used across the company. Unfortunately, most local managers felt their applications were unique; they made little effort to develop programs that could be used elsewhere and resisted adopting systems written in another location.

In Singapore, Victor only has a sales office and warehouse, and the local staff developed its own applications for order entry and inventory control. In addition to the AS/400, the different locations have access to a LAN and local PCs with connectivity to the Internet. The major issue facing Singapore is the demand of customers to place orders over the Internet as well as by phone, fax, and EDI connection.

Manchester, United Kingdom

Manchester is the European sales office, so many applications are similar to those in Singapore. As more and more original equipment manufacturers and contract manufacturers move to Asia to take advantage of lower wage rates, Victor expects that much of its European business will migrate to Asia. The AS/400 in Manchester also supports production control and plant accounting for a small manufacturing facility on the outskirts of the city.

Malaysia

The Malaysian plant came to Victor through the acquisition of another company. The plant is fairly autonomous, and Victor's IS group left it alone. Unfortunately, the plant is using rather obsolete technology that has not been updated in years; it runs DEC minicomputers with the VMS operating system. Compaq bought DEC and phased out most of its product lines. Now that Compaq and Hewlett-Packard have merged, the migration path for older DEC customers is even more murky. Nancy Scott knows that she must do something in Malaysia, but is afraid of making a local decision until she develops a plan for a global IT architecture for Victor.

Spain

The Spanish plant is another acquisition; this one has DEC equipment, with Alpha servers running Unix. DEC always had good technology, but it had management problems in sales and support, and it missed the PC revolution. A few years before the Compaq purchase, DEC engineers developed a high-speed, 64-bit chip called *alpha* and used it as the CPU for a series of servers running Unix. In the late 1980s and early 1990s, customers thought that "open" operating systems and software offered many advantages. Open contrasts with the closed or proprietary systems that individual vendors controlled, systems such as OS/390 and OS/400 at IBM. If you began using proprietary systems, you felt locked in to them because of the high costs of conversion.

The advantage of Unix is that it runs across a variety of computers, and no one vendor controls Unix. The hope was that all vendors would adopt a single version of this operating system, but unfortunately, they did not and different vendors have different versions of the system. However, the situation is far better than with single-vendor, proprietary operating systems.

The plant in Spain has no immediate needs to upgrade or change its software, so Nancy feels little pressure for a decision on where to go next. With the merger of HP and Compaq, the DEC alpha chip is going to be consigned to history. HP is committed to the Itanium 64-bit chip that it developed jointly with Intel. Nancy has yet to determine what might be involved in a conversion. The operating system should not be much of a problem because DEC and HP both feature variations of Unix. However, the applications programs for the alpha chip probably will not run on the Itanium chip, so to convert to Itanium will require compliers or conversion programs to move from the alpha chip. The major applications at the Spanish plant are manufacturing, inventory control, and accounting.

Maine

The plant in Maine has always been a bit unique. Nancy and John Roberts are not sure exactly why, but for some reason this plant was able to get approval to buy Sun servers that run Sun's version of Unix called Solaris. Although not fitting with the rest of the architecture at Victor, at least the equipment and applications are modern.

New Mexico

New Mexico has a small AS/400s and runs packaged software that the plant purchased, including an ERP package written in RPG. Even though Victor as a whole was never able to choose an ERP package, or to decide to go into ERP, New Mexico convinced someone at headquarters that it had the capability to implement ERP on the AS/400. The plant manager told Nancy Scott that he had sold the idea to headquarters as a prototype for acquiring the ERP software for all of the plants running AS/400s. However, he never formed any kind of task force from the other plants, and they all reacted with the well-known, "not invented here syndrome," showing complete disinterest despite the fact that the system works quite well in New Mexico.

Mexico, Puerto Rico, and Costa Rica

Victor built and equipped each of these small plants in the 1990s, and the IT group was convinced that the cheapest approach to technology was networked PCs with custom-written code. Four programmers and analysts worked in Puerto Rico to develop a system for tracking production through the plants, and then installed it in Mexico and Costa Rica. These plants receive shipments from other plants and do some finishing work, so scheduling production there is not particularly complex.

Communications and Networking

One of Nancy's major concerns is with the current telecommunications infrastructure at Victor. Most locations seem to be satisfied with their local area networks, PCs on the desktop, and Internet connections for office workers. However, the communications among plants and the sales offices are less impressive. For the most part, the plants communicate with the sales offices and with Rockville through dial-up and leased lines.

Each night local time, the IBM mainframe in Rockville and the AS/400s exchange information on the status of finished goods inventory in the United States, Asia, and

MANAGEMENT PROBLEM 12-1

Stardust Hotels has a mainframe reservations system that is fifteen years old and runs on IBM legacy mainframe computers. The system is one of the company's most important assets because it is the primary interface between Stardust and its customers. An increasing number of customers are accessing it through the Internet, while others call a toll-free number and talk to a reservations agent who also uses the system. The legacy computer is also connected to airline CRSs because the airlines often sell a hotel reservation with a plane ticket.

Mark Spencer, the Stardust CIO, admits that the reservations system is one of the applications that troubles him the most. "It is a little bit like having an old car that you really like, but you don't have the instruction manual anymore, and you worry that parts may not be available soon. In addition, the car has managed to become a part of your life and connects you to many activities. The system works well, but after fifteen years and a lot of changes, the code is really hard to

follow. We had to do modifications to interface with the airline CRS, and to enable customers to access the system through a Web interface."

Spencer continued, "It is hard to convince management to fix something that doesn't look to them like it is broken. Is the reservations system like a bridge that is slowly corroding, and someday will drop into the river without warning? I don't think it's that bad, but we have to monitor this system to be sure that it keeps working. We could start over again with a clean sheet to design a new system, but I'm not sure you'd see that much new functionality from a new design. So we might invest $20 million for a system that doesn't look much different from the one we replace. We would simply sleep better knowing that we could maintain the new one more easily than the old. That's a lot of money to ask for peace of mind."

What do you recommend to Mark and Stardust? Should they replace the legacy reservations system with something new?

Europe. The idea is to allow sales order representatives in each country to sell inventory that is at another location if they do not have any of a particular product a customer wants. It turns out that the company has some complex transfer pricing rules in effect, which discourage these kinds of sales. In addition, the actual steps the representative has to go through to arrange shipment from say, Rockville to Hong Kong, are much more difficult than selling from one's own inventory. Finally, the inventory information is not real-time because it is only updated once a day.

As a result, Victor rarely takes advantage of the fact that one region has inventory that would be useful to another. John Roberts learned about this problem shortly after he arrived at Victor, and he has asked Nancy for a solution. She realizes that the problem extends beyond technology to the attitudes of Victor employees in various countries, and to accounting procedures that discourage the development of a global inventory visible to sales representatives around the world. Both she and John are aware that the result of all of these problems is that Victor provides poorer service than it could, and encourages costly duplication when Europe manufactures a product that is in inventory in Singapore.

Web Site ASP

When the Internet began to capture everyone's imagination, Victor's previous management knew that it did not have the skills to develop a Web site. The company first went to a local entrepreneur who developed and hosted a site for Victor on a PC server that the local company owned. This first site was fairly crude, but it still attracted a number of visits. Engineers at Victor began putting product specifications on the site, and even developed a couple of innovative simulation programs that showed potential customers how some of its products worked.

As the demands on the site grew, it became clear that the local provider could not support a sophisticated Web presence for Victor. However, Victor itself still lacked the ability to develop and host its own site. It turned to an applications service provider (ASP), AmericaNet, one of the largest at that time. AmericaNet did set up an attractive site and built some Internet-based sales applications for Victor. Unfortunately, the ASP business experienced problems in the business downturn of 2001 and 2002, and AmericaNet went through a planned bankruptcy, reemerging as a much smaller company. Nancy's question now is whether the company will be an ongoing business and whether Victor can stay with them for Web hosting. Should Victor develop the capabilities to do this task itself? Should it turn its Web site over to a more established firm such as IBM?

Why This Architecture?

Victor developed an IT architecture that looks like Figure 12-1. Part of the reason for its disparate equipment and incompatible applications comes from the lack of planning and attention to IT. Victor's management has never been technologically oriented or sophisticated; they tended to look at IT as a cost and not an investment. John Roberts believes in the value of technology, which is the reason he hired Nancy Scott. Nancy, however, cannot start with a clean sheet of paper because of what she inherited in the way of equipment and systems.

Nancy sees the following issues based on her first review at Victor:

- Solving the connectivity problem and compatibility problems for global inventory (inventory that is kept on different systems in different databases)

- Whether to keep the legacy mainframe and the applications or convert to something else such as Unix or Linux, and whether to adopt an ERP package and production planning

- Whether to keep and upgrade the AS/400s and let them remain a standard for the plants

- How to take advantage of e-commerce and make greater use of the Internet

Table 12-1 presents some of the options that Nancy and Victor have for making a major improvement in the company's IT systems and operations.

Victor cannot simply start over, because it cannot afford to replace all of its equipment with new computers, and to build a new set of applications at one time. Even if it could hire enough qualified analysts and programmers, Nancy wonders whether the organization could handle that much change at one time. In addition, a task this massive would require a long development period, so that the benefits would come far into the future. Nancy is not ready to recommend the "do it yourself, begin again" option to John Roberts.

Victor could also look into outsourcing or "computing on demand." An outsourcer would take over Victor's IT operations, and Victor would negotiate a contract with a vendor such as IBM or HP to meet the company's computing needs. However, Victor would still have to upgrade its applications and go through some major conversions; just changing from owning its computers to having someone else provide computing power for current applications would not be much of an advance.

TABLE 12-1 Victor's options for turning around its IT.

Option	Pros	Cons
Start over	A complete new architecture, hardware, networks, new up-to-date applications	Far too costly and disruptive to Victor; would take a long period of time
Outsource	Obtain needed expertise quickly, outsourcer with highly professional staff	Need to manage outsourcing; ability of Victor to cope with major change
On demand computing	A relatively new approach that would reduce IT investment in equipment	Newness, lack of seasonality requiring unused capacity (What is the advantage of on demand here?)
Install a number of packages	Victor gets debugged programs that it can see in use other places; faster than writing own	Costly, implementation is not trivial, integrating packages, change management at Victor
Incrementalism	Make small improvements where possible, avoid major disruptions	The problems are so large that this approach is unlikely to provide a turnaround
Develop a vision for IT and a plan	The first step Victor should take, possibly with help from consultants	Will delay a solution, but should save time and money in the long term

Another possibility is to acquire a series of packages to accomplish all of Victor's processing. Certainly an ERP package would help automate many of the routine transactions, but it, too, would require a long time to implement. In addition, Victor badly needs production planning and scheduling systems, so it would have to implement a number of packages to meet its needs. These packages also would work in Rockville only; they do not solve the problems of coordinating with distributed locations, each having a different kind of computer.

One viable strategy is incrementalism; attack each small problem and try to make improvements. For example, work with a consulting firm to figure out how to implement global inventory visibility across the world. This project alone would be a major undertaking, because it involves organizational changes as well. Nancy's biggest fear here is that by attacking small problems, she will miss the larger picture. "We have a mish-mash of technology; if we go for small victories, we will still have no unified architecture. I don't want to make every location do the same thing, but there are real advantages to having some standards in place, as we are seeing with global inventory visibility. If we try to do a quick fix with the systems we have, then someone has to figure out how to have a query made in Rockville access data from the DBMS on the 3090 and at the same time send a query to Singapore and Manchester to access information about the same product on their AS/400s, which use a different database. And we are not done then, we have to make it easy for the sales order entry rep to arrange for something she found in Singapore to be shipped to a customer in the U.S."

Nancy went on, "I am thinking that we need a major planning effort at Victor. We need to start at the top and look at our strategy and see how technology enables that strategy,

MANAGEMENT PROBLEM 12-2

Victor Electronics has an IT architecture in place that is similar to many other firms. They began using computers years ago, and naturally have legacy systems. Victor also bought other companies, and these firms have their own IT in place, which may or may not be very compatible with Victor. Nancy Scott is faced with the problem of maintaining the architecture and the technology infrastructure of the company.

"We've got some time," she said, "but eventually I'll have to make a recommendation on how we develop our hardware and software. There are several clusters of different computing in the company. Of course, we have the IBM mainframe in Rockville; I have to find out more about the applications on that computer and to what extent we are tied into the legacy mainframe architecture because of our applications.

What if are planning to replace these applications, should we also move to a different platform? Then we have the AS/400 cluster. Do we want to stay with these machines and follow IBM's upgrade path, or would we be better off converting to servers running Linux? Again we have to look at the software on the 400s to see whether it runs under Linux. The last category is the oddballs: an alpha server here, a Sun machine there, and of course, the PC systems. These we will have to look at on a case-by-case basis."

How should Nancy proceed? What information does she need in order to develop a plan for the future IT infrastructure at Victor Electronics? Does it make sense to try and move to one family of computers? What happens when you buy another company that uses incompatible systems?

or how it suggests new strategies we might want to follow. After understanding strategy, we can begin to see what applications are important and how we should go about developing them. In a parallel effort, we can look at the IT architecture and see what kind of computers, databases, and communications networks we need to support the business. My feeling is that we'll want to rely heavily on the Internet for communications."

Ellen Collins, the VP of Finance, asked Nancy, "Why don't we just hire someone to do the whole thing—bring in IBM Global Solutions or Accenture and turn it all over to them? They can bring in a huge workforce and use their experience to get something up and running for us in a hurry."

Nancy responded, "Ellen, you may be right, and I'm sure that we'll outsource some part of what we come up with. However, we need to do our homework and set out the requirements for what we want. I don't trust other people to come up with our strategy, and we're the ones who know how to operate our business. John wasn't kidding when he called the IT architecture at Victor 'interesting.'"

What Does *Legacy* Really Mean?

Only the start-up can start with brand new technology, and soon its systems will be legacy systems as well. Companies tend to adopt the technology that is current at the time they are making purchasing decisions. As a result, a company like Victor, which has been in business for forty years or more, has ended up with a variety of technology. Some of this technology Victor developed itself, and some came with the acquisition of other companies and plants.

A look at the path the computer industry has followed provides some insights into the kind of IT architecture you are likely to encounter in firms that have been using technology for some time.

As mentioned earlier, the first computers were mainframes, and companies developed most of their applications themselves. Large numbers of systems analysts and programmers worked to develop custom systems that ran on these large computers. In the 1950s and 1960s, these applications were largely batch processing in nature. That is, clerks gathered all of the input at one point in time, and the computer programs updated a file with it and produced reports and other output. It involved no user interaction. After 1964 and the Sabre online reservations system, more and more applications moved online. Today, most applications that individuals use are online, but many updates are still done in batch mode. For example, a production system is likely to update some of its files in batch mode overnight.

In the 1960s the cost of fabricating the CPU dropped significantly, and minicomputer makers such as DEC were able to offer better price/performance ratios on smaller machines than mainframes offered. Of course, the smaller machines could not do as much, but they offered a lot of power for the money. Frequently these minicomputers ended up as time-sharing machines for users in a department.

In the early 1980s, IBM first offered a personal computer for sale, legitimizing the desktop computer. At first these machines were all stand-alone, but soon users wanted to share files and access corporate data. The local area network (LAN) developed in response to this need, and soon the LAN was connected to mainframes and other computers so that users on PCs could access and download data from them.

The next architecture that developed is client–server in which the desktop computer is a client to a larger server. This architecture was a natural evolution for companies such as HP, DEC, and Sun who manufactured computers that ran variations of Unix. The idea was to produce powerful networks of computers that would compare favorably with the power of a mainframe, but would not be as proprietary. One of Sun's advertisements claims that "the network is the computer."

In 1995 the government ended its funding for the Internet and it became available for profit-making use. The Internet sparked a real revolution in computing because it offers worldwide connectivity at prices that are a fraction of the cost of a private network. In addition, the Internet is widely accessible to anyone who has a personal computer and a connection to an Internet service provider. If a merchant establishes an online store on the Internet, well over 100 million people in the United States can access it. Despite the problems with dot-coms, firms have been aggressively moving to use the Internet in a variety of ways.

The past fifty years of history in the technology field saw companies take divergent paths to develop their IT architectures. Although it would be nice to have the newest and best technology, the costs of replacement and the changes to the organization involved often make this solution impractical. Instead, managers have to figure out how to update and renew the firm's technology as needed. Nancy Scott has the right idea in developing a plan for Victor Electronics; then she and management can decide how best to implement the plan or an acceptable version of it.

One popular alternative in dealing with legacy systems is to dress them up in a way that hides their age. A legacy mainframe system at one time ran on character-based terminals with no graphics. A quick solution is to replace the interface with a PC and some graphics to make the system more appealing. It is a little more involved, but you can redesign the online interactions so that they take place using a browser such as Internet Explorer, making it much easier and more intuitive to use the system. A firm can try different integration techniques with products sold by different vendors under the label enterprise applications integration (EAI); these products help you create a more integrated set of systems to users. Each of the host of alternatives to replacing a legacy system in its entirety has its pros and cons.

IT ARCHITECTURE QUESTIONS FOR MANAGEMENT

Victor Electronics illustrates some of the issues and questions about IT architecture facing management. For most firms, the following questions have proven difficult to answer:

1. *When do you replace a legacy system?*
   If company's legacy system is performing well, management must decide at what point to replace it. One company is facing this decision for its order processing system, a major application in the company. The current system is running well on IBM mainframes and is about fifteen years old, though it has been continually updated. Replacing the system is estimated to cost at least $15 million. Management will make a decision based on the limitations of the system, the difficulties of modifying it to meet new demands, the ability to obtain support from the vendor of the hardware and software and cost.

2. *What parts of the IT architecture/operations do you want to outsource?*
   Outsourcing is a common strategy for all or part of IT operations. However, you do not want to outsource with the idea that it eliminates the need to manage IT anymore. In fact, the opposite is likely to be the case because of the need to carefully monitor the outsourcer. One good argument for outsourcing is to bring a lot of resources to bear on a problem quickly, which is one reason the idea is appealing to Victor Electronics.

3. *What are the problems with a heterogeneous IT architecture?*
   A set of standard hardware and software makes it easy to share and move people among jobs and locations. Cisco, in the early 1990s, decided it needed to implement an ERP system partially to create a standard computing platform across the company. As a result, when the Internet opened up for profit-making use, Cisco was ready to move all of its applications onto the Web. The rest is history.

4. *How can a common architecture be planned and maintained as technology changes?*
   Even if Victor or another firm figures out a standard architecture, it faces the challenge of maintaining it given the pace of technological change. Today the recommendation is a client–server with a heavy reliance on the Internet, but that model may change in the next five years. In the 1950s the choice was a mainframe, and in the 1960s, a mainframe with distributed minis.

5. *What should strategy be for electronic commerce?*
   It is clear that electronic commerce is here to stay, and that companies should be figuring out how to take advantage of it.

6. *Should systems move to the Internet?*
   The answer today is Yes. Hopefully it will be the right answer in the future.

The most important message of this chapter is that legacy systems exist everyplace, and nothing is wrong with them per se. You might say it is a part of the natural aging process; any system you install today runs the risk of becoming a legacy system in the next few years. The challenge is to plan a technology architecture taking into account the history of the organization, the technology in place, and your vision for the future.

CHAPTER SUMMARY

This chapter examined the heterogeneous IT architecture that exists at Victor Electronics. Every firm that is not starting in business today deals with a legacy architecture, and the new firm will have it after it puts its first technology in place. Victor's problems come from a lack of attention and planning over the years; it has acquired firms and installed systems worldwide without much of a vision for how it wants to operate as a global company. A legacy architecture is inevitable; the question is how to manage it and how long before it is replaced. These are difficult issues for any manager and organization; the decisions depend on the context and the firm's business model. Instead of a single right answer, you try to find a solution that fits your vision for technology in the firm within the resources available at the time.

RECOMMENDED READINGS

Hackney, R. 1998. The expert's opinion. Journal of Global Information Management, 6(4), pp. 43–45. (Presents an anonymous interview of a chief information officer regarding information systems (IS) management in business, IS strategic roles in the business, views on IS participation within business function, and opinions on maintaining legacy systems.)

Holland, C. P., Light, B., and Kawalek, P. 1999. Focus issue on legacy information systems and business process change. Communications of the AIS, 2(9), pp. 1–11.

Kiely, T. 1996. Computer legacy systems. Harvard Business Review, 74(4), pp. 10–12. (Discusses the merits of upgrading and maintaining legacy systems over replacement of such systems.)

Prahalad, C. K., and Krishnan, M. S. 2002. The dynamic synchronization of strategy and information technology. Sloan Management Review, Summer, pp. 24–33. (A paper arguing that rigid IT infrastructures inhibit corporate strategy; the authors also make the point that legacy applications are fine if they still meet the business need.)

Schneidewind, N. F., and Ebert, C. 1998. Preserve or redesign legacy systems? IEEE Software, 15(4), pp. 14–17. (Discusses the functionality of legacy systems and the competition of dealing with these systems; challenges of keeping legacy systems updated; advantages and disadvantages of legacy systems; and information on the maintenance of legacy systems.)

DISCUSSION QUESTIONS

1. Define IT architecture. What does it include? What is a firm's IT architecture?

2. What are the characteristics of a mainframe computer?

3. Why are mainframes associated with legacy systems?

4. What was the advantage of minicomputers when they were first developed?

5. What motivated the development of LANs?

6. What made it possible for the Internet to be used for profit-making activities?

7. Why did Victor Electronics invest in AS/400 computers in Singapore and Manchester? What is the advantage of these computers?

8. Why does Victor have a network of leased lines instead of using the Internet?

9. What are the problems associated with Victor trying to have real-time global inventory availability information in all parts of the world?

10. Would a standardized package for order entry running all over the world solve the global inventory problem at Victor? If so, how?

11. What is an open system? What are its advantages over a closed or proprietary system?

12. IBM is moving in the direction of providing servers, many of which use Linux, a "free" version of Unix. Why do you suppose IBM is not just emphasizing its proprietary mainframe architecture?

13. What approaches are available to a company when it acquires another company that has a different, incompatible IT architecture?

14. What criteria should management use to decide on replacing a legacy system?

15. Do you think that mainframes will disappear in the next ten years? If so, why, and if not, why not?

16. Much of IT architecture is centered on hardware. Why is software a more important consideration in most cases?

17. If software is so important, then why be concerned about hardware? Is it not just a commodity product?

18. Why can you not run the software for one type of computer on another one without making any changes?

19. Do you agree that a firm needs to move toward e-commerce and should develop a strategy if it does not have one? Why or why not?

20. What kind of IT architecture do you see being dominant in the next five years? Ten years?

21. Design an IT architecture plan for Victor Electronics assuming that you can start over with a clean sheet of paper.

22. Design an IT architecture plan given that you have to migrate from its current architecture.

CHAPTER 13

THE FIRST COMPONENT: COMPUTER SYSTEMS

A Manager's Perspective

The computer is an amazing device. The first machines were small scientific computers that took up a good part of a room. They used punched cards to input programs and data, and different switches set on the console controlled parts of the program. The computers on most desks now are more powerful than an early mainframe. Advances in electronics are the reason for this remarkable evolution. The first computers used vacuum tubes, bulky and power-hungry devices that failed often. The second generation adopted transistors, a huge improvement over tubes in terms of speed, power consumption, and reliability. The third generation and subsequent computers employ integrated circuits. Chip manufacturers continually increased the number of transistors, and hence the number of circuits, on a chip. The more components on a chip, the cheaper the manufacturing cost, and the fewer chips needed to make a computer. Companies such as Dell use technology to manufacture highly affordable, powerful computers. The computer is literally the machine that changed the world.

THE COMPUTER CHANGED THE WORLD

The first component of the incredible technology available today is the computer itself. The breakthrough that led to computers was the development of electronics that could replace mechanical calculators. The second breakthrough leading to modern computing devices was the idea of having a program in computer memory along with data. The first electromechanical devices had external boards and programming involved wiring these boards. Storing programs in memory provided many more options and gave rise to complex software that controls computing.

In the early days, all computers were known as mainframes. At one time, eight different companies in the United States manufactured computers. Univac had the early lead in computing but soon lost it to IBM. (Later Univac became a part of Sperry, which merged with another computer vendor, Burroughs, to form the UNISYS Corporation.)

As IBM became the dominant vendor in the United States and abroad, the computer industry was sometimes described as "IBM and the Seven Dwarfs." In the 1950s and early 1960s, companies such as Apple, Digital Equipment Corporation (DEC), and Compaq did not exist. RCA and General Electric manufactured mainframe computers, eventually taking huge write-offs as they left the business. Today, minicomputer and mainframe vendors are reeling from dramatic changes in the cost/performance ratios of "commodity" processor chips versus systems based on proprietary circuit designs.

A number of trends in the technology created today's computer industry. The many different types of computers are each designed to do specific tasks.

The Rise of the Mainframe

Mainframes are large, general purpose machines. In the early days of the computer industry, one could run only batch programs (the staff collects all data into a batch that was processed at one time) on mainframe computers. Many organizations developed substantial applications on mainframe computers. Today this type of machine is likely to support a number of terminals and personal computers interacting with huge databases containing billions of characters of data. Mainframe computers are used extensively to process transactions and maintain vital data for access by various users. Examples of mainframe systems include order entry and processing at an electronics manufacturer, production planning and scheduling at Chrysler, and airline reservations at all the major air carriers

Mainframe computers feature proprietary hardware (instruction sets that in general are unique to and controlled by the vendor). Intel and Motorola make millions of chips a year; the demand for mainframe computers is far less. The proprietary architectures of mainframe computers cannot take advantage of economies of scale in production, and for this reason they have a worse cost/performance ratio than smaller computers built around commodity chips. Mainframe vendors are working to reduce the costs of their machines, for example, by designing multiprocessors using chips such as the PowerPC.

Mainframe systems represent a heavy investment, they process critical transactions, and they are difficult to change. These mainframe systems are capable of processing a huge volume of transactions. Even though the firm might be able to buy hardware that has a better cost/performance ratio, it would have to spend a large amount to develop new applications for this hardware. IBM's strategy is to continue mainframe development and to keep these machines competitive; it markets them as large servers. IBM updates the operating system regularly, the most recent edition features networking capabilities to help the mainframe become a giant server on a network, capable of hosting large electronic commerce applications. Over the past five years, mainframes have become smaller, faster, and cheaper as a result of using CMOS technology and the clustering of parallel processors to provide more computing power.

Organizations using mainframe computers generally process large amounts of data. The computers may access databases with billions of characters of data and control networks of hundreds or thousands of terminals. As a result, the computers need to be able to handle extensive telecommunications activities and input/output operations. This architecture created extremely fast mainframe computers that are used in database, transactions processing, and numerous other applications. IBM's largest mainframes are now called eSeries servers, "e" for enterprise.

Powerful Supercomputers

Mainframe computers are not fast enough for some applications. The mainframe computer was originally developed for business use. Its features enhance the processing of business data involving character manipulation and decimal arithmetic. Scientists and engineers need to solve computationally intensive problems, often involving numbers with many digits of significance. Examples include the simulation of airflow over an aircraft, weather forecasting simulations, analysis of geological data, and even predictions about the speed of a sailboat designed for the Americas Cup competition.

Supercomputers are the fastest computers today, with speeds measured in teraflops (1 trillion floating-point instructions per second). A parallel supercomputer at Los Alamos has a peak processing speed of 30 trillion instructions per second, or thirty teraflops. Some experts argue that the future of high-speed computing is in massively parallel machines or by combining the power of a number of individual workstations connected with a network. Of the twenty fastest computers in the world, only one uses *vector technology*, the original approach to supercomputing. Other fast machines are designed to be *massively parallel*, using a large number of individual chips operating in parallel.

The fastest supercomputer today, according to the rankings maintained by the Universities of Tennessee and Mannheim, is the Earth Simulator built by NEC in Japan. This computer has 640 supercomputer nodes connected through a high-speed network. Each node contains eight gigaflop/s (billion floating point operations a second) vector processors and sixteen gigabytes of high-speed memory, which provides a total of 5,120 processors (640 nodes with eight vector processors each) and ten terabytes of main memory. The Earth Simulator's world-record sustained performance is 35.86Tflop/s, or 35.86 trillion mathematical calculations per second. It might be noted that Seattle-based Cray is now offering a supercomputer that can do 52.4 teraflops. An estimated forty-seven supercomputers worldwide can do one teraflop or more.

Minis: The Beginning of the Revolution

The next type of computer to develop was the mini. Companies such as DEC found that with integrated circuits they could build a highly cost-effective small computer with an eight- or sixteen-bit word length. Minis became popular as stand-alone time-sharing computers and as machines dedicated to a department in a corporation.

Minicomputers evolved as manufacturers increased processing speeds and expanded word sizes to thirty-two bits. These computers can be classified as midrange. IBM claims to have sold more than 200,000 of its midrange AS/400 system. Companies use this midrange computer for a variety of processing tasks, some of which are similar to what a mainframe did a decade ago. A firm might use this computer for all of its processing. A geographically dispersed company could have AS/400 computers at various geographic locations connected to a larger machine at headquarters. Third parties have developed thousands of applications for the AS/400 as well.

As an example of the trends in medium and larger computers, in 1995 IBM introduced models of the AS/400 built around its PowerPC chip. IBM, Apple, and Motorola developed this RISC chip to compete with Intel. Using a customized version of this chip lets IBM get away from a proprietary architecture and reduce the cost of the computer. However, because a huge number of applications are available for this popular computer, IBM had to maintain compatibility with its original architecture. The computer translates existing applications software the first time it is executed on the new machine without the need to change the original program. The latest models in this line are called iSeries servers.

The Personal Computer Changed Everything

Next came the PC, or personal computer, which was first designed as an 8-bit computer. Apple introduced its famous PC in 1977. The original IBM PC, marketed in 1981, retrieved eight bits at a time from memory but performed computations on sixteen bits at a time. Soon IBM introduced the AT, which retrieved and processed sixteen bits at a time. The next generation is the thirty-two-bit PC or 386 (later the 486 as well) computer, which retrieves and processes thirty-two bits at a time. The Pentium is capable of retrieving and storing sixty-four bits at a time, though it does computations on thirty-two bits. The personal computer is used in countless ways today and many thousands of programs are available for it.

Workstations use high-performance thirty-two-bit computers for engineering and scientific work. The workstation features superior graphics and is often used for design tasks. Powerful Pentium personal computers running graphical user interfaces (GUIs) fall into the workstation class as well. These PCs have the computational power and software capabilities to become the same kind of personal productivity tool for the manager that the engineering workstation is for the engineer.

The Server

In the client-server model of computing, a user's client PC makes requests of a server computer that has data and programs on it. The server is responsible for the database and is likely to execute transactions to update and manage it. The server also has to extract data and provide it to the client. The user's client does various analyses of the data using its own processing power. At first, the server did not do much but let users download software and print reports in a local area network. However, as PC chips became more powerful, so did servers. They now challenge minicomputers and may soon go after the mainframe market. Intel is so optimistic about the server market that it is marketing complete boards for servers containing four Pentium chips. A vendor can use this board as the major component of a server. Vendors such as Sun Microsystems sell powerful servers based on their own chips like Sun's SPARC chip.

A large grocery store used to have a $250,000 minicomputer. Now it runs its business on a multiprocessor server that costs $25,000 to $50,000. One server containing four Pentium processors has been clocked at 600 transactions per second with standard database software compared to 200 transactions per second for some midrange computers. Server makers envision computers with up to thirty-two Intel Pentium processors achieving the performance of today's high-end mainframes.

The Network PC Versus the Under $1,000 PC

Competitors of Microsoft, along with the Internet, stimulated the development of a new kind of PC called the Net PC. The idea behind the Net PC is that a person connected to the Internet does not need a powerful PC; this individual can work quite happily with a device that has a relatively slow CPU, limited memory, and perhaps no disk drive. Advocates of this approach think it should be possible to build the Net PC for well under $1,000. Competitors to Microsoft envision the Net PC running an operating system (control program) other than Windows.

The Net PC has so far failed to displace sales of full-featured personal computers. These devices do look attractive as replacements for dumb terminals (terminals with minimal logic that connect to minis and mainframes), or for providing network access for students at a more affordable price than a standard PC for most school districts. The dramatic reductions in the price of full-featured PCs bring their costs closer to those of a Net PC, making the case for the latter less clear. In addition, many devices other than PCs connect to the Net; a Palm Pilot may be more valuable for many people than a Net PC as a way to access the Internet. When 3G cellular phone systems are in place, the cell phone will compete with other devices for Internet access.

It should be noted, however, that the cost of owning a PC goes well beyond its purchase price. The "total cost of ownership" for a PC in an organization has been estimated at two or three times the purchase price, primarily due to software and support requirements and the costs of networking PCs together. The Net PC, because it is simpler and takes most of its software from a server, should have a lower total cost of ownership than a full-featured PC.

The majority of desktop PC sales today are for a class of machines costing less than $1,000. It is not clear whether the Net PC will be attractive if one can buy a full-featured PC at these prices. Consumers may not be as sensitive to a few hundred dollars if it buys a much more capable computer that can do meaningful work when not connected to the Internet. Notebook computers also enjoy robust sales; they have become powerful enough to be a desktop replacement for many users. Tablet computers that use a stylus like a PDA are growing in popularity as well, especially if one has access to a wireless network. The tablets are light in weight and highly portable, yet they can run complex software packages.

Massively Parallel Computers

The highly parallel machine category includes a number of approaches to computer design. The approaches have in common the idea of trying to avoid the bottleneck in conventional designs where all instructions and data have to be retrieved from memory and brought to the CPU for processing. Some of these parallel computers have multiple processors that all execute the same instruction at once on the same data. Others execute multiple instructions on different data. Clearly, coordinating the execution of instructions and programming these machines is a challenge. As the physical limits of computation are reached, one way to gain increased performance is to compute in parallel.

Grid Computing

A recent strategy followed by some users who need extremely high-speed computing is to connect clusters of personal computers with special software that lets them attack the same problem. The idea is to make use of the extensive idle time on PCs when users are not actively working on them. Grid software assigns various parts of a complex computation to different computers on the network, generating considerable increases in processing power. It is possible for some applications that used to require a supercomputer to run on such a connected group of workstations. Monsanto installed grid software to tie together various computers from Compaq and Sun that were already on its St. Louis headquarters network. When the computers are idle, the grid software assigns them tasks to complete. Using the capabilities of the grid, Monsanto scientists are able to analyze thousands of genes a year, fifty times more than what they could do five years ago.[1] Novartis in Switzerland linked 2,700 personal computers to help create new drugs using software developed in Texas. The company plans to expand the system to its entire corporate network of 70,000 PCs. The European Union is starting two large grid projects, one linking 20,000 computers in seventy institutions to form an e-science grid, and the other, a distributed supercomputing project led by a research center in France.[2]

A grid system is under development to create a digital archive of mammograms to improve breast cancer diagnosis by comparing old and new X-rays. Eventually the grid will link thousands of hospitals in North America. Grid computing is being combined with new, digital mammogram machines that store X-rays digitally rather than producing film. Software developed at the University of Pennsylvania collects data from digital mammogram machines, encrypts it for transmission to a central database, and indexes the images so they can be retrieved by a physician. Eventually the archive is to include 2,000 hospitals with different hardware and software; grid software has to make all of these computers work in concert with each other. IBM provided the servers and database software for the project, seeing it as a test for grid computing.[3]

A Personal Assistant

The personal data assistant (PDA) began as super calculators able to store a user's calendar and phone book. Today these devices often weigh less than a pound, and some offer handwriting and voice recognition, fax and modem communications, and a pager. PDAs are inexpensive enough that firms will develop dedicated applications for them. For example, a sales representative might use a small PDA that has information on contracts. A longshoreman uses a PDA that has a bar-code reader and scanner to record the location of containers. A rental car company might have local maps and tour guides available in each city to be downloaded to your PDA. As wireless transmission technology expands and drops in price, PDAs will become more attractive.

In Orange County, California, real estate agents have the opportunity to use a PDA to remotely access, download, and store property information on a Sony Magic Link personal communicator. An agent can use it to communicate via fax, electronic mail, and paging, or access a commercial online service. The agent can select listings using different parameters such as location and special needs of the client. The PDA will replace printed property listings, which were published every two weeks.

A variety of PDAs is available, with the market leader being the Palm Pilot. A cellular phone now accesses e-mail and provides some of the features of a digital assistant. PDAs face competition from handheld computers that feature small keyboards to facilitate data entry, a process that is at best clumsy on a PDA. Most PDAs are able to easily upload and download or synchronize with programs that run on a PC. The smaller PDAs use proprietary operating systems. Microsoft promotes Windows CE for slightly larger PDAs that are more computer-like than the handheld models. Microsoft's long-term goal is to capture this market as well as the set-top cable controller market for Windows CE.

Mobile Computing

The latest excitement in technology is mobile computing through wireless communications. This approach is going in two directions simultaneously. The first is the use of wireless local networks, or WiFi, using an IEEE standard 802.11x, where x represents a series of letters each designating slightly different protocols offering various speeds for data transmission. With wireless, a user has connectivity to the Internet using radio waves rather than a direct connection. Airport lounges and gates might offer this service to passengers waiting for flights. Coffee shops have installed wireless systems, as have universities to let students connect to the Internet from anyplace in a building, or even outdoors on campus.

MANAGEMENT PROBLEM 13-1

Standard Foods is facing a decision on how to support its sales representatives around the world. Jaya Agarwal, the CIO, is faced with two problems working with sales management on the project. "We know that we have to provide a system to help the sales force, to provide information on the customers and what they have ordered in the past. The salesforce needs tools to help the rep analyze what is going on in a territory. Our second problem is figuring out how the rep should access any system. Do we put it on the Internet? If so, what kind of device should the sales rep carry, a notebook computer, a PDA, or a cell phone that is Web-enabled."

Standard is comparing an expensive, proprietary customer relationship management (CRM) package with salesforce.com, a system that follows the applications service provider model. That is, Standard only pays for what it uses, and does not have to own or maintain any software. Agarwal said, "I like the fact that we don't need to worry about owning or maintaining software. But will the company remain in business—after all it is a dot-com. In addition, we are entering into something that is a variable cost. What if our use really explodes? It could get expensive."

How should Standard go about making its decision on software? What factors should it consider? What about the hardware question? Make a list of the pros and cons of the different alternatives for sales reps to access either system.

This kind of wireless connection anticipates the use of a notebook PC as the computing device. However, interest is also strong for using other kinds of devices to connect to the Internet, including PDAs and cellular phones. DoCoMo, a cellular service in Japan, has been extremely successful by offering an e-mail service to its subscribers. Japanese teenagers seem to be fascinated by sending short e-mail messages to each other on cell phones. It remains to be seen whether others in the world will want to surf the Web or buy products using the limited keyboards and displays of cellular phones.

Conclusions

It is clear that the task of developing the architecture for an organization's computing system is difficult. If an organization is starting with no computing, one could conceive of buying a large midrange computer, a small mainframe, or a network of personal computers. The question of which option to choose may require a major study and considerable effort. The organization that already has a number of computers in place must decide how to manage and expand its systems as users come up with new needs and ideas for technology.

So Many Types of Computers

The text discusses a variety of different types of computers, but you may be quite happy with a desktop or notebook PC. The preceding discussion presented the different computers—supercomputers, mainframes, minis, and PCs—in order of their development. The major reason for the variety of computers is the applications users have programmed to run on them. Many applications are developed for mainframe computers. It would be expensive to convert to a new architecture, even though the new system could handle the processing volume of the mainframe, which explains why some companies have not adopted a client-server configuration or moved to the Internet and replaced their older configurations.

As the industry develops new types of computers, mainframes, minis, and PCs, users write custom applications for these computers. One large financial services firm recently reported having more than 75,000 active COBOL programs comprising some 70 million lines of code, a significant investment in one language and system. As a result, the company feels a great reluctance to throw away existing applications to adopt the latest trend in computing. Instead, companies put new applications on the latest computing platform, create new interfaces for their old mainframe systems, and plan to reprogram applications sometime in the future. You should not be surprised to see a variety of almost all types of computers in a company, nor should you think a firm is necessarily behind the times because it still has applications that run on mainframe computers.

FUTURE TECHNOLOGY

Predicting future trends in technology has always been a risky endeavor, because new innovations constantly offer new directions for applications. This section reviews new technologies that are expected to change the way computing is used or dramatically alter the cost/performance ratio of computation.

The Amazing Chip

Significant investments in research and development stimulated the revolution in information technology. In the 1950s you would find bulky vacuum tubes inside computers. The second generation moved to transistors, and the third to integrated circuits. Today, central processors consist of one or a few chips with incredible numbers of components on them. Intel is converting to a new production process, requiring a $12 billion investment in manufacturing technology. This technology allows Intel to include wireless networking on a processor chip. Intel is now able to produce chips with circuit lines that measure 130 nanometers (a nanometer is a billionth of a meter), and will soon begin to manufacture chips with ninety nanometer circuits. The process appears capable of producing fifty nanometer features, which would be 1/2,000th of the width of a human hair.[4]

The emphasis on small sizes results from the quest for faster chips. More circuits means that signals do not have to travel as far. Smaller chips use less power, which is important, because more and more devices are portable and spend some time running from batteries. Small size makes it possible to pack tremendous computer power in small devices. Most important, Intel and other chip makers' investments reduce manufacturing costs per chip, making computers more affordable, and making it more attractive to include chips in different products.

Servers: Small and Large

The general computer architecture of today is client–server. Your computer is a client and it connects over a network to a computer that is called a server. Often the server is a more powerful computer than the client because it is communicating with multiple clients at one time. On the Internet, you find all types of information on servers that you connect to by clicking on links or typing URLs into the search bar. Your university probably has an e-mail server (or multiple servers), and possibly a server that contains applications programs like those for statistical analysis. A business school is likely to have a server with financial databases for faculty and student research.

A company with an online store will have a Web server to interface with the customers accessing the store via the Internet (see Figure 13-1). It will have a server for the

FIGURE 13-1 An e-commerce client-server configuration.

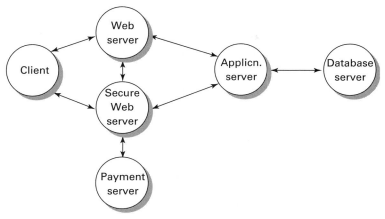

E-commerce site

actual e-commerce application, and probably a database server as well. A server handles secure payments by using some kind of encryption to receive information on a customer's credit card. Figure 13-1 shows just one server, but in reality an active site will have multiple servers doing the same function. In front of these servers will be a PC that acts as a load balancer; it assigns incoming requests to different servers in order to spread the load among them and keep response times to a minimum. Different kinds of firewalls also work to prevent unauthorized access to your network and servers, access that might be associated with malicious intent or fraud.

The mainframe model has a large number of tasks from different applications running on the same computer. Sometimes dedicated servers are used to do just one function. You can buy servers in many different sizes, and their cost/performance ratios are such that it is economical to have multiple servers rather than one large one to do a job. A modular design assigns a restricted set of functions to a dedicated server. Modularity makes it easy to add capacity incrementally by bringing in a new server. Modularity also makes it easier to diagnose problems. If something goes wrong with secure payments, you know to start the diagnosis at the secure payments server.

The Internet follows the client–server model, and most new applications in organization are client–server. Thus, this architecture is likely to be around for a number of years, but that expectation does not mean the architecture is static. Two interesting approaches are generally used in configuring servers. The first is called a "blade" server, a server that consists of a series of small computers each built on a card or cards that slide into a rack inside a cabinet. The servers are thin (like blades) and a number of them can be placed in the cabinet and linked together. These boxes provide the power of a large server at a fraction of the price.

The opposite approach is to take a large server and partition it to look like a number of smaller servers. IBM and Sun both offer machines in this category. For IBM, a large computer (maybe even a mainframe) can be partitioned by its operating system into multiple servers. In this case, the computer runs Linux, a shareware operating system that is similar to Unix. The buyer does not have to purchase an expensive proprietary operating system and can easily change the configuration of logical servers running on the larger computer.

Web Services

Firms have often built applications around a particular function, for example, order entry, customer service, production, and so on. These stand-alone applications have been referred to as *stove pipes* because they work vertically in a department, but have no horizontal connections to any other part of the organization. Large enterprise applications such as ERP come with connectivity among functions; when someone in customer service updates a customer's address, that information is available throughout the system. When a customer pays an invoice, that payment is reflected immediately in the credit limit seen by someone in order entry when the customer sends in a new order.

Most applications, however, are not that integrated. The data a sales representative on the road might want could be in different databases on different computers. The databases are likely to be from different vendors with different methods of creating a query. The Internet offers a way to tie all of a firm's computers together and provide remote access to them. What is lacking is integration among different programs and databases on these computers. The term *Web services* applies to a variety of software and programming techniques that foster integration among disparate applications. Many Web services are based on the use of Extensible Markup Language (XML) to describe data that is being exchanged on the Web.

The original standard for graphical information on the Web was Hypertext Markup Language (HTML). See Figure 13-2. A Web browser such as Netscape or Internet Explorer interprets the HTML commands and uses them to format content that appears on the screen. HTML provides no information about what the data being displayed mean. XML adds "tags" to fields of data describing what they mean. As a result, programs can access XML content and find a particular field, for example, model number and price for data at an online store. XML, then, provides semantic information; it communicates meaning rather than just formatting. XML is the basis for Web services and for the integration of applications across the Internet. See Figure 13-3.

Another component of Web services is Simple Object Access Protocol (SOAP), which is a message envelope for sending messages by Hypertext Transfer Protocol (HTTP). The Universal Description, Discovery and Integration (UDDI) format lets applications identify one another, and Web Services Description Language (WSDL) lets programs describe their capabilities.

When a Web services developer creates a service and sends it to a server; he or she creates a description of that service, which is published in a directory. A client process looks in a directory to find a service to solve its problem, and executes it.

As an example, suppose that you wish to obtain a transcript from your undergraduate college while in graduate school. You could send a request to the registrar at the graduate school. In today's environment, the request would probably come back saying that you must contact your undergraduate school directly. In a Web services world, the registrar's system would look for a Web service to find a transcript at your undergraduate school. If your college had such a service and published its location, the registrar's system would request the service, obtain the transcript, and send it to you.

Developers are creating Web services to try and hide the incompatibilities among computers and systems. The objective is to make computers and their applications interoperate seamlessly, so that a user only has to ask what he or she wants. The concept is great, but you can see that it requires a lot of effort involved in making it work.

FIGURE 13-2 The University of Maryland Home Page and part of the HTML that produced it.

```
<!DOCTYPE HTML PUBLIC "-
    //W3C//DTD HTML 4.01
    Transitional//EN">
<HTML>
<head>
 <title>The University of
    Maryland</title>
 <META http-
    equiv="Content-Type"
    content="text/html;
    charset=ISO-8859-1">
 <META name="Description"
    content="Welcome to
    the University of
    Maryland, College
    Park">
 <META name="KeyWords"
    content="University
    of Maryland, college,
    Maryland, College
    Park, research,           system, university, campus, school, Maryland Day, pub-
    lic, Terps, ZOOM, Terrapins, University       of Maryland, NCAA Champs">
 <META name="Description" content="Welcome to the University of Maryland">
 <META name="KeyWords" content="University of Maryland, University, Maryland,
    Technology, college,  Maryland, College Park, research, system, university,
    campus, school, public, land-grant">
 <LINK REL="shortcut icon" HREF="http://www.umd.edu/gr/favicon.ico">
```

Credit: Screenshot of University of Maryland homepage and programming HTML code. Used by permission.

FIGURE 13-3 An example of XML showing tag sets.

```
<?xml version="1.0" encoding="ISO-8859-1" ?>
 <!-- Edited with XML Spy v4.2 -->
- <breakfast_menu>- <food> <name>Belgian Waffles</name>
 <price>$5.95</price>
 <description>two of our famous Belgian Waffles with plenty of real maple
    syrup</description>
 <calories>650</calories>
 </food>- <food> <name>Strawberry Belgian Waffles</name>
 <price>$7.95</price>
 <description>light Belgian waffles covered with strawberries and whipped
    cream</description>
 <calories>900</calories>
 </food>- <food> <name>Berry-Berry Belgian Waffles</name>
 <price>$8.95</price>
 <description>light Belgian waffles covered with an assortment of fresh berries and
    whipped cream</description>
 <calories>900</calories>
 </food>- <food> <name>French Toast</name>
 <price>$4.50</price>
 <description>thick slices made from our homemade sourdough bread</description>
```

MANAGEMENT PROBLEM 13-2

Terry Anderson at Chicago Scientific is intrigued by grid computing. "We are a relatively small company, and a lot of our work is scientific and engineering. That means we do real calculations in addition to processing transactions. The engineers always want more computing power, but we can't afford to give them a supercomputer. We do have lots of PCs, and I have read about the idea of hooking them all together in a grid. I bet most of the PCs are inactive 80 percent of the day, and probably all night. But I hate to be the pioneer with a new technology.

"As I understand the grid concept, we wouldn't have to change our network, though we might upgrade the speed of some of our LANs. We would have a software program that controlled the grid and parceled out the work to be done to idle PCs. It sounds great and makes use of an asset that is underutilized. I wonder how the engineers would like the idea."

What are the pros and cons of grid computing? What should Anderson do to get started? Do you think that grids will become commonplace in a few years?

The Semantic Web

The original Web allowed users to search through links to find different documents. The format for representing documents, HTML, provided no information about the content of the document, it only described how a browser should format it. As described, the advent of XML allows someone preparing a document or data to identify its content, and begins to move toward an understanding of the semantics, the meaning of information.

Attaching meaning to the contents of the Web is a significant challenge. Even if users do some encoding of information as they enter it, programs need to use inference rules to draw meaning from this content. The complexity of a semantic Web is illustrated by the need to relate different types of data to each other; for example, a program must know if two terms on different computers mean the same thing. This requirement means someone has to define a relationship among different fields of data for different applications.

The semantic Web will be particularly valuable for personal agents or software robots that people use to perform tasks for them on the Web. Shopping agents today compare the prices offered on different Web sites. They require separate scripts for each Web site to know where the catalog number and price of each item are displayed on the Web page. In the semantic Web, the pages would be coded in XML tags that identify catalog item number and price, so that the agent could visit any site without the need for special programming.

It is unlikely that a semantic Web will appear all at once, but rather the Web will move in this direction as users encode more semantic information along with content, and as researchers represent inference rules and knowledge across the Web (see Berners-Lee, Hendler, and Lassila, 2002).

Moving Software to the Cloud

It has been suggested that no one really wants to own software, but you need it to get a computer to do something useful. The Internet presents the possibility for avoiding software ownership—for example, if someone could just execute a program when he or she needed it. Microsoft wants to link its programs to distributed services so as not to lose its valuable desktop franchise from Office. IBM and Sun would like to break Microsoft's monopoly; they will locate programs on the Internet that people can use as needed.

One of the barriers to this kind of distributed software is security and trust. Users want to know that the code they are using is sound and that hackers are not copying their data as they compute. No one seems to have specified a revenue model yet for this kind of computing. An author probably invokes Word twenty or thirty times for each chapter, which makes a fixed cost of a few hundred dollars look pretty attractive for word-processing software. No one will want to pay by the use, but possibly users would be willing to pay for a long-term license. By leasing the program users would never have to update their software; the company granting the license can update the program on the Web, and customers automatically invoke the updated program the next time they use it.

A system such as Hotmail is a precursor of this kind of software. A user performs all of the tasks associated with e-mail using only a browser. Servers run by Microsoft take care of providing the mail, storing it in a mailbox, and allowing a user many options for sending and replying to mail. It is likely this model will be extended; accessing an application through a Web browser seems natural compared to some of the complex interfaces to programs that run on PCs. The model works well for a generic program such as a word processor or spreadsheet, but applications that are unique to a firm provide an additional dilemma. Companies must decide whether to put a proprietary application in a software cloud on the Internet, even if access is restricted to its own employees.

Ubiquitous Computing

A modern automobile has a large number of microprocessors on board, computers that manage engine fuel, air, and emissions; control antilock brakes; provide dynamic stability control; and navigate for the driver. Except for the navigation computer, you can drive a car with no knowledge of the computers at work under the hood. Some researchers ask why other kinds of computing should be any different.

Some of the ideas behind ubiquitous computing were developed at the famous Xerox Palo Alto Research Laboratory. Suppose a firm creates a smart building with sensors and computers built into walls and furniture. A person wears an active name tag that sends identification information to the room. The system knows to route calls and queries to this location if the person is located there. If a person carries a PDA, a wireless connection makes it possible to process e-mail and communicate outside the building. Add voice recognition capabilities and computers might well shrink into the woodwork, just as they are well hidden in an automobile.

A Worldwide Computer

The grid computing network described earlier works in an organization. Other efforts tried to solve large problems by enlisting thousands of idle computers on the Internet and assigning each a small task. This scenario brings up the possibility of a worldwide computer. Two computer scientists proposed such a computing device (Anderson and Kubiatowicz, 2002). Such a worldwide operating system would run over the Internet and would be able to harness the power of the more than 150 million host computers on the network.

The system would consist of a thin layer of software or an agent running on each host computer; a central coordinating system would run on one or more server complexes. The central server would assign tasks, allocate resources, and handle payments to each of the computers involved in a task. As a simple example, a user might wish to backup files on the Internet. The central coordinating server would send pieces of those files to different computers for storage, and would arrange payment to those providing storage. The user would not know where the files were, but would have confidence that the coordinating server could retrieve them. Many computers connected to the Internet sit idle for most of the day; a worldwide operating system could put these machines' idle capacity to work.

Monitoring and Sensing

Generally it is cheaper and safer to fix a problem before it becomes worse. This approach is particularly appropriate for complex equipment such as airplanes. General Electric is a major manufacturer of airplane engines, and it offers a service that monitors the engines in-flight and arranges for repairs when the plane lands. For example, a GE engine might loose some of its insulating skin causing the temperature to drop in the combustion department. The drop in temperature is too small to show up on the pilots' instruments, but a thermocouple that monitors temperatures in the engine department registers the drop. Three hours into this flight, an onboard computer monitoring the engines uploads its data to a satellite, which relays the information to a computer near Cincinnati. The Ohio computer uses the report about a lower temperature, other sensor readings, and the engine's maintenance history to diagnose the problem and make a recommendation. The Ohio center phones the airline so that mechanics can repair the problem when the plane lands.

In the past, the problem would have worsened until a visual inspection caught it, and repairs would have been more expensive, possibly taking the plane out of service for days. Complex, costly equipment where safety is involved is an obvious choice for remote monitoring. However, as the cost of sensing devises and communications drops, many more self-diagnosing system will be developed. GE is a leader in the field of remote diagnosis. In addition to airplanes, the company monitors 300 locomotives that also relay sensor data via satellite to a GE service center. Monitoring is facilitated by the switch to electronic from mechanical controls, some two dozen microprocessors control a modern locomotive.[5]

New Chip Technologies

Chipmakers exhibited great creativity in improving the performance of chips based on silicon. However, new approaches may replace this material in the future. One of the ways to increase miniaturization and speed is a molecular-level computer. HP and UCLA patented a technique for making molecular-scale logic chips, which may eventually replace silicon chips. This early research produced sample logic circuits a hundred times smaller that the size of today's chips. Scientists create these small chips using chemical and electrical processes.[6]

Carbon nanotubes are also being applied to the design of electrical circuits. Researchers at IBM developed a thread-like nanotube that they draped over electrodes, producing two types of transistors, each a few nanometers (billionths of a meter) in diameter, which is 100 times smaller than today's transistors on computer chips. Currently, Intel gets 42 million transistors on a Pentium 4 chip, but it is becoming difficult to add more. Nanotube transistors could allow billions of transistors on a chip.[7]

Implications

Technology does not stand still; computers progressed from bulky vacuum tubes to tiny chips, and researchers are investigating new ideas for improved computational devices that will be smaller, take less power, and operate faster than today's processors. Rather than looking with disdain at legacy systems, it is important to recognize the steady progress of technology that is bound to create them. It is too early to forecast which of the innovations described are likely to be successful in the marketplace and to plan accordingly. Instead, it is necessary to learn how to manage legacy systems while simultaneously taking advantage of what new technology has to offer.

CHAPTER SUMMARY

1. Computer technology is marked by great changes. The early years were the era of the mainframe. They were followed by the development of the minicomputer and then the personal computer.

2. The mainframe computer is often criticized today, but it has a lot of features to recommend it. The most important is the large number of applications that currently run only on mainframes. The cost of redoing all of these systems is staggering! Mainframe technology is also well understood and the machines have achieved a high degree of reliability.

3. The minicomputer has evolved into a midrange system. These systems are merging with file servers that provide data and sometimes programs for PCs in a network.

4. A few manufacturers make supercomputers. It appears that the supercomputer of the future is most likely to be a massively parallel machine or a group of computers in a grid all working on the same problem when they are not busy.

5. The personal digital assistant has been very successful. Improvements in wireless communications and the capabilities of these machines should increase their appeal.

6. The revolution in computer technology came about because of the chip and the ability to put millions of electronic components on a small chip of silicon or other material. Chipmakers are continually developing new approaches to pack more transistors on a chip to improve its performance.

7. Many of the features of larger computers are incorporated into PC chips as these devices become more sophisticated.

8. Changes in the technology force changes in hardware and software architecture. The cost per MIP (millions of instructions per second) of a PC is much lower than for a mainframe. PC software is also easier to use and more appealing to the user than mainframe applications. These changes in the technology and the economics of computing prompted the client-server model in which data and some programs reside on servers, midrange computers, or mainframes while users work with PCs running programs to access and analyze the data provided by the various servers.

9. Computers are fast, but secondary storage is not. It takes much longer to access data on a disk than in primary memory. However, it is not practical (or possible) to keep gigabyte (billions of bytes) or larger databases in primary memory.

10. Efforts are underway to store content on the Web in such a way that programs can interpret content meaning, the so-called semantic Web.

11. Trends to watch include ubiquitous computing and software distributed around the Internet.

KEYWORDS

Batch	Laser printer	Semantic Web
Client	Minicomputer	Server
Disk file	Monitoring	Supercomputer
Graphics	Nanotubes	Ubiquitous computing
Grid computing	Online	Web services
Imaging	Proprietary hardware	XML

RECOMMENDED READINGS

Anderson, D., and Kubiatowicz, J. 2002. The worldwide computer. *Scientific American,* March, pp. 40–47.

Berners-Lee, T., Hendler, J., and Lassila, O. 2001. The semantic Web. *Scientific American,* May, pp. 35–43.

Foster, I. " 2003. GRID: Computing without bounds. *Scientific American,* April, pp. 78–85. (An article proposing the Web as the grid for a virtual worldwide supercomputer.)

IEEE Spectrum, January issues. (This publication features annual technology reviews and forecasts or a number of technologies.

Monthly issues generally offer articles on computer hardware and software and networks.)

Susarla, A., Barua, A., and Whinston, A. B. 2003. Understanding the service component of application service provision: An empirical analysis of satisfaction with ASP services. *MIS Quarterly,* 27(1), pp. 91–123.

Saha, D., and Mukherjee, A. 2003. Pervasive computing: A paradigm for the 21st century. *IEEE Computer,* March, pp.

25–31. (How computers will move into the background of everyday living.)

Walsh, K. R. 2003. Analyzing the application ASP concept: Technologies, economies, and strategies. *Communications of the ACM,* 46(8), pp. 103–107. (Discusses the advantages, economics, and technologies used by the application service provider (ASP) model; increased availability of software applications; improvement in network computing technologies; ASP infrastructure; and computer security and reliability.)

DISCUSSION QUESTIONS

1. Distinguish between computer hardware and software. Which most concerns a manager?

2. Why is the cost/performance ratio for a PC much better than for a mainframe?

3. What is grid computing? How does it work?

4. Why can conversion from one computer to another be a problem?

5. Why is it difficult to convert programs from mainframes to client-server platforms?

6. What are the implications of wireless communications for management?

7. What are the main limitations of a PDA?

8. What are the uses for a supercomputer?

9. What are Web services? How do they work?

10. What applications can you think of for a PDA that accesses the Internet?

11. What features should a high-end server have?

12. What are the main characteristics of the client-server model?

13. Why is a computer manufacturer interested in compatibility within its own line of machines? Does a manufacturer want its computers to be compatible with the computers of other manufacturers? What are the advantages and disadvantages of such a strategy?

14. What applications seem best suited to the use of a touch screen?

15. What issues are involved in making a massively parallel computer work?

16. What are the advantages and disadvantages of a cellular phone as an Internet access device?

17. What are the reasons for having secondary storage? Why not just add more primary memory?

18. What are the arguments for having data and servers in a central location?

19. How has IBM's hardware strategy evolved over the years since it generated most of its revenue through mainframe computer leasing and sales?

20. Compare and contrast Net PCs with inexpensive personal computers.

21. Why might an application use a two-tier client-server architecture in which one server provides program execution and another server holds the database?

22. Do you think that at some point in the future companies will no longer own computers, but will obtain computing services from an Internet utility, similar to the way they obtain electrical power?

23. Do you think companies made mistakes that led to the heterogeneous computing environments often encountered? Did they choose inappropriate computers to acquire in past years?

24. What is ubiquitous computing? Do you think it will become pervasive? Why or why not?

25. What are the implications for the use of the Web if efforts to make meaning more transparent are successful?

26. What are the pros and cons of partitioning a large computer to turn it into a series of smaller servers? What are the pros and cons of blade servers?

27. What new technologies are likely to dramatically increase the performance of computer chips?

28. What are Web services? What are users trying to accomplish with these services?

ENDNOTES

1. *Business Week,* June 3, 2002.

2. *New York Times,* November 10, 2003.

3. *Technology Review,* September 2002.

4. *Wall Street Journal,* August 13, 2002.

5. *Technology Review,* September 2001.

6. *InformationWeek,* February 4, 2002.

7. *Technology Review,* March 2002.

CHAPTER 14

THE SECOND COMPONENT: THE DATABASE

A Manager's Perspective

The database is the second component that creates the extraordinary power of modern information technology. Storage devices let the computer file and retrieve data and update information. In the early days of computing, programmers had to handle all of the design of storage files and write routines for accessing the data. Soon it became obvious that programmers were all doing just about the same thing, so why not automate it? Several companies, who were not computer vendors, developed database management systems for mainframe computers. These companies were successful, and they forced IBM to get into the database business. When you build an application in Access on your PC, you are benefiting from years of database development. Two decades ago only a skilled programmer could do what you do routinely on your PC!

THE IMPORTANCE OF THE DATABASE

Databases are one of the most significant parts of information technology, as well as one of the least understood components of systems. The database is the place where an organization stores content, which consists of data, documents, pictures, or anything that can be represented in a computer. The database not only stores all of this valuable content, it makes it possible to retrieve it instantaneously. Users easily understand a manual system with files in folders and filing cabinets, but often have trouble with the concept of storing data in a computer system. The information on what flights are available between two cities, on the balance in your checking account, and on the securities in your brokerage account has to be stored someplace in a system so that you can retrieve it by asking a question about flights between two cities, entering your bank account number, or inputting your brokerage account number.

A student working on her dissertation studied the way new employees in a consulting firm, most of whom were recently hired MBAs, learned how to use the IT tools the firm provided to help solve clients' problems. She found that the students had no trouble learning to use Excel models, and most of them knew word processing before they started. The application that provided the most problems was in understanding Access and the relational database model. In fact, the doctoral student found these new employees developing complicated Excel spreadsheets to solve problems that would have been far easier in Access.

Computers would be valuable even if all they could do is compute; certainly in a number of problems in science and engineering, the computer's key contribution is the ability to perform a huge number of calculations in an extremely short time period. But the database is what makes IT so valuable for organizations. The ability of a system to store and retrieve vast amounts of data is the second major component of the technology that has transformed business organizations. Any business organization depends on information to operate, and the database is one of its most valuable resources.

DATABASE MANAGEMENT SOFTWARE

The first computers stored information on paper tape, punched cards, and finally on magnetic tape. The development of the magnetic disk file changed processing dramatically. With a disk, it is possible to access data directly. One type of disk consists of a series of platters mounted on a spindle (see Figure 14-1). The top and bottom of each platter (except for the very top and bottom ones) are coated with a magnetic material like that on a music cassette tape. Read and write heads are fitted between the platters. They float on a cushion of air created by the rotation of the disk and do not actually touch the surface of the platter. Moving the heads in and out allows access to any spot on the rotating disk.

The total access time to read or write is about ten to twenty milliseconds. Because the internal processing speeds of the computer are measured in nanoseconds, processing that requires accessing the disk is up to a million times slower than processing data in primary memory. Because of the way in which all secondary storage devices work, the program must bring data from a disk or tape into primary memory before it can process it. Storage devices do not have processing logic, they organize and hold data under the direction of programs.

Enter DBMS Software

All programmers working with direct access files were going through the same process of developing schemes to store and retrieve data. It was also getting more and more expensive

FIGURE 14-1 Magnetic disk.

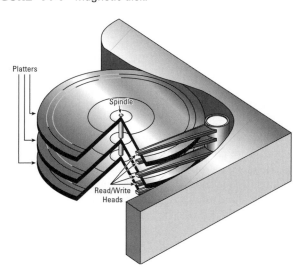

to change systems because these changes involved altering file structures and records. To address these two problems, software vendors developed database management systems (DBMSs) to automate many of the tasks associated with using direct access files. As with other types of software originally developed for large computers, a large number of sophisticated DBMSs now work on personal computers.

A DBMS helps solve the storage and retrieval problems in several ways. First, a database administrator describes the database and desired indexes, and the DBMS does the work of creating them. Second, the database administrator defines the records, and individual programs can ask for specific fields (pieces of data) without having to define the entire record. As a result, only programs that access a piece of data have to be changed when something about that data changes.

A DBMS must provide the following:

- A method for defining the contents of the database
- A way to describe relationships among data elements and records
- A mechanism to set up the database in the first place
- Ways to manipulate the data including:

  - Updating (adding, modifying, and/or deleting information)
  - Retrieval using complex criteria to select data

Benefits of the Relational Model

The *relational model* is the dominant structure for vendors writing DBMS. The underlying concept of a relational file system is simple: Data are organized in two-dimensional tables, such as the one in Figure 14-2. These tables are easy for a user to develop and understand. One virtue of this type of structure is that it can be described mathematically, a most difficult task for other types of data structures. The name is derived from the fact that each table represents a relation.

Because different users see different sets of data and different relationships among them, it is necessary to extract subsets of the table columns for some users and to join tables together to form larger tables for others. The mathematics provides the basis for extracting some columns from the tables and for joining various columns.

Relational database management systems offer many advantages. Most DBMSs for personal computers are based on the relational model because it is relatively easy for users to understand. This section presents an example of a relational database and shows how it would be processed by a personal computer DBMS. It also discusses some of the key issues in the design of relational databases.

An Example

The most common file structure is a record that consists of related data fields. For example, a student database might contain a record that consists of the following data fields: student number, student last name, student first name, address line one, address line two, city, state, ZIP code, and phone number. (See Figure 14-3.) Each field consists of one data element, and the size of the field is the same for each record. For example, a designer

FIGURE 14-2 A relational database.

Name	Address	Zip code	City	Department number
Smith	16 Main	92116	New York	302
Jones	37 Spencer	07901	Chicago	161
Morris	19 Old Way	83924	New York	302
Able	86 Fulton	10006	Denver	927
Charles	19 Hunter	11126	Chicago	161

Name	Profession	Income
Johnson	Bartender	$45,000
Martin	Programmer	$54,000
Jones	Systems Analyst	$78,000
Carson	Manager	$117,000
Smith	Systems Analyst	$89,000

Join:	Name,	Address,	Zip code,	Profession,	Income
	Jones	37 Spencer	07901	Systems Analyst	$78,000

Project:	City,	Department
	New York	302
	Chicago	161
	Denver	927

might allow fifteen characters for student last name. To simplify processing, for a student named Smith, that name would occupy fifteen characters in the record. Often a database system will ask the user to define an index or key field; in this example, the user would designate student number as a key. The database will build an index to make it faster to find records when someone enters a particular student number.

Figure 14-4 shows the results of creating two relations using a DBMS called Access, a part of Microsoft Office, and entering data in them. The first relation is Student; the key is student number, and the other fields are name, age, and year in school. The second relation is Class, and its key is also student number; the relation relates student number to class number.

Figure 14-5 shows how Access can be used to inquire about all students who are in year 1. The user fills out a table describing the inquiry and indicates each desired field for the answer, then indicates the criteria for selection. In this case, the criterion is that year = 1. Access places the answer on an output screen.

One of the most frequently used relational operations is the join, in which two relations are joined on some key. Figure 14-6 shows how the DBMS would be used to join the Student and Class relations. Note the line the user drew to indicate the relation between the student numbers. That line tells Access the common field on which the two relations are to be joined.

The Figure 14-6(a) shows the query form, and the results of the join are shown in Figure 14-6(b). Now a list indicates each student and his or her assigned classes. Note that Doe does not appear in the join because the Class relation for Doe had no record. Similarly, student 160 is listed as taking two classes, so Berman appears twice in the joined relation.

FIGURE 14-3 A record definition for a database table.

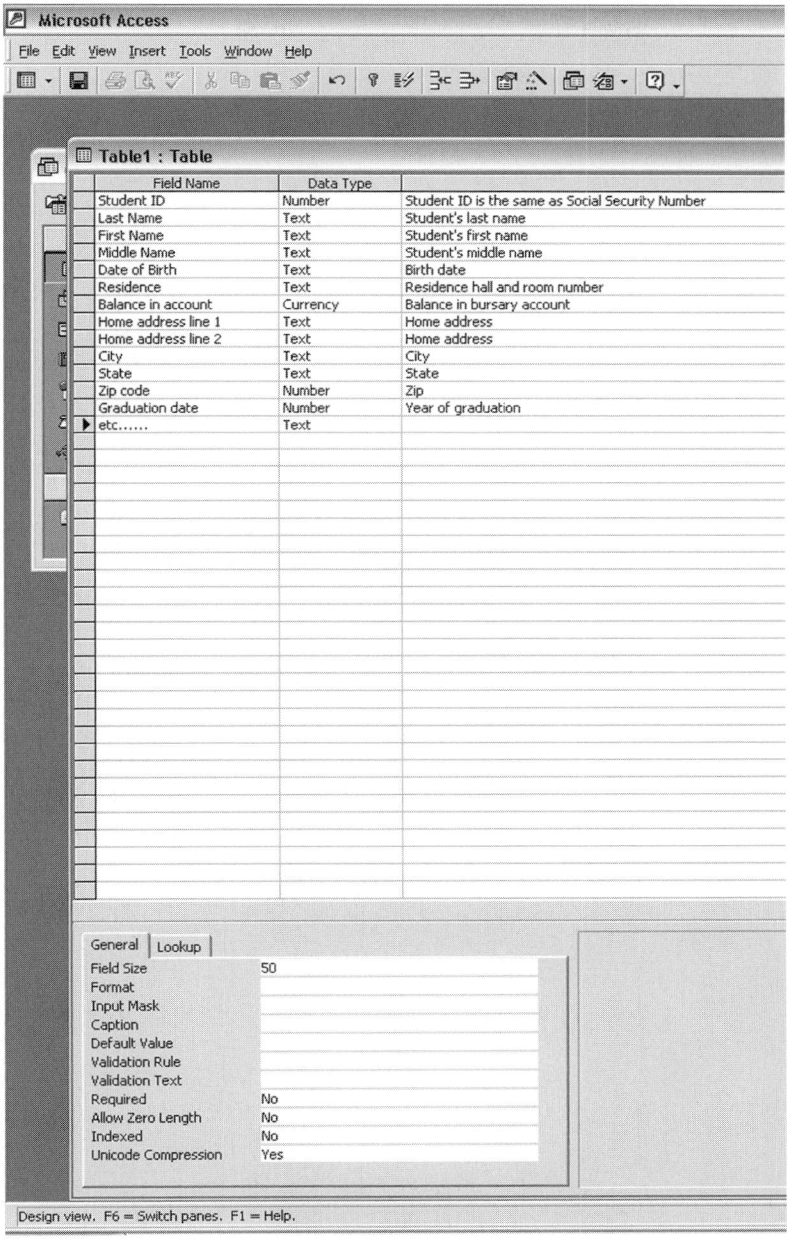

FIGURE 14-4 Setting up two relations.

FIGURE 14-5 Setting up an inquiry on year = 1. *(Continues)*

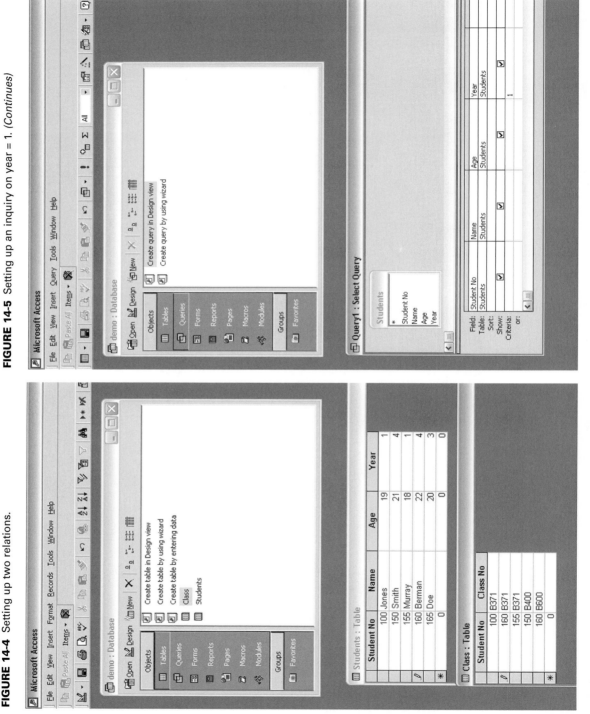

FIGURE 14-6 Setting up join of two relations. *(Continues)*

FIGURE 14-5 *(Continued)* Running the inquiry on year = 1.

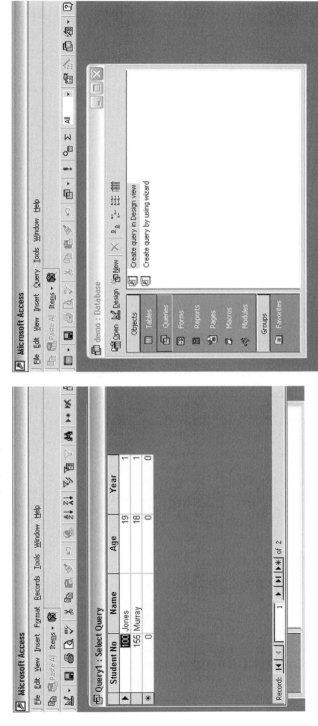

FIGURE 14-6 *(Continued)* Results of the join.

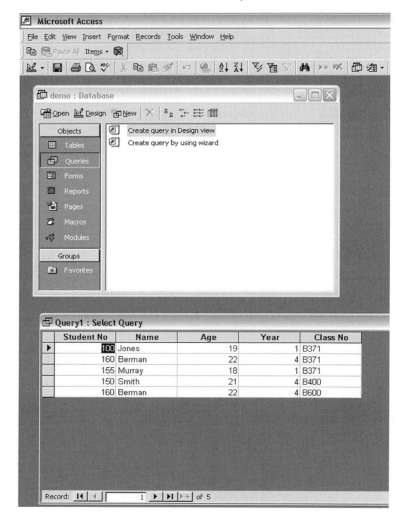

Object-Oriented Databases

Most relational databases support a limited number of data types, generally alphabetic (character), numeric (decimals and integers), dates, and time. A modern organization has many different kinds of data, such as graphics objects, audio sound clips, video segments, subscripted arrays, and complex data used for data mining. Different relational database management vendors developed extensions to their products in order to handle objects; this capability adds a great deal of power to database processing. One such provision allows the selection of data based on the content of an object. For example, you might express a query as:

```
SELECT *
FROM VISITOR
WHERE Reception_Photo LIKE Email_Photo
```

The system should look through photos (graphic objects) sent via e-mail to the company in advance and compare them to a photo just taken at the reception desk to be sure the visitor is the person who made an appointment. These extensions make a relational database more robust in meeting the needs of different kinds of users and their organizations.

SQL

IBM developed Structured Query Language (SQL) as a retrieval language for users, but it is somewhat complex, so few users are likely to work with it directly. SQL has been adopted by the major DBMSs and offers a mechanism for universal database access. For example, suppose that the DBMS you are using translates the query language you enter into SQL commands. It could then retrieve data on a different system as long as they both used the same SQL dialect.

1. The basic structure of a SQL expression has three parts. The select clause lists the attributes desired in answer to the query.

2. The from clause is a list of relations or tables that the query language processor should consult in filling the request.

3. The where clause describes the attributes desired in the answer.

As an example, consider the following SQL expressions taken from Korth and Silberschatz (1986):

```
select branch-name
  from deposit
```

This SQL expression obtains a list of all branch names from a bank table (branch-name) containing data about branches and customers. One might find all customers having an account in the Midtown branch with the following expression:

```
select customer-name
  from deposit
  where branch-name="Midtown"
```

SQL expressions can become complicated with qualified retrieval requests:

```
(select customer-name
  from deposit
  where branch-name="Midtown")
  intersect
(select customer-name
  from borrow
  where branch-name="Midtown")
```

The preceding query produces a table of all customers who have both a loan (from the borrow table) and an account in the Midtown branch.

For the proliferation of database management systems for all types of computers, SQL appears as the one common thread. Various vendors design their DBMS packages to translate queries using the package's interface into SQL commands to query a remote database. This feature can hold great interest for a user.

Suppose you are working with Access, a PC database system, and want to retrieve data located on an IBM mainframe in a DB2 database. You would like to enter Access queries and not have to learn about DB2. Using a SQL interface, Access could retrieve the data you want from the mainframe. Of course, Access must translate your queries into SQL and forward them to the DB2 for processing. You would have to know the names of the fields and the relations in the DB2 database.

The use of SQL as an intermediary and a standard in accessing a large number of different types of database systems should be of great help to users and to systems analysts. Although you may never formulate a query in SQL, you are likely to find it processing queries developed in other languages.

Oracle: An Enterprise DBMS

The Oracle Corporation is the leading vendor of databases at the enterprise or entire firm level, claiming to have the largest market share for server database systems. Today the company positions its primary database system called Oracle *n*, where *n* is the most recent version, as a database for network computing for the enterprise.

Oracle's view of hardware and software architecture is what they call *servercentric*. They mean that most of the heavy processing takes place on the server, with the client having limited logic. One of the arguments in favor of this architecture is control and the ability to respond to change. If databases are distributed across a number of clients, it is easy for data to be in conflict and it is difficult to ensure that changes reach each machine. Keeping a database centrally on one or more servers reduces the problems of managing the data.

Oracle offers an extended relational data model and uses SQL for queries. The first relational database systems supported alphabetic and numeric data types. Today, the many types of data include images, documents, audio, and video to name a few. Rather than create a separate system for each, Oracle extended its DBMS to support a variety of data types. Oracle models an object view, essentially to map data from a relational database so that it looks as if one is working with an object, which is the basis of object-oriented systems.

Oracle's latest version of its DBMS will support tens of thousands of users, according to the company. It also can process huge amounts of data, tens of terabytes or more, to support the kind of highly detailed, disaggregated data that companies like to analyze. The company also provides support for using Java in combination with its DBMS to develop applications. In addition to offering its DBMS as a product, Oracle used it to develop a number of applications packages consisting of thirty-five integrated software modules for tasks such as financial management, supply chain management, manufacturing, human resources, and sales force automation to form an enterprise resource planning (ERP) system.

Distributed Databases

Organizations are building more distributed databases in which different parts of the database are located on different computers in a network. This type of database raises a number of issues for the organization, including the following:

■ Will data be replicated across computers or will there be only one copy?

MANAGEMENT PROBLEM 14-1

One of the great things about a database system is data independence. The idea is to make data and the programs that access them as independent as possible so that a change in the database has a minimum impact on programs. The program only asks for the exact data it needs and is unaffected if data that it does not need are changed in the database. This approach works well in general, but it cannot guarantee that large changes can be avoided.

An example is a major change for retailers, which is coming on January 1, 2005, when twelve-digit bar codes go to thirteen digits because of a shortage of UPC codes. The thirteen-digit codes are used almost everywhere else in the world. One expert estimates that this change will cost at least $2 million for a chain of 100 stores with ten checkout lanes each to upgrade.[1] This number is probably conservative.

First, retailers must replace the readers, the scanners themselves unless they are capable of reading thirteen digits, which is the case only if they are less than three years old. Duane Reade, a chain of 200 drugstores in New York has 3,500 scanners that cost $1,000 to $2,500 each. And of course, that is just for the hardware. The software dealing with the database for scanner data will have to change to accommodate thirteen digits instead of twelve. The UPC code is a key field used to look up a price and record sales of an item. It is possible, but not certain that some programs using the code will have to be changed to reflect this new field. Any displays on a screen or printed reports will need one more digit displayed, so changes will be necessary in output programs, and screen and report formats.

As a consultant to Duane Reade, develop a plan for determining the extent of the changes required to go to thirteen digits in the UPC bar code. Itemize the changes that are likely to be required and the information you would need to estimate the total cost of the project.

- If data are replicated, how frequently must different versions be updated to reflect changes (different values for the same data will result if all copies of a file are not updated at once)?
- How will updates to the database be coordinated so that integrity is maintained?
- Who "owns" distributed data, and who has access to it?
- Distributed databases offer users easier access to data at the cost of higher overall complexity of the system.

Consider a company such as Victor Electronics with operations in the Americas, Europe, and Asia. You could design a system in which all data are stored at one location, say in Rockville, Maryland, in the United States. Another option is to have the Americas data on a database in Rockville, European orders and customer information on a system in Manchester, and keep Asian data on a system in Singapore. Each region would have control over its own data, and communications among regions would facilitate sales made in one place of product located in another. This distributed system makes it unlikely that all of Victor's systems and data would be lost if something happened to a network or data center. Each location could provide backup for the others, though it would entail increased coordination costs and complexity.

The Data Warehouse

Businesses collect a tremendous amount of transactions data as a part of their routine operations. Marketing departments and others would like to analyze these data to understand the business better. For example, you might ask to see a display of sales by region, for the current time period, compared to the same time last year. After seeing this display, you want to see the analysis by product group, then product group for the last six months, and finally the same data by sales team. Instead of the two dimensions associated with the relational model, you are asking for a multidimensional analysis.

To accommodate this kind of analysis, called online analytical processing (OLAP), firms offer multidimensional databases for data warehousing. You must define the various dimensions of your business so the system can provide summaries based on those dimensions. The idea is to let you ask questions involving a number of factors without having to be familiar with the underlying organization of data. See Figure 14-7 for an example of how a multidimensional view differs from a relational table. One strategy for creating the *data cube* associated with a multidimensional database is to create a *fact cube* through an *n*-way crossing of all the dimensions specified when defining the database.

Analysis of a data in a warehouse can help you understand your business better. This kind of technology, then, helps create a *learning organization*, an organization that is able to understand its market, customers, and itself better.

An Example: A Data Warehouse at Hudson's Bay Company

Hudson's Bay Company (Hbc), established in 1670, is Canada's largest department store retailer and oldest corporation. Even as competition in the Canadian retail market exploded over the past decade and the economy softened, Hudson's Bay Company has seen solid growth. It now has more than 500 stores and 70,000 employees at several retail channels, led by the Bay and Zellers chains.

Hbc's hundreds of stores generate a tremendous amount of data spread across a number of operational systems, which make it difficult to quickly access information. To make merchandising and product management decisions, merchandising associates relied on the IT group to produce reports. The reports could take as long as one week to generate and often were missing information or were too old to be useful by the time they were delivered. Inventory and buying decisions had to be made largely on instinct, not analysis. Management saw the data warehouse as a way to consolidate and share data.

The Hbc IT staff and a consultant built a data warehouse around the Teradata® database. Since initial installation, the Hbc data warehouse grew from 245 gigabytes to more than 1.7 terabytes of user data with Hbc adding two nodes to the system each year as new stores and more data are added and new applications are built. The system runs on a six-processor node NCR 5250 server; and currently requires 4 terabytes (10^9) of disk space.

The Teradata Warehouse stores both detail and summary sales and inventory data, with information refreshed nightly from more than 100 inputs from different operational systems. More than 400 users access the system to perform ad hoc queries and view standard reports.

The Teradata Warehouse provides Hbc users with a single view of the business for analyzing inventory and promotional programs, monitoring sales, and influencing ordering so they can make better, faster decisions. Even though measuring all the benefits of the system is impossible, Hbc has been able to quantify a 300 percent return on investment. Savings were identified through reduced excess inventory, lower labor costs (because answers are easier to find), and a reduction in lost sales during promotions. According to Mary Jane Jarvis-Haig, Senior Manager, Data Warehousing for Hbc, these factors are what the business users have been able to identify. "We have many tremendous softer intangible benefits that are difficult to quantify, such as better information, faster and better decision making."

FIGURE 14-7 Multidimensional Database Example.

A multidimensional database supports multiple views of data sets for users who need to analyze the relationships between data categories. For example, a marketing analyst might want answers to the following questions:

■ How did Product A sell last month? How does this figure compare to sales in the same month over the last five years? How did the product sell by branch, region, and territory?

■ Did this product sell better in particular regions? Are there regional trends?

■ Did customers return Product A last year? Were the returns due to product defects? Did the company manufacture the products in a specific plant?

■ Did commissions and pricing affect how salespeople sold the product?

■ Did particular salespeople do a better job of selling the product?

The analyst would use tools like Excel for online analytical processing or OLAP to answer these questions.

Data is stored in a multidimensional database as a cube of cells containing data values. Each data value is stored in a single cell in the database. You refer to a particular data value by specifying its coordinates along each standard dimension. Consider the simplified database in Figure 14.7a.

FIGURE 14.7a A multidimensional database outline.

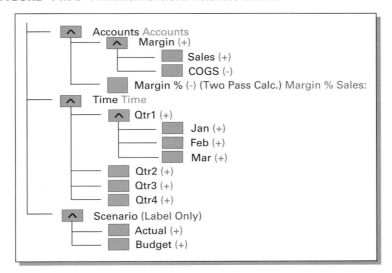

This database has three dimensions: Accounts, Time, and Scenario.

■ The Accounts dimension has four members: Sales, COGS, Margin, Margin%.

■ The Time dimension has four quarter members. Figure 14-7a shows only the members in Qtr1.

■ The Scenario dimension has two child members: Budget for budget values and Actual for actual values.

An intersection of members (one member from each dimension) represents a data value. The example in Figure 14-7a has three dimensions; thus, the dimensions and data values in the database can be represented in a cube, as shown in Figure 14.7b.

FIGURE 14.7b A three dimensional database.

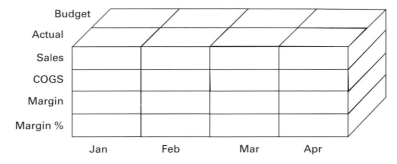

The shaded cells in Figure 14.7c illustrate that, when you refer to Sales, you are referring to a slice of the database containing eight Sales values:

FIGURE 14.7c Sales slice of the database.

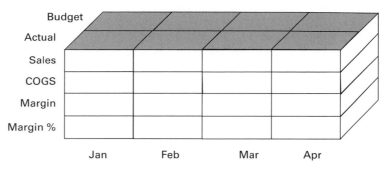

When you refer to Actual Sales, you are referring to four Sales values:

FIGURE 14.7d Actual Sales slice of the database.

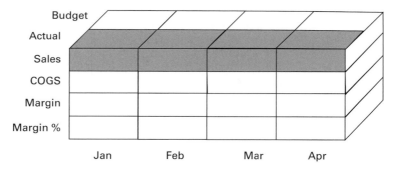

A data value is stored in a single cell in the database. To refer to a specific data value in a multidimensional database, you specify its member on each dimension. In Figure 14.7e, the cell containing the data value for Sales, Jan, Actual is shaded:

FIGURE 14.7e   Sales, Jan, Actual slice of the database.

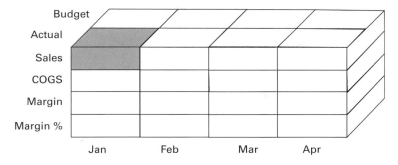

Slicing the database in different ways gives you different perspectives of the data. The slice in Figure 14.7f, for example, shows data about the month of February:

FIGURE 14.7f   Data for February.

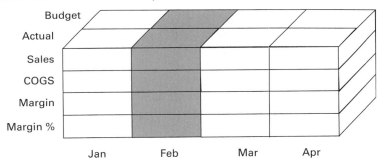

The slice in Figure 14.7g shows data for profit margin:

FIGURE 14.7g   Profit margin slice of the database.

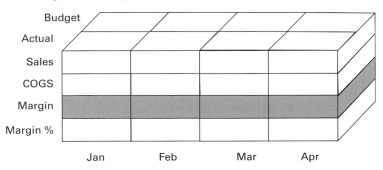

Slicing a database amounts to fixing one or more dimensions at a constant value while allowing the other dimensions to vary. The slice of February in Figure 14.7f, for example, examines all data values for which the Month dimension is fixed at February.

SOURCE: Adapted from http://www.essbase.com/, the maker of Hyperion Software Solutions.

As a product management system, the data warehouse is having an impact on Hbc's supply chain management processes. "The data warehouse is adding value both in the information it provides and in the support of more finely tuned and effective processes," says Jarvis-Haig. "The data warehouse began as just another information source, but the business has become very dependent on it." The importance of the data warehouse is evident in the promotions the retailer runs, and promotions are an important part of a retailer's strategy. Previously, merchandising associates relied on spotty reports or they made decisions based on instinct. Now users can query the system by SKU level for various stores to analyze promotions to ensure the right amount of inventory is in stock at each store when specific products are promoted. That capability means fewer lost sales and product markdowns. Promotions on seasonal items such as beach towels have seen significant reductions in lost sales with improved store allocations. Hbc is also using the data warehouse to better know its customers' needs through market basket analysis. Users can quickly query reams of transaction data to discover product affinities.

"We can see if customers are coming in and buying only what is advertised, or are also buying related products," explains Jarvis-Haig. "If we put toothpaste on sale, do we need to also promote toothbrushes or are they bought anyway? It may seem obvious, but when you're so close to the detail, sometimes you don't see the obvious. The ability to analyze shopping baskets really points to who our most profitable customers are and how we can reach them." Market basket analysis is also used to gauge the success of new line launches. By using a specific driver item, Hbc gets immediate feedback on the impact of the new line. In some cases, the analysis resulted in lines being discontinued before they seriously affected markdowns and customer satisfaction. Basket analysis also provides input on flyer effectiveness and allowed Hbc to reduce circulation costs by fine-tuning the distribution of flyers.

The IT group has a number of plans to further enhance the effectiveness of the data warehouse. It will be working to move the system to an active data warehouse through trickle feeds of data and further efficiency improvements from its operational systems. It will also attempt to further integrate operational systems with the data warehouse to accommodate event triggers. When a certain action occurs, the system will take action and notify appropriate personnel. This example demonstrates how one organization uses a data warehouse to improve its business in a number of different ways.[2]

Data Mining: Looking for Gold in the Data

The purpose of data mining is to discover interesting structure in large amounts of data. This structure consists of patterns, statistical or predictive models of the data, and relationships within the data (Fayyad and Uthurusamy, 2002). A pattern describes a relationship among a subset of the data, for example, "people who have computers at home shop online." One of the challenges in data mining is to figure out what "interesting" means, because it depends on the domain and the user. Algorithms that search data for interesting patterns and relationships need some sort of guidance from human decision makers.

Data mining is applied extensively to customer data from sources such as retail scanners that provide huge amounts of data about purchases, far too much for someone to analyze statistically. A chain of grocery stores might have a million purchases a week, and each purchase consists of a subset of thousands of products on the shelves. Correlating the items purchased with each other to look for patterns would require a great deal of computing power and would overwhelm a human with statistics. The objective of data mining in this arena is to look for relationships that maybe significant without performing a statistical analysis of all data points.

As an example, suppose that you had some way to systematically explore a large database of purchases from a chain of convenience stores. The analytical techniques that you apply to the data report that people who buy disposable diapers also tend to buy a six pack of beer at the same time. Why might these two items be purchased together? People who buy diapers obviously have young children and perhaps tend to watch television and have a can of beer rather than go out. The real reason does not matter; the fact that you discovered the relationship between purchasing two items allows you to take action. As the merchandising manager for the chain, you can place beer near disposable diapers to make it easier for the customer to purchase both items together.

SPSS is a vendor of statistical analysis software and the company offers products for data mining as well. Its Web site lists a number of reasons for undertaking data mining:

- Increasing business unit and overall profitability
- Understanding customer desires and needs
- Identifying profitable customers and acquiring new ones
- Retaining customers and increasing loyalty
- Increasing ROI and reducing costs on promotions
- Cross-selling and up-selling
- Detecting fraud, waste, and abuse
- Determining credit risks
- Increasing Web site profitability
- Increasing store traffic and optimizing layouts for increased sales
- Monitoring business performance

Approaches to Data Mining

Data mining encompasses a number of approaches to finding relationships in data. The first of these approaches is visualization. For many years people looked at graphs of data, seeking relationships and trying to determine whether two variables such as diaper and beer sales positively correlated, negatively correlated, or unrelated. A graph can tell a lot.

Visualization is closely related to different statistical techniques for analyzing data. Managers and analysts have used statistical packages for many years to look at different kinds of data and for prediction purposes. Sales forecasting is a well-developed area of practice featuring techniques from exponential smoothing to regression analysis. Factor analysis, principal components analysis, and discriminate analysis are all statistical procedures that you might use in data mining.

However, statistical techniques usually require the user to have some prior hypotheses about the variables involved, to have an idea of what you might be looking for. Other techniques for data mining are based on search and optimization methods from the management science field. A number of search algorithms can be applied to data mining. Artificial intelligence, which facilitates nonlinear analysis, provides yet another approach to data mining. A neural network can be used to help analyze a large amount of data to look for important relationships.

MANAGEMENT PROBLEM 14-2

Some organizations have systems with highly centralized databases, for example, airline, hotel, and car rental reservations systems. Other organizations with multiple locations around the world might have distributed databases, which is the case at Victor Electronics where the database of regional sales resides in the regions. A centralized database provides the most real-time coordination; an agent knows immediately if a seat on a flight is available. For example, you may be on the phone with a reservations agent and a seat opens up while you are talking. Another passenger just cancelled, the system updated the change immediately, and the newly available seat was yours to reserve.

Distributed databases often exist because when they were developed, companies felt little need to share data, which was the case at Victor. Now, however, Victor wants to share information about global finished goods inventory across regions and sales offices. Because the three systems involved use different and incompatible database managers, arranging the sharing may be difficult. Victor has asked you to help them understand the problem.

Why do you suppose that Victor developed separate databases on different computers in the first place? What reasons might justify having distributed databases today? Should a centralized database contain copies of distributed data? Why or why not? How should Victor solve its global inventory problem? Should it develop one centralized database or tie together the existing systems? If it chooses to tie the databases together, should it use a private network or the Internet?

Clementine

Clementine from SPSS is a popular product for data mining. A review of this package demonstrates the process a manager might use in trying to extract meaningful information from a large data set. Figure 14-8 comes from the Clementine Web pages. Clementine is one of several commercial products for data mining; an organization can employ this powerful technique to develop business intelligence without needing specialists in management science or artificial intelligence. Data mining is something to consider given the huge amounts of data that are now captured online via scanners, online stores, and companies with linked supply chains.

An Example of Data Mining at Credit Suisse

"Credit Suisse's data mining activities—analysis and modeling—have been fully integrated into our business processes and have proven their value in many different applications," said Dr. Alex Nippe, head of data analysis/data mining at Credit Suisse. "The demand for data mining within the bank is rising all the time, and the strategic component is becoming increasingly important."

The bank used data mining for a new Loyalty Based Management project. Bank customer consultants had limited resources and depended on information that enabled them to use these resources as efficiently as possible. The consultants' services were also costly, and their time needed to be used effectively. As a result of the success of the Loyalty Based Management project, Credit Suisse consultants began to see data mining's benefits and started to use it to sell specific customers targeted services. With SPSS's data mining tool, Clementine, Credit Suisse now identifies customers, typically the top 1 percent, who are extremely likely to buy a service, thus increasing the opportunities for cross-selling and retaining customers.

FIGURE 14-8 Clementine for Data Mining (http://www.spss.com/spssbi/clementine).

Leverage Your Firsthand Knowledge

As a manager, you need to know what you are doing with the valuable data that's flowing into your organization everyday. Clementine's powerful visual interface enables you to interact with this precise record of your operations and customer relationships to discover solutions you otherwise wouldn't.

Build Your Expertise into the Discovery Process

You search for a solution by creating and interacting with a stream—a visual map of the entire data mining process—through which your data flows. This visual approach makes it easy to see every step along the data mining journey and enables you to quickly explore hunches or ideas by interacting with the stream. Even Clementine's graphs are interactive, helping you to use discoveries made within a graph to get closer to your goal.

Explore Opportunities with Powerful Modeling Techniques

Clementine enables you to explore the opportunities in your data, backed by a comprehensive set of powerful modeling techniques to help you find the best result in the shortest amount of time. Even if opportunities for improving your business are hidden deep within massive datasets with millions of rows and hundreds of columns, Clementine scales up to the size of the challenge to produce fast results.

Get Answers from Your Data with the Interactive Discovery Process

See Your Solution Discovery Process Clearly

The interactive stream approach to data mining is the key to Clementine's power. Using icons that represent steps in the data mining process, you mine your data by building a stream, or a visual map of the process your data flows through. Start by simply dragging a source icon from the object palette onto the Clementine desktop to access your data flow. Then, explore your data visually with graphs. Apply several types of algorithms to build your model by simply placing the appropriate icons onto the desktop to form a stream.

Discover Knowledge Interactively

Data mining with Clementine is a discovery-driven process. Work toward a solution by applying your business expertise to select the next step in your stream, based on the discoveries made in the previous step. You can continually adapt or extend initial streams as you work through the solution to your business problem.

Build and Test Models Easily

All of Clementine's advanced techniques work together to quickly give you the best answer to your business problems. You can build and test numerous models to immediately see which model produces the best result. You can even combine models by using the results of one model as input into another model. These metamodels consider the initial model's decisions and can improve results substantially.

Understand Variations in Your Business with Visualized Data

Powerful data visualization techniques help you understand key relationships in your data and guide the way to the best results. Clementine's interactive graphs help in spotting characteristics and patterns at a glance. Then you can "query by mouse" to explore these patterns by selecting subsets of data or deriving new variables on the fly from discoveries made within the graph.

How Clementine Scales to the Size of the Challenge

The Clementine approach to scaling is unique in the way it aims to scale the complete data mining process to the size of large, challenging datasets. Clementine executes common operations used throughout the data mining process in the database through SQL queries. This process leverages the power of the database for faster processing, enabling you to get better results with large datasets.

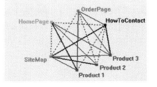

Detailed segmentation of its vast customer base allows Credit Suisse to develop targeted solutions for its customers. This segmentation is executed inductively using the cluster algorithm and the dimensions are tailored directly to customer requirements.

Each cluster serves as a starting point for individual marketing campaigns. This hierarchical system is advantageous because the system customer database is continually researched and monitored. As a result, changes in the cluster structure are quickly identified and appropriate responses are triggered.

It's not enough to know whether customers are interested in a product. Will they actually follow though and purchase it? Credit Suisse uses data mining to analyze situations where customer interest in a service did not correlate with a purchase. Many times, customers did not have good enough credit and were subsequently refused the service. Improved models factored in credit as a criterion. As a result, the percentage of customers interested in purchasing a service but who were refused due to bad credit was reduced by almost half in subsequent campaigns. The reductions allowed substantial cost savings. Dr. Nippe affirmed, "We recouped the total costs of the project within two years."[3]

DATABASES AND THE ORGANIZATION

The database is the second component of an information technology that provides the organization with incredible opportunities. The typical organization has many databases, some highly organized and others a loose collection of information. You can think of your firm's Web site as a database of content; for a large company you can be talking about thousands of pages of this content on a Web site. E-mail programs also provide a database, usually organized around file folders where users file their messages. The routine processing of transactions generates huge amounts of data, which the organization stores in a database. Many firms also collect data from external sources, such as the sales statistics for companies in one's industry. A manager is responsible for the creation, maintenance, and protection of these data. They are the firm's memory, and they allow it to remain in business.

CHAPTER SUMMARY

1. Organizations keep a tremendous amount of material in machine-readable form stored as files on a computer. This trend will continue as firms move away from the use of paper for records.

2. Data in files are stored in records. The most common form is a fixed-length record consisting of fields. Each field contains a group of characters that represent a value for the field (i.e., a social security number).

3. The database management system automates the tasks of setting up a database. It facilitates defining records and relationships among them, and it handles the updating and retrieval of data from the database.

4. The relational model in which data are stored in tables or relations is the dominant type of DBMS today.

5. SQL is an intermediate language that may offer a bridge among different DBMSs.

6. You can use one of a number of PC DBMSs to develop quite sophisticated applications for yourself and others to use.

7. Data warehouses facilitate online analytical processing, an analysis that helps better understand one's business and contributes to becoming a learning organization.

KEYWORDS

Character	File	OLAP
Database administrator (DBA)	From clause	Record
Database management systems (DBMS)	Join	Relation
	Key	Relational file
Data mining	Knowledge discovery	Select clause
Data warehouse	Logical view	Structured Query Language (SQL)
Entity relationship (ER) diagram	Multidimensional database	Where clause
Field	Object-oriented database	

RECOMMENDED READINGS

Cooper, B. L., Watson, H. J., Wixom, B. H., and Goodhue, D. L. 2000. Data warehousing supports corporate strategy at First American Corporation. *MIS Quarterly, 2*(4), pp. 547–567.

Embley, D. 1997. *Object Database Development: Concepts and Principles*. New York: Addison-Wesley. (A detailed introduction to object-oriented database technologies.)

Hernandez, M. 1997. *Database Design for Mere Mortals: A Hands-On Guide to Relational Database Design*. New York: Addison-Wesley. (A practical reference explaining the core concepts of design theory without technical jargons.)

Parent, C., and Spaccapietra, S. 1998. Issues and approaches of database integration. *Communications of the ACM, 41*(5), pp. 166–178. (An excellent paper exploring the issue of integrating different databases.)

Schach, S. 2000. *Introduction to Object-Oriented Analysis and Design with UML and the Unified Process*. New York: Irwin McGraw-Hill. (A clear explanation of object-oriented design.)

Silberschatz, A., Korth, H., and Sudershan, S. 1998. *Database System Concepts,* 3rd ed. New York: McGraw Hill. (A complete database textbook that covers everything from the basic to complex and provides theoretical underpinnings and practical implications.)

Wixom, B. H., and Watson, H. J. 2001. An empirical investigation of the factors affecting data warehousing success. *MIS Quarterly, 25*(1), pp. 17–41.

DISCUSSION QUESTIONS

1. Why do users have different logical views of their data requirements?

2. Why is direct access so much more flexible than sequential access?

3. How does a DBMS tend to make data and programs more independent? Can programs and data ever be totally independent?

4. What is OLAP? How does it contribute to the organization?

5. Why do most organizations use a DBMS for specific applications rather than attempt to define a comprehensive database for all applications?

6. How does a DBMS make it easier to alter the structure of a database?

7. Does a DBMS completely isolate the user from the underlying structure of the data?

8. Why does a relational database need to be normalized?

9. Why might you want a DBMS on your PC that could also communicate with a larger computer database?

10. What complications are added to a DBMS when distributed processing is involved?

11. What kind of security and controls are needed in a DBMS?

12. In an online environment, a common problem is to lock out access to a record while it is updated. Why do you think this practice would be necessary?

13. Recovery from a computer failure or other interruption of a system is a major consideration for organizations. What problems do you see in recovering from such a failure when using a DBMS?

14. How should one backup a database used for online processing?

15. How can accessing data in relational tables be speeded over a straight sequential search?

16. What evaluation criteria would you recommend be applied to a decision of what database management system to acquire?

17. Why is a database administrator needed in an organization using a DBMS?

18. How can the systems analyst use the facilities of a DBMS during the design process for a new system?

19. To what extent is performance (in terms of speed of access) a major consideration in database design?

20. Under what conditions is it better to program a retrieval option into a system, as opposed to providing a user with a general purpose query language?

21. Under what conditions would it be desirable to duplicate data in a database?

22. Think of an application such as student registration, and then design a relational database for the registrar.

23. Under what conditions might an organization want to have more than one vendor's DBMS? What problems do you foresee with the use of multiple database systems?

24. Why has the relational model come to dominate the DBMS market for personal computers?

25. What is object-oriented analysis? How does it differ from structured design approaches?

26. What considerations apply to the decision on whether a DBMS is on a server or on client computers?

27. What demands does object-oriented design place on a database and how would you expect an object-oriented database to differ from a relational one?

ENDNOTES

1. *New York Times,* August 12, 2002.

2. Information adapted from Teradata, available at http://www.teradata.com.

3. The information about Clementine was adapted from SPSS, available at http://www.spss.com.

APPENDIX 14-1

Designing Databases

One of the major design tasks in building an information system is determining the contents and structure of a database. The type of retrieval and reporting required by users and the availability of input determine what data to store. However, it is a complex task to specify these data, group them into records, and establish data structures for a system.

One approach is to create a data model to guide the design of a database. A data model is useful for a number of reasons. First, it helps us understand the relationships among different components in a systems design. Data models show users more clearly how a system will function. Users are concerned about data and information, and they want to know whether adequate data are available to perform their jobs.

The most common type of data model is the entity-relationship (ER) diagram. The ER diagram is easy for a user to follow and serves as an excellent communications vehicle. The ER diagram consists of object types and relationships. Figure 14-9(a) provides an example of two objects linked by a relationship: A customer purchases a product. The two entities here are *customer* and *product*; the relationship is *purchases*. Entities are represented by rectangles and a relationship by a diamond. Some analysts like to use a simple, straight line between entities and label the line with the relationship, (as shown in Figure 14-9b), though certain more complex relationships cannot be modeled in this manner.

Entities also have attributes, which are the fields to be included in a file record. A product has a product number, size, description, price, cost, and so on. The

ER diagram, then, can be used to show relationships while the conventional listing of the file contents contains the attributes of entities.

Figure 14-10 shows another example of an ER diagram. Here, the figure shows that a doctor sees a patient. He or she writes a prescription and the receptionist bills the patient. The numbers on the ER diagram describe the nature of the relationship. One doctor writes from 1 to n prescriptions. In this practice, one doctor sees n patients. The receptionist sends one bill at a time to many (n) patients. Many patients buy one or more prescriptions. The entities can have 1:1, 1:n, n:1, and m:n (many-to-many) relationships.

Another way to show the nature of relationships is to use arrows. A single arrow stands for a 1 relationship, and a double arrow represents a many-to-many relationship.

Figure 14-11 is a data model for a student applying to college. A student completes an application and the admissions staff decides about many applications. It notifies candidates by sending out a letter. The round circles in the ER diagram are attributes of an entity. The application entity has three attributes: an identification number, the decision (accept, reject, postpone), and a date. Figure 14-12 shows what happens when the student works with his or her adviser. The adviser counsels many students and these n students enroll in m different classes—an n:m relationship. Each student has a biography and can choose from many different majors.

Other views might be needed for different individuals. A professor might care only about a class list, not about a student's major or adviser. The department

FIGURE 14-9   (a) An entity relationship (ER) diagram. (b) An alternative ER diagram.

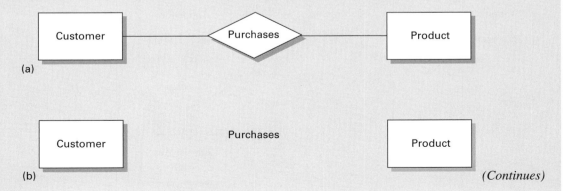

(a)

(b)   *(Continues)*

APPENDIX 14-1 *(CONTINUED)*

Designing Databases

chairperson wants to know something about majors in the department. These differences are called logical views of the data. It is likely that different users will have different logical views of data. A key task of design is to integrate these many potential views and create a physical database capable of supporting different logical views with adequate performance.

FIGURE 14-10 Doctor-patient ER diagram.

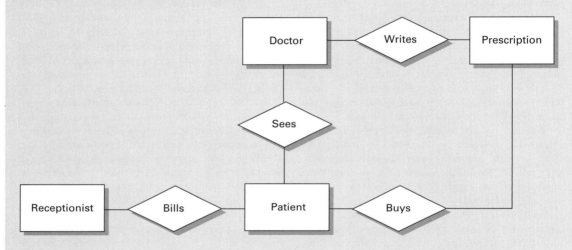

FIGURE 14-11 College application ER diagram.

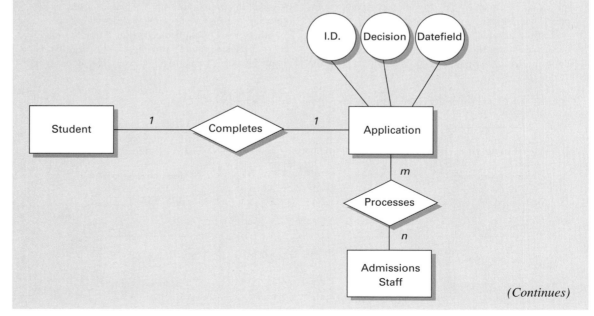

(Continues)

APPENDIX 14-1 *(CONTINUED)*

Designing Databases

FIGURE 14-12   Student-advisor ER diagram.

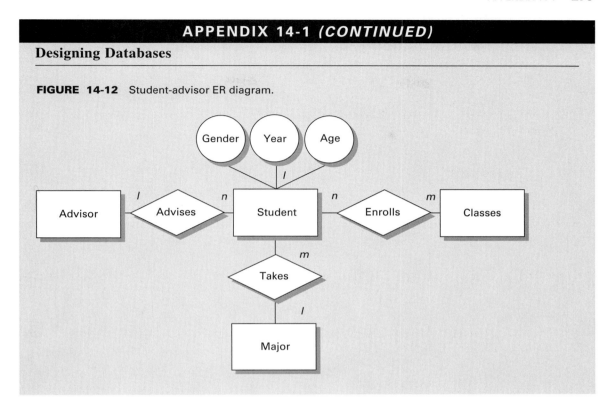

CHAPTER 15

THE THIRD COMPONENT: POWERFUL NETWORKS

A Manager's Perspective

This third component of IT, the network, has had a dramatic impact on organizations and commerce, particularly the Internet. If a medium-sized company a decade ago wanted a worldwide order entry system, its only choice would be for order entry personnel to take orders by phone, mail, or fax and enter those orders into a local computer system. A small or medium-sized firm simply could not afford a worldwide communications network that would provide online order entry for customers. The Internet changes all of that; an inexpensive Web site or services provider lets the small firm set up a global order entry system that hundreds of millions of people can access.

Networks are the information superhighways of a technologically based economy. They tie together people and organizations, and they remove the constraints of time and place on interaction. A "netcentric" organization is one that understands the potential of networks, and incorporates them into its structure and operations. It is the model of the future and the reason why you want to understand how networks work and what options they give the manager.

One of the most important developments in information technology is the evolution of the computer from a calculating engine to a communications tool. As a calculator, computers are extremely valuable. It is difficult to imagine businesses operating on the scale they do today without the capabilities of the computer. However, the computer's role as a communications device may dwarf its impact as a calculator. Computers, databases, and communications are allowing us to change the structure of organizations and the nature of commerce.

The first networks were used by business for electronic linking and communications and for electronic customer–supplier relationships. Most proprietary or private networks were developed for use within a single enterprise. For example, the first bank networks connected tellers in branches with a central computer that had information on customer checking accounts.

Electronic data interchange involves customers and suppliers. Here companies agree to standards for exchanging information. Railroads and their shippers agree on a standard to use for the data that must be exchanged for shipping products by rail. A new customer can begin exchanging data with the railroads by following this message standard.

Until the advent of the Internet and the ability to use it for profit-making purposes, virtually all data networks were private. The Internet is revolutionary in providing an international network that is available for little cost. It is easy to offer services on the

Internet; all one needs is a Web server. It is also easy to access the Internet with a computer or other device through a number of Internet service providers (ISPs).

THE IMPACT OF COMMUNICATIONS TECHNOLOGY

The telephone system is an example of a large, international network. This network provides a number of important features. First, it is ubiquitous, at least in the United States where almost all residences have a telephone. Even with a number of different phone companies, they all interoperate—a call from a regional Bell company can be made transparently to a phone from a different company. Through international standards organizations, telephones interoperate at the country level. You can direct dial phones in a large number of foreign countries. This phone network carries voice and data.

One of the nicest attributes of the telephone network is the fact it is there. We have a communications infrastructure that makes it simple to plug a new telephone or fax into the network. We can buy a telephone from a number of different sources and know that it will function on the network because of published standards that vendors use in the manufacture of their equipment.

BUILDING PRIVATE NETWORKS

Developing private computer networks is not as easy as adding a telephone. No single infrastructure is comparable to the voice network for data. Of course, one can simply use modems and dial-up voice lines, but for many applications this alternative is either too costly or infeasible because the voice lines are too slow for data transmission. Proprietary networks can be used for voice or data; the company designs these networks using various kinds of lines leased from common carriers. A network may consist entirely of land lines, or it may include satellite links. It is a major undertaking to design and set up such a network, but these nets are attractive in a number of situations. In the United States, companies developed two different kinds of private networks: electronic data interchange (EDI) and proprietary data networks.

A company that sells financial information to stock brokers transmits its data to a satellite antenna on the roof of the brokerage office; the data then go to a server to which each broker's client computer is connected. Despite the presence of the Internet, many private networks continue to be developed and operated, especially those dedicated to a particular application like the distribution of financial data. Private networks have much greater security than the Internet, and can provide guaranteed levels of service.

EDI refers to networks in which multiple parties agreed to follow a standard for exchanging data electronically. EDI networks exist in retailing, transportation, and insurance. The national standard in the United States is called ANSI X.12, and the European standard is called EDIFACT. Most EDI takes place in batch mode; a computer generates orders and sends them to a supplier. The supplier receives the order and processes it and other orders when convenient, possibly in a batch together. Little or no online interaction occurs between people compared to when you use the Internet to order a product and interact with a company's Web site.

In private industry and government, EDI is extremely popular for lowering costs while increasing accuracy and quality in purchasing goods. One objective of EDI is to reduce manual keying, therefore reducing errors and speeding up the order cycle. By exchanging data electronically, organizations can change their production cycles and the kind of services they offer.

Despite their achievements, EDI networks have less impact than one would expect because they cannot rely upon a common telecommunications infrastructure. As a result, to use EDI effectively takes expertise and resources. The high cost of networking gives larger firms an advantage over smaller competitors in using data networks.

Given the lack of a data network infrastructure in the United States, firms face a number of choices when considering the development of a network application. These applications are expensive to develop because of the amount of reinvention with each new network. For companies to exchange data they must completely agree on data formats. A firm sending a purchase order must put data in exactly the right place in the electronic message so the supplier can interpret it.

The ANSI X.12 standard is intended to facilitate this process, but a number of industry-specific networks do not conform to the standard. Due to incompatibilities, some press reports indicate that up to 50 percent of the data exchanged via EDI needs rekeying. A firm must change its internal computing systems or purchase special software to map the data from existing systems to an accepted EDI standard. Although some service companies can help a company get started, and PC EDI packages are available for smaller firms, the start-up and maintenance costs are too high for many companies. It is also difficult to get all trading partners to use EDI. Generally, large firms are more sophisticated technologically and can afford the development cost.

Before the Internet, firms could not rely on a national data infrastructure, therefore they developed elaborate private or proprietary networks, sometimes using common carrier facilities and other times bypassing them completely. Examples of familiar companies using proprietary networks include FedEx and UPS for package delivery, United and American Airlines for their reservations systems, Frito-Lay for distribution and decision support, Allegiance for supplying its customers, and many other nationally recognizable firms. These networks are proprietary because they do not follow any kind of industry standard.

Each of these firms must bear the expense of designing, implementing, and operating a proprietary data network. Some of these efforts even required inventing new technology. Frito-Lay undertook the development of a handheld computer for its drivers to use for placing orders and keeping records. If a firm operates in an industry without support for or tradition of EDI, today it has to decide to develop a proprietary data network for an application, use a service company's existing network, or develop its application on the Internet.

In the future, EDI will move gradually to the Internet so that users do not have to pay for proprietary value-added networks or dial-up long-distance charges. Wal-Mart is requiring all of its vendors to use an Internet EDI package known as AS2, sold by a company named Isoft. By early 2004, more than 98 percent of Wal-Mart's EDI exchanges took place via the Internet. This new technology forced EDI network vendors to drop their prices by more than 50 percent. The vendors using AS2 to communicate with Wal-Mart report that the package paid for itself in reduced communications costs.

The Virtual Private Network

The Internet provides one solution for the company that wants to design or replace a private network. This option is a virtual private network (VPN). A company replaces leased lines (or keeps them in place for backup) with interfaces to the Internet. One of the fears of the Net is that it is public, and less secure than a private network. VPN communications equipment converts the user's data to packets, encrypts the packets, and sends them to their desired destination. The user does not know the path the data follow, but they are encrypted so security worries are minimized. To the user, the communications appear to be traveling over a dedicated network from one point to the next, thus the term *virtual private network*.

The Typology of a Network

Most users connect to the Internet without seeing much of the network itself. In fact, the designers of the network want to keep it invisible so that it is easy to use. The Internet is a huge, global network, but the same design philosophy applies to a small private network and to the Internet. The purpose of a network is to connect organizations and individuals, so it is practical to assume that a network has a human user. That user may want to connect to a database to obtain information, or may want to connect and communicate with another individual who is located remotely.

The example of the phone network helps clarify how designers configured the Internet and private networks. When you make a phone call using a land line, a physical pair of wires connects your house to the telephone central office. Every phone reached through that central office has a unique, dedicated pair of wires connected to it. This dedicated line means that only one person at a time will ever use the connection to the central office, which is called the local loop. Multiple users do not share this line at the same time. For this reason, the line does not need a large capacity; it is only going to carry voice traffic, which is relatively slow. (At least that was the original designers' thought; now the local carriers would like to be able to provide broadband, or high-speed, data services to your home.)

Once your phone call reaches the central office, it must be routed to the central office that is connected to the phone of the person you are calling. The phone companies connect the central offices to each other with a network of high-speed, generally fiber-optic lines shared by all of the traffic between two given offices at the same time.

A data network such as the Internet operates the same way. The equivalent of the local office is your ISP; if you have a cable connection, then your cable company takes the signals from your cable and routes them to a backbone service provider such as MCI or AT&T. These backbone providers have global, fiber optic networks that carry traffic from a number of service providers. Figure 15-1 shows how a such a network is configured and Figure 15-2 shows how a North American backbone is connected to other countries; note how this network consists of lines of varying capacity, depending on the amount of traffic between nodes. As of this writing, the network in the figure has slow speed lines of 64Kbit/second (64,000) up to 10Gbit/second (10 billion).

With more than one backbone provider, a natural question is how traffic on one backbone network gets routed to another. Figure 15-3 shows Metropolitan Area Exchange (MAE) interchange points for Internet traffic. ISPs connect to the MAE points via routers, so that an e-mail message from someone using a Comcast cable modem in Washington, D.C., can reach a person using AT&T Worldnet in Los Angeles. Other network exchange points in addition to these MAEs, include MAEs in Paris and Frankfurt.

The Internet has the potential to create a revolution in the telephone business. Voice over Internet Protocol (VoIP) makes it possible for a subscriber to make a call over the Internet. Several companies offer unlimited calling in the United States for prices as low as $15 a month, dramatically undercutting the prices charged by local and long-distance

FIGURE 15-1 An example of a global backbone network.

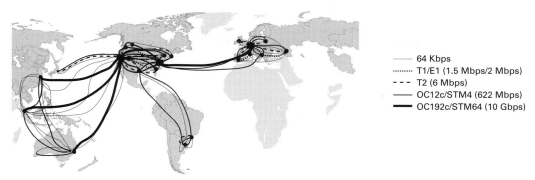

— 64 Kbps
···· T1/E1 (1.5 Mbps/2 Mbps)
– – – T2 (6 Mbps)
— OC12c/STM4 (622 Mbps)
— OC192c/STM64 (10 Gbps)

telephone operating companies. The VoIP carrier gives the customer a "black box" to plug into a cable or DSL connection; the subscriber's phone connects to the box, and he or she is ready to make calls. IP makes much more efficient use of a network than does the traditional circuit switching of the phone company, with a direct connection through the network from your phone to the person's phone you are calling. The major carriers are watching VoIP carefully and are updating their networks to offer similar services.

THE INTERNET TRANSFORMS BUSINESS AND COMMERCE

The Internet is a worldwide, interconnected collection of computer networks that really has changed the world. The Internet started in 1969 as the Arpanet, a military-sponsored research project on how to build reliable networks in the face of unreliable components. Over time, as additional research laboratories, universities, and even personal computer networks connected to it, the Internet became an infrastructure for scientific and educational computing in the United States and in a significant portion of the world.

One of the Internet's main virtues is the fact that it lets a variety of heterogeneous computers connect to the network using a number of different communications options.

FIGURE 15-2 A North American backbone connected to other countries.

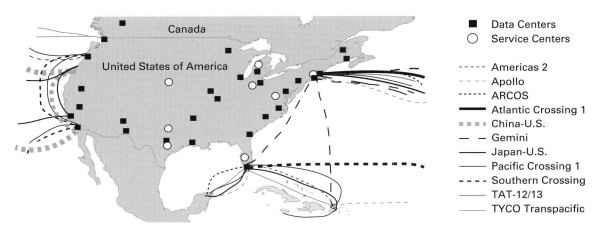

■ Data Centers
○ Service Centers

– – – Americas 2
– – – Apollo
···· ARCOS
— Atlantic Crossing 1
▪ ▪ ▪ ▪ China-U.S.
— — Gemini
— Japan-U.S.
— Pacific Crossing 1
– – – Southern Crossing
— TAT-12/13
— TYCO Transpacific

FIGURE 15-3 WorldCom MAE services.

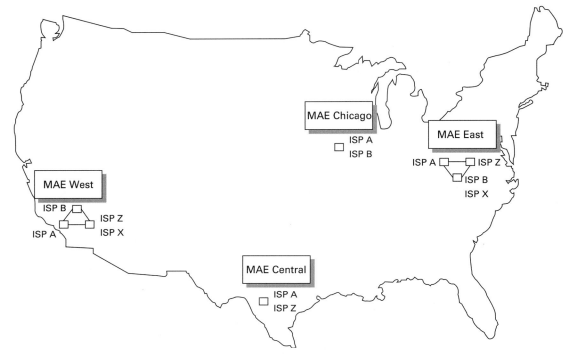

WorldCom MAE facilities are switching centers where ISPs may interconnect to exchange Internet traffic. WorldCom operates three of the major interconnect points for the Internet in the United States: MAE East, MAE West, and MAE Central. On October 1, 2001, WorldCom opened its newest MAE site - MAE Chicago. A significant amount of the traffic that flows between ISP networks passes through WorldCom MAE service facilities.

MAE West facility is located in California's Silicon Valley; MAE West® services provide a second interconnection point linking major ISPs in that area.

MAE Central facility is located in Dallas, Texas; MAE CentralSM services are the latest addition to our Tier 1 services and facilities.

MAE Chicago facility provides an FE interconnection point; MAE ChicagoSM services provide OC48 port speeds.

MAE East facility is located in the Washington D.C. metropolitan area; MAE East® services connect many of the major ISPs as well as European providers.

WorldCom MAE® Services provide traffic exchange facilities where ISPs connect to each other to exchange Internet traffic. The MAE facilities and services form part of the "Inter" in Internet.

SOURCE: http://www.mae.net/mae_services1.htm.s.

The network operates on two core protocols: Transmission Control Protocol (TCP) and Internet Protocol (IP). These protocols break a data stream into packets and give each packet a sequence number. IP is responsible for getting the packets from the sender to the receiver in the shortest possible time. TCP manages this flow of packets and verifies that the data are correct. More than 100 TCP/IP protocols are based on the core protocols

MANAGEMENT PROBLEM 15-1

Victor Electronics has a number of EDI connections with its customers. Typically the customer negotiates an annual contract with Victor, indicating that it will buy a specified amount of a particular product, say a resistor, that year. The customer may also agree that it will buy at least 75 percent of its resistors from Victor. The customer wants to negotiate a volume price for the year with Victor, as is the custom in the industry.

At the end of each week, customers send a forecast to Victor for the products and quantities they want shipped the next week using an EDI link. Unfortunately, customers change their minds! On Monday a flurry of EDI messages, faxes, and phone calls requests modifications of the forecasts submitted on Friday.

Nancy Scott is wondering about the impact of moving EDI to the Internet and making it more interactive. "What if we could give each customer a home page with all of the data about their annual purchasing agreements with us. They could update it with their forecasts, and go into the page and change the forecast whenever they wanted to. Of course we would have to set some kind of limits—we can't have them changing the forecast after we have shipped what the originally asked for."

What factors should management at Victor consider in making a decision about moving from batch EDI to the Internet? What kind of changes will be required at Victor? At customers' locations?

described earlier. As a result, computers from Sun workstations to personal computers to Macs can connect to the Net.

Although it is not known with any certainty how many users exist, nearly 200 million host computers operate on the Internet. One estimate is 600 million users in at least 150 countries. Scientists and engineers were early users, followed by academics, and today the Internet is available to commercial firms and to the general public. Figure 15-4 shows the tremendous growth in Internet hosts.

You can connect directly to the Internet through an organization's computers. The domain name identifies the type of organization, for example, an address is first initial

FIGURE 15-4 Growth of Internet hosts.

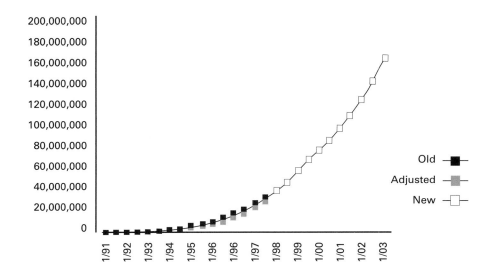

followed by last name@rhsmith.umd.edu. The suffix edu is an educational institution, com a commercial firm, gov the government, and mil the military. With this kind of address your organization has a computer connected directly to the Net. Internet service providers (ISPs) connect you with the Net; these access providers also contend with cable TV companies offering Internet access via cable modems, as well as companies offering digital subscriber line (DSL) access, which has higher speeds than a dial-up connection. High-speed satellite ISP is an alternative to cable or DSL service.

The Arpanet was originally designed so scientists and others could conduct research on the computer network itself and gain access to remote computers and files. The government also wanted to tie together diverse networks developed for the military by various low bidders, each providing different equipment. Within months of the opening of the Arpanet, however, interpersonal communication in the form of electronic mail and computerized bulletin boards became the dominant application.

At first, the Internet was criticized as difficult to use. The World Wide Web and graphical browsers represent major breakthroughs on the Internet. Researchers at CERN in Geneva developed the World Wide Web (WWW), which connected an estimated 30,000 network servers using the Hypertext Transfer Protocol (HTTP). The Web uses hypertext links produced with the Hypertext Markup Language (HTML) to link documents and files. Hypertext is created by placing links on words to reference other sections of text or other documents. Clicking a highlighted piece of text with a mouse retrieves a new file or document, allowing the user to browse through related pieces of information. The retrieved documents may all reside on different computers, but the Web makes all retrieval transparent to the user.

HTTP is a connectionless protocol, which means that each client-server connection is limited to a single request for information. This way, the network is not tied up in a permanent connection between the client and server. The Web is an excellent example of a client-server architecture—your computer is the client and you visit a variety of Web servers as you search for information. To see an example of hypertext source documents, run your Internet browser and click View and then Source.

To use the WWW, one needs an Internet browser. The development of a graphical Web browser is a second breakthrough, one made possible by the connections provided by HTML and the Web. These programs work by pointing and clicking with a mouse, which is a vast improvement over character-based terminal access to the Internet. A browser connects users to different services, helping them navigate around the confusing and disorganized structure of the Internet. One can also use browsers to create forms and facilitate the publication of data.

Host computers on the Internet generally provide some form of content, information that users access with their browsers. With millions of Web hosts, an incredible amount of content is available. To help you find information, more than thirty search engines are available on the Web. These services, funded by advertising, accept your search queries and look for matching content on the Web. Google, one of the most successful search engines, says that it is searching over 3 billion pages of content on the Web.

Search engines do not actually search the Web for each query; rather they search the Web at various times and build an index of terms. When you make a query, the engines search their indexes and give you the Universal Resource Locators (URLs) that look like http://rhsmith.umd.edu, plus a few lines of text from the page the URL references. It is

---

SIDEBAR 15-1

The Internet Connections at Maryland

The University of Maryland provides a number of connections to the Internet and is typical of a large research university in terms of its connectivity.

The College Park campus's multiple connections to the Internet include:

- 95Mbps of service to Qwest Communications for commodity internet traffic
- 150Mbps of service (with bursts to 1Gbps) to MAX (Mid Atlantic Crossroads), a consortium of local research institutions, through which Maryland has high speed connectivity to those institutions as well as the NSF vBNS network and the Internet2 Abilene Network
- An ATM connection to UMATS, the intercampus network of the University System of Maryland for connectivity with other USM schools

- A 45Mbps connection to UUnet for extra capacity and redundant Internet connectivity

To see the results of a traffic monitor for the University, go to http://noc.net.umd.edu/newoff campusrate.html.

Maryland is a member of Internet2, a high-speed research network (www.internet2.edu).

More than 200 universities are Internet2 members: http://members.internet2.edu/university/universities.cfm.

On campus, the Internet is available from local area networks and from a university wireless network.

The Internet is a major piece of infrastructure for universities around the world; it supports a huge variety of communications as well as administrative and research activities on campus. It is difficult to imagine a modern university without access to the Internet.

---

interesting to note that some of the advertisements on search engine sites are sensitive to the query you make; the search engine tries to show you ads that match your search. Google has been successful using the number of links pointing to a page as an indicator of the page's popularity and relevance to a user's search.

The interaction with the Web described so far depends on the user's initiative; you search for and decide what sites to access. "Push" technology refers to services on the Internet that come to you automatically. You can sign up with companies that send news and other information to your client computer on a continuous basis. Originally push technology developed on the Internet, but it is spreading to intranets as well. Wachovia Securities, a Richmond, Virginia, financial services firm, uses push technology to alert its stock brokers of important news and stock-selling opportunities from large blocks of shares the firm buys several times a day.

Currently a raging debate is going on between visionaries who see the Internet as the next era of computing, and those who see the Net as an important but not revolutionary advance. The visionaries argue that so much information, software, and multimedia content will be available through the Internet, especially given Java's ability to share programs easily and safely, that no one will need a PC. This group is the one that favors the development of Net PCs. Sun Microsystems, the developer of Java, encourages this view.

In summary, the Internet was launched with government subsidies for the network and terminals that helped it become established. For most early users, the network appeared to be a free good. Early use of the network focused on interpersonal communications and the sharing of programs and information. The Internet's open standards allowed many users and service providers to connect. The network has an open, decentralized, and extendible architecture. The Net's open culture and free exchange of software encourages users and providers. Products such as Web browsers (e.g., Netscape and the Internet Explorer) make it easy to use the Net. A spate of articles on the information superhighway, cyberspace, and the Internet (including a cartoon in the *New Yorker*) made a network connection highly fashionable. All of these factors led to the critical mass needed for the network to succeed.

Intranets and Extranets

Internet technology is having a major impact on companies through networks called *intranets* as opposed to Internet. A firm sets up servers and clients following Internet protocols and distributes a Web browser to its users. This information is likely to be proprietary so the company does not want other Internet users to have access to it. An intranet also provides a platform for developing and distributing applications that anyone with a browser can access.

A company can benefit from this kind of technology investment. Morgan Stanley is a major investment bank and a retail broker since its merger with Dean Witter. Morgan Stanley developed an extensive intranet containing the research information that various parts of the firm develop. By having it on the intranet, the information is available to anyone in the company. Members of the firm do not overlook research because it happens to be in someone's bottom desk drawer.

At Chrysler, an intranet replaced the company telephone directory; it provides a photograph and job descriptions in addition to phone numbers. The automaker expects to use its intranet to broadcast information around the company, monitor projects, and reduce the amount of time hunting for information. Vehicle program managers post car design changes to Chrysler's intranet so they are instantly available.

The engineering department invested $750,000 in its part of the intranet in an effort to link isolated systems. Using the same browser interface, engineers can move from its main software design system, CATIA, to regulatory manuals and home pages that describe how different projects are going. The minivan team home page links to a progress report on the design of a new vehicle's body. Executives can check progress without calling a meeting. The intranet should help Chrysler achieve its goal of reducing the cycle time for vehicle design to two years from the current four or five years.

Intranets offer the potential to tie together employees in an organization, as well as disparate information systems. As firms create links between intranet standards and legacy transactions processing systems, it is possible to envision an environment in which the major desktop application for each user is a browser. Using the browser and intranet, an employee accesses all types of corporate information along with the data from internal, proprietary information systems in the company.

It is also common to provide external access to an intranet so that customers and others can access your internal servers. An Extranet uses the Internet technology to provide online access to internal net servers, generally through a password for each external user. With an Extranet, you can create an online system quickly because it takes advantage of the existing worldwide Internet.

A Variety of Ways to Access the Net

Going Wireless

One of the most exciting options for connecting to the Internet is a wireless fidelity, or WiFi, network that is capable of speeds as high as eleven megabits per second. These

SIDEBAR 15-2

The Web Makes a Big Difference

In its November 24, 2003, issue, *BusinessWeek* identified the "Web Smart 50," fifty companies that demonstrate real benefits from their Web applications. We describe some of them here:

Company and Application	Benefits
Mattel uses the Web for designers in dispersed locations to collaborate on toy design.	In two years, Mattel cut the time to develop new products by 20 percent.
Alcoa has an online showroom to sell slow-growth businesses; the site includes balance sheets and profit and loss statements.	Alcoa sold three business from the Web and expects to save $200,000 in travel expenses with this method.
IBM developed a Web system for employee collaboration.	Web conferencing cut $375 million from the training budget and saved $20 million in travel.
Eli Lilly has a Web site for listing scientific problems with cash prizes for a solution (open to the public, not just employees).	Problem solving time dropped to months from two three years.
Homeland Security Department Web site helped emergency services coordinate responses to disasters, including secure instant messaging.	Disaster workers have quick access to shared data, replacing "frantic" phone calls.
Bovis Lend Lease has a Web site for builders, architects, and suppliers to collaborate on a $600 million remodeling of 10,000 BP America gas stations.	The site let the firm double the pace of renovation, to 200 gas stations each week.
General Motors uses electronic auctions to sell vehicles to auto dealers at the end of their leases.	Last year GM moved 303,000 vehicles through the auctions, saving an estimated $180 million.
JetBlue replaced paper pilot manuals with Internet-linked laptops that also handle preflight calculations.	The system helps reduce flight times, which cuts operating costs and increases customer satisfaction.
Landstar, a freight company using independent drivers, has an automated dispatch service that informs 8,000 drivers of available loads.	Retention of drivers increased from 36 percent to 51 percent, which is two or three times what comparable ompanies average.
BMW uses the Internet to allow buyers to create custom orders for most cars in Europe and about 30 percent in the United States. The Net links dealers, factories, and suppliers.	The system provides options for customers and cuts the time to deliver cars by a third as well as cutting overstocked inventories.
TaylorMade provided its sales representatives with handheld devices to connect to the Web for updated sale and inventory information.	Sales rep productivity is up 25 percent, and TaylorMade is the number one in golf club sales.
Wells Fargo tracks and analyzes every transaction from its 10 million retail customers.	The bank better targets products and sells nearly double the industry average per customer.
Bristol-Myers Squibb uses a Web system for managing and improving the speed of drug research and development.	The system helped reduce time to develop new medications by a third, saving money and boosting revenues by getting products to market faster.
Kinko's replaced a collection of more than fifty employee-training sites with three Internet learning systems.	The company saves about $10 million a year in training costs, and it can roll out new services more efficiently.

SOURCE: Adapted from "Web Smart 50," *BusinessWeek*, November 24, 2003.

MANAGEMENT PROBLEM 15-2

The major airlines, FedEx, UPS, banks, and a large number of companies have private networks. Yet the Internet offers similar capabilities at a much lower cost. These companies could reach 600 million people or more via the Internet, something that no one could afford to do with a private network. But these companies stay with their private networks.

What are the advantages of a private network compared to the Internet for the kind of mission critical applications one finds at the airlines, package carriers, and banks?

GE Global Exchange is a company that builds marketplaces and exchanges for its customers. The firm has its roots in EDI and is one of the large, value-added carriers that help companies exchange data using EDI standards. Despite all of the publicity about the Internet, GE Global has indicated that its EDI business is actually increasing rather than shrinking. Here is another example of the use of old technology, just as one sees with private networks.

Why might EDI transactions volume be increasing? Why is it not being replaced with XML exchanges on the Internet? What in general are the reasons a firm might continue with old technology, and even expand its use of that technology?

networks are based on an IEEE standard called 802.11. Corporations such as Merrill Lynch installed this technology so that workers can use laptops and other devices to access the Web from any place in a building. Service providers are setting up WiFi networks in airports and hotels, and charging customers a monthly fee for access to any of their networks. Even Starbucks is providing WiFi networks in their coffee shops.

Do-it-yourself Wi-Fi networks allow individuals to set up connections by leasing a high-speed DSL or cable line and plugging that line into a wireless base station with an antenna. Anyone within a few hundred feet who has a computer with a receiver card can connect to the Internet through this network. Some service providers, fearing a loss of revenue, forbid the use of their high-speed lines for this purpose, but it is a difficult movement to stop.

Some Internet users are trying to set up wireless clouds so that you could log on to the Internet from any location. Many of the home-based WiFi networks are not secured, so anyone can use them to connect to the Internet. As a result, one expert envisions cities with hundreds or thousands of small wireless networks, and people using whatever network they are closest to when they want to connect to the Net. This picture is somewhat disconcerting to cellular phone companies and others who want to charge for access to the Internet. Verizon is experimenting with a wireless network that covers New York City; subscribers to its DSL service will be able to use the wireless network when they are traveling in New York. Wireless has great promise for changing the way people interact with the Internet and the nature of the Web.

Computer vendors support the development of both subscription WiFi networks in cities and the spread of the technology. Intel is pushing its Centrino processors that have built-in WiFi capabilities, eliminating the need for an external wireless card. The reason, of course, is that wireless computing should stimulate demand for more computing devices because it makes the Internet ubiquitous.

Cell Phones, PDAs, and Refrigerators

Some experts predict that the majority of devices accessing the Internet in the future will not be personal computers, but instead will be a variety of devices that suddenly become intelligent. Consider the ability of cell phones to browse the Net. Today their speed is limited, as is the keyboard and screen. However, when 3G wireless networks arrive, they will offer high-speed surfing, though the problem of keyboard and display still remains.

More interesting is the proposition that all kinds of appliances will have Internet connections. Your refrigerator will have a bar code scanner that notes when items leave the refrigerator and do not come back, indicating they are finished. The refrigerator uses the Internet to access an online grocery store and place an order for resupply. This scenario sounds a little far-fetched, but you might be interested in a home security system connected to the Internet so that when away, you could change the pattern of lights displayed, monitor and control the temperature of the house, and manage your garden sprinkler system.

The Impact of the Internet

Books can and have been written about the impact of the Internet. In fact the chapters in this book are interwoven with the impact of the Net, especially on corporate strategy and for allowing new business models and electronic commerce. The following is a short summary of some of these impacts. (Try to add impacts that you think are missing.) The Internet has:

- Helped remove the constraints of time and space on communications.
- Leveled the playing field for small businesses that now have access to a worldwide network at a very reasonable cost.
- Created new business models, especially for business-to-consumer (B2C) and business-to-business (B2B) transactions.
- Established a network infrastructure that anyone can plug into with a server or a browser.
- Enabled companies to dramatically reduce transactions costs by linking together and reducing or eliminating paper transactions.
- Provided the means for companies to more closely integrate their supply chains.
- Fostered a great deal of information sharing among firms who do business with each other.
- Provided the communications links that encourage companies to outsource and create value networks among themselves.
- Encouraged the creation of other alternative forms of organizations such as the T-Form organization.
- Created new businesses such as eBay as well as network service providers.
- Allowed businesses to open a new channel to their customers, with the customers often doing their own self-service on the Web instead of talking to expensive customer service representatives.
- Provided new convenience and service to individuals, for example, the ability to make travel reservations, compare ticket prices, look for different itineraries, and comparison shop on the Web.
- Created a virtual library of information on a host of topics (little of which is verified).

- ■ Widened the divide between industrialized and developing countries, and the gap between the wealthy and poor.
- ■ Created a source of uncensored ideas that are difficult for any one government to control.

The list goes on and on, and ample evidence indicates that the Internet is truly a revolutionary change. The Net epitomizes the confluence of computer technology, database systems, and telecommunications. It is becoming more pervasive every day, and the most successful mangers will be the ones who figure out how to take maximum advantage of what the Internet has to offer.

CHAPTER SUMMARY

1. The telephone network offers great ubiquity and connectivity. Computer networks are striving to reach its level of ease of use.

2. A company that wants to develop a private network is faced with a variety of choices. In many instances large firms designed their own, proprietary networks.

3. Industries developed standards for EDI. The electronic interchange of information is expanding rapidly in industries such as retailing, transportation, and insurance.

4. The Internet, based in the United States, is a network of networks. The development of the World Wide Web and graphical browsers contributed to the exponential growth of the Internet.

5. Companies provide a great deal of content on the Web, ranging from information about themselves and their products to sites that allow customers to order products directly from them.

6. Intranets offer the firm the ability to make information and knowledge available to all employees. They also provide a platform for developing different kinds of applications that help coordinate activities in the organization.

7. Electronic commerce is a new and exciting way of conducting business. Electronic markets will become more common because of the Internet.

8. Networks provide connectivity. They help transform the organization by connecting it to customers, suppliers, and alliance partners. The impact of greater connectivity will be to increase the pace of change in organization structure.

9. The combination of computers, networks, and databases enables new models for business that offer many opportunities for managers. These new models are characterized by fast response times and high levels of efficiency.

KEYWORDS

ANSI X.12

Auction

Browser

Computer network

EDI

Electronic commerce

Home page

Hypertext Markup Language (HTML)

Hypertext Transfer Protocol (HTTP)

Microsoft Network

Netscape

Network

TCP/IP

Ubiquity

VPN

WiFi

World Wide Web

RECOMMENDED READINGS

Bailey, J. P., and Bakos, Y. 1997. An exploratory study of the emerging role of electronic intermediaries. *International Journal of Electronic Commerce, 1*(3), pp. 7–20.

Bakos, Y. 1998. The emerging role of electronic marketplaces on the Internet. *Communications of the ACM, 41*(8), pp. 35–42. (A major section of this issue is devoted to information systems and economics.)

Greenstein, S. 2001. Technological mediation and commercial development in the early Internet access market. *California Management Review, 43*(2), pp. 75–94.

Kwak, M. 2001. The offline impact of online prices. *Sloan Management Review, 42*(3), pp. 9–11.

Lewis, I. 2001. Logistics and electronic commerce: An interorganizational systems perspective. *Transportation Journal, 40*(4), pp. 5–13.

Zaheer, A. , and Zaheer, S. 1997. Catching the wave: Alertness, responsiveness, and market influence in global electronic networks. *Management Science, 43*(11), pp. 1493–1509. (An interesting article looking at the requirements for success in global currency trading, which amounts to more than $1 trillion a day, approximately 50 percent of which takes place over the Reuters network.)

DISCUSSION QUESTIONS

1. What advantages does the telephone system offer as a model for a network?

2. Why have companies developed so many proprietary networks?

3. Why are EDI standards difficult to develop? Why will one standard not serve across industries?

4. What industries are most likely to be able to take advantage of EDI?

5. How do networks contribute to the development of the T-Form organization?

6. What IT organization design variables are affected by networks?

7. What is the appeal of a mass market network?

8. What are the options for broadband connection to the Internet?

9. What are the problems with completing transactions over these networks (i.e., providing your credit card number after ordering merchandise)?

10. What are the major impacts of the Internet on business?

11. How do search engines work? How does Google work?

12. Describe the World Wide Web. How can a word or phrase in something you are reading on the screen result in your being connected to another computer that has more information about that term or phrase?

13. Why are people putting so much information on the Internet, information that they are not likely to ever receive payment for from readers? Is this behavior strange from an economic standpoint?

14. How do browsers contribute to the growth of the World Wide Web?

15. Pick a specific company and describe how it might make use of the Internet.

16. What is an intranet? What is its role in an organization?

17. Electronic filing of tax returns was originally plagued with fraud. How do you think one could defraud the system, and what could be done to prevent further fraud?

18. What is the role of the government in stimulating the development of a national network infrastructure?

19. The Internet reaches most countries in Europe and Asia and the Americas. Connections are more spotty in the Middle East and Africa. What are the implications today for a country that is "off the net"?

20. Pornography on the Internet raises a great deal of concern, while authoritarian countries worry about the free flow of ideas on the Net. How might it be possible to regulate information content the Internet? Is it desirable to do so?

CHAPTER 16

ELECTRONIC COMMERCE: CHANGING HOW BUSINESS IS DONE

A Manager's Perspective

Electronic commerce lost some of its aura as dot-com companies went bankrupt one after the other. Most of these firms classified themselves as e-commerce companies, and their business models stressed the role of the Internet in their operations. Mark Twain's comment that "reports of my death have been greatly exaggerated" applies here as well. Some of the dot-coms are dead, but electronic commerce is alive and well. And in the not-too-distant future, e-commerce will be considered ordinary and treated as an accepted part of doing business. Customers expect to be able to conduct their business electronically, so getting into e-commerce is not really an option in the twenty-first century, it is a necessity. The issues are how to go about electronic commerce, developing a business mode, and designing an online store for retail customers. For business-to-business (B2B) e-commerce, you have to worry about standards and interfacing with customers' systems. Managers also have to make decisions about whether to outsource e-commerce or develop it internally. For many companies right now, e-commerce represents change; in the future it will be the norm.

VALUE PROPOSITION

Investments in electronic commerce provide value on a number of dimensions:

- New channels for sales
- Reduction in personnel required to take orders and provide customer service
- Reductions in the cost of transactions
- Providing better customer service (e.g., electronic airline tickets and self-service check-in kiosks at airports)
- Broadening markets and providing more transparency of prices
- Creation of new markets (e.g., eBay and auctions for surplus industrial products)
- Development of more efficient supply chains
- Creation of more competitive markets for buyers

You can evaluate some of the contribution of e-commerce to the firm with the following metrics:

- Percentage of electronic transactions

- Percentage of customers ordering online
- Percentage of electronic business with suppliers
- Cost per order received
- Percentage of repeat business (customer retention)

Electronic commerce is the use of technology, in particular the Internet, to conduct business. In general *e-commerce* refers to buying or selling electronically, usually interactively. Some researchers include EDI as a part of e-commerce, even though EDI most frequently does not use the Internet and is not interactive. Ordering a book from Amazon.com is certainly an example of e-commerce, as is ordering repair equipment from Grainger.com.

THE NATURE OF MARKETS

In a free market economy, transactions take place where the downward-sloping demand curve intersects the upward-sloping supply curve. The intersection of these two curves determines both the price and the quantity sold. This simple model is powerful and enables decentralized decision making in a complex economy. The next few sections look at what happens when you add competition to the simple demand-supply model, and how e-commerce might be expected to influence prices. Transactions cost theory also helps explain the potential impact of e-commerce on the economy and on individual firms. Finally, e-commerce is facilitating another type of market, the auction.

THE LAW OF ONE PRICE

An early, simple model of competition in the 1880s explained commodity agricultural markets. *Bertrand competition* assumes that firms set their prices, and the market determines the amount sold. The question is what the selling price should be in a market with two firms selling identical products. Bertrand, a French economist, argued that price must equal marginal cost (where marginal cost includes a return on capital). If price is less than marginal cost, a firm could increase its profits by selling less. If price is greater than marginal cost, a firm can lower its price a small amount. If competitors do not change their prices, then customers will move to the firm that lowered its prices. The competitor must cut its prices or go out of business. The same logic holds if a firm raises its prices; customers will flock to the lowest-priced producer.

This model requires that customers are able to discover the prices of all competitors, a condition often met in commodity markets. The first predictions for electronic commerce were that products would obey the law of one price; that is, price would all tend to converge among suppliers because the Internet facilitates price discovery. You might not be willing to go to five physical stores to compare the price of a new pair of running shoes, but you might visit five Web sites to compare prices. Also, Web agents compare prices for a given product, so that you do not have to visit all the sites yourself.

A supplier views the commodity product business in a particular way. The supplier would like your business, but if all sellers offer the same commodity at the same price, a consumer has no particular reason to buy from a specific vendor. In this kind of market, a supplier will try to differentiate its product to attract customers, allowing the vendor to charge a higher price than the competition. The supplier will use advertising to try and create the impression of a difference in its product compared to competitors. The supplier may also provide additional features or services that competitors do not offer. Unless competitors are successful at differentiation, Bertrand competition suggests that the price of similar products should converge to the same amount. The results of research on electronic commerce are mixed; in many instances studies do not show convergence to one price as sellers try to avoid having their products sold as commodities.

TRANSACTIONS COST ECONOMICS

Another view of the impact of e-commerce on markets makes use of transactions cost economics. Transactions costs are the costs of obtaining goods and services in the market. Economic theory often ignores or assumes away these costs, but an economist named Oliver Williamson constructed an elaborate theory of transactions costs and argued that they are a significant factor in the marketplace.

The forms and amounts of transactions costs vary. For example, when a company mails an order for a replacement electric motor to Grainger, a large supplier of repair and maintenance products, both the buyer and seller encounter significant costs. The buyer must search to find the motor, looking at different suppliers to find the exact product and compare costs. The buyer has to complete an order form, and fax it to Grainger, the supplier that had the best price that day. The buyer generates a purchase order by entering information about the purchase into a computer system. At Grainger an order processing clerk enters the order into a computer system that handles order processing. Grainger notifies its warehouse to ship the order, and a warehouse staff member picks, boxes, and sends the motor, entering the shipping information into the computer. Another system at Grainger generates an invoice and sends it to the buyer, who, in turn, enters it into the purchasing and payables system to generate a check to Grainger.

One promise of electronic commerce is to reduce these transactions costs. First, the buyer can search among suppliers online. The buyer can order online with the order going directly to a Grainger computer, bypassing the step of faxing an order, and saving Grainger the cost of entering the order into its system. The Grainger system communicates electronically with the warehouse. Payment can be through a credit card, or Grainger can post the purchase price to a monthly statement for this customer. This scenario should offer substantial opportunities for savings in transactions costs across the entire economy.

Transactions costs theory is more elegant than it may appear at first. The theory also tries to explain how firms are organized and how they govern themselves. Williamson suggested that companies use markets to acquire goods when the goods can be easily described and many suppliers offer them. In contrast to the market, some firms become more of a hierarchy when the goods they need are not readily available in the market. If a product is highly specialized it is said to have high asset specificity. These assets also tend to have complicated product descriptions. Because of little demand for these products, a company wishing to purchase them may have a choice of only one or two suppliers. Instead of a market, the buyer must negotiate with these suppliers. At one extreme, a company might buy a supplier company to be sure that it has access to the parts it needs.

Ten years ago, General Motors resembled a hierarchy; it made 70 percent of the parts it used in cars. Toyota was a market-oriented firm and bought 70 percent of the components in its cars. Many years ago, automobile manufacturers built the chassis and supplied the engine and transmission; specialized companies manufactured bodies to be put on the chassis. To be sure of an adequate supply of bodies for its cars, GM bought Fisher body, moving from a market to a hierarchy. Thus, in some instances, a company may feel pressure to become more of a hierarchy in order to eliminate risks.

A company gives up a number of advantages with a hierarchy. If one continues to operate as a hierarchy, and a market develops for the products acquired through the hierarchy, the firm can lose the advantages of price competition in the marketplace. If a company makes a large number of components for its products, it may not price these same products in the market place or figure out what it actually costs the company to make them itself. For many years General Motors was the high-cost automobile producer, partly because of the high costs it paid for using a hierarchy rather than a market for parts. The Big Three Detroit automakers all spun off their parts operations into separate companies in order to move more toward a market and to encourage the parts companies to come up with more competitive pricing.

One of the effects of e-commerce on the economics of transactions is lower costs as companies link to each other electronically over the Internet. As described earlier, electronic ordering offers tremendous potential to save labor and cost. The predictions for e-commerce are that it will lead more to markets as it makes markets less expensive and more efficient to use. A firm can easily search for products it needs that are available someplace, and if not can look for multiple vendors who might be able to supply them. Electronic commerce should reinforce our market economy, and firms should move away from hierarchical arrangements to markets.

AUCTIONS

Economists feel that auctions present an efficient market, because winners in the auction pay what an item is worth to them; they get to decide on the price, and can decide to stop bidding if the price of the item exceeds its value to them. Picture an auction conducted by Sotheby's or Christies where the auctioneer attempts to obtain the highest price possible for the goods being offered for sale. In this English auction, the auctioneer announces an opening price and bid increments, and encourages higher and higher bids from the audience. When no one will raise the bid, the last person bidding wins the auction at his or her last bid. Another well-known auction is the Dutch auction, originally used to sell tulips, where the opening price is set high, and is *lowered* by small increments. The bidder "calling" out first wins the auction and gets the goods.

Although a bidder for an art auction at Christies may be present in person or on the telephone, for the most part auctions, before the Internet, required the bidders to be present in a particular place at a specified time. Internet auctions remove the constraints of place and time on an auction, and enable widespread participation.

Governments use the Internet to conduct multiround auctions, sometimes exceeding 100 rounds, for parts of the radio spectrum used for communications, especially cellular phone services. FreeMarkets is a company that helps clients design and then run procurement auctions. United Technologies uses FreeMarkets to conduct auctions for its suppliers, and the company expects to save about $1.2 billion in 2002.[1] General Electric moved to online auctions for most of its procurements, buying more than $6 billion in goods in 2000 (Pekec and Rothkopf, 2003). Companies also found they can auction off surplus inventory and equipment over the Internet, opening up a new way to extract value from goods that might have been totally written off before the auction market.

Priceline.com is a "demand aggregator," though some call it a "reverse auction." The buyer names the price, and sellers decide whether they want to provide a good or service at that price. Priceline has been most successful with airline tickets and hotels. The Internet and e-commerce enable and facilitate the creation of auction markets, and should stimulate the expansion of this approach to buying and selling merchandise.

Manheim Auctions

Manheim is a good example of an auction company that has grown up on the Internet. Manheim, a subsidiary of Cox Enterprises in Atlanta, is the largest automobile auction company in the world, having more than 35,000 employees in eighty-six physical auction sites in North America, twenty sites in the United Kingdom, and ten in Australia and New Zealand (Woodham and Weill, 2001). Some 9 million automobiles pass through Manheim with a gross value of nearly $55 billion, yielding nearly $1 billion in revenue for Manheim.

Manheim is relatively unknown to the public because it auctions used cars to dealers, not to individuals seeking to buy a car. A typical provider of cars for auction would be the leasing arm of a manufacturer such as Ford Credit, or a rental car company such as Avis or Hertz that sells its cars when they reach a certain mileage. Manheim has attractive locations, and it collects and reconditions cars before offering them for sale. The physical auction sites feature ten to fifteen lanes with cars rolling down each lane. An auctioneer stands at a podium by each lane and chants about the next car in the lane. If a dealer buys a car, Manheim provides back-office services to transfer ownership, collect payment, and deliver the vehicle to the dealer.

Manheim launched Manheim Interactive in February of 2000 as a separate, wholly owned subsidiary. See Figure 16-1. It is possible to argue both sides of the question of whether the company is cannibalizing its own business by moving auctions online. Certainly the electronic auction will have some impact on the physical auction. However, if Manheim did not enter the business, it is likely that someone else would. Manheim can realize a lot of advantages in starting an electronic auction; it can capitalize on an excellent brand name that buyers and sellers trust. Managers at Manheim also understand auctions and the used car business; as a result, they should be able to create an electronic business that reflects the needs of buyers and sellers.

The Internet provides several advantages for Manheim and it's buyers. A buyer does not have to visit a physical auction, but can participate from his/her desktop online in three ways. One option is that the buyer can visit an online inventory vehicles, where the consignor (seller) establishes a fixed price for each vehicle. The buyer can purchase the car

FIGURE 16-1 Manheim interactive Web site.

Courtesy of Manheim. Used by permission.

MANAGEMENT PROBLEM 16-1

Chicago Scientific faces an interesting dilemma. The company would like to open an online store to sell via the Internet, but it is concerned about relationships with the stores that currently sell its products. Mark Spencer talked about the situation, "Take West Marine, they have hundreds of stores and their own Web site for online sales. They sell our products at about 20 percent off full retail price, and we sell a lot of product through them. How will they respond if we open an Internet store? Of course our prices will be higher—will customers be upset when they buy from us at full retail and then see the same product for 20 percent less at West Marine?"

Spencer recalled an article he had read about a different approach taken by Black & Decker, the power tool manufacturer. Black & Decker has a tremendous amount of sales through Home Depot and Wal-Mart. It faced a similar problem in setting up a Web site; how could it alienate any of its large outlets? The solution was for Black & Decker to have an online store that does not sell anything! Instead, it offers information about products and provides links to retailers who carry its products. Black & Decker will only establish a link if the store has a page for their products, they won't send the customer to the retailer's home page where they might find a competitor's products.

What strategy do you recommend for an online store for Chicago Scientific? What do you think of Black & Decker's approach? In what other ways might companies establish online stores without cannibalizing their existing sales channels?

anytime, twenty-four hours a day, seven days a week. A second option, the buyer can bid over a set period of time in an online auction, in which the consignor sets a starting bid price, floor price, and incremental price changes. Finally, the buyer can participate in a live auction, bidding against other buyers, real-time (including visual of vehicle going through the sale lane and audio or auctioneer).

Manheim provides a number of services to customers. PowerSearch allows dealers to search online inventory, and physical auction presale lists for a vehicle that meets their specifications. The Manheim Market Report provides value to customers through wholesale pricing information on all vehicles sold by the company.

A key to the success of online auctions is trust. In the physical auction the buyer can see the car; in an online auction, he or she has to trust Manheim. When a vehicle arrives at auction, Manheim creates a complete physical description of standard features and takes digital photographs showing all aspects of the interior and exterior, including any damage. If a consignor requests the service, Manheim will conduct a mechanical inspection and provide a warranty on the vehicle.

E-COMMERCE

The question now is whether all commerce will be electronic in a few years. Some might consider e-commerce to be only another sales channel, but its impact is much greater than other channels. The scenarios described previously suggest substantial advantages for buyers and sellers with electronic commerce, and that this new channel has a dramatic impact on transactions costs. In addition, establishing the channel requires a substantial investment for many sellers on the Internet.

Managers face a number of issues in deciding on their approach to e-commerce, including the following:

■ What products and service should we sell electronically?

- How should we design our online store?
- How do we avoid cannibalizing our existing sales channels?
- What incentives should we provide for cooperation between those responsible for traditional and electronic sales and distribution?
- How much should we invest in e-commerce? What is the likely return?

In answering these questions, managers have some options to consider. Decisions on what products and services to offer depend on the company and its domain, as well as on what its competitors are doing online. The design of an online store is difficult, but many examples provide some guidance in choosing one's design. In addition, a number of software firms sell online store packages or provide consulting services to customize a package for a client.

In most cases, firms will cannibalize their existing channels, but with generally positive results. Many companies report that the average electronic order is larger than their average physical order. In Manheim's case, management must have been concerned that another company would start an online wholesale auto auction business if Manheim did not take the initiative. In the future, buyers are going to expect to be able to interact with sellers online; e-commerce will become an integral part of the economy, if it has not already. Fears of cannibalization, then, should be offset by fear of the competition and consumer demands for e-commerce.

The question of incentives within the company is a difficult one. Manheim developed an incentive scheme for managers in its physical auction based on the success of Manheim Interactive. More than one company provides a credit to a sales representative when his or her customer orders electronically. Managers need to be creative in developing incentives so that the organization works for the success of electronic commerce initiatives.

The question of how much to invest in e-commerce is difficult, as is the question of how much return one should expect from an investment. Referring to the framework for types of investments, it is quite likely that today electronic commerce falls into the category of competitive necessity. Customers expect to find online sales of some kind, and competitors may already provide it, or will in the near future. As a result, the firm may find little choice to adopting electronic commerce. As with any investment in this category of application, you will try to minimize costs with the constraint that you develop a system that is competitive, or that leads the competition.

Business-to-Consumer (B2C) E-Commerce

Business-to-consumer e-commerce received the most attention in the early days of the dot-com era as many individuals came up with exciting new business models for selling to consumers. In the discussion in Chapter 2 about strategy for electronic commerce, most of these models could not be protected in any way. It takes relatively little effort to establish a presence on the Internet and an online store; therefore, the first person with an idea for a business model did not even get much of a first mover advantage.

eToys came up with the idea of selling toys online, and soon Toys "R" Us went online as well. eToys had some problems fulfilling orders one Christmas, and eventually went out of business. Toys "R" Us was not making any profits from its online business, and eventually formed an alliance with Amazon.com in which it maintains the electronic store, and Amazon sells the toys from its Web site and handles fulfillment. Many defunct dot-com companies had great business models, but their inability to prevent competition meant not enough business to go around. No company was able to attain a critical mass of customers.

To some extent, these companies were ahead of their customers. Today, the estimate of the number of U.S. homes with Internet access is approaching 60 percent. When the dotcom era was at its peak, far fewer homes could access the Internet, though many people had access at work. The companies were also hindered by consumer fears about buying over the Internet; customers wondered whether the merchant would really deliver what was purchased. Also fears of stolen credit card numbers caused some reluctance to purchase online. Today, more and more homes have Internet access, and shopping at online stores is much more natural. In the future, many of the failed business models are likely to reappear and become successful as B2C electronic commerce matures.

The predictions earlier in the chapter on the impact of e-commerce included one that prices for the same product would converge. Mixed evidence in studies of the Internet fails to indicate definitively whether convergence is happening. As for the supplier side and whether companies are setting similar prices for comparable goods on the Internet, one study concluded that merchants for commodity computer accessories such as printers change their prices fairly regularly. By collecting price data from a sample of merchants, the researchers were able to track prices for the same products over time. The results demonstrated price differences within a given time period and over time. For most of the products, life cycles were short as manufacturers came up with new models; as a result, demand dropped over time. Instead of converging as demand dropped, the researchers found greater price dispersion. Price dispersion appeared to be less for high-priced items that presented significant gains from buyer search, because buyers are likely to spend more time searching for lower prices for expensive items than for inexpensive ones (Oh and Lucas, 2002).

The data also suggested that some vendors change their price strategies frequently to make it difficult for customers to know whether the vendor is a high- or low-priced outlet. This behavior is similar to the physical merchant who advertises an inexpensive "loss leader" to get you into the store, which is filled with more expensive items. The loss leader makes the merchant appear in its advertising to have low prices.

The conclusion from this research is that both buyers and sellers have tools on the Internet that facilitate price discovery. You can use a search engine to find stores selling a product you want to buy, and then visit the Web sites of a number of stores selling the given product to compare prices. You can also use comparison sites such as Mysimon.com or dealtime.com; their agents (shopbots) retrieve and compare prices for a specific product for you. A seller on the Web can do the same thing and adjust prices accordingly. Whether the buyer or the seller gains the most from B2C e-commerce may well depend on who is willing to do the most work in a search for prices.

Business-to-Business (B2B) E-Commerce

The market for business-to-business e-commerce dwarfs the B2C market; firms buy huge quantities of raw materials up and down the supply chain. U.S. businesses spent an estimated $482 billion in online transactions with other businesses in 2002, up more than 240 percent from the previous year. This number compares to an estimated $71 billion in B2C transactions that year. Dow Chemicals is one firm that has taken advantage of B2B ecommerce; some 15 percent of its transactions now occur online, up four to five times from 2000.[2]

Estimates are that GM spends $85 billion per year with its suppliers, Ford $80 billion, and DaimlerChrysler $73 billion. Some 30,000 suppliers make up the automobile industry, and a typical car has in excess of 10,000 parts. Many, many purchases take place between manufacturers and their suppliers during a year. The industry automated many of these purchases with EDI years ago, but EDI is a batch-oriented technology and does not tie the buyer and seller as closely together as the Internet. E-commerce and the Internet will capture an increasing share of these B2B transactions.

The value of B2B e-commerce is not in a relationship between one buyer and seller, but rather from transactions throughout the supply chain. The grocery and clothing industries have been two leaders in creating electronic links in their supply chains long before the Internet became available for profit-making purposes. In the apparel industry, the approach is called quick response (QR), and involves retailers communicating sales to their suppliers, who in turn are responsible for replenishing inventory shelves in the store. Grocery stores call their program efficient customer response (ECR) and use data from checkout scanners to reorder automatically from a company warehouse or from a manufacturer.

Much of the success of Wal-Mart is credited to its intensive use of IT to drive down its costs. Many Wal-Mart suppliers are responsible for the inventory of their products in each Wal-Mart store. This approach reduces Wal-Mart's costs for processing transactions and handling merchandise, and allows it to offer low prices. These examples deal with a retailer and manufacturers; it is difficult to know the extent to which the manufacturers reflect Wal-Mart's and other customers' demands through their supply chains.

To participate in B2B e-commerce and reflect that participation through the supply chain, a company faces a number of options. The first is to make arrangements with a firm's first-tier suppliers and encourage them to communicate their demands to their suppliers in turn. Over time this practice will provide everyone in the supply chain with accurate information on what is being consumed and ordered at the downstream end of the chain.

When the dot-com era ended abruptly and the sale of computer equipment seemed to stop, Cisco, the manufacturer of Internet communications equipment such as routers, ended up taking a $2 billion write-off for inventory that it could not use. This inventory was not at Cisco, but rather at the location of its second- and lower-tier suppliers. Cisco had good electronic connections with its first-tier suppliers, and they took Cisco's request for bids and sent them to their suppliers in turn. That supplier down two or more levels saw demand for, say 10,000 routers, coming from each of the three first-tier suppliers bidding on making the routers. The lower tier then saw demand for 30,000, not 10,000 pieces of equipment. Cisco is working on a system that will make its demand visible across the entire supply chain.

Instead of developing one's own supply chain and connections, industry efforts work toward facilitating electronic commerce in a particular industry. The home page of RosettaNet states its goal for encouraging widespread standards:

> A self-funded, non-profit organization, RosettaNet is a consortium of major Information Technology, Electronic Components and Semiconductor Manufacturing companies working to create and implement industry-wide, open e-business process standards. These standards form a common e-business language, aligning processes between supply chain partners on a global basis.

If all firms in an industry follow the same standards, they will find it much easier to establish electronic links among them.

MANAGEMENT PROBLEM 16-2

At the height of the dot-com economy, converts argued that most physical stores would go away; everyone would shop from a computer. Egghead software closed its physical stores and became a virtual store on the Internet, later merging with onsale.com. Experts told traditional merchants to fear Amazon, which would soon become the Wal-Mart of the Internet. As it turned out, these predictions were a bit overblown.

What kind of products and services seem most amenable to sale on the Internet?

Physical merchants struck back with appealing Web sites. Some merchants are putting kiosks in their stores so that a customer can order an item that is not in the store using the company's online site. While pundits offer the scenario of customers shopping in a store and using their cell phones' Web browser to check the price of the item on Amazon, so far the technology is not quite in place for this kind of electronic shopping.

Do you think physical stores have anything to fear from these predictions? How do you see physical and Internet stores competing in the next five years? How will each model develop? Why did Amazon, a pure Internet player, build physical warehouses around the country? What alternatives will be available for consumers in the next few years?

A third alternative is to purchase software designed to integrate trading partners and their supply chains. Both i2 Technologies and Manugistics offer such systems.

> i2 Global Network is an Internet collaboration space that enables buyers, suppliers, and marketplaces to rapidly connect to each other and use i2 Network Services for content, collaboration, and commerce. i2 Network Services allow the enterprise to extend its e-procurement and collaboration initiatives beyond Tier 1 suppliers. This unique service-based value chain integration approach enables your company to achieve greater return on investments in e-procurement and multi-enterprise collaboration initiatives. (www.i2.com)

The company's software is designed to interoperate among different customers so that they can link together to form a marketplace. Tradematrix is both a network and a suite of products from i2 for this purpose.

Exchanges

The exchange model is another form of B2B commerce that attempts to create a marketplace where buyers and sellers meet. An exchange may include a wide variety of firms, or it may focus on a single industry. So far, the latter have been more successful. In addition, exchanges that are successful have strong industry founders, who often agree to purchase a set amount of material through the exchange.

Avendra is an exchange established by five major hotel and lodging companies to purchase supplies. The company at times views itself as a contracting agent as well; it aggregates the demand for the hotel and restaurant properties, and negotiates yearly or longer purchasing agreements with suppliers. The members of the exchange have the option of purchasing through conventional purchase orders and fax machines or using the Internet to connect with suppliers.

Avendra has purchasing programs in different categories:

- Food and beverage
- Room operations
- Engineering and energy

- Administrative, financial, and legal
- Furnishings, fixtures, and equipment
- Building and construction
- Technology and telecommunications
- Golf and grounds maintenance
- Retail and spa
- Replenishment services

Covisint is another exchange, this one started by major automobile manufacturers. The auto industry suppliers actually asked for a single exchange so that they would not have to deal with five or six different exchanges with different formats and conventions. Covisint offers products and services in a number of areas:

- Collaboration
- Procurement
- Supply chain
- Quality

The exchange offers auctions and facilitates e-commerce among its members. (See Figure 16-2.)

A number of exchanges have failed, and the exchanges that are still in operation report difficulties with the model. Two firms acquired different parts of Covisint in 2004, and it will no longer operate as a consortium of automobile manufacturers. It will continue to sell supplies to the automakers under its new ownership. It is likely that both problems with cooperation among the fiercely competitive automakers, as well as antitrust concerns if they cooperate too much, doomed the original concept for Covisint.

Management at the early exchanges did not seem to understand how businesses purchase from each other. Although spot purchases do take place, much B2B commerce takes place under annual or longer contracts negotiated at one point in time. The buyer then orders products each day, week, or month that are "releases" under the blanket order. A number of suppliers are suspicious of exchanges, viewing them as a way to force down prices and destroy their profit margins.

The Japanese auto industry popularized the idea of working with one's suppliers to improve their operations and ultimately reduce their costs. The idea of establishing a long-term relationship with a supplier is contrary to trying to extract the best price from the supplier for a one-time purchase. To succeed in this kind of environment, an exchange has to provide more than cost savings. Covisint is addressing the entire value chain for an auto manufacturer, improving more than just the purchasing function.

Exchanges also seem to have suffered from a lack of trust. Buyers, forced by a parent company agreement, are suspicious that they are in fact not getting the best price. One exchange admits that it does not have the lowest price on each item, but claims that overall, if a customer buys all of its products through the exchange, it will save money. Even though an exchange may be able to demonstrate a cost savings when a company first joins, it can be difficult a year or two later to figure out what the customer would be paying if not in the exchange. The exchanges also must carefully safeguard information so that one customer does not see the data for a competitor. Exchanges must protect proprietary information and be sure that their customers do not inadvertently violate antitrust laws.

FIGURE 16-2 Covisint homepage.

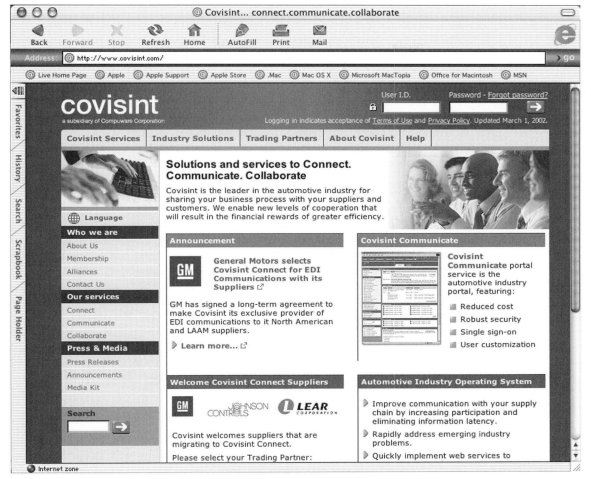

Courtesy of 2004 Compuware Corporation. Used by permission.

The concept of an exchange is powerful; companies pool their purchasing power and enjoy economies on product prices and in ordering efficiencies. However, the model has more complex dynamics than appear on first view, and it remains to be seen whether exchanges will ultimately be successful in advancing B2B commerce.

Technology makes it possible for customers to configure custom products online using the Web. Vendors such as Dell offer options for customizing a new computer, but the product can be made by snap together parts. More challenging is a totally custom product. Lands' End accepts a handful of measurements and produces a custom-fit pair of chinos. These special chinos and jeans cost 54 percent more than regular orders, but they account for 40 percent of online sales.[3] The company sent a mobile fitting studio to take customers' measurements with laser-based equipment. You can also order custom-colored M&Ms from Mars, albeit at a much higher price than the multicolored candies in the mass-produced packages.

What Happens to Intermediaries?

Early predictions were that the Internet would end the role of intermediaries in the economy. Realtors are intermediaries between buyers and sellers of homes; brokers are intermediaries between investors and the market, and faculty may be intermediaries between students and knowledge. Predictions were that the Internet would replace the intermediary, leading to vast disintermediation.

Many stock brokers still conduct trades, though an increasing number of investors do trade online without a broker. Realtors moved quickly to the Web and have the largest real estate site in the country. They have been successful in keeping a monopoly over multiple listings, though some sites help people buy and sell homes without a realtor. These sites say they can cut commissions because they automate many of the tasks performed by a human real estate agent, such as notifying prospective buyers that a house that meets their criteria has come on the market. These capabilities put considerable pressures on real estate commissions from the Internet, and the average commission has been falling.

It is likely that some intermediaries will continue to function on and off the Web; those who solve customer or producer problems are likely to do well. The exchanges discussed are a kind of intermediary; they provide value to the customer by negotiating low prices with suppliers, and through the convenience of "one site shopping."

Personalization is an example of how an intermediary can add value. By having customers rate their purchases and by having record of purchases of multiple products, a service provider can develop profiles of linked products. This intermediary can look through its database for people who fit a profile, and send them suggestions via e-mail for products they are likely to want. Amazon tells you what other books customers bought when they purchased the one you are interested in, and sends frequent messages of books related to your recent purchases. The site adds value in this way, and also stimulates further sales of its products.

Some Successes

We mentioned that a number of exchanges have failed, and the problems with dot-coms are a part of business history now. The way to reconcile these failures with an optimistic projection of having online connectivity with suppliers is to recognize that traditional firms are making use of e-commerce, and the amount of business they are doing through online stores is increasing all the time. An example of an of e-commerce success story may help.

Grainger

Grainger is a company that sells repair parts and industrial supplies. (See Figure 16-3.)

> Grainger sells the products every business and institution needs to keep its facilities and equipment running. We help customers get the job done by offering the broadest product selection in the industry. Finding the right products at competitive prices, backed by superior customer service and reliable information, is why customers turn to Grainger more than 100,000 times each day. (http://www.grainger.com)

Grainger actually sells more than 210,000 industrial supplies, and recent annual sales were more than $4 billion. The company has 500 stores and 1.5 million customers, but only sells to other companies, not to individuals.

FIGURE 16-3 Grainger homepage.

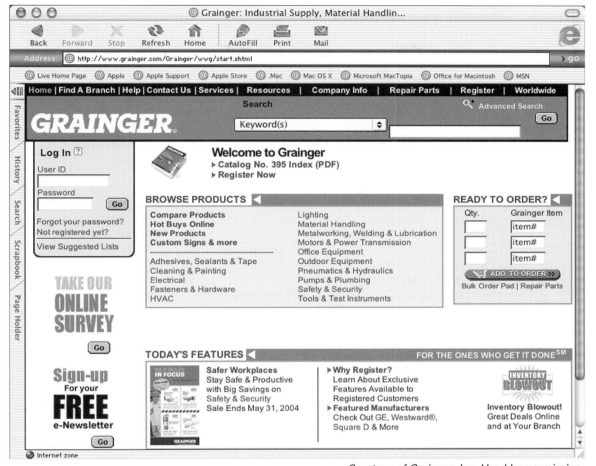

Courtesy of Grainger, Inc. Used by permission.

For a traditional company, Grainger was innovative in setting up an early Internet store for its industry, investing only $5 million in 1995 to test the concept. By 1999, Grainger was selling $100 million a year at the site. The next year sales hit $400 million and Grainger invested $120 million more in the online store. Grainger tried to rethink its business model for the Web, realizing that the online store was more than just a new toll-free 800 number. The store represented a new way of doing business and interfacing with its customers. For example, the company has a 4,000-page catalog; searching the catalog online is a much more pleasant activity than thumbing through actual pages. A customer can order online and pick up the order at a store if they would like.

In this case, a traditional firm saw the potential in the Internet and the importance of innovation. Grainger is well positioned to expand its electronic commerce business while continuing its physical business at the same time.

Southwest Airlines

Southwest is one of the few airlines making a profit, which is due to its low-cost business model and dedicated employees. The airline has competitive wages but a lower total labor cost than its competitors. Southwest flies nothing but Boeing 737 aircraft so that every pilot can fly every plane; no specialists or scheduling problems crop up because a pilot has not been certified to fly a particular type of aircraft.

Southwest flies from one location to another and avoids the popular hub-and-spoke system that seems to be causing more traditional airlines so much trouble in the aftermath of September 11. Southwest's fares are usually lower than those of the competition, and its fare structure is relatively simple.

The low-cost model extends to operations; Southwest can turn around a plane in twenty to thirty minutes after landing, which means that expensive aircraft spend more time flying rather than sitting on the airport tarmac. The cabin attendants clean up the passenger cabin after a flight, eliminating the need to wait for a crew of cleaners. Southwest does not assign individual seats; rather passengers receive a letter code when they check in at the airport indicating with which of three groups they will board. The airline assigns the letters in order of the passenger's check-in for the flight. The first to check-in get to board the aircraft first. As a result, boarding is a relatively fast process because passengers are looking for any seat, not one they have been assigned.

A Web site seems a natural way to make reservations on an airline such as Southwest. (See Figure 16-4.) The airline runs an easy-to-use site and offers lower fares on the Web to encourage passengers to make their own reservations, saving the airline the cost of having the passenger talk to an agent. As of this writing more than 57 percent of Southwest's revenue comes from its Web site bookings.

FedEx

FedEx is the largest express transportation business in the world with an estimated 30 percent market share and revenues of more than $19 billion. The company views IT as a strategic resource and continually invests in its technology infrastructure. The company handles more than 100 million transactions per day.

The Customer, Operations, Service, Master Online System (COSMOS) is a centralized computer system and the first in the industry used to track packages. The company also has a global operations control center that contains wall-sized screens that track weather patterns and the real-time movement of FedEx trucks and aircraft. The heart of the infrastructure is a mainframe database system in Memphis, which also features a data warehouse. A number of applications servers in different locations interact through the mainframe with the database. On top of all these computers is a data access tier that allows retrieval of information from the Web, dumb terminals, and radio data terminals.

This flexible infrastructure allowed FedEx to provide more services for customers, and to become more involved in their business processes by providing a range of logistics services. FedEx offers a number of eShipping tools to customers to facilitate their interactions with the company. Various programs let customers integrate FedEx into an e-commerce fulfillment operation. FedEx uses its IT capabilities to provide more services to customers in helping to manage their supply chains and to shorten order-to-delivery times. As an example, National Semiconductor formed an alliance with FedEx through which the shipping

FIGURE 16-4 Southwest Airline's homepage.

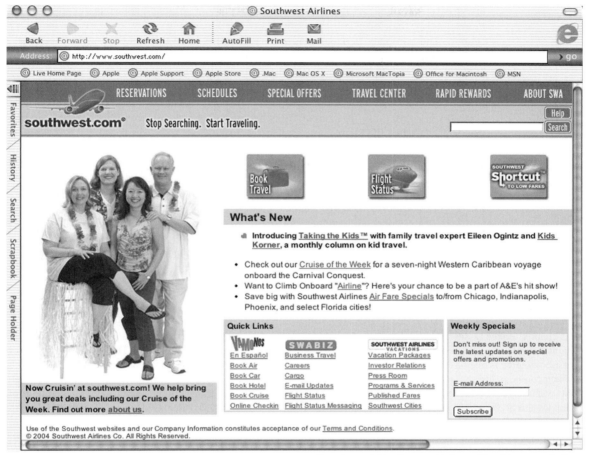

company acts as National's logistics department. National routes its orders to FedEx electronically, and the company takes over the delivery process. Each company has access to the other's systems in order to coordinate their efforts (Farhoomand, Ng, and Conley, 2003).

General Motors

One of the keys to success in the automobile business is design and a short time to market. Not too many years ago, it could take four to five years to go from the idea for a new vehicle to its introduction to dealers and the public. General Motors struggled for years with a declining market share and with designs that were dictated by financial considerations rather than by aesthetics. With a market share of nearly 60 percent in the 1960s, it slipped to less than 30 percent. A new chairman of GM is pushing the company to improve its design process and reduce the cycle time for creating a new vehicle.

One step in this process has been connecting fourteen GM engineering centers with a corporate intranet; all the centers use the same computer-aided design software and 3-D simulation tools. Before digital technology, various executives and committees required up to fifty redesigns before a car reached the market. Management can review designs more quickly than ever before, without the need to create a new clay model for every change. The company believes that these tools stimulated the creativity of its designers. GM is estimated to have invested more than $1.7 billion in Internet applications, which allowed the company to retire 3,500 older legacy systems.

The results are impressive: GM is creating new vehicles in eighteen to twenty-one months. Digital simulations dramatically reduced the time and cost of government-mandated crash testing programs. The company is becoming an innovator with technology, and IT lies at the heart of the chairman's strategy to make GM more competitive. The company sold 90,000 GM Celtas online in Brazil since 2000. GM figures that its new programs are saving $1.5 billion a year. Some 9,000 suppliers are linked in real time to GM via its GM Supply Power system.

GM has more than 360,000 employees. One executive commented that the company's goal was to make GM "feel like a small company" (Rifkin, 2002). One of the key roles technology can play in an organization is coordination, and GM offers an excellent example of how IT affects organization structures and processes. It will be interesting to see whether it is possible to make one of the largest companies in the world feel small to its employees.

CHAPTER SUMMARY

This chapter looked at different trends, some success stories, and some failed business models. The bottom line is that e-commerce is one of the most important innovations of the technology age that started in the middle of the last century. Home access to the Internet is steadily increasing in the United States and in other countries, and one of the major attractions of the Internet is electronic commerce. The technology has truly reached a critical mass; suppliers expect to make their products available through online stores, and buyers expect to find these stores and to shop from home. In the fall of 2001, fears of terrorism encouraged more and more people to shop at home rather than visit a physical mall. Suppliers are beginning to see the value of the Internet as a distribution medium, especially companies that sell information goods such as news, music, and videos.

On the B2B side, all experts expect the volume of e-commerce to dwarf B2C sales. The future of exchanges and innovative approaches to industrial purchases is still in doubt, but traditional firms are embracing the Internet, firms such as Manheim and Grainger. The attraction of integrating supply chains to increase efficiency is also great. By engaging in e-commerce a company improves efficiency, reduces costs, and provides better customer service. This value proposition is compelling. Over time, e-business will be a part of all business, so it is important to understand the contents of this chapter and Chapter 2 on strategies for the Internet and e-commerce.

KEYWORDS

Auction	Exchange	Markets
Channel	Hierarchy	Supply chain
B2B	Intermediaries	Transactions cost economics
B2C	Law of one price	

RECOMMENDED READINGS

Anderson, P., and Anderson, R. 2002. The new e-commerce intermediaries. *Sloan Management Review,* Summer, pp. 53–62. (A balanced look at the predictions and reality of intermediaries on the Web.)

Coltman, T., Devinney, T., Latukefu, A., and Midgley, D. 2001. E-business: Revolution, evolution, or hype. *California Management Review,* 44(1), pp. 57–86. (A well-balanced view of electronic commerce.)

Day, G. S., Fein, A. J., and Ruppersberger, G. 2003. Shakeouts in digital markets: Lessons from B2B exchanges. *California Management Review,* 45(2), pp. 131–150.

Ellis, C. 2003. Lessons from online groceries. *Sloan Management Review,* 44(2), p. 8.

Farmoomand, A., Ng, P., and Conley, W. 2003. Building a successful e-business: The FedEx story. *Communications of the ACM,* 46(4), pp. 84–87. (The story of technology at FedEx.)

McNealy, S. 2001. Welcome to the bazaar. *Harvard Business Review,* 79(3), pp. 18–19.

Pinker, E., Seidmann, A., and Vakrat, Y. 2003. Managing online auctions: Current business and research issues. *Management Science,* 49(11), pp. 1457–1484.

DISCUSSION QUESTIONS

1. Why do experts expect B2B e-commerce to dwarf B2C e-commerce?

2. Why do you think the online toy business had so much difficulty in getting established?

3. What factors have slowed the adoption of B2C e-commerce?

4. What problems are encountered in sending credit card information over the Internet?

5. How can consumers handle micro-payments, for example, buying a short newspaper article for 25 cents?

6. What factors account for eBay's tremendous success?

7. What does eBay do to encourage trust on both sides of the auction, the buyer and seller?

8. How has the Internet facilitated auctions?

9. What is transactions cost economics? Contrast a market and hierarchy.

10. What do you expect the impact of e-commerce to be on transactions costs?

11. What is the law of one price? Why has it not been strictly observed on the Internet?

12. How does price discovery affect both the buyer and seller in e-commerce?

13. What is an exchange? What particular problems emerge as organizations try to form exchanges?

14. How does B2B e-commerce affect the supply chain?

15. How did Grainger integrate e-commerce into its traditional business?

16. What do you think motivated Manheim International to set up Manheim Interactive?

17. What advantages does a *cyber* auction have over a physical auction?

18. How did Manheim Interactive address the issue of trust in selling used cars?

19. Why might some traditional firms have an advantage over start-ups when it comes to e-commerce?

ENDNOTES

1. *New York Times,* September 26, 2001.

2. *The Wall Street Journal,* November 20, 2003.

3. *BusinessWeek,* December 2, 2002.

CHAPTER 17

BUSINESS PROCESS: EXAMPLES FROM ERP AND CRM

A Manager's Perspective

Businesses execute a large number of processes. A typical business process is handling an order from a customer. The organization must acknowledge the order, find out if what the customer wants is in stock, ship the product or backorder it, bill the customer and finally process payment. The order process is far more complicated in most organizations than this brief description, and it is not the only process at a typical company. Processes and systems are similar—you are likely to find one or several systems that help carry out a process such as order entry. If a manager can understand business processes, and do the same for systems, he or she will know how that business really works. The way to understand a process is to walk through it and visualize it. Then draw a picture to document your understanding. When you have knowledge about all of the key processes and systems in the firm, you are in an excellent position to think of new innovations and better ways of doing business.

VALUE PROPOSITION

Information technology that is focused on business processes falls most often into the direct returns investment category. A company implements an enterprise resource planning (ERP) system to provide the following benefits:

■ Efficient processing, measured by indicators such as the number of transactions per employee, cycle time reductions, and supply chain efficiency

■ A level of process standardization, which leads to efficiencies for companies with many different locations

■ A platform for the development of new systems and to open options for the future

Customer relationship management (CRM) provides value in the following ways:

■ Improved customer relations leading to repeat business

■ Reduced costs for acquiring a customer

■ Reduced costs per customer service call

■ Greater customer satisfaction

■ Opportunities for cross-selling and for additional business from an existing customer

■ Increased revenue

You can measure the contribution of ERP with the following metrics:

- Transactions processed per employee
- Cycle time reduction in the production of goods or services and the development of new products
- As an option for other applications

CRM affects the following measures:

- Customer satisfaction
- Customer retention (amount of repeat business)
- Cost of acquiring a customer
- Cost per sales call
- Cost to process a customer support interaction

UNDERSTANDING BUSINESS PROCESSES

In the early 1990s, one of the most popular management topics was business process redesign, or *reengineering*. It turns out that reengineering as viewed by its proponents was difficult to accomplish; however, this management fad did serve to focus attention on business processes such as order processing and fulfillment as opposed to business functions such as the order entry department.

A good definition of reengineering is:

Reengineering is the fundamental rethinking and radical redesign of business processes to achieve dramatic improvements in critical, contemporary measures of performance, such as cost, quality, service, and speed. (Hammer and Champy, 1993.)

This framework has four key words:

1. *Fundamental*: Why does the firm do things a certain way?
2. *Radical*: Get to the root of a process. Look for reinvention as opposed to making superficial changes or minor enhancements to what is already in place.
3. *Dramatic*: Reengineering is not about marginal or incremental improvements, but rather it focuses on achieving quantum leaps in performance. Results that mean a 10 percent improvement are not reengineering.
4. *Processes*: Traditional design often is centered on tasks, jobs, people, and structures. Reengineering looks at a business process, which is a collection of activities that takes one or more kinds of inputs and produces some output of value.

The problem with reengineering was that finding a huge order of magnitude improvement was difficult to do. The term also became associated with downsizing and the reduction of staff, so that reengineering projects met with much employee resistance. The lack of success helped reengineering fade as an active program in most firms. What we can learn from this period is the importance of asking first whether a process needs to be undertaken at all before trying to improve it.

WHAT IS A PROCESS?

Most of the discussion to this point focused on the structure of the organization and how IT design variables can be used to change structures. This chapter looks at what a process is and how it is related to structure. A process is much like a system; it begins with some inputs, involves processing, and ends with an objective accomplished. A process may extend across many organization boundaries, involve a large number of individuals, and require many decisions and actions along the way.

One of the fundamental processes for a firm that sells a product is order fulfillment. Picture a mail-order firm in which operators take orders when customers call on a toll-free 800 number. The order entry department is responsible for talking to customers and entering their orders into a computer system. The system checks a *book* inventory to determine whether the goods requested are available. If so, it produces a picking list for the warehouse staff to use in completing the order. If the requested merchandise is out of stock, the system notifies the Purchasing Department that it is time to reorder, and it creates a backorder on the system so that the company can fill the order when a new shipment arrives. (We explore this process in more detail with Figure 17-7 later in the chapter.)

Note that the focus of this discussion is on the order and what happens to it as it moves through the organization, not on the individual departments involved in processing it. One way to improve this process would be to add an online order capability so that customers could enter orders from the Internet. Such a change would reduce the amount of manual effort required for an employee to enter an order into the computer system. You might also want to examine the backorder process to see if by giving suppliers access to your current orders and order history they could reduce stockouts.

AN EXAMPLE OF A PROCESS AT MERRILL LYNCH[1]

Merrill Lynch is the largest brokerage and financial services firm in the United States with more than 500 branch offices. This section presents both an old and a redesigned process to illustrate how a focus on a process can lead to major improvements. The objective of its securities processing operation is to receive certificates from customers, perform the proper processing of the certificates, and post data to customer accounts (Lucas, Berndt, and Truman, 1996).

A high-level process flow consists of the following steps:

1. The customer brings documents to a branch office.
2. The branch does preliminary processing.
3. Certificates are sent to a processing center.
4. The center verifies and checks the certificates.
5. The center processes certificates.
6. The center posts data to the customer's account.

On a typical day, Merrill Lynch offices around the United States receive some 3,500 securities that need processing of some kind. Some of the reasons customers bring securities to a branch office include the following:

1. The customer sold the stock and must surrender it so shares can be issued to the buyer.

2. A person inherited stock and must have the shares registered in his or her name.

3. A company reorganized and called its old stock to issue new shares.

4. A bond has been called by the issuer.

5. A customer wants Merrill to hold his or her securities.

The Original System

The customer brings the security plus other supporting documents to the branch office cashier. The cashier provides a receipt and batches all of the securities together to be sent for processing. Before the development of a new process, the branch would send these documents to one of two securities processing centers, either in Philadelphia or Chicago. (See Figure 17-1 for a diagram of this process.)

The objective of securities processing at the centers was to credit the customer's account as soon as possible, certainly within the twenty-four hours suggested by the Securities and Exchange Commission. Because of exceptions and the possible need to contact the customer again, sometimes it was not possible to achieve this goal. A good example of problems is in the area of legal transfers when someone inherits stock. Supporting documents such as a death certificate are required. If the customer does not bring the documents and the branch does not catch the fact that a necessary piece of paper is missing, the securities processing center must contact the branch and ask them to contact the customer.

Because many of the securities are negotiable, the security processing centers (SPCs) must be extremely careful in processing. Merrill Lynch is required to keep an accurate audit trail whenever it moves a security. This requirement led to frequent, repeated microfilming of securities as they moved around a center.

To the Merrill Lynch financial consultant (FC) or broker, the securities processing task seemed to require an inordinate amount of time and lead to numerous problems. (Approximately 15,000 FCs were employed at Merrill at the time of this study.) The branch operations staff had to continually monitor accounts to see whether securities were credited properly. FCs were forced to contact clients to obtain additional documents. A great deal of friction arose between the sales side of the business and securities processing department.

All of these reasons plus the labor intensive nature of processing led to a desire to improve securities processing. The most radical approach would be to eliminate the process entirely. Unfortunately, this option is out of Merrill Lynch's control. Although much publicity focused on *book entry* shares of stocks, a large number of physical shares of stocks and bonds remains in circulation. Obliterating the process would require industry-level and government cooperation to eliminate all physical certificates, replacing them with an electronic record. This solution would also require consumer acceptance and a massive effort to record electronically and eliminate all existing paper certificates.

After suggestions by the operations staff and extensive research, the systems group at Merrill proposed a new process using image technology to capture an image of the security certificate and related documents that accompany a transaction. The focus of the project was on workflow redesign, not just the use of image processing. Workflow redesign involved the closing of the two processing centers and the development of a securities processing department at a single site in New York (now in New Jersey).

FIGURE 17-1   SPC overview.

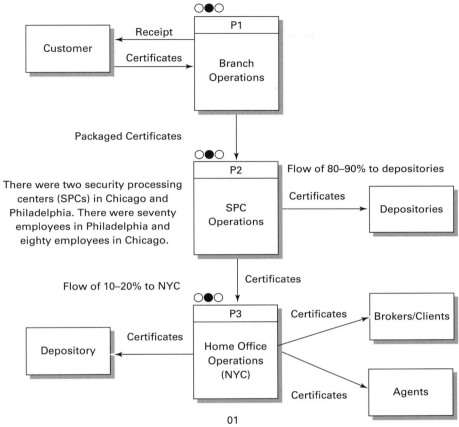

SOURCE: From Lucas, Berndt, and Truman, "A Reengineering Framework for Evaluating a Financial Imaging System", *Communications of the Association for Computing Machinery,* 39–5 (May 1996) pp. 86–96.

In this old process, customers brought securities and supporting documents to a branch office or sent them to Merrill through the mail. This set of documents will be referred to as a *certificate*, the terminology used at Merrill. After receiving the certificates, the branch conducted a manual review for negotiability. If this preliminary review verified that the security was negotiable, a clerk typed a receipt for the customer. If the certificates appeared not to be negotiable, the clerk told the customer what additional information was necessary to complete the transaction. (See Figure 17-2.)

During the day, several branch clerks accepted certificates and accumulated them. At the end of the day a courier took all certificates to one of two securities processing centers (SPCs) in Philadelphia or Chicago. The clerks attached a manually prepared manifest to the package summarizing its contents.

Normally the package arrived at the SPC the next day. Upon arrival, an SPC clerk inspected the package and checked that its contents balanced to the manifest. The clerk contacted the branch office to resolve any discrepancies. All certificates that matched the manifest continued to the next stage in processing. (See Figure 17-3.)

FIGURE 17-2 Branch operations.

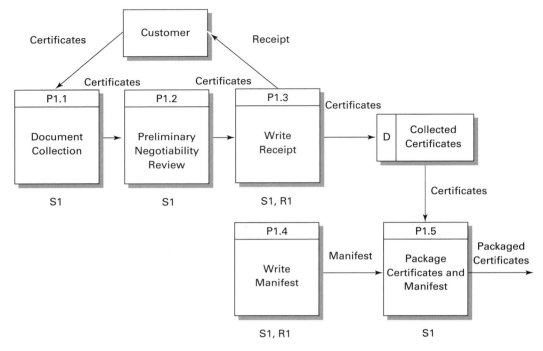

SOURCE: From Lucas, Berndt, and Truman, "A Reengineering Framework for Evaluating a Financial Imaging System", *Communications of the Association for Computing Machinery,* 39–5 (May 1996) pp. 86–96.

The first step after checking the packages was to microfilm all certificates. Next, clerks conducted a second negotiability review that was contingent on the type of transaction: legal or nonlegal. An example of a legal transaction is a stock transfer because the customer inherited the security. Regulations require that certain documents accompany the security, such as a death certificate for the person in whose name the security is currently registered.

If further review showed the certificate was not negotiable, it was segregated. A clerk logged this status into a Merrill Lynch securities control system. Once classified as negotiable, the certificate moved to a final holding area for distribution.

The SPCs sent 80 to 90 percent of the certificates directly to depositories. The remaining certificates were distributed to specialty departments in New York for further processing, for example, to a department that handles exchanges of stock necessitated by a stock split. Upon arrival at a depository or at a Merrill specialty department, the certificates were again microfilmed and staff members updated their status in the control computer system. Certificates were microfilmed yet again before consignment to their final holding area.

This process entailed so much microfilming because Merrill must carefully control securities and credit them to a customer's account as soon as possible. Given the volumes of paper involved, microfilming became an integral part of the control process. Merrill must also pass audits by the SEC, which checks controls on securities processing.

FIGURE 17-3   SPC operations.

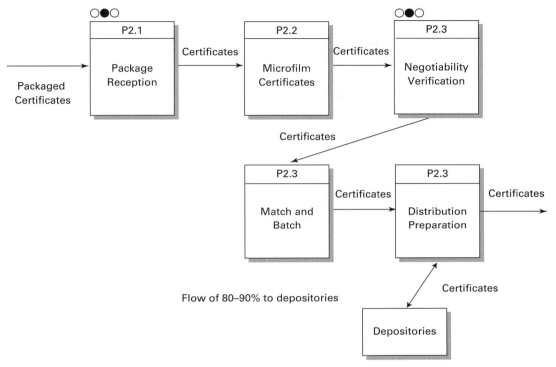

SOURCE: From Lucas, Berndt, and Truman, "A Reengineering Framework for Evaluating a Financial Imaging System", *Communications of the Association for Computing Machinery,* 39–5 (May 1996) pp. 86–96.

A New System

Merrill completely redesigned the SPC process. As in the old process, customers bring securities to a branch office or mail them to Merrill. The branch cashier conducts a preliminary negotiability review supported by an expert system. This system helps the cashier determine negotiability status. It also prints a customer receipt and generates a document control ticket that travels with the certificates. The expert posts a record of the certificate to a computer file, including a unique identifier number for the transaction.

At the end of the day, clerks package all certificates to be taken by courier to the single securities processing center in New Jersey. The system generates a manifest sheet for the package and updates a manifest file so that it contains information on the shipment.

At the SPC, the staff first wands a bar code on the package to verify receipt. Clerks check the package against the manifest; if a discrepancy is found, they update computer files and the system notifies the branch of the problem. Branch personnel can access to these files to check the status of processing of any security at any time. (See Figure 17-4.)

Negotiability must be verified in the new process, both for legal and nonlegal documents. However, the presence of the expert system in the branches reduced the number of

FIGURE 17-4 New system branch operations.

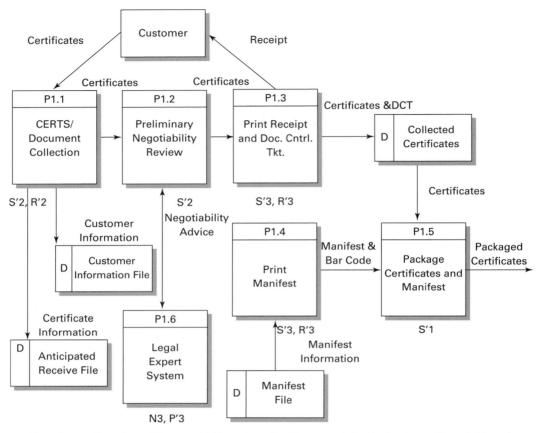

SOURCE: From Lucas, Berndt, and Truman, "A Reengineering Framework for Evaluating a Financial Imaging System", *Communications of the Association for Computing Machinery,* 39–5 (May 1996) pp. 86–96.

certificates arriving without the documents needed for negotiability by 50 percent for legals and 75 percent for nonlegals.

A major technological innovation in the process was the introduction of image scanning and character recognition for certain key fields on the stock certificate. The scanning system recognizes a reference number via the bar code on the control sheet accompanying the certificates. The system uses the reference number to access the computer record that shows the scanner operator the certificates included in the transaction. The operator scans the certificates and any legal documents. At this point the images and physical certificates diverge. (See Figure 17-5.)

The scanned certificate image undergoes a character recognition procedure to turn three areas of the image into characters that can be processed by a computer. (See Figure 17-6.) From a technical standpoint, this recognition employs a proprietary algorithm embedded in *firmware* in the imaging computer. This recognition process converts three

FIGURE 17-5 Image capture.

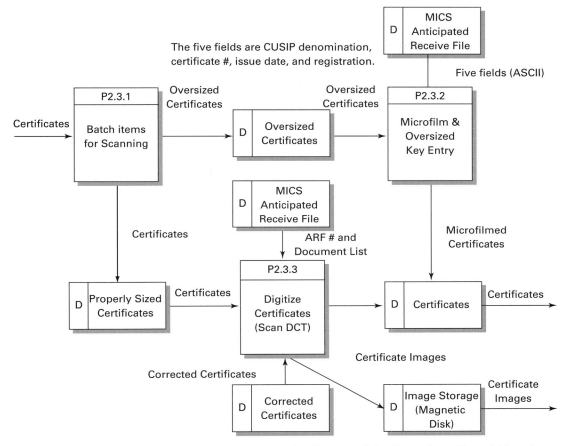

SOURCE: From Lucas, Berndt, and Truman, "A Reengineering Framework for Evaluating a Financial Imaging System", *Communications of the Association for Computing Machinery,* 39–5 (May 1996) pp. 86–96.

important fields from image to character format: the CUSIP number (a unique number for each security assigned by the securities industry), denomination of the security, and the security number. These three numbers are already recorded in the computer; recognition of the imaged fields is to establish rigorous control and provide assurance that the right documents have been scanned.

The recognition task is complicated by the lack of standard formats for securities. The three fields may exist any place on the security. The recognition algorithm needs to know where to look for the fields it is trying to convert. This information comes from a template database that indicates where the three fields are located on the security. Merrill developed a template for each CUSIP and date of issue combination. The scanning computer routes any certificate whose template is not yet in the database to a workstation operator. The operator uses a mouse to draw a box around each field, and the system records this location information in a new template for the security.

FIGURE 17-6 Character recognition.

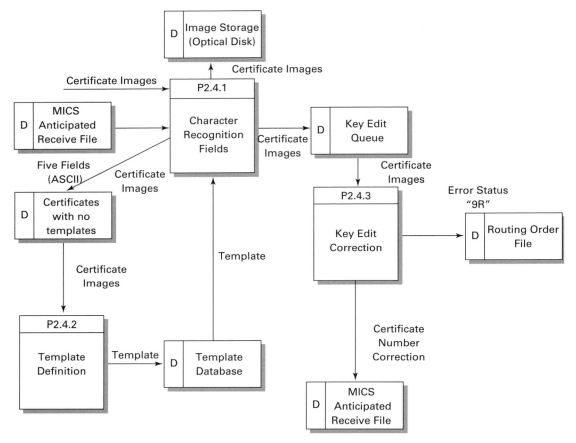

SOURCE: From Lucas, Berndt, and Truman, "A Reengineering Framework for Evaluating a Financial Imaging System", *Communications of the Association for Computing Machinery,* 39–5 (May 1996) pp. 86–96.

The system performs the image-to-character conversion by referencing the image, overlaying the template, and executing the algorithm. If the converted character fields match the same fields from the computer, the system updates the computer files to show scanning is complete and stores the images for this transaction permanently to optical disk. In the case of a mismatch between the converted characters and the computer record, or other nonrecognition, the system refers the transaction to key edit. There, operators examine the image and input data to unrecognized fields.

The staff takes the physical certificates for distribution to their final location. The system executes a procedure to provide routing orders for each certificate, and it specifies a destination box for the certificate.

When a user needs access to security information, he or she can retrieve the image of the security on a graphics workstation. It is no longer necessary to access the physical security, or to hunt through microfilm records, a process that could take as long as three days in the old process.

Evaluation

Table 17-1 lists the major changes from the Merrill Lynch SPC process and shows the value derived from this effort. The redesign effort resulted in the elimination of two process centers and the creation of a securities processing department at a central site. The process supports major changes in tasks and workflow, beginning with the receipt of securities at a branch office. The interface to the process for all groups having contact with it has also been changed.

TABLE 17-1   Evaluation of certificate processing.

Changes in organization structure
>   The major organizational change was the elimination of two securities processing centers and the consolidation of all securities processing in a central site.

Changes in workflows and functions performed
>   Branch office input changes
>   Branch office customer receipt
>   Anticipated receipt information
>   Package receipt and bar coding
>   Elimination of most microfilming
>   Legal negotiability workflow changes
>   Imaging operation; scanning and key edit
>   Retrieval of image rather than physical security

Interface changes
>   Branch office interface
>   Customer interface
>   Worker interface with scanning equipment
>   User interface retrieving images

Major changes in technology
>   Expert system to assist branch cashier receiving certificates
>   Incorporation of scanning to replace most microfilm and provide better control, including:
>>   Scanners
>>   Template definition
>>   Key edit
>>   Computer facility with optical disk jukebox
>>   Retrieval of scanned documents
>>   Modifications to existing control system

Impact
>   Improvements in customer service
>   Better customer receipt
>   More information captured at point of contact
>   Broker can query system for status of processing
>   Better control

Certificate-level control
High-quality images compared to spotty microfilm
Reduction in up to three-day searches for microfilm to instantaneous retrieval
Significant cost reduction
Reduction in research time

SOURCE: From Lucas, Berndt, and Truman, "A Reengineering Framework for Evaluating a Financial Imaging System", *Communications of the Association for Computing Machinery,* 39–5 (May 1996) pp. 86–96.

Technology changes include the expert system for the branch office input, scanners, a template library, character recognition from images, and optical disk storage. Significant increases in the level of customer service and the quality of support were realized in the securities processing provided to the branches. Much less handling of physical securities also resulted, and retrieval time for a certificate image is now nearly instantaneous. The time to research a security has been dramatically reduced, from up to three days in the old process to virtually instantaneously in the new.

The new securities processing system has had a dramatic impact on resources:

1. Reduction of occupancy from two locations to one
2. Reduction in depository fees
3. Interest savings on receivables
4. Reduction of microfilm costs
5. Savings in security services
6. Reduction in staff of 168 positions, leaving a current total of 165 including temporary staff

The new process required an investment of approximately $3 million. The return on the investment was calculated as a payback period of less than two years, which translates to a savings of about $1.5 million a year.

This example shows how one can execute a major redesign of a business process. Merrill used technology along with process redesign for *technological leveling* and reducing the number of processing centers and the number of managers needed to staff them. It applied information technology to automating the flow of certificates through the SPC, a form of *production automation.* The image system captures the certificates electronically and employees in different departments can retrieve the image of a certificate in seconds without the need to visit a vault. The certificate image can be routed to any terminal capable of displaying it within Merrill illustrating *electronic workflows.* (Subsequently, Merrill outsourced all securities handling to a third party; the simplification of securities processing made it possible to turn over all handling of securities to a separate firm that will use electronic linking and communications to work as a partner with Merrill Lynch.)

Improving Processes

The first question in looking at a business process is whether the process itself is necessary. The questions to ask include the following:

1. What are our key business processes?
2. Do we have to execute this process at all?
3. What totally new ways, taking advantage of information technology, exist to perform this process?
4. What does redesigning a process imply for the structure of the organization?
5. How can we use IT design variables in conjunction with process redesign to change the structure of the organization?

ENTERPRISE RESOURCE PLANNING SYSTEMS (ERP)

All businesses have basic transactions processing requirements. The example at the beginning of a chapter of processing an order looks similar for any company that sells a physical product, at least any company that sells to retail buyers. For many B2C companies the process is also the same. All companies need to collect payment from customers and to pay their suppliers. Thus you would expect to find accounts receivable and accounts payable processes in some form in any firm.

Figure 17-7 is a schematic of the basic transactions cycles in a typical manufacturing firm. This diagram represents a high level and does not include many details in order to make it more readable. A customer at the top of the figure consults a catalog and decides to place an order. The order may be sent over the Internet using XML, through an EDI

FIGURE 17-7 Enterprise resources planning: a schematic of a firm's transactions processing.

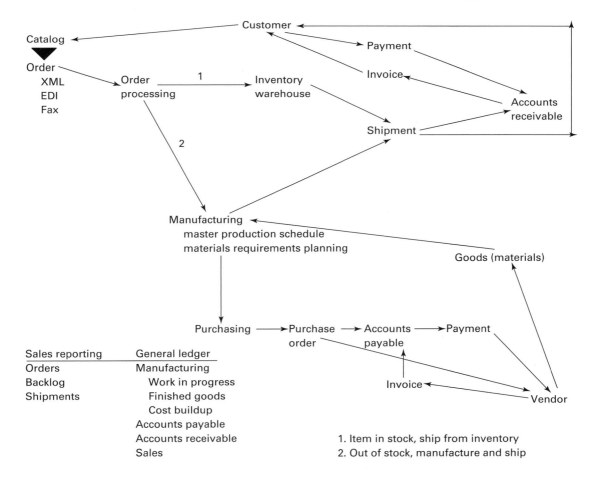

MANAGEMENT PROBLEM 17-1

ERP systems have a fair amount of controversy associated with them, as described a bit in this chapter. In the mid to late 1990s, these systems were extremely popular with many companies installing them to solve their Y2K problems. Y2K involved converting date fields for the change to a new century. In older systems programmers represented dates by the last two digits of the year, for example, 1998 as 98. Because a lot of calculations involve subtracting one date from another (e.g., to get the length of a loan), some action was necessary. The year 2000 – 1998 should have a result of 2. However, a program using two-digit dates would have 00 – 98, or a –98 as the answer. ERP systems were Y2K-compliant and offered a solution to this problem that did not involve reprogramming a lot of older, legacy systems.

Of course, some firms also wanted the functionality provided by ERP systems, and the degree of standardization they provided. Something called reengineering was a fad around this time, and management often viewed an ERP package as a way to reengineer their transactions systems. The ERP package providers moved to adapt their software to the Web so that the primary interface is a Web browser. They also feature e-commerce capabilities so that the firm uses the ERP system as the infrastructure for building e-business applications.

Given all of these considerations, the decision to adopt an ERP package is no easier today than it was in the 1990s. In fact, it may be more difficult because companies are not facing such pressing issues like Y2K. The failure of a number of these systems emphasizes that no company has any guarantee of a successful system no matter how much money is put into it.

Your CEO has asked you to do a study and to recommend whether your firm should implement an ERP system. The first part of your study is to look at the generic question of whether to go with an ERP, and the second is to choose an ERP vendor if the outcome of the first part is to go with ERP. What kind of information would you need for this study? What factors would influence your recommendation on whether to invest in an ERP system? If you recommend going with ERP, what criteria would you use to choose among ERP vendors? What would you want most in an ERP package?

link, or by phone or fax. The order arrives at an order processing function, which could be a department with human employees or a computer program. At this point the manufacturing firm checks inventory; if the items ordered are in inventory, the manufacturing firm sends the order to the warehouse with instructions to fill it.

If the items are out of stock, the firm routes the order to a manufacturing facility. This facility creates a master production schedule and includes the new order in this schedule. The plant uses materials requirements planning (MRP) as a part of its operations; this application "explodes" an item into its constituent parts so that they may be ordered or manufactured. The MRP output goes to the purchasing department to procure the raw materials needed for production. Purchasing places an order with the vendors that supply materials to the company. The vendor ships goods to the plant, and sends an invoice for payment through the manufacturing firm's accounts payable function.

Back at the warehouse, the ordered goods are available to be shipped, or they come in from manufacturing. The warehouse picks the goods, packs them, and sends them to the customer. It also notifies the accounts receivable department, which sends an invoice to the customer, who in turn sends payment. At the bottom left of the figure is a list of what a sales reporting system might include: orders, backlogs, and shipments (actual sales). The general ledger is affected by many of the processing steps in the figure. A manufacturing company needs to value all inventories including raw materials, work-in-process, and finished goods. Many manufacturing firms use cost accounting systems to do a *cost buildup* to show the value added to goods in the process of being manufactured.

Obviously the details of transactions processing differ among companies, but any manufacturing firm has some process to accept orders and fulfill them. A distributor follows much the same process, but does no manufacturing; all of the goods it sells come from others.

Considerable effort is required to develop systems for the processes in Figure 17-7. Long before the advent of ERP systems, companies developed applications for different functions in the figure, for example, an order processing system that recorded orders and checked warehouse inventory, either sending an order to manufacturing or picking instructions to the warehouse. Manufacturing was a separate system, with production control often done manually, and a computer program to do materials requirements planning. Separate accounts receivable and accounts payable subsystems would be set up as well. The company would have a financial and general ledger system to prepare financial statements.

Several reasons explain why a firm would develop separate systems. The first is that the systems often followed the functions of the organization; the manager of order processing was interested in a system for the tasks in the order processing department. No strong management guidance at the top suggested integrating the functions. In addition, the processing shown in Figure 17-7 is complex; few IT professionals would advocate developing one large system to do every step implied in Figure 17-7.

Rather than each company designing and programming its own version of basic transactions systems, software vendors created packaged systems for companies to purchase. Early packages handled a few processes; for example, over the years a number of vendors created packages for financials including accounts receivable, accounts payable, and general ledger. A few vendors expanded on this concept to include software to handle all of the basic transactions for different types of companies, and these larger software suites became known as enterprise resource management (ERP) packages.

Even though these packages are integrated, they are not a single, monolithic piece of software. Rather the ERP vendors sell modules that encompass the processing for major subsystems such as order processing, manufacturing, accounts receivable, general ledger, human resources, production planning, and so on. These modules differ from the ones that the manufacturing firm in Figure 17-7 might have developed itself over the years in an important way. The ERP package is integrated and provides a consistent interface. A company developing software for all the functions in the figure would require many years to complete the task. The technology changes, personnel turnover, and a system completed in the tenth year of a development effort would look a lot different from the original specifications for the system.

Also, these systems might or might not integrate well together. Perhaps a change in one system might not be reflected immediately in another. When an order is shipped, the warehouse system needs to immediately decrement on-hand inventory so that the order processing system sees what is available to ship. In addition, the manufacturing planning system needs to see the new inventory balance. Then when a customer pays an invoice, if the accounts receivable system fails to immediately update the customer's credit limit, any new order might put the customer over its limit.

A good ERP system should do all of these things; it should have a consistent interface, today using a Web browser, and it should be tightly integrated. The advantages of this system are that it exists with a program code that has been used and debugged already; it can provide a solution for most of a firm's transactions processing needs; and for better or worse, it creates a level of standardization in the company. Major ERP package vendors include SAP, Oracle, PeopleSoft, and J.D. Edwards (now merged with PeopleSoft).

Product Examples

The Web sites of these three vendors provide an idea of the size and complexity of ERP systems.

SAP

Recognizing that different industries have different requirements, vendors such as SAP created variations in their packages to apply to a specific industry. For example, a financial services firm probably is not interested in supply chain management or production scheduling software. SAP offers twenty different industry solutions. For example, for consumer products SAP offers specific packages for apparel, footware, and beverages. The key capabilities of this software as listed at the SAP Web site include the following:

Mass data processing: Lets you efficiently manage and manipulate the large volumes of complex data generated continuously in the apparel and footwear value chain, including sales orders, customer master data, and material master data.

Supply chain management: Enables you to see and control your entire supply chain, from suppliers and partners to retailers and end-consumers, helping you cut costs, remedy problems, and exploit opportunities.

Customer relationship management: Helps you deliver on commitments made to customers and to improve customer service.

Business intelligence: Gives you the critical information you need to set realistic budgets and map out future strategy.

E-business and enterprise portals: Lets you leverage online and e-business capabilities for both business-to-business and business-to-consumer scenarios with mySAP Enterprise Portals.

A further look at the supply chain management component of this software reveals its features:

mySAP Supply Chain Management (mySAP SCM) is the supply chain solution that delivers real business value. By dramatically improving your ability to plan, respond, and execute, mySAP SCM enables you to adapt to the inevitable exceptions that occur in the race to meet market demands.

That starts with visibility portals that allow your employees, partners, vendors, and customers to communicate and collaborate. So you can constantly check the pulse of plans, exceptions, and performance measures. And move from a linear, sequential supply chain to an adaptive supply chain network.

What's more, mySAP SCM offers the only complete supply chain solution. With capabilities that cover supply chain planning, execution, coordination, and networking. Enhanced by industry expertise and proven methodologies acquired through three decades of supply chain leadership.[2]

SIDEBAR 17-1

Integrating Production Planning with ERP

VF Corporation is a $5 billion apparel manufacturer whose brands include Lee and Wrangler jeans, North Face gear, and Vanity Fair lingerie. Seven years ago the company installed i2 supply chain planner software. Today this package is used to plan 90 percent of the company's domestic supply chain operations. The company adopted a slow and steady approach to move from multiple legacy systems in its five divisions to a common architecture based on packaged software.

VF cannot just manufacture its product. Retailers are expecting suppliers to know what is selling best and to deliver those garments when the store needs them. As an example, Penney's depends on VF's retail floor space management system, a program that analyzes climates, demographics, and historical sales patterns to suggest a product assortment for each of Penny's 1,100 stores. VF has been a leader in vendor-managed inventory. As early as 1991 it built a mainframe system that produced a daily inventory model of each client's stores by product, taking into account forecast sales, planned promotions, shipping and lead times, and retail floor space.

The company gained a great deal from i2, but a spokesperson described it as "the hardest piece of software I've ever dealt with." The staff did eventually learn the package and has been able to integrate it into VF's operations. Each night i2 processes more than 1 million records of demand forecasts for the next six months. The IT group wrote more than 80 programs so that i2 could retrieve data from all of its different systems, including older COBOL mainframe programs and SAP's ERP suite. VF had to work closely with SAP and i2 to develop systems for its requirements.

The chairman of VF said, "We believe technology will differentiate the winners from the losers in a highly competitive and consolidating industry."

Source: *InformationWeek,* May 26, 2000.

SAP developed software for a large number of business processes, and then it customized this software for particular industries. The supply chain software described was not written exclusive for the consumer products industry, rather SAP adapted it for this industry.

As e-commerce exploded in the late 1990s, ERP vendors adapted their software to the Internet so that companies could expand these packages to set up online stores and links to suppliers. You are likely to find that an ERP vendor now calls its software an e-business suite rather than an ERP package.

Oracle

Oracle's first products included a database management system that proved popular with customers. Using this DBMS as a core, Oracle developed applications packages for different business processes. Combining these processing modules into one package produced Oracle's version of an ERP system. This ERP system is integrated with the Internet, and Oracle promotes it as a solution to developing e-commerce capabilities. Their system includes functions in the follow areas:

- Marketing
- Sales
- Service
- Contracts
- Financials
- Human resources

- Supply chain
- Order management
- Procurement
- Project management
- Asset management
- Manufacturing

PeopleSoft

PeopleSoft is another vendor that offers ERP packages. A look at their Web site for offerings in consumer products finds that this vendor also offers supply chain management software. However, rather than develop its own software, PeopleSoft formed an alliance with another vendor to integrate its product into the PeopleSoft package. Here is what it says about supply chain software:

Market-Driven Supply Chain: Manage your business from product demand through your entire supply chain. PeopleSoft is the first vendor to offer you an integrated customer relationship management and supply chain management solution.

Adept Demand Planning: Use PeopleSoft to create a demand plan that ensures resources and schedules throughout your organization are targeted toward a well-defined and reliable market strategy.

PeopleSoft has partnered with Syncra Systems, Inc., the premier provider of inter-enterprise supply chain collaboration solutions and Collaborative Planning, Forecasting, and Replenishment (CPFR). Our joint solution combines the PeopleSoft Supply Chain Planning solution with Syncra's CPFR-based technology, resulting in inventory reduction, improved service levels, and increased sales.

Closed-Loop Promotions Management: PeopleSoft offers the only closed-loop solution for trade promotions that enables you to effectively target your retail merchandising activities. You can forecast accurately to ensure supply meets demand, reduce excess inventory, and decrease deductions while improving customer satisfaction.[3]

Great Detail and Complexity

ERP packages cover a large number of business functions and address the needs of customers who all think they are unique. The challenge for ERP providers is to convince a company to purchase a software package that is general enough to be used by a large number of firms. The major motivation for a customer is to reduce the time required and the risk of developing one's own ERP software. In theory, a customer should be able to implement more functions more rapidly through a package than by developing its own code.

A package vendor must address the differences among companies in their practices. The first approach they use is to customize the package for various industries, or at least to assemble different building blocks for these industries. The second tactic the vendor follows is to include a lot of options in the software, for example, if a university was looking at a package, the vendor might include the ability for the registrar to record and average grades using letters (A, B, C, D, F) or numbers (0–100). In setting up and installing the software, the university would indicate in a table in the software what grading scheme it used. For a complete ERP implementation, a client may be looking at more than 5,000 such decisions involving a large cross-section of managers in the firm.

A third strategy calls for custom coding; the client makes changes to the package, hopefully changes that affect the smallest part of the package as possible. Vendors generally dislike this approach because the customer will likely encounter problems when upgrading to new versions that become available. The customer must be able to identify the changes it made, and then recreate them in the new version of the package.

For this reason, the fourth strategy the vendor will suggest is for a customer to change procedures before thinking about changing the package. It is quite possible that the procedures implied by the packages are more efficient than the ones in place at a customer's site. It may in fact be easier to change procedures to accommodate the package rather than vice versa.

Business processes are complex and detailed, and management must understand that they can only be simplified to a certain point. The training manual for just the warehouse administration component of an ERP system for midrange computer users is more than 300 pages long. It includes information about the contents of the package's database that relate to the warehouse, and transactions such as receipt of goods, picking and shipping, taking inventory, and generating reports. Eight activities associated with the receipt of goods each requires the system to take some action. For example, when goods arrive at a warehouse, they have to be booked, physically received, and put away at an assigned location in the warehouse. The system must be able to handle scheduled as well as unscheduled receipts. A user also wants to keep track of the movement of goods in the warehouse.

The Implementation Challenge

Because of the complexity of business processes and the software that addresses them, the implementation of ERP packages has met with mixed success. Some noted disasters occurred at Hershey's Chocolates, Nike, and Whirlpool, and it is believed that ERP implementations have failed at an alarmingly high rate. Many successes also happened. In the early 1990s, Cisco decided to replace its stove-pipe systems with an ERP package. Management made it a priority for the year, and at one point, 10 percent of the company's employees were working on implementation. Cisco managed to move over to the package in nine months, but it was many more months until business operated routinely.

The nine-month implementation time is one of the shortest recorded for an ERP package implementation. Acquiring a package is certainly less time-consuming than programming a system yourself, but these packages are large and they involve many subunits in the organization. It is unrealistic to expect to implement an ERP package in a medium-sized or larger firm, especially one with multiple locations, in less than two years. Because implementation requires knowledgeable managers and users, the process ties up a lot of talent in the organization for a long time.

Several messages emerge from the implementation of ERP at Cisco and others. First is the importance of leadership from top levels of the organization. At Cisco, the chairman made successful ERP implementation one of the key goals of the company for the year.

MANAGEMENT PROBLEM 17-2

Boston City is a large commercial and retail bank in Boston. The bank has used IT for many years and has a number of systems. The major problem is that the systems are typical "stove pipes." The bank developed the loan system to process loans; at the time loan officers were not interested in mortgage business, so the mortgage department developed its own system. As a result, a good customer of the bank might exist in four or five systems. Because they lacked information, bank personnel were unable to tell whether a caller was already a good customer.

Boston City has been working for a year to develop a common system that is oriented around the customer, not a bank function. The bank wants a customer services representative to see all of a customer's relationships with the bank when that customer calls. The service rep should know whether the customer has a checking account, savings, owns certificates of deposit, has a personal or auto loan, uses a credit card issued by the bank, and holds a mortgage. Boston City is looking for a stock brokerage firm to purchase, and eventually would integrate brokerage account information with the bank data.

Why is the bank going to all of this trouble? Is this system just to provide better customer service, maybe to match what competitors are doing? What other alternatives does a customer relationship management system such as this one provide? What are the opportunities for revenue generation?

At Digital China, a computer sales company in China, senior executives made management bonuses and even continued employment dependent on the success of the ERP implementation. It should also be noted that despite the examples of ERP failures, sometimes, as in the case of Hershey's, a difficult implementation with all kinds of problems and labeled a failure turned out well because the company persevered and today is happy with the benefits it receives from an ERP system.

Second, you must expect to hire significant consulting help. Often the consulting budget equals the cost of the software. Other estimates put total implementation at three to ten *times* the cost of the software package alone. In addition to vendors, a number of consulting firms can help a company implement this software.

A key advantage and disadvantage of ERP software, or any major package, is the standardization it provides. Standardization offers many advantages for a company. Communications standards let networks and communications devices interoperate; the Internet works partially because of standards such as TCP/IP. On the other hand, convincing employees to change their procedures to adopt a standard is not easy, particularly if the standard is more difficult or cumbersome for them individually. It can be difficult to get long-time employees to change what they have been doing for years.

It is unrealistic to expect that SAP or any applications package will fit your business as it comes from the vendor. The organization needs to make a number of decisions in implementing such software. With SAP, the firm first configures the software by making entries in SAP tables that tell the software what functions to execute; thousands of such tables require configuring. An SAP consultant indicated that you could fit about 60 to 70 percent of your existing business processes through this configuration process. SAP fully supports this kind of input when it creates upgrades, so you do not have to go back and start over when you install a new version of the software. The software supports "best practices," and you can change your business processes to match the software. Of course, this strategy requires changes in the organization and in workflows. A company chooses this path to save money now, and later when upgrading the software.

SAP offers a second level of customization that it calls enhancements. In the actual SAP programs, a client can insert its own code at certain places. SAP determines where the code is to go, but the client writes the code. When you upgrade, you have to be sure that these custom-coded modules are installed in the new version of the software. A firm can meet an estimated 70 to 85 percent of its current processes through configuration and enhancement processes. At this point, you again decide whether to change business processes to match the system. If not, the choice is to modify the system, something that is not easy to do. After modification, SAP will not guarantee that the installation can be successfully upgraded when new releases come along.

A manager should not expect that buying an ERP package at all resembles the purchase and installation of Microsoft Office on a PC. A dedicated application such as ERP is intertwined with all of the basic and many of the advanced functions of a business. You are installing this package to change the way the firm processes transactions, and probably the way it executes some of its business processes. This change is going to be disruptive, and it needs management leadership to make it successful. ERP implementation failures tend to be customer management failures more than they are technology failures.

An Example

Geneva Pharmaceuticals is a division of Novartis, which manufactures generic drugs. The company's primary business activities are the manufacturing and distribution of generics. It has a 600,000 square foot facility in Broomfield, Colorado, and distribution centers in Broomfield and Knoxville, Tennessee. The manufacturing process for drugs requires careful attention to quality and to the standards set by the U.S. Food and Drug Administration. Geneva supplies about 250 customers including large drug distributors like McKesson and Cardinal Health, as well as drugstore chains such as Rite Aid, grocery chains with pharmacies, mail-order firms, and governmental agencies. Pricing involves negotiations with customers and generally features rebates, a standard of the industry. Most orders come through EDI, and software at Geneva filters those orders with a number of error checks.

Until 1996, Geneva used multiple software programs for different functions such as procurement, manufacturing, accounting, and sales, generally built for an IBM AS/400. Individual business units funded and developed systems generally without any concern for the enterprise. Geneva had situations in which different personnel keyed the same data into a system because systems did not interoperate. Management at Geneva decided to move to a standard platform that could support the entire organization, not just individual departments. After investigating two options, Geneva chose to implement SAP R/3 in a three-phase project.

The first phase focused on supply-side processes such as manufacturing planning and procurement planning. Phase II dealt with order management and customer service, and Phase III was to integrate supply and demand sides and to improve supply chain management.

Geneva employed ten IS staff members and ten full-time users, supplemented by ten part-time users on its R/3 team. A consulting firm provided technical assistance in the form of ten staff members who knew R/3 and could program modifications to it. After four months, Geneva found that it had made little progress. System requirements were not yet defined in sufficient detail, and a lack of coordination existed among team members. To get the project back on track, Geneva hired a new CIO with experience implementing R/3 at his former employer. The CIO viewed ERP as a change effort as much as a technical implementation project. As a result, he focused more on process and the changes that Geneva employees would encounter with the new system.

Phase II was more complicated than phase I, because customer orders tended to be unique and were often tracked manually. The company replaced its original consulting firm with two new firms for this phase, including one that was an expert in process design. Geneva expanded its team and spent considerable effort on business process redesign and improvement. This effort culminated in a conference room pilot or prototype to test the new ideas and R/3. Geneva equipped five rooms running R/3 and brought in trainers to work with users. The team targeted selected Geneva employees to act as change agents during implementation; training lasted three weeks and each user received an average of three to five days of instruction related to the employee's role in the new system. The company deemed the second phase a success, and began on the third at the time of this report (Bhattacherjee, 2000).

CUSTOMER RELATIONSHIP MANAGEMENT

The idea behind customer relationship management is to create a highly personalized relationship with each customer leading to greater customer satisfaction and a stronger, more profitable business relationship with him or her. USAA, the insurance company for armed forces members in Texas, follows a strategy of outstanding customer service. Long before CRM software packages became popular, USAA developed procedures to respond to the needs of its customers. The company was one of the first in the industry to develop a scanning system for correspondence from policy holders. The customer support system also provided a record of each telephone contact with a customer.

When an insured calls USAA, the service representative on the phone can see an image on the screen of all the correspondence the customer had with the firm. The customer service representative also had a record of phone calls. As a result, if the customer called back in five minutes, or five days, and was connected with a different customer services representative, that person also knew all about the issues of concern to the customer.

With the development of the Internet, marketing has focused on personalization. (Sometimes personalization is called *one-to-one marketing* or *relationship marketing*.) The goal is for a company to establish a personalized relationship with a customer so that it provides exactly the information and products the customer wants. Amazon.com offers personalized book recommendations based on your purchases. Amazon's software allows it to group books by content, and it maintains a record of all your purchases. When you make a purchase, Amazon recommends books that other people bought at the same time they purchased the book you just bought. Another approach is collaborative filtering, which is a way of grouping people together who purchased similar products. When a number of people in a group similar to you purchase a new book, the filtering algorithm indicates that this book might be of interest to you as well. Amazon sends you an e-mail recommending the book.

The best source of new business is from an existing customer. It is estimated to cost six times more to sell to a new customer than an existing one, and that the probability of a new customer making a purchase is 15 percent compared to 50 percent for an existing one. Personalization also can lead to cross-selling. Banks and other financial institutions have merged to provide combined banking and brokerage services. These financial institutions want to create databases with complete information on each customer so that a brokerage client who needs a loan will be convinced to bring that business to the financial firm rather than to some other loan provider.

Siebel Systems

Customer relationship management (CRM) is a popular type of packaged application. Thomas Siebel, founder of Siebel Systems, has written extensively about CRM and how it can help a company. He offers a series of marketing and sales principles for companies to follow as they become electronic businesses. His first saying is to know the customer by collecting data about him or her. These data include items such as customer name, address, and credit card information, transactions data about your interaction with the customer, and third-party data from research firms and other information providers. Siebel suggests that you develop customer profiles and segment customers on important criteria such as size or industry.

Next he suggests using multiple channels to interact with customers, something that has become especially important with the Internet. You also need to understand the cost structure of different channels. Siebel offers an example for a typical bank:

- A teller transaction costs $1.00.
- A call center transaction costs $0.50.
- An ATM transaction costs $0.25.
- An Internet transaction costs $0.01.

By knowing information about customers, channels, and costs, a firm can personalize the customer's experience. Popular Web sites such as Yahoo! let you design your own Web page, and customers with personalized Web sites tend to return many more times than others to that site. Dell, for many years, has provided large customers with their own custom-designed site for reviewing and ordering Dell products on the Web (Siebel, 2000).

Siebel Systems has been the leader in CRM and offers a number of products to enhance customer relations. Its CRM products are highly integrated with the Internet, and provide applications in sales, marketing, call center, interactive selling, partner relationship management, employee relationship management, and sales analysis. One of the core products is in sales. Its description for the Web site is:

Source: Siebel.com

Product Description

Siebel Sales enables field sales organizations to sell collaboratively across geographies, time zones, and currencies, and scales to meet the needs of even the largest global deployments. With Siebel Sales, field professionals can accurately forecast future business, generate customized presentations and proposals, and easily produce customer communications such as personalized invitations, thank you notes, letters, and other correspondence.

Sales organizations can use Siebel Sales to seamlessly share information across sales teams, manage sales pipelines, rapidly create customer quotes and proposals, easily configure products and services to meet the unique needs of each customer, and provide superior after-sales service and support.[4]

The company also sells applications to facilitate marketing activities in the firm. One product streamlines planning and budgeting for marketing campaigns by providing workflow and collaboration capabilities, along with financial modeling. The product has a command center to track campaigns across different market segments. The software provides ways to analyze the results of multiple campaigns.

The vendor's call center software coordinates customer interactions across all channels for contacting a company. Of particular interest is a product that assists a client in setting up a Web customer service operation. The objective is to establish a Web site so that customers can accomplish as much as possible of their own customer service by querying the site; Web services often provide a faster response (no telephone wait time) and are cost-effective for the company providing the service. The customer answers his or her own questions without the need for a costly customer service representative.

SIDEBAR 17-2

A Dissenting View on CRM

Not everyone is a fan of customer relationship management systems. A few academics question the rush toward these systems. They wonder whether customers really want a relationship with most of the products and services that they buy. People generally do not have time, the interest, and the emotional energy to form a relationship with a wide variety of companies. A company might eschew relationship programs to concentrate on offering high-quality products and services, so that customers are happy with the results of their purchases and come back again.

Clear examples indicate where interaction is desired; it makes a lot of sense, according to Grahame Dalton, for Harley-Davidson to create a relationship with its buyers. Consumers who purchase a Harley-Davidson motorcycle are buying into a subculture, and the company promotes values such as personal freedom, patriotism, and machismo.

One difficulty of loyalty schemes as a means to form a relationship is that your competitors can easily copy them. When American started the frequent flyers program, it did not take long at all for other carriers to follow suit. At first, analysts speculated that customers

chose airlines to increase their mileage totals, even taking out-of-the-way routings for this purpose. However, the success of low-cost airlines today suggests that for many customers, a low fare is more important than accumulating mileage on a full-service airline.

The bottom line for management is whether a customer relationship management program creates incremental revenue, or maintains or expands market share. A good way to create additional revenue is a CRM program that provides opportunities for cross-selling or selling up, rather than a program that is designed to increase customer loyalty.

The jury is still out on CRM programs. It is clear that management needs to carefully consider the nature of the products and services it offers, the CRM programs that competitors are offering, and what kind of program is most likely to counter the competition and deliver returns to the corporation.

SOURCE: G. Dowling, "Customer Relationship Management: In B2C Markets, Often Less Is More," *California Management Review,* 44(3) (Spring 2002), pp. 181–199.

Salesforce.com

Salesforce.com has taken a different approach to CRM; it acts as an application services provider. See Figure 17-8. Sales representatives can record information about their clients and sales calls anyplace they have an Internet connection. The salesforce.com Web site creates a database from this input and provides a number of options for reporting and looking at the data. For example, management can view by sales representative and customer. The site provides tools for sales forecasting as well. In addition to sales force automation, salesforce.com offers products to help plan and execute marketing campaigns and to provide customer service and support.

This Web-based CRM service is an interesting contrast to the package vendor that wants to sell its software. Salesforce.com had over 10,000 customers when it went public in 2004. The applications services providers and outsourcers see this system as the model for the future. The customer does not have to install software or worry about running it. However, the customer does have to adapt to the structure of the salesforce.com system's functions; the company cannot afford to make major modifications for each customer. However, the customer can make changes to the look and feel of the user interface using drag and drop menus. It is an open question whether or not the ASP model will replace purchased software.

FIGURE 17-8 Salesforce.com.

Some vendors of ERP software also offer CRM software for applying technology to this function, which is becoming popular. Because it is aimed at one or two functions, CRM software should be less difficult to implement than ERP. These packages are another example of how computers, databases, and Internet technologies offer new opportunities for companies to improve their business processes.

CHAPTER SUMMARY

The technology discussed in this chapter provides value that the firm can often measure. A CRM application should increase revenues. Improved business processes improve efficiency and reduce costs; you can calculate a direct return from implementing ERP software. But these packages do more than improve processes; they provide a base of standardized processes and software across the company. If a firm has multiple locations, implementing the same ERP system in all of them provides standardization and a platform for the development of other applications.

As an example, Cisco implemented an ERP package just before 1995 when the Internet became available for profit-making use. This standard set of programs made it much easier for Cisco to move its operations to the Internet; Cisco bought an option to move to the Net when it purchased the ERP system, though it may not have realized that fact at the time. A major package such as ERP or CRM thus has an options component to it in addition to the immediate benefits it provides. It is difficult to estimate the value of this option, because you do not know what opportunities lie ahead; it is a bonus that comes with the package.

KEYWORDS

Character recognition	Imaging	Process
CRM	Incremental improvement	Production automation
Electronic workflows	Obliterating a process	Reengineering
ERP	Oracle	SAP
Expert system	Peoplesoft	Technological leveling

RECOMMENDED READINGS

Bhattacherjee, A. 2000. Beginning SAP R/3 implementation at Geneva Pharmaceuticals. *Communications of AIS, 4*(2). (An interesting article that balances the technical and organizational aspects of ERP implementation.)

Goodhue, D., Wixom, B., and Watson, H. 2002. Realizing business benefit through CRM: Hitting the right target in the right way. *MIKS Quarterly Executive, 1*(2), pp. 79–94. (A good tutorial on CRM with six case studies.)

Hammer, M. 1997. *Beyond Reengineering: How the Processed-Centered Organization Is Changing Our Work and Our Lives.* New York: HarperCollins. (This is Hammer's newest book on business reengineering and covers many current issues and problems related to organizations' reengineering initiatives.)

Kopczak, L., and Johnson, E. 2003. The supply-chain management effect. *Sloan Management Review*, Spring, pp. 27–34. (A good overview of supply chain management.)

Lucas, H. C., Jr., Berndt, D., and Truman, G. 1996. A reengineering framework for evaluating a financial imaging system. *Communications of the ACM, 39*(5), pp. 86–96. (A discussion of the Merrill Lynch system.)

Mabert, V., Soni, A., and Venkataramanan, M. 1991. Enterprise resource planning: Common myths versus evolving reality. *Business Horizons*, May–June, pp. 71–78. (Some good advice on ERP systems.)

Siebel, T. 2000. *How to Become an eBusiness.* San Mateo, CA: Siebel Systems.

Rust, R., and Kannan, P. K. 2003. E-service: A new paradigm for business in the electronic environment. *Communications of the ACM, 46*(6), pp. 37–42. (This and other articles in this issue discuss how use IT to better service customers.)

Winter, R. 2001. A framework for customer relationship management. *California Management Review, 43*(4), pp. 89–105. (A good tutorial on CRM.)

DISCUSSION QUESTIONS

1. What is a business process? How does it relate to a function?

2. What is the role of the expert system for receiving securities in the Merrill Lynch branch office?

3. If the Merrill Lynch control computer has information from the expert system, why is it necessary to recognize three fields on the documents scanned in the SPC?

4. What are the major components of an ERP system?

5. Why have ERP systems proven difficult to implement?

6. What is the role of senior management in ERP implementation?

7. Why would one pay as much for consulting help as the software when buying an ERP system?

8. What does it mean when a software package is Web-enabled?

9. How does an ERP system offer the potential for cost savings?

10. What ways does a package vendor have to deal with a potential client's concerns that the client is "unique"?

11. Why do package vendors recommend that customers not modify their software?

12. Why is a dedicated application more difficult to implement than a general purpose piece of software such as Microsoft Office? Office offers a number of large programs that provide many functions to users. What is the difference between it and an ERP package?

13. What are the major functions of a CRM package?

14. How might a CRM package increase revenue?

15. What are the likely implementation problems with a CRM package? *Hint*: Think about the nature of sales representatives.

16. How does a package such as ERP provide the buyer with an option for some future application?

17. What is the best way to implement an ERP package, given the various modules that it contains? In what area of the company might you start?

18. How should a company with multiple locations implement an ERP package? Should it implement one function at a time at all locations, or implement one location completely to serve as an example and testbed?

19. Given that it can take a year or more to implement an ERP package, how does a company save time with a package compared to developing a custom system itself?

20. What are the advantages of having part of customer service delivered through the Web?

ENDNOTES

1. Description of the old and new systems at Merrill Lynch from Lucas, Berndt, and Truman, "A Reengineering Framework for Evaluating a Financial Imaging System", *Communications of the Association for Computing Machinery,* 39 –5 (May 1996) pp. 86–96.

2. www.sap.com.

3. www.peoplesoft.com.

4. www.siebel.com.

CHAPTER 18

DECISION AND INTELLIGENT SYSTEMS

A Manager's Perspective

Most managers can easily accept a decision support system based on data, particularly if it uses simple displays and graphs. It is more difficult to have faith in model-based systems and in systems that use artificial intelligence (AI) techniques because these approaches are hard to understand. You have to rely on the experts and believe that the systems have been tested and validated adequately. Experts developing mathematical or AI systems have a responsibility to explain clearly how these systems work so that a manager who lacks a degree in mathematics or computer science can become comfortable with them. Churchman pointed out years ago that the lack of mutual understanding between the management scientist and the manager was a problem that could lead to the rejection of management science solutions to problems. The same can be said for decisions that make use of artificial intelligence and model-based systems. The two are both incredibly powerful technologies, but their implementation often leaves something to be desired.

VALUE PROPOSITION

Decision and intelligent systems are risky to develop, with no guarantee of positive results. However, companies have obtained impressive benefits from these systems. They can lead to the following outcomes:

- Dramatically improved business processes that reduce costs
- Better coordination and support for individuals and groups in the firm
- The ability to capture and retain knowledge that exists in the organization

You can measure some of the contribution of decision and intelligent systems with the following metrics:

- Improvements in efficiency
- Better customer service
- Cost savings per project

DECISION SUPPORT SYSTEMS

A decision support system (DSS) is a computer-based system that helps the decision maker utilize data and models to solve unstructured problems. One of the most frequently used DSSs is a spreadsheet package. A decision maker builds a model and looks at the impact of changing certain variables or assumptions. You might look at the effects of a change in interest rates on a possible investment in a new manufacturing plant.

A simple framework for classifying different types of DSS divides these systems into (1) data-oriented and (2) model-based. A data-oriented system provides tools for the manipulation and analysis of data. Various kinds of statistical tests can be run, and data can be combined in different ways for display. A model-based system generally has some kind of mathematical model of the decision being supported. For example, the model might be an operations research optimizing model or a simple model represented by a balance sheet and an income statement for a firm.

Decision support systems offer tremendous power for managers who can generate and try many different alternatives, asking what-if questions and seeing the results. One manager said, "I'm not being forced to take the first solution that works, just because it takes so long to generate an answer; using a model and a spreadsheet program on a PC, now I can try different alternatives and choose the one that looks best."

EXAMPLES OF DSSs

This section examines decision support systems in some detail to illustrate the contribution they make to the organization.

Yield Management: How to Overbook Gracefully

American Airlines faces a problem common to the industry: how to maximize the revenue or yield from each flight. Yield management for an airline is like inventory control for a food manufacturer. If food items are left in inventory past a certain date, they must be discarded as spoiled. American estimates that without controls to allow for overbooking, 15 percent of its seats would be "spoiled" on sold out flights.

American estimated that solving the yield management problem using a nonlinear, stochastic, mixed-integer mathematical program would require approximately 250 million decision variables for its entire route system. Instead of developing a single model, American's operations research group developed a series of models to attack three more manageable subproblems (Smith et al., 1992).

Overbooking

The first of the models controls overbooking, the practice of intentionally selling more reservations for a flight than seats available on the aircraft. An airline overbooks because it knows that a certain number of passengers will cancel, and others will be no-shows at the gate. A second model helps American decide how many discount seats to offer on a flight. Finally, traffic management controls reservations by passenger origin and destination to maximize revenue. Because of the current hub-and-spoke system, the flights are interdependent; a passenger flying into the Dallas/Fort Worth hub may leave on any number of other flights to reach his or her final destination.

Overbooking allows the airline to accommodate more passengers, but penalties are associated with denying passengers boarding if they have a confirmed reservation. The airline must compensate "bumped" passengers, and it must provide an alternative flight for them. This cost of overbooking actually increases with the number of passengers denied seats. For example, the airline may have to offer more hotel and meal vouchers and may have to transport the bumped passenger on another airline's flights.

American developed an optimization model to trade off the added revenue from selling more seats through overbooking versus the added costs of compensating passengers when it did not have seats for all passengers with reservations. As the overbooking level increases, net revenue, which is passenger revenue minus overbooking costs, rises to a maximum value and then decreases as the cost of an additional oversale exceeds the value of an additional reservation. The overbooking model draws on data from the Sabre reservation system. The overbooking level has a constraint to prevent degrading passenger service too much. It relies on four forecasts: (1) the probability a passenger will cancel, (2) the probability of a no-show, (3) the probability that a bumped passenger will take another American flight, and (4) the oversale cost.

Discount Seats

The large number of special fares and discounts greatly complicates the problem of maximizing revenue from a flight. Because the number of seats on a plane is fixed, selling a seat at a discount that could be sold for a full fare reduces overall revenue. American cannot control fare classes independently, otherwise it could sell a low-fare seat while turning away a passenger willing to pay full fare. American uses a marginal revenue approach to determining how many seats to sell in a given fare class. The approach uses a heuristic that finds an acceptable, but not necessarily optimal, solution.

Traffic Management

With the hub-and-spoke traffic system, American's percentage of passengers flying into a hub to connect with another flight has gone from 10 percent to more than 60 percent. Consider a simple hub-and-spoke system with a single hub in Dallas and spokes to Portland, Los Angeles, New York, and Miami. A number of itineraries is possible even in this simple system. American's problem is to accept reservations in such a way as to maximize profits, given a huge variety of discount and full fares. Assume that the full fare from Portland to Dallas is less than the discount fare from Portland to Miami through Dallas. The airline has to consider multiple possibilities for trips and fares or it might accept a full-fare Portland to Dallas passenger while turning away a discount seat from Portland to Miami, a decision that would lower total revenue.

Ideally, the airline would control based on a market and fare class. However, the large number of markets and fares makes this computationally infeasible. American developed a method of clustering similar market/fare classes into groupings it calls *buckets* to make the problem more manageable. All the market/fare classes on each flight are clustered into eight buckets. First and business class go into separate buckets while coach market/fare classes are in the remaining buckets. As sales increase, the availability of seats is restricted first to low-value reservations regardless of market/fare class. Although this problem may seem simple, American currently has 150,000 market/fare classes.

American uses a dynamic programming algorithm to index the market/fare classes into buckets. The idea is to maximize the variability of market/fare class values between buckets while minimizing the variability within a given bucket. Every time a passenger requests a flight, the Sabre system accesses a condensed table containing bucket information. The system scans the bucket information until it finds the appropriate category for the reservation request, and then makes a decision on whether to offer the seat at that fare.

Results

American developed models to estimate the benefits of the DSS just described. The over-booking DSS has been in use since 1990 and it is estimated to have increased revenue by more than $200 million each year. The discount-seat allocation model is estimated to have obtained from 30 to 49 percent of the revenue opportunity from discount sales resulting in additional revenue of $200 to $300 million. In three years, the total yield management program produced quantifiable benefits of more than $1.4 billion for American. For that same three-year period, American had a net profit of $892 million.

This example shows that sophisticated operations research models within decision support systems can have substantial returns for the organization. This kind of DSS is possible only because American invested over the years in the Sabre reservations system; it has the data the airline needs to operate these models. All of these techniques fall into the category of *yield management*, which refers to the practice of trying to maximize the revenue from products and services. Hotels also practice yield management, constantly examining the number of reserved rooms and adjusting the room rates for rooms that are still available.

A Distribution Network at Pfizer

Pfizer is a *Fortune* 100 manufacturer of pharmaceuticals, animal health products, and consumer products; in 2000 it merged with Warner-Lambert to form a combined company with sales over $30 billion. Its more familiar consumer products include Schick and Wilkinson shaving products and over-the-counter drugs and beauty products. Pfizer integrated its distribution with a new decisions support system at Warner-Lambert.

The original Warner-Lambert U.S. distribution network consisted of two large distribution centers (DCs) in Illinois and Pennsylvania with a second echelon of thirty-five small distribution locations throughout the United States and run by third parties. Large consumer product orders went in truckloads from the factories to the customer, while small orders went from the DC to the local distributor to the customer. Courier services handled most of the delivery of pharmaceutical orders.

The need for better planning and a more efficient supply chain that would be responsive to customers led Warner-Lambert to develop a decisions support system to support strategic, tactical, and operational planning. The data needed for this effort included historical sales by SKU, transportation rates and data, transit times by city pair, inventory, manufacturing capability, purchasing costs for all inputs, tax data, accounts receivable information, and similar data. The main purpose of the DSS was to support decisions about the U.S. distribution network for distributing finished goods, including warehousing, transportation, and ultimate delivery to the customer.

Warner-Lambert and its consultants developed three linked simulation models:

1. Distribution center storage and capacity model
2. A DC picking and shipping model
3. A DC facility sizing model

These models made it possible for the company to evaluate capacity requirements over planning horizons of two and five years. A key use of the model was for sensitivity analyses. For example, analysts could try a variety of sales forecasts and assess their impact on inventories and distribution. In addition to the simulation models, Warner-Lambert created an optimization model of its U.S. network. This mixed integer programming model generated plans for the distribution of products over a given planning horizon. The output showed projected product flows through the network by individual location as goods moved from plants to customers. It could also forecast the future product volumes at each warehouse. The last model was one for inventory investments.

The total DSS was used for several long-range studies. The first of these determined whether Warner-Lambert should expand the first echelon of its network, for example, by adding another regional distribution center. The second study helped plan a new pharmaceutical delivery network. The third strategic use of the DSS was to help consolidate the Warner-Lambert distribution networks after the merger of the two companies (Gupta, Peters, and Miller, 2002).

This DSS involved a major commitment of time and resources; the result is a fairly complex system that requires skilled analysts to produce the input to the models and interpret the output. The returns from projects such as this one can be impressive, though they can be difficult to estimate in advance.

OnStar

General Motors employed a number of decision models when it decided to implement an onboard system in its cars called OnStar. The OnStar service is a two-way vehicle communication system offering a number of services for safety, security, and entertainment. It is based on satellite service and includes a three-button panel that is installed on the rearview mirror or dashboard of more than sixty models of cars and trucks built by seven manufacturers.

The vehicle communicates with an automated system known as the *virtual advisor*, or with a human being through a cell phone. The system automatically calls the OnStar center if the car's air bags deploy. GM also expanded the system so that it will call automatically if any of a network of sensors in the car indicates that an accident has occurred; this new option is called the automatic crash notification system (AACN). A built-in global positioning system (GPS) identifies the location of the vehicle and a human in the call center can dispatch emergency services to the scene. The system has been used to locate a number of stolen cars as well.

In addition to safety and security, customers can use OnStar to obtain information on real-time traffic from the virtual advisor. It is also possible to find content, such as a newspaper, through the service. The virtual advisor will read *The Wall Street Journal* to an OnStar customer. GM is planning other services to add to this successful system.

OnStar is the largest provider of vehicle telematics services; as of this writing OnStar has 2.5 million subscribers. The first year of service is included in the price of the car, and the cost for subsequent years is $199–799 depending on the features chosen. The company expects to sell 400,000 of the AACN systems in new models the first year it is offered.

GM tested a prototype of the system in 1996, but it was expensive and cumbersome to install. In 1997 GM had to make a strategic decision about developing and deploying OnStar. The conservative view was that OnStar was solely a vehicle option that would improve safety and security. A more expansive view was to see OnStar as a service business that could generate significant profits. In this model consumers would subscribe to OnStar, generating healthy monthly service fees for GM. The aggressive strategy would require more investment and carried more risk.

GM formed a project team to analyze its options; this team had to figure out how to model an industry that did not yet exist. No historical data were available to help in making predictions. The project team developed a simulation model that became the core analytical tool for investigating the potential of OnStar. This model had six sectors including customer acquisition, customer choice, alliances, customer service, finances, and dealer behavior. The customer acquisition part of the model simulated the acquisition and retention of customers by looking for causal mechanisms for acquisition and for customer churn. The product diffusion literature helped construct this part of the model. The model incorporated feedback loops to make the simulation more realistic; for example, the team represented the impact of third-party installers in expanding the market for OnStar applications.

The team employed a marketing science technique known as conjoint analysis with a sample of 621 new car buyers to estimate how many buyers would choose OnStar if offered the choice. Another part of the model evaluated a policy of offering OnStar to other vehicle manufacturers. This part of the model looked at the choices other manufacturers had, which include doing nothing, starting their own service, joining OnStar, or joining another service. Because no competing service was available at the time, and the cost of duplicating OnStar would be high, the team thought the service would appeal to other manufacturers.

Customer service turned out to be an important part of the project. An analysis showed that if GM skimped on service to save costs, the system would fail. OnStar depends on a capable, well-trained staff to provide excellent service during what, for the subscriber, is probably a major crisis such as an accident. OnStar adopted the policy of overstaffing the customer service facility in order to have capacity in advance of demand.

Another important decision was whether to factory-install OnStar or leave it as a dealer or third-party add-on. Dealer installation cost $1,300 and took two days; it was a significant deterrent to customers during the early trial. However, if the GM factory installed the system and the customer chose not to activate it, GM would be out the cost of the hardware and would receive no revenue. The evaluation team felt that factory installation would significantly increase the number of customers who subscribed to the service. The simulation showed that after the first few years, factory installation generated more profits than the alternatives, and this strategy was robust even under different assumptions.

By the end of 1997, the project team recommended an aggressive strategy to management, including factory installation on GM vehicles, offering the service to other manufacturers, and making the first year of service free. The team encouraged GM to pursue alliances with content manufacturers. GM has an 80 percent share of the telematics market, and by 2002, the project team estimated that OnStar had a market value of $4–10 billion. GM has partnerships with manufacturers that account for more than 50 percent of vehicle sales including Toyota, Honda, VW-Audi, and Subaru. The nearest competitor is a small independent company with about 80,000 subscribers. Looking back at the dynamic strategy model, GM gained a first mover advantage by continued investment in this telecommunications system, and it may have such a lead in knowledge and market share that no competitor will be able to match OnStar, certainly not in the short run (Barabba et al., 2002).

Merrill Lynch's Integrated Choice Account Structure

The previous discussion of organizational transformation noted that Merrill Lynch moved into online trading when Schwab's $25.5 billion market value exceeded Merrill's $25.4

MANAGEMENT PROBLEM 18-1

The literature offers many examples of successful applications of model-based decisions support systems; a significant number of these examples includes data on how much they saved a company or how much revenue they generated. The American Airline example is impressive when one looks at the savings from the system compared to airline profits; without these systems the airline would have had a loss during the period.

Given the demonstrated benefits of model-based systems, why aren't more of them used? In the 1960s and 1970s, many firms had management science or operations research departments to develop such systems;

today these departments are much more difficult to find. Some argued that managers have trouble understanding the mathematical models behind the systems, and therefore distrust them. Others suggested that it is possible to do so much with spreadsheets, that data-oriented DSSs dominate systems with more sophisticated mathematical models in them.

Why are not more model-based DSSs used? What kinds of problems do these systems address? What kind of business could make most use of them? How do they compare to spreadsheet modeling?

billion one crucial day. Investors thought that Schwab "got" the Internet, and that Merrill did not. Even though Merrill knew it needed to do something, the company was worried that it might make a costly mistake in responding to the threat from online brokers. Its chairman at the time described the decision to offer Integrated Choice as Merrill's most important since it introduced the cash management account in the 1970s.

The focus of attention was the U.S. Private Client (USPC) business at Merrill, which manages nearly $1.4 trillion, serving more than 5 million households and small and medium-sized businesses. USPC provides brokerage, banking, checking, ATM, and Visa cards. Asset services include stocks, bonds, mutual funds, and various complex securities products along with research on different companies. USPC also provides mortgages and home equity loans, securities-backed lines of credit, and commercial real estate financing. The key client contact is the Merrill Lynch financial consultant (FC).

Merrill turned to its Management Sciences group for help in coming up with new product structures and pricing options when it realized that the company must meet the competition from Schwab and other e-brokers. The first option was an account based on assets and a continuing relationship with an FC. The client would be charged a percentage of his or her assets at Merrill, and would no longer pay for trades individually. This option became known as the Merrill Lynch Unlimited Advantage (MLUA) account. With this new structure, the client fees to Merrill would be aligned with the appreciation of clients' assets; clients would pay more only if their wealth increased. The client and FC could adjust the client's portfolio without worrying about transactions fees, and clients would know in advance the cost of Merrill's services. The plan eventually featured three tiers with a percentage fee highest on the first $1 million (1 percent on equities, 0.3 percent on fixed income products), and lowest on assets over $5 million (0.5 percent on equities and 0.2 percent on fixed income products).

A second type of account would feature direct online pricing for clients who were self-directed and did not need the advice of an FC. This product became known as Merrill Lynch Direct and features trades at $29.95. The key task here was to establish the rate.

Some clients would choose to remain in a traditional transaction-based account, or they could choose a wrap account giving the FC discretionary power over the account. A question for the analysts was whether to restrict clients to only one type of account, or let them choose any of the four, the two existing or the two new accounts, in combination.

Management asked the Management Science group to design an appropriate account structure and pricing for this major transformation at Merrill. Part of the analysis had to consider the total revenue at risk, and estimate what accounts customers would choose, and the impact of their choice on revenues. The group was also supposed to identify the impact on each FC and indicate those who would be most dramatically affected. The firm had to worry about changes in FC compensation and the potential for a drop in morale and higher FC turnover.

The project team assembled a 200-gigabyte database of client information on 5 million clients, 10 million accounts, 250 million ledger records (containing sources of revenue for each account), 100 million trade records, and 16,000 FCs. The team had to consider eighty-two revenue sources that were applicable to the planning analysis. The basis for the analysis was to simulate client-choice behavior. The observed system data formed the baseline on which to try changes. This baseline consists of every revenue-generating component of every account of every client at Merrill. The output of the model includes the resulting revenue at the firm level, the compensation impact on each FC, and the percentage of clients that choose a new account option that decreases overall revenue for the firm. Changes tested with the model included different variations in the two new products, MLUA and ML Direct.

The team's first model assumed rational behavior on the part of investors; they would make decisions without consideration of a relationship with the FC; this model was the most severe and put an upper bound on the total amount of revenue at risk. The FC affinity model included rational considerations and qualitative factors of the client's relationship with his or her FC. One of these models included a Monte Carlo simulation of client behavior to estimate the impact of changes on total revenue and on individual FCs.

The team had extensive interactions with management, and to everyone's relief, the worst case revenue impact on the firm ($1 billion) did not exceed the benefits gained from a better position in the market, increased market share, and the better retention of clients. Management used the results of the pricing analysis in its decision to move ahead with the new accounts. The results were that Merrill seized the marketplace initiative by finding the "sweet spot" for pricing, improved its financial performance, and returned to a leadership position in the industry. One happy note was that the MLUA account proved exceptionally popular, and many FCs were very happy with the results of Merrill's new Integrated Choice account offerings. By 2000, Merrill had gathered $83 billion in assets into MLUA, $22 billion of which were new to the firm. Some 48 percent of MLUA enrollees in 2000 were new to Merrill while 60 percent of ML Direct investors were new to the firm. The number of MLUA accounts increased 80 percent between 1999 and 2000. Another $3 billion in assets flowed into ML Direct.

By 2001, Schwab was worth $40 billion, about 30 percent less than Merrill, and it is likely that gap will widen. Launny Steffens, the executive most associated with Merrill's transformation during the growth of online competitors, said, "The decision to implement Integrated Choice was an unprecedented change in strategy for us. Management Science and Strategic Pricing provided the modeling and analyses that enabled me and my executive management team to better understand the revenue risks. This is the kind of thing that kept me up at nights! We have moved forward like a bullet train, and it is our competitors that are scrambling not to get run over." (Altshuler et al., 2002.)

More Intelligent Pricing Decisions

Saks must constantly make decisions about when to mark down merchandise for clearance and how much to mark it down. If the firm discounts too early, it loses potential revenue from shoppers willing to pay the current price, or it angers customers by selling out. If it waits too long or does not mark merchandise down sufficiently, it risks becoming a warehouse of unwanted merchandise. A small number of companies offer systems that help managers make these decisions more scientifically instead of by feel.

Saks uses a system for price optimization from Spotlight Solutions. The program uses sales data from past years and the current season, and determines which goods to mark down to specific prices at each store. It also recommends the timing of the markdowns. The software makes it possible to take different markdowns and prices at individual stores. The system delivers recommendations to store merchandise managers over the Internet. Saks credits the program with improving its gross margins and reducing excess inventory levels for the first half of the year it used the software. Saks is planning to roll the system out to all of its stores.

The vendors claim that retailers could improve gross margins by 10 percent with such systems, which, if true, would be a dramatic gain from better pricing decisions. In today's economy, it is estimated that retailers end up with about one-third of their sales consisting of clearance goods. The vendors of price optimization software also think their products can be used to help set prices at stores that do not take frequent markdowns, such as supermarket chains and drug stores. For example, they can be used to help set prices on complementary goods such as crackers and dip. Because of the potential amount of savings, software vendors charge $1 million to $5 million for their price optimization systems.

Information technology is often associated with cost savings; price optimization systems are an example of how one can use technology to increase revenues as well as reduce costs. Justification for a $1–5 million investment in IT may be relatively easy for a company that expects to see a 5 percent gain in gross margins from implementing price optimization software.

SOURCE: *New York Times*, September 2, 2002.

The Promise of DSS

The systems described in this section provide information to support decisions; see Table 18-1 for a summary of the examples. A number of decisions are programmed into the systems. They also evaluate different alternatives and process information that is presented to and acted on by the decision maker. The American and Pfizer systems showed costs savings, something that is more difficult for other types of DSSs. The value of better planning remains largely unknown. It is difficult to know whether the decision makers using these systems performed better than under the previous manual systems. For many DSSs, justification is not done or is based on faith of the managers involved that the model is helping to solve a problem.

EXECUTIVE INFORMATION SYSTEMS

Companies build an executive information system (EIS) to bring to senior management information that needs its attention. An EIS requires access to data of interest to senior executives. However, the data are not easily accessible, and the EIS software must summarize data and make them available for downloading to a personal computer in the executive's

TABLE 18-1 Examples of successful decision support systems.

DSS Example	Characteristics
American Airlines	Yield management system to maximize revenue among fare classes on each flight; involves overbooking, discount seats, and traffic management
Pfizer	Simulation models of the entire distribution system used to figure out the lowest-cost configuration for distribution centers and to determine their capacity
OnStar	A simulation model for the system as proposed to help evaluate its potential and provide guidelines for its design
Merrill Lynch	Analysis of data on current clients to estimate the impact of creating a new structure for Merrill's accounts, called Integrated Choice

office. Because many managers do not like to type and are not comfortable with computers, EIS designers focus on providing an appealing interface and a system that is easy to use.

One characteristic of these systems is a *drill down* feature. The user first sees figures at a high, summary level. If these numbers look all right, the user continues. However, if some total looks unusual, for example, sales in the western region are lower than expected, the user puts the cursor on the suspicious figure, clicks the mouse button, and sees a display that contains more detail on just the western region. Depending on how the system is designed, the user might be able to drill down several levels to get to quite detailed data.

Senior managers who use these systems praise them highly. A power company president reports that he can view a series of corporate indicators with one keystroke. He can create a personal menu to look at the indicators he needs to review on a daily basis. This executive feels that the system has improved communications throughout the organization.

Another executive uses the system to look for trouble spots and find out why a division's expenses are higher than anticipated. He gets a quick snapshot of his competitor's financial position through the system as well. Another manager uses the firm's EIS to check for exceptions, such as shipments to customers that are taking too long. Setting up the system forced his company to think about its business and what indicators it wanted to monitor.

A number of ways can be used to develop an EIS. Several vendors offer software designed to access mainframe databases and provide a graphical user interface (GUI) for executives. General Electric is one of the earliest users of an Internet-based "digital dashboard or cockpit." Senior executives in its eleven major divisions log into the company intranet to review their division's financial data. The Plastic's Division display shows three categories: manufacturing, selling, and procurement. Each category contains a small number of important statistics compared to a threshold. If a number deviates from the threshold, it is shown in red. Clicking on a number brings up more details about the statistic. If a number is far enough from the accepted range, the system generates e-mails to a group of executives.[1]

GROUP DECISION SUPPORT SYSTEMS

Interest in using information technology to support workgroups is high. A workgroup consists of individuals who have some need to work together. Theoretically, any number could be involved, but typically such groups consist of two to twenty people who must work on some problem.

One way IT can support such a workgroup is with a group decision support system (GDSS). A GDSS consists of special software and physical facilities, such as a conference room containing PCs for each person in the room. The software helps identify issues and evaluate alternative decisions and actions. A GDSS might also contain a model whose solution provides participants in the group with insights into their problem.

Workgroup decision making may also be supported using technology when the workgroup is dispersed. Electronic mail allows members of a group to exchange messages at any time of the day or night and is insensitive to time zones. An extension of e-mail is the electronic conference. Individuals can all be online to a computer at the same time for a conference, or they can join the conference whenever they like, reading and responding to the comments of others at their leisure. Microsoft offers its NetMeeting product to facilitate group meetings using the Internet. It is also offering a product called Live Meeting, a data and application sharing program for business.

Existing computer packages can be used in a group setting. A network of personal computers might be used to share data on a problem or to share a spreadsheet. A database management package on the network server could provide common data for each participant in a group at his or her own personal computer connected to the LAN.

Technology-Assisted Meetings

A number of companies use specially equipped meeting rooms with GDSS software to conduct meetings. IBM installed a number of electronic meeting rooms based on a room developed at the University of Arizona. A typical meeting room has participants seated at a horseshoe-shaped table, each with a personal computer connected to a network and file server. A projection screen is placed at the open end of the horseshoe to show what is on the discussion leader's (facilitator's) PC.

The role of the leader is particularly important in setting the pace of the meeting and in helping to form a consensus. A typical meeting might begin by stating the problem to be addressed. Participants brainstorm at their PCs for some period of time, say, fifteen minutes to an hour. Each comment appears on all workstations, but without attribution; that is, no one knows who typed a particular entry. This anonymity is one of the features that makes an electronic meeting different from a conventional one. It is felt that participants will be less reticent, particularly around superiors, if their comments are anonymous.

Next, another piece of software can be used to group alternatives into categories generated in the first stages of the meeting. Each participant could then numerically rank suggested alternatives. The meeting room software would average the ranks and sort the suggestions according to their average. Different software packages offer a variety of features designed to facilitate achieving a consensus about some issue or problem.

The opinions about whether electronic meeting rooms work have been positive. Participants in meetings generally seem enthusiastic about their experiences. Some claim that the use of these facilities and software reduce meetings by a factor of 10. It has also been argued that solutions are better because no one will be intimidated by a superior when contributions are anonymous.

These claims need careful review. Similar results can be achieved without a special room and elaborate software system. Certainly what the computer system does could be done manually by a facilitator and an assistant. The computer helps to automate this process, but one could also simply write ideas on a blackboard for all to see. The use of the computer and a high-tech meeting room may make participants feel better about the results of the meeting. Also, the act of using such a room says that the topic being discussed is important.

Of course, some drawbacks also come with electronic meeting rooms. In one case, participants generated about 1,000 alternatives in half an hour. It is not clear how a group can deal with this number of suggestions! It seems likely that the appropriateness of this type of meeting depends on the subject matter. If the goal is a number of creative suggestions to a problem or the generation of a lot of alternatives, the room could be especially useful.

INTELLIGENT SYSTEMS

Artificial Intelligence

Expert systems, case-based reasoning, neural networks, and genetic algorithms represent an applied branch of the computer science field of artificial intelligence (AI). Workers in AI try to develop machines and programs, the behavior of which might be considered intelligent if viewed by humans. Consider the activities at which humans are very good. Men and women are able to learn from experience, they can make sense out of contradictions, and they can reason to come to a conclusion. People are also able to reason inductively—to look at evidence and generate a hypothesis about the process that generated the evidence.

The question is whether a machine can do any of these things. Certainly, no one machine can do them all. In looking at AI systems, their domain—the area in which the system functions—must be considered. A program to diagnose tumors may work well with tumor information, but it would be hopelessly lost if asked about viral infections.

Alan Turing, a British mathematician, proposed a test to assess whether a program or device actually demonstrates intelligent behavior. *Turing's test* is to place a computer and a human in two separate rooms. An interviewer in a third room, who cannot see the human or the computer user, asks questions that are passed to the computer and to the human. If the interviewer cannot tell the difference between the answers from the computer and the human, the machine is said to exhibit intelligent behavior.

AI versus Traditional Programs

Just as the goals of AI programming differ from those of a conventional information processing system, so do the characteristics of these programs. First and most important, in AI one is manipulating symbols rather than numbers. A program to diagnose diseases does not need to compute arithmetic expressions. Instead it has to manipulate logical symbols, just as someone solving a geometry problem would manipulate symbols rather than numbers.

SIDEBAR 18-1

IT for Homeland Security

Intelligence agencies are used to closely guarding their information and its sources. Yet it appears that a lack of coordination among these agencies can be a serious impediment to countering the threats of terrorism. IT can provide assistance in a number of ways. First, the technology can help share and protect data. One can build security "wrappers" around different databases to protect sensitive information while sharing critical data. A wrapper around a medical database might let a health agency query the database for summaries of data, for example, the number of people who have gone to a hospital emergency room with unusual symptoms in a particular city. However, if anyone at the agency tried to inquire about the health records of a specific person, the wrapper would deny access.

Other uses of IT include processing information to look for threats. Intelligence agencies are looking at a program—called Non-Obvious Relationship Awareness (NORA) program—for preventing corporate theft. This program correlates millions of transactions per day and extracts information such as the applicant for a casino job has a sister who shares a telephone number with a known underworld figure. It is easy to imagine how such a program could be adapted to intelligence use.

A company in Cambridge, England, developed a graphical program called Analyst's Notebook. This program creates timelines that illustrate related events unfolding over days or even years. It also generates transaction analysis charts that show relationships or patterns, for example, in the flow of cash among bank accounts. The program produces link analysis charts that resemble an airline route map. The crisscrossing lines are not cities, but symbols that represent people, organizations, and bank accounts. Each element is hyperlinked to the evidence that supports it.

Tools can help the intelligence community prevent terrorist plots from succeeding if such tools are used to their fullest potential.

SOURCE: *Technology Review,* March 2003.

It is also claimed that AI programs are nonalgorithmic. An algorithm is defined as an effective procedure for solving a problem. If the algorithm is followed, one is usually guaranteed of finding a solution to the problem. As opposed to algorithmic programming, AI programs often employ heuristics, or rules of thumb, for finding problem solutions.

Many AI programs are concerned with pattern recognition. In fact, some of the early work in AI is responsible for successful optical-scanning devices, because these devices must read input symbols and match them with patterns already in the scanning device to identify the input. Pattern matching is an important human capability that allows individuals to make sense out of many varied patterns.

EXPERT SYSTEMS: APPLIED AI

Currently, few applications in business could be called AI. Instead, organizations take advantage of an applied branch of artificial intelligence called expert systems—advisory programs that attempt to imitate the reasoning process of human experts (Turban, 1995).

One of the purposes for building such systems is to make the expertise of an individual available to others in the field. One company built an expert system to help diagnose and solve the problem of oil exploration rig drills getting stuck. The knowledge of the firm's best drilling expert became available on all rigs through the expert system.

Another motivation for creating an expert system is to capture knowledge from an expert who is likely to be unavailable in the future, perhaps because of an impending retirement. An expert system also provides for some consistency in decision making.

Imagine a brokerage house in which the compliance department must see that brokers follow the firm's and the SEC's rules. If the firm uses an expert system to help advise its analysts, each case of suspected rule violations will be evaluated consistently.

This kind of knowledge discovery differs from the knowledge bases one can build with groupware like Notes in a significant way. Both kinds of applications have the same goals, but the groupware solution does simple searches on word matches. Expert systems feature more sophisticated approaches to search; they can discover new patterns and relationships in the data, something that a search on keywords is unable to do.

Components of Expert Systems

An expert system (ES) consists of the following components:

- The user interface
- The knowledge base
- The inference engine

Research indicates that the user interface is an extremely important component of an expert system. Possibly because users are not accustomed to systems that provide advice, they are more demanding. Also, if the advisory system is used frequently, it becomes an important part of the user's daily activities. A good interface makes the system much more pleasant to use and helps promote its acceptance.

The knowledge base in an expert system differs from a database. One important way to represent an expert's knowledge is through the use of rules. An example of a rule might be as follows:

IF the broker sold stock in an account on one day

AND bought the same stock for the same account the next day,

THEN investigate the transaction p=10

This hypothetical rule indicates that the probability of an investigation is to be increased if the broker sold stock one day and bought it back the next. The broker might be trying to generate commissions without a valid investment reason for the transactions.

A database stores numbers and symbols. It might show a simple relationship among the data because they are stored together or defined as connected in some way. A rule in a knowledge base, however, contains some of the logic of an application. This rule implies something about when an investigation should be undertaken. An ordinary database makes it difficult to figure out the logic of the application. A knowledge base contains more information about logic than a conventional database.

The Inference Engine

The inference engine is the reasoning part of the expert system. An example will help illustrate how the inference engine might work (Luconi, Malone, and Scott Morton, 1986). Figure 18-1 contains several production rules for personal financial planning. Suppose the client's tax bracket is 33 percent and liquidity is more than $100,000. This client has a high tolerance for risk. Forward chaining involves going through the rules one at a time to infer that exploratory oil and gas investments are the best recommendation.

FIGURE 18-1   Expert system example.

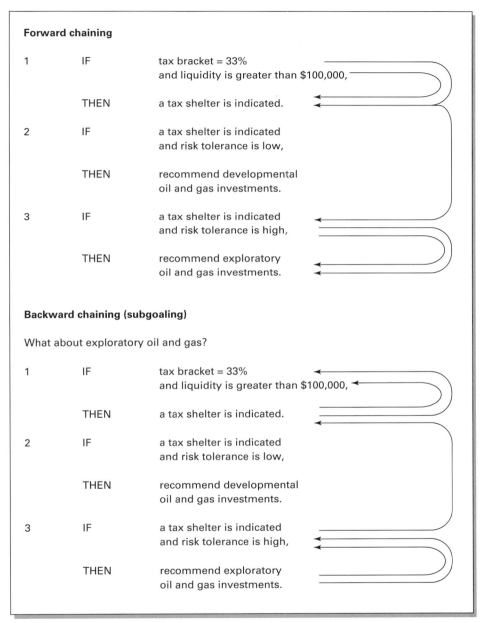

If an adviser is interested only in whether exploratory oil and gas investments are the best recommendation and is not interested in other possible investments, backward chaining is more efficient. In backward chaining, the system begins with a goal. In this case, the goal is to show that the client needs exploratory oil and gas investments. At each stage, the inference engine establishes subgoals that, if achieved, would indicate the client needs exploratory oil and gas investments.

Look at Figure 18-1 and assume that the THEN condition of the third rule is the goal. To conclude that the exploratory shelter is recommended, an adviser needs to know whether the risk tolerance is high (which is already known), which means a rule is needed to show a shelter is recommended. By checking other rules, the inference engine finds if rule 1 is true, it can achieve its subgoal of having a shelter recommended. The IF conditions of rule 1 are true, so the subgoal is attained and rule 3 is true.

Systems Development

Expert system development lends itself naturally to prototyping and learning through test cases. Sometimes the individual designing the system is called a *knowledge engineer* to distinguish him or her from a traditional systems analyst. The development process is different because advice is far more tentative than the numeric solution of a problem or the processing of transactions.

Note, however, it can be quite difficult to conduct knowledge engineering. In the AESOP example presented next, many hours were spent in meetings with the expert. Although the expert was extremely knowledgeable, it was difficult for him to explain his logic because he was not conscious of his decision-making steps.

In some instances, experts are reluctant to reveal their expertise to systems developers. In many cases, systems are developed as an experiment and never fully implemented. The kind of systems described in this chapter may be some of the most difficult to implement successfully.

Some Examples

AESOP: A System for Stock Options Pricing

A stock option is a security giving the holder the right to buy or sell an asset at a specified time. A stock option call is the right to buy a share of stock at a certain price at a future date, a put is the right to sell a share of stock. The price at which one may purchase or sell the stock is called the strike price. On the American Stock Exchange (AMEX), options have an expiration date at which time they may be exercised. A position in an option may be closed out by purchasing an offsetting contract. All options expire on the third Saturday of the month of exercise.

Table 18-2 is an example of a call option for XYZ stock. The price of a May option to buy a share of XYZ at $40 (the *ask* price) is $3 and seven-eighths. (Options below $3 are priced in one-sixteenths, and above $3 are priced in one-eighths.) The *bid* price for the May 40 is $3 and five-eighths. The quote for the May 50 call option is *no bid*, one-eighth asked. The price is given for an option to buy or sell one share of the stock, however, contracts on the AMEX are for 100 shares. An option for a stock at a certain strike price is called an options series.

TABLE 18-2 An Example of a Call Option.

	XYZ Calls Stock Price $42					
	40 Bid	Ask	45 Bid	Ask	50 Bid	Ask
May	3 5/9	3 7/8	0 5/16	0 4/8	0 0/8	0 1/8
June	4 1/8	4 3/8	0 13/16	1 0/8	0 0/8	0 1/8

Assume that the current price of a share of XYZ is $42. A May 40 call is said to be "in the money" because if the stock price holds until expiration, an option owner has the right to buy a share for $40 and can sell it immediately for $42. The May 45 and 50 calls are "out of the money." For puts, the opposite logic holds. A May 40 put is out of the money because if the $42 stock price holds until the option expires, no gain will come from having the right to sell a share of stock at $40 when the market price is $42. The May 45 and May 50 puts are in the money.

The Specialist

The options specialist is a market maker in an option. He or she is responsible for posting the bid and ask quotes for the stock option at the options post on the floor of the exchange. Only one specialist works on the exchange for each stock option. The specialist maintains an inventory of options and can trade from his or her own account. Specialists also maintain a position in the underlying stock as a hedge on their inventory of options. The role of the specialist is to ensure a fair and orderly market. The specialist buys and sells from his or her own account to prevent price changes from being unduly erratic.

If the specialist posts an incorrect price, he or she does not obtain the maximum return on invested capital and runs the risk of incurring a large loss. Investors, noting a discrepancy between the price of the option and the underlying stock, will arbitrage against the specialist. Errors in pricing provide the investor with an opportunity for nearly risk-free profits. (The specialist's exposure is limited because a public quote is good for only a limited number of contracts.)

An important role of the specialist is to represent limit orders. The limit order is a bid to buy or sell an option at a particular price. The specialist is responsible for executing a trade for the limit order when the option price reaches the price on the limit order, assuming that a customer takes the other side of the trade or that the specialist handles the trade from inventory. For example, assume the specialist has a customer who puts in a limit order to buy at 4 and two-eighths and the current bid price for the option is four and three-eighths. The specialist can lower the quotation so that the public bid price is four and two-eighths. However, the specialist cannot lower it to four and one-eighth because of the limit order from a buyer willing to pay four and two-eighths.

The specialist involved in this project used the Black-Scholes options pricing model for a number of years and was reluctant to change models. The specialist provides the parameters for the model. His most frequent change is in the underlying stock price. The stock for his options is traded on the New York Stock Exchange, and the monitor at his posts displays the bid and ask prices as well as the last sale price of the underlying stock at the NYSE. The specialist also changes the interest rate for the model and inputs new volatilities for the stock.

The output of the Black-Scholes model is of invaluable assistance to the specialist. Due to the assumptions of the model and the unique situation of the specialist, however, he must modify the theoretical prices. The problem domain of the specialist requires that he take the following constraints into consideration when pricing:

1. The model outputs point estimates and the specialist must put a bid-ask spread around the theoretical price. (The specialist has a desired spread, which is one of his decision variables. The stock exchange also has guidelines for spreads, which are a constraint on the decision process.)

2. The specialist cannot price through limit orders. He must constantly check his book of limit orders.

3. Various exchange rules apply to pricing. For example, on the maximum spread allowed between bid and ask prices, the requirement to price is one-sixteenths below $3 and one-eighths above.

4. The specialist's own inventory position in a series.

5. The possibility that certain quotations when combined provide an opportunity for someone to arbitrage against the specialist. (The theoretical price prevents arbitrage, but some of the constraints cited in this section force the specialist to post prices that differ from the theoretical price and therefore create opportunities for arbitrage.)

6. The level of current trading activity in the option.

The Expert System

AESOP integrates the Black-Scholes mathematical model with an expert system and attempts to provide recommended quotations for the specialist that are closer to what he can post than the theoretical prices produced by the mathematical model alone. The AMEX sponsored the development of the system with a research grant. Its objective was to assess the use of expert systems technology at the exchange. A major goal of this project was to show such a model could succeed in a challenging environment like the floor of a stock exchange.

Many expert systems are advisory and operate with loose time constraints. The options pricing specialist must function in close to real time as the market changes. AESOP would have to function on the floor of the exchange and provide recommendations whenever the specialist changed input parameters. The recommended prices would have to appear quickly enough to be posted to the public quote board before a trader could take advantage of an old price.

The expert system was developed over a two-year period with a senior options specialist at the AMEX as the human expert. The ES uses rules to represent the knowledge of the specialist. This particular approach to knowledge representation seemed natural given the environment. The American Stock Exchange has a series of rules that apply to options prices. The heuristics used by the expert specialist also seemed to follow an if-then structure: "If I am long on contracts, then reduce the asking price by one increment."

Figure 18-2 presents an overview of the AESOP system. The specialist interacts with the system through the user interface managed by AESOP's control module. When the

FIGURE 18-2 The AESOP model.

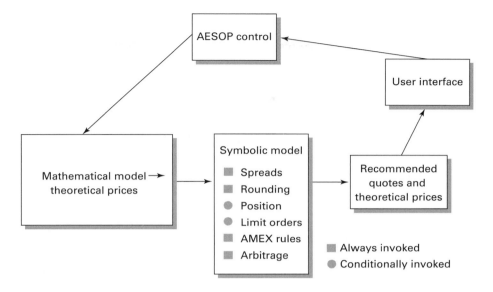

user changes any parameter, the control module invokes the Black-Scholes mathematical model to generate theoretical prices for each series. If the specialist has four different strike prices for each month for four months for both puts and calls, thirty-two theoretical values must be computed (four strikes $\times$ four months for puts and calls). The expert always considers the specialist's desired spreads (the difference between bid and ask prices) and always applies the specialist's rounding rules. (Public quotations must be stated in sixteenths and eighths of a dollar.)

If the specialist's position in any series exceeds a threshold level, the expert model adjusts the price of that option to encourage (specialist is long) or discourage (specialist is short) trading. The symbolic model also looks for limit orders and adjusts the bid-ask prices based on the presence of these orders. Limit order adjustments are the most complicated and potentially the most valuable feature of the symbolic model.

The expert system always checks the AMEX rules to be sure exchange regulations are not violated. The model also scans for arbitrage possibilities. In almost all cases, arbitrage arises because bid-ask prices are adjusted away from the theoretical price for some reason, most often because of the presence of a limit order.

The user interface presents the recommended quotations of the symbolic model along with the theoretical prices generated by the mathematical model. The user is free to override any recommendations, ask for an explanation or trace of the symbolic model, or change parameters and rerun the entire system. The user of the system can use the interface for the following:

- Entering and processing limit orders
- Invoking a system for updating contracts, positions, and so on
- Changing parameters in the Black-Scholes model or bid-ask spreads

MANAGEMENT PROBLEM 18-2

The technology field has had a number of fads, and one of the most fun fads was expert systems. The technology that used computers as symbol processors rather than number crunchers elevated the way in which we think about machines. Imagine a computer being able to offer advice to managers! The Japanese were so taken with expert systems that they started a "fifth-generation" computer project to produce a computer that would actually process symbols rather than do calculations; its speed would be measured in logical inferences per second rather than the number of calculations per second.

A lot of the ideas behind expert systems have turned up in other applications, particularly in situations where a series of rules are easier to express in logic than in mathematics. However, the world of technology did not turn away from conventional processing or abandon it in favor of expert systems.

Today we find expert systems in the form of intelligent agents on the Web. If you want to purchase a product, you can go to mysimon.com or dealtime.com, and the intelligent agents on these sites will search online stores to find the lowest price. These agents or shopbots employ artificial intelligence techniques, as do expert systems. AI has also become a part of data mining where it helps to have some intelligence in looking for relationships in data.

The manager to whom you report has asked you to look for applications of intelligent agents in the company. Imagine that you work in a financial services and consulting firm. What is the role for agents here? What might they do for consultants? For financial analysts and planners?

- Explaining the reasoning behind each recommended quotation and alerting the user to arbitrage possibilities
- Manually overriding any recommended price
- Posting recommended quotations to the Current Board columns on the screen
- Displaying the position or changing the threshold position for position rules to apply
- Turning a log on or off
- Running the Black-Scholes model

A specialist used AESOP on an experimental basis for two months. The developers compared AESOP's recommendations with the actual quotes posted by the specialist for calls with an ask price in eighths. The results: 269 times the specialist posted the ask price in eighths recommended by AESOP; 151 times the specialist raised the recommended bid by one-eighth; and 256 times he lowered it by one-eighth. Further analysis of puts and calls showed that AESOP performs best on calls. AESOP is successful in demonstrating an expert system can improve the ease of use of a mathematical model and it can do so in a demanding, semi-real-time environment.

The Port of Singapore Authority

Singapore has long had government policies promoting economic growth and employment. Because trade is vital to Singapore's economy, applying technology to processing trade-related information was a natural choice. In addition, Singapore knew that its main rival as a port, Hong Kong, was developing an EDI system for trade. Trade involves many entities in Singapore, so the effort to reengineer trade information processing included representatives of the Economic Development Board (EDB), the National Computer Board (NCB), the Trade Development Board (TDB), and various statutory boards involved with trade such as Customs, the Port of Singapore Authority (PSA), and the Civil Aviation Authority.

It was clear that automating present procedures and documents would produce few gains; it was necessary to reduce the twenty plus forms involved in trade to a few, or even one form. The design effort for TradeNet resulted in a single, long, formatted computer screen to serve nearly all trade documentation for Singapore. The development effort led to the creation of Singapore Network Services (SNI) to establish the EDI system. SNI purchased a mainframe EDI engine from IBM to serve as the core of the trade system; a local Singapore firm wrote the custom interfaces, monitoring and billing subsystems among others. Other subcontractors developed the user interface software for the trading companies that would use TradeNet (King and Konsynski, 1994).

The TradeNet EDI system links the TDB, Customs, shipping agents, the ports, freight forwarders, traders, and others together. When implemented in January 1989, the $10 million plus system was a tremendous success. Customer response was much greater than anticipated, and by 1991 the use of TradeNet became mandatory. Several freight forwarders reported savings of 25 percent or more in handling trade documentation. An evaluation of TradeNet showed that the TDB staff handling trade documentation and procedures fell from 144 before the system to thirty-eight afterwards. After the system, turnaround time for documents that took two days under manual processing dropped to fifteen minutes while documents that used to require four days now normally take four hours (Teo, Tan, and Wei, 1997).

At the Port

TradeNet greatly facilitated document processing, and it removed time considerations for most of the parties who use it. Port operations, on the other hand, impose severe, real-time requirements on information processing. The objective of outstanding customer service, which is measured by minimum ship turnaround time and error-free container handling, imposes significant constraints on information processing and port operations. PSA, in combination with various partners, developed an integrated set of traditional and expert systems to provide exceptional customer service to shipping lines. It is estimated that more than 300 applications are used in all facets of the Port's operations (Tung and Turban, 1996). Two major systems and many subsystems allow the port to provide superb service despite its handicap in land area for storing and moving containers.

PortNet and MAINS

Two major systems provide information to Port customers and PSA staff. PortNet is a nationwide system connecting PSA to users; it is linked to TradeNet. The Maritime Information System (MAIN) collects data from shipping agents, shippers, truckers, and others about a vessel, its contents, schedule, cargo, and other pertinent information. MAIN provides a central database of information that other systems access (Tung and Turban, 1996).

Prior to the arrival of a ship, shippers notify the Port Authority of the containers that will be loaded using PortNet, an online system with about 1,500 subscribers. PSA replies with a window of time for the shipper's trucks to appear at an entry gate to the Port. The objective is to have trucks go to the right stack of containers and to have a yard crane available to offload the container from the truck. Such scheduling minimizes the need to handle containers.

CITOS

The Computer Integrated Terminal Operations System, or CITOS, supports planning for and managing all operations of the port. The subsystems in CITOS process information for allocating berths to ships, planning the stowage of containers, the allocation of resources in general, and reading container numbers and operating trucking gates. The first prototype of CITOS appeared in 1988; it was converted to a production system in 1989, and won an Artificial Intelligence Innovation Award shortly thereafter. Four subsystems handle berth allocation, stowage planning, yard planning, and resource allocation, and a neural network application is used for gate automation.

Berth Planning

The assignment of ships to berths is complex given the large number of ships handled daily (forty or more), priorities, weather constraints, changes in schedules, and the need to allocate resources such as quay cranes. The expert system relaxes some of the constraints on the problem using different heuristics. The system provides about 80 percent of the solution, and planners use it as a starting point. The planner works with a graphic user interface to drag and drop vessel icons in different berths. The system reduces the planning time by up to 90 percent and has improved the utilization of berths (Tung and Turban, 1996). (SPA has not put this system into operation.)

Stowage Planning

The planner assigns containers to cranes and to bays on a ship; he or she determines the containers to be removed and loaded. Each ship is different and has a unique template showing its holds and the locations of containers. Planners must balance the load on the quay cranes subject to safety and ship balance constraints. (There are twenty to thirty berths and ten quay cranes.)

This problem is complex because ships typically carry cargo for several destinations, and it is important to minimize handling by loading containers in the right sequence. As an example, one of the new large container ships, the 6,600 TEU[2] *Sally Maersk*, recently made its maiden voyage to Singapore. PSA achieved a rate of 203 container moves per hour for this vessel, exceeding its 1997 average of 88 moves per hour (the fastest in the world). The Port handled 1,700 boxes and turned the ship around in less than eight and one half hours. The ship loaded containers from forty-four other vessels and discharged containers to another thirty-eight during the vessel's visit.

Yard Planning

Singapore is a small island with limited space. PSA stacks containers up to nine high, which is much higher than other ports with more land. If a container that is needed is on the bottom of a stack, a lot of handling and time are required to retrieve it. The Yard planner determines the placement of containers to support the rapid turnaround of ships. Its objectives are to use space efficiently and keep yard activities orderly.

Resource Allocation

This system helps deploy operations staff and container handling equipment with the exception of quay cranes. Users work with a graphical tool to deploy resources and produce a deployment plan. Employees use their staff passes, which are smart cards, in a machine that provides them with instructions.

Gate Automation

As trucks carrying containers arrive at the entry gate to the port, the container number recognition system reads and interprets the container's number. The system uses a video camera for each letter and number of the eleven-character container ID that is painted on each container. A neural net recognizes each character and the system checks it against its record of the container that was expected. The gate automation subsystem also records the weight of the vehicle and directs the driver to the container's desired location within forty-five seconds. This system reduced the number of individuals manually checking IDs from sixteen, one per lane, to three.

CIMOS

The Computer-Integrated Marine Operations System helps to manage shipping traffic and the activities of the port. It includes a vessel traffic information subsystem that watches the Singapore Straits and approaches. This information is available in a database that shippers access via PortNet to learn the status of vessels in the port.

Five expert systems are used for planning, including applications to assign ships to anchorages, schedule the movement of vessels through channels to terminals, deploy pilots to tugs and launches, route launches, and deploy tugboats.

- **Vessel Traffic I and II**. This expert system provides surveillance of the port approaches including the Singapore Straits. It uses a computer-aided radar tracking system with five radars in place. The system relays vessel movement information to a control center where it is displayed on high-resolution, color graphics terminals. The second vessel traffic system has four radars to monitor port waters. The information from this system is used to deploy pilots, tugs, and launches, and to assign anchorage space.

- **Port Traffic Management.** This system provides a central database integrating all information from other subsystems. It is also linked to PortNet so that customers and others can obtain status information.

- **Marine Radio System.** This system is installed on PSA vessels and transmits operational data using wireless technology. The system is installed on tugs and launches; all pilots carry radios.

- **Planning Systems.** Five expert systems help plan resource allocations for the port:
    1. Anchorage Utilization assigns anchorage slots to vessels according to the ship's characteristics.
    2. Channel Utilization plans and schedules movements of container vessels calling at terminals (more than 45,000 a year).
    3. Pilotage Deployment assigns pilots to tugs and launches.
    4. Launch Deployment produces routes for the launches that serve vessels and employees.

5. Tug Deployment allocates tugs to meet service demands (Tung and Turban, 1996).

This example from PSA shows the power of integrating expert systems technology with more traditional applications. The Port has achieved impressive results that contribute to Singapore's overall strategy for trade and commerce.

KNOWLEDGE DISCOVERY

Knowledge discovery is an area of active research and application; it combines AI techniques with large databases. By combining the resources of a large database with AI-based knowledge discovery programs, you may be able to learn valuable facts from the data. For example, suppose that you had a database of the credit card charges for thousands or even millions of card users. A knowledge discovery program would look for patterns in the data and report the results to the user. One pattern might include young professionals with an income over $50,000 who eat out at least once a week. You might target this group for a special restaurant promotion.

Today transactions systems routinely generate billions of characters of data. Credit card charges are one example, but they are small compared with the data grocery and retail store scanners generate each day. The combination of AI and database technologies has great potential for extracting useful information from massive amounts of transactions data.

NEURAL NETWORKS

This approach to AI was first suggested many years ago but only recently became fashionable. The first neural networks were loosely based on how the brain functions. The brain consists of neurons, which can be thought of as small processing units. Outside stimuli or other neurons provide input for a given neuron. The neurons are connected in a large, complex network.

The network has dendrites that transmit messages across various paths. The dendrites are like highways connecting the network. A synapse exists where the network connects with a particular neuron. Many dendrites (thousands) may lead to a single neuron. In the brain the neurons function through a chemical or electrical impulse. These impulses can either excite the neuron and it can "fire," sending a message across the network, or the impulses can inhibit a neuron to keep it from firing. This output goes across a single axon that transmits the neuron's signal to the network. Estimates put the number of neurons in the human brain in the trillions (possibly 10^{12}) (Zahedi, 1993).

The most popular type of neural network is used to classify input into different categories. Figure 18-3 shows the basic building blocks for a neural network: neuron i connected to neuron j. The weight w_{ij} represents the strength of the connection between the two neurons. A neural network contains at least two layers of neurons. The input layer receives input from the external environment. The output layer consists of neurons that communicate the output of the system to the user. Figure 18-4 shows a neural network consisting of three layers.

The input to a neuron consists of a weighted sum of all the neurons (that fired) connected to it. For example, in 18-4 the input to neuron x consists of the output from neurons a, b, and c (assuming that they fired), multiplied by their respective weights. If the

FIGURE 18-3
Neural nodes.

FIGURE 18-4 A three-layer neural network.

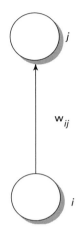

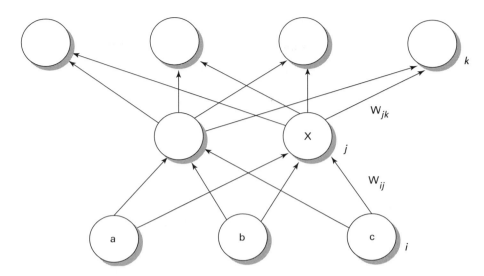

sum of this output exceeds some threshold value, neuron x will fire and send its output to the next layer according to the weights connecting it to layer k. The network has to be trained to establish the weights for the connections.

In the simplest network, neurons in one layer are connected only to neurons in the next layer. More complex networks feature neurons that are connected within a layer. Probably the most common business uses of neural nets feature feed-forward networks; the neurons in one layer receive inputs from the layer below and send outputs to the layer above. In a feed-forward network the flow of inputs is in one direction, from the input layer, through intermediate layers, and finally to the output layer.

Neural networks have proven to be quite robust in classification problems. For example, suppose that your firm wants to classify new customers into four types: those who are likely to pay their bills on time, those who may take between two and three months to pay, those taking three to six months, and those who are not likely to pay at all. You might design a neural network to try to classify potential customers. The input to the network would be information about the customer, and the output would be a classification into one of four groups corresponding to the likely payment categories.

First you must design the network and then train it. Typically you would choose a feed-forward network with at least three layers: an input layer and an output layer plus one or more hidden layers in between. The layers have connections from the input to the hidden to the output layers. Backward connections are only used for training the network.

To train the network, you present it with past cases, data on customer attributes, and how these former customers paid their bills. Learning is through back propagation, because the learning program looks at the output and then works backward to adjust the weights for the connections between neurons. Various learning rules are used to adjust the weights during training. For example, the delta training rule attempts to minimize the sum of squared errors between the actual output of the system and the correct output. If, during the training, your network misclassified a former customer, the delta rule would adjust the weights to try to minimize the error. After training with a large number of cases, the weights should stabilize and the network is ready for use. At this point, you begin to use the network to classify new customers based on the same kind of input information you used to train the network.

Case-Based Reasoning

Case-based reasoning (CBR) captures lessons from past experience and uses them to find solutions to a new problem. CBR is both a problem-solving approach and a model of how some experts think individuals learn, remember, and think about problems. A case-based model is particularly appropriate when rules cannot express the richness of the knowledge domain. CBR is described as most useful in situations of rich experience, but little knowledge.

A case-based system needs cases, a similarity index, a case retrieval mechanism, and an explanation module. A case is similar to the cases you study in school: it has a set of features, attributes, and relations, and an associated outcome. A case is specific to a given situation, unlike a general rule in a rule-based expert system. The PERSUADER is a case-based system for mediating management and labor disputes. For this CBR program, a case is a past labor dispute similar to the one it now faces. A repository of past cases is crucial. The more cases and the greater the variety of experiences they represent, the better are the recommendations from the system.

A set of indexes is the mechanism through which cases similar to the one under consideration are located. The indexing process stores cases and generates similarity indexes to be used in retrieving cases similar to the one at hand. The task of developing robust indexes is one of the biggest challenges facing developers of case-based systems. Another component, the retrieval mechanism, must retrieve cases with the closest match between attributes of past cases and the current case on which advice is sought. The explanation module allows the system to explain its analysis of the current problem and a proposed solution. It should describe why and how the present problem is similar to past cases.

A user presents the system with a problem and the system indexes its attributes, features, and relations based on standards built into the system. The system uses these indexes to retrieve a set of similar past cases and their solutions based on the indexes created when the cases were originally added to the knowledge base. The system examines the cases retrieved from memory to find the best fit with the current problem. It also examines the solution to past cases until it can generate a proposed solution to the problem at hand. If the system's proposed solution is accepted, it incorporates the current case into its knowledge base to be used again in the future.

Genetic Algorithms

The traditional approach to solving problems in artificial intelligence involves looking at a single candidate for a solution and interactively manipulating it using various heuristics or rules of thumb. Genetic algorithms work on a population of candidates at the same time. This population of candidate solutions may be as few as ten to several thousands. Figure 18-5 describes these evolutionary computations. In general the approach involves generating a population of possible problem solutions (the unrated population in the figure) and rating them based on some fitness function. The next step is to apply a selection function

FIGURE 18-5   General procedure for all evolutionary computations. A complete cycle from unrated population to unrated population represents one generation of the search.

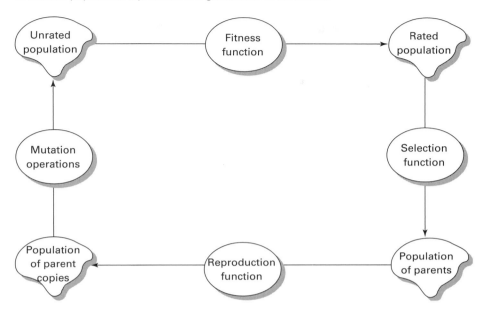

to the unrated population to select "parents" for the next generation of solutions. A reproduction function generates copies of the parents. These copies go through mutation operations to create the next generation of solutions for evaluation, closing the loop in the figure at the "unrated population" in the upper left-hand corner.

To start, a genetic algorithm rates how good each solution is for the problem under consideration by using a fitness function. This function is similar to a cost function used in other search techniques. The function returns a number denoting the worth of the solution just evaluated. The objective of the genetic algorithm is to minimize (or maximize, depending on the problem) the value returned by the fitness function.

Once the fitness function evaluates all candidates, the genetic algorithm selects a subset of the population to form parents for a new population. The algorithm chooses parents based on the relative worth of the candidates in the population as determined by the fitness function. Genetic algorithms feature a variety of selection methods to designate the parents. As an example, a simple strategy would be to take the best half of the current population to be the parents for the next generation. Most of the time, the selection of the better part of the population is augmented with lesser fitness scores to promote diversity.

To create a new generation of possible solutions, the genetic algorithm applies operators known as mutations to copies of the parents it has selected. These mutations alter the content of the parents. As shown in Figure 18-6 genetic algorithms represent problem solutions as fixed-length vectors containing features of the solution. Genetic algorithms mimic the manipulation of DNA and gene sequences. The mutations include inversion, point mutation, and crossover as shown in the figure. The inversion operation reverses the order of randomly selected, contiguous portions of the vector. A point mutation alters a single feature, replacing it with a randomly chosen value. The crossover operator randomly

FIGURE 18-6 (a) Inversion, (b) point mutations, and (c) crossover operations used in genetic algorithms.

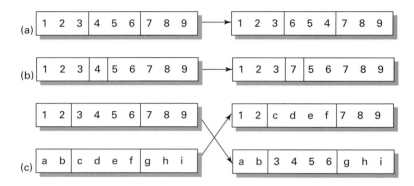

selects a sequence of features and swaps them between two parents. This later mutation is the most popular and most frequently used. The creation of populations stops after a set number of generations or after the fitness function reaches a predetermined value.

A rule-based expert system will show the rules that fired and allow the user to trace through the solution. Like neural networks, genetic algorithms do not provide the user with an understanding of how they reached a solution. Both of these techniques provide good solutions to a variety of problems despite the drawback that their solution mechanism is not obvious.

Intelligent Agents

If you combine AI with networks, the resulting innovation is an intelligent agent. An agent is a piece of software that performs a task for its owner. Some developers call agents *softbots*, a play on the mechanical robot. An intelligent agent must exhibit some kind of behavior observers would consider to be intelligent. Suppose you could send an agent over the Web armed with a request to obtain the four lowest prices it could find for a certain kind of appliance, say a VCR, and have it return with the information. This behavior might be considered intelligent. The first applications for intelligent agents have been for consumer tasks such as shopping. A pioneer in developing these applications created a Web site to provide recommendations on music. A user indicates a music type preference, and an agent matches that profile with those of others in the database. It recommends music, liked by those with similar profiles, to the user.

CHAPTER SUMMARY

Many of the systems discussed in this chapter, applications such as ERP, process transactions for the firm; they support decision making, but they do so with straightforward information. The system shows that it is time to ship an order requested by a customer. The applications described show the range and diversity of information technology; it can do more than process transactions and help people communicate. Some of the applications need to be justified as a research and development expenditure because they carry high risk. But in the cases reviewed here, those risks led to substantial rewards at American Airlines and the Port of Singapore. Many other opportunities await knowledgeable managers and firms willing to balance development risk against possible returns.

KEYWORDS

Artificial intelligence (AI)	Fitness function	Mutation
Back propagation	Forward chaining	Neural network
Backward chaining	Genetic algorithm	Neuron
Case-based reasoning (CBR)	Group decision support system (GDSS)	Optimization
Crossover		Stock option
Decision support system (DSS)	Heuristic	Synapse
Dendrite	Inference engine	User interface
Evolutionary computations	Inversion	Weight
Executive information system (EIS)	Knowledge base	Yield management
Expert system	Knowledge discovery	
Feed-forward network	Knowledge engineering	

RECOMMENDED READINGS

Communications of the ACM, 45(8), August 2002. (A special issue on data mining.)

Dhar, V., and Stein, R. 1997. *Seven Methods for Transforming Corporate Data into Business Intelligence.* Englewood Cliffs, NJ: Prentice-Hall. (A book illustrating several methods for making organizations more intelligent.)

Fayyad, U., and Uthurusamy, R. 2002. Evolving data mining into solutions for insights. *Communications of the ACM, 45*(8), pp. 28–31.

Gordon, Lee, and Lucas. 2003. "A System of Resources for Competitive Advantage: A Case Study of the Port of Singapore." College Park, Robert H. Smith School of Business Working Paper.

Gupta, V., Peter, E., and Miller, T. 2002. Implementing a distribution network decision support system at Pfizer/Warner-Lambert. *Interfaces, 32*(4), pp. 28–45. (An article describing the DSS in the examples section of this chapter.)

Hand, D., Mannila, H., and Smyth, P. 2001. *Principles of Data Mining.* Cambridge, MA: MIT Press.

Jackson, J. 2002. Data mining: A conceptual overview. *Communications of AIS, 8*(19). (A good tutorial on data mining.)

Smith, B. C., Leimkuhler, J., and Darrow, R. 1992. Yield management at American Airlines. *Interfaces, 22*(1), pp. 8–31. (A detailed description of the DSS discussed in this chapter.)

Stohr, E., and Konsynski, B. (eds.). 1992. *Information Systems and Decision Processes.* Los Alamitos, CA: IEEE Computer Society Press. (An excellent collection of articles about organizational support systems by some of the leaders in the field.)

Tung, L. L., and Turban, E. 1996. Port of Singapore Authority: Using AI technology for strategic positioning. In N. Boon Siong (ed.), *Exploiting Information Technology for Business Competitiveness.* Singapore: Addison-Wesley.

Trippi, R., and Lee, J. 1996. *Artificial Intelligence in Finance and Investing: State-of-the-Art Technologies for Securities Selection and Portfolio Management.* Homewood, IL: Irwin. (A clearly illustrated book introducing the artificial intelligence applications in finance.)

DISCUSSION QUESTIONS

1. What is a decision support system?

2. How does a DSS differ from a traditional system?

3. How does a DSS involve users in its design?

4. For what types of systems might the user need assistance in building a DSS?

5. How are electronic spreadsheet packages used on a PC for building a DSS?

6. What kind of DSS is a manager most likely to build, a model-based or data-based system? Why?

7. Why is an EIS likely to be data as opposed to model based?

8. What are the objectives of group decision support systems? How do they differ from an individual DSS?

9. What do graphics capabilities contribute to a DSS?

10. Should users actually write programs? Is building a DSS programming?

11. How does prototyping contribute to a DSS?

12. What are the pros and cons of electronic meeting rooms as a DSS?

13. What is the role of a model in a model-based DSS?

14. Why do managers want to be able to change values and run a DSS again?

15. What features distinguish an executive information system from a DSS?

16. What is a drill down facility, and why is it important for an EIS?

17. How has technology changed the cost–benefit ratio for decision support systems since the early ones developed in the late 1960s?

18. What are the reasons for developing an expert system?

19. In what ways does an expert system resemble a decision support system?

20. Why are production rule systems popular for advisory systems in business?

21. Why is a mistake costly for American Express in authorizing credit card purchases?

22. Why is prototyping a good approach for the development of an ES?

23. What is the purpose of the inference engine in an expert system?

24. Why is the user interface an important component of an expert system?

25. How does one go about identifying the expert to be used in developing an expert system?

26. What benefits can knowledge discovery systems provide to the organization?

27. What kinds of problems are best suited to the use of a neural network?

28. What steps are involved in creating a neural net?

29. Explain the way a genetic algorithm functions. What is the underlying model for this approach to intelligent systems?

30. How do expert systems contribute to the Port operation in Singapore? How does the technology help Singapore implement its economic strategy?

31. What is data mining?

32. What are the major approaches to data mining?

ENDNOTES

1. *New York Times,* July 29, 2002.

2. A TEU is a twenty-foot equivalent unit, a standard measure of the number of containers on a ship. A forty-foot long container would equal two TEUs.

CHAPTER 19

KNOWLEDGE MANAGEMENT: BENEFITING FROM CORE COMPETENCIES

A Manager's Perspective

During the last bull market, CEOs became similar to royalty in other countries. They received huge salaries, many perquisites, and stock options whose value exceeded the GDP of some small countries. No one questions whether CEOs are important, but many question whether they are worth all that is lavished on them. Louis Gerstner turned around IBM when it was at its lowest point, and led it charging into services to generate revenue. Jack Welch built the modern General Electric. Yet no chairperson could run a company alone. And no single person at the top of the corporation has enough knowledge to centralize all decision making and attend to the smallest details. One person cannot hope to have the knowledge to run a complex organization. In fact, knowledge is distributed throughout the organization, and a business needs to tap into and manage that knowledge to succeed. From the lowest-paid to the highest-paid employee, in postindustrial economies such as the United States, Europe, and Japan, knowledge is a major resource and constitutes a core competence of the firm.

VALUE PROPOSITION

Knowledge management is a key activity for managers, and certain kinds of knowledge are capable of providing a sustainable competitive advantage for the organization. Technologies can assist the manager in storing, retrieving, and disseminating knowledge, yet much of knowledge management remains a human task. These technologies contribute in the following ways:

- Help coordinate individuals working in different locations.
- Provide a way for staff members to find out if someone else in the organization has knowledge they need.
- Provide repositories for knowledge so that it accumulates over time.
- Reduce the costs of providing customer service when a firm makes its knowledge available on the Web.

You can measure some of the benefits from knowledge management with the following metrics:

- Number of new products and services
- Costs to develop new products and services

- Percentage of products sold and percentage of sales from new products/services
- Time to market
- Response time to customer support requests

THE NATURE OF KNOWLEDGE

Knowledge of something means possessing information about it, but knowledge is more than information. One useful definition is that knowledge is "information plus know-how" (Kogut and Zander, 1992). Know-how is the ability to apply and use information, and to accumulate more information and ways of using it based on experience. A doctor has information about different diseases, and the knowledge about how to diagnose them based on symptoms. You have information about bicycles and how they operate, and knowledge about how to ride a bicycle.

Organizations can also have knowledge, but organizational knowledge is the accumulation of the knowledge of its members. An organization, itself, is not a sensing or thinking being, it is an aggregation of individuals who are affiliated with the organization. An individual working for the organization develops specialized knowledge about how to do a job. The question then becomes whether that knowledge belong to the individual or to the organization that has paid the individual to develop the knowledge. The ultimate answer is not obvious. Often when a senior executive leaves a company, he or she is asked to sign a noncompete clause saying that for some period of time, the executive will not start or work for a competing company. The firm the manager is leaving is trying to protect itself so that the departing executive cannot use his or her knowledge to compete against it.

Knowledge on the Plant Floor

Blackmer/Dover Resources is a company that makes industrial pumps. This task involves great precision and a small error can make a pump useless. One twenty-four-year employee, Bill Fowler, is known for the accuracy of his cutting, and he is also faster than any other worker in the plant at preparing his giant cutting machines to shift from one type of pump shaft to another. Although management would like to benefit from his knowledge, Fowler will not say much, "If I gave away my tricks, management could use (them) to speed things up and keep me at a flat-out pace all day," he told a reporter for the *The Wall Street Journal* (July 1, 2002).

Blackmer's pumps move commodities such as refined oil and propane gas. The company made an effort to include information on how to make parts on the specification sheets for different pumps. However, this "tribal knowledge" as one manager puts it, is difficult to write down. One worker tells the difference between Teflon and neoprene O-rings without looking at them by their feel in his hand. This same worker can often diagnose what is wrong with a malfunctioning pump by listening to it. The plant manager agrees that this kind of knowledge defies written description. Workers who operate the same machine for years develop intimate, detailed knowledge about how to run the machine.

About 20 percent of the workers in the plant are unwilling to share information with management for fear that the company might use it to move jobs to a lower-wage country or try to force them to speed up their work. Other workers seem quite willing to share information. One employee is known for running his cutting machine at top speed without doing any damage to the machine. The worker says that his trick is to determine the hardness of the steel he is machining into rotors; if the steel is too hard, running the machine at high speed damages its expensive cutting tools.

The knowledge these workers have enables the plant to operate; it is knowledge that managers do not possess, and which would be difficult to write down and give to another worker. It is the kind of knowledge that one learns by doing, not by reading about it. Knowledge exists on the plant floor, in engineering, marketing, sales, and throughout the organization, across all functions and levels. Knowledge management is the task of creating, maintaining, and utilizing all of this knowledge that employees bring to the organization.

From Information to Knowledge

Knowledge is a strategic resource for organizations. Information alone is not enough to produce knowledge; managers must also understand the best way to use information to solve a problem, contribute to a product or service, or make a similar contribution to the organization. Knowledge builds over time in the heads of employees in the form of past decisions, processes in the organization, characteristics of products, interests of customers, and similar experiences.

One New England company decided to move its operations to the South. It offered all current employees jobs, but would only pay the moving expenses of employees above a certain management level. When the company left for its new location, most of the staff stayed behind. Within a year, the company was bankrupt. It had lost the knowledge that the staff possessed on how to run the business. Customers did not like dealing with new order processing and customer service staff members who did not know their business and needs. These customers began to place their orders with competitors, and the firm could not survive its loss of knowledge from the staff it left behind.

Highly developed countries are in a postindustrial age; they have far more employees in the services industry than in manufacturing. Most of these people work with information and rely on their knowledge to earn income; employees in this sector are often called *knowledge workers.* For such organizations, knowledge is a strategic resource; it is valuable and difficult to imitate. Imagine a company such as Accenture with more than 45,000 employees worldwide. When a new client approaches Accenture with a problem, someone at the consulting firm is likely to have relevant knowledge to help solve the problem. Accenture's consultants represent a huge investment in knowledge; the firm's challenge is to capture that knowledge and make it available throughout the world. Accenture uses information technology, including groupware and an intranet, to help meet this challenge.

It is instructive to look at different types of knowledge. Nonaka (1994) distinguishes between *explicit* and *tacit* knowledge. Explicit knowledge is represented by facts. Formal education provides a great deal of explicit knowledge. This text is an example of an attempt to present explicit knowledge to you, knowledge about information technology and how to manage it in an organization. Tacit knowledge is something individuals understand, but have difficulty explaining. A good example of tacit knowledge is the how to ride a bicycle. Many people can ride a bicycle, but it is difficult to put in words to someone how to master this skill; knowledge about bike riding is tacit.

Internalizing explicit knowledge turns it into tacit knowledge. If you are able to articulate tacit knowledge, you may be able to convert it to explicit knowledge for others to use. Tacit knowledge is an important source of competitive advantage because it is difficult

MANAGEMENT PROBLEM 19-1

When people speak of a "learning organization" or "knowledge workers," often the vision that comes to mind is a highly educated professional. The Blackmer plant, however, shows how knowledge exists everywhere in the organization. One of the jobs of any manager, then, is to see that this knowledge grows and is applied to achieving the goals of the organization. As the Blackmer experience demonstrates, some employees are eager to share their knowledge, and others are deeply suspicious of management and have an attitude of "by helping you I'm probably putting myself out of a job."

In the early days of IT, many applications did result in layoffs because the technology was applied to transactions processing systems. Automating these systems reduced the need for clerical and other hourly workers.

At Blackmer, it is unlikely that the skilled workers in the plant would be laid off if they shared their knowledge, but some of them obviously feel threatened.

The question of whether knowledge gained on the job belongs to the employee or the employer remains. Most organizations ask R&D employees to sign a statement acknowledging that any patents the employee files based on working on company time belong to the corporation. The same principle arguably applies to knowledge gained on the job.

Present the arguments pro and con on the question of who owns knowledge developed on the job. What are the implications of your conclusions for knowledge management systems?

---

for competitors to imitate. Intel considers its knowledge of how to build and operate a chip fabricating plant, today a multi-billion dollar investment, as one of its key competitive advantages.

The most obvious way in which companies acquire knowledge is through experience working with products, services, customers, and suppliers. In this way, knowledge becomes embedded in practice, just as in the case of the factory workers at Blackmer/Dover Resources earlier in the chapter. Knowledge often comes from beginning to understand cause-and-effect relationships. Almost everything that one does in an organization presents a learning opportunity. Research and development departments, new product groups, engineers, and special task forces are formal efforts of the firm to create and acquire knowledge. One important job for a manager is to foster the development of organizational knowledge and to create an organization that learns as it operates.

Diffusing Knowledge

Managers want to see that knowledge is available and applied where it is needed in the organization. At Blackmer/Dover, some workers willingly share their knowledge, and others do not. In some cases, workers develop knowledge that management does not approve of. For example, one worker mentally rearranges the sequence of orders for a machine to make similar parts together rather than have to keep changing the setup on the machine. The policy of the company is first-in, first-out for orders, though this worker is actually increasing personal productivity by mentally resequencing the orders.

In another case, workers found that sleeves that fit inside the pump were too thick and that the pumps would not work, even though the sleeves were within the tolerances specified for the pumps. The workers, on their own, make the sleeves thinner, but they have not told management or engineering to reflect the changes on pump drawings. A new employee would turn out sleeves that do not work following the specifications unless an experienced worker told the new worker what to do.

SIDE BAR 19-1

Knowledge Management at DaimlerChrysler

Before the merger of Daimler-Benz and Chrysler Corporation in 1998, Chrysler had an active knowledge management program in place. The company established teams with cross-functional responsibilities for building vehicle platforms for small cars, large cars, minivans, and jeeps. However, the reorganization caused some problems when the teams lacked knowledge that they needed on how to build cars.

Engineers undertook the task of finding where information existed and then finding ways to integrate it. The head of engineering established "tech clubs" to facilitate the interaction of engineers and designers working on similar problems in areas such as engineering, body, chassis, electrical, interior powertrain, thermal, and similar areas. Corporate vice presidents sponsored the clubs that met informally to exchange best practices.

The company also developed an *Engineering Book of Knowledge* to capture the knowledge generated in the tech clubs. The book identified subject matter experts and contained leading practices. Each of eight functional areas in engineering was responsible for maintaining a section of the book.

Daimler, due to its German origins, had different knowledge management needs when it merged with Chrysler. Due to a strong vocational program for educating engineers, Daimler engineers progressed through an educational system designed to pass tacit knowledge from one generation of engineers to the next.

Daimler set up a number of postmerger projects to integrate the two companies. One of these projects focused on sharing knowledge between engineers at Chrysler and at Daimler. Working together, the two groups of engineers reduced by half the number of new car prototypes needed by developing a new vehicle through the use of CAD simulation tools. The engineers found that Chrysler was better at 3-D modeling and simulation, while Daimler was better at crash simulation. The groups set out to transfer knowledge in these areas between company engineers.

Senior management assigned managers to a series of issues resolution teams, each focused on a specific area such as global sales and marketing, corporate finance, or procurement and supply. The teams used Lotus Notes to coordinate its activities.

Daimler also copied the idea of tech clubs in Germany, calling them communities of practice. The company also developed a worldwide intranet to help share knowledge throughout the company.

A merger presents many challenges to the newly created company; it needs to quickly take advantage of the knowledge of employees from each of the merged companies. A knowledge management program is one way to facilitate the task of finding and sharing knowledge.

SOURCE: C. Johnston, "DaimlerChrysler Knowledge Management Strategy" (Boston: Harvard Business School Press, 2001).

Information technology can help store and distribute some kinds of knowledge, but it will not solve the problems of employees who do not want to contribute their knowledge to the firm or to others. Although it is possible to record some tacit knowledge for distribution, it is likely that technology will contribute the most to the dissemination of explicit knowledge. IT platforms can also provide links to those individuals who have the tacit knowledge needed by someone else in the organization.

THE NATURE OF INFORMATION

Information is a key part of knowledge, and much information takes the form of data or facts. Information must go beyond raw data to include some interpretation or understanding of the data. One role of information is to reduce uncertainty about some state or event. As an example, consider a weather forecast predicting clear and sunny skies tomorrow. This information reduces uncertainty about whether an event such as a baseball game will be held. Information that a bank just approved a loan for a firm reduces management uncertainty about whether the firm will be in a state of solvency or bankruptcy next month. Information derived from processing transactions reduces uncertainty about a firm's order backlog or financial position. Information used primarily for control in the organization reduces uncertainty about whether the firm is performing according to plan and budget. Another definition of information is: "Information is data that has been processed into a form that is meaningful to the recipient and is of real perceived value in current or prospective decisions" (Davis and Olson, 1985, p. 6).

How People Interpret Information

A classic article on information systems suggested in part that an information system serves an individual with a certain cognitive style faced with a particular decision problem in some organizational setting (Mason and Mitroff, 1973). In addition to these variables, personal and situational factors are important in the interpretation of information. (See Figure 19-1.)

Clearly, the nature of the problem influences the interpretation of information. The seriousness of the decision, the consequences of an incorrect decision, and the benefits of a correct decision all affect an individual's view of information. An important decision may require more care in analyzing data than would a minor decision. For example, a bank's decision to merge with a stock brokerage firm is more important than its decision to lease additional office space.

The organization itself affects the interpretation of information. Studies show that the individual becomes socialized by the organization. Over time, employees are influenced by organizations in the way they approach problems. Thus, in most instances, the attitudes of a new employee will differ substantially from those of members of the board of directors. As the new employee associates over the years with other employees of the firm, he or she is

FIGURE 19-1 Influences on the interpretation and use of information.

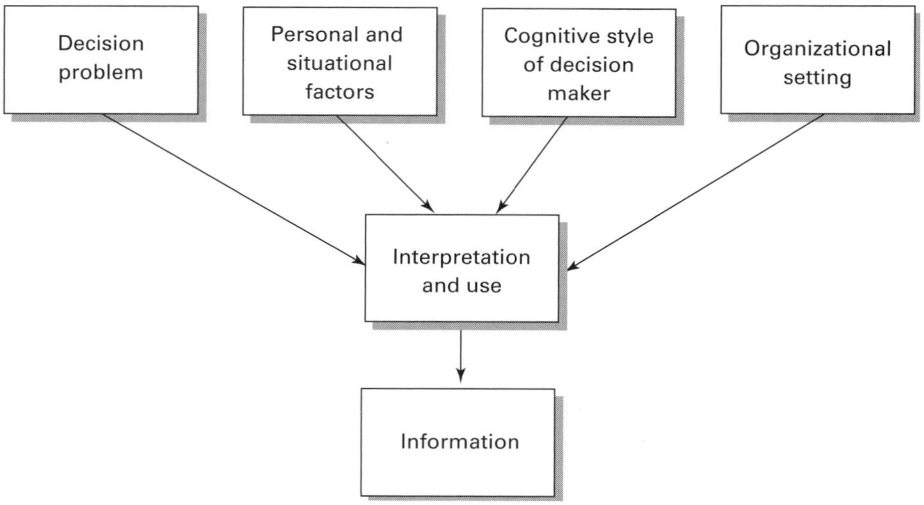

influenced by their attitudes and by the environment of the workplace. Gradually, new employees begin to change their attitudes to be more consistent with those of their associates.

People who have different ideas interpret information differently. Again, many of a person's ideas are influenced by peers and by the socialization process in the particular organization where the individual works. Several individuals trying to influence the government to regulate prices in an industry may use the same information. However, the head of a corporation in the industry, the leader of a consumer group, and a government decision maker in a regulatory agency will interpret the same information differently.

Personal and situational factors also influence the interpretation of information. One study done many years ago showed that given comparable information, decision makers interpreted a problem differently depending on their position. In this exercise, finance executives saw financial problems, sales executives recognized sales problems, and so forth. In all the given scenarios, the information was the same—it was just interpreted differently (Dearborn and Simon, 1958). A more recent study found managers are getting less parochial, though many managers are heavily influenced in problem diagnosis by their backgrounds and position.

Psychologists studying the thought patterns of individuals developed the concept of cognitive style. Although psychologists do not agree on exactly how to describe or measure different cognitive styles, the concept is appealing, because people do seem to have different ways of approaching problems. One of the simplest distinctions is between analytic and heuristic decision makers. The analytic decision maker looks at quantitative information. Engineering is a profession attractive to an analytic decision maker. The heuristic decision maker, on the other hand, is interested in broader concepts and is more intuitive. Most researchers believe that individuals are not analytic or heuristic in every problem but that they do have preferences and tend to approach the same type of problem with a consistent cognitive style.

Characteristics of Information

Information can be characterized in a number of ways; some kinds of information are more suitable for decision making than others. The time frame for information can be historical or predictive. Historical information can be used to design alternative solutions and to monitor performance. Information may be expected or it may be unanticipated. Some information systems experts feel that information is worthless unless it is a surprise to the recipient. However, information that confirms something also reduces uncertainty. Surprise information often alerts us to the existence of a problem; it is also important in developing and evaluating different alternatives. Information may come from sources internal to the organization or from external sources, such as government agencies.

In general, different types of decisions require different kinds of information, and providing inappropriate information is one common failing of information systems. (See Table 19-1.) Operational control decisions are characterized by historical information. Usually the results are expected and the source of the information is the internal operations of the organization. The data (e.g., production control data, inventory status, and accounts receivable balances) must be detailed. Because operational control decisions involve day-to-day operations of the firm, information often must correspond closely to real time. This information is often highly structured and precise.

TABLE 19-1 Information characteristics versus decision types.

Characteristics	Operational control	Managerial control	Strategic planning
Time frame	Historical	⟶	Predictive
Expectation	Anticipated	⟶	Surprise
Source	Largely internal	⟶	Largely external
Scope	Detailed	⟶	Summary
Frequency	Real time	⟶	Periodic
Organization	Highly structured	⟶	Loosely structured
Precision	Highly precise	⟶	Not overly precise

Information for strategic decisions, on the other hand, is more predictive and long range in nature. Strategic planning may uncover many surprises. Often, external data on the economy, the competition, and so forth are involved in strategic decision making. Summary information on a periodic basis is adequate; highly detailed or extremely precise information is usually not necessary. Strategic planning decisions are usually characterized by loosely structured information. The requirements for managerial control decisions fall between operational control and strategic planning. Obviously, information can be classified in a number of ways, which complicates the decision maker's problem in expressing what output is desired from an information system.

GROUPWARE, INFORMATION, AND KNOWLEDGE

One of the most difficult questions to answer is, "What do managers do?" For the first three or four decades of information technology, IT did little to help managers in their day-to-day tasks, often because IT staff did not understand managers. Few management information systems existed, though many companies claimed to have them. The last decade witnessed the development of groupware, designed to support both the daily tasks of management and coordination, and to provide a repository of organizational intelligence.

More than thirty years ago, Henry Mintzberg (1973) conducted a classic study of managers. He observed their behavior by living with them for a week. Based on his observations, Mintzberg identified a number of roles that a senior manager plays in an organization. One role of management that seems to be universally agreed upon is leadership: the manager is, and should be, a leader for the organization. In this role, the manager sets direction, acts as a public spokesperson, and tries to see that the resources of the organization are employed to achieve the objectives set forth.

Management researchers have emphasized the decision-making nature of management since the 1950s. Certainly, managers are expected to make decisions in many different domains. Important decisions include funding R&D, product development, and the decision to introduce a new product. Many managerial decisions revolve around issues of resource allocation. Almost every organization is confronted with limited resources and competing demands for them.

A role that managers often face is as a disturbance handler. Disputes and problems in the organization find their way to a manager who is in a position to resolve them. These disturbances may come from inside the firm, or they may be prompted by problems with suppliers or customers.

Managers also deal with information in their jobs and function as the spokesperson for the firm. A good manager scans the environment for competitive actions, threats, and new opportunities. Today, companies are also dependent on government regulations and actions.

The discussion so far has been about managerial roles, but not about what a manager actually does during the day. Mintzberg divided observations about managers' activities into five categories. The first of these was scheduled meetings, which consumed more than half of the day for the CEOs he studied. Next came unspecified desk work. Unscheduled meetings took 10 percent of the day while phone calls consumed 6 percent of the managers' time. Finally, managers spent a small amount of time on "tours," or "management by walking around."

This distribution of time begins to get at the tasks managers perform. Two activities cut across all of the roles and tasks: communications and information processing. As a leader, spokesperson, decision maker, disturbance handler, and in most other roles, the manager is communicating with others. He or she disseminates the strategy and goals of the firm. The manager receives communications from subordinates, customers, suppliers, the financial community, and many others. Meetings, both scheduled and unscheduled, involve communications as do phone calls and tours. Much of desk work involves letters and memos, another form of communication.

Many communications and much purposeful managerial work revolve around information processing. Individuals frequently communicate to obtain new information. When making a decision, the manager must process information to determine the appropriate course of action to take. Suppliers and customers want information. The securities industry seeks information about company plans and performance.

The technology described next is designed to support people in the organization in the tasks they are expected to perform. This technology lets managers and other workers redesign their tasks. It provides a great deal of flexibility and a number of alternatives for the flow of work, communications, and coordination. Groupware is aimed at what a manager does: It supports members of the organization who have a common task and who operate in a shared environment.

Groupware is sometimes called coordination software because it helps managers coordinate the work of others in the firm. To *coordinate* means to assure that the resources of the firm are applied to achieving its objectives. Coordination means managing dependencies, that is, seeing that individuals or groups that depend on each other or on common resources function effectively.

With groupware, it is difficult not to focus on Lotus Notes, the original groupware product. Groupware and Notes are not easy to define. Even the vendors have difficulty describing the nature of the products. First, Notes is based on client–server computing; the product assumes that users or clients are connected on a local area network with a server. Databases to be shared are kept on the server, though you may have a local database on your own PC. One of Notes' major features is its ability to replicate databases across departments and organizations. You can tell Notes how often to synchronize databases. If offices in New York and Rome use Notes, the system could be set up to automatically update databases at, say, 9 P.M. U.S. time. Notes will update both databases to add new information without losing existing data. Thus, team members in New York and Rome can make changes during the day with impunity. The software replicates those changes on both copies of the database. (If two individuals change the same information, Notes flags the changes and leaves it to the people involved to resolve the conflict.)

This database replication feature is one of the Notes coordination features. The software coordinates diverse workgroups and allows them to share information without worrying about updating anomalies. Just having the same database easily available to multiple individuals working on a project, regardless of replication, promotes coordination as well. Notes also has its own e-mail system so Notes users can communicate with each other.

Notes aggressively integrated its products with the Internet and World Wide Web. Lotus modified its original Notes software so that a Notes Domino server is also a Web server. The software automatically translates information on the server into HTML format if a Web browser requests it, or in Notes format for a Notes client. Lotus believes that Notes is a natural authoring environment for Web information. More than that, Notes is positioned for easy applications development on the Web. Companies want to conduct transactions over the Web and need software that does more than retrieve static information. You must interact with the person using the client. For example, a magazine publisher wants to have a button on its Web site that a person visiting the site clicks on to get a form for subscribing to the magazine. The publisher wants to accept that person's credit card, search its database to see whether this person is a new subscriber, and send a message welcoming a new reader or welcoming back an old subscriber.

Today Notes offers instant messaging to the corporation as well as Web conferencing that facilitates sharing information among participants. IBM describes some current Notes applications on its Web site:

- A global *Fortune* 100 investment fund company uses both Lotus Instant Messaging and Lotus Web Conferencing to streamline its meeting process and rein in what had been its high cost of travel. Now the solution has grown to where the company is now hosting 1,500 internal and external Web conferences per month, many of which support up to 15,000 attendees.

- A leading European bank offered its trader community Lotus Instant Messaging for securely sharing real-time information. By archiving the messages, they not only share worldwide in real time, brokers/dealers are able to retain and track customer correspondence. The company is able to integrate Lotus Instant Messaging easily with little training costs. By using Lotus Instant Messaging, the bank greatly increased the effectiveness of their traders.

Other significant adopters of the system include General Motors Europe, major consulting firms, and several major accounting firms including Peat Marwick and Coopers & Lybrand. A study of how one consulting firm used the technology revealed that Notes was not used extensively to manage customer engagements. Rather, the firm used Notes internally to improve administration.

Just as with any other company, a consulting firm has to manage itself. This consultant, with revenues in excess of $2 billion a year, has to administer personnel, manage billings and collections, administer contracts, and perform a wide variety of administrative tasks. The practice manager for the Northeast described how Notes improved his operations. The

MANAGEMENT PROBLEM 19-2

In one study, Orlikowski worked with a group of consultants to understand how groupware supported their activities. The consultants were supposed to use Lotus Notes to help manage knowledge developed on their projects. The consulting firm was large and wanted to have a knowledge base that recorded clients' experiences. When a new client approached the firm, the idea was that a consultant could search the knowledge base and find out whether any other consultants had worked on a similar engagement. Because the consulting firm is selling knowledge and expertise, having access to knowledge developed throughout the firm could be especially valuable in selling and executing assignments for clients.

It turned out that the Notes application was not as successful as management had hoped. A lot of junior consultants did not use the system heavily, and they certainly did not use it to its potential. Although many factors affect how people use systems, Orlikowski concluded that the firm rewarded consultants for individual success, but the Notes system benefited groups, not individuals. For a junior consultant, the system provided few benefits, and using it did not advance an individual's career.

What kind of incentives do managers need to create for knowledge management systems to be successful? How can one of these systems benefit those who are expected to contribute information as well as those who make use of the contributions?

firm had developed a number of administrative applications. His group of direct-reports from around the region was able to dramatically reduce the number of meetings through the use of groupware.

J.P Morgan Chase is another major Notes site with thousands of users across a highly distributed network. Lynda Applegate and Donna Stoddard (1993) reported on the use of Notes at Chemical Bank prior to its merger with Chase. At Chemical, it was the Corporate Systems Division (CSD) that first became interested in groupware. The senior VP of corporate systems was launching a productivity program to generate more output from the design and programming staff at the bank. He felt that the division's work was communications intensive and that it was breaking down using conventional forms of communicating. His estimate was that Notes would allow a 15 percent productivity improvement for a staff whose salaries totaled $15 million a year. The VP also viewed a test in CSD as a good preview for rolling out Notes to the rest of the bank.

The bank brought in a groupware consultant and offered training in the use of Notes in anticipation of its implementation. The VP hired a full-time Notes specialist and formed a Notes support group to assist users. Rollout began with twenty senior managers and their secretaries. In a period of less than two years, 300 CSD employees were using Notes and the bank developed more than ninety applications with Notes.

In the middle of this effort, Chemical decided to centralize IT resources, and then initiate a 40 percent reduction in IT staff. Shortly thereafter, Chemical Bank announced its merger with Manufacturer's Hanover Bank. During this period, turmoil ruled the systems division. One major application the VP initiated was the "rumor mill." Concerned employees could post rumors to the rumor mill database, and senior managers would respond. The VP felt that this simple technique helped create a feeling of trust and openness in the group.

One manager remarked that Notes let developers create applications quickly to respond to a business need. It also helps create geographic independence. In one application a group in New York worked with developers at a Texas bank owned by Chemical. Notes also helps make work independent of time because it reduces the need for face-to-face communications.

A *Wall Street Journal* staff writer found that groupware tended to erode the hierarchical nature of organizations. In some cases, however, groupware created problems for management. The Chemical VP resigned after the Manufacturer's Hanover merger and his successor eliminated the rumor mill. It seemed that the forum became "unruly" and began to receive a number of cutting criticisms of management.

The thrust of the report, however, was more positive. The reporter talked to various managers who felt that groupware helped dissolve corporate hierarchy by making it easy to share information. The rank and file can join discussions with senior management if given access to groupware.

One major contribution of groupware is providing organizational knowledge where it is needed. A worldwide consulting firm such as Accenture, with thousands of employees, has a great deal of expertise. A consultant in Japan needs a way to find out if the company solved a problem similar to the one in some other country; Accenture uses groupware to provide this knowledge base. An important role of groupware is to capture organizational knowledge and make it available anyplace in the firm.

Of course, a few cautions are needed. Like the phone or any other network, the system works only if everyone who needs to be involved has access. Networks only become useful to service providers and consumers when they reach a critical mass. Another major threat to Notes is the World Wide Web; a number of companies are posting information to the Web rather than using a groupware system. Morgan Stanley uses an intranet to present information such as telephone directories, equity analysis reports, and SEC filings. These applications could also be implemented with Notes. It will be interesting to see whether Lotus and IBM are able to coopt the threat of the Internet with their Domino Internet Notes server.

THE OPTIONS

Groups of people can work together electronically in a number of ways. Figure 19-2 is a useful framework for thinking about the options. When people work at the same time in the same place, then a group decision support system and an electronic meeting room can provide support for their shared tasks. Working from different locations at the same time leads to an increasing interest in videoconferencing, especially using the Internet. Chat rooms are another possibility, though they do not seem all that popular in business. If those with a

FIGURE 19-2 Framework for electronic coordination.

		Time	
		Same	**Different**
Place	**Same**	Group decision support systems, electronic meeting rooms	Groupware e-mail
	Different	Videoconferencing, chat rooms	Groupware e-mail

shared task are only able to communicate at different times, then location is not as important. Groupware and e-mail are two technologies that facilitate asynchronous communications.

Building Knowledge Bases

The chapter began with a discussion of knowledge; one of groupware's features is its ability to create knowledge bases that you can use to search and retrieve organizational knowledge. Zeta Corporation used Notes to build a database of customer problems and their resolution; after a few months this database became the first place customer service personnel looked when a customer called in with a problem. Many companies today are creating customer service databases using a variety of software, and these databases represent a vast knowledge base that is growing on the Web.

Hewlett-Packard has been experiencing paper feed problems with one of its popular printers. A customer visiting its Web site is quickly directed to an order form for a free repair kit to replace the pads feeding the paper. Raymarine makes a variety of electronics and instruments for commercial and recreational boats. It has a simple knowledge base on the Web that consists of the familiar FAQs—frequently asked questions—about its products. The database is searchable, so an individual can enter keywords describing a problem and the Web site returns related answers. A caller with a problem concerning marine growth fouling the impeller on a speedometer quickly found a recommended solution. He should use a water-based anti-fouling paint that does not interfere with the electrical signals in the instrument.

Customer service applications that make firm knowledge available to customers with problems represent a high-return investment for companies. These knowledge bases become more knowledgeable over time as more and more questions and their resolution are added. Second, customer service is better because the customer does not have to wait on the phone for someone to provide help. Finally, the company saves money because it does not have to employ as many customer service representatives or maintain as much phone equipment for callers.

CHAPTER SUMMARY

This chapter explored knowledge, information, and the role of managers in the organization. In the earlier discussion of strategy, knowledge was described as a key resource. It is also the basis for theories of core competence in business organizations. Knowledge is difficult to identify, explain, and process in a computer system. It is easy to describe data; turning data into information requires that someone interpret its meaning. Information is a part of knowledge, but know-how must be added to create knowledge.

Most information technology has been directed to tasks that are not key to a manager. Groupware and knowledge repositories come closer to helping a manager in daily work. Making knowledge available in the organization can be a great competitive edge for companies such as consulting and accounting firms. One of the products they sell is experience and knowledge, and they want to "reuse" some of this experience by making it available to new clients with similar problems. Knowledge bases for customer service offer better service at a lower cost.

Developing an application that supports knowledge management is a different kind of task than implementing an ERP package. However, the payoff from knowledge, given that it is pervasive from the factory floor to the CEO's office, is likely to be high.

KEYWORDS

Coordination	Interpretation	Management by walking around
Decision maker	Know how	Scheduled meetings
Disturbance handler	Knowledge	Spokesperson
Explicit knowledge	Knowledge base	Tacit knowledge
Groupware	Leader	Unscheduled meetings

RECOMMENDED READINGS

Davenport, T. H., and Glasser, J. 2002. Just-in-time delivery comes to knowledge management. *Harvard Business Review*, *80*(7), pp. 107–112.

Davenport, T. H., Harris, J. G., and Kohli, A. K. 2001. How do they know their customers so well? *Sloan Management Review*, *42*(2), pp. 63–73.

Hansen, M., Nohria, N., and Tierney, T. 1999. What's your strategy for managing knowledge? *Harvard Business Review,* March–April, pp. 106–116. (Some sound advice on knowledge management strategies.)

Management Science, *49*(4), April 2003. (An issue devoted to research papers about knowledge in organizations.)

Purvis, R., Sambamurthy, V., and Zmud, R. 2001. The assimilation of knowledge platforms in organizations: An empirical investigation. *Organization Science*, *12*(2), pp. 117–135. (A study of the diffusion of a knowledge platform in organizations, in this instance, a tool to support systems development; the article addresses some of the problems in encouraging employees to use an IT tool for knowledge management.)

Soo, C., Devinney, T., Midgley, D., and Deering, A. 2002. Knowledge management: Philosophy, processes, and pitfalls. *California Management Review*, *44*(4), pp. 129–150.

DISCUSSION QUESTIONS

1. What is information? How does it differ from raw data?

2. What is knowledge? What are the two types of knowledge discussed in this chapter?

3. What are a manager's roles according to Mintzberg?

4. Given the current attention focused on CEOs and boards of directors, which of these roles seems most important for the senior managers of the firm?

5. What kind of knowledge do workers on the factory floor possess?

6. How might managers encourage hourly workers to share their information?

7. Does workers' knowledge of their jobs belong to the organization, the worker, or both?

8. What are the various ways in which groupware can be used?

9. How does groupware help with a manager's coordination tasks?

10. How can knowledge be considered a competitive advantage? What kind of knowledge provides an advantage?

11. How can knowledge be a part of the core competence of an organization?

12. Are the knowledge needs of a consulting firm any different from those of a manufacturing company?

13. How does a firm increase its stock of knowledge? Can technology help?

14. How is a knowledge base used in customer service?

15. It has been suggested that the Web is one of the world's largest knowledge bases. Do you agree? Why or why not?

16. How can knowledge management applications reduce costs for a firm?

17. What are the capabilities of a product such as Lotus Notes?

18. Does Notes provide any functions that one cannot obtain from Web tools?

19. How can the firm protect its knowledge and keep it from competitors?

20. Do you think it is possible to communicate tacit knowledge? If so, how?

21. How might someone turn explicit knowledge into tacit knowledge?

CHAPTER 20

TECHNOLOGY HAVES AND HAVE NOTS: THE DIGITAL DIVIDE IN THE U.S. AND THE WORLD

A Manager's Perspective

If the digital divide exists, a manager might be interested in it for a number of reasons. One good reason is customers: If you have an online store and a significant proportion of your potential customers cannot access it, then the store will be less successful than it could be. Also, jobs in the United States increasingly require some knowledge and use of information technology. Although workers may be exposed to some of this technology in schools and libraries, it is a good idea for them to reinforce these experiences with technology at home. A look at the world as a whole reveals that developing countries are falling further behind the developed countries in technology. If you believe that technology is going to be a key feature of all successful economies, then less-developed countries are likely to continue to face problems associated with poverty, and they certainly will not be major players in the world economy. Think about the digital divide in terms of customers and workers, and in terms of the instability that is often associated with developing countries that lag far behind the postindustrial democracies.

As you might expect, the first families to purchase personal computers tended to be well educated and in the upper income ranges in the United States. As computers became more important in education, data supported the view that children from poor families, especially minority children, were falling behind their more affluent peers. Particularly as technology became more pervasive in the workplace, children leaving school with little exposure to computers would be at a tremendous disadvantage in finding employment and succeeding on the job.

The U.S. government noticed the technology and Internet revolution, and undertook a number of programs to provide greater access to computers and the Net for students. For example, the Clinton administration had the goal of connecting all schools in the country to the Internet. An Education Department program subsidized community technology centers for students and for adult education, and the Commerce Department's Technology Opportunities Program provided money and services to organizations that would benefit from technology.

Two reasons explain why the digital divide is important for business: customers and employees. On the customer side, a retailer would like to reach as many potential shoppers as possible; if a substantial number of people do not have Internet access, an online store can only achieve part of its potential. The more people with Internet access, the greater is the opportunity for sales. Retail sales create the demand for a variety of products and help drive the economy. The second reason the digital divide is of concern to managers is the quality of the workforce. Technology is everyplace in business, from the corner drugstore to the factory with computerized manufacturing equipment. In the economy of the twenty-first century, a skilled worker must be knowledgeable about information technology.

THE DIVIDE IN THE UNITED STATES

A recent report sponsored by the Ford Foundation and prepared by Leslie Harris and Associates in July 2002 found that the divide, even though it still exists in the United States, has narrowed in the past few years. That report stated the following:

> [A]lmost 90 percent of school age children now use computers, and rates of use between children of different backgrounds are narrowing. These gains can be attributed to federal programs like the E-rate, which has made Internet service affordable for 95 percent of public libraries and 98 percent of public schools.

> [T]he data in the report demonstrates that not everyone is adopting these tools at the same speed and identifies the groups that are progressing at a slower rate. Significant divides still exist between high- and low-income households, among different racial groups, for people with disabilities, as well as between northern and southern states and rural and urban areas.

By September 2001, nearly 90 percent of all school-aged children use computers and 58.5 percent use the Internet, mainly to complete school assignments.[1] Just over 80 percent of children (ages ten to seventeen) in the lowest income category were using computers at school, little difference from the 88.7 percent of children at the highest income level. In the lowest income category, however, only 33.1 percent of children use computers at home, in contrast to 91.7 percent of children in the highest income category. (See Figure 20-1.) The gap in computer use narrows, however, from almost sixty points between the

FIGURE 20-1 Computer use among ten- to seventeen-year-olds by race origin and location, 2001.[2]

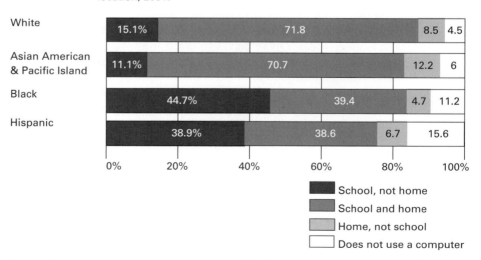

SOURCE: Information based on data from the U.S. Department of Commerce, *A Nation Online.* February 2002. www.ntia.doc.gov/ntiahome/dn/html/anationonline2.htm.

highest and lowest income children's use at home to a twelve-point gap in computer use when home and school are combined.

- *Schools are closing the gap for minorities without computer access at home.* Hispanic and Black children—who have lower computer use rates at home—approach computer use rates of Whites and Asian American/Pacific Islanders largely due to their computer use in school. A far higher percentage of Hispanic (38.9 percent) and Black (44.7 percent) children rely solely on schools to use computers than do Asian/Pacific Islanders (11.1 percent) and White children (15.1 percent). The availability of school computers makes overall computer use rates among children of different racial and ethnic backgrounds comparable.

- *Libraries play critical role in Internet access for low-income families.* Ten percent of Internet users access the Internet at a public library. Reliance on Internet access at public libraries is more common among those with lower incomes than those with higher incomes. Just over 20 percent of Internet users with household family incomes of less than $15,000/year use public libraries. As household income rises, not only does the proportion of public library Internet users decline, but also the percentage of Internet users without alternative access points also declines. In sum, the data in the report make clear that schools and libraries are helping to equalize the disparities that would otherwise exist in computer and Internet use among various household income categories and racial groups. The success in expanding access in schools and libraries has not however, solved the problem of home access.

- *The Income Gap: Rates of adoption rise more slowly for low-income users.* Although computer and Internet use is rising for all Americans across income, large gaps remain between low-income and high-income consumers. For many, cost remains the most important reason not to acquire Internet access at home. Not surprisingly, as income levels drop, the importance of cost rises. (See Figure 20-1 and Table 20-1.)

- Seventy-five percent of people who live in households where income is less than $15,000 and 66 percent with incomes between $15,000 and $35,000 are not yet using the Internet. In contrast, 67.3 percent of Americans making $50,000–75,000/year and 78.9 percent of people making over $75,000/year use the Internet. (See Figure 20-2.)

- *Children in low-income households have significantly less access to Internet.* While computers in schools have been critical to narrowing the technology gap for low-income children, they remain significantly behind in Internet access. Nearly four times as many children (ages ten to seventeen) go online only at school when they live in a household in the lowest income category (20.8 percent) than at the highest income level (5 percent). Additionally, home Internet use is much higher for those who live in high-income households. Children in families at the lowest income level have an overall Internet use rate about half that of children at the highest income level.

- *The Racial Gap: Blacks and Hispanics trail far behind.* In September 2001, computer use rates were highest for Asian American/Pacific Islanders (71.2 percent) and Whites (70 percent). Among Blacks, 55.7 percent were computer

TABLE 20-1 Percent of U.S. households with Internet access by income.[3]

Family income	1997	1998	2000	2001
Less than $15,000	9.2	13.7	18.9	25.0
$15,000–$24,999	11.6	18.4	25.5	33.4
$25,000–$34,999	17.1	25.3	35.7	44.1
$35,000–$49,000	22.8	34.7	46.5	57.1
$50,000–$74,999	32.3	45.5	57.7	67.3
$75,000 and above	44.5	58.9	70.1	78.9

users. Less than half of Hispanics (48.8 percent) were computer users. During the same year, Internet use among Whites and Asian American/Pacific Islanders hovered around 68 percent, while Internet use rates for Blacks (30 percent) and Hispanics (32 percent) trailed behind. (See Table 20-2.)

■ *The gap is even greater for Spanish-speaking households.* In September 2001, only 14.1 percent of Hispanics who lived in households where Spanish was the only language spoken used the Internet. In contrast, 37.6 percent of Hispanics who lived in households where Spanish was not the only language spoken used the Internet.

■ *Native Americans have little access to even basic communications technology.* Of rural Native households, only 22 percent have cable television, 9 percent have personal computers, and of those, only 8 percent have Internet access.

■ *The Disability Gap: People with disabilities are online 50 percent less than the population average.* People with disabilities tend to use computers and the Internet at rates far below that of the average population. On average, only 25.4 percent of the population ages three and above with at least one disability uses the Internet.[4] Of senior citizens (over age sixty), 30 percent report having a disability—making

FIGURE 20-2 Percent of U.S. households with Internet access by income.[5]

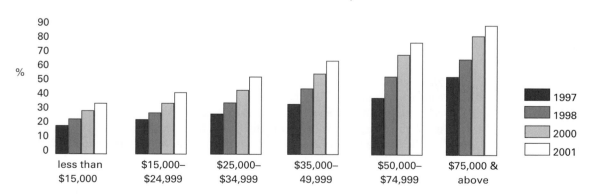

SOURCE: Information based on data from the U.S. Department of Commerce, *A Nation Online.* February 2002. www.ntia.doc.gov/ntiahome/dn/html/anationonline2.htm.

TABLE 20-2 Percent of U.S. households with Internet access by race, 2001.[6]

Location	White	Black	Asian American/ Pacific Islander	Hispanic
U.S.	55.4	30.8	68.1	32.0
Rural	51.0	24.4	68.2	29.9
Urban	57.2	31.6	68.1	32.2
Central cities[7]	54.8	27.4	63.1	29.8

SOURCE: Information based on data from the U.S. Department of Commerce, *A Nation Online.* February 2002. www.ntia.doc.gov/ntiahome/dn/html/anationonline2.htm.

them the most represented age group within the population reporting a disability and the least likely to have access to a computer at home or out of the home.[8]

■ *Blue-collar and unskilled workers have little access and few opportunities to develop technology skills.* In 2001, 73.2 percent of employed people (age sixteen and older) were computer users and 65.4 percent were Internet users.[9] And although nearly 57 percent of adults use a computer at work (and 74 percent of these use the Internet), computer use is concentrated in white-collar jobs. The proportion of people using a computer at work was 80.5 percent for people in managerial and professional specialty occupations and was 70.5 percent for people in technical, sales, and administrative support occupations. At the other end of the spectrum, only about one in five persons used a computer at work in the occupation categories for operators, fabricators, and laborers as well as for farming, forestry, and fishing.

A Cause for Optimism

The preceding report and other government data offer some cause for optimism in the United States. Schools and libraries are helping to close the digital divide among wealthy and poor children, and among the races. Clear inequalities still remain, but it appears that most children are exposed to computers at school, and that Internet use is increasing. It will take a concerted effort by the government, business, and local schools to increase computer use and Internet access at home for those with lower incomes and for minorities.

THE GLOBAL DIGITAL DIVIDE

The digital divide among nations is larger than the divide in the United States. As discussed in this section, the gap between wealthy and poor countries is widening, and the consequences of this gap can be quite severe. The Internet and information technology (IT) represent a revolution that may well have an economic impact corresponding to waves of innovations that began with England's Industrial Revolution more than two centuries ago. Because these waves of innovation occurred and were most exploited in relatively few parts of the world, they dramatically increased global economic inequalities. Economic inequalities became associated with discrepancies in political power among nations. During the nineteenth and the first half of the twentieth centuries, these discrepancies led to imperialism and

MANAGEMENT PROBLEM 20-1

Morgan Mining is thinking about buying a mining company in a South American country. The company is concerned about a variety of problems in the country, including political instability, an insurgency, and vast poverty among the country's Indian population. The CEO said, "The stereotype of a miner as a huge, hulking worker with a pick and shovel is pretty outdated. In open pit mining we use global positioning system (GPS) receivers to map out ore pockets and direct the equipment on where to operate. We use fairly sophisticated computer programs to help us run all aspects of the mine. One of the reasons we think we can turn around this money-losing mine is because of our technology."

The CEO went on, "But we've got real concerns about the ability of the population to work in our environment. We try to pay fair wages and to minimize environmental damage from mining, but workers have to adapt to the way we run a mine, and that involves using technology. Does it make sense for us to buy this mine?"

The CEO has asked you for an analysis of the country and the potential for Morgan Mining if it buys this property. What actions would you recommend the company take if it does establish a base in this South American country? Does it have a responsibility to help improve the level of technological literacy for its workers? For the country in general? What can one company do?

large-scale warfare. The last half of the twentieth century brought concerted efforts to reduce global economic inequalities, with mixed results at best.

Web Inequality

The estimate of more than 600 million users of the Internet worldwide today is expected to more than double by 2005. A U.N. Human Development Report (1999) noted that the lead of the United States in Internet development resulted in 80 percent of Web sites being in English and 26 percent of Americans using the Web, whereas only 3 percent of Russians, 0.04 percent of South Asians, and 0.02 percent of people in Arab states do so. A United Nations summit in late 2003 focused on the problem that much of the content of the Internet is meaningless to people outside of English-speaking countries. The challenge is not just to get technology into people's hands, it is to get them to use it. Because more purchasing power resides in the West, private firms build sites for the developed countries. The statistics are not good: 1.5 billion villages have no access to phones and the Internet, and 70 percent of users live in countries that constitute only 16 percent of the world's population. Many potential users are illiterate, though projects are underway to translate text into speech.

The United States has more computers (potential Web access) than the rest of the world combined. Moreover, an American can buy a computer with a month's salary, a Bangladeshi would need eight years' income to buy one. Nielsen estimates that 58 percent of U.S. homes have Internet access as of July 2002. By implication, the reduction in worldwide economic inequality that occurred in the last half of the twentieth century is being reversed, contrary to the rosier scenarios of some economists who argue that the recent reductions in inequality are likely to continue in the twenty-first century.

An optimistic scenario has developing countries adopting the Internet to stimulate economic growth. Many stories describe artisans in poor countries marketing their products worldwide through a Web site. The Internet is promoted as a technology that will enhance education and expand commerce, allowing developing countries to make rapid advances.

The Internet is a kind of technological infrastructure, however, and developing countries are notoriously short of infrastructure. The Internet also requires a level of education and training to use, and educational opportunities in poorer countries are generally inferior to those in wealthy countries. Unfortunately, data show that poor countries are almost "off the screen" as far as Internet capabilities. The data suggest that what appear to be key determinants of the Internet's penetration in more developed country settings have almost no explanatory power for developing countries. If this situation persists, most of the continued diffusion of Internet technologies will occur in wealthy countries, and the likelihood increases—based on the historical impacts of earlier network technologies—that economic inequality and political and social instability will increase in the world.

New Technologies and Economic Inequality Among Nations: Historical Perspectives

Two to three centuries ago the world's major regions and societies knew far less economic inequality than today. From then to the present, as is evident from Table 20-3, the gap in average income per person between rich and poor societies became much wider. In 1700, the United Kingdom was the richest country shown in the table, and its gross domestic product (GDP) per person was about three times that of a person in Africa, the poorest region, and about twice that of the other countries and regions in the table, as well as about twice the world average in 1700. Even in 1820, GDP per person in the United Kingdom was only two times the world average and but three times that of China and India, and four times that of Africa.

Contrast the 1700 and 1820 figures with those for 1998, when the United States was the richest country with a GDP per person almost five times the world average (and nearly six times the world average excluding the United States). In 1998, the U.S. figure is approximately nine times that for China, sixteen times that for India, and twenty times that for Africa as a whole. At the extremes, U.S. GDP per person in 1998 was thirty to forty times the level of many individual countries in Asia and Africa, and more than fifty times the level in Afghanistan and Chad.

What raised the gap between rich and poor nations from a ratio of 2 or 3 to 1 to a gap of 30, 40, or 50 to 1 in two centuries? No one knows for sure whether to expect the gap to be narrowed in the years, decades, and century ahead. Economists and economic historians

TABLE 20-3 Real GDP per capita relative to world average, selected countries/regions, 1700–1998. (World average GDP = 100 at each date.)

Year	U.K.	U.S.	France	Japan	China	India	Africa	Latin America
1700	203	86	160	93	98	89	65	86
1820	256	188	184	100	90	80	63	100
1870	368	282	216	85	61	61	51	81
1913	326	351	231	92	37	45	93	100
1950	327	452	249	91	21	29	40	121
1973	293	407	320	279	20	21	33	110
1998	328	479	343	358	55	31	24	102

SOURCE: From Lucas and Sylla, "The Global Impact of the Internet: Widening the Economic Gap Between Wealthy and Poor Nations?" *Prometheus Journal*, www.tandf.co.uk. Derived from Maddison (2001), Table B-21, p. 264.

are far from agreement on the answers to these questions. Some espouse a traditional view that major technological innovations associated with the Industrial Revolution for the past two centuries catapulted some nations and world regions ahead of others. Moreover, they suggest, history gives us reasons for optimism about eventually closing the gaps opened by the Industrial Revolution. Nations such as the United States and Japan were once relatively poor, but they became relatively rich. And more recently, nations such as India and China, by growing faster than the world economy as a whole, have reduced the gap between themselves and a steadily increasing world average of GDP per person. Proponents of this traditional view see advantages in being a latecomer to industrialization. Latecomers often grow faster than industrial pioneers, whose innovations they can implement without having to develop them on their own.

A newer view of modern economic history reaches more pessimistic conclusions about the possibilities for reducing gaps between the rich and the poor. In this view, the great economic gaps that emerged over the past two centuries resulted not from industrial technologies that can relatively easily be implemented by latecomers, but from waves of network technologies and network innovations. The innovators who took advantage of network effects or externalities rapidly moved far ahead of others so that gaps in relative incomes grew rather than declined. To the extent such network technologies continue to develop, the rich innovative nations increase their lead, and the world becomes less, not more equal. The United States is the prime example. Already the world's richest nation a century ago, the United States has since increased its lead over most of the rest of the world, as Table 20-3 demonstrates. Now, as the prime innovator of Internet and IT, that lead is likely to increase.

The Traditional View: Advantages of Latecomers

In a recent article, Robert Lucas, a prominent economic theorist and Nobel laureate, utilized these stylized facts of economic history to develop a model predicting that economic inequality in the world would be far lower 100 years from now than it is today (Lucas, 2000). Latecomers to industrialization in Lucas's model grow faster than earlier industrializers by a factor proportional to the average income gap between the two groups, eventually eliminating the gap, and all industrialized countries grow at the same rate. As more and more of the world's countries industrialize, world economic growth slows down, and income gaps among countries are greatly reduced. According to Lucas, this phenomenon has been happening since the middle of the twentieth century, and it is likely to continue over the coming century as more or less the whole world becomes industrialized.

If Lucas is right, the worry of the U.N.'s 1999 Human Development Report, that the tendency of the Internet and other new information technologies increase inequality, is unfounded. They, too, will be incorporated into the world's stock of technology, and with some lag will be adopted by latecomers even more rapidly than by today's leaders. Eventually—maybe in 100 years—all or most countries will be at similar levels of income.

Other reasons, however, support doubt for such a rosy scenario. The model, which does seem to capture some important facts of economic history, is deficient in others. It appears to assume that the world's stock of state-of-the-art technology is relatively unchanging or changing slowly, so that latecomers can avoid the costs incurred by pioneers, and then by growing faster than the pioneers, eliminate the income gaps between them.

The Internet and related IT are epochal innovations such those of the British Industrial Revolution two centuries ago, or the related railroad technologies that came along in the middle decades of the nineteenth century, or the electrical and automotive technologies that were developed in the late nineteenth and early twentieth centuries. If so, these new technologies, like the older ones just mentioned, might well increase inequality in the world for decades, with political and social consequences that do not differ from those that came with inequalities brought by industrialization after 1800.

A New View: The Power of Networks and Network Externalities

A new interpretation of the economic history of the past two centuries puts the possibility that world economic inequality may increase in historical perspective. This new interpretation, while not denying the importance of the great inventions and innovations of the industrial era, gives more emphasis to the importance of network innovations and network externalities in shaping the modern economic world.

In the new view, the Internet and IT are examples of fundamental network technologies that promoted and sustained industrialization where it took place. The earlier network technologies, in order of their appearance, were modern financial systems in the seventeenth and eighteenth centuries (before the Industrial Revolution), early transportation networks (road, canal, ocean and waterway shipping, and, most prominently, railway networks) from the late eighteenth to the late nineteenth centuries, and, finally modern transportation (highway, airway), communication (telegraph, telephone), and electrical networks, which began in the late nineteenth and early twentieth centuries.

Each of these historical network breakthroughs can be associated with the industrialization of the modern world and the income gaps among nations and world regions to which "selective" industrialization led. Financial systems were the first (and least recognized) of the great network technologies of the modern world. The pioneers in financial systems were the Dutch Republic, the British, and the United States. These three countries early in their modern histories had what some have termed *financial revolutions*. In all three, financial networks—banking systems and securities markets, for example—were in place to mobilize and allocate capital before the Industrial Revolution, so that the revolution could advance rapidly without capital-supply constraints.

The early transportation technologies of the nineteenth century, particularly the railways, which developed rapidly from their start in the late 1820s, were classic network technologies. Constructing railway networks was costly and relied on financial system networks already in place for funding. Countries (and individual entrepreneurs) that built and used the new railway network technologies earliest and to the greatest extent prospered the most, while others were left to catch up later or left in the dust. Inequality widened.

Just as the range of applications of industrial technologies increased over time, so too did the range of network technologies. A third wave of network development occurred from the mid nineteenth through the early twentieth century. First came the communications networks represented by the telegraph and the telephone. Then the automobile, followed by the airplane, created the need for new transportation networks, highways on land, and air traffic systems for flight. Simultaneously, electrical networks spread and spawned a host of industrial and consumer applications. These innovations led to more inequalities of income and wealth between the rich and the poor of the world.

From the early decades of the twentieth century to the IT revolutions at its end, no great breakthroughs occurred in network technologies. Without such technological developments, the have-nots of the world could adopt older technologies already developed by the haves and catch up with them, as Robert Lucas predicts. In other words, the poorer countries could install the infrastructure necessary to join the networks established earlier by the richer countries, and disproportionately benefit from doing so when they became members of large networks previously developed by others. By enlarging the network their membership created network externalities for existing participants, who could now reach more members.

With the Internet and other IT advances that arrived in recent years, the world appears to be on the edge of an era when economic inequalities again increase, as they did in the wake of earlier financial, transportation, communication, and electrical network innovations. These past network developments bypassed many people and large areas of the world for long periods of time. Making the rich richer and leaving others behind seems to be a general characteristic of networks technologies.

The Growth and Distribution of the Internet

Which countries are using the Internet today? What is the extent of Internet use among developing countries? What factors predict the intensity of Internet use in a particular country? The answers to these questions are important in formulating policies to assist developing countries in taking advantage of technology.

Data from the World Bank on 1998 economic development indicators, at the time the most recent numbers available, provide some insights on Internet use worldwide. One can add to these data information about the number of Internet hosts in each country from the Internet Software Consortium (ISC) at www.isc.org/ds. A country with a large number of hosts or servers is indicative of more Internet penetration and activity than a country with fewer hosts. The host data were adjusted to take into account some known errors.

No accepted number of hosts has been set as a standard for a country to be considered as having a major Internet presence. The sample of countries is divided at the median host count for 1998, 632 hosts. Countries without much presence on the Internet may be found in Africa, the Middle East, and parts of Asia.

Table 20-4 contains descriptive statistics on the two host subsamples in terms of the development indicator variables in the study. These variables describe and compare countries with a well-developed presence on the Internet with those lacking such a presence, and illustrate the relationship between conventional measures of economic development and Internet presence.

The variables include population and gross domestic product per capita adjusted for purchasing power and recorded in U.S. dollars. Also included is an estimate of the percentage of the average income earned by females in a country; it is a measure of gender equality in the workplace. Life expectancy is a measure of health while literacy rate is indicative of educational levels in a country. The percent of paved roads is a measure of physical infrastructure. In its 1999 *Knowledge for Development Report*, the World Bank uses the number of phones per 1,000 people as a measure of information access. PCs per 1,000 people is an indicator of technology diffusion, but unfortunately, too many missing observations make this variable unusable in statistical analysis of the data.

Comparing countries with fewer than the median number of hosts with those equal to or greater than the median, the adjusted GDP in the first group is 54 percent that of countries having 632 or more hosts. The percentage of average income earned by women is nearly

TABLE 20-4 Descriptive statistics.

Name	Definition	Number of hosts <632		Number of hosts >=632	
		N	Mean	N	Mean
Pop	Population	107	9,451,217	92	50,391,809
Adjgdp	Adjusted GDP PPP$	91	$2,758	83	$5,093
% income/ females	% average income to females	80	33%	83	33%
Lifeexp	Life expectancy	91	60 years	83	72 years
Litrate	Literacy rate	91	68%	83	90%
Roadpav	Paved roads	87	35%	80	61%
Phone1000	Phones/1,000 people	111	92	91	275
PCs1000	PCs/ 1,000 people	25	16	70	78
Hosts95	Internet hosts 1995	46	6	87	55,755
Hosts98	Internet hosts 1998	147	96	94	389,921
Host98Adj	Adjusted hosts 1998	147	105	94	380,738

NOTE: The World Bank's Knowledge for Development Report 1999 uses phone density as a measure of a population's ability to access information.
SOURCE: From Lucas and Sylla, "The Global Impact of the Internet: Widening the Economic Gap Between Wealthy and Poor Nations?" *Prometheus Journal*, www.tandf.co.uk. Derived from Maddison (2001), Table B-21, p. 264.

the same in each group. However, life expectancy and literacy rates are lower in the less-than-632-host group. This group with fewer hosts also has fewer paved roads, PCs, and phones per 1,000 people than countries with 632 or more hosts.

The growth rate of hosts between 1995 and 1998 in the two groups of countries favors countries with less than the median number of hosts. However, the low host group grew from a small base, averaging 6, to 100. This figure compares with more than 380,000 hosts in the greater than median group. The countries with fewer than 632 Internet hosts in 1998 average three orders of magnitude fewer hosts than the countries having more than 632 hosts. OECD data confirm that developed countries, especially the United States, are experiencing greater growth in Internet hosts than poorer nations. OECD data show that between September 1999 and March 2000, the United States added 25.1 Internet hosts per 1,000 inhabitants, the United Kingdom 5.5, Japan 4.1, Germany 3.0, and France 2.7.[10] A significant gap opens up between the countries with little presence on the Internet and countries that have a more substantial presence. Countries with fewer than the median number of hosts on the Internet are a long way behind those with a substantial Internet presence.

Predicting Internet Hosts

To identify what characteristics of a country are associated with a presence on the Internet, the data described in Table 20-4 predict the number of Internet hosts by country in 1998 divided by population. A regression analysis found that adjusted gross domestic product, literacy rate, and phones per 1,000 people explained 61 percent of the variance in the dependent variable, number of Internet hosts divided by population. As others predicted, wealth, education, and infrastructure are associated with a greater presence on the Internet.

The Internet is growing rapidly and the analysis only captures a cross-section at a time when economic and demographic statistics were available. Although countries with fewer hosts are increasing their hosts at a high rate, they are dominated in absolute numbers by countries with a significant Internet presence. It appears from these data that the gap among nations on Internet participation continues to grow. (See Table 20-5.)

The Implications

The analysis demonstrates clear differences between countries that have embraced the Internet and those that have not. Economists argue that wealth is necessary to produce capital and that education and gender equality are important for economic growth. These data support several conditions for development and extend them to technology infrastructure. Higher levels of gross domestic product, higher levels of literacy, and communications infrastructure are associated with greater Internet presence for all countries combined. In those countries having fewer than the median number hosts, the independent variables have little predictive power. However, some evidence indicates that wealth and communications infrastructure are important here. The results on wealth and communications infrastructure are much stronger for countries at or above the median number of Internet hosts. These disparities appear to be growing over time, not diminishing.

The Controversy

Developing countries collect economic statistics infrequently or sometimes not at all, so obtaining accurate estimates of any digital divide are difficult. One recent paper focuses on the African continent, and finds that there, technology poses a real dilemma for its countries (Sonaike, 2004). This article shows that even though all fifty-four African countries have Internet access, at least in their capitals, the impact remains insignificant. If the divide is serious enough, these countries risk becoming irrelevant in the new world.

This chapter identifies a digital divide within and between countries. One side argues that the divide, if it ever existed, is shrinking. However, it is easy to find statistics to support both sides of the argument. When in 2004 a visiting academic from the capital of Azerbaijan has no broadband Internet connection at his office, it suggests huge disparities among countries and individuals in their ability to utilize modern technology. If you believe that technology, especially the Internet, is vital to economic development, then statistics and anecdotes suggest cause for concern.

TABLE 20-5   Average hosts by group over time.

	Hosts in 1995	Hosts in 1998	Hosts in 2001
Hosts < median in 1998	6	134	721
Hosts >= median in 1998	55,756	389,921	1,298,205

SOURCE: From Lucas and Sylla, "The Global Impact of the Internet: Widening the Economic Gap Between Wealthy and Poor Nations?" *Prometheus Journal,* www.tandf.co.uk.

MANAGEMENT PROBLEM 20-2

Although the evidence of a digital divide between the industrialized countries and developing countries is ample, the case for a domestic digital divide within the United States is less clear. Federal and local programs to wire schools and libraries have made Internet access more readily available to the population, especially those of school age. The statistics suggest that marked differences remain in home access to the Internet among different income and ethnic groups in the United States.

Should a lack of Internet access at home for a little under half the population be a concern for a manager?

What advantages come to a company from having a large number of people able to access the Internet? Why might it be enlightened self-interest for a company to find ways to encourage Internet access for the population? What do you think is the maximum percentage of the population that would ever have Internet access from home? How important is the Internet in developing a skilled workforce in the United States?

Modest Progress

Many experiments are taking place to bring IT to underdeveloped countries. Simputer Trust in India created a simple, handheld computer and software that can be used by rural villagers, many of whom are illiterate. The name stands for "simple, inexpensive, multilingual computer," and it has been designed for India, Malaysia, Nigeria, and Indonesia. It will sell for $250–300, which seems expensive for these countries. However, the Trust feels that one Simputer could be used by an entire village to access the Internet. The computer has a simple user interface with limited commands on each screen; a text-to-speech program will help the user make a choice if he or she cannot understand what is on the screen. A farmer in a village could use the device to check cotton prices and sell a crop at the best time. A neighbor could check property records online instead of making a trip to the city. Competing with the Simputer will be wireless Internet access via cell phones.[11]

The government of Thailand embarked on a program to place 50,000 PCs with ordinary citizens, and then expand the total to a million or more. The government approached local electronics firms and asked them whether they could make a $199 computer like the one Wal-Mart was selling on its Web site. It turns out the Wal-Mart computer had a tiny disk drive and no monitor. The government minister guaranteed the purchase of 100,000 machines and asked the Thai Computer Manufacturers trade group to make a much more full-featured computer for $260. The government would take care of delivery and ongoing service. Citizens who get the "people's PC" pick it up at their local post office.

Some fourteen manufacturers are building the machines that have a Celeron processor and twenty-gigabyte hard drive. The computers have open source software and run Linux. Microsoft, threatened already by Linux, offered its software for $36, an incredibly low figure. Now, for a slightly higher price, a user can get a Windows PC instead of the Linux machine.[12] It will be interesting to see whether just putting computers in users' homes is enough. The bigger issue is whether they learn to take advantage of the machine, or whether a training program is needed as well.

Different private companies have programs to help diffuse technology to underdeveloped countries. Hewlett-Packard provides many discounts to developing countries. The company also enters into partnerships with other agencies to reach rural communities around the world. The company is working with a partner that plans to house computers in recycled shipping containers; solar power and satellite communications mean that the units can operate without any kind of electrical or local communications system.

What seems to be lacking is an organized and concerted effort to close the digital divide among nations.

Some Recommendations

The Internet and its associated technologies are important for economic growth. The Litan and Rivlin (2001) study discussed earlier suggests that they are. Another study estimates a 10 percent increase in the relative number of Web hosts in a country is associated with 1 percent greater trade in 1998–1999 (Freund and Weinhold, 2000). If the Internet is an important, transforming technology, then the policy implications need consideration. Various factors inhibit the adoption of the Internet. Some countries tend to see the Internet as an American-dominated technology and therefore, as something to be distrusted. In addition to cultural issues, the Internet requires a group of knowledgeable users to diffuse the technology to others. Many developing countries lack such a corps of dedicated IT professionals.

A number of developing countries have undemocratic governments that are concerned with limiting the free flow of information. Governments may be worried about the ease with which dissident groups can communicate with each other through Web sites and e-mail. The ability to access the Internet opens up a world of Web sites, more than 3 billion pages of information at last count, some of which is critical of nondemocratic forms of government.

Developing countries lack the funds for investing in a telecommunications infrastructure, purchasing computers, and providing education on how to use the technology. The lack of infrastructure, phones, and PCs is a major impediment to Internet adoption. Where the infrastructure exists, Internet access is considerably more expensive in poor countries than in wealthy ones relative to income.

Proposals for Assistance

Specific policy measures might dramatically increase the adoption of the Internet and help poorer nations narrow their substantial technology gap with wealthier countries, but their justification is another matter. If the gap identified between wealthy and poor countries continues to accelerate, and the Internet and IT revolution suggest that it will, poor countries will see stagnating living standards and incomes, while the wealthy countries become wealthier. This phenomenon occurred before in modern history. An increased gap between the rich and poor tends to lead to an environment that encourages political instability, wars within and between nations, and a continuing cycle of misery for the people in affected countries.

Policy measures that might reduce such possibilities by diffusing more rapidly the benefits of Internet technologies throughout the world include:

1. A sustained effort by the United Nations and individual, wealthy countries to build the most appropriate communications infrastructure in developing countries.

2. The dedication of sufficient satellite transponders for two-way Internet access for poor countries using technology now available from DirectPC.

3. An Internet Corps within the U.N. or individual countries modeled after the Peace Corps. This group of aid workers would have as its primary responsibility

SIDE BAR 20-1

Utah Takes Broadband into Its Own Hands

Salt Lake City and seventeen other Utah cities are planning to build the largest, ultrahigh-speed digital network in the United States. If the cities can raise the money, they plan to start construction of the Utopia project in the spring of 2004. The network would be able to supply Internet access to homes and businesses at speeds 1,200 times faster than current commercial services. The network will offer digital television and telephone services over the Net. This project will bring fiber optics to the home or office, eliminating the need for dial-up or the use of slower DSL and cable connections. The estimated total price is $470 million, and it is one of the most ambitious efforts in the world today to deploy fiber-optic cables. It will cost an estimated $1,100 per house to connect to the network with fiber.

Such a project is bound to be controversial, raising questions about the role of the government versus private industry. The cities claim that reliable access to the Internet is vital to their goals of improving education and advancing economic growth. As a result, the proposed fiber-optic network is similar to the role of the government in building roads, bridges, schools, and sewers. It is also common in the Midwest and western United States for municipalities to provide electric power.

Utah views this infrastructure project as key to its future success; it should help attract sophisticated companies and well-educated, high-tech professionals. The network will reach 723,000 residents in 248,000 households and 34,500 businesses. Basic service should cost about $28 a month. Naturally, companies such as Comcast, which reach 80 percent of Utah's residents (to become 90 percent by the end of 2003), are not strong supporters of the Utopia project. Comcast is working to increase its cable modem speeds to three megabits per second, and is investing $350 million in Utah. This speed pales when compared to fiber-optic speeds of 100 megabits per second and higher.

This level of bandwidth is significant. Television needs about six megabits per second to deliver DVD-quality programs over the Internet, and more like eighteen megabits for high-definition TV. Based on state laws, Utopia cannot deliver services directly. It will be a wholesaler that leases space on fiber to companies providing retail digital services. The Utopia project, if successful, could be the stimulus needed to move the country toward really high-speed broadband Internet access.

SOURCE: *The New York Times,* November 17, 2003.

establishing connectivity and training people in less-developed countries on how to access the Internet and how to build Web sites. Part of the aid would be devoted to developing native language Web sites and content.

4. A concerted effort by aid agencies to encourage government policies in developing countries that favor innovation, venture capital, investments in research, and education about technology.

5. A $1 per month surcharge on the Internet accounts of every user in wealthy nations to fund the preceding activities, similar to the surcharge on U.S. phone bills to connect schools to the Internet and provide phone service for low-income subscribers.

6. A 1 percent tax on all electronic commerce dedicated to expanding Internet use in developing countries.

7. An International Developing Countries Venture Capital Fund to allocate the capital raised in points 5 and 6; some of the capital should be applied to infrastructure, and some to new ventures that involve the Internet.

Although taxes and surcharges such as those mentioned in points 4 and 5 would not be popular, they can be justified on economic grounds. Substantial network externalities from the Internet and World Wide Web mean that both buyers and sellers benefit from increasing the number of users of the Net around the world. The more users connected to the Net, the more valuable the Internet is to content providers, who in turn, attract more users. Subsidies from rich to poor countries to increase the Internet network can be justified on grounds that the benefits of expansion of the network, initially at least, may be greater for existing members than for new ones.

The Internet phenomenon is as dramatic a revolution as were the Industrial Revolution and financial, transportation, communication, and electrical network breakthroughs that occurred during the past three centuries. The choices wealthy countries make with regard to the Internet and the communications infrastructure of developing countries may well determine the economic future of half the world's population and the stability of large regions of the globe. The kind of assistance suggested here has the possibility of contributing as much to the countries offering aid as those receiving it.

An Important Consideration

A researcher who visited a number of programs to close the digital divide among nations offers some words of caution (Warschauer, 2003). Many of those attempting to help developing countries fall under the spell of "technological determinism," which is the belief that all one needs to do is provide technology and the problem will be solved. This researcher believes that you cannot solve complex social problems by focusing on equipment. Warschauer describes a number of programs that failed and others that saw limited success. One project in New Delhi was aimed at one of the poorest areas in the city. The city government and a private company set up computers with dial-up Internet access inside a locked booth with monitors and keyboards available through holes in the booth. The idea was for children to learn at their own pace, without any teachers. The Internet connection rarely worked, and the children, with no instruction, generally played games or used the computer to draw.

The point is the need for support and social services as one tries to bridge the digital divide. Providing nothing but hardware will fail in most settings. One must design a system just as for any other IT application. Systems design involves requirements analysis, learning what the users' needs are for the technology. Then you must determine what resources are available and come up with an appropriate design, which depends on whether you are dealing with children in school or with a village of farmers with a low literacy rate or with some other group. Implementation is a key variable here as it is with corporate IT. Technology exists in a complex social setting, and you need to work with intended users of the technology to see how they can best utilize it. Giving people or groups of people a computer is unlikely to accomplish your objectives.

CHAPTER SUMMARY

This chapter discussed two gaps between haves and have-nots, in the United States and between the United States and the rest of the world, focusing on the Internet. Network externalities or effects mean that as additional people make use of a network, its value increases for those who are already users. Significant benefits for business around the world come from having more people using the Internet. Computer and Internet users in general also provide a more skilled workforce. Because the gap is being reduced in the United States, some parties feel that the government should not try to reduce it further. Others argue that both equality of opportunity and the benefits of network externalities mean that an investment in reducing the digital divide in the United States makes sense.

The international gap among nations is troubling, especially if the network analysis is correct in this chapter and technologies such as the Internet continue to widen the differences between wealthy and poor countries. This kind of a gap does not just result in inequality, but it can lead to instability in regions of the world and significant antagonism toward wealthier countries. Right now some international efforts by the United Nations and others are aimed at improving the situation, but these programs are limited.

KEYWORDS

Computer use

Disability gap

Economic development

Externalities

Income gap

Industrial Revolution

Innovation

Instability

Internet access

Latecomers

Network effects

Racial gap

Technology revolution

RECOMMENDED READINGS

Barabasi, Albert-Laszlo. 2002. *Linked: The New Science of Networks*. Cambridge, MA: Perseus Publishing.

Harris, Leslie, and Associates. 2002. *Bringing a Nation Online: The Importance of Federal Leadership.*

Hart, S., and Christensen, C. 2002. The great leap: Driving innovation from the base of the pyramid. *Sloan Management Review*, Fall, pp. 51–56. (The authors present compelling arguments for improving the conditions for people in developing countries.)

Kedia, B., and Bhagat, R. 2002. Cultural constraints on transfer of technology across nations: Implications for research in international and comparative management. *Academy of Management Review*, *13*(4), pp. 559–571.

Landes, D. 1998. *The Wealth and Poverty of Nations: Why Some Are So Rich and Some So Poor.* New York: W.W. Norton & Co.

Litan, R., and Rivlin, A. (eds.). 2001. *The Economic Payoff from the Internet Revolution*. Washington, DC: Brookings Institution Press.

Lucas, H. C., Jr., and Sylla, R. 2003. The global impact of the Internet: Widening the economic gap between wealthy and poor nations? *Prometheus*, Spring. (The article providing much of the data on the digital divide among nations.)

Lucas, Robert E., Jr. 2000. Some macroeconomics for the 21st century. *Journal of Economic Perspectives, 14,* pp.159–168.

Maddison, A. 2001. *The World Economy: A Millenial Perspective.* Paris: OECD.

Sonaike, S. A. 2004. The Internet and the dilemma of Africa's development. *International Journal for Communication Studies*, *66*(1), pp. 41–60.

Petrazzini, B., and Kibati, M. 1999. The Internet in developing countries. *Communications of the ACM*, *42*(6), pp. 31–36.

UNDP. 1998. *Human Development Report, 1998.* New York, Oxford University Press.

UNDP. 1999. *Human Development Report, 1999.* New York, Oxford University Press.

Warschauer, M. 2003. Demystifying the digital divide. *Scientific American*, August, pp. 42–47.

World Bank. 1999. *Knowledge for Development.* Washington: World Development Report.

DISCUSSION QUESTIONS

1. What is a digital divide?

2. Why might minority children have less home access to computers than others?

3. What is the major deterrent for Internet home access?

4. What roles do schools play in reducing the digital divide?

5. What do libraries contribute to a reduction in the divide?

6. What are the major factors that help a country improve the wealth and well-being of its citizens?

7. Why is literacy so important in reducing the digital divide among countries?

8. Why would gender equality help a country's economy?

9. What kind of infrastructure is needed for Internet access in a country?

10. What are the solutions for Internet access in a country that lacks roads, electricity, and phone service?

11. Just providing a computer and Internet connection may not be enough. What other help does a developing country need to close the digital gap with wealthier nations?

12. How could schools and libraries in developing countries help spread the Internet?

13. What are network effects, and what is their implication for the digital divide?

14. Do you feel that the digital divide is sufficiently closed in the United States, and that the federal government does not need to address it any longer?

15. In what ways might the wealthy countries help finance the expansion of the Internet in poor countries?

16. How is the Internet revolution similar to the Industrial Revolution? How are they different?

17. What are the possible outcomes of a tremendous inequality between poor and wealthy countries?

18. Why do you think the United States has adopted the Internet so extensively?

19. Do you think the U.S. government or industry should subsidize broadband Internet access for poor families? For those over sixty or sixty-five years old?

20. What can an individual manager or company due to reduce the digital divide?

ENDNOTES

1. Unless otherwise indicated, all charts and graphs are based on data from U.S. Department of Commerce, A Nation Online, February 2002. Available at www.ntia.doc.gov/ntiahome/dn/ index.html.

2. www.ntia.doc.gov/ntiahome/dn/html/anationonline2.htm.

3. www.ntia.doc.gov/ntiahome/dn/html/anationonline2.htm.

4. Disability as defined for this purpose includes: blind or severe vision impairment, deaf or severe hearing impairment, difficulty walking, or difficulty typing.

5. www.ntia.doc.gov/ntiahome/dn/html/anationonline2.htm.

6. www.ntia.doc.gov/ntiahome/dn/html/anationonline2.htm.

7. A central city is the largest city with in a metropolitan area, as defined by the Census Bureau. Additional cities within the metropolitan area can also be classified as central cities if they meet certain employment, population, and employment/residence ratio requirements.

8. Part of the reason only 25.4 percent of people with disabilities use the Internet is because the population of people with disabilities is heavily weighted towards older Americans.

9. In contrast, only 40.8 percent of people who were not employed were computer users and 36.9 percent were Internet users.

10. *The Wall Street Journal,* June 21, 2000.

11. *Scientific American,* October 2002.

12. *The Wall Street Journal,* August 14, 2003.

CHAPTER 21

ETHICAL ISSUES AND A LOOK AHEAD

A Manager's Perspective

A professor teaching in an ethics program was often asked whether anything could be done about ethics by the time someone is an adult. Learning ethics takes place as one grows up. Events in the early twenty-first century make it clear that some managers did not learn ethics early on, and that some guidance about what is ethical behavior is necessary. Consider a man who chaired the audit committee of a well-known company that is now in bankruptcy. He went from an accounting professor to dean of a business school. His early actions were always ethical and beyond reproach. Yet the audit committee permitted some of the behavior that led to the company's downfall. It had to relax standards and the corporate code of ethics to allow the actions that ultimately doomed the company. Perhaps board members became too close to management. Or maybe the board did not understand the likely outcome of its actions. As a result of these scandals, more rules and guidelines now dictate what is permissible in corporate governance. Ethics is an issue throughout the organization and life itself. The easiest test is to ask how you would explain a particular decision to your closest family members, and how it would look if presented on page one of a newspaper.

CORPORATE GOVERNANCE AND IT

The beginning of the twenty-first century witnessed a crisis of confidence in corporate governance in the United States. Several large companies went bankrupt, contributing to a lack of confidence in the financial statements of all companies and a large decline in the stock market.

- Enron, a large energy company, filed for bankruptcy under accusations of improper and misleading accounting. The firm's accountant, Arthur Andersen, appears to have agreed to improper accounting and misleading financial statements because of the tremendous amount of business Enron represented for the accounting firm. Enron established special partnerships that had the effect of removing debt from its balance sheet, hiding it from investors. As this saga unfolds, it appears that major banks such as Citibank and Chase structured complex transactions that made debt look like operating expenses so that it did not have to appear on the balance sheet. As a result of Enron's failure:

  - Arthur Andersen lost many of its clients, lost its license to practice in several states, and disbanded as a firm.

- Investors lost billions of dollars as Enron's stock tumbled and eventually became worthless.

- A significant number of Enron employees lost all of their pension funds, which were required by the company to be in Enron stock.

- A number of Enron senior managers sold stock and exercised stock options worth millions of dollars, while they publicly encouraged people to purchase Enron stock.

- Global Crossing, a communications firm that built or leased a huge network of fiber-optic cables, filed for bankruptcy. The head of the company made tens of millions of dollars by selling stock, while investors ended up with stock having no value.

- WorldCom reported that its chief financial officer had been capitalizing certain expenses, and that its financial statements had overstated profits by $3.8 billion. The CFO scattered charges, such as those for leasing capacity on other carriers' lines, through different capital accounts. These charges were clearly for ongoing operations; they were not a capital investment. Because of this misstatement and suspicion over other WorldCom statements, the company found itself unable to borrow. As a result, it filed for the largest bankruptcy in U.S. history, more than $100 billion. Subsequent investigation raised questions about a total of $11 billion that may have been accounted for improperly.

- Tyco, a large conglomerate, found itself unable to continue growing when its stock price dropped, and the company explored breaking itself up into five smaller units. Shareholders objected and Tyco dropped the plan. Then its CEO was arrested and charged with evading sales taxes and obstruction of justice involving expensive artwork he purchased. He has also been tried for "looting" the company, using corporate funds for personal expenditures. The company appears to be sound, but is in turmoil as new leadership tries to establish its direction.

- The founder of Adelphia Communications, a cable TV firm, and two of his sons were arrested and charged with systematically looting the company of more than $2 billion.

Hearings and investigations of these companies turned up a number of questionable accounting practices. Investors lost confidence in companies' financial statements and fled from investing in the stock market, leading to significant declines during the summer of 2002.

Proposals for Reform

Demands for reforms in corporate governance came from Congress, the SEC, and the stock exchanges, particularly the New York Stock Exchange (NYSE) and the NASDAQ. The Sarbanes-Oxley Act required significant changes in the practice of corporate governance. In theory, the shareholders of a publicly held firm elect the board of directors to represent them. The first duty of the board member is to protect the interests of the stockholders. Company management reports to the board and managers should see themselves as working for the directors. Two principal-agent relationships function here. First, the board is an agent of the stockholders, and second, management is an agent of the board.

Reality may fail to match theory, however. In most instances, management, generally the CEO, chooses board members and proposes them to the shareholders for election. A CEO is likely to nominate board members he or she knows from a personal or business relationship. A CEO wants someone who will be helpful, but not overly critical of the CEO's actions and the firm. Rarely do the shareholders nominate their own slate of directors, nor do nominations come from the floor at the company's annual meeting.

Most of the proposals for reforming corporate governance call for strengthening the independence of boards. Table 21-1 offers a summary of changes the NYSE made in the requirements for companies listed on the exchange as a result of the scandals. An estimated 75 percent of the nearly 3,000 NYSE-listed companies have a majority of independent directors on their boards. However, it is also possible that what the company considers to be independence differs from the NYSE and the shareholders!

TABLE 21-1   NYSE key regulations for corporate governance.

- Requiring independent board members to meet alone without management on a regular basis and establishing the position of a lead independent director to chair these meetings

- Increasing the responsibilities of board audit committees including requirements that they meet alone, with the members of the company's audit firm both with and without management, and with management alone

- Mandating that shareholders vote on all equity-based compensation plans, including stock option plans

- Requiring audit, nominating, and compensation committees to consist solely of independent directors, with a requirement that the chair of the audit committee have accounting or financial management experience

- Tightening the definition of an independent director, a former employee of the firm or its audit firm is not considered independent for five years after his or her employment ends

- Mandating that director compensation represent the sole remuneration from the listed company for audit committee members

- Granting the audit committee sole authority to hire and fire auditors and to approve any significant nonaudit work by the auditors

- Requiring the CEO of NYSE-listed companies to attest to the accuracy, completeness, and understandability of information provided to investors

- Mandating that listed companies adopt and publish corporate governance guidelines and a code of business conduct and ethics

- Establishing a Directors' Education Institute to assist directors in their responsibilities

- Allowing the NYSE to impose additional penalties, including public reprimand letters, in addition to suspension and delisting

- Requiring non-U.S. issuers to disclose how their practices differ from NYSE rules and procedures

Are the Proposals Enough?

The requirements from the NYSE are one example of many calls for the reform of corporate governance. Other suggestions include regulating stock options, because some observers feel stock options motivated managers to manipulate earnings so share prices would keep rising, increasing the value of their options. Congress also passed a bill—the Sarbanes-Oxley Act—which increased penalties for fraud. The SEC is requiring all CEOs and CFOs of publicly held firms to sign and certify the accuracy of their financial statements. Certifying an incorrect statement would open the manager to fraud charges.

Many of these reforms aim directly at the composition of the board of directors and its independence. The NYSE requires that the nominating committee for new board members consist only of current, independent members, eliminating the presence of the CEO. Still, this change may not be enough to assure independence. It is most likely to be the CEO who will make suggestions, so that even an independent nominating committee will be influenced by the CEO, reducing the chances for an independent board.

One suggestion is for the stock exchanges, in conjunction with the SEC, to create a National Directors Board (NDB) that would maintain a database of qualified board members. The NDB would review materials submitted by potential board members and certify that they are qualified. When selected as a candidate for a particular board of directors, the NDB would verify their independence. For example, it would look for business relationships between the potential board member and the company nominating him or her. Nominating committees for different boards could search the NDB database for qualified candidates having particular areas of expertise or characteristics the committee would like to add to its board. Although technology is not the whole solution to the corporate governance problem, it can provide the infrastructure for choosing boards that are more responsive to shareholders and who are free from conflicts of interest involving a firm's CEO.

This proposal is not intended to bypass the CEO completely. The CEO and other managers could and should interview board candidates, and no CEO should be forced to accept a candidate he or she finds objectionable. However, the source of candidates would be removed from company management and really turned over to an independent nominating committee. With this mechanism in place, boards would be more likely to represent shareholders, boards would see a clear role in providing guidance to the company, and managers should see themselves as working for the board rather than vice versa.

Corporate Codes of Ethics

Regulations now require a firm to have a code of ethics, though many firms have had such a code for a long time. It is interesting to note that Enron has a code of ethics, and that the board agreed to suspend it to allow some of Enron's executives to participate in the partnerships that removed debt from the balance sheet. A code is only useful if it is followed.

Raytheon, a large defense contractor, has an extensive Web site devoted to ethics. Its comprehensive ethics statement follows:

Our Reputation—A Foundation Built on Personal Integrity and Ethical Principles

Throughout its history, Raytheon has been a global leader in technology and systems development. Our continued growth, profitability, and prosperity are linked to our employees' ability to make decisions that are consistent with Raytheon's business values and core ethical principles. By embedding these business values and principles in our policies and practices, Raytheon has established an ethical business culture that is accepted by its employees and woven into the fabric of the ways in which we work. We are an exceptional company, committed to:

Integrity. We are honest and forthright in our dealings with employees, customers, suppliers, teammates, competitors, shareholders, and the community. We conduct our business with respect for laws and regulations, and we promote individual responsibility to ensure that all actions are based on the highest ethical standards.

Respect. We treat others as we would want to be treated—attentive to personal dignity and receptive to diversity of ideas. We recognize the value that comes from respecting individuality, personal experience, and varied heritages.

Teamwork. We value teams because they promote trust, openness, challenge, opportunity, and growth. We join with each other, our customers, and our suppliers to provide high-value solutions to complex problems, requirements, and demands.

Quality. We believe that quality and continuous process improvement are fundamental to the way we develop, manufacture, and support our products and services. We are customer-driven—striving to meet and exceed expectations in all that we do.

Innovation. We build on our heritage of technological excellence through creative thinking, novel ideas, and practical solutions. Customer success is enhanced through our technology leadership and program execution. We encourage, recognize, and reward our employees for being creative, resourceful, and productive.

Citizenship. We give back to the communities where we live and work. We serve as stewards of the environment and strive to leave the world better for having been a good corporate citizen in the global marketplace.

These principles support and guide our leadership in establishing the strategic direction of the company. Our employees, representatives, and suppliers are expected to conduct their business in accordance with these ethical principles. We must do more than be compliant with laws, regulations, and policies; we must work according to our ethical principles and endeavor to conduct ourselves in a manner beyond reproach. Raytheon's reputation is based on the personal integrity of each of its employees and those with whom we do business. Sound judgment must be exercised in the service of our reputation as a global business leader, employer of choice, and good corporate citizen.[1]

Many corporations have codes of ethical conduct, and some are quite extensive. A statement of corporate ethics provides guidelines for managers and is a valuable part of corporate governance.

The Role of IT in Corporate Governance

Much of the crisis in corporate governance comes from false and misleading information and the consequent loss of investor confidence in companies and the stock market. The number of accounting rules arises because of the variety of businesses with different kinds of transactions. However, many of the problems described here could have been prevented if managers and their auditors followed the principle that *the purpose of financial statements and disclosure is to provide investors with as much information as possible about the true condition of the company.* Some evidence indicates that the SEC is moving from a reliance on pure technical compliance with generally accepted accounting principles (GAAP), to a requirement that managers see that statements fairly present and give an accurate and complete picture of the business. If Enron's managers and accountants followed this simple guideline, no "off the books" partnerships would have developed to remove debt from the balance sheet. Similarly, WorldCom would not have inflated its profits by capitalizing what should have been treated as operating expenses.

What happened in these companies is partially an information problem, but not an information systems problem. To date, information systems and technology do not appear to share the blame for any of the scandals. Whether technology could have prevented false and misleading earnings reports remains to be determined. Most accounting and financial software assumes that the organization has procedures in place to prevent incorrect and fraudulent entries. You could certainly build software that requires one person to login and make an entry, and a second person to login and verify that entry. The vast majority of companies where such an independent check is not needed would probably ask to have that feature of the software disabled.

Technology can be used to facilitate corporate governance. The first suggestion is the database required for the National Directors Board as proposed earlier. This database would contain information about potential board members and their business relationships and possibly family ties. (The stock exchanges maintain a database of corporate officers, family members, and associates as a part of their efforts to discourage and detect insider trading.) Nominating committees could use a search engine to retrieve potential candidates based on a variety of conditions. For example, a nominating committee might want to locate a board member with expertise in information technology or the life sciences. The database would be available on the Internet, protected by a password provided to a nominating committee for some window of time.

The next contribution of technology is its ability to support communications and collaboration. The independent directors of the firm are to meet regularly, and the audit committee, consisting of independent board members, also must have frequent meetings. Independent board members are likely to be in many different locations; IT can help remove time and space limits on meetings. Boards will, in addition to physical meetings, hold a number of virtual meetings making use of videoconferencing, teleconferencing, and Internet meetings. One concern is that the workload being placed on board members will discourage qualified people from serving; information and communications technology can ease some of the demands that are increasingly being placed on boards.

A company can also set up an Extranet with information for directors. A vice president at Enron, Sharon Watkins, first raised concerns about the firm's accounting practices in a letter to its chairman. Her fears turned out to be justified. An internal auditor at WorldCom discovered the CFO's efforts to put expense transactions in capital accounts. One valuable contribution from information technology would be an anonymous re-mailer that would send comments from employees to the lead independent director. Employee comments could then be anonymous if the employee did not want to be identified as the source of information.

The U.S. capital markets and relationships among business in general rely on trust. When one individual or a group of people violate that trust, creating mechanisms in order to restore trust is necessary. Table 21-2 summarizes the preceding suggestions. Society,

TABLE 21-2   IT and corporate governance.

IT in corporate governance	Contribution
Corporate directors database	Help boards nominate truly independent directors based on their qualifications
Support communications	Facilitate frequent meetings among boards and board committees without requiring participants to be in one location
Directors' Extranet	Provide up-to-date information for board members to peruse at their leisure
Anonymous re e-mailer	To encourage individuals in a company to take their concerns to the board without fear of retribution

business, and financial markets represent a closely coupled system. Unethical behavior by a few managers can lead to bankruptcy for their firm, the loss of thousands of jobs, workers with pensions that are now worthless, and a steep decline in the stock market. Hopefully these experiences will lead to a new awareness of ethics and the responsibilities of management that go beyond the executive suite.

THE ETHICAL USE OF TECHNOLOGY

Well before the corporate governance scandals of 2002, a number of ethical issues concerned information technology. These issues relate to privacy, data collected online, especially from individuals visiting different Web sites, the piracy of digital content, workplace monitoring, security, and spam.

Privacy

The present basis of personal privacy protection is the U.S. Constitution, various Supreme Court rulings, and laws such as the 1971 Fair Credit Reporting Act, the 1978 Right of Financial Privacy Act, and the 1974 Privacy Act, which deals with the release of government records. More recently the Children's Online Privacy Act of 1998 was passed; it prohibits collection of children's information from those thirteen years and younger from Web sites without permission from their parents. Certain Web sites must obtain parental consent before collecting personal information from children. With some exceptions, sites also must obtain parental consent before collecting, using, or disclosing personal information from children (E-Ethics Center, Colorado State University).

The United States and Europe have quite different views of privacy. The European Union has a law that prohibits the purchase and sale of personal data, something quite common in the United States. The law basically makes it illegal to use information about a customer in ways the customer never intended, which means that a firm cannot sell data to another company to use for marketing purposes. A key provision of the law is a prohibition for any company doing business in the European Union from transmitting personal data to a country that does not guarantee comparable privacy protection—namely the United States. The United States has a much more relaxed policy, relying primarily on industry self-regulation. One fear is that this legislation could have a chilling effect on electronic commerce.

The difficulty is in determining at what point the right to privacy conflicts with other rights. Society certainly has the need and the right to have certain kinds of information that contributes to the general welfare. Demographic information and information on income levels are vitally important in establishing national policy. Information on wages and financial conditions, however, is considered to be extremely sensitive by most individuals.

Individuals should have the right to ascertain whether information held about them is correct and to enforce the correction of errors. However, less agreement surrounds the issue of penalties imposed for misuse of private information maintained in some type of data bank. Other questions arise as to whether individuals should have the right to know who requested information about them from a data bank because this requirement forces a great deal of costly record keeping on the part of the owner of the data.

Some legislators in the United States are concerned about the practice of state governments selling data. A number of states sell access to automobile registration data. Direct-mail marketing organizations use auto registration information to target mailings. In other instances, individuals obtain the license plate numbers of a group attending a meeting and use that information to harass the attendees.

The Web introduces another privacy concern: companies collecting information about people who visit their Web site without the visitor's knowledge. The Federal Trade Commission (FTC) conducted a recent survey; a group of agency lawyers surfed the Web for two weeks, visiting some 1,400 sites. Of these sites, more than 90 percent collected personal information from visitors, but only 14 percent of them disclosed how the information would be used. The FTC concluded that some form of formal regulation is needed and that self-regulation of the Internet had largely failed.

A Japanese committee studied privacy issues in Japan and suggested the following guidelines:

- Personal data may only be collected with the consent of the individuals concerned. For example, the recommendation applies to the use of cookies, because using cookies to gather historical information on personal Web access patterns is "possible without the consent of the individuals concerned."

- An individual should have the right to veto the use of personal data, so that personal data already available to an online service provider cannot be used or transferred to a third party without the consent of the individual concerned.

- To ensure the proper management of personal data, a manager within the organization who understands the objectives of the guidelines and who is capable of implementing them should be appointed to manage the personal data. (E-Ethics Center, Colorado State University.)

A number of suggested ethical codes of conduct concerns privacy. The Computer Professionals for Social Responsibility offer the following guidelines from the Code of Fair Information Practices.

- *Promote Information Privacy:* Computer Professionals for Social Responsibility (CPSR) and Privacy International.

- *Stop Data Misuse:* Personal information obtained for one purpose should not be used for another purpose without informed consent.

MANAGEMENT PROBLEM 21-1

Cookies are necessary to make use of many of the features of the Internet. When your browser is set to accept cookies, Web sites you visit will send information to your browser to be stored in the cookies file. Remember that the http protocol is connectionless; the basic protocol does not have a provision for a server keeping track of a connected client. When you access a Web page, the server sends to your computer what you have requested and forgets that you ever made a connection. If you are using the Web to look at different documents, this protocol works fine.

However, if you want to buy something on the Web, the server to which you are connected needs a persistent connection, one that it can use to track your session. A cookie is what allows you to browse Amazon and choose different books to add to your shopping basket. When you connect to different pages, Amazon's server needs some way to associate your request with the market basket it is creating for you. The Amazon server sends identifying information to your browser, which stores that information in the cookies file. If you wonder how some sites greet you by name, it is because the last time you were there the site saved information about you through your browser.

All of this sounds quite useful and innocent. However, given the ability to write cookies on your personal computer, different Web sites could track your use of the Internet and might even be able to tell a competitor about your visit to Amazon. The cookie file could be used to violate your privacy.

What kind of safeguards should companies put in place when they need to use cookies? Should a firm have a code of conduct for how it uses the Internet to deal with customers and suppliers? Do you feel threatened by cookies?

- *Encourage Data Minimization:* Collect only the information necessary for a particular purpose. Dispose of personally identifiable information where possible.

- *Promote Data Integrity:* Ensure the accuracy, reliability, completeness, and timeliness of personal information.

- *Allow Data Inspection:* Notify record subjects about record-keeping practices and data use. Allow individuals to inspect and correct personal information. Do not create secret record-keeping systems.

- *Establish Privacy Policies:* Establish and enforce an information privacy policy. Make the policy publicly available.

As a manager you may be in a position to either collect or purchase data from customers or suppliers. In such a position, you will be concerned about privacy and any other ethical issues involved. You may want to ask how the data you collect could be misused, and how it could damage the customer and your company.

Protection of Intellectual Property

Advances in information technology, especially the Internet, create new opportunities for the piracy of content, a violation of what is often referred to as intellectual property rights. The first concerns about piracy involved illegal reproduction of software and movies. The Asia/Pacific region is considered by most companies to be the largest center of piracy. Estimates of piracy in the People's Republic of China run as high as 98 percent. The score for Russia and Latin America is estimated to be 90 percent. An attorney for Microsoft estimated that the company is losing half its revenue worldwide to piracy. By his calculation, pirates are stealing another whole Microsoft.

The violation of intellectual property rights is not confined to individuals selling pirated copies of software. Anytime you borrow a program a friend purchased with a licensing agreement and install it on your computer, you probably violated the licensing agreement. (Many programs are available without charge on the Internet and through various shareware bulletin boards.) For the software vendor, the misappropriation of its intellectual property rights is a major problem.

The Internet created a significant challenge for companies that sell digital content; for example, entertainment companies are threatened by piracy through illegal downloading. The recording industry resorted to court action to shut down Napster, a site for sharing music without paying royalties. (See Chapter 4.) Other peer-to-peer programs are available, and they accomplish the same kind of sharing without requiring a central site such as Napster. This kind of architecture is much more difficult for the recording industry to influence. In 2003, the Recording Industry Association of American began suing individuals identified as heavy users of peer-to-peer downloading services.

A number of music download services now exist so that music fans can download music, either on a subscription basis or by paying for individual pieces of music. Apple has been successful selling songs for 99 cents each. Usually these services allow a subscriber to make a limited number of copies of the downloaded music. It looks likely that in the near future, the Internet will be the vehicle of choice for most music distribution.

Hollywood is concerned that the same kind of distribution without payment will happen with movies. Some in the technology field feel that the recording industry followed the wrong strategy and should instead figure out how to take advantage of systems like Napster to distribute their products. Content providers might be better off by taking advantage of what technology has to offer rather than trying to stop innovation. Movie distributors fought videotape players, and then found that they made a lot of money from video sales and rentals. The same may be true for distributing content over the Internet.

Monitoring

Some systems offer the opportunity to monitor worker performance closely. An insurance company can determine how long it takes a representative to serve a customer on the telephone. An airline can tell how long a reservations agent takes on each call and how many calls the worker handles in each shift. On the production line, errors are traced back to the individual making them. Control systems also track individual worker productivity. One employee sued her employer for monitoring her e-mail messages.

Many individuals respond negatively to such monitoring. It is possible employees will refuse to work with or try to sabotage systems that closely monitor their work performance. One solution adopted by an automobile manufacturer formed workers into teams; the firm publicizes the performance of the entire team rather than that of individual workers. Team members discuss the team's performance and try to figure out how to do better. Coupled with a team bonus system, this approach to monitoring lets management keep track of production without a severely negative effect on individuals who resent having their performance measured by a computer system.

Security

Closely related to problems of privacy is the issue of system security. Threats to the security and integrity of computer systems are potentially infinite, particularly those systems

SIDEBAR 21-1

Radio Frequency Identification (RFID)

One of the technologies that shows great promise is radio frequency identification. This system is used for automatic toll machines such as E-Z Pass on the U.S. East Coast. A car has an RFID tag mounted on the windshield. As it approaches the toll booth, a reader at the booth generates an alternating magnetic field that serves as a power source for the tag. A charge accumulates in a capacitor in the tag, increasing the voltage in the unit, which then triggers a circuit to transmit its identity code.

The tags are getting smaller and smaller, some are as tiny as a grain of rice. They can be placed in ID cards, wristbands, and purchase tokens. They are beginning to appear in auto key chain antitheft devices and toys. A number of organizations would like to adopt these tags. Airlines think they have great potential for routing and tracking luggage. Carriers such as UPS and FedEx see an RFID tag on every package to make tracking and sorting easier. (The price has to drop to pennies or fractions of a cent for this application to be economical.) Hitachi in Japan claims to have tags small enough to be embedded in paper currency to allow governments to track the movements of cash.

The tags, when molded into product packaging, may eventually replace the UPC code on items in stores. In addition, it is possible to store information on the tag whenever a reader interrogates it. Other ideas call for the tags to be placed in offices and ID badges to track workers. They could also be embedded in buildings as strain gauges deep within a structural element. When interrogated, they would send data on the stresses acting on the building. It appears that their functionality is limited only by users' imaginations in figuring out new uses for RFID devices.

SOURCE: R. Want, "RFID, A Key to Automating Everything," *Scientific American,* January 2004, pp. 56–65.

with widespread accessibility by individuals external to the organization. A number of well-publicized penetrations of various computer systems include a major cancer research hospital's online system. Computer viruses are a major annoyance and cause huge losses of productivity through time spent repairing damage and disinfecting computers. Early in the days of electronic commerce, concerns over the security of credit card data was a major factor inhibiting growth. Today, with secure payments servers and browsers that encrypt credit card information, most online shoppers seem to have accepted the idea of sending a card number over the Internet.

As a manager, you need to ensure that your systems are secure. A major breach of security could cause huge losses for the organization and damage to your customers.

Spam

It has been estimated that well over half the e-mail sent in the world is spam. Of course, one person's spam is another's legitimate promotion of a product for sale. Experts fear that e-mail, one of the great communications and productivity tools from the technology revolution, will be rendered useless by the amount of spam delivered to mailboxes. Spam presents a classic case of the trade-off between an individual's rights to unfettered speech and the desire to be left alone. A tremendous amount of time and resources is devoted to detecting and trying to block spam, imposing a large cost on society. In addition, individuals waste time reading or deleting the spam that arrives with other e-mail. As of this writing, Congress is considering legislation to regulate and reduce spam, just as regulatory agencies are promoting "do not call" lists to reduce the number of phone calls from telemarketers. This legislation is being criticized as too weak to dramatically reduce spam.

MANAGEMENT PROBLEM 21-1

The current corporate governance environment is moving toward more independence on the part of boards of directors. All signs point to a reduction in power for CEOs of publicly held corporations. Audit committees will consist of all independent directors, and their responsibilities have grown. For example, one CEO was very upset when the audit committee of his board became more active; it actually questioned some accounting moves that he wanted to make. As a result, he rearranged the membership of that committee to make it more compliant.

It will be interesting to see whether this CEO is happy with this change now that he and the CFO in the company have to sign the firm's financial statements certifying that the results are accurate. He will be subject to prosecution and a jail sentence for fraud if it later turns out that the company has to restate earnings that he certified.

As a CEO with today's more stringent rules for corporate governance, how do you feel about independent boards? Why should today's CEO view the audit committee that asks a lot of questions as an ally rather than an irritant? What technology should the CEO put in place to help the board meet its responsibilities? How important is the attitude (and humility) of the CEO in bringing about effective corporate governance?

You will have to decide whether a marketing campaign you are planning to launch with thousands of e-mail messages to customers is a service or spam.

ETHICS FOR IT PROFESSIONALS

A professional code of conduct for computer professionals was developed by the Association for Computing Machinery, a society of individuals who teach and work in the field. This code applies peripherally to users and managers who may work with technology, but who do not consider themselves professionals.

Ethical considerations include the following concerns:

- Data in the organization are used for their intended purpose and the intended purpose is legitimate.
- Monitoring of workers is undertaken with their consent, and the data are used to help rather than punish the workers involved.
- Systems and services made available to individuals external to the firm behave as specified and cause no harm to others.
- Systems within the firm are not guilty of harassment.
- Appropriate privacy is maintained, for example, e-mail files are not read by individuals not involved in the exchange of messages.
- Appropriate software copyrights are observed and intellectual property is respected.
- Systems are secure and well controlled.

Ethical decisions arise frequently when dealing with information technology. Mason suggested how to identify and approach a situation where ethical considerations arise.

The crucial point occurs when a moral agent—one that by definition has choices—decides to change the state of information or information technology in a human system.

Changes in hardware, software, information content, information flow, knowledge-based jobs, and the rules and regulations affecting information are among the many things that agents do that affect others. [W]e must use our moral imagination to guide our choices so that we can contribute positively toward making the kind of ethical world in which we want to live and want to bequeath to our future generations. How can we do this? [F]unda-mental is our conscience, aided by our understanding and expertise in information technol-ogy. If we have an inkling our behavior . . . might in some way harm others, we probably should examine our decisions a little more carefully and from an ethical point-of-view.

The facts of an ethical situation can be summarized by four factors. The first factor is to clearly identify the moral agent. Whose actions will bring about the technology-induced change? The next factor is the set of alternative courses-of-action available to the agent. These are the real world acts that will have an effect on the human system under consideration. Acts have consequences, hence the third factor:…delineation of the results that are expected to occur if each act is taken. Finally, it is essential to identify the stake-holders who will be affected by the consequences of the acts…stakeholders have an inter-est in what the agent does. (Mason, 1995, p. 55)

It is easy to choose ethical behavior in a classroom setting when discussing a case study. It is much more difficult when working in an organization and facing budgetary constraints and pressure from peers, customers, top management, and stockholders. Kallman and Grillo (1993) suggest several informal guidelines for ethical behavior:

- ■ *The family test.* Would you be comfortable telling your closest family members about your decision or action?

- ■ *The investigative reporter test.* How would your actions look if reported in a newspaper or on a television news program?

- ■ *The feeling test.* How does the decision feel to you? If you are uneasy about a decision or action but cannot understand why, your intuition is telling you it is not the right thing to do.

- ■ *The empathy test.* How does this decision look if you put yourself in someone else's position? How would it look to another party affected by your actions?

Significant lapses in business ethics in the United States and around the world create a new awareness of the need for ethical behavior in highly interdependent societies and economies. The ethical issues surrounding technology are probably easier than most and knowledge helps you make the right decisions.

THE FUTURE WITH INFORMATION TECHNOLOGY

With more than half of capital investment in the United States in information technology, innovation occurs at a rapid pace. In the early part of the twenty-first century, spending on technology took a serious downturn, accompanied by a dip in the employment of IT pro-fessionals. As the economy improves, both of these trends are likely to turn in the other direction. Technology is the vehicle for increasing productivity at most organizations, and businesses are unlikely to stop investing in IT anytime soon.

- ■ Globalization demands better communications and linking among the distrib-uted parts of an organization. IT and the Internet provide the capability to man-age the global firm across time and space.

■ Networked organizations rely heavily on their partners to undertake tasks that a traditional organization does in-house. IT facilitates the management of network organizations by linking partners together and making all parts of the supply chain visible to its participants.

■ All commerce will have an electronic commerce component. Today, customers expect to find products at an online store. B2B commerce will increasingly move to the Internet, away from phones, fax, and EDI.

■ Managers are increasingly mobile; 58 percent of Americans older than twelve years own a mobile phone.[2] Managers increasingly use tools such as Blackberry for wireless e-mail, Palm Pilot PDAs, and they frequently carry notebook computers. Business hotels are providing high-speed Internet service in their rooms. WiFi networks suggest that in the future, people will be able to connect to the Internet from a variety of locations, from the corner park to their favorite restaurant to an airport lounge. Third-generation cell phones will provide relatively fast Internet access. Satellite providers offer an alternative for anytime, anyplace connection to the Internet.

■ Businesses are expanding their communications links with customers and suppliers as competition and the Internet drive communications costs downward. New developments in fiber-optics promise almost infinite capacity. Business would change dramatically if communications costs essentially disappeared.

These and other trends have some important implications. First, technology will become even more pervasive in organizations and industries, as well as in our personal lives. Firms will continue to invest heavily in new technologies, and managers will confront a number of decisions about IT during their careers. Much of your success will depend on how well you manage information technology, even if you do not consider yourself to be in the IT field. This text illustrates the extent to which technology is the "glue" that holds the organization together, including basic transactions processing systems such as ERP and CRM, systems that allow customer self-service (e.g., through e-commerce online stores), applications that help manage and disseminate knowledge, systems that let you communicate electronically with suppliers and customers, and applications that help support decisions in the organization. One of the most important managerial skills in the twenty-first century is the ability to manage information technology.

Key Management Decisions

This text discussed a number of important decisions related to the management of information technology, which are summarized here:

■ *Strategy.* IT is an important component of corporate strategy. With the Internet and electronic commerce, the firm must invest in IT in order to achieve a critical mass and enjoy the benefits of network externalities. As new opportunities arise and the technology advances, further investments are required.

■ *Value of Investing in IT.* Many different kinds of value come from IT investments. The manager must evaluate proposals for IT initiatives, assign priorities, and allocate resources.

- *Legacy Applications.* The decision whether and when to replace a legacy application challenges organizations over and over again as systems age.

- *Deciding on Applications.* The major applications in organizations include ERP, CRM, and knowledge management applications. Some include intelligent and decisions support applications as well. A firm must decide which applications are important for the organization and how to implement them in the most effective way.

- *The Role of Knowledge.* Knowledge is a core competence of the organization and a resource for competitive advantage. The firm needs technology to support knowledge management.

- *E-Business.* Electronic business is becoming a component of all business; the firm needs to have a strategy and plan for e-commerce.

- *Providing IT Services.* The organization can adopt a centralized or decentralized approach to IT management, or some point between. It can also outsource some or all of its IT operations.

- *Managing Change.* Organizations implement new technology in order to change the firm; management has to lead this change effort. It appears that this kind of major change is most effective when senior management of the firm takes a leadership role.

- *Managing Value Networks.* As business moves toward a network model of the kind employed by Cisco, managers will have to become adept at managing network relationships. Managers will use influence rather than directives to achieve the organization's goals.

- *IT Vision and Plan.* It is important to have a vision for how the firm will operate in five years, and of the kind of technology that will achieve the firm's goals. This vision translates into an operational plan for information technology in the organization.

Looking to the Future

The last half of the twentieth century witnessed a revolution in information technology. After seeing the first mainframe computers, no one seriously considered the possibility of having a machine that was more powerful sitting on a desk or in a briefcase. It has taken many years for information technology to make dramatic changes in organizations and society. However, the pace of change increased dramatically with innovations like the Internet. No one is completely sure what new applications of information technology will look like and how they will change the way people work and live.

The most recent and fastest-growing innovation is the Internet and the World Wide Web. New models for business generally involve the Web and include ideas such as electronic commerce, streamlined supply chains, electronic markets, and even Web-enabled appliances. The Internet provides, for the first time, a worldwide network infrastructure. More than 600 million people around the world can access applications and information placed on the Web.

This same technology allows knowledge workers to access vast amounts of corporate information online using an intranet. Extensive amounts of information are available through a single program, your Web browser. No longer is it necessary to create or use a custom interface for each application. By allowing customers and suppliers to access firm data, organizations change their business models.

The technology offers options for designing new organization structures, especially networked organizations that concentrate on core competencies and outsource other activities. These organizations have the potential for great efficiencies, but they must coordinate with other companies in their network that provide them with goods and services. Novel organization structures enabled by technology present new challenges for the manager; traditional bases of authority do not work in this environment where the company depends on the performance of managers and workers at a partner company it does not control. In a networked environment, managers must develop ways of influencing others rather than directing them or assigning tasks to them.

The combination of computers, databases, and telecommunications, especially the Internet, provide the manager with an incredible number of options for improving the way organizations function. Your challenge is to innovate, to develop strategies in which technology will contribute to the firm's competitive advantage. Then you must choose appropriate technology, implement it successfully, and continually manage change. It is likely that technology will play a major role in the design of your organization and the way in which it does business. As a result, management of the organization means the management of information technology. Those who understand this role of IT, and how to manage it in the organization, are the managers who will succeed in the twenty-first century.

KEYWORDS

Clients	Intellectual property	Monitoring
Control	Internet	Multimedia
Ethics	Legislation	Privacy
Governance	Misuse of information	Spam

RECOMMENDED READINGS

Banerjee, D., Cronan, T., and Jones, T. 1998. Modeling IT ethics: A study in situational ethics. *MIS Quarterly,* 22(1), pp 31–60. (This article offers valuable implications regarding the misuse of computers that has caused huge negative effects on business and society.)

Ermann, M., Williams, M., and Shauf, M. 1997. *Computers, Ethics and Society,* 2nd ed. New York: Oxford University Press. (An excellent reference covering the issues of possible threats of IT on privacy, freedom, and democracy.)

Fusaro, R. 2000. Forethought: Chief privacy officer. *Harvard Business Review,* 78(6), pp. 20–21. (An interview with Richard Purcell of Microsoft on the role of a chief privacy office in an increasingly technology-driven corporate world.)

Hart, J. 1997. *Ethics and Technology: Innovation and Transformation in Community Contexts.* Cleveland, OH: Pilgrim Press. (A short, but great text analyzing the benefits and costs of technology from the business point of view.)

Kallman, E., and Grillo, J. 1993. *Ethical Decision Making and Information Technology.* New York: Mitchell/McGraw-Hill. (An interesting book on ethics with a number of cases to discuss.)

Kreie, J., and Cronan, T. P. 2000. Making ethical decisions. *Communications of the ACM,* 43(12), pp. 66–71. (Focuses on an ethics survey conducted in the United States, which supports the idea that businesses can influence their employees' behavior; the concept of an individual's perceived importance of an ethical issue; a list of scenarios involving the use of information technology; a company's code of ethics; and the importance of providing ethical training.)

Ross, P. F. 2002. Whatever became of integrity? *Communications of the ACM,* 45(9), pp. 27–28. (Discusses the responsibility of those in the computing profession to practice moral integrity, as well as the author's account of lack of protocol on the Web and intellectual copyright violation.)

DISCUSSION QUESTIONS

1. What has happened to make business and government concerned with corporate governance?

2. What is the role of the board of directors for a publicly held company?

3. What should the relationship be between the board and senior management, especially the CEO?

4. What are the reasons for wanting the majority of board members to be independent of the company?

5. What can technology do to help improve corporate governance?

6. What are the key ethical issues for management to consider with respect to IT?

7. Is there such thing as a right to privacy?

8. Does technology make it easier to violate an individual's privacy?

9. Is fraud easier with a computer system than with its manual predecessor?

10. What are the ethical responsibilities of an IS professional?

11. Do employers have a responsibility to retrain workers replaced by information technology?

12. How is a highly technological society such as the United States vulnerable to "electronic aggression"?

13. What kind of safeguards can a company or group of companies adopt to protect vital technology?

14. What are the drawbacks of workplace monitoring? Why might management want to monitor worker productivity?

15. What are a manager's responsibilities for information technology?

16. What strategy would you recommend recording companies and movie distributors adopt for dealing with the Internet and programs like Napster?

17. What guidelines do you recommend for a company in collecting data from customers who visit its Web site? What is a legitimate use of cookies?

18. The NYSE wants companies to come up with a code of ethical conduct. What do you think should be in such a code?

19. Could the scandals described in this chapter have been prevented if managers had acted more ethically? What should they have done?

20. Describe how a National Directors Board might operate. What kind of systems does it need?

ENDNOTES

1. From www.raytheon.com.

2. *PC Magazine,* March 12, 2002.

BIBLIOGRAPHY

Adam, N., Awerbuch, B., Slonim, J., Wegner, P., and Yesha, Y. 1997. Globalizing business, education, culture, through the Internet. *Communications of the ACM*, *40*(2), pp. 115–121.

Agarwal, R., and Sambamurthy, V. 2002. Principles and models for organizing the IT function. *MIS Quarterly Executive*, *1*(1), pp. 1–16.

Altshuler, S., Batavia, D., Bennett, J., Labe, R., Liao, B., Nigam, R., and Oh, J. 2002. Pricing analysis for Merrill Lynch Integrated Choice. *Interfaces*, *32*(1), pp. 5–19.

Andal-Ancion, A., Cartwright, P., and Yip, G. 2003. Digital transformation of traditional businesses. *Sloan Management Review*, Summer, pp. 34–41.

Anderson, D., and Kubiatowicz, J. 2002. The worldwide computer. *Scientific American*, March, pp. 40–47.

Anderson, P., and Anderson, R. 2002. The new e-commerce intermediaries. *Sloan Management Review*, Summer, pp. 53–62.

Applegate, L. 1993. "Frito-Lay, Inc.: A Strategic Transition (A) (Updated)." Boston: Harvard Business School.

Applegate, L., Austin, R., and McFarlan, F. W. 1999. *Corporate Information Strategy and Management*, 6th ed. Homewood, IL: Irwin McGraw-Hill.

Applegate , L., and Stoddard, D. 1993. "Chemical Bank: Technology Support for Cooperative Work." Boston: Harvard Business School.

Austin, R. D., and Darby, C. A. R. 2003. The myth of secure computing. *Harvard Business Review*, *81*(6), pp. 120–126.

Bailey, J. P., and Bakos, Y. 1997. An exploratory study of the emerging role of electronic intermediaries. *International Journal of Electronic Commerce*, *1*(3), pp. 7–20.

Bakos, Y. 1998. The emerging role of electronic marketplaces on the Internet. *Communications of the ACM*, *41*(8), pp. 35–42.

Banerjee, D., Cronan, T., and Jones, T. 1998. Modeling IT ethics: A study in situational ethics. *MIS Quarterly,* *22*(1), pp. 31–60.

Barabasi, Albert-Laszlo. 2002. *Linked: The New Science of Networks*. Cambridge, MA: Perseus Publishing.

Barabba, V., Huber, C., Cooke, F., Pudar, NJ., Smith, J., and Paich, M. 2002. A multimethod approach for creating new business models: The General Motors OnStar project. *Interfaces*, *32*(1), pp. 20–34.

Barney, J. 1991. Firm resources and sustained competitive advantage. *Journal of Management*, *17*(1), pp. 99–120.

Barthelemy, J. 2001. The hidden costs of IT outsourcing. *Sloan Management Review*, Spring, pp. 60–69.

Bartlett, C., and Ghoshal, S. 1989. *Managing Across Borders*. Cambridge, MA: Harvard Business School Press.

Benaroch, M., and Kauffman, R. 1999. A case for using options pricing analyses to evaluate information technology project investments. *Information Systems Research*, *10*(1), pp. 70–86.

Berners-Lee, T., Hendler, J., and Lassila, O. 2001. The semantic Web. *Scientific American*, May, pp. 35–43.

Bhattacherjee, A. 2000. Beginning SAP R/3 implementation at Geneva Pharmaceuticals. *Communications of the AIS*, *4*(2).

Black, F., and Scholes, M. 1973. The pricing of options and corporate liabilities. *Journal of Political Economy*, *81*(3), pp. 637–654.

425

Bozeman, B. 2002. "Government Management of Information Mega-Technology: Lessons from the Internal Revenue Service's Tax Modernization." The PricewaterhouseCoopers Endowment for the Business of Government.

Bragg, S. 1998. *Outsourcing: A Guide to ... Selecting the Correct Business Unit... Negotiating the Contract... Maintaining Control of the Business.* New York: John Wiley & Sons.

Brown, C., Clancy, G., and Scholer, R. 2003. A post-merger IT integration success story: Sallie Mae. *MIS Quarterly Executive, 2*(1), pp. 15–27.

Brown, C., and Magill, S. 1998. Reconceptualizing the context-design issue for the information systems function. *Organization Science, 9*(2), pp. 176–194.

Brown, C., and Vessey, I. 2003. Managing the next wave of enterprise systems: Leveraging lessons from ERP. *MIS Quarterly Executive, 2*(1), pp. 65–77.

Brynjolfsson, E. 1993. The productivity paradox of information technology. *Communications of the ACM, 35*(12), pp. 66–77.

Capelli, P. 2001. Online recruiting. *Harvard Business Review, 79*(3), pp. 139–146.

Carmel, E., and Agarwal, R. 2002. The maturation of offshore sourcing of information technology work. *MIS Quarterly Executive, 1*(2), pp. 65–77.

Chan, Y. E. 2002. Why haven't we mastered alignment? The importance of the informal organizational structure. *MIS Quarterly Executive, 1*(2), pp. 97–112.

Chesbrough, H. W., and Teece, D. J. 2002. Organizing for innovation: When is virtual virtuous? *Harvard Business Review, 80*(8), pp. 127–135.

Cohen, M., March, J., and Olsen, J. 1972. A garbage can model of organizational choice. *Administrative Science Quarterly, 17*, pp. 1–18.

Coltman, T., Devinney, T., Latukefu, A., and Midgley, D. 2001. E-business: Revolution, evolution, or hype. *California Management Review, 44*(1), pp. 57–86.

Conner, K., and Prahalad, C. K. 1996. A resource-based theory of the firm: Knowledge versus opportunism. *Organization Science, 7*(5), pp. 477–501.

Cooper, B. L., Watson, H. J., Wixom, B. H., and Goodhue, D. L. 2000. Data warehousing supports corporate strategy at First American Corporation. *MIS Quarterly, 24*(4), pp. 547–567.

Darwall, C. 2001. *Cisco Systems, building leading Internet capabilities.* Boston: Harvard Business School Press.

Davenport, T. H., and Glasser, J. 2002. Just-in-time delivery comes to knowledge management. *Harvard Business Review, 80*(7), pp. 107–112.

Davenport, T. H., Eccles, R., and Prusak, L. 1993. Information politics. *Sloan Management Review, 34*(1), pp. 53–65.

Davenport, T. H., Harris, J. G., and Kohli, A. K. 2001. How do they know their customers so well? *Sloan Management Review, 42*(2), pp. 63–73.

David, J. S., Schuff, D., and St. Louis, R. 2002. Managing your IT total cost of ownership. *Communications of the ACM, 45*(1), pp. 101–106.

Davis, G. B., and Olson, M. 1985. *Management Information Systems: Conceptual Foundations, Structure, and Development,* 2nd ed. New York: McGraw-Hill.

Day, G. S., Fein, A. J., and Ruppersberger, G. 2003. Shakeouts in digital markets: Lessons from B2B exchanges. *California Management Review, 45*(2), pp. 131–150.

Dearborn, O., and Simon, H. 1958. Selective perception: A note on the departmental identification of executives. *Sociometry, 21*, pp. 140–144.

Dhar, V., and Stein, R. 1997. *Seven Methods for Transforming Corporate Data into Business Intelligence.* Englewood Cliffs, NJ: Prentice Hall.

DiRomualdo, A., and Gurbaxani, V. 1998. Strategic intent for IT outsourcing. *Sloan Management Review, 39*(4).

Dos Santos, B. 1991. Justifying investments in new information technologies. *Journal of MIS, 7*(4), pp. 71–90.

Dowling, G. 2002. Customer relationship management: In B2C markets, often less is more. *California Management Review, 44*(3), pp. 181–199.

Dutta, A., and McCrohan, K. 2002. Management's role in information security in a cyber economy. *California Management Review, 45*(1), pp. 67–87.

Earl, M., and Feeny, D. 1994. Is your CIO adding value? *Sloan Management Review*, Spring, pp. 11–20.

Ellis, C. 2003. Lessons from online groceries. *Sloan Management Review, 44*(2), p. 8.

Embley, D. 1997. *Object Database Development: Concepts and Principles*. New York: Addison-Wesley.

Ermann, M., Williams, M., and Shauf, M. *Computers, Ethics, and Society*, 2nd ed. New York: Oxford University Press.

Ewusi-Mensah, K. 1997. Critical issues in abandoned information systems development projects. *Communications of the ACM, 40*(9), pp. 74–80.

Farmoomand, A., Ng, P., and Conley, W. 2003. Building a successful e-business: The FedEx story. *Communications of the ACM, 46*(4), pp. 84–87.

Fayyad, M., and Uthurusamy, R. 2002. Evolving data into mining solutions for insights. *Communications of the ACM, 45*(8), pp. 28–31.

Feeny, D. 2001. Making business sense of the e-opportunity. *Sloan Management Review, 42*(2), pp. 41–51.

Foster, I. 2003. The GRID: Computing without bounds. *Scientific American*, April, pp. 78–85.

Frei, F. 2002. "eBay (A): The Customer Marketplace." Boston: Harvard Business School.

Freund, C., and Weinhold, D. 2000. "On the Effect of the Internet on International Trade," Federal Reserve International Finance Discussion Paper No. 693.

Fusaro, R. 2000. Forethought: Chief privacy officer. *Harvard Business Review, 78*(6), pp. 20–21.

Galal, H. 1995. "Verifone: The Transaction Automation Company (A)." Boston: Harvard Business School.

Garud, R., and Lucas, H. C. Jr. 1997. "Virtual Organizations: What You See May Not Be What You Get." Working paper, Stern School, New York University.

Ghoshal, S., and Gratton, L. 2002. Integrating the enterprise. *Sloan Management Review*, Fall, pp. 31–38.

Goodhue, D., Wixom, B., and Watson, H. 2002. Realizing business benefit through CRM: Hitting the right target in the right way. *MIS Quarterly Executive, 1*(2), pp. 79–94.

Gordon, J., P. Lee, and H. Lucas, Jr. 2003. "A System of Resources for Competitive Advantage: A Case Study of the Port of Singapore." Working paper, College Park, Robert H. Smith School of Business.

Greenstein, S. 2001. Technological mediation and commercial development in the early Internet access market. *California Management Review, 43*(2), pp. 75–94.

Gupta, V., Peters, E., and Miller, T. 2002. "Implementing a distribution-network decision-support system at Pfizer/ Warner-Lambert." *Interfaces, 32*(4), pp. 28–45.

Gwynne, P. 2001. Information systems go global. *Harvard Business Review, 42*(4), p. 14.

Hackney, R. 1998. The expert's opinion. *Journal of Global Information Management, 6*(4), pp. 43–45.

Hagel, J. III, and Brown, J. S. 2001. Your next IT strategy. *Harvard Business Review, 79*(9), pp. 105–113.

Hammer, M. 1997. *Beyond Reengineering: How the Processed-Centered Organization Is Changing Our Work and Our Lives*. New York: HarperCollins.

Hammer, M., and Champy, J. 1993. *Reengineering the Corporation*. New York: HarperCollins.

Hand, D., Mannila, H., and Smyth, P. 2001. *Principles of Data Mining.* Cambridge, MA: MIT Press.

Hansen, M., Nohria, N., and Tierney, T. 1999. What's your strategy for managing knowledge? *Harvard Business Review,* March–April, pp. 106–116.

Harris, Leslie, and Associates. 2002. *Bringing a Nation Online: The Importance of Federal Leadership.*

Hart, J. 1997. *Ethics and Technology: Innovation and Transformation in Community Contexts.* Cleveland, OH: Pilgrim Press.

Hart, S., and Christensen, C. 2002. The great leap: Driving innovation from the base of the pyramid. *Sloan Management Review*, Fall, pp. 51–56.

Hernandez, M. 1997. *Database Design for Mere Mortals: A Hands-On Guide to Relational Database Design.* New York: Addison-Wesley.

Hirschheim, R., and Lacity, M. 2000. Myths and realities of information technology insourcing. *Communications of the ACM, 43*(2), pp. 99–107.

Holland, C. P., Light, B., and Kawalek, P. 1999. Focus issue on legacy information systems and business process change. *Communications of the AIS, 2*(9), pp. 1–11.

Ives, B., and Jarvenpaa, S. 1992. Global information technology: Some lessons from practice. *International Information Systems, 1*(3), pp. 1–15.

Jackson, J. 2002. Data mining: A conceptual overview. *Communications of the AIS, 8*(19).

Jap, S. D., and Mohr, J. J. 2002. Leveraging Internet technologies in B2B relationships. *California Management Review, 44*(4), pp. 24–38.

Johnston, C. 2001. "DaimlerChrysler Knowledge Management Strategy." Boston: Harvard Business School Press.

Kallman, E., and Grillo, J. 1993. *Ethical Decision Making and Information Technology.* New York: Mitchell/McGraw-Hill.

Kambil, A., Henderson, J., and Mohsenzadeh, H. 1993. Strategic management of information technology investments: An options perspective. In R. Banker, R. Kauffman, and M. Mahmood (eds.), *Strategic Information Technology Management.* Harrisburg, PA: Idea Group Publishing.

Kambil, A., and Lucas, H. C. Jr. 2002. The board of directors and the management of information technology. *Communications of the AIS, 8*(26).

Kedia, B., and Bhagat, R. Cultural constraints on transfer of technology across nations: Implications for research in international and comparative management. *Academy of Management Review, 13*(4), pp. 559–571.

Kiely, T. 1996. Computer legacy systems. *Harvard Business Review, 74*(4), pp. 10–12.

King, J., and Konsynski, B. 1994. "Singapore TradeNet: A Tale of One City." Boston: Harvard Business School.

Kirkman, B. L., Rosen, B., Gibson, C. B., Tesluk, P. E., and McPherson, S. O. 2002. Five challenges to virtual team success: Lessons from Sabre Inc. *Academy of Management Executive, 16*(3), pp. 67–79.

Kogut, B., and Zander, U. 1992. Knowledge of the firm, combinative capabilities, and the replication of technology. *Organization Science, 3*, pp. 383–397.

Kopczak, L., and Johnson, E. 2003. The supply-chain management effect. *Sloan Management Review*, Spring, pp. 27–34.

Korth, H., and Silberschatz, A. 1986. *Database System Concepts.* New York: McGraw-Hill.

Kraemer, K., and Dedrick, J. 2002. "Dell Computer: Organization of a Global Production Network." CRITO Working Paper, Irvine.

Kreie, J., and Cronan, T. P. 2000. Making ethical decisions. *Communications of the ACM, 43*(12), pp. 66–71.

Kumaraswamy, A. 1996. "A Real Options Perspective of Firms' R&D Investments." Unpublished Ph.D. dissertation, Stern School, New York University.

Kwak, M. 2001. The offline impact of online prices. *Sloan Management Review*, *42*(3), pp. 9–11.

Lacity, M. 2002. Lessons in global information technology sourcing. *IEEE Computer*, August.

Lacity, M., and Hirschheim, R. 1993. The information systems outsourcing bandwagon. *Sloan Management Review*, Fall, pp. 73–86.

Landes, D. 1998. *The Wealth and Poverty of Nations: Why Some Are So Rich and Some So Poor.* New York: W.W. Norton.

Lederer, A., and Prasad, J. 1992. Nine management guidelines for better cost estimating. *Communications of the ACM*, *35*(2), pp. 50–59.

Lewis, I. 2001. Logistics and electronic commerce: An interorganizational systems perspective. *Transportation Journal*, *40*(4), pp. 5–13.

Litan, R., and Rivlin, A. (eds.). 2001. *The Economic Payoff from the Internet Revolution.* Washington, DC: Brookings Institution Press.

Loh, L., and Venkatraman, N. 1992. Determinants of information technology outsourcing: A cross-sectional analysis. *Journal of MIS*, *9*(1), pp. 7–24.

Lucas, H. C., Jr. 1996. *The T-Form Organization: Using Information Technology to Design Organizations for the 21st Century.* San Francisco: Jossey-Bass.

Lucas, H. C., Jr., and Baroudi, J. 1994. The role of information technology in organizational design. *Journal of MIS*, Spring, pp. 9–23.

Lucas, H. C., Jr., Berndt, D., and Truman, G. 1996. A reengineering framework for evaluating a financial imaging system. *Communications of the ACM*, *39*(5), pp. 86–96.

Lucas, H. C., Jr., Ginzberg, M., and Schultz, R. 1991. *Implementing Information Systems: Testing a Structural Model.* Norwood, NJ: Ablex.

Lucas, H. C., Jr., Oh, W., Simon, G., and Weber, B. 2002. "Information Technology and the New York Stock Exchange's Strategic Resources from 1982–1999." Working paper, College Park, Smith School of Business.

Lucas, H. C., Jr., and Sylla, R. 2003. The global impact of the Internet: Widening the economic gap between wealthy and poor nations? *Prometheus,* Spring, pp. 3–22.

Lucas, R. E., Jr., 2000. Some macroeconomics for the 21st century. *Journal of Economic Perspectives, 14*, pp.159–168.

Luconi, F. L., Malone, T., and Scott Morton, M. S. 1986. Expert systems: The next challenge for managers. *Sloan Management Review,* Summer, pp. 3–14.

Mabert, V., Soni, A., and Venkataramanan, M. 1991. Enterprise resource planning: Common myths versus evolving reality. *Business Horizons*, May–June, pp. 71–78.

Maddison, A. 2001. *The World Economy: A Millenial Perspective.* Paris: OECD.

Mason, R. 1995. Applying ethics to information technology issues. *Communications of the ACM*, *38*(12), pp. 55–57.

Mason, R., and Mitroff, I. 1973. A program for research in management information systems. *Management Science*, *19*(5), pp. 475–487.

Mbarika, V., Jensen, M., and Meso, P. 2002. Cyberspace across sub-Saharan Africa: Moving from technological desert toward emergent sustainable growth. *Communications of the ACM*, *45*(12), pp. 17–21.

McAfee, A. 2003. When too much knowledge is a dangerous thing. *Sloan Management Review*, Winter, pp. 83–89.

McFarlan, W., and Nolan, R. 1995. How to manage an IT outsourcing alliance. *Sloan Management Review,* Winter, pp. 9–23.

McNealy, S. 2001. Welcome to the bazaar. *Harvard Business Review*, *79*(3), pp. 18–19.

Meinel, C. 1998. How hackers break in…and how they are caught. *Scientific American*, October.

Merchand, D. A., Kettinger, W. J., and Rollins, J. D. 2000. Information orientation: People, technology, and the bottom line. *Sloan Management Review*, *41*(4), pp. 69–80.

Mintzberg, H. 1973. *On the Nature of Managerial Work*. New York: Harper & Row.

Montealegre, R., and Nelson, H. J. 1996. "BAE Automated Systems (A): Denver International Airport Baggage-Handling System." Boston: Harvard Business School Press.

Moon, Y. 2002. "Online Music Distribution in a Post-Napster World." Boston: Harvard Business School.

Mukhopadhyay, T., and Kekre, S. 2002. Strategic and operational benefits of electronic integration in B2B procurement processes. *Management Science*, *48*(10), pp 1301–1313.

Nadler, D., and Tushman, M. 1988. *Strategic Organization Design*. New York: HarperCollins.

Newell, S., Pan, S. L., Galliers, R. D., and Huang, J. C. 2001. The myth of the boundaryless organization. *Communications of the ACM*, *44*(12), pp. 74–76.

Nonaka, N. 1994. A dynamic theory of organizational knowledge creation. *Organization Science,* *5*(1), pp. 14–37.

Oh, W., and Lucas, H. C., Jr. 2002. "Information Technology and Pricing Decisions: Price Adjustment and Price Rank in On-Line Computer Markets." Working paper, Smith School of Business.

Orlikowski, W. 1996. Improvising organizational transformation over time: A situated change perspective. *Information Systems Research*, *7*(1), pp. 63–92.

Parent, C., and Spaccapietra, S. 1998. Issues and approaches of database integration. *Communications of the ACM*, *41*(5), pp. 166–178.

Pekec, A., and Rothkopf, M. 2003. Combinatorial auction design. *Management Science*, *49*(11), pp. 1485–1503.

Peteraf, M. 1993. The cornerstones of competitive advantage: A resource-based view. *Strategic Management Journal*, *14*, pp. 179–191.

Petrazzini, B., and Kibati, M. 1999. The Internet in developing countries. *Communications of the ACM*, *42*(6), pp. 31–36.

Pinker, E., Seidmann, A., and Vakrat, Y. 2003. Managing online auctions: Current business and research issues. *Management Science*, *49*(11), pp. 1457–1484.

Porter, M. 1985. *Competitive Advantage.* New York: The Free Press.

Prahalad, C. K., and Hamel, G. 1990. The core competence of the corporation. *Harvard Business Review*, May–June, pp. 79–91.

Prahalad, C. K., and Krishnan, M. S. 2002. The dynamic synchronization of strategy and information technology. *Sloan Management Review*, *43*(4), pp. 24–33.

Purvis, R., Sambamurthy, V., and Zmud, R. 2001. The assimilation of knowledge platforms in organizations: An empirical investigation. *Organization Science*, *12*(2), pp. 117–135.

Quinn, J. B., and Hilmer, F. G. 1994. Strategic outsourcing. *Sloan Management Review*, Summer, pp. 43–55.

Randall, D., Hughes, J., O'Brien, J., Rodden, T., Rouncefield, M., Sommerville, I., and Tolmie, P. 1999. Banking on the old technology: Understanding the organizational context of 'legacy' issues. *Communications of the AIS*, *2*(8).

Rangan, V. K., and Bell, M. 1998. "Dell Online." Boston: Harvard Business School Press.

Rifkin, G. 2002. GM's Internet overhaul. *Technology Review*, October, pp. 62–67.

Roche, E. 1992. *Managing Information Technology in Multinational Corporations*. New York: Macmillan.

Ross, P. F. 2002. Whatever became of integrity? *Communications of the ACM*, *45*(9), pp. 27–28.

Rust, R., and Kannan, P. K. 2003. E-service: A new paradigm for business in the electronic environment. *Communications of the ACM*, *46*(6), pp. 37–42.

Saha, D., and Mukherjee, A. 2003. Pervasive computing: A paradigm for the 21st century. *IEEE Computer*, March, pp. 25–31.

Sambamurthy, V., and Zund, R. 2000. Research commentary: The organizing logic for an enterprise's IT activities in the digital era—A prognosis of practice and a call for research. *Information Systems Research*, *11*(2), pp. 105–114.

Sawhney, M., and Prandelli, E. 2000. Communities of creation: Managing distributed innovation in turbulent markets. *California Management Review*, *42*(4), pp. 24–54.

Schach, S. 2004. *Introduction to Object-Oriented Analysis and Design with UML and the Unified Process*. New York: Irwin McGraw-Hill.

Schneider, M. 2002. A stakeholder model of organizational leadership. *Organization Science*, *13*(2), pp. 209–220.

Schneidewind, N. F., and Ebert, C. 1998. Preserve or redesign legacy systems? *IEEE Software*, *15*(4), pp. 14–17.

Scott, J. E., and Vessey, I. 2002. Managing risks in enterprise systems implementations. *Communications of the ACM*, *45*(4), pp. 74–81.

Shapiro, C., and Varian, H. R. 1999. *Information Rules: A Strategic Guide to the Network Economy*. Boston: Harvard Business School Press.

Siebel, T. 2000. *How to Become an E-Business*. San Mateo, CA: Siebel Systems.

Silberschatz, A., Korth, H., and Sudershan, S. 1998. *Database System Concepts*, 3rd ed. New York: McGraw Hill.

Smith, B. C., Leimkuhler, J., and Darrow, R. 1992. Yield management at American Airlines. *Interfaces*, *22*(1), pp. 8–31.

Sonaike, S. A. 2004. The Internet and the dilemma of Africa's development. *International Journal for Communication Studies*, *66*(1), pp. 41–60.

Soo, C., Devinney, T., Midgley, D., and Deering, A. 2002. Knowledge management: Philosophy, processes, and pitfalls. *California Management Review*, *44*(4), pp. 129–150.

Steinbart, P., and Nath, R. 1992. Problems and issues in the management of international data communications networks: The experiences of American companies. *MIS Quarterly*, *16*(1), pp. 55–76.

Stohr, E., and Konsynski, B. (eds.). 1992. *Information Systems and Decision Processes*. Los Alamitos, CA: IEEE Computer Society Press.

Straub, D. 1994. The effects of culture on IT diffusion: E-mail and fax in Japan and the U.S. *Information Systems Research*, *5*(1), pp. 23–47.

Stywotsky, A. 2001. Revving the engines of online finance. *Sloan Management Review*, *42*(4), p. 96.

Susarla, A., Barua, A., and Whinston, A. B. 2003. Understanding the service component of application service provision: An empirical analysis of satisfaction with ASP services. *MIS Quarterly*, *27*(1), pp. 91–123.

Sylla, R. 1998. U.S. securities markets and the banking system, 1790–1840. *Federal Reserve Bank of St. Louis Review, 50*, pp. 83–98.

Sylla, R. 1999. Emerging market in history: The United States, Japan, and Argentina. In Ryuzo Sato et al. (eds.), *Global Competition and Integration*. Boston: Kluwer Academic Publishers, pp. 427–446.

Sylla, R. 2002. Financial systems and economic modernization. *Journal of Economic History, 62*(2), pp. 277–292.

Teece, D. 1987. Profiting from technological innovation: Implications for integration, collaboration, licensing, and public policy. In D. Teece (ed.), *The Competitive Challenge*. New York: Harper & Row.

Teece, D., Pisano, G., and Shuen, A. 1997. Dynamic capabilities and strategic management. *Strategic Management Journal*, *18*(7), pp. 509–533.

Teo, H, Tan, B., and Wei, K. K. 1997. Organizational transformation using electronic data interchange: The case of TreadeNet in Singapore. *Journal of MIS*, *13*(4), pp. 139–165.

Townsend, A. M., DeMarie, S. M., and Hendrickson, A. R. 1998. Virtual teams: Technology and the workplace of the future. *Academy of Management Executive*, *12*(3), pp. 17–29.

Trippi, R., and Lee, J. 1996. *Artificial Intelligence in Finance and Investing: State-of-the-Art Technologies for Securities Selection and Portfolio Management*. Homewood, IL: Irwin.

Tung, L. L., and Turban, E. 1996. Port of Singapore Authority: Using AI technology for strategic positioning. In N. Boon Siong, (ed.), *Exploiting Information Technology for Business Competitiveness*. Singapore: Addison-Wesley.

Turban, E. 1995. *Decision Support and Expert Systems*, 4th ed. New York: Macmillan.

Tyson, L. D. 1999. Old economic logic in the new economy. *California Management Review*, *41*(4), pp. 8–16.

UNDP. 1998. *Human Development Report*. New York: Oxford University Press.

UNDP. 1999. *Human Development Report*. New York: Oxford University Press.

Venkatesh, V., Morris, M., Davis, F., and Davis, G. 2003. User acceptance of information technology: Toward a unified view. *MIS Quarterly*, *27*, pp. 425–478.

Venkatraman, N., and Henderson, J. C. 1998. Real strategies for virtual organizing. *Sloan Management Review*, *40*(1), pp. 33–48.

Walsh, K. 2003. Analyzing the application ASP concept: Technologies, economies, and strategies. *Communications of the ACM*, *46*(8), pp. 103–107.

Want, R. 2004. RFID, A key to automating everything. *Scientific American*, January, pp. 56–65.

Warschauer, M. 2003. Demystifying the digital divide. *Scientific American*, August, pp. 42–47.

Weber, R. 1999. *Information Systems Control and Audit*. Upper Saddle River, NJ: Prentice Hall.

Weill, P. 1990. *Do Computers Pay Off?* Washington, DC: ICIT Press.

Weill, P., Subramani, M., and Broadbent, M. 2002. Building IT infrastructure for strategic agility. *Sloan Management Review*, *44*(1), pp. 57–65.

Weill, P., and Vitale, M. 2001. *Place to Space*. Boston: Harvard Business School Press.

Weill, P., and Vitale, M. 2002. What IT infrastructure capabilities are needed to implement e-business models? *MIS Quarterly Executive*, *1*(1), pp. 17–34.

Winter, R. 2001. A framework for customer relationship management. *California Management Review*, *43*(4), pp. 89–105.

Wixom, B. H., and Watson, H. J. 2001. An empirical investigation of the factors affecting data warehousing success. *MIS Quarterly*, *25*(1), pp. 17–41.

Woodham, R., and Weill, P. 2001. "Manheim Interactive: Selling Cars Online." Working paper, Boston and Melbourne: MIT and Melbourne Business School.

World Bank. 1999. *Knowledge for Development*. Washington, DC: World Development Report.

Zack, M. H. 1999. Modifying codified knowledge. *Sloan Management Review*, *40*(4), pp. 45–58.

Zahedi, F. 1993. *Intelligent Systems for Business: Expert Systems with Neural Networks.* Belmont, CA: Wadsworth.

Zaheer, A., and Zaheer, S. 1997. Catching the wave: Alertness, responsiveness, and market influence in global electronic networks. *Management Science, 43*(11), pp. 1493–1509.

INDEX

Page locators shown in **Bold** type indicate Figures, Management Problems, Side Bars, and Tables.

technology transformation,
189

world economic development,
402–04

Port of Singapore, 38–39,
364–86

portals, 46–47, 54–55, 57

Porter, Michael, 25–29

Priceline.com, 38, 57

privacy protection, 413–15

private network, 49–50, 282–85,
292

process control, 209–10

processing systems
automated, 16, 113
ERP, 332–34
organizational redesign and,
78, 84, 319–28
reengineering, 318–19
routine, 15
. *see also* business process

procurement, 26–27

product introduction, 93

product management, 266–70

production planning, **333**

productivity paradox, 113–17

programmed activities, 19

programming
applications packages and,
156–61
database, 255
ERP, 334–37
legacy systems, 225–26,
420–22
outsourcing, 95–96

project management, 214, 222

proprietary data networks,
282–83, 290

protocols, network, 248–50,
286–90

prototypes, 181

purchasing, 58–59, 93, **186**,
307–10

R

racial groups, IT and, 390–93

radio frequency identification
(RFID), **86**, **417**

rationalized manufacturing, 93

Red Hat software, 161

reengineering, 318–19

regulation
antitrust laws, 309
code of ethics and, 410–11
Foreign Corrupt Practices
Act, 215
global systems, 99–100
governance and corporate,
215, 408–10
intellectual property rights,
415–16
Internet, 294
investment opportunities
matrix and, 119–21
privacy protection, 413–15
Sarbanes-Oxley Act, 216,
408–10
securities trading, 48
spam, 417
telecommunications, **58**
. *see also* government

relational database, 257–62
. *see also* databases

relationship marketing. *see* customer relationship management
(CRM)

resources
competitive advantage, 23–25
core competencies as, 29–30
dynamic model/modeling of,

31–39
investment opportunities
matrix and, 117–26
knowledge as strategic,
377–78
maintaining competitive
advantage, 38–39
managing IT, 196–98,
200–204
systems implementation, 181
. *see also* assets

retail sales model, 50–51

retail stock markets, 64–70

return on investment (ROI)
conversion effectiveness and,
132–33, 137–38
infrastructure, 113–17
investment equation and,
133–37
investment opportunities
matrix, 117–26
value equation and, 137–38

revenue model, 43, 57

reverse auction, 57, 301

rewards, management control
through, 210, 212

risk
exchange rate, 93
investment decision-making,
129
management control of, **213**
NPV, 139, 144
OPM, 143–44
outsourcing, 96

S

sales forecast, 209

SAP, 160, 332–33, 343n.2

Sarbanes-Oxley Act, 216,
408–10